Manichaeism and Early Christianity

Nag Hammadi and Manichaean Studies

Editors

Jason D. BeDuhn
Dylan M. Burns
Johannes van Oort

Editorial Board

A.D. DECONICK – W.-P. FUNK – I. GARDNER
S.N.C. LIEU – H. LUNDHAUG – A. MARJANEN – L. PAINCHAUD
N.A. PEDERSEN – T. RASIMUS – S.G. RICHTER
M. SCOPELLO – J.D. TURNER † – G. WURST

VOLUME 99

The titles published in this series are listed at *brill.com/nhms*

Manichaeism and Early Christianity

Selected Papers from the 2019 Pretoria Congress and Consultation

Edited by

Johannes van Oort

BRILL

LEIDEN | BOSTON

The Library of Congress Cataloging-in-Publication Data is available online at http://catalog.loc.gov
LC record available at http://lccn.loc.gov/
Library of Congress Cataloging-in-Publication Data

Names: Manichaeism and early Christianity (Conference) (2019 : University of
   Pretoria), author. | Oort, J. van (Johannes), editor.
Title: Manichaeism and early Christianity : selected papers from the 2019 Pretoria
   congress and consultation / edited by Johannes van Oort.
Description: Leiden ; Boston : Brill, [2021] | Series: Nag Hammadi and Manichaean
   studies, 0929-2470 ; volume 99 | Includes bibliographical references and index.
   | English and French.
Identifiers: LCCN 2020045264 (print) | LCCN 2020045265 (ebook) |
   ISBN 9789004445451 (hardback) | ISBN 9789004445468 (ebook)
Subjects: LCSH: Christianity and other religions–Manichaeism–Congresses. |
   Manichaeism–Relations–Christianity–Congresses. | Gnosticism–Congresses.
Classification: LCC BT1410 .M317 2019 (print) | LCC BT1410 (ebook) |
   DDC 273/.2–dc23
LC record available at https://lccn.loc.gov/2020045264
LC ebook record available at https://lccn.loc.gov/2020045265

Typeface for the Latin, Greek, and Cyrillic scripts: "Brill". See and download: brill.com/brill-typeface.

ISSN 0929-2470
ISBN 978-90-04-44545-1 (hardback)
ISBN 978-90-04-44546-8 (e-book)

Copyright 2021 by Koninklijke Brill NV, Leiden, The Netherlands.
Koninklijke Brill NV incorporates the imprints Brill, Brill Hes & De Graaf, Brill Nijhoff, Brill Rodopi,
Brill Sense, Hotei Publishing, mentis Verlag, Verlag Ferdinand Schöningh and Wilhelm Fink Verlag.
All rights reserved. No part of this publication may be reproduced, translated, stored in a retrieval system,
or transmitted in any form or by any means, electronic, mechanical, photocopying, recording or otherwise,
without prior written permission from the publisher. Requests for re-use and/or translations must be
addressed to Koninklijke Brill NV via brill.com or copyright.com.

This book is printed on acid-free paper and produced in a sustainable manner.

Contents

Preface VII
Notes on Contributors IX

1 The Religious Innovator Tatian: A Precursor of Mani in Syrian Christianity? 1
   Josef Lössl

2 Antithèses en mutation, de Marcion à Mani 24
   Michel Tardieu

3 The Diatessaronic Sequence of Mani's Sermon on the Life of Christ in the Berlin *Kephalaia* 35
   Zsuzsanna Gulácsi

4 The Strange Case of 'Quire A' in the Dublin *Kephalaia* Codex: Further Thoughts on Mani's *Book of Mysteries*, M281 and the *First Apocalypse of James* 51
   Iain Gardner

5 Mani's *Book of Mysteries*: A Treatise *De anima* 70
   Dylan M. Burns

6 A Manichaean Reading of the *Gospel of Thomas* 98
   René Falkenberg

7 "For only our lord the Paraclete is competent to praise you as you deserve" (P.Kell.Gr. 63): Identifying a Roman-Egyptian Patron of the Manichaeans in Kellis 128
   Mattias Brand

8 Les *Acta Archelai* et ses principaux personnages: Notes historiques et lexicales 152
   Madeleine Scopello

9 Snakes in the Garden and Tares in the Wheat Field: Ephrem of Nisibis' Polemic of Lineage against the Manichaeans 186
   Robert Morehouse

10 Manichaeism in John Chrysostom's Heresiology   225
      Chris L. de Wet

11 Augustine's *De pulchro et apto* and its Manichaean Context   253
      Johannes van Oort

12 Thing and Argument: On the Function of the Scenario in Augustine's *De beata vita*   288
      Therese Fuhrer

13 Augustine, Faustus, and the Jews   302
      Jason David BeDuhn

14 Pelagius against the Manichaeans: Real Opponents or Clichéd Heresiology?   324
      Nils Arne Pedersen

15 Evodius of Uzalis and the Development of Manichaeism in Roman North Africa   351
      Aäron Vanspauwen

16 The 'Children' of the Manichaeans: Wandering Extreme Ascetics in the Roman East Compared   374
      Rea Matsangou

17 The Afterlife of Manichaeism in Neoplatonic Education   401
      Byard Bennett

Index of Antique and Modern Personal Names   433

Preface

This volume contains the selected papers from the 2019 congress and subsequent consultation 'Manichaeism and Early Christianity' which was organized as part of the research project 'Augustine and Manichaeism' at the University of Pretoria. Nine contributions were read and discussed at the Congress that took place from 21–23 March 2019 in Brooklyn, Pretoria; the other contributions came from project participants unable to attend in Pretoria but happily willing to shed their specialist light on parts of the theme. All chapters have been thoroughly peer-reviewed by the best experts worldwide. The result is a book that uniquely explores the relationship between Mani's religion (once again it turned out to be essentially a 'Gnostic' form of heretic Christianity) and diverse expressions of early mainstream and also other 'Gnostic' types of Christendom. In fact, this publication is the first major exploration of a largely undeveloped field of research that aims to study the relationship between Manichaeism and varied Early Christianity. Nevertheless, all experts in the discipline will agree that still much can and should be done in this important field. To name just a few major research wishes: how was the relationship between Mani's Church and the Jewish-Christian Elkesaites originally and later on?; to what extent was Athanasius acquainted with Mani's religion and probably with Manichaeans in his immediate environments?; to what extent did Manichaean questions influence the development of the dogmata and confessional formulas of mainstream Catholic churches?; what about the enigmatic writing *Ad Iustinum Manichaeum contra duo principia Manichaeorum et de vera carne Christi*, often ascribed to the—in fact not much less enigmatic and still understudied—Roman rhetor and Christian Marius Victorinus? Etc.!

These last observations may not only indicate how many results can still be expected in our new and rich field of research: they may also implicate to what extent wonderful results can already be reported. This book bears witness to in-depth research into Mani's predecessors; new light on some of his own writings; surprising results when comparing Manichaean texts with a number of the Nag Hammadi documents; a new analysis of some of the recent Kellis finds; thorough examination of writings by mainstream Christian authors who—whether or not attesting to unique knowledge of Manichaean thought or writ—dealt with Manichaean principles and practices: (Pseudo-)Hegemonius, Ephrem the Syrian, John Chrysostom, Augustine, Pelagius, Evodius of Uzalis, later Greek ecclesiastical writers and even a Neoplatonic inspired philosophical instruction published here for the first time with analysis of its ecclesiastical setting in the manuscripts. The philosophical and theological questions emphatically raised by the Manichaeans have dominated the discussions for centuries, and not least the writings of Church Father Augustine provide an example in this regard that has had a great and even lasting influence on Western thought.

Thinking about the contents of this book, the bright days of March 2019 come to mind again. From entirely different places in the world, a unique band of researchers came together for two days of intensive discussion of a dozen in-depth research papers. From the outset this conference had been called a 'congress', but perhaps better—if this would not have triggered possible misunderstandings among those who go for the literal meaning of a word—a 'symposium'. Anyway, the delicious discussions completed with delicious meals and drinks, and finally a visit to the Cradle of Mankind with a lion park game drive, have become unforgettable for many.

The editor of this collection would like to express his special gratitude not only to all who made their scientific contributions then and later, but also to the Dean of University of Pretoria's Faculty of Theology and Religion, Prof. Jerry Pillay, for his support, and to its Deputy Dean and Supervisor of Research, Prof. Ernest van Eck, for opening the conference. The Board of the International Association of Manichaean Studies was so kind as to accept the 2019 Pretoria meeting as one of its congresses and both its President, Nils Arne Pedersen, and Vice-President, Jason BeDuhn, were present and actively participated in the deliberations. Our highly esteemed colleague Chris de Wet from the University of South Africa (UNISA) in Pretoria gave many valuable advice. Wilma de Weert was once again a great support at Brill, as was Louise Schouten, who even attended our conference. The young Leuven doctor Aaron Vanspauwen was of great help in compiling an Index.

> Brooklyn, Pretoria,
> the 13th of November 2020, *JvO*

Notes on Contributors

Jason David BeDuhn
is Professor of Religious Studies at Northern Arizona University. Among his recent publications are *Augustine's Manichaean Dilemma*: 1: *Conversion and Apostasy, 373–388 C.E.* and 2: *Making a 'Catholic' Self, 388–401 C.E.*, University of Pennsylvania Press, 2010 and 2013.

Byard Bennett
is Emeritus Professor of Historical and Philosophical Theology at Grand Rapids Theological Seminary/Cornerstone University. His publications have focused on Greek Christian philosophical texts of the patristic, Byzantine, and post-Byzantine periods.

Mattias Brand
is a postdoctoral fellow at the Zürich Institute for the Study of Religions. He received his PhD at Leiden University (2019) on 'The Manichaeans of Kellis: Religion, Community, and Everyday Life in Late Antiquity'. His research interests include late antique religion, Manichaeism, Early Christian diversity, as well as method and theory in the study of religion.

Dylan M. Burns
is a research associate at Freie Universität Berlin. He has published several books and many articles on Gnosticism, later Greek philosophy, early Christianity, and their modern reception, recently including *New Antiquities* (Equinox, 2019) and *Did God Care?* (Brill, 2020).

René Falkenberg
(Aarhus University) is associate professor of New Testament Studies. He has published on Paul, Manichaeism, and texts from Nag Hammadi. Currently he works in the Biblia Manichaica Project and on a monograph on *Eugnostos the Blessed* (NHC III,3 and V,1) entitled *Immortal among Mortals* (Brill).

Therese Fuhrer
holds the Chair of Latin at the Ludwig-Maximilians-Universität Munich. She is the author and editor of several books such as (with Martin Hose) *Das antike Drama*, München: Beck 2017 and (with Simone Adam) *Augustinus, Contra Academicos, De beata vita, De ordine* (Bibliotheca Teubneriana 2022), Berlin/Boston: De Gruyter 2017.

Iain Gardner
is Professor of the History of Religions at the University of Sydney, and a Fellow of the Australian Academy of Humanities. His recent publications include *The Founder of Manichaeism. Rethinking the Life of Mani*, Cambridge: Cambridge University Press 2020.

Zsuzsanna Gulácsi
is Professor of Art History and Asian Studies at Northern Arizona University, Flagstaff. She is the author of *Manichaean Art in Berlin Collections* (Brepols 2001), *Mediaeval Manichaean Book Art* (Brill 2005), and *Mani's Pictures: The Didactic Images of the Manichaeans from Sasanian Mesopotamia to Uygur Central Asia and Tang-Ming China* (Brill 2015).

Josef Lössl
is Professor of Religious Studies and Theology at Cardiff University, specializing in the study of early Christianity, patristics and Late Antiquity. He is co-editor of *A Companion to Religion in Late Antiquity* (Wiley Blackwell 2018) and currently working on a commentary on Tatian's *Oratio ad Graecos* in the series *Kommentar zu frühchristlichen Apologeten* (*KfA*).

Rea Matsangou
is a member of the Department of History, Archaeology and Social Anthropology, University of Thessaly, Greece, and PhD candidate at the University of Leiden. Most recent publication: 'Real and Imagined Manichaeans in Greek Patristic Anti-Manichaica (4th–6th centuries)', in: *Manichaeism East and West* (CFM. Analecta Manichaica 1), Turnhout: Brepols 2017, 159–170.

Robert Morehouse
is an adjunct professor of Arabic at Liberty University (USA).

Johannes van Oort
(em. Prof. Utrecht University and Radboud University Nijmegen) is an extraordinary Professor of Patristics at the University of Pretoria. Among his most recent publications is *Mani and Augustine. Collected Essays on Mani, Manichaeism and Augustine*, Leiden-Boston: Brill 2020.

Nils Arne Pedersen
(Aarhus University, Denmark) is an associate professor of Church History. Among his most recent publications (as senior author) is *The New Testament Gospels in Manichaean Tradition: The Sources in Syriac, Greek, Coptic, Middle*

Persian, Parthian, Sogdian, Bactrian, New Persian, and Arabic, Turnhout: Brepols 2020.

Madeleine Scopello
FAHA, Correspondent of Institut de France (Académie des Inscriptions et Belles-Lettres), is em. Director of research at Centre National de la Recherche Scientifique (Paris) and em. Director of studies at École Pratique des Hautes Études (chair of Gnose et Manichéisme).

Michel Tardieu
is emeritus Professor at the Collège de France (Paris), Histoire des syncrétismes de la fin de l'Antiquité (1991–2008). He has published many books and papers on Gnosticism, Manichaeism, and Greek philosophy.

Aäron Vanspauwen
is a postdoctoral researcher (FWO—Research Foundation Flanders) at KU Leuven. His research focuses on the polemics between mainstream Christianity and Manichaeism in North Africa. Recent publication: *In Defence of Faith, Against the Manichaeans. Critical Edition and Historical, Literary and Theological Study of the Treatise* Aduersus Manichaeos, *Attributed to Evodius of Uzalis* (IPM 79), Turnhout: Brepols, 2020.

Chris L. de Wet
is Associate Professor of New Testament and Early Christian Studies at the University of South Africa, Pretoria. He has written two monographs, *Preaching Bondage: John Chrysostom and the Discourse of Slavery in Early Christianity* (California, 2015) and *The Unbound God: Slavery and the Formation of Early Christian Thought* (Routledge, 2018).

1

The Religious Innovator Tatian: A Precursor of Mani in Syrian Christianity?

Josef Lössl

Abstract

Tatian the Syrian, author of an *Oration to the Greeks* and the *Diatessaron*, who flourished in the second half of the second century (150–180+), has long been looked at in the context of the study of the early Christian sources of Manichaeism. In the past attempts were made to draw direct links between Tatian, early Syriac Christianity, and early Manichaeism. F.C. Burkitt, for example, suggested that the name "Tatian" might be the Greek version of the apostle "Addai", protagonist of the Syriac *Doctrine of Addai*, which H.J.W. Drijvers later proposed to be a Christian appropriation of a Manichaean tradition. Yet later, J.C. Reeves found many elements that occur in Tatian's *Oration* recurring in third-century Mesopotamian literature and thus feed into an emerging Manichaean tradition. This paper does not attempt to draw a direct link between Tatian's second century teaching and Mani's teaching but looks at some of Tatian's teachings as put forward in the *Oration*. It asks to what extent these show characteristics that may be found later in Mani's teaching. The focus will be on three areas: 1) Tatian's concept of Pneuma, the working of which Tatian seems to explain (in some places) in surprisingly materialistic terms; this will be compared with a Manichaean text; 2) Tatian's assumed "leanings" towards Encratism; and 3) in connection with (2), passages in the *Oration* that deal with issues related to women and gender. Overall, Tatian's original thinking in some of these areas is analysed with a view to the concept of "innovation" in late-antique religion.

Introduction: Innovation and Innovators in Ancient Religion

In relation to Mani and his teaching the question has recently been asked how scholars of ancient religions work with concepts such as innovation and invention in religion.[1] At what point will they recognize a religion as a "new" religion?

---

[1] See e.g. N. Baker-Brian, "A New Religion? The Emergence of Manichaeism in Late Antiquity,"

When is a religion a new religion in antiquity? *What* is a new religion in antiquity?[2] Mani (216–ca. 274) of course did found a new religion, consciously so; and he was confirmed by a tradition (even a Church) that lasted for centuries. In that respect he was in a sense a predecessor of Muhammad, another religious founder figure of late antiquity, in seventh century Arabia, who was even less coy about being an innovator than Mani was.[3]

But being innovative in religion is not necessarily the same as inventing, creating, or founding a (new) religion. Many small innovative steps were taken by many figures in the run-up to the momentous steps that Mani took during his life-time, or his followers took in his wake. One could think of a number of strong individual characters, figures with revolutionary ideas, highly innovative designs and impressive literary oeuvres, who found themselves nevertheless sidelined by the reception process, or who never thought of themselves as founder figures. In connection with that we need to consider the link between innovation and tradition.[4] Many great figures slotted into traditions, enriching them from inside, while others breached the traditions in which they were originally situated, whether intentionally or unintentionally, via reception processes, thus creating new traditions, sometimes superseding older ones.

---

in: J. Lössl and N. Baker-Brian (eds.) *A Companion to Religion in Late Antiquity* (Hoboken, NJ: Wiley, 2018), 318–343 at 337–340, who refers to A. Houtman a.o. (eds.), *Empsychoi Logoi. Religious Innovations in Antiquity. Studies in Honour of Pieter Willem van der Horst* (Leiden: Brill, 2008); A. DeConick, "The Countercultural Gnostic: Turning the World Upside Down and Inside Out," *Gnosis: Journal for Gnostic Studies* 1 (2016) 7–35; and J. BeDuhn, "Mani and the Crystallization of the Concept of Religion in Third Century Iran," in: I. Gardner a.o. (eds.), *Mani at the Court of the Persian Kings. Studies on the Chester Beatty* Kephalaia *Codex* (Leiden: Brill, 2015), 247–275.

2   Some altogether deny the existence of religions in antiquity, e.g. B. Nongbri, *Before Religion: A History of a Modern Concept* (New Haven, CT: Yale University Press), discussed in Baker-Brian, "A New Religion?" (n. 1), 321. In relation to Mani, Baker-Brian defends the use of the concept of "religion" to "characterize the totality of Mani's activities."

3   On this observation see e.g. G. Fowden, *Before and After Muhammad. The First Millennium Refocused* (Princeton: Princeton University Press, 2014), 188–190; A. Al-Azmeh, *The Emergence of Islam in Late Antiquity. Allah and His People* (Cambridge: Cambridge University Press, 2014), 360–402; and A. Al-Azmeh, "Paleo-Islam: Transfigurations of Late Antique Religion," in: Lössl and Baker-Brian (eds.), *Companion* (n. 1), 345–368 at 354–363. The crucial common external factor in the emergence and rise of the new religion in each case is its link with empire building (the Persian empire in Mani's, an Arab empire in Muhammad's case).

4   E.g. through a continuing issuing of prophecies and the reception of such prophecies through exegesis and the development of canonical scriptures, or the building of church structures, without or within wider and "harder" external political (e.g. imperial) structures. See for this G.G. Stroumsa, *The Making of the Abrahamic Religions in Late Antiquity* (Oxford: Oxford University Press, 2015); and *idem*, "The Scriptural 'Galaxy' of Late Antiquity," in: Lössl and Baker-Brian (eds.), *Companion* (n. 1), 553–570.

The usual approach in scholarship is to link figures within a tradition back to the beginnings of that tradition, while founder figures (and often also those close to them) tend to be more openly studied in both directions, in view of the tradition from which they emerged and in view of the tradition which they founded. For example, Jesus of Nazareth, Paul of Tarsus and indeed many known figures in first century Christianity are studied from both Jewish and early Christian perspectives, while second century Christian figures tend to be seen already much more firmly as representatives of an early Christian tradition.[5] This is certainly true of the second century apologists and among them in particular the figure with whom the present paper is concerned, Tatian, a pupil of Justin Martyr and author of an extant *Oration to the Greeks*.[6] The argument of this paper is that Tatian may be a figure who might be interesting in the present context, the study of Manichaeism and early Christianity, as (what has perhaps been formulated somewhat provocatively in the title) a 'precursor of Mani', a figure whose life and work anticipates in some respects Mani's and may contribute to a better understanding of the pre-history of Manichaeism in the late second and early third century.

Although Jesus, Christ, or Christianity are not mentioned once in Tatian's *Oration*, which is in fact his only extant work from which we can reconstruct his thought,[7] it is nevertheless firmly identified as an early Christian work, ironically; for it is also often seen (and was seen traditionally) as a source of some

---

5   Problems of this approach have been famously (and controversially) highlighted by Daniel Boyarin in *Border-Lines: The Partition of Judaeo-Christianity* (Philadelphia, PI: University of Pennsylvania Press, 2004), who argues that border-lines between Judaism and Christianity remain blurred well into the fourth century and sharp distinctions were mainly drawn by heresiologists with the intention to shape a Christian identity. For a nuanced approach based on second-century sources, which in some respects relativizes but in other respects also confirms Boyarin's observations, see T. Nicklas, *Jews and Christians? Second Century 'Christian' Perspectives on the 'Parting of the Ways'* (Tübingen: Mohr Siebeck, 2014).

6   See the new edition and translation with notes by H.-G. Nesselrath, *Gegen falsche Götter und falsche Bildung. Tatian, Rede an die Griechen* (Tübingen: Mohr Siebeck, 2016).

7   Tatian himself mentions several other works (besides *or.*) which he claims to have written or which he still planned to write, but none of them is extant. In *or.* 15.4 he refers to a work *On Animals* (περὶ ζώων), in *or.* 16.2 to several occasions or places (ἐν ἄλλοις) where he discussed questions concerning the human soul, in *or.* 40.4 he mentions a work entitled *To those who explained the matters pertaining to God* (πρὸς τοὺς ἀποφηναμένους τὰ περὶ θεοῦ). Perhaps half a generation after Tatian, Clement of Alexandria, *strom.* 3.81.1–2 cites from a work of Tatian's entitled *On perfection according to the saviour* (περὶ τοῦ κατὰ τὸν σωτῆρα καταρτισμοῦ). Eusebius, *h. e.* 5.13.8 reports that Tatian's pupil Rhodon knew of a work by his teacher entitled *Book of difficult questions* (προβλημάτων βιβλίον); *h. e.* 4.29.2 he cites Irenaeus, *haer.* 1.28.1, where the bishop of Lyons reports on a teaching of Tatian's which cannot be verified from his *Oration* and which may therefore have been contained in a different work; *h. e.* 4.16.7 he reports that Tatian left many memorable teachings in his writings; *h. e.* 4.29.6 he refers to

strongly heretical views, Gnostic and Encratic.[8] The proposal of the present paper is on the one hand to follow some of these strands of investigation, i.e. to what extent Tatian held Gnostic, Encratic, or other positions, and on the other to look at his thought in its own right, his individual, original creation, as it could potentially be the basis of a new religion. My findings might then serve as a basis for further investigation, e.g. in what way Tatian's thought in a sense anticipates (or bears at least some similarities to) some of the ideas which we find also emerge in Mani's work and in late-antique Manichaeism.[9]

To give just one example: In *Kephalaion* 331 in the recently published volume of the *Kephalaia Codex*,[10] Goundesh, Mani's Indian interlocutor, shows

---

Tatian as author of the influential *Diatessaron*, a Gospel Harmony that was still in use in the Syrian church during Eusebius' lifetime; for further details on Tatian's works see Nesselrath, *Gegen falsche Götter* (n. 6), 7–8; for the *Diatessaron* see W.L. Petersen, *Tatian's Diatessaron. Its Creation, Dissemination, Significance, and History in Scholarship* (Leiden: Brill, 1994), and, for recent developments in *Diatessaron* research, U.B. Schmid, "The Diatessaron of Tatian," in B.D. Ehrman and M.W. Holmes (eds.), *The Text of the New Testament in Contemporary Research. Essays on the Status Quaestionis. Second Edition* (Leiden: Brill, 2013), 115–142; M.R. Crawford, "The Diatessaron, Canonical or Non-canonical? Rereading the Dura Fragment," *NTS* 62 (2016), 253–277, and the contributions in M.R. Crawford and N.J. Zola (eds.), *The Gospel of Tatian: Exploring the Nature and Text of the Diatessaron* (London: Bloomsbury, 2019), in particular those by Crawford and Zola, T. Baarda, J. Joosten, N. Perrin and I.N. Mills.

8   For a discussion of such views as they allegedly occur in the *Oration* see E. Hunt, *Christianity in the Second Century. The Case of Tatian* (London: Routledge, 2003), 20–51 (for links to Valentinianism); J. Trelenberg, *Tatianos. Oratio ad Graecos. Rede an die Griechen* (Tübingen: Mohr Siebeck, 2012), 204–219. Trelenberg concludes that it is not the task of modern critical scholarship to defend Tatian against the early Christian charge of heresy. This began with Irenaeus, *haer.* 1.28.1 (reported by Eusebius, *h. e.* 4.29.2) and Clement of Alexandria, *strom.* 3.89.1. But neither Irenaeus' nor Clement's charges can be unequivocally verified from the extant text of the *Oration*. See for this emphatically N. Koltun-Fromm, "Re-Imagining Tatian: The Damaging Effects of Polemical Rhetoric," *JECS* 16 (2008) 1–30; and more recently M.R. Crawford, "The *Problemata* of Tatian: Recovering the Fragments of a Second-Century Christian Intellectual," *JTS* 67 (2016) 542–575.

9   Such lines have been drawn for some time. F.C. Burkitt, for example, even suggested that the name "Tatian" might be a Greek version of the apostle "Addai", protagonist of the Syriac *Doctrine of Addai*, which H.J.W. Drijvers later proposed to be a Christian appropriation of a Manichaean tradition; cf. F.C. Burkitt, "Syriac-Speaking Christianity," in *The Cambridge Ancient History, vol. 12: The Imperial Crisis and Recovery AD 193–324* (Cambridge: Cambridge University Press, 1939), 492–496; and already *idem*, "Tatian and the Dutch Harmonies," *JTS* 25 (1924) 113–130 at 130; and *idem*, *Early Eastern Christianity* (London: John Murray, 1904), 69; H.J.W. Drijvers, "The Abgar Legend," in W. Schneemelcher (ed.), New Testament Apocrypha 1: Gospels and Related Writings (Cambridge: James Clarke, 1990), 492–499, esp. 495; see also the reports in Hunt, *Christianity* (n. 8), 14–15 (with n. 50) and 144–145 (with n. 8).

10 I. Gardner, J. BeDuhn and P.C. Dilley (eds.), *The Kephalaia Codex. The Chapters of the*

the Apostle an egg and points out how smooth it is.[11] He asks how it should be possible for a sparrow's soul (ψυχή) to escape from it, should the sparrow die in it, since the egg has no openings.[12] Mani informs him that the egg is porous, like "these sponges" (σπόγγος), which are apparently also at hand. Only, in the case of the egg, Mani continues, the pores are too tiny for the human eye to see.[13] After the conversation has covered a few further points he adds that "the soul (ψυχή) is a spiritual thing (πνευματικόν) coming also out from inside this egg spiritually (πνευατικῶς)."[14] He then continues with a comparison. A person shouting aloud inside a house with all doors and windows shut can still be heard outside, because sound, too, is a spiritual thing (πνευματικόν) penetrating the walls through vibration. In the same way the sparrow's soul (ψυχή) comes out of the egg.[15]

Obviously, the "soul" (ψυχή) as a "spiritual thing" (πνευματικόν) is here understood in a materialistic sense. For Tatian, this could not have been the whole story. For him, "Pneuma that penetrates matter is inferior to the more divine Pneuma,"[16] which alone can guarantee the soul eternal life and bliss.[17] However, it could be part of the story. Tatian accepted that there was a material dimension to πνεῦμα and a transition from cruder to more refined areas of the

---

Wisdom of my Lord Mani. Part III: Pages 343–442 (Chapters 321–347) (Leiden: Brill, 2018); hereinafter the source text will be abbreviated as "*2 Ke*" (followed by number of chapter, page and line numbers of the codex, and page numbers of the edition in brackets); the title of the edition is abbreviated as "*GBD*".

11   *2 Ke* 331, 372.29–30 (*GBD* 64–65).
12   *2 Ke* 331, 373.1–3 (*GBD* 66–67).
13   *2 Ke* 331, 737.4–7 (*GBD* 66–67).
14   *2 Ke* 331, 737.28–29 (*GBD* 66–67).
15   *2 Ke* 331, 373.29–374.7 (*GBD* 66–69).
16   Tatian, *or.* 4.4: πνεῦμα γὰρ τὸν διὰ τῆς ὕλης διῆκον, ἔλαττον ὑπάρχον τοῦ θειοτέρου πνεύματος.
17   Cf. e.g. Tatian, *or.* 13.3–4: The soul (ψυχή), if it is connected with the divine Pneuma (πνεῦμα) as in a harness (συζυγία), rises up (ἀνέρχεται) to the places to which the Pneuma guides it, i.e. (probably) the "higher / mightier aeons" (αἰῶνες κρείττονες), which are filled with an inaccessible light (φέγγος, *or.* 20.4). From the beginning, the soul is in a symbiosis with the Pneuma: γέγονεν μὲν οὖν συνδίαιτον ἀρχῆθεν τῇ ψυχῇ τὸ πνεῦμα (*or.* 13.4). It squanders it by refusing to follow the Pneuma's lead (ἕπεσθαι μὴ βουλομένην αὐτῷ) upon which the Pneuma abandons it (ταύτην ... καταλέλοιπεν). However, it retains a "spark" (ἔναυσμα) of the Pneuma's power, which still enables it to follow the "many gods" (πολλοὺς θεούς) and the "demons" (δαίμοσι). But these behave towards it in sophisticated and deceptive ways (ἀντισοφιστεύουσι δαίμοσι). Most of humanity is reduced to this fate. Only to a few, who live just lives (δικαίως πολιτευμένοις), the Pneuma will return, reconnect them with the soul (συμπεριπλεκόμενον) and announce (ἀνήγγειλε) to the remaining souls through prophetic proclamations (διὰ προαγορεύσεων) that which is hidden (τὸ κεκρυμμένον, *or.* 13.5). Tatian seems to have seen himself in the latter role when he referred to himself at one point as "herald of the truth" (κῆρυξ τῆς ἀληθείας, *or.* 17.2).

universe. For example, on one occasion he tries to explain what happens when one person speaks and others listen: As the sound carries the rational arguments formed in the speaker's mind from the mouth to the ears of the listeners, and as they penetrate the latters' hearing, they also affect their thinking.[18]

The latter example bears at least some similarities with Mani's parable of the person shouting from inside a shut building in *Kephalaion* 331, while overall, too, Tatian's thinking about concepts such a ψυχή and πνεῦμα may be worth looking at in view of later developments in the history of religion including the emergence of Manichaeism.

In what follows Tatian's "pneumatology" will therefore be of special interest. Other foci will be on his apparent encratic leanings (if not outright Encratism) and his gnostic tendencies (or Gnosis). His self-professed (indeed loudly protested) Syrian identity, too, will be of interest, not least in view of the impact of his teaching in third-century Syrian Christianity. However, the intention of the paper is not to draw direct lines from Tatian to Mani or to Manichaean sources but to explore more widely aspects of the pre-history of Manichaeism in the work of and reports on a late second century apologist, who was (although writing in Greek) a self-professed Syrian Christian author and whose teaching was not only identified (by "western" ecclesiastical authors starting from Irenaeus and Clement of Alexandria) as Encratic and Gnostic (and therefore heretical), but seems to have had a strong impact in third-century Syrian Christianity, too.

Beyond that, what will hopefully also emerge from this exploration, is that Tatian was an original and innovative religious author and practitioner, who although being in many respects a marginal figure is nevertheless worth investigating—especially in the present context—in his own right.

1 The Syrian

Tatian (ca. 120–180+)[19] is one of the earliest known Syrian Christian authors. He has been included before in line-ups of early Syrian Christian writers (and authors writing in Syriac), who are sometimes considered in connection with

---

18 Cf. Tatian, *or.* 5.5: καὶ γὰρ αὐτὸς ἐγὼ λαλῶ, καὶ ὑμεῖς ἀκούετε, καὶ … διὰ τῆς μεταβάσεως τοῦ λόγου … προβαλλόμενος … τὴν ἐμαυτοῦ φωνὴν διακοσμεῖν τὴν ἐν ὑμῖν ἀκόσμητον ὕλην προῄρημαι.—"For I am speaking now and you are listening and through the transmission of my speech, as I project my voice, I intend to order in you the yet unordered matter."

19 For the dating see J. Lössl, "Date and Location of Tatian's *Ad Graecos*: Some Old and New Thoughts," *Studia Patristica* 74 (2016), 43–56; see also Nesselrath, *Gegen falsche Götter* (n. 6), 4–7.

the intellectual and religious background of Mani, in particular Bardaisan (154–222).[20] But regard for him is usually not very high. In a recent account on Greek influences on the literary culture of Roman Syria William Adler has reiterated some of these stereotypes: Tatian's anger against and hate of everything Greek; his apparent disappointment with Greek culture, perhaps due to lack of success as a sophist in Rome; his Syrian nativism and advocacy of barbarian philosophy, despite his continued use of Greek and exuberant display of knowledge of Greek myth, art, literature and philosophy.[21] Tatian's extant work, moreover, is meagre compared, for example, to that of Bardaisan—a mere 42 chapters, less than fifty pages in modern print editions—and it apparently lacks coherence, though this latter point is disputed.[22] As already mentioned, from his lifetime onwards (beginning with Irenaeus and Clement of Alexandria)[23] it was seen by some as contaminated by Gnosis. Others found in it Encratism. Generally, it is not easy to fit into an emerging "proto-orthodox" tradition unlike, for example, Justin Martyr, Athenagoras, or Theophilus of Antioch.

Tatian refers to himself as a native of the "land of the Assyrians" (γεννηθεὶς μὲν ἐν τῇ τῶν Ἀσσυρίων γῇ, *or.* 42.1). For the likely time of his birth, ca. 120 CE,[24] this

20   See e.g. J.C. Reeves, *Heralds of that Good Realm: Syro-Mesopotamian Gnosis and Jewish Traditions* (Leiden: Brill, 1996), on Tatian's self-reference in *or.* 17.2 as "herald of the truth" (similar to a widespread *topos* in third-century Syriac Christian literature); discussed in J. Lössl, "Hermeneutics and Doctrine of God in Tatian's *Ad Graecos*," Studia Patristica 45 (2010), 409–412; or now also I. Ramelli, *Bardaisan of Edessa: A Reassessment of the Evidence and New Interpretation* (Piscataway, NJ: Gorgias Press, 2009) and A. Bellettato, *Greek and Syriac in Dialogue: Identity Construction in Tatian's* Oratio ad Graecos *and in the Bardesanite* Liber Regum Regionum (PhD, University of Padua, 2019).

21   For details see W. Adler, "The Creation of Christian Elite Culture in Roman Syria and the Near East," in: D.S. Richter and W.A. Johnson (eds.), *The Oxford Handbook of the Second Sophistic* (Oxford: Oxford University Press, 2017), 899–917 at 900. For Tatian's "barbarism" see also S.E. Antonova, *Barbarian or Greek? The Charge of Barbarism and Early Christian Apologetics* (Leiden: Brill, 2019), 146–162.

22   For a discussion see Nesselrath, *Gegen falsche Götter* (n. 6), 9–14.

23   See above n. 8.

24   This approximate date is justified by several pieces of evidence. Irenaeus, *haer.* 1.28.1 (*apud* Eusebius, *h. e.* 4.29.2–3) relates that Tatian was a follower (literally "hearer," ἀκροατής) of Justin Martyr in Rome, who became a heretic after Justin's death (in 165). Epiphanius, *pan.* 1.46.1.7–8 adds that not long after he was excluded from the Roman church, left for the east (Syria [Antioch/Daphne], Cilicia, and Pisidia) and after some wandering around founded a school in Mesopotamia. Jerome's chronicle (p. 206 Helm) dates Tatian's expulsion from Rome in the year 172. Tatian himself states *or.* 1.4, 42.1, 35.1 that after training as a sophist and wandering the earth (πολλὴν ἐπιφοιτήσας γῆν) he came to Rome. If we allow some years give or take, he would have been in his 20s when he arrived in Rome (between 140 and 150), in his 40s around Justin's death, and in his 50s when he left Rome and went back to the East.

does not mean "beyond the Euphrates," let alone "outside the Roman Empire".[25] Lucian of Samosata, a contemporary of Tatian's, too, calls himself an Assyrian,[26] and Samosata was definitely a city on the western banks of the Euphrates and well within the Roman Empire. But like Lucian, Tatian makes much of his Syrian origins and his origin from the geographical and cultural margins of the Graeco-Roman world. He repeatedly says that he excelled in Greek *Paideia*, Sophistic, and Philosophy,[27] but his obsession with the Greek language including correct pronunciation suggests that Greek may not have been his first language and he may have spoken it with a foreign ("barbarian") accent.[28] By the time he writes the *Oration* he distances himself from his "Greek" achievements. They are "yours," the Greeks, he writes, i.e. not mine, the Syrian's.[29]

At one level this antagonism can be explained by way of Tatian's conversion to what is obviously Christianity. One could argue that "Greek" in the *Oration* stands for pagan, "Barbarian" for Christian. But things are more complicated. It is significant, as has already been mentioned, that Tatian does not explicitly

---

25   In this regard I follow Nesselrath, *Gegen falsche Götter* (n. 6), 5 against Trelenberg, *Tatianos* (n. 8), 1 and other earlier scholarship, notably M. Whittaker, *Tatian. Oratio ad Graecos and Fragments* (Oxford: Clarendon, 1982), ix.

26   See Lucian, *Dea Syr.* 1: γράφω δὲ Ἀσσύριος ἐών. In Lucian, *Bis. Acc.* 27 personified rhetoric reports that she first met young Lucian in Ionia, when he was still wearing a *kandys* the Assyrian way (κάνδυν ἐνδεδυκότα εἰς τὸν Ἀσσύριον τρόπον). Lucian, *Pisc.* 19 and *Hist. Conscr.* 24 relate that Samosata was Lucian's home town.

27   See Tatian, *or.* 42.1: "I was first educated in *your* [i. e. Greek] Paideia (παιδευθεὶς δὲ πρῶτον μὲν τὰ ὑμέτερα);" 1.5: "I rejected *your* [i. e. Greek] wisdom, even though I once excelled in it (τούτου χάριν ἀπεταξάμεθα τῇ παρ᾽ ὑμῖν σοφίᾳ κἂν εἰ πάνυ σεμνός τις ἦν ἐν αὐτῇ);" 35.1: "... after I acquired *your* Sophistic arts (σοφιστεύσας τὰ ὑμέτερα)."

28   Tatian, *or.* 1.4 attacks the existence of entrenched dialects in classical Greek (Koine Greek was not acceptable among the educated): there is no harmony (ὁμοφωνία) among the Greeks when they speak with each other. Dorian, Attic, Aeolian and Ionian Greek are very different from each other. But worse still, it is the height of fashion among Greeks to spike their speeches with barbarian phrases (or accents), and these are often used wrongly, which makes the confusion perfect: βαρβαρικαῖς τε φωναῖς ἔσθ᾽ ὅτε καταχρώμενοι συμφύρδην ὑμῶν πεποιήκατε τὴν διάλεκτον. In *or.* 26.1 he seems to condemn this latter practice as a form of cultural appropriation: "Stop parading foreign expressions ... One day, when each city demands its own speech back, your sophistries will become untenable (παύσασθε λόγους ἀλλοτρίους θριαμβεύοντες ... ἑκάστη πόλις ἐὰν ἀφέληται τὴν ἰδίαν αὐτῆς ἀφ᾽ ὑμῶν λέξιν, ἐξαδυνατήσουσιν ὑμῖν τὰ σοφίσματα)." The plight of Sophists speaking with foreign accents (e.g. when speaking in front of native audiences in Rome) is also addressed by Lucian, e.g. *merc. cond.* 24 (βαρβαρίζειν); also ibid. 10 (κακῶς συρίζειν, though this reference is to a Syrian doorkeeper, not a Sophist); further references and discussion in L. Nasrallah, *Christian Responses to Roman Art and Architecture. The Second-Century Church Amid the Spaces of Empire* (Cambridge: Cambridge University Press, 2010), 63–64.

29   See above n. 27.

refer to Christianity or, for that matter, to anything Christian. Christian "jargon" (e.g. references to Christ, church, apostles, prophets, scriptures etc.) hardly occurs in the *Oration*.[30] Instead Tatian refers to his new-found way of life as "barbarian philosophy" and a "law-based barbarian way of life."[31] This suggests that it would be wrong to interpret Tatian's use of the barbarian motif purely as a metaphor for a religious conversion. The antagonism addressed in the *Oration* is not just one of religious faith—"barbarian" is not just code for "Christian"— it is also cultural, even in a nativist sense:[32] Tatian the Assyrian has found a way of life for himself emerging right from the culture of his birth.

It is also geographical. Tatian makes much of the fact that after he was trained in the foreign wisdom[33] he had to "travel the earth,"[34] and not just geographically. His journey was also a formative one. He claims that he personally witnessed all manner of strange phenomena (e.g. the practice of human sacrifice in certain pagan cults) and got initiated in mystery cults.[35] Against the background of the concept of *Paideia* that was dominant in the culture of the Second Sophistic, this description of an educational journey is of course

---

30 What does occur, e.g. passages on the λόγος, as in *or*. 5.1, had later (probably in the fourth century) to be amended to fit better with orthodox doctrine, other expressions, e.g. a reference to the Logos as ἔργον of the Father in *or*. 5.2, proved problematic and cause "irritation" to scholars even today because of their unorthodox, potentially heretical, nature; see Trelenberg, *Tatianos* (n. 8), 34–40 at 37.

31 For the theme of "barbarism" generally see Antonova, *Barbarian or Greek?* (n. 21), 146–162. For a first explicit mentioning of "barbarian philosophy" and "barbarian wisdom" see *or*. 31.1; but see already 12.10 a reference to a law-based barbarian way of life (βαρβαρικῇ νομοθεσίᾳ), with which Tatian identifies.

32 This is why Richard Kukula's otherwise ingenious translation of "Greeks" (ἄνδρες Ἕλληνες, *or*. 1.1, 4.1, 12.6 and frequently) with "Bekenner des Griechentums" ("people who profess Greek culture") does not quite work. For Tatian, to be a true barbarian and adherent of a barbarian philosophical way of life is not just a matter of conversion and confession but also of descent; cf. R.C. Kukula, "Tatians des Assyrers Rede an die Bekenner des Griechentums," in: *Frühchristliche Apologeten und Märtyrerakten aus dem Griechischen und Lateinischen übersetzt*, 1. Bd. (BKV 12; Munich and Kempten: Kösel, 1913).

33 Tatian, *or*. 42.1: παιδευθεὶς πρῶτον τὰ ὑμέτερα.

34 Tatian, *or*. 35.1: πολλὴν ἐπιφοιτήσας γῆν.

35 Tatian, *or*. 29.1: "After I had seen all these things, took part in mystery cults (μυστηρίων μεταλαβών), assessed worship (θρησκεία), occurring everywhere, that is conducted by effeminate and androgynous priests, and witnessed among the Romans that Iuppiter Latiaris takes delight in human blood and in the bloodshed that results from the killing of humans, and that Artemis, not far from the great city, elevated the same practices to become her cult ..." For the credibility in particular of witnessing practices of human sacrifice in the second century see Nesselrath, *Gegen falsche Götter* (n. 6), 165 n. 445, and, specifically on the cult of Iuppiter Latiaris on Mons Albanus, I. Gradel, "Jupiter Latiaris and Human Blood: Fact or Fiction?" *Classica et Mediaevalia* 53 (2002), 235–253.

a trope.³⁶ Not every detail that Tatian relates about his journey is credible. But given that he came from a marginal region in the Roman empire and is reported to have travelled from there all the way to Rome and back again³⁷—and that in the course of this journey he found the religious tradition which, as it turned out, had been, so to speak, "his" all along, from his birth—his wanderings are an essential part of his identity.

Tatian identifies himself as an Assyrian, descendant of an ancient barbarian culture, which he has found again for himself through his discovery of the "barbarian scriptures" (*or.* 29.2), i.e. the Bible, after a long journey, and which he now intends to demonstrate in his *Oration* to be the one true, oldest and most eminent cultural (including religious) tradition.³⁸ With this enterprise he also questions Roman imperial claims. In *or.* 4.2 he states that he accepts his status as a subject of the Roman emperor (δουλείαν γινώσκω) but then immediately qualifies his statement: human beings ought to be honoured in a human way, only God ought to be feared.³⁹ Again, these are motifs which are known from other early Christian sources,⁴⁰ but with Tatian's project of a Syrian Christianity they take on a new quality. The area to which Tatian will eventually be returning, was forever contested between Rome and Persia. As a loyal subject of the Roman emperor he could easily find himself one day forced to flee a Persian invasion, stay and become a Persian subject, or flee Roman persecution and escape across to Persia.

The source of Tatian's new-found barbarian wisdom, by the way, is none other than Tatian himself, and he alone. After recounting his world-wide travels and encounters of various religions he states: "Then I turned inwards, to myself (κατ' ἐμαυτὸν γενόμενος), and sought (ἐζήτουν) how I could find the truth; and as I pondered (περινοοῦντι) these serious questions, I chanced upon (συνέβη ἐντυχεῖν) certain barbarian writings …"⁴¹ No mention here of the influence

---

36   However, this does not mean that religious travel was not extensively practised in the age of the Second Sophistic; see e.g. I.C. Rutherford, "Pilgrimage," in: Richter and Johnson (eds.), *Handbook of the Second Sophistic* (n. 21), 841–857.
37   For details see above n. 24.
38   Notably, his first mentioning of the word "barbarian philosophy/wisdom" *or.* 31.1 occurs at the outset of his chronological "proof" of the superior antiquity of this culture; see for this aspect also M. Wallraff, "The Beginnings of Christian Universal History. From Tatian to Julius Africanus." *ZAC* 14 (2011), 540–555; and Adler, "The Creation" (n. 21), 901–903.
39   Tatian, *or.* 4.2: τὸν μὲν γὰρ ἄνθρωπον ἀνθρωπίνως τιμητέον, φοβητέον δὲ μόνον τὸν θεόν. Cf. 1 Peter 2:17: τὸν θεὸν φοβεῖσθε.
40   See e.g. Matthew 22:15–22; Mark 12:13–17; Luke 20:20–26; Romans 13:6–7; Justin, *1Apol.* 17.1–2; cf. Trelenberg, Tatianos (n. 8), 93 n. 44.
41   Tatian, *or.* 29.1–2.

of a teacher, despite evidence that Tatian was a pupil of Justin Martyr and himself a teacher while in Rome.[42] For his Syrian project these links are broken. Something new is beckoning, and Tatian himself is its only author.

As was mentioned earlier (above n. 23), after leaving Rome in 172,[43] or having been expelled from there as a heretic, Tatian went to the east, to "Mesopotamia" according to Epiphanius,[44] but more probably to Antioch in the first instance to spread his teaching there and in the surrounding areas.[45] The case has been made to consider the *Oration*, so to speak, as a "taster" or "descriptor" of his teaching programme.[46] If Epiphanius can be trusted in principle and Tatian founded a school in Mesopotamia at some point in time, it is not impossible that a Syriac version of his teaching too emerged at some point. This is also suggested by the attested influence of the *Diatessaron* in the Syrian church down to the fifth century and the persistence of a Syriac version of the *Diatessaron* even after that period.[47]

---

42 Tatian himself acknowledges Justin in *or.* 19.2 where he writes that the Cynic Crescens tried to have them both killed (probably by denouncing them to the authorities as Christians). I follow here the text of Nesselrath, *Gegen falsche Götter* (n. 6), 74 and n. 304: οὕτως αὐτὸς [= Κρίσκης] ἐδεδίει τὸν θάνατον ὡς καὶ Ἰουστῖνον καθάπερ καὶ ἐμέ ... Irenaeus, *haer*. 1.28.1 refers to Tatian as a "hearer" of Justin. There is strong evidence that Tatian in his *Oration* used Justin's works as a source; cf. Trelenberg, *Tatianos* (n. 8), 195–203. In turn, Eusebius, *h. e.* 5.13.1/8 knows of a pupil of Tatian's called Rhodon (probably in Rome), who later distanced himself from his teacher; see P. Lampe, *From Paul to Valentinus. Christians at Rome in the First Two Centuries* (Minneapolis: Fortress Press, 2003), 285–291.

43 Eusebius/Jerome, *chron. an.* 172 (204.7; 206.13 Helm): *Romanorum xiiii regnavit Marcus Antoninus qui et Verus, et Lucius Aurelius Commodus ann. Xviiii et mens i. ... an. xii* [= 172] *Tatianus haereticus agnoscitur*; Epiphanius, *pan.* 1.46.7: ἀπὸ Ῥώμης γὰρ μετὰ τὴν τοῦ ἁγίου Ἰουστίνου τελείων διελθὼν ἐπὶ τὰ τῆς ἀνατολῆς μέρη καὶ ἐκεῖσε διατρίβων. See also the following two footnotes. Epiphanius suggests that Tatian was first expelled from Rome, then went to "the East" and wandered about there, establishing "first" a school in Mesopotamia and then spreading his teaching in Antioch and its wider vicinity towards the west (Cilicia and Pisidia). The reverse order is more likely: first Antioch and the western areas, then, if at all, Mesopotamia.

44 Cf. Epiphanius, *pan.* 1.46.6: τὸ δὲ αὐτοῦ διδασκαλεῖον προεστήσατο ἀπ᾽ ἀρχῆς μὲν ἐν τῇ Μέσῃ τῶν ποταμῶν.

45 Cf. Epiphanius, *pan.* 1.46.8: τὸ δὲ πλεῖστον τοῦ αὐτοῦ κηρύγματος ἀπὸ Ἀντιοχείας τῆς πρὸς Δάφνην καὶ ἐπὶ τὰ τῶν Κιλίκων μέρη, ἐπὶ πλεῖον δὲ ἐν τῇ Πισιδίᾳ ἐκράτυνεν. A journey from Rome to Antioch, by boat (via Alexandria), is also more plausible in historical terms; cf. Lössl, "Date" (n. 19), 53.

46 Cf. Kukula, "Tatians Rede" (n. 32), 192; see also J. Lössl, "Zwischen Christologie und Rhetorik—zum Ausdruck 'Kraft des Wortes' (λόγου δύναμις) in Tatians 'Rede an die Griechen,'" in: F.R. Prostmeier & H.E. Lona (eds.), *Logos der Vernunft—Logos des Glaubens*. FS Edgar Früchtel (Berlin & New York: De Gruyter, 2010), 129–148 at 131.

47 For references see above n. 7.

But no matter whether Tatian really emerged as a founder figure of an early Syrian, or even Syriac, theological tradition or not, there is evidence in his *Oration* that this is how he might have liked to present himself, and there is evidence in the early reception of his work (which included not just the *Oration* and was therefore broader than what is accessible today) that this is how others (Irenaeus, Clement of Alexandria, Tertullian, [Pseudo-]Hippolytus, Epiphanius, Theodoret and, later, Theodore bar Koni or Agapius of Hierapolis)[48] saw him too, though not necessarily always in a positive light.[49]

2   The Encratite

The earliest author accusing Tatian of heresy is Irenaeus.[50] As mentioned earlier, the heresiological accounts (assuming that they are *bona fide* reports of Tatian's views at all) seem to be based on sources other than the *Oration*.[51] They cannot be corroborated from the *Oration*. But whether true or not, they are reflections of Tatian's reputation as an original, innovative and influential religious thinker, a leading Encratite and Gnostic of the late second century.[52] This also confirms what was said in the first section about Tatian's potential role as a religious innovator and in the second section about his self-stylisation as a pioneering, foundational Syrian ecclesiastical author.

Irenaeus' report does not yet fully reflect this reputation.[53] Irenaeus in fact initiates another tradition regarding Tatian, namely of belittling him and presenting as a secondary figure. Irenaeus' entire report reads as follows:

---

48   For numerous references see Trelenberg, *Tatianos* (n. 8), 218 n. 109; and A.M. Ritter, "Spuren Tatians und seiner *Oratio ad Graecos* in der christlichen Literatur der Spätantike," in: Nesselrath, *Gegen falsche Götter* (n. 6), 287–303.

49   As Trelenberg, *Tatianos* (n. 8), 218 n. 109, following Hunt, *Christianity* (n. 8), 154, observes, Tatian tended to be considered a heretic in the "West" (i. e. in the orthodox Latin and Greek world) but not in the (Syriac) East, where gnostic and encratic views remained mainstream for longer. In the Syriac churches he was known as "the Greek" (cf. Theodore bar Koni in his *liber scholiorum* dating from 791). The first eastern author referring to him as a heretic was Agapius of Hierapolis, *Kītab al-ʿUnwan* (ca. 942).

50   Irenaeus, *haer.* 1.28.1; cited by Eusebius, *h. e.* 4.29.2–3.

51   See above n. 8.

52   On the basis of Irenaeus' account this reputation grew massively; by the fourth century Tatian was not merely seen as a heretic but as a "heresiarch"; see Jerome, *in Amos* 2.12: *T. Encratitarum princeps*; *in ep. ad Tit. praef.*: *T. Encratitarum patriarches*; *in ep. ad Gal.* 6.8: *T. Encratitarum acerrimus haeresiarches*; for further references see Trelenberg, *Tatianos* (n. 8), 7 n. 38.

53   Importantly, Irenaeus does not yet see Tatian as the founder of the Encratites (cf. above

The so-called Encratites take their beginning from Saturninus and Marcion. They proclaim the non-married life. Thus, they reject what was originally formed by God and obliquely accuse Him who created man and woman for the procreation of men. They also introduced abstinence from things which they believe possess a soul. This is ungrateful against God, who created everything. They also deny that he who was created first [i.e. Adam] is saved. This has come up among them only very recently. It was a certain Tatian who first introduced this blasphemy. He was a hearer of Justin and never expressed such a view while he was still with the latter. But after Justin's death as a martyr he apostasised from the church. Believing in his presumption to be a teacher in his own right he became proud and self-important, as if he was superior to the rest. He developed a teaching with its own unique character. He mythologized regarding certain invisible *aeons* similar to those postulated by Valentinus; and very much like Marcion and Saturninus he rejected marriage as rape and prostitution and denied Adam's salvation, though the latter was his own idea.[54]

Tatian's characterisation in this report is ambivalent. He is secondary to Saturninus, Marcion and Valentinus. As a hearer (ἀκροατής) of Justin he did not develop a profile of his own during the latter's lifetime but remained meekly within the church's fold. But after Justin's death there was a radical change. For Irenaeus these events lay only ca. ten years in the past, at most,[55] while the impact of Tatian's new teaching is "now" (νῦν). Tatian in his view is a con-

---

n. 52 and below n. 54). It is Eusebius, *h. e.* 4.28–29, who first reports that Encratism only emerged in Tatian's time and that Tatian himself is said to have been its founder: ἧς παρεκτροπῆς ἀρχηγὸν καταστῆναι Τατιανὸν λόγος ἔχει. Jerome in his judgement (n. 52) probably follows Eusebius.

54 Irenaeus, *haer.* 1.28.1: ἀπὸ Σατορνίνου καὶ Μαρκίωνος οἱ καλούμενοι Ἐγκρατεῖς ἀγαμίαν ἐκήρυξαν, ἀθετοῦντες τὴν ἀρχαίαν πλάσιν τοῦ θεοῦ καὶ ἠρέμα κατηγοροῦντες τοῦ ἄρρεν καὶ θῆλυ εἰς γένεσιν ἀνθρώπων πεποιηκότος, καὶ τῶν λεγομένων παρ' αὐτοῖς ἐμψύχων ἀποχὴν εἰσηγήσαντο, ἀχαριστοῦντες τῷ πάντα πεποιηκότι θεῷ. ἀντιλέγουσί τε τῇ τοῦ πρωτοπλάστου σωτηρίᾳ, καὶ τοῦτο νῦν ἐξευρέθη παρ' αὐτοῖς, Τατιανοῦ τινος πρώτως ταύτην εἰσενέγκαντος τὴν βλασφημίαν. ὃς Ἰουστίνου ἀκροατὴς γεγονώς, ἐφ' ὅσον μὲν συνῆν ἐκείνῳ, οὐδὲν ἐξέφηνεν τοιοῦτον· μετὰ δὲ τὴν ἐκείνου μαρτυρίαν ἀποστὰς τῆς ἐκκλησίας, οἰήματι διδασκάλου ἐπαρθεὶς καὶ τυφωθεὶς ὡς διαφέρων τῶν λοιπῶν, ἴδιον χαρακτῆρα διδασκαλείου συνεστήσατο. Αἰῶνάς τινας ἀοράτους ὁμοίως τοῖς ἀπὸ Οὐαλεντίνου μυθολογήσας, γάμον τε φθορὰν καὶ πορνείαν παραπλησίως Μαρκίωνι καὶ Σατορνίνῳ ἀναγορεύσας, τῇ δὲ τοῦ Ἀδὰμ σωτηρίᾳ παρ' ἑαυτοῦ τὴν ἀντιλογίαν ποιησάμενος.

55 See above nn. 43–45 for the complementary reports by Eusebius and Epiphanius. Irenaeus wrote *haer.* in the early 180s.

temporary upstart with far too high an opinion of himself.[56] Unsuitable as a teacher he was quickly jettisoned from the Roman church. But this is only half the story. For Irenaeus acknowledges at the same time that Tatian was in fact capable of producing a body of teaching with its own unique, original, characteristics (ἴδιον χαρακτήρ διδασκαλείου). Irenaeus probably did not mean this as a compliment. What Tatian taught was blasphemy (βλασφημία) in his opinion. But he had to admit: Tatian was a religious innovator with a momentous impact.

The teaching that Adam was beyond salvation (ἀντιλέγουσί τε τῇ τοῦ πρωτοπλάστου σωτηρίᾳ) constituted a radicalisation and dogmatisation of Encratite teaching. Irenaeus, who discussed it once more in Book 3 of *Adversus haereses*,[57] rightly recognised that it was undermining the doctrine of creation, in particular regarding man (cf. Genesis 1:26–28), pushing harder towards a more radical dualism. That Tatian should have denied the doctrine of creation is inconsistent with certain passages in the *Oration*, where Tatian, as one of the first Christian authors ever, edges towards formulating a theory of *creatio ex nihilo*,[58] and it is also difficult, if not impossible, to corroborate from the *Ora-*

---

56 In his pride, thus Irenaeus, Tatian thought of himself as different (i. e. superior) to the rest, ἐπαρθεὶς καὶ τυφωθεὶς ὡς διαφέρων τῶν λοιπῶν. Does "the others" here refer to Justin's other pupils, several of whom are possibly known by name? If one assumes (as not everyone does) that the *Acts of Justin Martyr* provide historical evidence for the martyrdom of Justin (and indeed of some of his pupils, of whom six are named, including a woman named Charito; cf. *Acta Iust.* 4.2 rec. A and B; the names of the others are Euelpistos, Chariton, Hierax, Paion and Liberianus), it is interesting that Tatian's name is missing from that list. For further details see Lampe, *From Paul to Valentinus* (n. 42), 276–278.

57 Irenaeus, *haer.* 3.23.8 refers to the teaching mainly as mendacious. He calls Tatian a liar (*mendax*) for introducing it. In his view it distorts the biblical evidence which overwhelmingly points to Adam's (and humanity's) salvation. For Irenaeus this is central because in *haer.* 3—with the help of countless biblical references—he develops a Pauline Adam-Christ soteriology. Tatian's teaching, which, as Irenaeus has to admit, is also based on Pauline exegesis (e.g. 1Corinthians 15:22: "in Adam we all die" [Irenaeus uses the first person]), is not compatible with this. Its foundations are different. For Tatian, it seems, following Irenaeus' interpretation, Adam's death (and the death of all those "in Adam") means their irredeemable eternal damnation. There is an unbridgeable gap between the damned and the saved. Tatian's outlook is, according to this interpretation, strictly dualistic. Because of the compelling nature and the impact of his systematic teaching particularly on the damnation of Adam and its soteriological implications, Irenaeus refers to Tatian as the "link between all heretics," *connexio ... omnium haereticorum*.

58 See e.g. Tatian, *or.* 5.6–7: ... οὔτε γὰρ ἄναρχος ἡ ὕλη καθάπερ καὶ ὁ θεός, οὔτε διὰ τὸ ἄναρχον καὶ αὐτὴ ἰσοδύναμος τῷ θεῷ, γενητὴ δὲ καὶ οὐχ ὑπὸ τοῦ ἄλλου γεγονυῖα, μόνου δὲ ὑπὸ τοῦ πάντων δημιουργοῦ προβεβλημένη.—"For neither is matter without beginning as God is, nor is it because of its being without beginning of equal power with God, but it 'became' [scil. originated] at some point, and it was created by none other than He who brought it forth

tion, as Naomi Koltun-Fromm has convincingly shown.[59] However, it is possible that Tatian formulated such views (as are attributed to him by Irenaeus) in other works, which are no longer extant. That this is not necessarily idle speculation is suggested by another ancient testimony. In *Stromateis* 3.12.80–81 Clement of Alexandria writes as follows:

> ... One ought not to assume ... that the tying of wife to husband is understood [in 1 Corinthians 7:39] as an entanglement of the flesh with corruption ... I believe that Tatian the Syrian dared to formulate such a doctrine. For he writes in his work *On Perfection According to the Saviour*, and I quote: 'Agreement [on abstinence from sexual intercourse in marriage] facilitates prayer [cf. 1 Corinthians 7:5], while being united in corruption corrodes prayerful behaviour. Thus, [Paul, in 1 Corinthians 7:6], by issuing a concession, is most insistently advising against [sexual intercourse]. For by conceding that [husband and wife] may come together again [i.e. after a period of abstinence] "because of Satan and lack of self-control" [1 Corinthians 7:5] he made it clear that those who follow [this concession] are wishing "to serve two masters" [Matthew 6:24], namely through the agreement God and through the disagreement lack of self-control, fornication and the Devil.'[60]

This passage dates ca. twenty, perhaps thirty years after Irenaeus' and thirty, perhaps forty years after Tatian's *Oration*.[61] Interestingly, while Irenaeus still referred to Tatian as "a certain Tatian", Clement is already using the expression "Tatian the Syrian", as if Tatian, as a Syrian writer, had now become a known quantity. The context of Clement's comments is a discussion of Paul's

---

as the creator of all." For details G. May, *Creatio ex nihilo: The Doctrine of 'Creation out of Nothing' in Early Christian Thought* (London: SPCK, 2004), 119.150–155.

59 Koltun-Fromm, "Re-Imagining Tatian" (n. 8), especially 3, 5, 9, 13 (on Tatian's Encratism).

60 Clement of Alexandria, *strom*. 3.12.80 f.: ... οὐ γὰρ ... δέσιν γυναικὸς πρὸς ἄνδρα τὴν σαρκὸς πρὸς τὴν φθορὰν ἐπιπλοκὴν μηνύεσθαι ὑποτοπητέον ... Τατιανὸν οἶμαι τὸν Σύρον τὰ τοιαῦτα τολμᾶν δογματίζειν. Γράφει γοῦν κατὰ λέξιν ἐν τῷ Περὶ τοῦ κατὰ τὸν Σωτῆρα καταρτισμοῦ· "συμφωνίαν μὲν οὖν ἁρμόζει προσευχῇ, κοινωνία δὲ φθορᾶς λύει τὴν ἔντευξιν. πάνυ γοῦν δυσωπητικῶς διὰ τῆς συγχωρήσεως εἴργει· πάλιν γὰρ ἐπὶ ταὐτὸ συγχωρήσας γενέσθαι διὰ τὸν σατανᾶν καὶ τὴν ἀκρασίαν, τὸν πεισθησόμενον δυσὶ κυρίοις μέλλειν δουλεύειν ἀπεφήνατο, διὰ μὲν συμφωνίας θεῷ, διὰ δὲ τῆς ἀσυμφωνίας ἀκρασίᾳ καὶ πορνείᾳ καὶ διαβόλῳ" ... The passage can also be found as Tatian, fragment 5, in Whittaker, *Tatian* (n. 25), 78–81.

61 For the date of Clement's *Stromateis* see E. Osborn, *Clement of Alexandria* (Cambridge: Cambridge University Press, 2005), 5–15. Osborn's conclusions are based on the assumptions that Clement lived from ca. 150 to 215 and that the *Stromateis* were a late work, based on Clement's mature teaching.

teaching on marriage and sexual abstinence in 1 Corinthians 7. The passage which Clement cites from Tatian's work *On Perfection* is clearly commentarial in nature. Tatian comments in particular on 1 Corinthians 7:5 and 6 and also seems to allude at one point to Matthew 6:24.[62] There is no reason to assume that Clement might have fabricated this reference. Rather, it is likely that we have here indeed a very small fragment from an otherwise lost work by Tatian.

In Clement's opinion Tatian takes a much more negative view of marriage—and in particular of the practice of sexual intercourse within marriage—than is warranted by Paul's teaching. Already the apostle himself, Clement argues, blamed irreligious (ἄθεοι) men to attribute the invention of marriage to the devil, "an opinion," thus Clement, "by which the lawgiver himself is in danger of being blasphemed."[63] Based on his commentary of Paul in *On Perfection* Clement takes Tatian to be such a man: He "dares to dogmatize" (τολμᾶ δογματίζειν) that Paul's concession regarding sex in marriage is in fact a "concession" (συγχώρησις), i.e. an extremely reluctant permission on Paul's part to weak couples to do something which they should rather not do. This proves that what they *do* is evil, i.e. something due to lack of self-control (ἀκρασία) and in the service of Satan.

Clement does not mention Irenaeus' contention that Tatian taught that the first man, Adam, was excluded from salvation, but he understood Tatian's text in *On Perfection* that all those who practised sexual intercourse in marriage *and* continued to worship as Christians were trying to serve two masters (God and the Devil), even in such a way that for Tatian God and the Devil were in fact two equal masters struggling with each other. He underlined this understanding in at least two more passages. In the first, *strom.* 3.12.82, he claims that Tatian argued for the abolition of the Old Testament ("the Law") as if it were from "another God" (ἄλλου θεοῦ). Without mentioning Marcion's name, Clement thus associates Tatian with Marcionism. But it has to be considered that in the context of Clement's discussion the issue is dogmatic Encratism, of which Tatian is accused, i.e. the idea that Satan is the creator of a realm of evil and everything

---

62   Clement himself concludes his citation with the words: "[Tatian] says this by way of commenting on the apostle," Clement of Alexandria, *strom.* 3.12.81: ταῦτα δέ φησι τὸν ἀπόστολον ἐξηγούμενος. That Tatian was a competent biblical commentator is confirmed by the testimony of his pupil Rhodon. The work *On difficult questions* (προβλημάτων βιβλίον) mentioned by Rhodon was exegetical in nature; for references see above nn. 7 and 42.

63   Clement of Alexandria, *strom.* 3.12.80: ... τῶν γὰρ ἄντικρυς διαβόλῳ προσαπτόντων τὴν τοῦ γάμου εὕρεσιν ἀθέων ἀνθρώπων ἐπίνοιαν κατηγορεῖ, καὶ κινδυνεύει βλασφημεῖσθαι ὁ νομοθέτης. Clement's argument here is implicitly referring to Genesis 1:27–28 and thus akin to Irenaeus' at the outset of *haer.* 1.28.1: ἀχαριστοῦντες [scil. the Encratites] τῷ πάντα πεποιηκότι θεῷ; see above n. 54.

that follows from this, especially the condemnation of sexual intercourse in marriage and the enjoyment of good food and other comforts in life.[64] The fact that Marcion also subscribed to this doctrine (as Irenaeus reports) is secondary for Clement.

The second further point that Clement makes—it is related to the first—is a bit more complicated. It questions Tatian's commitment to the idea of the creator God's oneness and omnipotence and enforces the impression that for Tatian it was in principle possible for the creator God and his creation to succumb to the powers of darkness. Such a view would make Tatian's sense of urgency regarding the need for sexual abstinence and his radical stance in that respect more understandable.

In *Prophetic Eclogues* 38 Clement writes: "To Tatian who said that [God's word in Genesis 1:3] 'Let there be light' was said in the optative mood we must reply: If God had knowledge of the supreme God (ὑπερκείμενον θεόν) in prayer, how does he say, 'I am God and there is no other but me'?"[65] Later in the third century Origen adds to this account that because Tatian did not realise that "Let there be" (γενηθήτω) is not always optative but can also be Imperative, he developed the "utterly impious" (ἀσεβέστατα) notion that the creator in Genesis 1:3 prayed (presumably to a yet higher God) when he said "Let there be light", "'because,' as he adds in his godless reasoning (ἀθεῶς νοῶν), 'God was sitting in darkness.'"[66]

That Tatian—again, in a Marcionite manner—taught the existence of a Demiurge who was subordinate to a supreme, transcendent God (ὑπερκείμενος θεός) cannot be corroborated from the *Oration*. However, the *Oration* does refer to the creator God as δημιουργός and it does conceive of the creation of the universe as a process in which the Logos and the Pneuma, subordinate to the transcendent Father, play central parts.[67] It is possible that the relevant passages in the *Oration*, which are still open to several possible interpretations, were later developed into a more Gnostic cosmogony.

---

64   Clement discusses this doctrine in several other places in *strom.* without mentioning Tatian, see e.g. 3.6.45–53, 3.18.105–110.
65   Clement of Alexandria, *eclog. proph.* 38: πρὸς δὲ Τατιανὸν λέγοντα εὐκτικὸν εἶναι τὸ 'γενηθήτω φῶς' λεκτέον· εἰ τοίνυν εὐχόμενος ᾔδει τὸν ὑπερκείμενον θεόν, πῶς λέγει 'ἐγὼ θεὸς καὶ πλὴν ἐμοῦ ἄλλος οὐδείς'.
66   Origen, *orat.* 24: μὴ συνιδὼν δὲ ὁ Τατιανὸς τὸ 'γενηθήτω' οὐ πάντοτε σημαίνειν τὸ εὐκτικόν, ἀλλ' ἔσθ' ὅπου καὶ προστακτικόν, ἐσεβέστατα ὑπείληφε περὶ τοῦ εἰπόντος 'γενηθήτω φῶς' θεοῦ ὡς εὐξαμένου μᾶλλον ἤπερ προστάξαντος γενηθῆναι τὸ φῶς, 'ἐπεί', ὥς φησιν ἐκεῖνος ἀθεῶς νοῶν, 'ἐν σκότῳ ἦν ὁ θεός'.
67   For the creation of the world (including matter) by the δημιουργός see Tatian, *or.* 5.6–7 cited above n. 57.

Both Irenaeus and Clement, the earliest extant witnesses of Tatian's literary legacy, thus seem to confirm that Tatian's strategy—namely to style himself in the *Oration* as a Syrian Christian philosopher and to impart on his audience a teaching of a distinct character (cf. Irenaeus' ἴδιον χαρακτήρ)—seems to have been successful. A radicalised and intellectualised version of Encratism, the origins of which Irenaeus attributed to Saturninus and Marcion, was now, at the end of the second century, associated with "Tatian the Syrian." It is possible that in the third century it also experienced a reception history in Syrian Christianity. It just also became clear that Tatian's intellectual Encratism may have had certain affinities to Gnosis too. This aspect will now be explored further.

3   The Gnostic

It was Pier Franco Beatrice who in his remarkable monograph, *Tradux Peccati*, of 1978 discussed the links as well as the differences between Encratism and Gnosis.[68] He saw a fundamental difference in perspective between the two movements. Encratism's focus was (in theory and practice) on what Encratites identified as the root corruption of the world. This ran so deep that the world was fundamentally divided in two: one that was essentially corrupt and irredeemably damned,[69] the other saved and purified to perfection through intellectual (philosophical), ascetic and ritual practice. Regarding the latter Beatrice saw baptism as a ritual designed to cleanse that root corruption transmitted through sexual procreation, from second-century Encratism to late-antique Augustinianism.[70]

The Gnostic perspective, according to Beatrice, is slightly different. Gnosis is not so much concerned with analysing the roots of corruption and the paths of its transmission in the physical world but rather with the spiritual paths in and out of this corrupt world. Nevertheless, there is a link between Encratism and Gnosis, which Irenaeus at one point even saw to some extent personified in Tatian and his teaching, when he called him the "link between all heretics."[71] Following Irenaeus' and Clement's reports, only a radical Encratite could also

---

68   We rely here on the excellent translation by Adam Kamesar, P.F. Beatrice, *The Transmission of Sin. Augustine and the Pre-Augustinian Sources* (Oxford: Oxford University Press, 2013), 191–219.

69   This is why Tatian might indeed have been able to speak of Adam as being in a sense excluded from salvation, as reported by Irenaeus; see above n. 54.

70   Beatrice, *The Transmission* (n. 68), 193.

71   Irenaeus, *haer.* 3.23.8: *connexio quidem factus omnium haereticorum* …; see also above n. 57.

be a true Gnostic for Tatian. Moreover, because of Adam's damnation humanity would be radically divided between saved and damned, Encratite Gnostics and "the rest".[72]

Beatrice's study with its extremely wide scope and sweeping observations may have many weaknesses. But for the purpose of this paper it helps to appreciate the important position that Tatian may hold as a late second-century linchpin in the history of Gnosis, Encratism and Syrian Christianity, which makes him also an important figure in the run-up to the emergence of Manichaeism. The linking of Encratism and Gnosis through the dogmatic grounding of his new teaching makes Tatian stand out both in Irenaeus's and Clement's reports; and evidence for this can also be found in the *Oration*.

Already Irenaeus' report makes it clear that at the root of Tatian's Encratism is not a quest for purification from some original sin. This aspect is only secondary. However, at the root of Tatian's Encratism is a theoretical position that clearly separates the saved from those excluded from salvation, i.e. those who are (spiritually) dead in Adam and from whom the life-giving divine Pneuma has withdrawn due to their transgression.[73] Those who are saved bear witness to their status by abstaining not only from sexual activity within marriage but also from eating animal products and other contaminating activities.[74] They form a separate group and inhabit a 'layered' spiritual universe. Different types of Pneuma[75] and different levels of intensity of being united with the holy

---

72 Cf. Irenaeus, *haer*. 1.28.1 the observation that Tatian in his arrogance thought he was "different from the rest." This could also be interpreted in the direction of spiritual elitism.
73 See Tatian, *or*. 13.4–5 as discussed above n. 10.
74 This Encratite behaviour is only attested in Irenaeus, *haer*. 1.28.1. Tatian, *or*. 13.5 speaks of those who have retained the holy Pneuma only as "living justly" (δικαίως πολιτευμένοι). But his use of πολιτεύομαι could suggest that he is thinking of a separate group, who "live as members / 'citizens' of a community (a πολίτευμα) of the just". For the wider background of the concept (also with a view to Manichaeism) see J. van Oort, *Jerusalem and Babylon: A Study into Augustine's* City of God *and the Sources of the Doctrine of the Two Cities* (Leiden: Brill, 1991, ²2013), 93–163, 212–221 and 274–350.
75 See the fundamental distinction in Tatian, *or*. 4.4 between a lower Pneuma, which permeates matter, and a superior, divine, Pneuma: πνεῦμα γὰρ τὸ διὰ τῆς ὕλης διῆκον, ἔλαττον ὑπάρχονω τοῦ θειοτέρου πνεύματος. The two are related, however. The higher Pneuma does not directly work within matter (οὐ διήκων διὰ τῆς ὕλης, *or*. 4.3) but apparently indirectly, through the lower Pneuma. E.g. in *or*. 5.5 Tatian argues that when he speaks to his addressees (i. e. directs his λόγος towards them), he intends to restore order to the disorderly matter in their minds in the same way as the divine Logos orders the universe in the creation process. But the Logos does this only insofar as he is identical with the divine Pneuma (cf. *or*. 7.1: λόγος γὰρ ἐπουράνιος, πνεῦμα γεγονὼς ἀπὸ τοῦ πατρός) and the divine Pneuma works together with the "hylic Pneuma" (πνεῦμα ὑλικόν, *or*. 12.3) which is present in all aspects of the material world (cf. *or*. 12.8; for the Stoic and Middle-Platonic back-

Pneuma enable them to ascend to higher aeons[76] and thus offer means of explanation and spiritual techniques and processes for various stages of transition from a frail and corrupt bodily existence to a life in both physical and spiritual perfection.[77]

Clement's report additionally suggests that the Divinity is at some level involved in this process. For example, there is a lower Demiurge, who creates everything including matter and is therefore instrumental in the perfection process. But he is himself relying on the higher transcendent God.

The *Oration* does not strictly and unequivocally contain this teaching, but there are traces. For example, Tatian distinguishes the Father and the Logos.[78] At the same time he tries to avoid speaking of the Father and the Logos as two separate beings (as Justin had done).[79] Therefore, when he refers to God "in the ultimate sense", τέλειος θεός,[80] or to the Demiurge,[81] it is not always clear whether he means the Father or the Logos. But it is clear that he sees the Logos as subordinate to the Father[82] and as instrumental in the creation process. It is therefore likely that when he speaks of τέλειος θεός, he means the Father, and when he speaks of the Demiurge, he means the Logos. At one point he even speaks of the Logos as "the firstborn work" of the Father.[83] It is therefore not totally out of the question that he could have conceived of creation as a process

---

ground of this concept see Trelenberg, *Tatianos* [n. 8], 43), a kind of "world-soul". If the divine Pneuma is withdrawn from the hylic Pneuma, the universe (including humanity) descends to death and darkness; if the two work together, it ascends to perfection. This is how Tatian also imagines the resurrection of the body (*or.* 6.1) and this is why he is against the use of purely natural remedies in medicine (*or.* 18.1): without reference to God's power in the holy Pneuma, medicine is purely hylic and therefore prone to demonic interference.

76   See the discussion above n. 10 and Tatian, *or.* 13.5 in combination with 20.4.
77   Note that the title of Tatian's work cited by Clement of Alexandria, *strom.* 3.12.81 is Περὶ τοῦ κατὰ τὸν Σωτῆρα καταρτισμοῦ, *On Perfection According to the Saviour.* Literally, καταρτισμός is not primarily "perfection", but "reconciliation" and "restoration." From Clement's excerpt one would assume that the understanding of "saviour" in this work is also primarily spiritual, or Gnostic.
78   E.g. Tatian, *or.* 5.1–2.
79   As Roman Hanig has shown, Tatian modifies Justin's teaching, in which the Logos is quasi a second God, and develops a more monarchian model; e.g. he focuses on the "one-ness" of the Logos and the Father (*or.* 5.2) and emphasizes that there is no separation (ἀποκοπή, literally "a cutting off" of the Son from the Father) but just a "sharing" of functions (μερισμός; *or.* 5.3). R. Hanig, "Tatian und Justin: Ein Vergleich," *VChr* 53 (1999), 31–73; see also Trelenberg, *Tatianos* (n. 8), 195–203.
80   Cf. Tatian, *or.* 4.4; 12.7; 15.4; 17.6; 25.4.
81   Tatian, *or.* 5.7.
82   Tatian, *or.* 5.1–2.
83   Tatian, *or.* 5.2: ἔργον πρωτότοκον τοῦ πατρός.

in which the Logos (as the Demiurge) created the universe following a prayerful interaction with the Father, as Clement's report suggests.[84] The Logos, as already mentioned, is also identified with the holy Pneuma,[85] which in turn is linked to the human soul. It holds the human soul (ψυχή) and with it the entire human being, "God's image and likeness" (Genesis 1:26), in a state of immortality.[86] The "first-formed" (πρωτοπλάστης) human, Adam, created in a syzygy with the divine Pneuma, was the first who gained this privilege[87] and lost it again out of his own fault (αὐτεξουσίον).[88] Again it is not entirely clear in the relevant passages in the *Oration* whether Tatian believes that for Adam this loss is irreversible. This is because Adam's fate seems strangely entangled with that of the first demon.[89] It is possible to interpret the relevant passages in the *Oration* in a way that makes them compatible with a 'proto-orthodox' doctrine such

---

84   For Clement's and Origen's reports see above nn. 65 and 66. Tatian, *or.* 5.1–2 might allow for such an interpretation: "In the beginning," before creation, God was alone (μόνος). But the "power [or 'potential,' δύναμις, in the Aristotelian sense] of the Logos" was already with Him, which included the "potential" of the universe to exist. The "power of the Logos" was going to realise this potential. To this end "the Logos emerges by the will of God's oneness" (θελήματι δὲ τῆς ἁπλότητος αὐτοῦ προπηδᾷ λόγος). However, not into emptiness, but it becomes the "firstborn work" of the Father; i.e. it becomes so to speak 'God on the side of creation,' to facilitate creation. All creation, including that of matter, happens through the Logos, or Demiurge (*or.* 5.7), but—one may assume—if the Demiurge is on the side of creation, he does his work in communication with the transcendent Father. In such a scenario it would indeed be imaginable that the Demiurge prayed to the transcendent God and was "sitting in darkness," as Origen suggests, at the point at which he embarked on the creation of the universe out of nothing, asking his transcendent counterpart to "let there be light." According to this model, divinity would also extend to the lowest level of matter in a continuum and matter would be present at the highest levels of divinity, while divinity itself would not be material (cf. *or.* 25.4).

85   Tatian, *or.* 7.1; see the discussion above n. 75.

86   Ibid.; cf. also *or.* 12.1; 15.3–4: the soul (ψυχή) on its own is hylic Pneuma; God's image and likeness is the human being endowed with the divine Pneuma.

87   Tatian, or. 13.3–4; see the discussion above n. 10.

88   Tatian, *or.* 7.2–3; 11.4 (on freedom, αὐτεξουσία, and freedom of choice, ἐλευθερία τῆς προαιρέσεως); 7.5 on the first man's loss of immortality.

89   Tatian, *or.* 7.3–5: Regarding "angels and men" things are as follows (7.3): "men followed one whose intellect was superior due to his status as 'first-born'. They declared him to be God, even though he had rebelled against God's law. Upon this the power of the Logos banned him who had started this madness and those who had followed him from God's presence" (7.4). "He who was God's likeness, after being separated from the more powerful Pneuma, became mortal. Because of his transgression and folly the first-born became a demon. Those who followed and imitated him became a host of demons and were handed over to their folly out of their own free choice" (7.5). "Humanity became for them the primary purpose [or 'target', 'raw material', 'playing field'] of their apostasy" (8.1).—In this argument it is not always entirely clear who is referred to. Two groups of agents are involved,

as Irenaeus'. In that case Irenaeus would have mis-represented Tatian's position in *haer.* 1.28.1 and 3.23.8, be it because of a mis-understanding or bad faith. However, they can also be interpreted in such a way that they can—at least potentially—be developed into a position in which Adam's fate and that of the 'first-born' angel are inextricably linked and both are irredeemably excluded from salvation.[90] Moreover, Irenaeus could of course have had access to other works of Tatian's (no longer extant) in which Tatian had developed his position in that direction.

4 Conclusion

Expressions such as ἔναυσμα, συζυγία or κρείττονες αἰῶνες occur in the *Oration* not only 'accidentally' (because they happen to be Greek words). Tatian is often using them in a vaguely Gnostic sense, reminiscent of the way Irenaeus reports Valentinus to have used them.[91] Tatian's entire soteriological discourse in the *Oration* can be read along Gnostic lines. For Tatian, σωτηρία is identical with γνῶσις. Γνῶσις and related expressions occur numerous times in the *Oration*.[92] Salvation, for Tatian, means Gnosis of God and creation. Tatian presents himself as someone who has achieved this goal and is therefore in a position to help others attain it.[93] On the reverse side: A soul that has not recognised the truth (μὴ γινώσκουσα τὴν ἀλήθειαν) dies and is dissolved into nothing (λύεται) together with the body.[94]

---

angels (ἄγγελοι) and men (ἄνθρωποι). Men followed the 'first-born' (πρωτόγονος), who was presumably an angel. He is the one who is said to have been banned from God's presence at the end of 7.4. "He of God's likeness" (ὁ κατ' εἰκόνα τοῦ θεοῦ γεγονώς) is presumably the first man, Adam. He lost his immortality. The 'first-born' became a demon and attracted a host of demons as followers, for whom humanity became the primary target of their mischief. But what happens to Adam in the end is not clear. Is he as "God's image and likeness" (cf. *or.* 15.3) among the "just ones" who are saved (13.5), or will the "higher aeons" remain forever inaccessible to him (20.4)? If we believe Irenaeus, Tatian taught the latter.

90 See above nn. 54–57.
91 For ἔναυσμα in *or.* 13 as remaining pneumatic "spark" that enables the abandoned soul to find again the kindred Pneuma (τὸ πνεῦμα συγγενές), see Trelenberg, *Tatianos* (n. 8), 215; for συζυγία also Hunt, *Christianity* (n. 8), 23. Here the rhetoric used in or. 13.4 and 15.1 reminds of the way Irenaeus, *haer.* 1.7.1 describes mystical union in Valentinian Gnosis. For κρείττονες αἰῶνες (*or.* 20.4) see Trelenberg, *Tatianos* (n. 8), 213.
92 Cf. *or.* 12.7, 19.3: γνῶσις; 13.1, 40.1: ἐπίγνωσις; 13.1, 42.2: γιγνώσκειν; 19.10: ἐπιγιγνώσκειν; 14.1: γνώμη, and many more.
93 Tatian, *or.* 42.2: γινώσκων δὲ λοιπὸν τίς ὁ θεὸς καὶ τίς ἡ κατ' αὐτὸν ποίησις, ἕτοιμον ἐμαυτὸν ὑμῖν πρὸς τὴν ἀνάκρισιν τῶν δογμάτων παρίστημι.
94 Tatian, *or.* 13.1.

One may argue that Tatian, as one of the major second-century Greek apologists, can also be read as a representative of the 'proto-orthodox' tradition (including Justin, Irenaeus, Clement and similar authors). It can also be argued that he should rather be counted among the heretics (Saturninus, Marcion, Valentinus), as Irenaeus and Clement of Alexandria suggested. In any case, he presents an unusual example of a Christian author in the late second century: original and innovative; classically, philosophically and biblically educated; a professed Syrian with strong Encratic and Gnostic leanings. He may not be strictly a 'precursor' of Mani, as the subtitle of this paper, perhaps somewhat provocatively, asks. Nevertheless, as a Syrian writer with a lasting impact in third-century Syrian Christianity he may also be seen as playing a part in the pre-history of Manichaeism.[95]

---

95 One aspect of this impact, much discussed already in the past (cf. n. 9) as well as more recently (cf. n. 7) but not pursued in this paper, is his influence through the *Diatessaron*, the dominant canonical Gospel tradition in Syriac until the fourth century and also relevant for early Manichaeism. Although research in the *Diatessaron* is of course also pertinent to Tatian's potential 'precursor-ship' of Manichaeism, it has proved difficult to relate to the *Oration* and the heresiological testimonies discussed in this paper, as these deal on balance more with Pauline rather than Gospel traditions. The studies contained in Crawford and Zola, *The Gospel* (n. 7) may provide a basis for further research in this direction; and see now also I.N. Mills, "Zacchaeus and the Unripe Figs: A New Argument for the Original Language of Tatian's Diatessaron," *New Testament Studies* 66 (2020), 208–227 on Greek as the original language of the Diatessaron.

2
Antithèses en mutation, de Marcion à Mani

Michel Tardieu

Résumé

La règle de vie et la loi sont des opposés, passés des antithèses d'Ænésidème à celles de Marcion. Ils se redéploient chez Mani (Adda, *CMC*) en annexant d'autres figures d'argumentation, comme le montrent en rapport avec Adda l'allégorie des deux cités (*Traité* chinois) et en rapport avec Marcion les stances d'hymnes abécédaires sur la rétribution des hypocrites (M281).

Le sens spécifiquement philosophique de l'antithèse en tant qu'opposition enracinée dans la distinction des objets métaphysiques en phénomènes et noumènes n'apparaît pas avant le XVIIIe siècle dans le cadre de la dialectique transcendantale de Kant.[1] L'antithèse kantienne traduit un conflit interne de la raison avec elle-même, alors que celle dont il sera question ici, c'est-à-dire l'antithèse marcionite-manichéenne, est essentiellement un instrument rhétorique d'argumentation destiné à faire apparaître le conflit externe de deux puissances opposées. L'histoire concrète d'une telle pratique n'est pas écrite. On considère souvent à tort le jeu de telles oppositions comme répondant à un système rigide, figé. Mais, comme nous le allons le voir, il est l'occasion aussi de belles créations poétiques. De ce fait, mon propos se limite à pouvoir éclairer un aspect de l'histoire ancienne de la catégorisation antithétique par la prise en compte de notions propres à la philosophie du langage à l'époque de la seconde sophistique.[2] Celle de Marcion et de Mani.

J'exprime ma reconnaissance à Johannes van Oort et à l'Université de Pretoria, à celles et ceux qui ont organisé cette rencontre et encouragé nos échanges.

---

1 E. Kant, *Critique de la raison pure*, Traduit et présenté par Alain Renaut, Paris, Flammarion/GF, 2006, p. 294.
2 Les aspects doxographiques et hellénistiques de cette philosophie du langage sont traités dans mon étude: «Basilide "prédicateur chez les Perses"», in Fl. Ruani et M. Timuș (éd.), *Quand les dualistes polémiquaient: zoroastriens et manichéens*, Paris, Éditions de Boccard, 2020, p. 179-200 (collection Orient et Méditerranée, 37).

1 La relation aux contraires

«Personne n'ignore, écrit Philon, que rien, ou presque, de ce qui existe n'est perçu par soi et en soi, mais est apprécié par comparaison avec son contraire, comme le petit par rapport au grand, le sec par rapport à l'humide, par rapport au froid le chaud, par rapport au lourd le léger, le noir par rapport au blanc, le faible par rapport au fort, peu par rapport à beaucoup».[3] Dans l'art de la persuasion, l'antithèse rapproche les séquences en opposition de contrariété, parce qu'elles présentent des situations en conflit. La tension duelle est dialectique, en ce sens qu'elle ne met pas fin à la disparition du conflit, mais le déplace ou en crée un nouveau. Tel est, sommairement dit, le type d'opposition autour duquel se construisent contes et récits qui parsèment les productions littéraires et religieuses de la seconde sophistique.

Le premier emploi connu du terme ἀντίθεσις est attesté par Platon comme figure signifiante par opposition des contraires, beau/non-beau.[4] Les espèces qu'Aristote distingue dans le genre de l'ἀντίθεσις sont de quatre sortes: la contradiction (ἀντίφασις), la contrariété (ἐναντίωσις), la relation (πρός τι) et la possession/privation (ἕξις/στέρησις).[5] La démonstration (ἀπόδειξις) est l'art d'argumenter par oppositions spécifiques. C'est le mode privilégié de l'enseignement. Il est aussi bien grec philosophique que juif rabbinique: "On vous a dit" / "Moi je vous dis". La brutalité binaire de l'antithèse est omniprésente dans les fables ésopiques comme dans les paroles et paraboles synoptiques prêtées à Jésus, et chez Marcion. L'usage très répandu de ce raisonnement par oppositions n'a cependant pas conduit un seul auteur antique à rédiger un traité d'*Antithèses*. Sauf Marcion.[6] Comment cela s'explique-t-il?

Il y a deux facteurs à prendre en compte. Le premier est la réorganisation des modes de l'antithèse dans l'école péripatéticienne. Au IIe siècle de notre ère, Alexandre d'Aphrodise adopte l'ordre suivant: contraires (τἀναντία), privation et possession (στέρησις καὶ ἕξις), relations (τὰ πρός τι), affirmation et négation (κατάφασις καὶ ἀπόφασις).[7] Notons que les contraires apparaissent ici en tête, et

---

3 Philon d'Alexandrie, *De ebrietate*, 186.
4 Platon, *Sophiste*, 257 E.
5 Aristote, *Topiques*, II 8, 113b15-114a25; *Métaphysique*, Δ 10, 1018a20–b8.
6 Cette exception est soulignée par A. von Harnack, *Marcion. Das Evangelium vom fremden Gott*, 2e éd., Leipzig, Hinrichs, 1924, p. 74, n. 2, qui parle des *Antithèses* de Marcion comme d'un «titre audacieux» (*der kecke Titel*); pour l'édition française (Paris, Cerf, 2003, p. 97, n. 2). Un intitulé similaire est, cependant, attesté dans l'école pythagoricienne, peu avant Marcion, par Archytas qui composa un Περὶ ἀντικειμένων (synonyme d'antithèses), cf. H. Thesleff, *An Introduction to the Pythagorean Writings of the Hellenistic Period*, Åbo, Akademi, 1961, p. 9.
7 Alexandre d'Aphrodise, *In Aristotelis Metaphysica*, ed. M. Hayduck, Berlin, 1891, p. 380, 12-13;

les contradictoires en dernière position sous la dénomination d'affirmation et négation. Le second et principal facteur qui selon moi amène Marcion à rédiger un instrument de lecture biblique par oppositions est la transformation et la diffusion du système des antithèses dans la philosophie alexandrine à partir d'Énésidème, un contemporain de Cicéron.[8] Ses tables d'oppositions, munies d'un grand nombre d'exemples empruntés à la culture grecque – on peut les lire chez Philon, Sextus Empiricus et Diogène Laërce – montrent la pluralité des modes de l'antithèse pour tout questionnement, selon que telle règle de vie ou bien telle coutume s'opposent à une législation, à une croyance légendaire, à un mythe, à une opinion dogmatique. Pour Énésidème, les contraires font apparaître la complexité des choses et énoncent les lois de l'existence, comme le faisait déjà Héraclite.[9] Empédocle soumet les éléments à l'opposition de la Haine et de l'Amour (Νεῖκος / Φιλότης)[10]. C'est en rapport avec cette théorie, et non avec l'héraclitisme, que l'auteur de l'*Elenchos* (Hippolyte de Rome ?) situe le modèle absolu des antithèses marcionites.[11] Celles-ci constituent désormais une œuvre, *opus*, comme le souligne Tertullien au livre IV du *Contre Marcion*. Elles sont un instrument de lecture à la façon des tropes d'Énésidème.

> Et ut fidem instrueret, dotem quandam commentatus est illi, opus ex contrarietatum oppositionibus Antithesis cognominatum et ad separationem legis et euangelii coactum, qua duos deos diuidens proinde diuersos, alterum alterius instrumenti, uel, quod magis usui est dicere, testamenti, ut exinde euangelio quoque secundum Antithesis credendo patrocinaretur.[12]

> Besides that, to work up credence for it he has contrived a sort of dowry, a work entitled *Antitheses* because of its juxtaposition of opposites, a work

---

G. Movia, *Alessandro di Afrodisia e Pseudo Alessandro, Commentario alla "Metafisica" di Aristotele*, Milano, Bompiani, 1996, p. 933.

8   Tout ce qui subsiste du refondateur du scepticisme pyrrhonien (Ier siècle avant J.-C.) est rassemblé par Roberto Polito, *Aenesidemus of Cnossus. Testimonia*, Cambridge, Cambridge University Press, 2014. Le mouvement de la pensée est restitué par Carlos Lévy, « Philon d'Alexandrie est-il inutilisable pour connaître Énésidème ? Étude méthodologique », *Philosophie Antique*, 15 (2015), p. 5-26.

9   Héraclite, in H. Diels-W. Kranz, *Die Fragmente der Vorsokratiker*, fr. 62 (Immortels mortels) et 88 (Le même qui est là, vivant et mort).

10 Empédocle, ibid., fr. 16 (cité par l'auteur de l'*Elenchos*, VII 29, 9-10).

11 Hippolyte (?), *Elenchos*, VII 29, 2 (p. 210, 12 Wendland) : « les causes de toutes choses sont duelles ».

12 Tertullien, *Contre Marcion*, IV 1, 1, 4-10, ed. Cl. Moreschini 2001, Sources Chrétiennes 456, 2001, p. 57/58.

strained into making such a division between the Law and the Gospel as thereby to make two separate gods, opposite to each other, one belonging to one instrument (or, as it is more usual to say, testament), one to the other, and thus lend its patronage to faith in another gospel, that according to the *Antitheses*.[13]

D'autre part, pour étayer la foi en celui-ci (= en son évangile), il (Marcion) l'a comme doté d'un commentaire de son cru: l'ouvrage qu'il a appelé les *Antithèses* à cause de la mise en face à face de contradictions, et qu'il a orienté de force vers la séparation de la Loi et de l'Évangile en ce sens qu'il a distingué deux dieux, pareillement opposés, relevant chacun d'un des deux "instruments" – ou "testaments" comme il est plus habituel de dire –, afin de patronner ensuite un évangile auquel il faudrait croire aussi, dans le droit fil des *Antithèses*.[14]

Au livre I, l'*instrumentum* marcionite est qualifié de *summum*. Les traducteurs mettent l'adjectif en contexte codicologique: "en tête" du livre, "au début" du livre, "livre souverain". Le substantif *instrumentum* en tant que désignation métaphorique de "livre" est un terme de mécanique, désignant l'outillage ou le dispositif qui sert à construire, à bâtir. La logique des oppositions fait de cet *instrumentum summum* une sorte d'équipement de pointe, nécessaire pour aborder toute lecture critique comparée.

Separatio legis et euangelii proprium et principale opus est Marcionis, nec poterunt negare discipuli eius quod in summo instrumento habent, quo denique initiantur et indurantur in hanc haeresim. Nam hae sunt 'Antithesis' Marcionis, id est contrariae oppositiones, quae conantur discordiam euangelii cum lege committere, ut ex diuersitate sententiarum utriusque instrumenti diuersitatem quoque argumententur deorum.[15]

The separation of Law and Gospel is the primary and principal exploit of Marcion. His disciples cannot deny this, which stands at the head of their document, that document by which they are inducted into and confirmed in this heresy. For such are Marcion's *Antitheses*, or Contrary Oppositions, which are designed to show the conflict and disagreement of the Gospel

---

13 Traduction d'E. Evans, *Tertullian. Adversus Marcionem. Books IV-V*, Oxford, 1972, p. 257.
14 Traduction de R. Braun, *Tertullien. Contre Marcion*, Sources Chrétiennes 456, p. 57/59.
15 Tertullien, *Contre Marcion*, I 19, 4, 24-31; texte identique chez R. Braun (SC 365, 1990, p. 188) et chez E. Evans, *Tertullian. Adversus Marcionem. Books I-III*, 1972, p. 48.

and the Law, so that from diversity of principles between those two documents they may argue further for a diversity of gods.[16]

La séparation entre la Loi et l'Évangile constitue l'œuvre propre et principale de Marcion; ses disciples ne pourront renier ce qui constitue pour eux le livre souverain, par lequel en effet ils sont initiés et endurcis dans leur hérésie. Il s'agit des *Antithèses* de Marcion, c'est-à-dire «les oppositions contradictoires», qui essaient d'établir un désaccord entre la Loi et l'Évangile, afin de conclure de l'opposition de pensée des deux livres à l'opposition des dieux.[17]

Les auteurs antimarcionites ou antimanichéens peuvent donner l'impression que la relation aux contraires se résume à du ping-pong exégétique, comme si pour obtenir une opposition il suffirait de retourner par antijudaïsme tel verset de l'Ancien Testament par tel verset du Nouveau. Ainsi que le reconnaît Tertullien, les antithèses font sens, parce qu'elles mènent de la *diuersitas sententiarum* à la *diuersitas deorum*. Il s'agit de constructions plus subtiles qu'il n'y paraît. La Transfiguration en est un exemple frappant, si du moins l'on croise latin et syriaque, Tertullien et Éphrem.[18] La narration du tête-à-tête entre Jésus et les gardiens de la montagne, Moïse et Élie, est structurée par des paliers successifs de contraires. D'un côté, le créateur par ses médiateurs Moïse-Élie est censé remettre au fils de l'étranger, c'est-à-dire à Jésus, les âmes des hommes pour les purifier, mais de l'autre, en contrepartie, comme sorte de prix à payer, c'est la mort sur la croix qui est mise en perspective. La formulation même de l'antithèse finale par un troc n'est transmise que par Éphrem: au Sinaï le créateur a dit: un feu s'est allumé dans ma colère, il brûlera jusqu'au shéol d'en bas, dévorant la terre et ses rejetons,[19] mais Jésus, le fils de l'étranger, a gravi la montagne pour éteindre ce feu et racheter au créateur les âmes souillées en les purifiant par l'exode qu'il devrait accomplir à Jérusalem.

---

16 Traduction d'E. Evans, *Tertullian. Adversus Marcionem. Books I-III*, 1972, p. 49.
17 Traduction de R. Braun, SC 365, p. 189. Les *Antithèses* de Marcion définies comme *contrariae oppositiones* sont, ainsi que traduit Evans, des *Contrary Oppositions*, et non pas des «oppositions contradictoires» (Braun).
18 Voir mon étude «La Transfiguration, ou les antithèses de la colère et de la gloire», dans l'édition française collective de Adolf von Harnack, *Marcion. L'évangile du Dieu étranger*, Paris, Cerf, 2003, p. 441-450.
19 Cf. Deutéronome 32, 22.

2   La relativité des contraires

Dans les antithèses de Mani à la suite de celles de Marcion, les contraires sont inégaux, déséquilibrés. Pour répondre à cette inégalité, le principe général est que la règle de vie doit prévaloir sur la loi, ainsi que l'explique Mani devant le collège presbytéral des Baptistes en arguant qu'Alkhasaios ni ne labourait ni ne cuisait le pain.[20] En conséquence de quoi, la non-violence l'emporte sur le travail agricole ;[21] l'homme sur le sabbat, c'est-à-dire le sujet sur l'objet ;[22] les pratiques ascétiques sur les prescriptions alimentaires, autrement dit la règle de vie sur la coutume.[23] Chez Énésidème, en revanche, les éléments s'opposent sans que l'un l'emporte sur l'autre, il y a équilibre des contraires, d'où la tranquillité du sceptique suspendant tout jugement, alors que chez Marcion et Mani le résultat de l'inégalité est le questionnement permanent qui commence avec la dualité des principes[24] car mettre les contraires en rapport avec un principe unique serait créer des contradictoires, donc tout ramener à de l'absurde. Telle est la leçon de la parabole des deux arbres, en remploi chez Marcion et omniprésente chez les manichéens : « sur des épines on ne cueille pas de figues, ni sur des buissons on ne vendange de raisin ».[25]

Le théoricien manichéen des antithèses fut, comme on vient de le voir, le disciple immédiat de Mani, Adda, de langue et de culture araméennes. Il est au manichéisme ce que Paul est au christianisme : un refondateur et un théologien. Aucun traité d'Adda n'est conservé, mais Augustin lui consacre un traité entier, le *Contra Adimantum* (rédigé en 394-395), dont la construction logique reste, pour moi du moins,[26] assez obscure. Les antithèses du traité ne recoupent pas entièrement celles des *Capitula* de l'évêque manichéen africain, Faustus de Milev. Les formulations de Faustus sont intéressantes pour l'histoire des controverses car elles émanent d'un auteur, aux dires mêmes de son adversaire, « d'une intelligence aiguisée et d'un langage châtié » (*acutum ingenium et lingua expolita*), rompu à l'exercice quotidien de la palabre (*cotidiana ser-*

---

20   *Codex manichéen de Cologne* (CMC), éd. L. Koenen et C. Römer, 1988, p. 96, 18-97, 17.
21   Adda dans Augustin, *Contra Adimantum*, 4, p. 122-123, éd. J. Zycha, CSEL 25/1, 1891.
22   Adda dans Augustin, *C. Adim.*, 22, p. 181 Zycha.
23   Adda dans Augustin, *C. Adim.*, 14, p. 148 Zycha.
24   Affirmée en tête des antithèses d'Adda, dans Augustin, *C. Adim.*, 1, p. 115-116 Zycha.
25   Luc 6, 44. Chez Marcion, les deux arbres forment un bloc antithétique avec la parabole des deux maîtres (Luc 16, 13) et celles du vieux et du neuf (Luc 5, 36-37), voir Harnack, *Marcion*, 2ᵉ éd., 1924, p. 260*-261*.
26   L'étude littéraire du dossier a beaucoup avancé avec J.A. van den Berg, *Biblical Argument in Manichaean Missionary Practice*, Leiden, Brill, 2010, en particulier p. 123-175 (Nag Hammadi and Manichaean Studies, 70).

mocinandi exercitatio).[27] Faustus est un rhéteur professionnel. Il a été formé à la lecture de Cicéron et de Sénèque. Ce que son apologétique anti-catholique a de très remarquable tient à la problématique *questio/argumentum*. Chaque *Capitulum* est un chef-d'œuvre de logique sous la forme d'un dialogue fictif entre un adversaire catholique qui pose une question à laquelle répond le manichéen. C'est le jeu rhétorique de ce qui est à prouver et de ce qui prouve. Topique manichéenne des preuves contre topique catholique des questions. Ces controverses sont organisées de façon rigoureuse selon la disposition des lieux dialectiques (*loci dialectici*), définis et exemplifiés par Cicéron et les commentateurs latins d'Aristote.[28]

Chez les manichéens d'Asie centrale, l'absence de conflit exégétique et de milieu scolaire philosophique n'a plus rendu nécessaire le recours systématique aux antithèses dans les exposés religieux. Elles ne disparaissent pas pour autant mais changent de modes en fonction de la variété des sujets/objets et des circonstances/dispositions. J'en signale deux exemples, l'un en rapport avec Adda, l'autre avec Marcion.

Un sermon manichéen interne au *Traité* chinois, introduit par l'incise: «Vous tous, écoutez attentivement, Listen carefully all of you[29]», s'ouvre par l'allégorie de deux cités.[30] Cette figure rhétorique célèbre, en raison de sa reprise dans la première moitié du Ve siècle comme structure littéraire et théologique d'une œuvre majeure d'Augustin (*De civitate dei*), a été l'objet d'une analyse exhaustive de la part de Johannes van Oort.[31] Cette démonstration permet de bien marquer la mutation manichéenne des antithèses du plan de la logique à celui de la symbolique.

Selon le *Traité* chinois, l'une de ces cités est dite celle de l'erreur: ses quartiers tortueux et anciennes demeures sont détruits par l'Envoyé du Νοῦς-Lu-

---

27 Augustin, *Confessions*, V 6, 11.
28 Cela ne vaut, en réalité, que pour les *Capitula* des livres II à XI. Ceux du livre I et du livre XII mettent en jeu d'autres figures antithétiques. Les lieux dialectiques sont associés: en V 1, l'argument *a consequentibus* (l'évangile affranchit du corporel) suppose l'argument *ab effectis* précédent (IV 1) sur ce qui prouve (l'adéquation du corporel à l'Ancien Testament).
29 E. Chavannes et P. Pelliot, «Un Traité manichéen retrouvé en Chine, traduit et annoté», *Journal Asiatique*, 10e série, 18 (1911), p. 556, 15; S.N.C. Lieu et G.B. Mikkelsen, *Tractatus Manichaicus Sinicus*, Turnhout, Brepols, 2017, p. 37 (*Corpus Fontium Manichaeorum, Series Sinica* I 1).
30 «Die einleitende Fiktion einer Belehrung des Jüngers Adda durch Mani ist längst vergessen!» (W. Sundermann, *Der Sermon vom Licht-Nous*, Berlin, Akademie Verlag, 1992, p. 94, Berliner Turfantexte 17). Adda est nommé dans le prologue du *Traité* chinois comme le destinataire de l'enseignement du *Traité* (Chavannes-Pelliot p. 509, Lieu-Mikkelsen p. 3).
31 J. van Oort, *Jerusalem and Babylon. A Study of Augustine's City of God and the Sources of his Doctrine of the Two Cities*, Leiden, Brill, 1991, 2013².

mière (Mani); l'autre cité est qualifiée également d'impure, remplie de fumée et de brouillard, mais pas totalement. Sa réalité est le mélange. Une fois parvenus à son sommet, les partisans de l'Envoyé aperçoivent vers le bas de la ville sept pierres précieuses, brillant d'un éclat incomparable en dépit des souillures alentour. Après quoi, l'Envoyé se choisit une terre grasse et fertile pour y semer ses propres graines. L'antithèse, élaborée par Mani et juxtaposant cité mauvaise et cité mélangée, sert à décrire symboliquement la situation des manichéens dans le monde en relais des expériences missionnaires pré-manichéennes. Symbolique analogue, dans la similitude initiale d'Hermas, où s'opposent pareillement deux cités, celle d'ici-bas qui est une terre étrangère, et celle qui appartient en propre aux serviteurs de Dieu.[32] Autre mise en confrontation, de plus grande ampleur, la parabole des deux cités dans les *Actes de Pierre et des Douze Apôtres* (Nag Hammadi Codices, VI 1).[33] Dans la cité ingrate où abordent les apôtres, il y a un marchand de perles ambulant, portant étui à papyrus et bâton de marche; l'autre cité est plus attrayante, c'est la patrie du même vendeur de perles, qui a revêtu l'apparence d'un ange et porte une cassette de médicaments. Il révèle le nom de sa ville: «9 portes + 1», puis sa fonction: il est Lithargoel, l'ange guérisseur, enfin son identité: il n'est autre que Jésus. La pointe prophétologique de cette parabole amène à penser que la tradition des deux cités, particulière au *Traité* chinois, est aussi une allégorie de fondation, en réemploi pour le manichéisme. Les débats qui dans le CMC opposent le jeune Mani aux autorités de la communauté baptiste sont transposés allégoriquement dans le *Traité* en métaphores architecturales: quartiers tortueux, anciennes demeures, palais, portes et rempart. Les images urbaines anticipent une décision de rupture pour signifier l'altérité religieuse, le passage d'un ordre ancien à un monde nouveau. Les sept pierres précieuses que les disciples de l'Envoyé voient briller de tout leur éclat dans la cité mélangée désignent l'heptateuque de Mani. Quant à l'image de la terre fertile ensemencée, par laquelle se poursuit le sermon, elle est la reprise de la parabole synoptique du semeur.[34] Antoine Guillaumont a observé que des séquences analogues, relevant du processus de changement de religion (cité étrangère, missionnaire déguisé en marchand ou en médecin, porteur de perles qui sont des livres), sont entrées dans la structure romanesque des multiples versions de *Barlaam et Ioasaph*.[35]

---

32 Hermas, *Pasteur*, III 1,1-2. Contextualisation comparée de la tradition des deux cités propre à Hermas: J. van Oort, *Jerusalem and Babylon*, p. 301-312.
33 Sur ces Actes, dans la perspective des deux cités: J. van Oort, ibid., p. 320-321.
34 Matthieu 13, 3b–8; Marc 4, 3-8; Luc 8, 5-8.
35 A. Guillaumont, «De nouveaux actes apocryphes: les Actes de Pierre et des Douze Apô-

Même dépourvues, comme on vient de le voir, d'arrière-plan scolaire philosophique, les controverses manichéennes sont propices à la construction d'antithèses poétiques. C'est le cas des hymnes abécédaires du M 28 I, dont l'exploration est continue.[36] Mon choix s'est porté sur les quatre stances ci-dessous (M 28 I Rii29-Vi9) en raison de leur particularité contextuelle. Elles sont l'unique document manichéen direct où il y a une référence explicite à une personnalité historique du christianisme primitif post-néotestamentaire : Marcion. Par là le débat s'enrichit autant qu'il s'obscurcit. Je reproduis la transcription qu'en a donné François de Blois 2001 (p. 13-14), suivie de son interprétation puis de la mienne.

2.1   *Lamed*

rasend dādīhā / druwandān ō dušox / če-šān xwad kird bazzagīh / ud wanyūdīh īg bazzakkarān

"According to the law the evil ones go to hell". (Thus speak) those who themselves have committed sins and (all) the destructive deeds (?) of sinners!

"Ils vont comme il se doit, / les hypocrites, en enfer!" / Mais eux aussi ont fait le mal / et (ils connaîtront) la perdition des pécheurs!

---

tres», *Revue de l'histoire des religions*, 196 (1979), p. 145, n. 6. J'ajouterai aux séquences relevées la parabole synoptique du semeur, reproduite intégralement par toutes les versions, y compris par les rédactions arabes prébyzantines.

36 M. Boyce, *A Reader in Manichaean Middle Persian and Parthian. Texts with Notes*, Leiden, Brill, 1975, p. 174-175 (Acta Iranica III/2/9); P.O. Skjærvø, «The Manichaean Polemical Hymns in M 28 I», *Bulletin of the Asia Institute*, N.S., 9 (1995), p. 239-255; W. Sundermann, *Iranian Manichaean Turfan texts in early publications (1904-1934). Photo Edition*, London, 1996, Plate 32-33 (Corpus Inscriptionum Iranicarum, Suppl. Series, Vol. III); Fr. de Blois, «Review of W. Sundermann 1996», *Journal of the Royal Asiatic Society*, 3[d] s., 8 (1998), 481-485; Id., «The Turfan Fragment M 28 I», in 'A.A. Ṣādeghi (ed.), *Tafazzoli Memorial Volume*, Tehran, Sokhan Publishers, 2001, p. 9-15; D. Durkin-Meisterernst, «Abecedarian Hymns, a Survey of Published Middle Persian and Parthian Manichaean Hymns», in S.G. Richter *et alii* (eds.), *Mani in Dublin*, Leiden, Brill, 2015, 116 [110-152] (Nag Hammadi and Manichaean Studies, 88); Cl. Leurini, «The Temple Tabernacle in M28/I/: An Anti-Judeo-Christian Polemic Strophe», *Iran and the Caucasus*, 22 (2018), 1-7; Fr. de Blois, «Manichaean Polemics: M 28 and the Book of Mysteries», in Fl. Ruani et M. Timuş (éd.), *Quand les dualistes polémiquaient: zoroastriens et manichéens*, Paris, Éditions de Boccard, 2020, p. 155-172 (Orient et Méditerranée, 37) [*non uidi*, non encore paru]; I. Gardner, «The Strange Case

2.2 Mem

mānāg hān če-šān kird / ōy yazad ī Markiyōn / če-š nīd hān ī nē xwēš / u-šān grift ud ōzad

Like what they did (to) that god of (whom) Marcion (spoke), because he led away what was not his own, and they seized him and killed him.

C'est comme ce qu'ils firent / au dieu de Marcion, / parce qu'il prit ce qui ne lui appartenait pas : / "Et ils s'en saisirent et le tuèrent" !

2.3 Nun

narm, xwaš ud nēmōš / kird-ušān gēg ud duz / u-š xwānend kirbakkar / wimarzāg ī zahag ī abārīgān

They treated the meek, good, and innocent one like a thief and a robber, but they call 'beneficent' the one who destroys (?) the child of others.

L'humble, le doux, le clément, / ils en firent un voleur et un brigand ! / Et ils nomment bienfaiteur / le massacreur de la progéniture d'autrui !

2.4 Samekh

sahmēn hān ī-š guft / ka-š marg nē čašt ānād / udranzid-uš ō kunišnkar / kū-t čim kird ubdār ?

(Behold) that terrifying (word) that he spoke, when he had (– as it seems, though) not (in reality –) tasted death, (and with which) he condemned the perpetrator, (namely:) 'Why has thou crucified (me) ?'

Terrible ce qu'il a dit, / alors qu'il ne goûta pas la mort / et condamna le Créateur : / pourquoi as-tu fait (que je sois) crucifié ?

Ces stances sont du marcionisme bon teint. François de Blois va plus loin : il les considère comme un texte marcionite, que les manichéens se seraient

---

of 'Quire A' in the Dublin *Kephalaia* Codex: Further Thoughts on Mani's *Book of Mysteries*, M28I and the *First Apocalypse of James* », Pretoria Conference, *supra*.

approprié pour leur propagande. Jean de Menasce était déjà de cet avis: « Il se pourrait que certains documents soient marcionites, qui passaient aux yeux des manichéens tardifs, et qui passent aux nôtres, pour manichéens ».[37] Ma réticence vient surtout de la stance *mem*. Il est bizarre qu'un marcionite appelle "dieu de Marcion" une entité centrale de la théodicée. D'autre part, la même stance est construite sur la parabole des vignerons homicides.[38] Or, l'*Évangile de Marcion* ne comporte pas ce récit, exclu en raison de la présence d'éléments matériels vétérotestamentaires (vigne, clôture, pressoir, tour) et du comportement violent du propriétaire et de ses serviteurs. Le "dieu de Marcion" ne désignerait pas, selon moi, « the good god, the Stranger », mais le démiurge biblique, le Messie et ses partisans, juifs, judéochrétiens, chrétiens: ils ont détourné l'évangile et seront jugés en fonction du principe de rétribution des actes (*lamed*). Le Christ du créateur est celui qui meurt (*mem*), le fils de l'étranger est celui qui échappe à la mort (*samekh*): le moi divin ne peut être crucifié. Selon l'exégèse chrétienne, la parabole des vignerons homicides était comprise pour prouver l'unité des deux Testaments.[39] En opposition de contrariété face au Christ du créateur, la stance *nun* évoque l'épisode de l'arrestation de Jésus, assimilé à un brigand;[40] le qualificatif de "bienfaiteur" est, par dérision, la dénomination biblique des rois des nations et de ceux qui ont le pouvoir:[41] est visée ici probablement l'histoire d'Élisée.[42] Des petits enfants qui se moquaient de la calvitie du prophète sont maudits au nom de Dieu, puis quarante-deux d'entre eux sont dévorés par des ourses. *Satis impudens antithesis*!

---

37 J. de Menasce, *Une apologétique mazdéenne du IXe siècle: Škand-Gumānīk Vičār, La Solution décisive des doutes*, Fribourg, Librairie de l'Université, 1945 p. 208.
38 Matthieu 21, 33-46; Marc 12, 1-12; Luc 20, 9-19; Évangile selon Thomas, *logion* 65.
39 Irénée, *Contre les hérésies*, IV 36, 1-2.
40 Luc 22, 47-53.
41 Luc 22, 25.
42 2 Rois 2, 23-24.

3

The Diatessaronic Sequence of Mani's Sermon on the Life of Christ in the Berlin *Kephalaia*

Zsuzsanna Gulácsi

Abstract

Previous scholarship has demonstrated that a significant part of Christian themes in early Manichaean text and art deal with the life of Christ. This study centers on one example in the form of a sermon, purportedly given by Mani and preserved in Coptic translation from the late 4th or early 5th century in the first chapter of the Berlin *Kephalaia* (*Kephalaion 1*, 12.21–13.11). The 22-line passage under consideration is a brief summary of Jesus' life narrated in sixteen events from Incarnation to Ascension. By focusing on the question of the sourcing of these sixteen events, this study maps their correlation to the canonical gospels and to Tatian's *Diatessaron*. It demonstrates that these sixteen events do not accord with any *one* particular gospel, nor with a straightforward combination of the four gospels collectively. Instead, they follow a chronology unique to the *Diatessaron*—the earliest known gospel harmony dating from the late 2nd century and attributed to Tatian—that was used in the place of the four gospels until the end of the 5th century across Syro-Mesopotamia. This comparative assessment thus suggests that the ultimate source behind Mani's sermon was most likely the *Diatessaron*, which in turn leads to a dual conclusion: (1) Mani and the early Manichaeans in 3rd-century southern Mesopotamia learned about the life of Christ from Tatian's gospel harmony; and (2) this passage of the Berlin *Kephalaia* constitutes a Late Antique, Coptic Manichaean witness to the *Diatessaron*.

The *Kephalaia* (Copt./Gr. *kephalaia* 'chapters') is one of the earliest surviving pieces of Manichaean literature both in preservation and content. As a physical object, the *Kephalaia* consists of two large volumes of papyrus codices, measuring about 35 cm in height and 21 cm in width[1] and forming a continu-

---

1 These measurements are deduced from the size of an associated wooden cover (unnumbered item) and a papyrus folio (LS 10.16) of the *Kephalaia* housed in the Chester Beatty Library, Dublin.

ous set with of a thousand pages in total. They constitute the bulkiest ancient codices known to date, with over 250 folia (500 pages) of text in each. They were produced in Egypt sometime during the late 4th and early 5th century as confirmed by carbon-dating.[2] They were discovered at Medinet Madi in the Fayyum oasis of Egypt during the early 20th century, sold separately on the antique market, and are preserved today in Berlin (volume 1 with an introduction plus chapters 1–201) and in Dublin (volume 2 with chapters 220–347 plus an epilogue) as loose papyrus sheets framed between glass panels.[3] The Coptic text of the *Kephalaia* is a translation from a lost work written originally in Syriac in southern Mesopotamia sometime during the late 3rd century, likely after Mani's death (274 or 277 CE), by unnamed disciples in order to preserve Mani's oral instructions. The two volumes are formatted uniformly into continuously numbered chapters, each of which are labeled with an explanatory sentence given below the chapter number. The chapters themselves start with a formulaic opening and present their material as the verbatim teaching of Mani, often in response to a question. Based on this presentation, the *Kephalaia* is considered today a unique genre of religious literature. Its content is apocryphal. Nevertheless, it is regarded as a highly authoritative primary Manichaean textual source, in which Mani's words take the reader back to Sasanid Mesopotamia of Late Antiquity.[4] The ongoing labor of the editions and translations of these two volumes has been gradually making the vast and valuable content of the *Kephalaia* accessible.

The Berlin volume of the *Kephalaia* bears the title *The Chapters of the Teacher*. It retains over 261 folia (i.e., 522 pages), including the last numbered chapter 201 that originally was followed by a few additional chapters now lost from the end of its codex. This is indicated by the first surviving chapter number 220 in the Dublin volume that misses some chapters from the start of its codex. Replacing the initial German translation from the 1940s, an English translation of the well-preserved bulk of the Berlin text (from the Introduction

---

2 A carbon-dating project conducted on the Medinet Madi codices by Jason BeDuhn and Greg Hodgins (2017, 10–28) argued that the *Kephalaia* was produced in Egypt sometime during the late 4th and early 5th century. Although the *Kephalaia* itself could not be sampled due to its preservation, two other Manichaean papyrus turfs (associated with the *Psalm Book* and the *Synaxeis Codex*) found together with the *Kephalaia* at Medinet Madi could, yielding a 60-year range for the entire corpus.

3 Gardner, BeDuhn, Dilley, 2018, 3.

4 Gardner 1995, xviii–xix. Timothy Pettipiece notes that although it is probable that some authentic details of Mani's teachings are preserved in it, the *Kephalaia* itself is heavily reworked and incorporates other textual material beyond the oral memory of the community concerning its founder and his revelation (2009, 8–9). For an overview, see Gardner 2018.

to Chapter 122) was published in 1995 by Iain Gardner. The more fragmentary part of the Berlin codex (Chapters 123–201) has been edited and translated into German by Wolf-Peter Funk in 3 fascicles that were published between 1999 and 2018.

The diatessaronic passage at the focus of this study is found in the first chapter of the *Kephalaia*, titled "Concerning the advent of the Apostle." In it, Mani explains how human messengers of God—called prophets in religious studies and "apostles" in the text—come to the world by using a long analogy to farming that references seasons of planting and harvesting. Before getting to his own story of prophethood, Mani lists prior human messengers, including numerous Jewish prophets (Adam, Sethel, Enosh, Enoch, Noah, and Shem) as well as the historical Buddha, Zarathustra, and Jesus.[5] When he comes to Jesus, Mani summarizes the life of Christ in 22 lines (*Kephalaion 1*, 12.21–13.11), which read as follows:

> The advent of Jesus the Christ our Master: He came [... / ...] in a spiritual one, in a body [... / ...] as I have told you about him. I [...] him; for he came without body! Also, his apostles have preached in respect of him that he received a servant's form, an appearance as of men. He came below. He manifested in the world, in the sect of the Jews. He chose his twelve [and] his seventy-two. He did the will of his Father, who had sent him to the world. Afterwards the evil one awoke envy in the sect of the Jews. Satan went into Judas the Iscariot, one among the twelve of Jesus. He accused him before the sect of the Jews with his kiss. He gave him over to the hands of the Jews, and the cohort of the soldiers. The Jews themselves took hold of the Son of God. They gave judgment on him by lawlessness in an assembly. They condemned him by iniquity, while he had not sinned. They lifted him up upon the wood of the cross. They crucified him with some robbers on the cross. They brought him down from the cross. They placed him in the grave. After three days he arose from the dead. He came towards his disciples and was visible to them. He laid upon them a power. He breathed into them his Holy Spirit. He sent them through the whole world that they would preach the greatness. Yet he himself rose up to [the heights ... / ...].[6]

In this passage, Mani's prose takes the form of a list that succinctly outlines Jesus' life story event by event from Incarnation to Ascension.

---

5 *Kephalaion 1*, 12.9–20 (Gardner 1995, 18).
6 Gardner 1995, 18–19.

An analysis based on the standard academic classification of episodes in the life of Christ reveals that this narration contains a total of sixteen events distributed unevenly across the four cycles (**Table 3.1**). The greatest attention is given to the Passion, occupying more than half of the text (events #4–11). The other three cycles are noted with increasing attention (#1, #2–3, and #12–16). The *Incarnation* is referenced in one event that mentions (#1) Manifestation, that is, how Jesus "received a servant's form, an appearance as of men. He came below. He manifested in the world, in the sect of the Jews." The *Ministry* is also discussed briefly, but in two events: (#2) Choosing the disciples and, what might be best classified as (#3) Ministry, stating that Jesus "chose his twelve [and] his seventy-two. He did the will of his Father, who had sent him to the world." The *Passion* cycle has eight events. It starts with (#4) Satan inhabits Judas: "Afterwards the evil one awoke envy in the sect of the Jews. Satan went into Judas the Iscariot, one among the twelve of Jesus"; and continues with (#5) Betrayal and (#6) Arrest: "He accused him before the sect of the Jews with his kiss. He gave him over to the hands of the Jews, and the cohort of the soldiers." Next is (#7) Trial: "They gave judgment on him by lawlessness in an assembly. They condemned him by iniquity, while he had not sinned"; followed by the two events of the Crucifixion that mention (#8) Christ's body and (#9) robbers with it: "They lifted him up upon the wood of the cross. They crucified him with some robbers on the cross." The passion narrative concludes with (#10) Deposition and (#11) Entombment: "They brought him down from the cross. They placed him in the grave." The last cycle, the *Resurrection*, contains five events. It starts with (#12) Resurrection: "After three days he arose from the dead"; it continues with (#13) Appearance and (#14) Bestowal of Spirit: "He came towards his disciples and was visible to them. He laid upon them a power. He breathed into them his Holy Spirit"; followed by (#15) Commission: "He sent them through the whole world that they would preach the greatness"; and finally it concludes with (#16) Ascension: "Yet he himself rose up to [the heights … / …]."

TABLE 3.1 Mani's sermon on the life of Christ in the Coptic Manichaean *Kephalaia*

Kephalaion 1, 12.21–13.11 (Gardner 1995, pp. 18–19)	Sixteen events & four cycles
The advent of Jesus the Christ our Master: He came [… / …] in a spiritual one, in a body [… / …] as I have told you about him. I […] him; for he came without body! Also, his apostles have preached in respect of him that …	**Title & Mani's introduction**
… he received a servant's form, an appearance as of men. He came below. He manifested in the world, in the sect of the Jews.	**Incarnation** 1. Manifestation
He chose his twelve [and] his seventy-two. He did the will of his Father, who had sent him to the world.	**Ministry** 2. Choosing the disciples 3. Ministry
Afterwards the evil one awoke envy in the sect of the Jews. Satan went into Judas the Iscariot, one among the twelve of Jesus. He accused him before the sect of the Jews with his kiss. He gave him over to the hands of the Jews, and the cohort of the soldiers. The Jews themselves took hold of the Son of God. They gave judgment on him by lawlessness in an assembly. They condemned him by iniquity, while he had not sinned. They lifted him up upon the wood of the cross. They crucified him with some robbers on the cross. They brought him down from the cross. They placed him in the grave.	**Passion** 4. Satan inhabits Judas 5. Betrayal (with a kiss) 6. Arrest 7. Trial (in an assembly) 8. Crucifixion 9. Crucifixion (with robbers) 10. Deposition 11. Entombment
After three days he arose from the dead. He came towards his disciples and was visible to them. He laid upon them a power. He breathed into them his Holy Spirit. He sent them through the whole world that they would preach the greatness. Yet he himself rose up to [the heights … / …].	**Resurrection** 12. Resurrection 13. Appearance 14. Bestowal of Spirit 15. Commission 16. Ascension

These sixteen events do not correspond with what is discussed in any one of the four canonical gospels (**Table 3.2**). The least correlation is with the *Gospel of Mark* that contains four events from Mani's sermon: (#8) Crucifixion, that is, lifting Jesus upon the cross (Mk. 15:24), (#9) Crucifixion with robbers (Mk. 15:27), (#10) Deposition (Mk. 15:46a), and (#11) Entombment (Mk. 15:46b). The *Gospel of Matthew* discusses five events: (#6) Betrayal with a kiss (Mt. 26:49), (#8) lifting Jesus upon the cross (Mt. 27:35), (#9) Crucifixion with robbers (Mt. 27:38), (#11) Entombment (Mt. 27:60), and (#15) Commission (Mt. 28:19). The *Gospel of John* covers seven events: (#1) Manifestation (Jn. 1:14), (#3) Ministry (Jn. 6:38), (#5) Satan inhabiting Judas (Jn. 13:17), (#7) Arrest (Jn. 18:12), (#8) Crucifixion, that is, lifting Jesus upon the cross (Jn. 19:18), (#10) Entombment (Jn. 19:41–42), and (#14) Jesus' breathing the Holy Spirit into the disciples (Jn. 20:22). The greatest match is with the *Gospel of Luke*, where eleven out of Mani's sixteen events are mentioned. These include (#2) Choosing the disciples (Lk. 6:13 and 10:1), (#4) Satan inhabiting Judas (Lk. 22:3), (#5) Betrayal with a kiss (Lk. 22:28); (#7) Trial in an assembly (Lk. 22:16), (#8) lifting Jesus upon the cross (Lk. 23:33a), (#9) Crucifixion with robbers (Lk. 23:33b), (#10) Deposition (Lk. 23:53a), (#11) Entombment (Lk. 23:53b), (#12) Resurrection (Lk. 24:7), (#13) Appearance (Lk. 24:13 and 24:36), and (#16) Ascension (Lk. 24:51).

The four canonical gospels together constitute an unlikely direct source of Mani's sermon (see Tab. 2). With its four events (#8–11), the *Gospel of Mark* does not contribute anything that was not already mentioned in the *Gospel of Luke*. Between the *Gospels of Luke and John*, Mani's sermon still contains one event, (#15) the Commission, that is found only in the *Gospel of Matthew* (Mt. 28:19). Although it is not entirely impossible, it is unlikely that Mani (or his disciples) compiled these sixteen events directly from the four gospels in a way that their harmonized account coincidentally matched an already existing and widely circulated gospel harmony known to be used by the early Manichaeans.

Instead of following any one canonical gospel or any obvious combination of them, Mani's account of Jesus' life in the *Kephalaia* compares favorably to the *Diatessaron*, in terms of its content and sequence (see Tab. 2). Only the *Diatessaron* contains all of the events in Mani's sermon. More significantly, the sequence of events related by Mani follows exactly the order in which Tatian already had assembled elements from the four gospels into a harmonized account. That Mani might have coincidentally harmonized elements of Jesus' life story in exactly the same way Tatian did is historically implausible. The plausible and most parsimonious explanation of their identical sequence is that Mani based his outline of the life of Christ on the *Diatessaron*, the use of which is well attested in early Manichaean context.

TABLE 3.2 Correlation of the sixteen events of Mani's sermon in the *Kephalaia* with the four gospels and the *Diatessaron*

#	*Kephalaion 1, 12.21–13.11*	*Gospels of Matthew, Mark, Luke, and John*				*Diatessaron*
1	He manifested in the world.	∅	∅	∅	1) Jn. 1:11	1) Diat. 3:53
2	He chose his twelve [and] his seventy-two.	∅	∅	1) Lk. 6:13–Lk. 10:1	∅	2) Diat. 8:19 & Diat. 15:15
3	He did the will of his father, who sent him to the world.	∅	∅	∅	2) Jn. 6:38	3) Diat. 19:32
4	Satan went into Judas the Iscariot.	∅	∅	2) Lk. 22:3	3) Jn. 13:17	4) Diat. 44:6
5	He accused him … with his kiss.	1) Mt. 26:49	∅	3) Lk. 22:47–Lk. 22:48	∅	5) Diat. 48:25
6	He gave him over to … the cohort of soldiers.	∅	∅	∅	4) Jn. 18:12	6) Diat. 48:44
7	They gave judgment on him by lawlessness in an assembly.	∅	∅	4) Lk. 22:66	∅	7) Diat. 49:19
8	They lifted him up upon the wood of the cross.	2) Mt. 27:35	1) Mk. 15:24	5) Lk. 23:33a	5) Jn. 19:18	8) Diat. 51:25
9	They crucified him with some robbers.	3) Mt. 27:38	2) Mk. 15:27	6) Lk. 23:33b	∅	9) Diat. 51:28
10	They brought him down from the cross.	∅	3) Mk. 5:46a	7) Lk. 23:53a	∅	10) Diat. 52:30
11	They placed him in the grave.	4) Mt. 27:60	4) Mk. 15:46b	8) Lk. 23:53b	6) Jn. 19:41–19:42	11) Diat. 52:30
12	After three days he arose from the dead.	∅	∅	9) Lk. 24:7	∅	12) Diat. 52:55 & Diat. 53:15
13	He came towards his disciples and was visible to them.	∅	∅	10) Lk. 24:13–Lk. 24:36	∅	13) Diat. 53:39 & Diat. 54:1
14	He breathed into them his Holy Spirit.	∅	∅	∅	7) Jn. 20:22	14) Diat. 54:15
15	He sent them through the whole world that they would preach.	5) Mt. 28:19	∅	∅	∅	15) Diat. 55:5
16	… he himself rose up to the heights.	∅	∅	11) Lk. 24:51	∅	16) Diat. 55:13

The *Diatessaron* (Gr. διὰ τεσσάρων, lit. 'through four') is the earliest known gospel harmony, dating from the 170s CE. Attributed to the early Christian writer Tatian (ca. 120–180 CE), this text was composed in either Syriac or Greek.[7] In its Syriac form it was used as the standard gospel text across the Syriac-speaking part of the Christian world until the late fifth century.[8] This text occupies a unique position in the early dissemination of the gospels in Syro-Mesopotamia. Although it is not the only gospel harmony that existed in Syriac, there is abundant evidence for its early use in both the Roman- and Iranian-controlled parts of the region. Today, the *Diatessaron* is considered to be the form in which the gospels first appeared in Syriac during the early third century. Its use is reflected in the gospel quotations of Ephrem (ca. 306–376 CE), and Aphrahat (late third century-ca. 345 CE), which could only happen if the *Diatessaron* had been circulating in the eastern part of the Christian world from the beginnings of Syriac Christianity.[9] The "Persian sage" Aphrahat, in particular, is connected with the Persian side of the frontier region of Christianity in southern Mesopotamia that was shared with Mani, separated from the latter's time by only a couple of generations.[10] The earliest direct evidence on the use of the *Diatessaron* in the region is provided by a fragment of a parchment scroll found at Dura-Europos. Dating from before the mid-250s CE, this fragment is one of the earliest Christian manuscripts known today. It contains fourteen Greek lines from a harmonized Passion of Christ narrative. It preserves linguistic traces of a Syriac language original, suggesting that it is a translation of Tatian's work.[11] As such, the Dura fragment provides an extremely early date for the circulation of the *Diatessaron* in the region—a date that coincides with the activities of Mani.

---

7   For the assessment of the available sources, see Petersen's summary (1994, 65–67), who notes that aside from the Arabic *Diatessaron* (discussed below), all witnesses were transmitted without a title or author's name. In addition, little is known about Tatian. His biography is alluded to in his only other extant work, the *Oratio ad Graecos*, stating that he was "born in the land of the Assyrians" (1994, 68). Born to middle- or upper-class class parents with means to travel, Tatian became a wandering student and converts to Christianity in Rome round 150 CE, where he spends an extended period with Justin Martyr (d. 165 CE) and starts teaching. He returns to his homeland probably around 172 CE and founds a school. His teachings became influential and (unlike in the West) were never regarded to be heretical by the Eastern churches (1994, 72).

8   Petersen 1994, 1 and note 5; and 39. Its Syriac title, *Euangelion da-Meḥalleṭē* (lit. *Gospel of the Mixed*) is first attested from the 5th century (1994, 39). Since the first pages of the Ephrem's manuscript in Dublin do not survive.

9   Petersen 1990, 403, 405, and 407.

10 For Aphraates and the *Diatessaron*, see Burkitt 1904, 180–186.

11 The Dura Fragment (Yale University Library, Dura Parchment 24; 9.5×10.5 cm; damaged

The *Diatessaron* survives through what are called "witnesses," the two most extensive of which transmit Tatian's text from different times and stages of transmission, copied into relatively late manuscripts. The earliest is a biblical commentary written by Ephrem Syrus (d. 373 CE) in Syriac—the language associated with the *Diatessaron* in Syro-Mesopotamia. Its full text survives only in Armenian translation from the late eleventh century (1195 CE),[12] while a partially preserved version in the original Syriac is estimated to date from the late 5th or early 6th centuries.[13] Working with a 4th-century edition of the *Diatessaron*, Ephrem quotes and comments upon only select passages. For this reason, his *Commentary* cannot be used for identifying a complete diatessaronic sequence.[14] A witness suited for such a purpose must preserve the intact text of the complete *Diatessaron*. The only such text known today is an Arabic Christian translation prepared by Abul-Farag Abdallah ibn at-Tayyib (d. 1043 CE), who rendered a Syriac edition (now lost) available to him into Arabic during the first half of the eleventh century.[15] Since it preserves the full original con-

---

on four sides, verso blank) contains a very early Greek translation of a Syriac *Vulgate*. See Petersen 1990, for its text (197) and summary of scholarship (196–203); as well as Kraeling 1935, for its first publication.

12 The Armenian translation of Ephrem's *Commentary* survives in two versions, including one (manuscript A) written in a more archaic and the other (manuscript B) in a more recent Armenian script. They were produced independently from each other in geographically separate and ideologically distinct locations, but in the same year 1195 CE (644 of the Armenian calendar). Louis Leloir's critical edition of the Armenian translations was published in 1953 based on both manuscripts (McCarthy 1993, 23–24).

13 The Syriac text of Ephrem's *Commentary* is housed in the Chester Beatty Library under the accession number MS 709. Prior to its discovery in 1956 and first publication in 1963, Ephrem's text was accessible only in Armenian translation. In the introduction to his critical edition of the Syriac text, McCarthy discusses its preservation (noting that about 80% of it has been identified scattered in various other manuscripts); as well as its relation to the Armenian versions (1993, 25–34). Leloir's dating of MS 709 was based on its Estrangela script. For details, see McCarthy 1993, 28 and note 4.

14 Petersen (1990, 408–409) considers Ephrem's extensive commentary to be the most important Eastern witness of the *Diatesseron* due to its early date and diction, since Ephrem quotes and/or discusses the contents of a fourth century version of Tatian's text. Nevertheless, in her introduction to the critical edition of the Syriac manuscript (see below), McCarthy notes the problems of sorting out abbreviations, citations, allusions, and paraphrases between Ephrem's commentary in relation to Tatian's *Diatessaron* and some of Ephrem's gospel citations. She explains: "even if one were to undertake a vast text-critical study in identifying the scriptural texts used by Ephrem one might not always succeed in achieving certainty, since Ephrem is basically commenting on a *Diatessaron* text and not on a Syriac form of the four separate gospels" (1993, 35–36).

15 The critical edition of this Arabic translation was published in French by A.S. Marmarji

tent of Tatian's harmony, the Arabic *Diatessaron* is used as the primary point of comparison in this study (see **Table 3.2**).[16]

The Manichaean witnesses from the Latin-speaking part of the Roman Empire are isolated passages. Nevertheless, they are highly valued for they reflect an earlier stage of transmission to the extent that they document the *Diatessaron* before its text became vulgatized; that is, in their prose, standard gospel quotations were not adopted in place of the genuine diatessaronic variants, as is the case with the Arabic *Diatessaron*. Gilles Quispel argues that it was the Manichaeans who preserved the most authentic version of Tatian's *Diatessaron* in the West.[17] Unlike the *Diatessaron* in Syriac Christian setting, where its content was gradually brought into greater alignment with the standard texts of the Greek gospels, the Manichaean version of the *Diatessaron* in the Latin West remained "archaic" and "wild," since the Manichaeans were under no pressure to "domesticate," that is, to vulgatize it.[18]

From across the Iranian cultural region, Manichaean witnesses to the *Diatessaron* are also early, in the sense that they, too, rely on likely 3rd-century editions of Tatian's harmony that survive copied into medieval manuscripts. They include three fragmentary texts with passages from the *Diatessaron* in Parthian translation written in the Manichaean script housed in the Turfanforschung of the State Library in Berlin. They are preserved copied onto folia of paper codices produced between the 8th and 10th centuries during the Uygur era of Manichaean history. Torn pages of these books survive today. The two smaller fragments quote from the Passion. In one, Jesus addresses his disciples before his death, while in the other, the women arrive to Jesus' tomb (M 6005 and M 18, respectively).[19] The largest fragment (M 4570), famously identified by Werner Sundermann in one of his first publications on Iranian Manichaean literature, also concerns the Passion. It is titled by its header as a *Sermon on the Crucifixion*

(1935). The first English translation was published by Hamlyn J. Hill (1910, reprinted in 2001), being based on the Latin translation that appeared as the preface to the first publication of the Arabic text in the late nineteenth century (Ciasca 1888). Hill's chapter and verse numbers are identical with that of the French text in Marmarji. For an overview, see Petersen 1994, 133–140.

16   This Arabic translation is considered to be the most reliable witness to the original sequence of Tatian's text. The colophons in several of the six manuscripts state that the text was translated in medieval times, suggesting that the translator's Syriac exemplar was already vulgatized (Petersen 1990, 409).

17   Quispel 1993, 374–378.

18   For a summary of Quispel's argument, see Petersen 1994, 282, 336, and 441.

19   Petersen 1988, 187–192 (M 18); and Sundermann 1973, 106–108 (M 6005).

and compares Mani's death to that of Jesus.[20] The Parthian language of these texts imply an early origin, most likely within the era of Mesopotamian and West Central Asian Manichaeism, sometime during the mid-third and fourth centuries. Parthian was the vernacular spoken from what is now northern Iraq, across northern Iran, to the Afghan border until its gradual disappearance from everyday use under the dominance of the Persian language in the Sasanid period (224–651 CE).[21] After the 7th century, Parthian was no longer a living language. It remained, however, a *lingua sacra* in the Manichaean Church during the Uygur era.[22] The earliest record of the southern Mesopotamian version of the Aramaic script that later became associated exclusively with the Manichaeans, is also attested from Mani's time, for it is used on Mani's rock crystal sealstone to identify its owner in Syriac as *Mānī šelīhā d-Išōʿ mešīhā*, that is, 'Mani, apostle (lit. messenger) of Jesus Christ (lit. messiah).'[23]

Quite remarkably, a visual witness to the *Diatessaron* also survives from the above noted Iranian Manichaean context in the Turfan Collection of the Asian Art Museum in Berlin. In a series of studies, I have catalogued and described this fragmentary work of art (III 4976a)[24] and interpreted its codicology and pictorial content, arguing that in original condition it contained a marginal illustration that depicted of the life of Christ in at least 24 or 28 vignettes. The events—conveyed pictorially in these vignettes—follow a distinctly diatessaronic order. Concerning the preservation of these vignettes, I have confirmed that they are found on a torn folio fragment that once belonged to a luxurious, illustrated edition of an Iranian (Parthian or Middle Persian) Manichaean hymnbook made during the Uygur era sometime during the 8th and 10th cen-

---

20 Sundermann 1968, 398; and 1981, 76 and plate 33. For a comparative table, see Gulácsi 2012, 155–157; or 2015, 382–383.
21 Although it is unconfirmed whether Mani himself spoke Parthian, a variety of documentary evidence records his initiative to have church materials rendered into Parthian for missionary work among Parthian speakers, as suggested for example in *Kephalaia* 5.25: "… the writing which I [Mani] wrote on account of the Parthians [i.e., the *Book of Giants*] (Gardner 1995, 11; Tardieu 2008, 51, Fig. 3); and M 2: "And when the Apostle of Light was" in the provincial capital of Holvān, he let the teacher Mār Ammō come, who knew the Parthian script and language and was familiar with … He sent him to Abarshahr" (Gulacsi 2015, 74–75). Boyce notes about prince Ardabān that he belonged to the house of the Parthian Arsacids, and thus was a kinsman of Mani's (1975, 40).
22 Lieu 1992, 106–107.
23 Mani's sealstone (INT. 1384 BIS), housed in the collection of the Département des Monnaies, médailles et antiques of the Bibliothèque nationale de France in Paris, is the only Manichaean work of art known today from late ancient Mesopotamia (Gulácsi 2013 and 2014).
24 Gulácsi 2001, 124–125 and 237.

turies. The textual content on the verso retains just enough Manichaean script lines from a cantillated hymn to verify the paintings' physical context. Likewise, the damaged pictorial content on the recto is just enough to confirm two narrative vignettes, one depicting "Judas paid in advance by Caiaphas" (Matt 26:14) and next to it another portraying the "Washing of the Feet" (John 13:1), but not the content of additional, more damaged, adjacent vignettes. The events these vignettes depict are unconnected to one another in the canonical gospels, but are discussed together in Tatian's gospel harmony (Diat. 44:6–9 and 44:11–21), interrupted in the *Diatessaron* only by a brief reference to Judas hanging himself (Diat. 44:10).[25] Concerning the origin of these vignettes, I have argued that these images could not have been invented during the Uygur era. Their iconographic clues (e.g., lack of halo around Jesus' head) and codicological clues (e.g., sideways orientation of images in relation to the direction of the writing on a vertical codex folio) indicate that the Manichaean prototype of these vignettes was most likely first portrayed in Mani's *Book of Pictures*—the only pictorial medium attested among the Manichaeans in 3rd-century Mesopotamia.[26] This claim is supported by other analogous cases of survival, when scenes attested in textual sources from Mani's *Book of Pictures* are later adapted to other pictorial mediums (e.g., manuscript illustration) and thus are preserved from the Uygur era.[27]

The identification of a diatessaronic structure in Mani's 22-line sermon on the life of Christ in *Kephalaion 1* (12.21–13.11) allows us to add this text as an additional Manichaean witness to Tatian's *Diatessaron*, and by far the earliest. Although transmitted in Coptic translation from the late 4th or the early 5th century, the content of this sermon originates about 100–150 years earlier in southern Mesopotamia. Thus, this newly identified witness is most closely connected to two others: an Iranian Manichaean witness and a Mesopotamian Christian witness. Among the Manichaean witnesses, the sermon at the focus of this study is most akin to the Iranian visual witness. Both are attributed to

---

25   Gulácsi 2012, 150–155; or 2015, 374–380.
26   Gulácsi 2015, 297–305 and Figs. 5/40–5/42; and 374–386 and Fig. 6/19. In order to see clearer the surviving pictorial content, the two vignettes were subjected to a digital restoration that enhanced their lapis-lazuli blue background and gilded frame; but left the pairs of figures untouched in each.
27   Gulácsi 2015, 308–312, Figs. 5/44 and Tab. 5/5. The best documented example involves a textual record (*Kephalaion 92*, describing Mani teaching catechumens about soteriology with the aid of a complex scene in the *Book of Pictures* used as a prop) and a full-page soteriological illustration preserved adopted to an Uygur Manichaean service book (III 4959 verso) as a sideways-oriented image, see Gulácsi 2015, 296–300 and Figs. 5/38–5/39.

Mani and contain diatessaronic patterns of events, since Mani narrates Jesus' life according to Tatian's harmony in both: visually in the painted image, which was originally part of the *Book of Pictures* and later transmitted via a book illustration in an Iranian hymnbook (8th/10th cc); and verbally in the sermon that was purportedly once spoken by Mani, recorded by his disciples, and subsequently included in the first chapter of the Coptic *Kephalaia* (4th/5th cc). Based on its association with Mani, the sermon in the *Kephalaia* also shows close temporal and geographic ties to the Greek fragment found in the church building at Dura-Europos. Much like the Dura fragment, Mani's sermon attests the circulation of the *Diatessaron* in and around Ktesiphon, the megapolis of which was located about a ten-day walking distance south from Dura along the local trade routes. Both date from the middle of the 3rd century, since the Greek fragment was in use prior to the destruction of the city sometime around 256 CE, while Mani's activities, including his use of the *Diatessaron*, took place between 240 and 274 (or 277) CE.

Bibliography

BeDuhn, Jason and Greg Hodgins
2017. "The date of the Manichaean codices from Medinet Masi, and its significance," in *Manichaeism East and West*, edited by Sam Lieu in association with E. Hunter, E. Morano, and N.A. Pedersen, Turnhout: Brepols Publishers, 10–28.

Burkitt, Francis Crawford
1904. *Evangelion Da-Mepharreshe: The Curetonian Version of the four gospels, with the readings of the Sinai palimpsest and the early Syriac patristic evidence*, Cambridge, Cambridge University Press.

Funk, Wolf-Peter
1999. *Kephalaia I*. Manichäische Handschriften der Staatlichen Museen Berlin, Band 1, 2. Hälfte, Lfg. 13/14, Stuttgart: Kohlhammer.
2000. *Kephalaia I*. Manichäische Handschriften der Staatlichen Museen Berlin, Band 1, 2. Hälfte, Lfg. 15/16, Stuttgart: Kohlhammer.
2018. *Kephalaia I*. Manichäische Handschriften der Staatlichen Museen Berlin, Band 1, 2. Hälfte, Lfg. 17/18, Stuttgart: Kohlhammer.

Gardner, Iain
1995. *The Kephalaia of the Teacher: The Edited Coptic Manichaean Texts in Translation with Commentary*, Leiden: Brill.

2018. "Kephalaia," *Encyclopaedia Iranica*, online edition, available at http://www.iranica online.org/articles/kephalaia

Gardner, Iain, Jason BeDuhn, and Paul Dilley
2015. *Mani at the Court of the Persian Kings: Studies on the Chester Beatty Kephalaia Codex*, Leiden: Brill.
2018. *The Chapters of the Wisdom of My Lord Mani. Part III: Pages 343–442 (Chapters 321–347)*, Leiden: Brill.

Gulácsi, Zsuzsanna
2001. *Manichaean Art in Berlin Collections: A Comprehensive Catalogue*, Corpus Fontium Manichaeorum: Series Archaeologica et Iconographica 1, Turnhout: Brepols.
2005. *Mediaeval Manichaean Book Art: A Codicological Study of Iranian and Turkic Illuminated Book Fragments from 8th–11th Century East Central Asia*, Leiden: Brill.
2012. "The Life of Jesus according to the *Diatessaron* in Early Manichaean Art and Text," *Bulletin of the Asia Institute* 22 (2008): 143–169 (published in 2012).
2013. "The Crystal Seal of 'Mani, the Apostle of Jesus Christ' in the Bibliothèque Nationale de France," in N.A. Pedersen and J.M. Larsen, *Manichaean Texts in Syriac*, Corpus Fontium Manichaeorum: Series Syriaca 1, Turnhout: Brepols, 245–267.
2014. "The Prophet's Seal: A Contextualized Look at the Crystal Sealstone of Mani (216–276 CE) in the Bibliothèque Nationale de France," *Bulletin of the Asia Institute* 24 (2010): 161–185 (published in 2014).
2015. *Mani's Pictures: The Didactic Images of the Manichaeans from Sasanian Mesopotamia to Uygur Central Asia and Tang-Ming China*. Nag Hammadi and Manichaean Studies 90. Leiden: Brill.

Hill, J. Hamlyn
2001. *The Earliest Life of Christ Ever Compiled from the Four Gospels: Being The Diatessaron of Tatian, Literally Translated from the Arabic Version and Containing the Four Gospels Woven into One Story*, Edinburgh: T. & T. Clark, 1910; reprint, Piscataway: Gorgias Press.

Kraeling, Carl H.
1935. *A Greek Fragment of Tatian's Diatessaron from Dura* with contributions by A.R. Bellinger, F.E. Brown, and A. Perkins. London: Christophers.

Leloir, Louis
1953. *Saint Ephrem. Commentaire de l'évangile concordant: version arménienne*. Corpus Scriptorum Christianorum Orientalium 137. Louvain: L. Durbecq.

Lieu, Samuel N.C.
1992. *Manichaeism in the Later Roman Empire and Medieval China*, Tübingen: Mohr.

Marmarji, A.S.
1935. *Diatessaron de Tatien: texte arabe établi, traduit en français, collationné avec les anciennes versions syriaques, suivi d'un évangéliaire diatessarique syriaque et accompagné de quatre planches hors texte*, Beyrouth: Imprimerie Catholique.

McCarthy, Carmel
1993. *Saint Ephrem's Commentary on Tatian's Diatessaron: An English Translation of Chester Beatty Syriac MS 709 with Introduction and Notes*. Oxford: Oxford Univ. Press.

Petersen, William L.
1988. "An important unnoticed Diatessaronic Reading in Turfan Fragment M 18." in *Text and Testimony: Essays on New Testament and Apocryphal Literature in Honour of A.F.J. Klijn*, ed. T. Baarda et al., Kampen: Kok, 187–192.

Petersen, William L.
1990. "Tatian's *Diatessaron*." in *Ancient Christian Gospels: Their History and Development*, ed. H. Koester, London: SCM Press, 403–430 (note: in this publication the author's name was misprinted as "Peterson").

Petersen, William L.
1994. *Tatian's Diatessaron: Its Creation, Dissemination, Significance and History in Scholarship*. Leiden.

Pettipiece, Timothy
2009. *Pentadic Redaction in the Manichaean Kephalaia*, Leiden: Brill.

Quispel, Gilles
1993. "A Diatessaron Reading in a Latin Manichaean Codex," *Vigiliae Christianae* 47.4: 374–378 (repr. with additional Note in *Gnostica, Judaica, Catholica: Collected Essays of Gilles Quispel*, edited by Johannes van Oort, Nag Hammadi and Manichaean Studies 55, Leiden: Brill 2008, 77–82).
1975. "Mani the Apostle of Jesus Christ," *Gnostic Studies*, vol. 2, Istanbul: Nederlands Historisch-Archaeologisch Instituut 1975: 230–237.

Sundermann, Werner
1968. "Christliche Evangelientexte, in der Überlieferung der iranisch-manichäischen Literatur." *Mitteilungen des Instituts für Orientforschung* 14.3:386–405.

1973. *Mittelpersische und parthische kosmogonische und Parabeltexte der Manichäer.* Schriften zur Geschichte und Kultur des Alten Orients: Berliner Turfantexte, vol. 8. Berlin.

1981. *Mitteliranische manichäische Texte kirchengeschichtlichen Inhalts.* Schriften zur Geschichte und Kultur des Alten Orients: Berliner Turfantexte, vol. 11. Berlin.

Tardieu, Michel
2008. *Manichaeism*, Urbana: University of Illinois Press (tr. of *Le manichéisme*, Paris: Presses universitaires de France, 1981).

4
The Strange Case of 'Quire A' in the Dublin *Kephalaia* Codex: Further Thoughts on Mani's *Book of Mysteries*, M281 and the *First Apocalypse of James*

Iain Gardner

Abstract

In 2009 I read a paper at the ARAM Conference in which I attempted to imagine what the contents of Mani's *Book of Mysteries* might have been. The bases for the speculation were primarily the section headings for the lost work as preserved by Ibn al-Nadīm, together with some other primary sources of relevance. I remain convinced that the basic trajectory of the argument was correct, even if the details are difficult to establish. Recent advances regarding three texts I hold to be relevant make it apposite to return to the topic once again. These are:

1. Quire 'A' in the Dublin Coptic *Kephalaia* codex, for which I completed in 2018 a draft edition as part of my on-going work in collaboration with Jason BeDuhn and Paul Dilley;
2. The polemical hymns in the Middle Persian text M281, of which François de Blois has made a detailed study with reference to the *Book of Mysteries* (in press);
3. The (*First*) *Apocalypse of James* (hereafter *James*), about which we now know considerably more due to the second Coptic version recovered in the Tchacos codex and most recently a Greek text of the work identified from Oxyrhynchus as announced late in 2017 by Geoffrey Smith and Brent Landau (edition in preparation).

All this work is very much in process, but I am in the unique position of being able to survey the material, with the kind assistance of the named scholars. This paper is a speculative first attempt to unravel the interrelations between the various texts. These suggest a number of important avenues for new research. The present discussion limits technical discussion of the texts due to its provisional nature.

The ultimate purpose of this research project, for which this paper is a kind of tentative and speculative interim report, is to recover as much as possible about the contents of Mani's lost *Book of Mysteries*; together with the work's continuing influence upon the teachings and practices of the community that held it as scripture. Here it is shown that *James* was an important source accessed and utilised by Mani in his writing; and also that two later productions extant now in Coptic and Middle Persian demonstrate the enduring impact upon Manichaean literature.

1 The *Book of Mysteries*

In 2009 I read a paper at the *ARAM* Conference held in the Oriental Institute of the University of Oxford, in which I attempted to imagine what the contents of Mani's *Book of Mysteries* might have been. The bases for the speculation were primarily the section headings for the lost work as preserved by Ibn al-Nadīm, together with such relevant information as was then available. Although the paper was published with others from the Conference[1] it attracted little attention, no doubt due to its hypothetical orientation and the limited audience. Nevertheless, I remain convinced that the basic trajectory of the argument is correct, even if the details are difficult to establish and individual suggestions I made at that time may well be improved upon.[2] Indeed, recent advances regarding three texts make it apposite to return to the topic once again.

The basic findings of my prior research as relevant here can be summarised in brief. Ibn al-Nadīm's *Fihrist* (Arabic, late tenth century but utilising earlier sources) lists eighteen section headings or chapter titles from this lost work by Mani. See the appended list.[3] Although there are a number of serious problems with the readings in the manuscripts available, and the bare titles are famously enigmatic, it was my thesis that they can be used in two important ways. One is to understand the sort of content and source-material Mani as author was interested in discussing in his book; the other is to sketch out the broad outline of his argument. It is apparent that he accessed a number of 'texts' that were known to him, with a notable focus on traditions about Jesus in the early part

---

1   See Gardner 2010.
2   In the following discussion I introduce a number of revisions or improvements upon the findings of my earlier research. In this present volume Dylan Burns also argues that chapters 6–8 of Mani's work did not concern cosmology (as per Gardner 2010), but continued the exegesis of early Christian apocalypses I had identified in the previous sections. Further, his paper has a valuable focus on the Bardesanite context for the *Book of Mysteries* as a whole, which leads him to suggest an overarching rationale or theme for the entire narrative. It is helpful to read both our papers in conjunction as approaches to the problem of reconstructing the lost scripture.
3   Following Gardner 2010, where further discussion of the textual problems, variant readings, and reference to editions and commentaries can be found. I reproduce the previous translations unchanged, although the research and conclusions of the current study might suggest some improvements. De Blois' forthcoming paper also supplies a list with some detailed notes on the Arabic text.

of his work. The question of the form in which these were available is of obvious importance for research, as we must be talking about the apostle's career in the decades between when he left the 'baptists' of his youth and his final sufferings (i.e. ca. 240–270 C.E.). It seems that when the chapter titles refer to *The testimony of* ... (for example nos. 2. 3, 5) they are referring to some kind of authoritative textual tradition, oral or written; works that it may be possible to identify in the known corpus of literature. Since Mani's cultural world was that of the Aramaic-speaking population of Sasanian Mesopotamia, the opportunity is provided to learn something about the circulation of such literature at that time and place. In the *ARAM* paper I made a number of suggestions about what these works might have been, which included *inter alia* such as the *Oracles of Hystaspes* (no. 2); *Apocalypse of James* (no. 3); *Gospel of Judas* (no. 5).

At the same time, it is evident that Mani was utilising these authorities in his on-going debates with other communities present in his life, notably the Bardaisanites (referred to explicitly as the Daysaniyya in nos. 1, 12 and 13); but quite probably others such as Marcionites. Finally, it seemed to me unlikely that the lost book was simply a ragged collection of bits and pieces, although this is the first impression given by the titles; but rather that as author Mani would have made all this material subject to his own presentation of a revealed wisdom, the general outline of which can be reconstructed with due caution and accords with his known teaching elsewhere. This would have included the familiar narrative of the history of the soul, the construction of the universe, transmigration and the degradation of the body, eschatology and the future hope. In all of this it is notable that the figure of Jesus is central, and Mani's accessing of pseudepigraphic and non-canonical sources (including hints of so-called Sethian literature and suchlike) are bound to fascinate modern scholars.

2   James

Whereas the *Book of Mysteries* must be counted a lost work, the contents of which we are only beginning to understand, *James* is a known text about which we have learnt a great deal more in the last decade. A second Coptic version to that from Nag Hammadi was recovered in the Tchacos codex, although it was the *Gospel of Judas* that received the major publicity at the time of that remarkable story. This has made it possible to gain a much better understanding of passages in the first-recovered version that had been difficult to comprehend, whether because of their fragmentary preservation or the state of the scribal redaction. The availability of the two copies, which have significant differences and contexts,[4] enables substantial advances to be made; whilst the announcement of Greek fragments of the composition identified in the Oxyrhynchus papyri, and thus a third context (which the editors suggest might have been as a teacher's model), makes it certain that this work will be the subject of major interest in the decade ahead.[5]

In view of these advances it is now fairly obvious that my original speculative suggestion regarding Mani's access of *James* was correct, and indeed that it was more central to the content of the *Book of Mysteries* than I had supposed. Whereas in my first research I had noted linkages with sections 3–4 as preserved by Ibn al-Nadīm, it now seems probable that they extended at least as far as section 8, and perhaps even further. The association of *James* with the *Gospel of Judas* in the Tchacos codex is also suggestive (see sections 5 and 9 for the latter). It is conceivable that the range of revelatory traditions under discussion may have reached Mani in a similar kind of collected corpus, just as NHC V also brought a series of apocalypses into association with each other. However, I will focus here on *James* as it is the intertextuality between that work and 'quire A' of the Dublin *Kephalaia* codex that will be of most interest at this time.

In order to explain my reasoning it is necessary to make a brief account of the content of *James* especially as regards the 'seven women' and the 'seven spirits'. The meaning and significance of this passage towards the conclusion of the work has become much clearer since the recovery of the Tchacos version, due to a better-preserved Coptic text. Indeed, if we leave aside for the moment the narrative and quasi-historical frames within which the actual revelatory teaching is presented and conveyed, it has long been recognised that *James* has a particular concern with femaleness.[6] Like much of its genre it is focussed on the issues of descent, loss and ignorance with their converse in ascent, reintegration and wisdom; working at multiple levels as regards theogony, cosmology, psychology, social legitimacy, praxis and so on. In this instance the question at issue is hooked upon the status of the feminine as instantiated in the naming of seven female disciples of Jesus, their identity with the seven spirits and consequently their authority relative to the twelve. We can see how the text operates

---

4 See the discussion by Jennot 2017, with a strong defence of the value of such scribal variants together with the importance of redactional histories and the study of the artefacts themselves (rather than the pursuit of some idealised *ur*-text); for evaluation and rejection of a Valentinian origin for *James* see Thomassen 2013.
5 E.g. the doctoral dissertations of Edwards 2015 and Haxby 2013.
6 See especially the study by Marjanen 2009; insightful comment by Funk 2009: 523–525. The teaching about the 'seven spirits' is explicitly derived in *James* from scripture, i.e. Isaiah 11:2–3.

and shifts between the Lord's approval or induction of different groups of his disciples in the gospel story (7, 12 and 72);[7] the communities and practices with which they are associated as regards the composition and circulation of the work we know of as *James*; the rulers of the planets and the stars through whose heavens the Son of God has descended, and whose power and judgement in the world the hearer must negotiate.

If we foreshadow what can be thought a Manichaean interpretation of the discourse, we can see how the multivalent nature of this would correspond well with their own method and concern with taxonomies. For example, in *Kephalaion* 337 Mani engages in complex numerological calculations as he seeks to explain to Goundesh the mysteries of the twelve and the seventy-two chosen by Jesus; the guides and angels established in the heavens; the numbers of the teachers and the leaders he has appointed as shepherds and guardians for his own church. Further, whereas the issue in *James* concerns the status of the seven spirits who have preached through the prophets in advance of the coming of the Lord and the fulfilment that he has brought, this would now be tailored to fit the relationship between Mani's own community and those other prior religions and laws that had partial access to the truth now fully incarnated in the body of his church. There is also something of this in Mandaeism, where Jesus is identified with Mercury and so forth.

There is a great deal to be explored about *James*, but my purpose here can only be to prepare the ground for future research with reference to what I understand to be the evidence for its use by Mani and his followers; and, most especially, for what I will demonstrate as an example of such intertextuality in 'quire A'. With that in mind, I detail two episodes or topics. The first is the curious pericope found in both Coptic versions where the Lord relates to James an episode from his descent through the archontic realms concerning Adōnai.[8] I translate from the Tchacos codex:

> When ⟨I⟩ passed by the earth of the great ruler called Addōn I went in to him and he was without knowledge; but when I came away from him he was thinking about me that I am his son, and he favoured me as his own son.

In this passage the purpose is clear: To demonstrate the ignorance and lowly status of the biblical God, whilst at the same time to provide a kind of origin-

---

7 See further Funk 2009: 525–533.
8 CT 2. 26, 11–19; NHC V, 3. 39, 8–18. Cf. the commentary in Brankaer and Bethge 2007: 237–238.

story for the title 'Son of Adōnai' (and thus suggesting to us something of interest about the context out of which this tradition developed).

The second topic is that of the seven female disciples. There has been considerable debate about the exact numbers, the list of names and their standing according to the teaching in *James*. Again, the Tchacos codex has been of substantial assistance in clarifying these matters and in its clear identification of the women with the seven spirits. In brief summary, there is found here a teaching concerning four women who were perhaps grouped as witnesses of the empty tomb, who are primary and considered in a positive way (however qualified or imperfect); and another group of three who are secondary and may be regarded more negatively. The first list consists of Mariam, Salōmē, Arsinoē and I think Martha (rather than "the other Mary"); the other of Sappira, Susanna and Jōanna.[9] As I already noted in my *ARAM* paper,[10] the only known references to Arsinoē other than in *James* are in Manichaean literature; that is in the Coptic *Psalm-Book*[11] and the Parthian fragment M 18. I will return to this topic when I discuss 'quire A'.

3   M 281

However, before that I must turn to the Middle Persian text M 281. It has long been recognised that this piece contains polemical material that corresponds to some of the teachings evident in the *Book of Mysteries*. For instance, Ibn al-Nadīm provides a gloss to section header no. 4 (*The son of the widow*) by saying that here Mani means the Messiah who was crucified by the Jews; whilst in M 281 there are striking remarks about the God of Marcion, the one who was seized and killed, the one who was crucified but did not taste death. Such references can be associated with other hints in the literature, notably a quotation ascribed to Mani's *Fundamental Epistle* (or: *Letter of the Foundation*) preserved by Evodius, that the enemy who had hoped to crucify the saviour was himself

---

9   This outline, as with all my comments on *James*, is necessarily abrupt; I have sought to avoid engagement with difficult problems as the content of this work is not the point of my argument. It is also obvious that I am influenced in my presentation of *James* by what I see in the Manichaean texts, where an interpretative lens has certainly been applied. For example, I presume Mariam is the Magdalene (cf. the Psalms of Heracleides at PsBk2 187, 2–35 and 192, 21–24 with John 20:1–18); but one is conscious of the problems as discussed in Jones 2002, particularly the papers by Shoemaker and Marjanen.

10   Gardner 2010: 325 n. 20.

11   PsBk2 192, 24; 194, 22.

crucified; all such pointing to the unveiling of a mystery that it was 'another' upon the cross.[12] This was a topic that I first explored in my PhD thesis at the very start of my career almost forty years ago! However, no complete edition of M 281 was available until one was published by Skjaervø in 1997, utilising photographs made available by Sundermann;[13] but despite this major advance the contents have remained difficult and obscure. In recent years de Blois has continued working on the text and has made a number of presentations both oral and written about it. Since this is very much his own research, with his major study at present in press, I will here only make a very brief summary of why this is important for our purposes.[14]

M 28 is a bifolium from Turfan containing hymns in Middle Persian. One leaf (M 28II) contains hymns to Jesus; the other (M 28I) preserves polemical content in abecedarian form. Here are found what de Blois describes as the final three stanzas of hymn 1, the complete 22 stanzas of hymn 2, and the first six of hymn 3. In the second hymn he identifies six sections attacking individual religious communities, that he lists as the Jews, Magians, Elchasaites ("Petrine Christians"), Marcionites, Bardaisanites and pagans. De Blois is clear that the hymn is not itself the *Book of Mysteries*, but asserts that it touches on many of the same themes in a versified, compact form. I agree with this, although with regard to detail I may understand both Mani's work and the composition from Turfan in rather different ways. I do think that we can use some of the stanzas in this hymn 2 for our purposes, and with even more precision than de Blois in his commentary; but whether all sections in that work are directed to the canonical scripture is more problematic and open to further research.[15]

As with *James*, for the present I will be brief and draw attention to a couple of phrases in order to progress our discussion towards the goal of 'quire A'. We can begin with:[16]

---

12   Cf. Gardner 2010: 324–325 with further references; also Sundermann 2002 for a summary of sources and discussion.

13   See the account in Skjaervø 1995 [1997], with details of previous partial editions and substantial commentary. Another interesting Manichaean text in Middle Persian (M 627) with polemic against the Christians was published by Sundermann 2009.

14   I was present at F. de Blois' presentation in Paris (June 2015), and the following summary is based substantially on the in-press article kindly provided to me by him in advance of publication.

15   For instance it is not clear to me whether the *Book of Mysteries* contained the sort of anti-Zoroastrian material found here in the four stanzas de Blois groups as against the Magians.

16   M 28I, ri, 19–23. All the following translations of the text are those of de Blois, with minor formatting changes. Skjaervø 1995: 245 has 'perplexed' for 'weary'.

> I made Adonay and his foul offspring weary and ashamed, saying: 'If God is one, who then deceived Gēhmurd (Adam)?'.

Although de Blois does not exactly explain his reasoning, he regards this section as against the Jews; presumably because of the reference to Adōnai and the Genesis story, and also he translates the following stanza as against the sabbath and circumcision. Interestingly, the difficulties in the text are evidenced in that Leurini in a recent article[17] understands that second stanza very differently, with reference to the tearing of the temple curtain. I do not find her interpretation convincing, nor am I persuaded that this material is specifically anti-Jewish; it seems to me more probable that the context (Adōnai and his offspring) relates to the sort of demiurgic and archontic preoccupations evident in texts such as *James* and other Nag Hammadi apocalypses. The deception of Adam may not simply be that of the overt biblical story (i.e. the serpent) to which we naturally default. Instead, does it allude to the many accounts of the mockery and confusion of the ignorant rulers in that literature? In the preceding and opening lines to hymn 2 (listed simply by de Blois as 'Introduction') one must surely expect a governing phrase and the theme for the entire production, and it is notable that this is what is found there.[18] This brings it closer to my understanding of the content of the *Book of Mysteries* (see section 9, *Laughter*).

This reading of Adōnai and the context for this polemic is reinforced by a later stanza in which he is again named, and which in its format is a kind of duplicate to the one regarding Adam:[19]

> They call Bar Maryam the seventh son of Adonay. If he is the lord of everything, who then crucified his son?

---

17 Leurini 2018.
18 M 281, ri, 14–18. De Blois declines to give a full translation ("I ... his and I ... his teaching and I laughed at him with the biting laughter of men"), although he notes that it must be someting like "I mocked/refuted/destroyed his teaching". On this theme of the descent through the archontic realms and the mockery of their ignorance, see the text of P. Macq. I 1. 9, 7–14, with references in Choat and Gardner 2013: 94–95. Although that late ritual codex is at a remote distance to this present text and to *James*, the parallel phrasing is striking.
19 M 281, rii, 24–28. There is a notable parallel in PsBk2 56, 31–57, 14 ("Who then led Adam astray and crucified the Saviour?") where the role of Adōnai is taken by 'the God of this aeon'.

The subject is certainly the false Jesus, the son of Mary in contrast to the son of God, described as the 'son of the widow' in the *Book of Mysteries* (no. 4). I doubt de Blois' explication of the numbering in terms of what he describes as the 'true prophet' teaching of the Elchasaites; it is more likely to be related to the archontic hebdomads (see above on the 'foul offspring' of Adōnai).

Two stanzas later there is the renowned statement about the 'God of Marcion':

> That thing which they did (is) like (what) Marcion's God (did), when he led away that which was not his own, and they seized and killed (him).

De Blois explains that this figure is the 'Stranger', that being the technical term used by the Marcionites (known from a variety of sources) for their newly-revealed God who redeems the souls of mankind from the creator through the sacrifice of his son. Thus "that which was not his own" refers to these souls. As we will see this very topic receives a remarkable commentary in 'quire A', to which I will turn in a moment; and where we will also need to think about how the phrase can be tracked to that pericope in *James* where Adōnai is deceived into thinking that the son of the true God is his own. We keep returning to that same theme of deception and counterfeit. The point is made explicit in the M 281 hymn two stanzas later, where this series of utterances about the crucifixion culminates in the following:

> Terrifying is that (word) that he spoke, when he had not (in fact) tasted death. He condemned the perpetrator (saying): "Why hast thou crucified me?".

In sum, hymn 2 in M 281 is closely related to the content of the *Book of Mysteries*, but its interpretation still needs to be re-thought. The passages we have considered are governed by the theme declared in the opening stanza, the mockery that is made of those archontic powers characterised by foolishness and ignorance. I doubt de Blois' neat grouping of six target communities, which tends to control his own understanding of the verses and the discussion provided in his commentary. The translation of a number of passages needs further research; and I think the theme of truth and appearance, defined by the mystery of the cross, is fundamental.

4 'Quire A'

Let me now introduce what I have termed the strange case of 'quire A' from the Dublin *Kephalaia* codex. The on-going project to edit the Coptic text of *The Chapters of the Wisdom of My Lord Mani* as it is preserved in the Chester Beatty Library is a collaborative endeavour with Jason BeDuhn and Paul Dilley. The first fascicle to be completed was published by Brill in 2018. In fact this is Part III of our planned edition, a section of a hundred pages (pp. 343–442) that cover the final chapters of the work itself (nos. 321–347), prior to the account of Mani's 'Last Days' that is appended in the Coptic codex after the conclusion of the actual *Kephalaia*. The publication utilised the pages conserved and put under glass by Hugo Ibscher as quires B–F and numbered from 1–60; followed directly by quires X–VIII (part way through which the sequence of chapters concludes), which had been worked through later by his son Rolf Ibscher. It will be apparent that the very first pages conserved by the father as quire A were not included here; but their special status is indicated by their not being listed within his sequence from 1–60.

The second fascicle (Part II) is now under preparation and corresponds to quires V–I conserved by Rolf Ibscher. This begins in the approximate middle of the original codex and is the remnants, often rather poorly preserved, of a coherent set of eighty pages of material that ends somewhat before the start of that edited in Part III. In other words, there appears to be a substantial portion of the original manuscript that is now lost between what was conserved as quire I (concluding this eighty-page section) and where Hugo Ibscher began his work on the preserved part of quire B at codex page 343. In our codicological reconstruction as it currently stands we calculate this missing portion as three full quires plus the first six pages of B (i.e. 54 pages total); but this is a theoretical calculation based on the average length of chapters in this part of the original work.

A substantial section of Part II is made up of material that I have glossed the 'Jesus-Book'.[20] This begins at chapter 295 and concludes probably at number 304. It is a relatively extensive unit extending through several quires and for over fifty pages of text. It conforms to the *kephalaia*-genre in that each chapter is presented as a discourse by the apostle, or dialogue with an interlocutor; but it demonstrates a contained sequence in that it begins with discussion of the

---

20 This was first outlined in a paper read at the Society of Biblical Literature Annual Meeting in San Antonio, November 2016. It has recently been published in Appendix C yo my *The Founder of Manichaeism: Rethinking the Life of Mani*. Cambridge University Press, Cambridge (2020).

advent of Jesus, then proceeding across the standard elements of the gospel story from the birth through miracles, wisdom-sayings, the passion, empty tomb and ascension. The format of the 'Jesus-Book' is not that of a narrative of the life of Jesus; rather it is a repository of community traditions and teachings arranged across the arc of the life from the advent to his ascension, and all put into the mouth of Mani as the ultimate authority who uses the opportunity to expound his own revealed wisdom. Within all this there is certainly evidence of those streams of tradition to which the Manichaeans were heir, such as Jesus' laughter; his multiplicity; the way that he changed himself upon the cross. In this sense it has some parallels with what I understand to have been the content of the *Book of Mysteries*, but here woven into a very different literary form and I think at some considerable distance to the canonical work.

However, of more immediate value in our task is the material conserved as quire A. This is much closer to what I understand to have been the specific topics of the lost work and the texts that I think Mani was engaged with there. Indeed, when I first began to read the Coptic text I wondered whether it might actually belong to the *Book of Mysteries*. In his discussion of the codicology, Rolf Ibscher states that Hugo had started on what he knew as codex C by removing four leaves from the back ("... die 4 Blaetter, die mein Vater zuerst von hinten des Codex C abgehoben hat ..."), which he labeled C.1–4.[21] These are the four leaves or eight pages now assigned to quire A.[22] Since Hugo Ibscher subsequently began numbering at 1 again for his quire B we must suppose quire A to be a loose set of uncertain placement within the original book. Indeed, Rolf believed, noting what he describes as their faded and reddish ink,[23] that the folios of quire A might not have belonged to the *Kephalaia* at all, but to have formed part of another unknown text such as he thought he could identify in certain layers of the codex-remains.

I have entitled this paper "The Strange Case of 'Quire A'" due to these issues. These pages show no immediate evidence of having belonged to the *Kephalaia*, in that there is no trace of chapter numbers or titles, nor obvious instances of the characteristic style. The ink does indeed look somewhat different, with

---

21 Typed memorandum by Rolf Ibscher from October 1955, entitled "Buchtechnisches zu den Restlagen des Psalmenbuches und con [*sic*] Codex C", p. 4. On p. 5 he refers to the 'Rueckseite'. However, given that Rolf was recalling actions at second hand from more than two decades before, and also that it is not clear in what state Hugo Ibscher had first encountered the codex remains (but probably not as we now understand it), this statement is of limited assistance for any reconstruction.

22 To be exact, Rolf Ibscher states that C.1 was the last folio of one quire, and C.2–4 are what remains from 'quire A'; but the status of this is difficult to determine.

23 Memorandum dated 29th November 1955: "verblassten Tinte, die ins roetliche spielt".

a distinct reddish tinge to it; and there are these curious comments by Rolf Ibscher. However, after very careful autopsy during 2018 in the Chester Beatty Library, focussed on the extremely poor traces of the page headers, I now think that these leaves must indeed belong to the Dublin *Kephalaia* codex. Nevertheless, this does not remove the possibility that their content may have been closely associated with the *Book of Mysteries*. There are examples, for instance, where exegesis or discussion of one or other of Mani's works formed the basis for individual chapters; e.g. the *Treasure of Life* (nos. 293 and 332). There are also many instances where extraneous literary material has been subjected to the kephalaiac genre with only the most minimal adaptation; e.g. fables such as the vanity of the peacock or the lion and the fox (appended to nos. 331 and 335). Indeed, there is even the example of the version of the literary cycle concerning Mani's last days that has simply been included into the codex, complete with the standard running headers (*The Chapters of the Wisdom | of My Lord Mani*), but in this instance without any of the constraints of being made to conform to the artifice of individual chapters. In other words, although we cannot know where the pages conserved as quire A belonged in the original codex, there are a number of possibilities for their subject-matter to be closely related to the *Book of Mysteries*.

In order to understand why I might think this it is necessary to outline some of the content. It must be emphasised that the condition of the pages is very poor. Only one leaf displays a substantial amount of preserved text, and that primarily on one side (facs. ed. 341). For the remainder it has been a struggle to ascertain much about their subject matter, although I have made some progress of interest. Further, due to the codicological problems already described, the sequence of the pages is by no means certain. One cannot even be sure if they form a consecutive series of leaves. For all these reasons and more, I will not provide any kind of draft edition; but rather summarise in brief some of what I understand to be the principal topics discussed insofar as they can be clearly ascertained. There are more points of interest than these, but the following is sufficient for present purposes.

The sequence to focus on begins with facs. ed. 344. Here a number of the female disciples of Jesus are named: Marihammē, Martha, Salōmē and Arsenoē. The inclusion of the last immediately recalls *James*, the only non-Manichaean text where the name is recorded; and, of notable interest, this new occurrence carries the suggestion of a narrative context in which she has her individual part to play. There is mention of "these four", so it is possible that a reference to Maria in the following line should be set apart from the women listed before. In chapter 295, where the 'Jesus-book' opens with a discussion of the advent of the saviour, it is clear that the 'son of Mary' must be kept distinct from the 'son of God'; perhaps the apparent naming of Maria here is something similar, but that is not yet clear.

The next content that can be read runs from the bottom of this page to the better-preserved facs. ed. 341. It concerns "three spirits" whose trickery, it seems, is established in the world today. There follows a series of polemical attacks against the assertions of various laws (*nomos*) through whose proponents these spirits speak. If it is valid to link these topics together, which is necessarily speculative, we can summarise: A tradition regarding groups of gospel women and series of spirits, four of which are positive and three are negative, is followed by an explication of the errors worked by the negative spirits in the teachings and presumably the communities that Mani opposed. The use of the term *nomos* is very interesting in Manichaean literature, where it is used for what we might think of as a religion, equivalent to the Iranian *dēn*. Thus, in my reading of this complex text, I identify a topic of exegesis that draws its ultimate inspiration from the revelations in *James* that we have seen Mani accessed in his *Book of Mysteries*, noting especially sections 7 and 8 on the seven spirits and then the four.[24] Presumably what we read here in the Dublin codex is a secondary expansion upon what has been lost to us in the canonical source.

If this sounds a little tenuous, details of the teachings attacked here may help to reinforce my argument. There are two in sequence on this page that are well-enough preserved and speak directly to those themes we have discussed already, as regards M 281 but also the pericope in *James* about the descent to the realm of Adonai. The first is an attack upon what must be Marcion's teaching, although he is not named. We read of the one who descends from an outer place to Adonai, coming for that which is not his own, and for this reason is said to be a 'stranger' who is called "the taker of what is not his". It is astonishing that here we have explicit, in Coptic, both the technical term for that newly-revealed 'God of Marcion' (i.e. 'stranger') and what must now be regarded as a catch-phrase preserved in the Middle Persian hymn.

The second false teaching follows directly on the first, in that it continues to talk about the advent of the son of God. This error is ascribed to the law of the spirit of forgery (*plastographia*). It is to say that he "is the son of Adonai", the

---

24 There is an evident problem in the description of the four spirits in Ibn al-Nadīm's section header no. 8: *The discourse on the four transitory (?) spirits*. See the discussion in Gardner 2010: 327–328, utilising prior comments on the Arabic text by de Blois (see also his entry in de Blois and Sims-Williams 2006: 51b–52a). My earlier attempt to understand the possible content of this section has been superseded by the realisation that Mani was discoursing on *James*, and I now suppose that the difficulty here relates to the issue of the ambivalent status of these four.

one who came from him and did his will, because he (i.e. Adonai as creator) is the God who has made everything, both the light and the darkness. This builds to a fierce critique of such demiurgic error, that it could be God who is the cause of every killing and so on.

5   Conclusions

Inevitably, this has been a speculative paper as many of the texts under discussion are difficult, poorly preserved, and still in the process of being edited. Nevertheless, the intertextuality demonstrated here suggests a number of important avenues for new research on two topics of considerable interest: Mani's lost *Book of Mysteries* and *James*. As regards the first of these, it has been argued that significant details about the content of the canonical work, and its use by the Manichaean community, can be derived from two texts that do survive, albeit only in fragmentary form. These are the polemical stanzas in the Middle Persian text M281 (building upon the research of François de Blois and earlier scholars) and the pages from the Chester Beatty Coptic *Kephalaia* codex conserved in what we know as 'quire A'.

If I can be permitted a brief excursus here. The situation is rather the same as with another of Mani's lost canonical works: the *Treasure (thēsauros) of Life*.[25] Editorial work on the Dublin codex is enabling us to inch towards a better understanding of its content. Already in the Berlin codex (chapter 91) Mani is given to comment that he has already written about this before in the *Treasure of Life*: A catechumen who will not pass further through transmigration is like a pearl without price, whereas for the others each will be liberated according to their deeds and their entry to the church.[26] These asides might hardly be noticed, but now their significance becomes clear. In chapter 293 from the Dublin codex the apostle is depicted in the assembly whilst his book is being read, whereupon there is a discourse with a catechumen about a pearl worth one hundred denarii. These elements suggest that the story is related to the parable of the pearl-borer, known from the introduction to *Kalīla wa Demna* (i.e. the collection of tales circulated in the west as the *Fables of Bidpai*) but also recorded in two Manichaean Sogdian manuscripts edited by Henning.[27] In *Kephalaion* 293 the point of the story, the telling and details of which are unfortunately very poorly preserved, is about the fear of transmigration. In the

---

25   For a recent study of all that is known about this book see Stein 2016.
26   1Ke 230, 7–11 and 20–24.
27   Henning 1945.

Sogdian versions it is certain that this is indeed the well-known fable, and in M 135 it is contextualised within a kephalaiac structure (incidentally one of the clearest instances of the circulation of this genre in the Middle Iranian literatures of the Manichaean East). In the other manuscript (So 18300 = T i T M 418) the allegorical interpretation is given: the pearl-borer is the body; the denarii are a hundred years of life; the owner of the pearls is the soul; the boring of the pearls represents piety.

In chapter 332 the apostle is again listening to a reading from his own *Treasure of Life*, but on this occasion his interlocutor is the sage Goundesh. The latter proceeds to tell a lengthy parable about a wonderful, precious stone with all sorts of special qualities. Interestingly, the specific designation of a pearl (*margarites*) seems only to occur in some kind of secondary analogy to the stone,[28] which itself is a kind of magical object. Nevertheless, the theme of it being beyond price is clear, and Goundesh compares it to the great book.

Thus, the repetition of these same *topoi* enables us to gain a clearer sense of what the lost book must have contained. Canonical scriptures in any tradition provide a reservoir of phrases, images and references that are continually replayed in all the productions of that community. Since modern scholarship is in the curious position of possessing substantial Manichaean literature whilst at the same time being almost entirely devoid of the works of the apostle himself, it is difficult to recognise those instances of intertextuality that would have been obvious to believers. However, each recovery of a topic from one of these lost books has a cumulative effect as one can then see the multiple occasions when it is referenced, as here with this complex of intertwined teachings and symbols (pearl/piety/catechumen/liberation). I suspect it would be worth pursuing these same throughout the available corpus in order to learn more about the *Treasure of Life*. That must wait for another project; but at least the web of allusions behind the title of Mani's book has become evident and point to the *Gospel of Thomas* as its proximate source.[29]

Thus, to return to our primary thesis, I suggest that we have uncovered a similar group of literary topoi related to the spirits who speak through those false teachings promulgated by the religious communities that Mani rejected. By his coming as the spirit of truth and his revelation their errors are exposed. As we look at this we can identify echoes and repeated phrasing about the descent of the son of God through the archontic realms, the way that he changed his

---

28 2Ke 376, 20–21.
29 Thomas log. 76; cf. Matthew 6:19–21 and 13:44–46 etc. The rich imagery and citations in P. Kellis v Copt. 32, referencing the good catechumen Eirene, demonstrate this complex of ideas; but the literature on the pearl is of course enormous.

appearance, the issues of truth and illusion. I suggest that through this we can uncover a better understanding of what was in the *Book of Mysteries*. We can identify important details about the apostle's source-material, and that may tell us a great deal about the evolution of his thought and the context within which he worked; and also about the way in which all this shaped the community of believers and was utilised by them in their future productions.

Finally, this also has important potential for a rather different avenue of research, that regarding the circulation and reception of *James*, perhaps even the development and understanding of its text. Three copies of this work have been identified from Egypt. However, the primary trajectory of its influence was in the Syriac-speaking communities of the Christian East. This is made apparent by the preserved text which, quite remarkably, contains its own commission narrative. It tells how the revelations were transmitted by Jesus, second only to the One-Who-Is, to James; then by a lineage established from Addai through the figures named as Manael and Levi to a second son of Levi. There are clear hints about who these figures were, the times and the locations within which they taught.[30] At a certain point this tradition was accessed by Mani in Sasanian Mesopotamia, who used it to promulgate his own revelation and define his church against its rivals and opponents. What can we know or reconstruct about the prior history of *James*?

6 Appendix: Mani's *Book of Mysteries*, section headers from Ibn al-Nadīm's *Fihrist*

1. *An account of the Daysaniyya*
2. *The testimony of Yastasif on the Beloved*
3. *The testimony of … about himself given to Yaʿqub*
4. *The son of the widow*
5. *The testimony of Jesus about himself as given to Judas*
6. *The commencement of the testimony of the right (hand) / righteous (one) as given after his victory*

---

30 Edwards 2015: 144–179 makes a sustained effort to identify as much as possible from the text and evident parallels (such as traditions about Addai). This is valuable, if only partially successful, and more work needs to be done. See also the detailed study of Pedersen 2018, who emphasises the legendary features to the chain of transmission but is tentative in his conclusions. On the thesis by Han Drijvers that interprets Addai traditions by means of Mani's disciple Mar Addā (and ignores the evidence of *James*) see Drijvers 1996: 164–165; Edwards 2015: 158; Funk 2009: 512 n. 11; Pedersen 2018: 189–191 and *passim*.

7. *The seven spirits*
8. *The discourse on the four transitory (?) spirits*
9. *Laughter*
10. *The testimony of Adam regarding Jesus*
11. *The fall from religion*
12. *The discourse of the Daysaniyya on the soul and the body*
13. *Refutation of the Daysaniyya on the living soul*
14. *The three trenches*
15. *The preservation of the world*
16. *The three days*
17. *The prophets*
18. *The resurrection*

7 Abbreviations, Texts and Editions

1Ke   *Kephalaia*, (Manichäische Handschriften der Staatlichen Museen Berlin I), ed. H.J. Polotsky, A. Böhlig and W.-P. Funk, Kohlhammer, Stuttgart, 1940, 1966, 1999, 2000, 2018.

2Ke   *The Chapters of the Wisdom of My Lord Mani. Part III: Pages 343–442 (Chapters 321–347)*, Brill, Leiden-Boston 2018. ed. I. Gardner, J. BeDuhn and P. Dilley.

James   Nag Hammadi Codex (NHC) V, 3 and Codex Tchacos (CT) 2, synoptic edition of the Coptic text in Brankaer and Bethge 2007; notes on the Greek text from Oxyrhynchus by B. Landau and G. Smith, "Nag Hammadi at Oxyrhynchus: A New Discovery" (paper read to the SBL Annual Meeting November 2017, unpublished).

M 281   With reference to F. de Blois, "Manichaean Polemics: M 28 and the *Book of Mysteries*" (In press: to be published in Flavia Ruani, Mihaela Timus (eds.). 2020. *Quand les dualistes polémiquaient : Zoroastriens et Manichéens. Actes du colloque international, 12–13 juin 2015. Collège de France* [coll. Orient et Méditerranée vol. 34], Peeters, Leuven).

'Quire A'   Unpublished pages of 2Ke (= Chester Beatty Coptic Manichaean Codex C), from work in progress by Gardner, BeDuhn and Dilley; cited here according to the order of the plates in the facs. ed. prepared by S. Giversen 1986.

PsBk2   *A Manichaean Psalm-Book, Part II* (Manichaean Manuscripts in the Chester Beatty Collection II), ed. C.R.C. Allberry, Kohlhammer, Stuttgart 1938.

Acknowledgements

I acknowledge with thanks the generosity of the following scholars who have shared unpublished work without which this paper would not have been possible: Brent Landau and Geoffrey Smith for their research on the Oxyrhynchus text of *James*; François de Blois for his research on M 281, and in the past on the Arabic text of Ibn al-Nadīm's account of the *Book of Mysteries*; Jason BeDuhn and Paul Dilley for their ongoing collaboration on the Chester Beatty *Kephalaia* project; Wolf-Peter Funk for much assistance over the years, including access to his provisional readings of the Dublin *Kephalaia* codex. All opinions presented here are my own.

Bibliography

de Blois, F. and Sims-Williams, N. 2006. *Dictionary of Manichaean Texts. II: Texts from Iraq and Iran*, Brepols, Turnhout.

Brankaer, J. and Bethge, H.-G. 2007. "(Die erste Apokalypse des) Jakobus", in *Codex Tchacos. Texte und Analysen*, Walter de Gruyter, Berlin-New York, 81–254.

Choat, M. and Gardner, I. 2013. *A Coptic Handbook of Ritual Power*, Brepols, Turnhout.

Drijvers H.J.W. 1996. "Early Syriac Christianity: Some Recent Publications", *Vigiliae Christianae* 50, 159–177.

Edwards, R.M. 2015. *The Three Lives of James: From Jewish-Christian Traditions to a Valentinian Revelation, Preserved in Two Late Antique Attestations* (PhD. University of Ottawa).

Funk, W.-P. 2009. "The Significance of the Tchacos Codex for Understanding the *First Apocalypse of James*", in *The Codex Judas Papers: Prceedings of the International Congress on the Tchacos Codex*, ed. A.D. DeConick, Brill, Leiden-Boston, 509–533.

Gardner, I. 2010. "Mani's *Book of Mysteries*: Prolegomena to a New Look at Mani, the 'Baptists' and the Mandaeans", *Aram* 22, 321–334.

Giversen, S. 1986. *The Manichaean Coptic Papyri in the Chester Beatty Library. I. Kephalaia*, Patrick Cramer Éditeur, Genève.

Haxby, M.C.G. 2013. *The First Apocalypse of James: Martyrdom and Sexual Difference* (PhD. Harvard University).

Henning, W.B. 1945. "Sogdian Tales", *Bulletin of the School of Oriental and African Studies* 11, 465–487.

Jennot, L. 2017. "Reading Variants in *James* and the *Apocalypse of James*: A Perspective from New Philology", in *Snapshots of Evolving Traditions. Jewish and Christian Manuscript Culture, Textual Fluidity, and New Philology*, ed. L.I. Lied and H. Lundhaug, De Gruyter, Berlin-Boston, 55–84.

Jones, F.S. (ed.). 2002. *Which Mary? The Marys of Early Christian Tradition*, Society of Biblical Literature, Atlanta.

Leurini, C. 2018. "The Temple Tabernacle in M28/I/: An Anti-Judeo-Christian Polemic Strophe", *Iran and the Caucasus* 22, 1–7.

Marjanen, A. 2009. "The Seven Women Disciples in the Two Versions of the *First Apocalypse of James*", in *The Codex Judas Papers: Prceedings of the International Congress on the Tchacos Codex*, ed. A.D. DeConick, Brill, Leiden-Boston, 535–546.

Pedersen, N.A. 2018. "The Legendary Addai and the *First Apocalypse of James*", in *Ägypten und der Christliche Orient. Peter Nagel zum 80. Geburtstag*, ed. H. Behlmer, U. Pietruschka and F. Feder, Harrassowitz Verlag, Wiesbaden, 187–211.

Skjaervø, P.O. 1995 [1997]. "The Manichaean Polemical Hymns in M 28 I. A Review Article", *Bulletin of the Asia Institute* 9, 239–255.

Stein, M. 2016. *Manichaica Latina. Bd. 4: Manichaei Thesaurus*, Westdeutscher Verlag, Opladen.

Sundermann, W. 2002. "Das Leiden und Sterben Jesu in manichäischer Deutung", in *Religionsbegegnung und Kulturaustausch in Asien. Studien zum Gedenken an Hans-Joachim Klimkeit*, ed. W. Gantke, K. Hoheisel and W. Klein, Harrassowitz Verlag, Wiesbaden, 209–217.

Sundermann, W. 2009. "Ein manichäischer Traktat über und wider die Christen", in *Exegisti monumenta. Festschrift in Honour of Nicholas Sims-Williams*, ed. by W. Sundermann, A. Hintze and F. de Blois, Harrassowitz Verlag, Wiesbaden, 497–508.

Thomassen E. 2009. (Review of Brankaer and Bethge 2007), *Zeitschrift für Antikes Christentum* 13, 536–541.

Thomassen, E. 2013. "The Valentinian Materials in *James* (NHC V,3 and CT,2)", in *Beyond The Gnostic Gospels. Studies Building on the Work of Elaine Pagels*, ed. by E. Iricinschi, L. Jenott, N.D. Lewis and P. Townsend, Mohr Siebeck, Tübingen, 79–90.

5

Mani's *Book of Mysteries*: A Treatise *De anima*

Dylan M. Burns

Abstract

My contribution to this volume takes up Iain Gardner's investigation of the contents of Mani's *Book of Mysteries* as related by an-Nadīm, particularly vis-à-vis exegesis of Gnostic apocalypses such as the (*First Apocalypse of*) *James* and the *Gospel of Judas* and the traditions they contain concerning the crucifixion of Jesus and the human soul. It extrapolates on Gardner's argument by taking up an-Nadīm's statement that chapters one, twelve, and thirteen of Mani's *Book of Mysteries* criticizes the views of the followers of Bardaiṣan about the nature of the soul and its relationship to the body. Ephrem the Syrian in his *Discourse Against Bardaiṣan* is a problematic but valuable witness for Bardaiṣan's psychology, and, I argue, Ephrem's evidence may be used to reconstruct a much more clear picture of the Bardaiṣanite views Mani so strongly opposed—and, thus, a more clear picture of the corresponding chapters of Mani's *Book of Mysteries*. On my reading, Mani's *Book of Mysteries* may then have been a treatise concerned chiefly with the soul—a kind of *De anima*—and its relationship to the fall of Adam, the incarnation and crucifixion of Jesus, and the post-mortem fate of individual souls, where Mani opposed to the teaching of Bardaiṣan traditions he knew from authoritative pseudepigrapha whose contents recall the *Oracles of Hystaspes* and the (*First Apocalypse of*) *James*.

Introduction

Canons of the works written by Mani, self-proclaimed "Apostle of Jesus Christ," include a text with the title *Book of Mysteries*.[1] True to its name, it remains one of the most mysterious of Mani's texts. No identifiable excerpts from it survive in our Manichaean primary sources. However, al-Bīrūnī does offer three quotations from the work in his treatise *On India*, and in the *Fihrist*, Ibn an-Nadīm offers a celebrated summary of Mani's *Book of Mysteries*, as follows:[2]

---

1 On Manichaean canon-lists in general, useful remains the survey of Reeves, *Jewish Lore*, 9–19.
2 Ibn an-Nadīm, *Fihrist*, tr. Laffan in Gardner and S. Lieu, *Manichaean Texts*, 155 (§ 45), slightly

Mānī wrote seven books, one in Farsi (i.e. Persian) and six in Syriac, the language of Syria. Among them are the *Book of Mysteries*, which contains (a number of) chapters, (including) 'An account of the Dayṣāniyya (i.e. the followers of Bardaiṣan of Edessa),' 'The testimony of Yastāsif on the Beloved', 'The testimony of ... about himself given to Yaʻqūb', 'The son of the widow' (who according to Mānī was the anointed and crucified one, crucified by the Jews), 'The testimony of Jesus about himself as given to Judas', 'The commencement of the testimony of al-Yamīn as given after his victory', 'The seven spirits', 'The discourse on the four transient spirits', 'Laughter', 'The testimony of Adam regarding Jesus', 'The fall from religion', 'The discourse of the Dayṣāniyya on the soul and the body', 'Refutation of the Dayṣānites on the soul of life', 'The three trenches', 'The preservation of the World', 'The three days', 'The prophets', (and) 'The resurrection'. This is what is contained in the *Book of Mysteries*.

While some words of this translation are open to dispute—for example, "to Judas" may possibly be read as "Judea" or "on the Jews," while "laughter" could also be read as "mockery"—the language of an-Nadīm here is relatively clear.[3] Yet his meaning is at first sight obscure, and the summary covers many different topics. Consequently, scholarship has hitherto regarded the contents of Mani's *Book of Mysteries* as a sort of 'black box,' and the table of contents in the *Fihrist* as describing, most charitably, a work where Mani attacked contemporary rivals on a variety of topics.[4]

However, Iain Gardner argued in 2010, and again in his contribution to this volume, that chapters three and four of Mani's *Book of Mysteries* probably dealt in some way with Mani's exegesis of a copy of the (*First Apocalypse of*) *James* or a document related to it. The parallels Gardner points out between the *Book of Mysteries* and *James* are striking indeed, and the present contri-

---

modified, per Gardner, "Mani's *Book*," 323 n. 4. For other translations, see e.g., Dodge, '*Fihrist*', 797–798; Adam, *Texte*, 7–9; Reeves, *Prolegomena*, 106–107; de Blois, "Manichaean Polemics." For a useful discussion of an-Nadīm's Syriac and Arabic sources, see de Blois, "New Light." For al-Bīrūnī's quotations of the *Book of Mysteries*, see below.

3 For "Judea" instead of "to Judas," see Laffan, in the previous note, as well as Dodge, '*Fihrist*', 798; Reeves, *Prolegomena*, 107; de Blois, "Manichaean Polemics." I follow Gardner as preferring "to Judas" to be "the better reading" ("Mani's *Book*," 323; also Adam, *Texte*, 9 n. 5). For "mockery" instead of "laughter," see Tardieu, *Manichaeism*, 39; as I argue below, the latter distinction is of minimal importance to the present argument.

4 Tardieu, *Manichaeism*, 41; Reeves, *Prolegomena*, 105 ("a number of topical discourses"). Even more restrained is Adam, *Texte*, 8: "Da wir keine rechte Vorstellung von dem Inhalt der einzelnen Kapitel haben, kann keine eindeutige Übersetzung des Fihrist-Textes gegeben werden."

bution humbly seeks to expand on his remarks. My sense is that the middle chapters of the *Book of Mysteries* are concerned with exegesis of traditions we know from extant Coptic Gnostic apocalypses on the crucifixion and body of Jesus—as well as the soul. I will support this contention by pursuing a second line of investigation, namely an-Nadīm's statement that chapters one, twelve, and thirteen of the *Book of Mysteries* addressed the followers of the second-century Syrian philosopher Bardaiṣan, particularly concerning the nature of the soul and its relationship to the body. If we take the description of these chapters by an-Nadīm as well as the testimony of al-Bīrūnī seriously, then the Daiṣanite *Book of Mysteries* dealt in some way with Bardaiṣan's psychology, and Mani responded to that. For this we have some evidence from Ephrem the Syrian, especially in his *Discourse Against Bardaiṣan*, as Alberto Camplani observed several years ago.[5] If we consider Ephrem's testimonia alongside the analysis initially pursued by Gardner, then a much more coherent picture of the contents of the *Book of Mysteries* emerges, where Mani rejected the views of the competing school of Bardaiṣan on the soul, the meaning of the fall of Adam, Jesus' incarnation on earth, the crucifixion, and the fate of the soul after death. Mani made his arguments against Bardaisan through critical reference to authoritative pseudepigrapha of his milieu, works with contents recalling those of *Oracles of Hystaspes* and above all, the *(First Apocalypse of) James*.

1 Mani's 'Book of Mysteries' and (the First Apocalypse of) 'James'

Gardner's central contribution in his 2010 article is to demonstrate that chapters three, four, and nine of the *Book of Mysteries* recall traditions about James the 'brother of the Lord,' as well as the *Gospel of Judas*; given the presence of a *James*-apocalypse as well as *Judas* in the Codex Tchacos, this invites further investigation of this relatively recently-published Coptic Gnostic manuscript and Manichaeism. This section outlines Gardner's argument, with chief reference to his updated reflections on this material printed in this volume.

First, "Yastasif" refers, as Gardner notes, to Hystaspes, a 'great king' converted to Zoroastrianism who figures prominently in Manichaean sources.[6] Gardner follows John Reeves in taking this chapter to have probably responded to the so-called *Oracles of Hystaspes*, an apocalypse from the Hellenistic Near East which enjoyed a vibrant reception-history in Christian circles in the first cen-

---

5 Camplani, "Bardaisan's Psychology."
6 Reeves, "Enochic Citation," 269–270, followed by Gardner, "Mani's *Book*," 323–324; see further Pedersen, *Studies*, 327–330.

turies CE.[7] Meanwhile, the "Ya'qūb" of chapter three could refer to the patriarch Jacob, but also to the figure of James, who is a more well-attested figure in Manichaean literature.[8] More importantly, Gardner notes, the (*First Apocalypse of*) *James* discusses themes like the contents an-Nadīm ascribes to *Book of Mysteries* chapters four, six, and nine.[9] Chapter four's mention of the 'son of the widow' likely refers to the crucifixion of "the material Jesus bar Maryam, in contrast to the Son of God."[10] The question of Manichaean Christology is tricky and I do not wish to be detained by it here, but it is safe to agree with Eugen Rose in his classic work on the subject that the evidence from Augustine's *Against Faustus* and the Berlin *Kephalaia* appears to distinguish between the historical Jesus who was crucified and the cosmic Christ, the light-*nous*.[11] Moreover, the *Fundamental Epistle* gives us something like a docetic reading wherein the crucifixion-event is a trick, and "the enemy" only crucifies himself.[12] In other words, to the extent we can piece their views together, Manichaeans seem—no pun intended!—to have held that the divine Christ is not exactly the son of Mary who was crucified.

As Gardner notes, we also find some kind of docetic Christology in the (*First Apocalypse of*) *James*, which I here cite from the Tchacos version, which is significantly better-preserved than that from Nag Hammadi Codex V. Prior to the crucifixion, Jesus tells James that "for [this reason] shall I [appear], for the

---

[7] Reeves, "Enochic Citation," 270–272; Gardner, "Mani's Book," 324, 333; also Tardieu, *Manichaeism*, 38. For a *Forschungsbericht* on the *Oracles*, see Sundermann, "Hystaspes." I agree with Reeves and Gardner in taking the chapter to have likely marked a pivot where Mani turns to his own interpretation of Jesus and his crucifixion. Worth noting is the witness of Justin Martyr (*1 Apol.* 20.1), who states that according to the *Oracles* the destruction of the world will be total, the implication being that it will include the annihilation of the souls who inhabit it—a view with which Mani agreed only in part (see the below discussion).

[8] For Jacob the patriarch, see Tardieu, *Manichaeism*, 38–39. For the figure of James in Coptic Manichaica, see 2 *Ps* 142.25–26; 194.10, 194.14, cit. Gardner, "Docetic Jesus," 61 n. 26; see also idem, "Mani's Book," 324 n. 13; Richter, *Exegetisch-literarkritische Untersuchungen*, 201–202.

[9] Cf. also the remarks of Reeves, *Prolegomena*, 106 n. 145.

[10] Tardieu, *Manichaeism*, 39; Gardner, "Mani's Book," 325.

[11] See Rose, *Manichäische Christologie*; also Franzmann, *Jesus*, 11–12, emphasizing rather the unity of Manichaean understandings of Christ.

[12] In Gardner and S. Lieu, *Manichaean Texts*, 171 (§ 53). For survey of materials and general remarks on the problem of Docetism in Manichaeism, see Gardner, "Docetic Jesus"; Franzmann, *Jesus*, 53–57, 71–81. A further relevant passage may be the 'polemical hymn' of M28 I verso i, 6–9, tr. Skjærvø, "The Manichaean Polemical Hymns," 246: "That frightening one [i.e., Jesus—DMB] who said—while he had not [actually] tasted death—[and so] condemned the doer of the deed: why did you crucify me?"

shaming of the archons (ⲉⲡⲉⲭⲡⲓⲟ ⲛ̄ⲛⲁⲣⲭⲱ[ⲛ])."[13] Following the crucifixion, Jesus appears to James privately, on the mountain Galgelam:

> [For] I did not suffer [from anything], nor did I die (ⲙ̄ⲡⲓϩⲓⲥⲉ ⲅ[ⲁⲣ] ϩ[ⲛ̄] ⲗⲁⲟⲩ[ⲉ] ⲟⲩⲇⲉ ⲙ̄ⲡⲓⲙⲟⲩ). And this very people did not do any evil. Now, this (group of people) is established as the type of the archons, as ⟨is fitting⟩ to be prepared. It is the archons who prepared it. Then it was finished. So, guard yourself, because the just god has grown angry (ⲁⲡⲛⲟⲩⲧⲉ ⲛ̄ⲇⲓⲕⲁⲓⲟⲥ ⲛⲟⲩϭⲥ̄)![14]

Still later, Jesus states: "but, I, [I] came and died—[and] (yet) I have not [died.] ([ⲁ]ⲛⲟⲕ ⲇⲉ [ⲁⲉ]ⲓⲉⲓ ⲁⲉⲓϫⲱⲕ ⲉⲃⲟⲗ [ⲁ]ⲩⲱ ⲙ̄ⲡⲓⲭ̣[ⲱⲕ ⲉⲃⲟⲗ])."[15] Gardner is also struck by the mention of "Judas" in *Book of Mysteries* chapter five, since the *Gospel of Judas* is of course also preserved in the Tchacos Codex, and also toys with the meaning of the crucifixion body.[16] Lacunae in the manuscript rob us of the context, but Jesus tells Judas: "[… it shall wipe out] the entire race of Adam, the man of earth. The one who [bears] me will be [tortured] tomorrow. Truly, I [say] unto you: no hand [of mortal] man [shall sin] against me! … But you, you shall do more than them all! For you shall sacrifice the one who bears me."[17] As Johanna Brankaer notes, "Jesus's torture seems somehow associated with the destruction of the earthly man Adam. In both cases it is the product of the archons that is destroyed. Like the bodily substrate of Jesus, the purely earthly Adam is mortal. Both are destroyed in physical death. The eschatological destruction of the entire race of the purely earthly Adam coincides with

---

13 *1 Apoc. Jas.* CT 16.15–17 = NHC V 30.2–3, text in Brankaer and Bethge, *Codex Tchacos*, 100, tr. mine.

14 *1 Apoc. Jas.* CT 18.8–17 = NHC V 31.18–31, text in Brankaer and Bethge, *Codex Tchacos*, 104, 106, tr. mine.

15 *1 Apoc. Jas.* CT 27.3–4 (the passage is not preserved in NHC V), text in Brankaer and Bethge, *Codex Tchacos*, 120, tr. mine. Brankaer and Bethge, op. cit., 239, read the passage in terms of cosmic eschatology. The phrasing, however, closely recalls the so-called "Amen hymn" (*2 Ps* 191.4–8), which, to my eyes, supports Richter's statement that "die Ansicht, daß sich die Amen-Hymnen des koptisch-manichäischen Psalmenbuches auf eine frühchristlich-gnostische Tradition beziehen lassen, ist voll zuzustimmen" (*Exegetisch-literarkritische Untersuchungen*, 111; cf. also ibid., 269, re: *1 Apoc. Jas.* NHC V 25.7–9, 28.16–20, 31.17–20). On the "Amen hymn," see also Gardner, "Docetic Jesus," 83–85; Franzmann, *Jesus*, 76.

16 Gardner, "Mani's *Book*," 326. 'Judas (Thomas)' has also been suggested as the referent of "Judas" (Tardieu, *Manichaeism*, 39; also entertained by Gardner, op. cit.).

17 *Gos. Jud.* CT 56.4–22, text in Nagel, *Codex apocryphus gnosticus*, 302, tr. mine. On this key passage in *Gos. Jud.*, see now Wurst, "L'avant dernier feuillet."

the destruction of the archons."[18] We shall return to this point below. Finally, according to an-Nadīm, Mani's *Book of Mysteries* chapter six refers to "the commencement of the testimony of al-Yamīn as given after his victory." "Al-Yamīn" could mean the "right hand" and so perhaps the 'Living Spirit' in Manichaean cosmology, but just as easily "the just, righteous one," an epithet used for Enoch and James alike.[19]

Gardner has now expanded upon these remarks, with special reference to the tremendous work that has been done on the version of *James* in Codex Tchacos, particularly regarding chapters seven and eight.[20] Now, Gardner sees the "seven spirits" of *Book of Mysteries* chapter seven as referring to the seven spirits of prophecy in a passage from the Tchacos *James*, who are present in seven female disciples:

> (*JAMES:*) "Still, I would ask you about this: who are the seven women who became your disciples? As for them, all the generations bless them. And I, I am astonished that, although they are in weak vessels, nonetheless[21] they have found powers and insights."

---

18   Brankaer, *Gospel of Judas*, 214. This reading appears to me to conflict, however, with her immediately subsequent statement that "Jesus' death [in *Judas*—DMB] is stripped of any soteriological value" (ibid., 215; similarly 217 n. 353). However, she is right to point out that Judas's theology of the crucifixion is rather vague, and does not explain why the torture and death of "the one who bears me" is necessary to destroy the Archons (unlike, say, *Apoc. Pet.* NHC VII 83.4–8, which explicitly ties the death of Jesus's body to the release of the living Christ from it; cf. the discussion below, n. 52). Rather, one must infer as much from Jesus's own articulation of the typology of earthly Adam-race of earthly humans-earthly Jesus. If correct, this reading would agree (*not* disagree, *pace* Brankaer, op. cit. 215, n. 343) with the *Second Treatise of the Great Seth*'s notion that the Archons only destroy the body which they themselves create, and which the 'real' Jesus has already abandoned (NHC VII 51.20–52.10; cf. on this point Gardner, "Docetic Jesus," 79–80).

19   For simply "the just," see Adam, *Texte*, 9 n. 6. Enoch: Tardieu, *Manichaeism*, 39; Enoch or James: Gardner, "Mani's Book," 326–327. For the Living Spirit as the "right hand," see 2*Ps* 2.5; *Acta Archelai* 7.4 (cit. Gardner, op. cit. 327 n. 30; see additionally Reeves, *Prolegomena*, 107 n. 147). For the title δίκαιος as referring to James in Patristic literature, see Hegesippus, ap. Euseb. *Hist. eccl.* 2.23.4 *passim*; for the title with reference to James in the Nag Hammadi texts, see *Gos. Thom* NHC II 34.25–30; *2 Apoc. Jas.* NHC V [44].13–15, 59.21–22; 60.10–13; 61.13–14 (Brankaer and Bethge, *Codex Tchacos*, 214, n. 212).

20   Gardner, "Strange Case," 54 (with reference to idem, "Mani's Book," 327–328): "whereas in my first research I had noted linkages with sections 3–4 as preserved by Ibn an-Nadīm, it now seems probable that they extended at least as far as section 8, and perhaps even further."

21   ⲁⲩⲱ that introduces narrative or statement (Crum, *Coptic Dictionary*, 20a).

(*JESUS:*) "James, rightly are you astonished! ... As for these very seven women, these ones are seven spirits (cf. Is 11:2).[22] It is in [this list][23] that they are brought forward: a spirit of wisdom [and] sagacity, a spirit of counsel [and power, a] spirit [of] mind and [thought], a spirit of awe."[24]

Meanwhile, the "discourse on the four transient spirits" an-Nadīm says was the subject of chapter eight of the *Book of Mysteries* may also recall another tradition known from the Tchacos *James*-apocalypse. When James asks Jesus if he favors any of these seven female disciples, Jesus answers:

> Be persuaded, now, of this other matter—Salōmē and Maria and Arsinoē, those whom I shall bring together with you, [because they] are worthy of He Who Is. For they became sober and [were freed] from [the blindness] which is in their heart. And they recognized me—namely, what I am.[25]

Gardner observes that Arsinoē not only appears as a disciple in the Manichaean *Psalm-Book*,[26] but also in hitherto unpublished Dublin *Kephalaia*.[27] Mani then appears to have knowledge of some kind of tradition where the 'seven spirits' of Isaiah 11:2–3 LXX are interpreted with respect to seven female disciples, including Arsinoē.[28]

---

22 On the 'seven spirits' vis-à-vis the seven female disciples, see further Brankaer and Bethge, *Codex Tchacos*, 235; Funk, "Significance," 524; Marjanen, "Seven Women." This all-important passage is not readable in NHC V.

23 A rare use of ⲅⲣⲁⲫⲏ, assuming the restoration is correct. See the Mudil-Codex (dialect M), 290.18–291.1 (Ps 86:6).

24 *1Apoc. Jas.* CT 25.17–26.10, text in Brankaer and Bethge, *Codex Tchacos*, 118, 120, tr. mine. Cf. Isa 11:2–3. I translate ϩⲟⲧⲉ as "awe," since it is here associated with good things; in the list of seven spirits in Isa 11:2–3 LXX, the final spirit is a πνεῦμα φόβου θεοῦ. For ϩⲟⲧⲉ as rendering Grk. φόβος, which is well-attested with the sense of "awe, reverence" (LSJ 1947a, s.v. 2.a), see Crum 720b. Brankaer and Bethge's "Furcht" is appropriately ambiguous and can have the sense of religious awe which is probably meant here (cf. *Gottesfurcht*).

25 *1Apoc. Jas.* 27 CT.24–28.5, text in Brankaer and Bethge, *Codex Tchacos*, 122, tr. mine.

26 *2 Ps* 192.24, 194.22, cit. "Mani's *Book*," 325, n. 20; on these passages, see also Richter, *Exegetisch-literarkritische Untersuchungen*, 211–214; Brankaer and Bethge, *Codex Tchacos*, 243–244. Cf. Tardieu, *Manichaeism*, 39, preferring the "four spirits" as referring to four directions (winds).

27 Gardner, "Strange Case," 62–63.

28 Cf. Gardner, "Strange Case," 63: "a tradition regarding groups of gospel women and series of spirits, four of which are positive and three are negative, is followed by an explication of the errors worked by the negative spirits in the teachings and presumably the communities that Mani opposed." It is difficult to ascertain whether the latter three female disciples in *1Apoc. Jas.* are less than benevolent, or, as Marjanen suggests, simply a group

A second feature of *James* which Gardner highlights is Jesus's statement that when he descended to earth, he eluded and mocked the demiurge Addōn:

> When ⟨I⟩ passed through the land of the Great Archon—the one who is called "Addōn"—I went right up to him, and he was unaware! And when I went away from him, he thought about [me] that I was his son, and he was gracious to me, as though I were his son![29]

One of the Middle Persian 'polemical hymns' from Turfan, M28 I, similarly features Jesus humiliating "Adonay and his brats."[30] It asks, "They call the son of Mary the seventh son of Adonay. If he is lord of all who crucified his son?"[31] The hymn may presuppose an engagement with Marcionite thought here, and François de Blois has suggested that it derives from the *Book of Mysteries*.[32]

---

of converts to the Jesus movement subsequent to the first four, putatively senior, female disciples ("Seven Women," 540–543; Brankaer and Bethge, *Codex Tchacos*, 246–247 eschew the question). How one answers this question is incumbent on restored text (particularly to CT 29.3) and interpretation of a tricky clause (CT 28.21–26; Funk, "Die erste Apokalypse," 1177, n. 89, remarks of the passage: "syntaktische Struktur dieses ganzen Passus unklar"). I hope to return to this problem in a future publication; fortunately, the issue is immaterial for the present argument.

29 *1 Apoc. Jas.* CT 26.11–19 = NHC V 39.8–18, text in Brankaer and Bethge, *Codex Tchacos*, 120, tr. mine.
30 M28 I recto i, 19–23, tr. Skjærvø, "The Manichaean Polemical Hymns," 245.
31 M28 I recto ii, 24–28; tr. Skjærvø, "The Manichaean Polemical Hymns," 246.
32 De Blois, "Manichaean Polemics." I thank Professor de Blois for sharing his paper with me in advance of its publication, and regret that the recent publication of Leurini, "Temple Tabernacle" (a rather different interpretation of M28 I) was not available to me at the time of writing this paper. See further Gardner, "Strange Case," 63–64 suggesting that 'Quire A' of the Dublin *Kephalaia* may even attack Marcionite Christology in similar terms. It is apposite that *1 Apoc. Jas.* denotes the "Great Archon" Addōn as "the Just God," and characterizes him by his wrath (*1 Apoc. Jas.* CT 18.8–17 = NHC V 31.18–31, quoted above)—a hallmark of Marcionite exegesis (for a useful overview with reference to related exegetical issues of the first two centuries CE, see recently J. Lieu, *Marcion*, 343–349). For patristic Greek sources referring to the "just God" as the lower deity in Marcionite exegesis, see PGL 368, s.v. δίκαιος, A.2.

Brankaer and Bethge do not regard the notion of the lower god's "wrath" as 'Marcionite' but 'Gnostic,' referring to Ptolemy's *Letter to Flora* (ap. Epiph. *Pan.* 33.3–7) and *Ap. John* NHC II 24.19–25 (on "Yave" and "Eloim" viz. Cain and Abel as just and unjust, respectively); *Orig. World* NHC II 106.11–17, 110.2–6 (on Sabaoth as a just deity and the creation of Paradise). The latter two references are somewhat misleading: *Ap. John*'s exegesis of Cain and Abel as "just" and "unjust" is intriguing, but too brief to be a useful *comparandum* with Marcionite exegesis; *Orig. World* denotes Sabaoth as "just" not in any sense of Marcionite exegesis, but because Sabaoth has repented and come under the tutelage of Pistis Sophia, unlike his evil father, Yaltabaoth (NHC II 103.32–104.31).

Meanwhile, Gardner points us in the direction of the theme, attested in other early Christian apocalypses, of *Christus descensus absconditus*.[33] And in fact, the theme of Jesus descending to his worldly incarnation while adopting disguises is attested in the *Psalm-Book* as well as the Berlin *Kephalaia*.[34] Gardner is right that these passages are concerned with "the mockery that is made of those archontic powers characterized by foolish ignorance."[35] In any case, the "laughter" (or if one prefers, "mockery") of chapter nine dovetails nicely with the docetic Jesus's ability to shape-shift during his descent, and his subsequent laughter at the archons' attempt to crucify him. This mocking or 'laughing savior' is a mainstay of heresiographical lore,[36] but no fiction, since it is attested in a number of extant primary sources from diverse Gnostic literary traditions, such as the *Gospel of Judas* and the Macquarie *Coptic Handbook of Ritual Power* (P. Macq. I 1), as well as works which appear to derive from the school of Basilides: the *Second Treatise of the Great Seth* (NHC VII,2) and the *Gospel of Peter* (NHC VII,3).[37] Yet what seems significant about the 'laughing/mocking' motif to me is that to the best of my knowledge, the combination of the theme

---

33 Gardner, "Strange Case," 58 n. 18, re: P. Macq. I 9.7–14; cf. idem, "Docetic Jesus," 67, 82, a reading more akin to that of de Blois. For the polymorphic, pre-incarnate Jesus descending to earth, see Burns, *Apocalypse*, 57.

34 *2Ps* 193.27–194.3, 196.10–33 (the crucifixion and harrowing of hell by use of a ⲥⲭⲏⲙⲁ); *1Ke* 61.17–28. For discussion, see Gardner, "Docetic Jesus," 69, 75–76, 81–82; Richter, *Exegetisch-literarkritische Untersuchungen*, 231–273; Franzmann, *Jesus*, 32, 53. As Franzmann notes, one of the points the hymn of M28 I makes is that Jesus the Apostle was sent by none other than Jesus the Splendor, not Adonai, who crucified him (*Jesus*, 52).

35 Gardner, "Strange Case," 59.

36 Already recognized by Adam, *Texte*, 9 n. 7 ("gnostisches Thema"), although his reference is spurious (Ir. *Haer.* 1.4.2, which refers to Sophia's laughter in a discussion of her passionate character, not mockery of the archons; more apposite would be e.g. ibid., 1.24.4, Irenaeus's account of Basilides's teaching that Christ had Simon of Cyrene crucified in his place, and ridiculed his would-be tormentors). Cf. Gardner's assessment of the theological significance of the motif of the laughing or mocking Jesus ("Docetic Jesus," 70): "for the believer the vital emphasis was on mockery, laughter, and secret power. For the more deep-thinking Gnostic groups there was a real spiritual expression in all this, though the crucifixion accounts show how piety could easily degenerate into farce and crude games of superiority. For instance to substitute a neutral character, such as Simon of Cyrene, for Jesus on the cross eliminates all sense or value from the account."

37 *Gos. Jud.* CT 34.2, 34.7; *Treat. Seth* NHC VII 55.9–24, esp. 55.30–57.7; *Apoc. Pet.* NHC VII 81.3–83.3; P. Macq. I 1 9.4–14, noted by Gardner, "Docetic Jesus," 80; idem, "Mani's Book," 328 n. 39. For a recent survey on Jesus's laughter focusing on *Gos. Jud.*, see Clivaz, "What is the Current State of Play." On the continuity of themes between *Gos. Jud.* and Manichaean sources indicating the possibility of Manichaean knowledge of the former text, see Sala, "Christ's gift-Gift to Judas." On the probable indebtedness of *Treat. Seth* and *Apoc. Pet.* to Basilidean teachings, see Dubois, "Les gnostiques basilidiens."

of Jesus's mockery of the archons with his polymorphism during his descent to the body is distinctive to Manichaean sources—with the exception of the (*First Apocalypse of*) *James*.[38]

An-Nadīm's chapter ten, meanwhile, refers to 'the testimony of Adam regarding Jesus.' Gardner recalls a number of mythologoumena where Adam meets a pre-existent Christ-figure: the Manichaean Jesus Splendour who instructs Adam, a legend also discussed by an-Nadīm and others; the Mandaean 'uthra who appears to Adam; the *Apocryphon of John*, whose long recension refers to Jesus as awakening Adam; the Nag Hammadi *Apocalypse of Adam*, where the protoplast receives instruction from three celestial men.[39] An-Nadīm says that chapter eleven concerns 'the fall from religion,' and Gardner avers that this deals with the fall of Adam, despite Jesus's teaching. The following chapters return to the Dayṣāniyya and then eschatological themes.[40] Gardner's conclusion is that in the *Book of Mysteries*, Mani engages pseudepigraphic authorities

---

38   It is worth noting in passing that another theme from *James* that holds a strong parallel in Manichaean sources is the use of correct answers by the soul as it navigates its way pass the celestial toll keepers (*1Apoc. Jas.* TC 14.6–16.2 = NHC V 27.13–29.13; for use of the formula among the Marcosians, see Ir. *Haer.* 1.21.5; for analysis of this tradition, see recently Thomassen, "Valentinian Materials"). A very similar scene (albeit with slightly different phrasing) appears in the Manichaean *Sermon of the Soul* (frg. 3, §§ 12–13, tr. Sundermann, *Der Sermon*, 75, cit. BeDuhn, *Manichaean Body*, 85):

> Und ein Mensch, der diese wundervolle und große Sache nicht kennt, der gleicht einem unverständigen Manne, der des Weges geht und den jemand fragt: "Woher bist du gekommen, und wo gehst du hin, was willst du, zu welchem Zweck bist du gekommen, wohin bist du gesandt, und was ist dein Name?" Und jener Mann sagt: "Von dem, was du mich fragst, weiß ich auch nicht eins."

Sundermann himself gives a Zoroastrian parallel (*Yasna* 44; Sundermann, op. cit. 24).

39   Gardner, "Mani's *Book*," 329–330. An-Nadīm's account is similar to that of Theodore bar Konai (tr. Jackson, *Researches*, 249–254; see further BeDuhn, *Manichaean Body*, 73; Franzmann, *Jesus*, 36):

> And he (Mānī) says: Jesus the Luminous approached Adam the Innocent and woke him from the sleep of death ... And he woke him and took hold of him and shook him; and he drove away from him the seductive Demon and bound away from him the great female Archon. Then Adam examined himself and recognized what he was. And He (i.e. Jesus) showed him the Fathers in the Height, and His own self thrown in all into the teeth of leopards and into the teeth of elephants, and swallowed by the voracious and devoured by the gluttons and eaten by dogs, and mixed and imprisoned in all that exists and bound in the pollution of Darkness.

Tardieu prefers a reference to the *Apocalypse of Adam* mentioned in the CMC, whereby Mani ostensibly buffered his prophetological credentials (*Manichaeism*, 39); similarly Reeves, suggesting the *Testament of Adam* (*Prolegomena*, 107, n. 148).

40   See Tardieu, *Manichaeism*, 40–41; Gardner, "Mani's *Book*," 331–333. On "the three trenches" (chapter fourteen), see further Pedersen, *Studies*, 148, esp. n. 351.

such as the *Oracles of Hystaspes* and the *(First Apocalypse of) James* and establishes his prophetic credentials, much as the Cologne Mani Codex shows him doing.⁴¹

Now, I am entirely persuaded by Gardner that we should look to the *(First Apocalypse of) James* and other Gnostic apocalypses in reconstructing the materials with which Mani engaged in the middle chapters—that is, chapters three through ten—of the *Book of Mysteries*. (It is worth adding in passing that the discovery that Mani knew some form of the *James* apocalypse and perhaps *Judas* as well reinforces our picture of him as a reader of Jewish and Christian apocalypses, not just a participant in discourse about them; thus, the titles and quotations of the apocalypses given in the Cologne Mani Codex likely refer to texts which are no longer extant, rather than books that never existed in the first place, as David Frankfurter has argued.⁴²) However, I want to push this reconstruction further, on two fronts. First, can we be any more specific about which Adam tradition was found in chapter ten? Secondly, how can Gardner's hypothesis lead us to re-think our understanding of Mani's *Book of Mysteries* as a whole, particularly as a polemic against the followers of Bardaiṣan?⁴³

2 Why the Dayṣāniyya? Jesus, Mani—and Tertullian, 'On the Soul'

Here, it may help to return to the Dayṣāniyya and see where that takes us. We have two good reasons for prioritizing our evidence about Bardaiṣan and Mani's *Book of Mysteries*. First, Bardaiṣan wrote his own work entitled 'the *Book of Mysteries*,' and Mani probably used the same title so as to respond to that of the Syrian philosopher.⁴⁴ Second, our two extant quotations from Mani's

---

41 Tardieu, *Manichaeism*, 40–41; Gardner, "Mani's *Book*," 331–333. Some Islamicate testimonia also highlight that the *Book of Mysteries* rejected other prophetic claims: e.g. Yaʿqūbī, *Taʾrīkh* (Mani rejected the claims of the Prophets); Abū Ḥātim al-Rāzī, *Kitāb aʿlām al-nubuwwa* (Mani alleged that Moses was an agent of the satans and disparaged Jewish authorities between the time of Abraham and that of Jesus); Ms. Or. Brit. Mus. 8613 fol. 16b–17a (Mani in the *Book of Mysteries* impugns the miracles of Moses); all in Reeves, *Prolegomena*, 105–106, 108.

42 *Pace* Frankfurter, "Apocalypses."

43 Cf. Gardner, "Mani's *Book*," 330, 334.

44 Drijvers, *Bardaiṣan*, 202; S. Lieu, *Manichaeism in the Later Roman Empire*, 58; Tardieu, *Manichaeism*, 38; Camplani, "Bardesane et les bardesanites," 29; idem, "Bardaisan's Psychology," 259; idem, "Traces de controverse religiuese," 54; idem, "Bardaisan and the Bible," 708; de Blois, "Elchasai," 37; Ramelli, *Bardaiṣan*, 53; Gardner, "Mani's *Book*," 323; Reeves, *Prolegomena*, 105.

Book of Mysteries attack the followers of Bardaiṣan.[45] It is worth reading the quotations—from al-Bīrūnī, in his work *On India*—in full:

> He (Mani) says in the *Book of Mysteries*:
>
> Since the disciples knew that souls are immortal and that they can repeatedly undergo transformation into any likeness of any form which it can wear, shaped as an animal[46] or like any form cast from a hollow mold, they asked Christ about the fate of those souls who did not accept the truth or learn about the reason for their existence. He said, 'Every infirm soul which does not obey its summons from Truth will perish (and) have no repose.'
>
> He [Mani—DMB] means by its 'perishing' its 'punishment,' not its annihilation. For he says also:
>
> The Dayṣāniyya are of the opinion that the ascension and purification of the Living Soul takes place in the human body.[47] They do not know that the body is the enemy of the soul and that it (the body) forbids it (the soul) to make ascent, for it (the body) is a prison and an instrument of torture for it (the soul). If this human form was associated with Truth, its creator would not let it wear out or experience harm, and he would not need to propagate sexually by means of semen in wombs.[48]

I will return to this passage later, but for now it suffices to observe that when we read an-Nadīm and al-Bīrūnī together, the most sure thing we know about Mani's *Book of Mysteries* is that it responded to the school of Bardaiṣan on the subject of the soul and personal eschatology, with reference to apocryphal literature.

In fact, a few pages earlier in *On India*, al-Bīrūnī gives us a third quote of Mani, who himself cites some kind of post-resurrection 'Gnostic dialogue' on the soul:

---

45   Drijvers, *Bardaiṣan*, 204–205; Browder, "Al-Bîrûnî's Manichaean Sources," 20–21; BeDuhn, *Manichaean Body*, 89; Tardieu, *Manichaeism*, 40; Camplani, "Bardesane et les bardesanites," 29; idem, "Traces de controverse religieuse," 54; Gardner, "Mani's *Book*," 330–331.
46   De Blois emends *dābba* ("animal") to *ḏā'iba* ("molten things")—"Manichaean Polemics."
47   Lit. "corpse," as noted by Adam, *Texte*, 10 n. 13.
48   Tr. Reeves, *Prolegomena*, 107–108. On al-Bīrūnī's reports on Manichaeism and its sources, see Browder, "Al-Bîrûnî's Manichaean Sources," and now, most thoroughly, de Blois, "Manichaean Polemics."

> The apostles asked Jesus (upon whom be peace!) about the life of inanimate things, and he said to them, "(As for the) dead thing, when the life that is mixed with it departs and separates itself, it returns to an inanimate state (and) no longer lives; but the life which departed from it never dies."[49]

Browder and de Blois rightly argue that this passage is also from Mani's *Book of the Mysteries*—it provides the proper narrative frame for the leading clause "since the disciples knew ..." in the first quote of Mani above, in this section.[50] Additional support for this view may be adduced by the content of the apocryphal dialogue Mani quotes. The context of Jesus's remarks appears to be a syllogism attributed to the putative founder of Stoicism, Zeno of Citium, which attempts to demonstrate the soul's corporeal character. It is preserved by Tertullian, in his work *On the Soul* (*De anima*):

> For Zeno, in defining the soul to be a congenital spirit (*consitum spiritum* < σύμφυτον πνεῦμα), draws up the argument in this manner: "Whatever causes," he says, "a living thing to die by departing from it, is a body. Now, it is through the departure of some congenital spirit that a living thing dies. Therefore, the congenital spirit is a body; therefore, the soul is a body (*ergo corpus est anima*)."[51]

In the apocryphal dialogue on which Mani comments, Jesus apparently flips the scenario proposed by Zeno. Jesus tells the disciples that scenes of the soul's departure from the body indicate not the corporeality of the soul (as Zeno and Tertullian would have it), but the lifeless character of a soulless body, and the vivifying character of the bodiless soul as it wanders from body to body.[52] Here,

---

49 Tr. Reeves, *Prolegomena*, 126. On Mani's 'exotericization' of esoteric teaching from Gnostic apocalypses, see Gardner, "Docetic Jesus," 77–78.

50 Browder, "Al-Bîrûnî's Manichaean Sources," 21–22; de Blois, "Manichaean Polemics" cf. also Adam, *Texte*, 26. Cf. Reeves, who declines to identify the work in question (*Prolegomena*, 126–127, n. 294).

51 *An.* 5.3 = SVF 1:137, text Podolak, *Soranus*, 111, tr. mine. A related but distinct form of the syllogism, also assigned to Zeno, is transmitted by Calcidius (*Comm. Tim.* 220 = SVF 1:138). For discussion of the syllogism and attendant scholarship, see Waszink, *Quinti Septimi*, 128–129; Podolak, op. cit. 46–48, 132–133.

52 Jesus also discusses the soul's activity at the scene of bodily death in several extant Gnostic apocalypses, although their accounts do not precisely map on to the text quoted by Mani here: *Gos. Jud.* CT 43.14–23 (the souls of the elect will not perish with the body, but be made alive and brought to heaven); *Apoc. Pet.* NHC VII 83.4–10 (Jesus's own soul was not killed, but escaped the body of the man who was crucified).

too, Mani's *Book of Mysteries* engages Christian revelatory pseudepigrapha on the subject of the soul's relationship to the body and its consequences for the post-mortem fate of the soul.

The natural question, then, is: what do we know about Bardaiṣan's psychology, and how can it help us understand the contents of Mani's *Book of Mysteries* as laid out by an-Nadīm and al-Bīrūnī?

3 Ephrem Syrus on Bardaiṣanite Psychology and Christology

As Camplani observes, our primary evidence for our understanding of Bardaiṣan's views on the soul and its relationship to the body and the afterlife are to be found in Ephrem the Syrian's criticisms of him.[53] In the *Hymns Against Heresies*, for instance, Ephrem claims that Bardaiṣan denies the resurrection of the flesh, but does not elaborate.[54] Our only source for the details of Bardaiṣan's views is to be found in Ephrem's work entitled *A Discourse Against Bardaiṣan*.[55] Indeed, Ephrem declares Bardaiṣan's ostensible denial of the resurrection of the flesh in the very first stanza: "Bardaiṣan, you see, declares—that even without the transgression of Adam—the Body would turn back to its earth,—that Flesh does not cleave to Spirit,—that the waste runs downward—and the pure substance upward,—and [...]—the one its zenith, and the other its abyss."[56] The body, Bardaiṣan avers, decays because bodies are perishable, not because of the death (or "sin") of Adam.[57] Already, two Pauline exegetical issues are on

---

[53] I here bracket the evidence of the *Dialogue of Adamantius* for reconstructing the views of Bardaiṣan. While some kind of Bardaiṣanite perspective is clearly voiced by the *Dialogue*'s character Marinus (Pretty, *Adamantius*, 7–8; Ramelli, "Origen, Bardaisan," 162–163; followed by McGlothlin, "Contextualizing," 320–321), the work is a hostile witness indeed (Possekel, "Bardaisan of Edessa on the Resurrection," 11; Ramelli, op. cit., 163 n. 114) and merits all the requisite caution.

[54] "How truly envious the evil one became of the body of Bar Dayṣān / With his mouth he cut down his hope; he was reviling his half / He drew his tongue and denied his own resurrection" (*Hymns Against Heresies* 1.9, tr. Morehouse, "Bar Dayṣān," 186; see also Drijvers, *Bardaiṣan*, 153; McGlothlin, "Contextualizing," 323).

[55] I use this title to refer to the work among Ephrem's so-called 'Prose Refutations' that carries the titular superscript "A Discourse Against Bardaisan" (*me'mrā' dluqbal bardaiṣan*—text Mitchell, *S. Ephraim's Prose Refutations*, 2:143, tr. ibid., 2:lxvi), henceforth *C. Bar.* Aland (Ehlers) rightly points out that here, Ephrem directly addresses Bardaiṣan, without explicit reference to Marcion and Mani ("Bardesanes von Edessa," 359).

[56] *C. Bar.* 1, text Mitchell, *S. Ephraim's Prose Refutations*, 2:143, tr. ibid., 2:lxvi, modified. Cf. further *C. Bar.* 13.

[57] See further Drijvers, *Bardaiṣan*, 154; Possekel, "Bardaisan of Edessa on the Resurrection," 11;

the table: one is the meaning of the Adam-Christ typology (Rom 5:12–19), the other concerning what Paul meant when he said that the flesh and blood would not inherit the kingdom of God (1 Cor 15:50).[58] Tellingly, Ephrem's reply is that resurrection is bound to Christology, so it comes down to one's stance on the character of the body Christ was in when he was crucified, died, and raised.[59] Ephrem accuses Bardaiṣan of docetism:

> For even if [...]—proclaims that our Lord was clothed with a Body,—Strife stops up its ears[60]—and in a contrary way proclaims something else,—that our Savior did not put on the Flesh.—And should his contrariness truly justify us—how much more will straightforwardness[61] justify us?[62]

Particularly invaluable are several stanzas where Ephrem actually quotes Bardaiṣan himself.[63] In stanza 74, "'Our Lord also,' says Bardaiṣan, 'who was raised,—why did He not raise all Bodies,—seeing how their destruction is by Adam—their reconstitution should be by our Lord?'"[64] Here, Bardaiṣan

---

Jurasz, "Résurrection," 401–402; McGlothlin, "Contextualizing," 327–328. Cf. also *Dialogue of Adamantius* 5.16–25, where Marinus argues that the body is "a substance in a state of flux," i.e., unstable. Made out of four elements, the body will decompose after death (so how, then, could God put them back together?—see Possekel, op. cit., 11–12; McGlothlin, op. cit., 321–323). For Bardaiṣan's philosophical views on the status of bodies and incorporeals, see recently the treatment of Jurasz, "Éphrem, Bardesane et Albinus."

58   See e.g. the discussion in *Dialogue of Adamantius* 5.22; cf. also the Manichaean evidence ap. Augustine, *Contra Fortunatum disputatio*, 1.19, discussed in Franzmann, *Jesus*, 57; Decret and van Oort, *Sanctus Augustinus*, 63–65.

59   *C. Bar.* 10; see also rightly Jurasz, "Résurrection," 402, and esp. *C. Bar.* 13, text in Mitchell, *S. Ephraim's Prose Refutations*, 2:146, tr. ibid., 2:lxviii: "For lo, by myriad trials—the affair of our Lord is learnt,—that in the Body He died and was raised,—and His Birth and His Death have become a test—for the very Body which He put on,—that not in appearance and fraud did He put it on."

60   With hesitation I follow Mitchell (*S. Ephraim's Prose Refutations*, 2:lxviii, n. 4) here in reading *mskr 'dnwhy* for MS *msbr 'rzwhy*.

61   Eschewing Mitchell's emendation to *taqnuteh* "*his* correctness" (*S. Ephraim's Prose Refutations*, 2:lxviii, n. 5), which appears to me to distort the sense of the passage. Ephrem's point is that, if Bardaiṣan's teaching justifies even though it is based upon contrary and backwards speculations, it would justify all the more if it were not backwards, but straightforward.

62   *C. Bar.* 15, text in Mitchell, *S. Ephraim's Prose Refutations*, 2:147, tr. ibid., 2:lxviii, significantly modified.

63   *C. Bar.* 74, 79, 80–83, rightly highlighted by Ramelli, *Bardaiṣan*, 229; Jurasz, "Résurrection," 415.

64   *C. Bar.* 74, text in Mitchell, *S. Ephraim's Prose Refutations*, 2:162, tr. ibid., 2:lxxv, modified.

appears to have asked the reasonable question, if Christ redeemed bodies as well as souls, why do Christian bodies keep dying?[65] Thus stanza 80, with reference to John 8:51–52: "[He finishes] his word with another,—'for you see,' writes Bardaiṣan, 'our Lord says—"Every one who keeps my word—death for ever he shall not taste,"—and you see, all those who have kept it have died. [...] death is sin.'[66] For he has confused and flowed together words—to the confusion of the inexperienced ear."[67] The answer, Bardaiṣan supposes, must be that bodies are too heavy to ascend. Consequently, Christ must have only liberated souls, not bodies, and accordingly Ephrem depicts Bardaiṣan as maintaining that Adam's disobedience caused the descent of the soul into bodies, not the perishability of bodies:

> Bardaiṣan has claimed that if it is the case—that these bodies died by Adam,—it was fitting for our Lord who came—that He should raise up the bodies from the grave;—but if it was not the bodies that he revived,[68]—it is clear[69] that the death of the soul—Adam brought in by his sins,—for the souls which he cast down to Sheol—did our Lord bring up with Him.[70]

Rather, writes Ephrem:

> According to the doctrine of Bardaiṣan—the death that Adam brought in—was an obstacle for the souls—for they were blocked at the passageway—because the sin of Adam [blocked] them,—"and the life," [Bardaiṣan says], "that our Lord brought in—is that He taught the truth and was taken up,—and He brought them across into the kingdom."[71]

---

65 Thus also Burkitt, "Introductory Essay," 2:cxxv, re: stanzas 2, 74, 79–80; Possekel, "Expectations," 69–70; eadem, "Bardaisan of Edessa: Philosopher," 454–455; Jurasz, "Résurrection," 416; Camplani, "Bardaisan's Psychology," 268–269; idem, "Bardaisan and the Bible," 709; McGlothlin, "Contextualizing," 324–325, re: stanza 74, 79–80.
66 [...] ' mwt' ḥth' hw. Mitchell does not translate this sentence.
67 C. Bar. 80, text in Mitchell, S. Ephraim's Prose Refutations, 2:164, tr. ibid., 2:lxxvi, modified. I accept Mitchell's emendation (ibid., n. 6) of MS l'wrbl' d'bn' b't' to l'wrql' d'dn' šbrt'.
68 Taking law to negate not the main verb (as Mitchell translates), but the object of the verb, pgr' (see further Nöldeke, Compendious Syriac Grammar, § 329).
69 Accepting Mitchell's emendation of dyn' to ydy".
70 C. Bar. 79, text in Mitchell, S. Ephraim's Prose Refutations, 2:164, tr. ibid., 2:lxxvi, modified. On this passage, see also Drijvers, Bardaiṣan, 155; Jurasz, "Résurrection," 416–417.
71 C. Bar. 82, text in Mitchell, S. Ephraim's Prose Refutations, 2:164–165, tr. ibid., 2:lxxvii, slightly modified. Possekel rightly points to this stanza as a summary of Bardaiṣan's view of the resurrection ("Bardaisan of Edessa: Philosopher," 454). It may indicate Zoroastrian

Earlier in the work, Ephrem digresses by answering an exegesis which disturbs the Adam-Christ typology by identifying Abel as the first human to die a physical death, which may have been a proof-text for Bardaiṣan in developing his own views.[72] In any case, Ephrem concludes that "because out of all the bodies that die—only the body of our Lord rose up—Bardaiṣan erred and supposed—that it was the souls that our Lord revived,—and he did not consider that also the death of Adam—in Adam reigned first and thus after nine hundred years—the leaven of it had spread in all generations."[73]

Ephrem responds with reference to the distinctively Syriac tradition that after death, the soul rests in a state of 'sleep' until the resurrection of the flesh.[74] Rather, Ephrem believes, the body and soul are both dependent on the same source of life, i.e. God; in fact, everything Bardaiṣan says about the priority of the soul actually shows that the body has priority.[75] Scholars today disagree about whether Ephrem's evidence indicates that Bardaiṣan denied the res-

---

influence on Bardaiṣan's thought (eadem, "Bardaisan of Edessa on the Resurrection," 17–18, followed by Jurasz, "Résurrection," 417).

72 In stanzas 37–39, Ephrem counters the view that God is accountable for the killing of Abel by virtue of His foreknowledge of the event (text in Mitchell, *S. Ephraim's Prose Refutations*, 2:152–153, tr. ibid., 2:lxx–lxxi). Ephrem apologizes for the digression in stanza 40 (also noted by Jurasz, "Résurrection," 400), but explains in stanza 41 that he brings it up because Abel died before Adam, so the parallelism between Christ's death and Adam's death is somewhat disturbed by the fact that while Adam is the first man, he is not the first man to die. Commentators reasonably assume that Ephrem here responds to Bardaiṣan himself (Burkitt, "Introductory Essay," 2:cxxv; Drijvers, *Bardaiṣan*, 154; Possekel, "Expectations," 68; eadem, "Bardaisan of Edessa: Philosopher," 454; Ramelli, *Bardaiṣan*, 228; Jurasz, "Résurrection," 403; Morehouse, "Bar Daysān," 152; Camplani, "Bardaisan's Psychology," 268; idem, "Bardaisan and the Bible," 709; McGlothlin, "Contextualizing," 324). Yet this is not explicit in the text, and in fact the immediately preceding stanzas concerning the responsibility inherent in divine foreknowledge answer an Epicurean argument which Tertullian and Jerome claim was used by Marcion (useful remains the discussion of Gager, "Marcion and Philosophy"). It is worth asking whether the argument concerning Abel made in *C. Bar.* stanza 41 answers Marcionites, rather than Bardaiṣan, or how the Marcionite argument concerning God's providential foreknowledge in stanzas 37–39 may color the Bardaiṣanite exegesis discussed in stanza 41. In any event, Ephrem's response is that Adam's death is the natural death God allots to all human beings, while Abel died due to human wickedness, which the crucifixion does not solve.

73 *C. Bar.* 91, text in Mitchell, *S. Ephraim's Prose Refutations*, 2:167, tr. ibid., 2: lxxviii–lxxix, slightly modified.

74 *C. Bar.* 32, text in tr. Mitchell, *S. Ephraim's Prose Refutations*, 2:151, tr. ibid., 2:lxix. For early witnesses to this tradition, see Euseb. *Hist. eccl.* 6.37; Aphrahat, *Demonstrations*, 8.19–23; cit. Camplani, "Bardaisan's Psychology," 260 n. 6. Ephrem's argument here presumes that Bardaiṣan does not think that the soul will be rejoined to a body in Paradise.

75 See *C. Bar.* 43, 60, respectively.

urrection of the flesh or not, but Camplani correctly observes that the later stanzas of Ephrem's *Discourse Against Bardaiṣan*, particularly stanza 82, clearly quote Bardaiṣan as stating that the soul will not be united with the body in Paradise.[76]

Finally, we can return to al-Bīrūnī's quotations of Mani in *On India*. According to al-Bīrūnī, Mani's *Book of Mysteries* highlighted that souls transmigrate after death; Ephrem, meanwhile, relates that Bardaiṣan claimed that immediately after corporeal death, souls either go to Sheol or ascend. It is reasonable to infer that Mani differed with Bardaiṣan on the question of metempsychosis. Mani likely claimed that the soul does not go straight to Sheol or Paradise after death; rather, he probably gave an account something like what we find about Manichaean personal eschatology in the *Fihrist*, where the soul of a deceased member of the Manichaean elect ascends directly to the Kingdom of Light.[77] The catechumens return to the cosmos and are reincarnated in a superior body,

---

[76] "The author of this text has denied the resurrection of the body in the clearest terms. The resurrection, therefore, is the process of purifying the soul that has kept the word of the Lord ... It consists in the rising of the soul from the underworld, or from the world, through the planetary spheres" ("Bardaisan's Psychology," 269; similarly idem, "Bardaisan and the Bible," 710; Pretty, *Adamantius*, 9; Possekel, "Bardaisan of Edessa on the Resurrection," 8–13). Jurasz is more hesitant ("Résurrection," 425): "Si rien n'indique que Bardesane aurait effectivement nié la résurrection des corps, il la concevait différemment de la résurrection de l'âme. C'est l'âme qui, selon Bardesane, devient mortelle à cause du péché d'Adam et ressuscite par la résurrection du Christ ..." Ramelli, meanwhile, argues that Ephrem must have misunderstood the resurrected (spiritual, purified) body of Bardaiṣan to not be a body at all (since it has no material component—Ramelli, *Bardaiṣan*, 225). Later sources from Ephrem onwards which attribute such denial to him refer not to Bardaiṣan, but his later followers (ibid., *Bardaiṣan*, 162). Rather, she hypothesizes that Bardaiṣan took the resurrection body to consist of a bodily substance purified of darkness, no longer mixed with evil substance (ibid., 162). Camplani notes that this is possible, but not based on any of the sources ("Bardaisan's Psychology," 267). Ramelli's interpretation derives in part from her reading of Ephrem's *Carmina Nisibena*, particularly 51.4 and 51.13, which ostensibly denote Adam's Fall as the cause not only of the perishability of the soul, but of the body (Ramelli, *Bardaiṣan*, 224–225). Camplani prefers the evidence from *C. Bar.* presented here (op. cit., 267 n. 28). These passages are obscure and merit closer treatment elsewhere, but it appears to me that Ephrem only ascribes Bardaiṣan's hermeneutic, not Adam's Fall, as depriving the body of the resurrection. Thus *Carmina Nisibena* 51.4, tr. Beck, *Des heiligen Ephraem des Syrers*, 60: "Die Lesung [Bardaisans—DMB] betrübte * gleicherweise Seele und Körper.—Denn sie legte zwischen die Freunde * eine Trennung ohne Hoffnung.—Den Körper beraubte sie der Auferstehung * und die Seele ihres Gefährten.—Und den Schaden, den die Schlange brachte, * nannte Bardaisan einen Nutzen."

[77] Camplani goes further, taking Mani's reference to the "ascension and purification of the Living Soul" in the body to refer to "not only the condition of a single soul in relation to its body, but also the place of the soul in the material universe and its relation with corporeality" ("Bardaisan's Psychology," 260–261).

the better to be purified and contribute further to the grand salvific plan, while the souls of sinners will, upon the destruction of the world, be condemned to an existence outside of the Kingdom of Light.[78]

Al-Bīrūnī's second quotation of Mani's *Book of Mysteries*, on the other hand, raises an interesting problem: Mani's account here of Bardaiṣan's teaching on the soul appears, at first glance, to disagree with that given by Ephrem. Mani in the *Book of Mysteries* states that the followers of Bardaiṣan claim the soul is purified while it is in the body. I quote it again:

> The Dayṣāniyya are of the opinion that the ascension and purification of the Living Soul takes place in the human body. They do not know that the body is the enemy of the soul and that it (the body) forbids it (the soul) to make ascent, for it (the body) is a prison and an instrument of torture for it (the soul).[79]

Yet according to Ephrem, Bardaiṣan claims that the soul's salvation has nothing to do with the body. Rather, following the body's death, the soul is in a perishable state outside of the body, until it is permitted to enter the Bridal Chamber thanks to Christ's intervention. Some commentators have taken Mani (*apud* al-Bīrūnī) at his word, regardless of Ephrem's remarks.[80] I would prefer to assume the veracity of both accounts, on which reading, the problem must have been

---

78   In Dodge, '*Fihrist*', 795–797. For the present reading of this evidence, see Pedersen, *Studies*, 352–353. On metempsychosis and personal eschatology on Manichaeism, see esp. the survey of Casadio, "Manichaean Metempsychosis"; further, BeDuhn, *Manichaean Body*, 80–82.

79   Tr. Reeves, *Prolegomena*, 107–108. On al-Bīrūnī's reports on Manichaeism and its sources, see Browder, "Al-Bîrûnî's Manichaean Sources."

80   Thus Drijvers: "this discussion of Mani with Bardaiṣan indirectly confirms our view of Bardaiṣan … Bardaiṣan has a positive attitude towards matter, and consequently towards sexuality, which is a form of purification" (Drijvers, *Bardaiṣan*, 205; similarly on the latter point, BeDuhn, *Manichaean Body*, 89; Ramelli, *Bardaiṣan*, 53–54). Similarly de Blois: "Bar Dayṣān believed (at least according to Manes) that the purification of the Soul of Life 'takes place in the human body', presumably through continual procreation and reincarnation; in other words, the spiritual substance is filtered and purified by passing through multiple bodies" ("Manichaean Polemics"; similarly idem, "Elchasai," 38). The impulse for this reading of Bardaiṣan is the testimony of Moshe bar Kepha that Bardaiṣan believed the mixture of the elements and Darkness "is being cleansed and refined by conception and birth until it is perfect" (Burkitt, "Introductory Essay," cxxiii). In other words, Mani (*apud* al-Bīrūnī) and bar Kepha have a roughly similar view of Bardaiṣan's psychology. Yet I hesitate to assign to Bardaiṣan a doctrine of metempsychosis, given the apparent absence of even a hint of such teaching from Ephrem's discussion in *C. Bar*. The stakes of the question are underlined by de Blois's recent argument that some passages of the 'polemical hymn'

the following: Mani claimed that it is the body which is in the way of the soul's ascent, while according to Ephrem, Bardaiṣan did not blame the body for keeping the soul from ascending. Rather, Bardaiṣan blamed the sin of Adam. While the body is perishable for Bardaiṣan, it is not responsible for the mortal state of the soul; Adam is.[81] Mani believed, on the contrary, that the soul is immortal, and the material body (literally, the "corpse") is the source of all perishability and death.

4   Conclusion: the 'Book of Mysteries,' a Manichaean 'De anima'?

While scholars have previously regarded Mani's *Book of Mysteries* as a kind of a grab-bag directed against various competing authorities, the reconstruction I propose here provides a clear line of argument for the text, as follows: the work began with a discussion of Bardaiṣan's teaching on the soul, proceeded to questions of the crucifixion and its implications for personal eschatology, returned in chapter twelve to the Daiṣanites, and finally pivoted to the chapters on cosmic eschatology which an-Nadīm describes as comprising the end of the work. Mani's *Book of the Mysteries* was then most likely a kind of a treatise *De anima*, in the sense that Tertullian used the title: a book concerned with the soul, its relationship to the body, and the question of what part of us exactly gets saved, all directed against competing philosophical and theological authorities.[82]

As is widely recognized, Mani pursued this argument with reference to pseudepigraphic, revelatory authorities and an engagement with Jewish and Christian prophetology, a modus operandi also evidenced by the Cologne Mani Codex. This would explain the appeal of *James* and other Gnostic apocalypses concerned with docetic Christology in the long mid-section of the treatise, sandwiched between chapters on the Daiṣanites—the latter of which, an-Nadīm states, was specifically concerned with personal eschatology. Taking Bardaiṣan's psychology and Christology as his point of departure, Mani dug into revelatory authorities and contrasted his beliefs with their views, before circling back to the Daiṣanites and presenting his own eschatological schema:[83]

M28 I (verso i, 10–31) may include Manichaean criticism of Bardaiṣanite psychology along the lines of al-Bīrūnī's testimony ("Manichaean Polemics"). The problem merits further investigation.

81   Tertullian argues along similar lines in his *De anima*, chapters 40–41.
82   On Tertullian's positioning of the argument of his *De anima*, see Waszink, *Quinti Septimi*, 7.
83   Cf. Camplani's recent suggestion that on such occasions, Mani engages in his own kind of 'heresiology' ("Traces de controverse religiuese," 55). On this reading, not only Bardaiṣan-

5 New Glosses on an-Nadīm's summary of Mani's 'Book of Mysteries'

1. An account of the Dayṣāniyya (→ against Bardaiṣan's *Book of Mysteries*, contents resembling the Bardaiṣanite psychology attacked by Ephrem Syrus, *Discourse Against Bardaiṣan*)
2. The testimony of Yastāsif on the Beloved (→ *Oracles of Hystaspes*, on the destruction of the soul after death)
3. The testimony of ... about himself given to Ya'qūb (→ *1Apoc. Jas.*)
4. The son of the widow (→ *1Apoc. Jas.*; the crucifixion)
5. The testimony of Jesus about himself as given to Judas (→ *Gos. Judas?*)
6. The commencement of the testimony of al-Yamīn as given after his victory (→ *1Apoc. Jas.*; James's martyrdom and subsequent ascent of the soul)
7. The discourse on the four transient spirits (→ *1Apoc. Jas.*)
8. The seven spirits (→ *1Apoc. Jas.*)
9. Laughter (→ *1Apoc. Jas.*, *Gos. Judas*)
10. The testimony of Adam regarding Jesus (→ Jesus the Splendor [the 'cosmic soul'] awakens Adam ...)
11. The fall from religion (→ ... against Bardaiṣan's reading of the Fall of Adam and the Adam-Jesus ['death of the soul']-typology critiqued by Ephrem)
12. The discourse of the Dayṣāniyya on the soul and the body (→ Bardaiṣanite psychology per Ephrem Syrus, *Discourse Against Bardaiṣan*, and al-Bīrūnī)
13. Refutation of the Dayṣānites on the soul of life (→ Bardaiṣanite psychology per Ephrem Syrus, *Discourse Against Bardaiṣan*, and al-Bīrūnī)

(Mani shifts from personal to cosmic eschatology)

14. The three trenches
15. The preservation of the World
16. The three days
17. The prophets
18. The resurrection (→ against Bardaiṣan per Ephrem Syrus, *Discourse Against Bardaiṣan*)

If Ephrem's testimony regarding Bardaiṣan's views on the resurrection and the soul can be trusted, we can be still more specific. According to Ephrem, Bardaiṣan rejected the resurrection of the flesh, and affirmed docetism. We cannot ascertain the veracity of the latter charge, but we do know that for Ephrem, the value of Bardaiṣan's teaching on personal eschatology hinges on interpretation

---

ite evidence but the testimony of some extant Coptic Gnostic apocalypses can teach us much about Mani's 'heresiology.'

of the crucifixion-event. Now, Mani certainly agreed with Bardaiṣan that the eschaton would not unite soul and flesh. This may be the topic with which he opened his *Book of Mysteries*. Gardner's ingenious work shows us that for Mani, interpretation of the crucifixion, with reference to works like the *Oracles of Hystaspes* and the (*First Apocalypse of*) *James*, were also central to his conception of personal eschatology, as discussed in chapters three to nine of the *Book of Mysteries*. However, as al-Bīrūnī tells us, Mani disagreed with Bardaiṣan about what personal eschatology is and how it works. This is likely what he discussed in chapters twelve and thirteen of the *Book*. Al-Bīrūnī's evidence permits us some specificity here: Mani took Bardaiṣan to task regarding the doctrines of metempsychosis and the living soul, particularly opposing Bardaiṣan's account of the effects of the fall of Adam.

Such a reading helps us solve a problem left open in the reading of the *Fihrist*'s description of the *Book of Mysteries* from the first part of this paper: the contents of chapters ten and eleven, concerning Adam and "the fall from religion." I suggest that here, Mani not only discussed his own teachings regarding Adam and his fall, but did so in order to respond to Bardaiṣan's teaching that Adam's fall resulted in the perishability of the soul. This may also explain part of the appeal of the *Gospel of Judas* to Mani's attack on Bardaiṣan's teaching about Adam, for *Judas* specifies that Jesus's crucifixion destroys the archons through disposing of the entire race of Adam, "the man of earth." Finally, if the reading given here is correct, an-Nadīm's testimony regarding the contents of the eighteenth and final chapter of Mani's *Book of Mysteries*—"on the resurrection"—may be clarified as well. This evidence may suggest that Mani's *Book of Mysteries* closed as it opened—with an attack on the followers of Bardaiṣan, who, Ephrem tells us, did affirm the resurrection after a fashion, but of the soul, without flesh.[84] Given the proximity of their view to Mani's own, the prophet of light had all good reason to close his *Book of Mysteries* by distinguishing his view from that of the Daiṣanites.

One might object that our later evidence about the Dayṣāniyya is very confused. It is difficult, if not impossible, to tell whether the Dayṣāniyya became influenced by Manichaeism, or if their teachings were conflated with Manichaean teachings in the heresiographical record. This is not much of an issue for the present analysis. What an-Nadīm reports when he refers to "an account of the Dayṣāniyya" etc. is that Mani responded to Bardaiṣan's followers of his own day, that is, the mid-late third century CE. If we base our reconstruction

---

84 Cf. Gardner's earlier suggestion that the title heading is an Islamicate gloss ("Mani's *Book*," 332). While others also translate "resurrection" here (e.g. Spuler in Adam, *Texte*, 9), Tardieu translates instead "final judgment" (*Manichaeism*, 41).

upon that to which what Mani responded, then we are on safer ground. Yet this raises a second problem, which is more serious: our information about Bardaiṣan's teachings in the third and fourth centuries is shadowy. The best index would be the *Book of the Laws of the Countries*, but this tells us relatively little about the problem in question, namely personal eschatology and the character of the crucifixion. Ephrem speaks directly to these themes in his *Discourse Against Bardaiṣan*, which is used liberally here, but he is hardly an impartial source and may confuse the teachings of Bardaiṣan with those of his later followers.[85] However, the present goal is not to reconstruct the teaching of 'the historical Bardaiṣan' with reference to the evidence about Mani's *Book of Mysteries*. Rather, the goal is the opposite: reconstructing the teaching of Mani's *Book of Mysteries* with reference to Daiṣanite evidence. Given this trajectory of investigation, it does not matter whether Ephrem's evidence tells us much about the teaching of Bardaiṣan himself or his third-century followers, because it does map on to the complex of issues Mani responded to in his own *Book of Mysteries*, according to the Arabic witnesses.

In any case, what I have hoped to show is that our Daiṣanite evidence is worth probing further in order to divine the contents of Mani's *Book of Mysteries*. Moreover, if Gardner is right that the middle chapters of Mani's work responded to the (*First Apocalypse of*) *James*, the *Gospel of Judas*, or other Gnostic apocalypses regarding the descent of the soul and a (quasi-)docetic interpretation of the crucifixion, then our evidence from Ephrem's *Discourse Against Bardaiṣan* supplies us with a substantial continuity of theme for the first two-thirds of the work: the soul, its relationship to the body, and its implications for our understanding of the crucifixion and salvation. The *Book of the Mysteries*, then, would have been a book on souls, and the fates of souls after they depart from the body—a treatise *De anima*.

Acknowledgements

This paper was briefly discussed in Pretoria (*in absentia*, March, 2019) and then presented in Dublin in October, 2019. I thank those present for their discussion

---

85 A useful discussion of this issue may be found in Ramelli, *Bardaiṣan*, 157–158. Despite this complicating factor, both she and Camplani speculate that the issues of the soul and its relationship to the crucifixion and resurrection were the subjects of Bardaisan's *Book of Mysteries* (Camplani, "Bardesane et les bardesanites," 45, 48; more explicitly at idem, "Bardaisan's Psychology," 262, 268; idem, "Bardaisan and the Bible," 708; Ramelli, *Bardaiṣan*, 224 n. 393).

and criticism of its contents. I particularly would like to express my gratitude to Alberto Camplani and Iain Gardner for offering feedback and criticisms regarding a written draft of this study. The judgments made and any errors therein remain, of course, my own.

Bibliography

Adam, Alfred, ed. *Texte zum Manichäismus*. Kleine Texte für Vorlesungen und Übungen 175. Berlin: De Gruyter, 1954.

Aland (Ehlers), Barbara. "Bardesanes von Edessa—ein syrischer Gnostiker. Bemerkungen aus Anlaß des Buches von H.J.W. Drijvers, *Bardaiṣan von Edessa*." Pages 355–374 in *Was ist Gnosis? Studien zum frühen Christentum, zu Marcion und zur kaiserzeitlichen Philosophie*. Edited by Barbara Aland. Wissenschaftliche Untersuchungen zum Neuen Testament 239. Tübingen: Mohr Siebeck, 2015.

Beck, Edmund, ed. and tr. *Des heiligen Ephraem des Syrers Carmina Nisibena*. 2 vols. Corpus Scriptorum Christianorum Orientalium 240, 241. Leuven: Peeters, 1961–1963.

BeDuhn, Jason David. *The Manichaean Body: In Discipline and Ritual*. Baltimore: Johns Hopkins University Press, 2000.

Brankaer, Johanna, ed. and tr. *The Gospel of Judas*. Oxford Early Christian Gospel Texts. Oxford: Oxford University Press, 2019.

Brankaer, Johanna and Hans-Gebhard Bethge, eds. and trs. *Codex Tchacos: Texte und Analysen*. Texte und Untersuchungen zur Geschichte der altchristlichen Literatur 161. Berlin: De Gruyter, 2007.

Browder, Michael H. "Al-Bîrûnî's Manichaean Sources." Pages 19–28 in *Manichaean Studies*. Edited by Peter Bryder. Lund: Plus Ultra, 1988.

Burkitt, F.C. "Introductory Essay." Pages 2:cxi–cxliv in *Ephraim's Prose Refutations of Mani, Marcion, and Bardaisan. Of Which the Greater Part has been Transcribed from the Palimpsest B.M. Add. 14623 and is Now First Published*. Edited and translated by Charles W.S. Mitchell. 2 vols. London; Oxford: Williams and Norgate, 1912.

Burns, Dylan M. *Apocalypse of the Alien God: Platonism and the Exile of Sethian Gnosticism*. Divinations. Philadelphia: University of Pennsylvania Press, 2014.

Camplani, Alberto. "Bardaisan and the Bible." Pages 699–715 in *Gnose et Manichéisme. Entre les oasis d'Égypte et la route de la soie. Hommage à Jean-Daniel Dubois*. Edited by Anna van den Kerchove and Luciana Gabriela Soares Santoprete. Bibliothèque de l'École des Hautes Études, Sciences Religieuses 176. Turnhout: Brepols, 2017.

Camplani, Alberto. "Bardaisan's Psychology: Known and Unknown Testimonies and Current Scholarly Perspectives." Pages 259–278 in *Syriac Encounters: Papers from the Sixth North American Syriac Symposium, Duke University, 26–29 June 2011*. Edited by Maria E. Doerfler, Emanuel Fiano, and Kyle Richard Smith. Eastern Christian Studies 20. Leuven: Peeters, 2015.

Camplani, Alberto. "Bardesane et les bardesanites." *Annuaires de l'École des hautes études* 112 (2003): 29–50.

Camplani, Alberto. "Traces de controverse religieuse dans la littérature syriaque des origines: peut-on parler d'une hérésiologie des 'hérétiques'?" Pages 9–66 in *Les controverses religieuses en syriaque*. Edited by Flavia Ruani. Études syriaques 13. Paris: Geuthner, 2016.

Casadio, Giovanni. "The Manichaean Metempsychosis: Typology and Historical Roots." Pages 105–130 in *Studia Manichaica: II. Internationaler Kongreß zum Manichäismus, 6.–10. August 1989, St. Augustin/Bonn*. Edited by Gernot Wießner and Hans-Joachim Klimkeit. Studies in Oriental Religions 23. Wiesbaden: Harrassowitz, 1992.

Clivaz, Claire. "What is the Current State of Play on Jesus' Laughter? Reading the Gospel of Judas in the Midst of Scholarly Excitement." Pages 213–242 in *Judasevangelium und Codex Tchacos. Studien zur religionsgeschichtlichen Verortung einer gnostischen Schriftensammlung*. Edited by Enno Edzard Popkes and Gregor Wurst. Wissenschaftliche Untersuchungen zum Neuen Testament 297. Tübingen: Mohr Siebeck, 2012.

Crum, Walter Ewing. *A Coptic Dictionary*. Oxford: Clarendon Press, 1962.

de Blois, François. "Elchasai—Manes—Muḥammad. Manichäismus und Islam in religionshistorischem Vergleich." *Der Islam* 81 (2004): 31–48.

de Blois, François. "Manichaean Polemics: M28 and the *Book of the Mysteries*." Forthcoming.

de Blois, François. "New Light on the Sources of the Manichaean Chapter in the *Fihrist*." Pages 37–45 in *Il Manicheismo. Nuove prospettive della ricerca*. Edited by Alois Van Tongerloo and Luigi Cirillo. Louvain; Naples: Brepols, 2005.

Decret, François and Johannes van Oort. *Sanctus Augustinus, Acta contra Fortunatum Manichaeum*. Corpus Fontium Manichaeorum Series Latina 2. Turnhout: Brepols, 2004.

Dodge, Baynard, tr. *The 'Fihrist' of al-Nadīm: A Tenth-Century Survey of Muslim Culture*. 2 vols. New York: Columbia University Press, 1970.

Drijvers, Han J.W. *Bardaiṣan of Edessa*. Assen: van Gorcum & Co., 1966.

Dubois, Jean-Daniel "Les gnostiques basilidiens et les textes du codex VII de Nag Hammadi." Pages 385–404 in *Nag Hammadi à 70 ans. Qu'avons-nous appris? Nag Hammadi at 70: What Have We Learned? (Colloque international, Québec, Université Laval, 29–31 mai 2015)*. Bibliothèque Copte de Nag Hammadi Section "Études," 10. Leuven: Peeters, 2019.

Frankfurter, David. "Apocalypses Real and Alleged in the Mani Codex." *Numen* 44 (1997): 60–73.

Franzmann, Majella. *Jesus in the Manichaean Writings*. London; New York: T&T Clark, 2003.

Funk, Wolf-Peter. "Die erste Apokalypse des Jakobus (NHC V,3 / CT 2)." Pages 1152–1180 in

Antike christliche Apokryphen in deutscher Übersetzung. I. Band: Evangelien und Verwandtes. Edited by Christoph Markschies and Jens Schröter, with Andreas Heiser. 2 vols. Tübingen: Mohr Siebeck, 2012.

Funk, Wolf-Peter. "The Significance of the Tchacos Codex for Understanding the First Apocalypse of James." Pages 509–533 in *The Codex Judas Papers: Proceedings of the International Congress on the Tchacos Codex held at Rice University, Houston, Texas, March 13–16, 2008*. Edited by April D. Deconick. Nag Hammadi and Manichaean Studies 71. Leiden; Boston: Brill, 2009.

Gager, John. "Marcion and Philosophy." *Vigiliae Christanae* 26 (1972): 53–59.

Gardner, Iain. "The Docetic Jesus: Some Interconnections Between Marcionism, Manichaeism, and Mandaeism." Pages 57–85 in *Coptic Theological Papyri II: Edition, Commentary, Translation. With an Appendix: The Docetic Jesus*. Edited and translated by Iain Gardner. Mitteilungen aus der Papyrussammlung der Österreichischen Nationalbibliothek 21. Wien: Verlag Brüder Hollinek, 1988.

Gardner, Iain. "Mani's *Book of the Mysteries*: Prolegomena to a New Look at Mani, the 'Baptists' and the Mandaeans." *ARAM* 22 (2010): 321–334.

Gardner, Iain. "The Strange Case of 'Quire A' in the Dublin Kephalaia Codex: Further Thoughts on Mani's *Book of Mysteries*, M281 and the *First Apocalypse of James*." In this volume, 51–69.

Gardner, Iain, and Samuel Lieu, eds. *Manichaean Texts from the Roman Empire*. Cambridge: Cambridge University Press, 2004.

Jackson, A.V. Williams. *Researches in Manichaeism. With Special Reference to the Turfan Fragments*. New York: AMS Press Inc., 1965.

Jurasz, Izabela. "Éphrem, Bardesane et Albinus sur les incorporels. Une confrontation entre le platonisme et le stoïcisme en milieu syriaque." *Philosophie antique* 17 (2017): 169–204.

Jurasz, Izabela. "Résurrection de l'âme chez Bardesane." *Chōra. RÉAM* 9–10 (2011–2012): 399–427.

Leurini, Claudia. "The Temple Tabernacle in M28/I/: An Anti-Judeo-Christian Polemic Strophe." *Iran and the Caucasus* 22:1 (2018): 1–7.

Lieu, Judith. *Marcion and the Making of a Heretic: God and Scripture in the Second Century*. New York: Cambridge University Press, 2015.

Lieu, Samuel N.C. *Manichaeism in the Later Roman Empire and Medieval China*. Wissenschaftliche Untersuchungen zum Neuen Testament 63. Tübingen: Mohr Siebeck, 1992.

Marjanen, Antti. "The Seven Women Disciples in the Two Versions of *the First Apocalypse of James*." Pages 535–546 in *The Codex Judas Papers: Proceedings of the International Congress on the Tchacos Codex held at Rice University, Houston, Texas, March 13–16, 2008*. Edited by April D. Deconick. Nag Hammadi and Manichaean Studies 71. Leiden; Boston: Brill, 2009.

McGlothlin, Theodore D. "Contextualizing Aphrahat's *Demonstration* 8: Bardaisan, Origen, and the Fourth-Century Debate on the Resurrection of the Body." *Le Muséon* 127:3–4 (2014): 311–339.

Mitchell, Charles W.S., ed. and tr. *S. Ephraim's Prose Refutations of Mani, Marcion, and Bardaisan. Of Which the Greater Part has been Transcribed from the Palimpsest B.M. Add. 14623 and is Now First Published*. 2 vols. London; Oxford: Williams and Norgate, 1912.

Morehouse, Robert Joseph. "Bar Dayṣān and Mani in Ephraem the Syrian's Heresiography." Ph.D. Diss., Catholic University of America. Washington, 2013.

Nagel, Peter, ed. and tr. *Codex apocryphus gnosticus Novi Testamenti. Band 1. Evangelien und Apostelgeschichten aus den Schriften von Nag Hammadi und verwandten Kodizes. Koptisch und Deutsch*. Wissenschaftliche Untersuchungen zum Neuen Testament 326. Tübingen: Mohr Siebeck, 2014.

Nöldeke, Theodor. *Compendious Syriac Grammar*. Translated by James A. Crichton. London: Williams & Norgate, 1904.

Pedersen, Nils Arne. *Studies in 'The Sermon on the Great War': Investigations of a Manichaean-Coptic Text from the Fourth Century*. Aarhus: Aarhus University Press, 1993.

Podolak, Pietro. *Soranus von Ephesos, ΠΕΡΙ ΨΥΧΗΣ. Sammlung der Testimonien, Kommentar und Einleitung*. Beiträge zum Altertumskunde 279. Berlin; New York: De Gruyter, 2010.

Possekel, Ute. "Bardaisan of Edessa on the Resurrection: Early Syriac Eschatology in its Religious-Historical Context." *Oriens Christianus* 88 (2004): 1–28.

Possekel, Ute. "Bardaisan of Edessa: Philosopher or Theologian?" *ZAC* 10:3 (2007): 442–461.

Possekel, Ute. "Expectations of the End in Early Syriac Christianity." *Hugoye* 11 (2008): 65–80.

Pretty, Robert A., tr. *Adamantius: Dialogue on the True Faith in God*. Edited by Garry W. Trompf. Gnostica 1. Leuven: Peeters, 1997.

Ramelli, Ilaria L.E. *Bardaiṣan of Edessa: A Reassessment of the Evidence and a New Interpretation*. Piscataway: Gorgias Press, 2009.

Ramelli, Ilaria L.E. "Origen, Bardaiṣan, and the Origin of Universal Salvation." *Harvard Theological Review* 102:2 (2009): 135–168.

Reeves, John C. "An Enochic Citation in *Barnabas* 4.3 and the *Oracles of Hystaspes*." Pages 260–277 in *Pursuing the Text: Studies in Honor of Ben Zion Wacholder on the Occasion of his Seventieth Birthday*. Edited by John C. Reeves and John Kampen. Sheffield: Sheffield Academic Press, 1994.

Reeves, John C. *Jewish Lore in Manichaean Cosmogony. Studies in the 'Book of Giants' Traditions*. Monographs of the Hebrew Union College 14. Cincinatti: Hebrew Union College Press, 2016.

Reeves, John C. *Prolegomena to a History of Islamicate Manichaeism*. Comparative Islamic Studies. Sheffield: Equinox, 2011.

Richter, Siegfried. *Exegetisch-literarkritische Untersuchungen von Herakleidespsalmen des koptisch-manichäischen Psalmenbuches*. Arbeiten zum spätantiken und koptischen Ägypten 5. Altenberge: Oros Verlag, 1994.

Rose, Eugen. *Die manichäische Christologie*. Wiesbaden: Otto Harrassowitz, 1979.

Sala, Tudor. "Christ's gift-Gift to Judas." Pages 155–171 in *From Gnostics to Monastics: Studies in Coptic and Early Christianity*. Edited by David Brakke, Stephen J. Davis, and Stephen Emmel. Orientalia Lovaniensia Analecta 263. Louvain: Peeters, 2017.

Skjærvø, Prods Oktor. "The Manichaean Polemical Hymns in M 28 I." *Bulletin of the Asia Institute* 9 (1995): 239–255.

Sundermann, Werner. "Hystaspes, Oracles of." *Encyclopaedia Iranica* 12:6 (2004). Available online at http://www.iranicaonline.org/articles/hystaspes-oracles-of. Accessed 27 September 2019.

Sundermann, Werner, ed. and tr. *Der Sermon von der Seele. Eine Lehrschrift des östlichen Manichäismus. Edition der parthischen und soghdischen Version mit einem Anhang von Peter Zieme, Die türkischen Fragmente des 'Sermon von der Seele'*. Berliner Turfantexte 19. Brepols: Turnhout, 1997.

Tardieu, Michel. *Manichaeism*. Translated by M.B. DeBevoise. Champaign-Urbana: University of Illinois Press, 2009.

Thomassen, Einar. "The Valentinian Materials in *James* (NHC V,3 and CT,2)." Pages 79–90 in *Beyond the Gnostic Gospels: Studies Building on the Work of Elaine Pagels*. Edited by Edouard Iricinschi, Lance Jenott, Nicola Denzey Lewis, and Philippa Townsend. Studien und Texte zu Antike und Christentum 82. Tübingen: Mohr Siebeck, 2013.

Waszink, Jan Hendrik, ed. *Quinti Septimi Florentis Tertulliani 'De Anima'*. Supplements to Vigiliae Christianae 100. Leiden; Boston: Brill, 2010.

Wurst, Gregor. "L'avant dernier feuillet de l'*Évangile de Judas*." Pages 51–56 in *Gnose et Manichéisme. Entre les oasis d'Égypte et la route de la soie. Hommage à Jean-Daniel Dubois*. Edited by Anna van den Kerchove and Luciana Gabriela Soares Santoprete. Bibliothèque de l'École des Hautes Études, Sciences Religieuses 176. Turnhout: Brepols, 2017.

6
A Manichaean Reading of the *Gospel of Thomas*

René Falkenberg

"Manichaeans even wrote a *Gospel According to Thomas* that, with a sweet smelling gospel-like title smacked on, destroys the souls of the simple ones."[1]

CYRIL OF JERUSALEM (*Catechesis* 4,36)

∴

Abstract

Recently, the second volume in the Biblia Manichaica series from the *Corpus Fontium Manichaeorum* (Brepols) has been published by Nils Arne Pedersen et al., *The New Testament Gospels in Manichaean Tradition* (Turnhout 2020). This reference work presents biblical allusions and quotations from edited Manichaean and anti-Manichaean sources in the Greek, Coptic, Semitic, and Iranian languages. The volume also contains an appendix on the *Gospel of Thomas*, where 30 new parallels are listed among the 73 instances of the Manichaean use of that apocryphal gospel. This chapter first presents a complete list of all these parallels including short analyses of the quotations and allusions, of which the majority is found in the Coptic material. Based on the sheer number of parallels it becomes clear that Manichaeans surely knew and used the *Gospel of Thomas*, even in its Coptic version. I then aim to take these conclusions to the next level, asking the hypothetical question: How would Manichaeans have read the *Gospel of Thomas*? As an experiment, I therefore engage in a Manichaean reading of logia 49 and 50, which may shed new light on old exegetical problems within the two logia that have puzzled scholars for a long time.

---

[1] Ἔγραψαν καὶ Μανιχαῖοι κατὰ Θωμᾶν εὐαγγέλιον, ὅπερ, εὐωδίᾳ τῆς εὐαγγελικῆς προσωνυμίας ἐπικεχρωσμένον, διαφθείρει τὰς ψυχὰς τῶν ἁπλουστέρων (text from Migne, *Patrologia Graeca* 33.500, as presented in Attridge 1989, 105). All translations in the present contribution are my own, unless stated otherwise.

1   Introduction

In his *Catechesis* to catechumens in Palestine, Cyril of Jerusalem warns Christian newcomers not to read a so-called *"Gospel According to Thomas,"* since he is sure that it was not written by one of Jesus' twelve apostles, but by one of Mani's disciples instead (6,31). Thus, when writing the *Catechesis* in AD 348, Cyril commences a long-enduring tradition, among Patristic writers, of associating the composition of this 'heretical' gospel to Mani and his followers.[2] Today we know, of course, that the *Gospel of Thomas* did not arise within Manichaeism, even if it, after Cyril, was often deemed Manichaean. However, that he twice in the *Catechesis* (4,36; 6,31) needs to address a *Gospel According to Thomas* may indicate that some members of his flock knew it. In addition, that he both times relates it to Manichaeans may indicate that they used it.

If we move on from Palestine to Egypt, the exact same year of the composition of the *Catechesis* is found in a documentary text that was later reused as cartonnage to strenghten the cover of Nag Hammadi Codex (NHC) VII.[3] This specific year not only offers a dating range for the production of that codex, but also of the rest of the Nag Hammadi codices, including NHC II, where we find the Coptic version of the *Gospel of Thomas*.[4] Therefore, the probable time range of the production of the Nag Hammadi codices (4th–5th century), their location (Egypt), their language (Coptic), and their religion (with a close relationship to Christianity)—all concur with the two discoveries of the Medinet Madi codices and a large part of the Kellis texts, which are Manichaean in origin.[5] Hence, Cyril's observation, made in Palestine, of the Manichaean connection to the *Gospel of Thomas* finds strong confirmation, as we shall see, in contemporary Egypt.

My point of departure will be the recent reference work *The New Testament Gospels in Manichaean Tradition* (2020), which also includes an appendix on

---

[2] Cf. *Decretum Gelasianum* 5,3 (5th or 6th century); Pseudo-Leontius of Byzantium, *De sectis* 3,2 (6th century); Timothy of Constantinople, *De receptione haereticorum* (*Patrologia Graeca* 86 1.21C; 6th century); John of Damascus, *Orationes de imaginibus tres* 2.16 (8th century); *Acts of the Second Council of Nicaea* 6,5 (8th century); George the Sinner, *Chronicon breve* 3,162 (9th century); the *Long Greek Abjuration Formula* 3 (9th century); Peter of Sicily, *Historica Manichaeorum seu Paulicianorum* 67–68 (9th or 11th century), etc.; cf. the lists in Attridge 1989, 107–109; Gathercole 2014, 40–51.

[3] Cf. Barns, Browne, and Shelton 1981, 57–58.

[4] Accordingly, the Nag Hammadi codices may have been produced in the last half of the 4th century, perhaps even as late as the first half of the 5th century; cf. Lundhaug and Jenott 2015, 9–11, *passim*.

[5] Cf. Falkenberg 2018, 264.

the *Gospel of Thomas*.[6] The reference work springs from the Biblia Manichaica Project, where biblical allusions and quotations in Manichaean sources are detected and analysed, in a wide array of ancient languages. The Project is located at Aarhus University and concerns the edited Manichaean as well as anti-Manichaean sources in Syriac, Greek, Coptic, Arabic, and the Iranian languages; for practical reasons, the Project does not include the Manichaean material in Chinese, Turkic, and Latin.[7] Nils Arne Pedersen leads the Project, where participants also are Claudia Leurini (in charge of the Iranian sources), John Møller Larsen (the Semitic sources), and myself (the Coptic and Greek sources).[8] The *Gospel of Thomas*-appendix lists six quotations and 67 allusions in Manichaean texts.

In the first part of the present contribution, I will present a list of all 73 instances of the Manichaean use of the *Gospel of Thomas*; then, analyse how specific logia from the *Gospel of Thomas* were quoted in Manichaean texts; and, finally, present a selection of Manichaean allusions, with a focus on the Coptic material. In the second part of the contribution, I aim to take our conclusions from these findings to the next level, asking the question: Exactly *how* may Manichaeans have read the *Gospel of Thomas*? As an experiment, I will therefore engage in a Manichaean reading of logia 49 and 50, which may help scholars solve two exegetical problems.

2 Part I: The *Gospel of Thomas* in Manichaean Sources

Any current list of examples of the Manichaean use of the *Gospel of Thomas* cannot be complete, since large amounts of the Coptic and Iranian material still await publication in edition. The publication of the relevant texts are an ongoing enterprise, wherefore we can expect an increase in such parallels in

---

6 Cf. Pedersen, Falkenberg, Larsen, and Leurini 2020, 371–393.

7 Especially the Latin material is of great importance since it includes, i.a., the whole Latin translation of the Greek *Acta Archelai* and, not least, the anti-Manichaean writings of Augustine. We have a well-known parallel between the prologue plus logion 1 of the *Gospel of Thomas* in Augustine's polemical *Contra Epistulam Fundamenti* 11 (see also his *Contra Felicem* 1,1); cf. Attridge 1989, 104–105. If Augustine here quotes one of Mani's own letters (i.e. *Epistula Fundamenti*), it may indicate that Mani himself was familiar with some early version of the *Gospel of Thomas*; cf. Quispel 2008, 655.

8 The outcome of the Project is a three-volume work on the Manichaean use of the Bible: Vol. 1 on their use of the Old Testament, vol. 2 on the New Testament gospels (including the *Gospel of Thomas* and Diatessaron), and vol. 3 on the New Testament Acts, Letters, and Revelation. Until now, the first two volumes have been published: Pedersen, Falkenberg, Larsen, and Leurini 2017 and 2020.

future scholarship. For the same reason, the appendix of the *Gospel of Thomas* in *The New Testament Gospels in Manichaean Tradition* can be viewed to represent a 'snapshot' of parallels that scholars have been able to find in available editions until 2013.[9] On this basis, the following list shows the 73 plausible examples of the Manichaean reuse of the *Gospel of Thomas*.[10]

Prologue (NHC II 32,10–12 [Coptic]; P. Oxy. 654,1–3 [Greek]): *Psalm-Book* II 55,17–18[11] [Coptic]; Ibn al-Nadim, *Fihrist* 328.11[12] [Arabic].

Logion 1 (NHC II 32,12–14; P. Oxy. 654,3–5): *Psalm-Book* II 185,20–25;[13] M5815/I/V/i/27–IV/ii/1–4[14] [Parthian]; So 14441+/R/6–19[15] [Sogdian].

Logion 3 (NHC II 32,19–33,5; P. Oxy. 654,9–21): *Psalm-Book* I pl. 189,25–26[16] [Coptic]; II 155,33–39;[17] 160,20–21;[18] M7/I/V/ii/27–28[19] [Middle Persian]; M1848/R/1–7[20] [Parthian]; M8287/A/11–13[21] [Parthian]; So 14441+/V/17–20[22] [Sogdian].

Logion 4 (NHC II 33,5–10; P. Oxy. 654,21–27): *Psalm-Book* II 192,2–3.[23]

---

9 Cf. Pedersen, Falkenberg, Larsen, and Leurini 2017, xvi; 2020, xi. For practical reasons, it has not been possible to include all the newest editions in the reference work. Thus, the year 2013 was chosen to draw a line regarding which Manichaean texts to include or not; therefore, we do not use later, but nevertheless important, contributions such as Funk 2018; Gardner, BeDuhn, and Dilley 2018; Leurini 2018.

10 Almost all data in the list are from Pedersen, Falkenberg, Larsen, and Leurini 2020, 371–393, and therefore based on the efforts of all four members of the Biblia Manichaica Project.

11 First suggested by Gärtner 1961, 98; cf. also Funk 2002, 69 n. 7. The following notes 12–83 in the list mainly refer to scholars who have suggested the parallels.

12 Cf. Puech 1978d [1960–1972], 212–215, 222–229; Hammerschmidt 1962, 122–123; Drijvers 1989, 291–292, 302–303.

13 Cf. Doresse 1959, 121; Ménard 1975, 78; Mirecki 1991, 255 n. 39; Helderman 1999, 484.

14 Cf. Puech 1978b [1956–1960], 74; 1978c [1957], 39 n. 2, 55; Doresse 1959, 121; Blatz 1987, 98 n. 3; Klimkeit 1991, 156; Helderman 1999, 484–485.

15 Cf. Pedersen, Falkenberg, Larsen, and Leurini 2020, 372.

16 Cf. Wurst 1996, 154–155. Since almost all of *Psalm-Book* I remains to be edited (only single psalms have been published yet), we can probably expect more Manichaean parallels to the *Gospel of Thomas* from there.

17 Cf. Puech 1978d [1960–1972], 271.

18 Cf. ibid., 271; Gärtner 1961, 214; Ménard 1975, 43; Nagel 2008, 279–280; 2010, 513–515.

19 Cf. Pedersen, Falkenberg, Larsen, and Leurini 2020, 373.

20 Cf. ibid., 373.

21 Cf. ibid., 374.

22 Cf. ibid., 374.

23 Cf. Puech 1978b [1956–1960], 83; 1978c [1957], 38, 55; Doresse 1959, 128; Gärtner 1961, 225; Ménard 1975, 2, 6, 45, 84; Blatz 1987, 99 n. 7, 322; Mirecki 1991, 255 n. 39; Helderman 1999, 485; Richter 1998, 68.

Logion 5 (NHC II 33,10–13; P. Oxy. 654,27–31): Berlin *Kephalaia* 163,26–29[24] [Coptic].

Logion 13 (NHC II 34,30–35,14): Ephrem Syrus, *Hypatius* V 175.33–176.4[25] [Syriac]; Berlin *Kephalaia* 5,21–33;[26] 90,18–19;[27] *Psalm-Book* II 201,27–28.[28]

Logion 14 (NHC II 35,14–27): So 18224/R/16–17[29] [Sogdian].

Logion 17 (NHC II 36,5–9): *Psalm-Book* II 172,30–31;[30] M789/R/4–7[31] [Parthian]; So 18220/R/19–24[32] [Sogdian].

Logion 19 (NHC II 36,17–25): *Psalm-Book* II 161,17–18;[33] 185,20–25;[34] So 18248/II/V/10–17[35] [Sogdian].

Logion 22 (NHC II 37,20–35): P. Kellis Copt. 34,9–15[36] [Coptic]; *Psalm-Book* II 155,33–39;[37] M105b+/R/3[38] [New Persian].

Logion 23 (NHC II 38,1–3): Berlin *Kephalaia* 187,32–188,1;[39] 285,24–25;[40] *Psalm-Book* II 4,19–20;[41] M635/I /R/1–2[42] [Sogdian]; M763/R/ii/24–28[43] [Parthian]; M5805/B/6–7[44] [Parthian].

---

24 Cf. Puech 1978a, 60–61 [1955]; 1978b [1956–1960], 85; 1978c [1957], 53, 55; Doresse 1959, 131; Ménard 1975, 6, 85; Blatz 1987, 99 n. 9, 322; Funk 2002, 69; Nagel 2008, 288–289; 2010, 506–507.
25 Cf. Pedersen, Falkenberg, Larsen, and Leurini 2020, 375.
26 Cf. Gärtner 1961, 123–124; Ménard 1975, 32, 99.
27 Cf. Doresse 1959, 202.
28 Cf. Pedersen, Falkenberg, Larsen, and Leurini 2020, 376.
29 Cf. ibid., 376.
30 Cf. Mirecki 1991, 255 n. 39.
31 Cf. Puech 1978c [1957], 55; 1979 [1960], 156–157; Doresse 1959, 147; Sundermann 1981, 38 n. 6; Blatz 1987, 101 n. 24; Puech and Blatz 1987, 322; Otero 1989, 52; Klimkeit 1991, 153; Helderman 1999, 485; Nagel 2008, 280–281; 2010, 503–504.
32 Cf. Sundermann 1981, 38 n. 6.
33 Cf. Doresse 1959, 149, 152; Puech 1978d [1960–1972], 100; Ménard 1975, 107; Helderman 1999, 485.
34 Cf. Doresse 1959, 121; Ménard 1975, 78; Mirecki 1991, 255 n. 39; Helderman 1999, 484.
35 Cf. Pedersen, Falkenberg, Larsen, and Leurini 2020, 378.
36 Cf. ibid., 379.
37 Cf. Gärtner 1961, 221.
38 Cf. Pedersen, Falkenberg, Larsen, and Leurini 2020, 379.
39 Cf. Funk 2002, 87; Nagel 2010, 504–506.
40 Cf. Funk 2002, 87; Nagel 2008, 278–279; 2010, 504–506.
41 Cf. Funk 2002, 85–86; Nagel 2010, 504–506.
42 Cf. Funk 2002, 87 n. 47; Coyle 2009, 131.
43 Cf. Klimkeit 1991, 155; Klimkeit 1998, 194; Helderman 1999, 485; Funk 2002, 87; Nagel 2008, 278–279; 2010, 504–506; Coyle 2009, 131.
44 Cf. Pedersen, Falkenberg, Larsen, and Leurini 2020, 380.

Logion 24 (NHC II 38,3–10; P. Oxy. 655 frag. d,1–5): L/A/1–2[45] [Parthian].

Logion 28 (NHC II 38,20–31; P. Oxy. 1,11–21): Berlin *Kephalaia* 37,3–5;[46] *Psalm-Book* II 39,19–22;[47] 56,15–16;[48] 172,28–29;[49] M219/V/17–21[50] [Middle Persian].

Logion 30 (NHC II 39,2–5; P. Oxy. 1,23–27): *Psalm-Book* II 162,9–10;[51] 171,13.[52]

Logion 33 (NHC II 39,10–18; P. Oxy. 1,41–[?]): Berlin *Kephalaia* 205,10–12.[53]

Logion 37 (NHC II 39,27–40,2; P. Oxy. 655 i,17–ii,1): *Psalm-Book* II 64,23–24;[54] 76,9–15;[55] 99,26–30;[56] 164,30.[57]

Logion 38 (NHC II 40,2–7; P. Oxy. 655 ii,2–11): *Psalm-Book* II 187,24–29.[58]

Logion 40 (NHC II 40,13–16): Berlin *Kephalaia* 288,3–5.[59]

Logion 44 (NHC II 40,26–31): Dublin *Kephalaia* 416,12–16;[60] 417,25–29[61] [Coptic].

Logion 47 (NHC II 41,12–23): *Psalm-Book* I pl. 179,27–29;[62] II 223,1–7.[63]

Logion 50 (NHC II 41,30–42,7): Berlin *Kephalaia* 195,18–19.[64]

---

45 Cf. ibid., 380. The fragment is only recorded in Müller 1904, 108.
46 Cf. Pedersen, Falkenberg, Larsen, and Leurini 2020, 381.
47 Cf. ibid., 382.
48 Cf. Doresse 1959, 164–165; Ménard 1975, 122.
49 Cf. Pedersen, Falkenberg, Larsen, and Leurini 2020, 382.
50 Cf. ibid., 382.
51 Cf. Doresse 1959, 166; Ménard 1975, 125.
52 Cf. Doresse 1959, 166.
53 Cf. Ménard 1975, 130.
54 Cf. Doresse 1959, 170; Mirecki 1991, 256; Helderman 1999, 485.
55 Cf. Mirecki 1991, 256.
56 Cf. Doresse 1959, 170; Gärtner 1961, 250–251; Mirecki 1991, 253–260; Helderman 1999, 485; Richter 1998, 24.
57 Cf. Mirecki 1991, 256.
58 Cf. Puech 1978c [1957], 56; 1978d [1960–1972], 263; Doresse 1959, 171; Gärtner 1961, 116; Ménard 1975, 8, 31, 138; Puech and Blatz 1987, 322.
59 Cf. Funk 2002, 76–79.
60 Cf. Funk 2002, 79–85; Nagel 2008, 282–284; 2010, 515–517. Only recently, the edition of the Dublin *Kephalaia* has commenced (cf. Gardner, BeDuhn, and Dilley 2018); unfortunately, it was published after 2013 and thus not included in *The New Testament Gospels in Manichaean Tradition* (see n. 9). However, the relevant Coptic text that parallels logion 44 was published earlier in an article by Wolf-Peter Funk (2002) and therefore included in the reference work.
61 Cf. Funk 2002, 79–85.
62 Cf. Nagel 2008, 285–288.
63 Cf. Blatz 1987, 107 n. 60.
64 Cf. Pedersen, Falkenberg, Larsen, and Leurini 2020, 386.

Logion 56 (NHC II 42,29–32): *Psalm-Book* II 63,21–28.[65]
Logion 60 (NHC II 43,12–23): *Psalm-Book* II 172,15–27.[66]
Logion 71 (NHC II 45,34–35): *Psalm-Book* II 194,23;[67] M42/V/i/13–20[68] [Parthian]; M4570/V/i/6–V/ii/20[69] [Parthian].
Logion 75 (NHC II 46,11–13): *Psalm-Book* II 217,13–17.[70]
Logion 76 (NHC II 46,13–22): *Psalm-Book* II 63,9–10.[71]
Logion 77 (NHC II 46,22–28; P. Oxy. 1,27–30): *Psalm-Book* II 54,25–28;[72] 120,25–28;[73] 155,33–39.[74]
Logion 82 (NHC II 47,17–19): *Psalm-Book* II 39,23–24;[75] 155,33–39.[76]
Logion 84 (NHC II 47,24–29): *Psalm-Book* II 203,14–17.[77]
Logion 89 (NHC II 48,13–16): *Psalm-Book* II 160,8–9.[78]
Logion 90 (NHC II 48,16–20): *Psalm-Book* II 97,27–28.[79]
Logion 98 (NHC II 49,15–20): M4577/A/ii/22–23–B/i/1–23[80] [Parthian].
Logion 99 (NHC II 49,21–26): M5860/I/V/i/3–6[81] [Parthian].
Logion 111 (NHC II 51,6–10): So 14441+/R/6–19[82] [Sogdian]; So 18155/V/14–15[83] [Sogdian].

With the exception of one parallel in Syriac (logion 13) and one in Arabic (the prologue), the list consists entirely of parallels in Iranian languages (22 instances, i.e. less than one third of the 73 parallels) and in Coptic (49 instances, i.e. a little more than two thirds of all parallels). In the Iranian languages, we have one parallel in New Persian (logion 22), two in Middle Persian (logia 3

---

65 Cf. Blatz 1987, 108 n. 69.
66 Cf. Doresse 1959, 180–181; Gärtner 1961, 168; Ménard 1975, 38, 161.
67 Cf. Pedersen, Falkenberg, Larsen, and Leurini 2020, 387.
68 Cf. ibid., 387.
69 Cf. ibid., 388.
70 Cf. ibid., 389.
71 Cf. Ménard 1975, 177.
72 Cf. Puech 1978d [1960–1972], 254, 257.
73 Cf. Pedersen, Falkenberg, Larsen, and Leurini 2020, 390.
74 Cf. Puech 1978d [1960–1972], 257.
75 Cf. Pedersen, Falkenberg, Larsen, and Leurini 2020, 390.
76 Cf. ibid., 390.
77 Cf. Doresse 1959, 193.
78 Cf. Pedersen, Falkenberg, Larsen, and Leurini 2020, 391.
79 Cf. Doresse 1959, 195.
80 Cf. Pedersen, Falkenberg, Larsen, and Leurini 2020, 392.
81 Cf. ibid., 392.
82 Cf. ibid., 393.
83 Cf. ibid., 393.

and 28), eight in Sogdian (logia 1, 3, 14, 17, 19, 23, and 111 [twice]), and eleven in Parthian (logia 1, 3 [twice], 17, 23 [twice], 24, 71 [twice], 98, and 99). Of the 22 Iranian examples are the two quotations (logia 17 [M789] and 23 [M763]), whereas 20 are allusions.

In Coptic, we have one single parallel from the Manichaean Kellis texts (logion 22), whereas the rest is from the Medinet Madi codices. Of these are eleven from the *Kephalaia*, two from the text in Dublin (logion 44 [twice]) and nine from the text in Berlin (logia 5, 13 [twice], 23 [twice], 28, 33, 40, 50). From the Medinet Madi texts are also 37 parallels from the *Psalm-Book*, two from Part I (logia 3 and 47) and 35 parallels from *Psalm-Book* Part II (the prologue and logia 1, 3 [twice], 4, 13, 17, 19 [twice], 22, 23, 28 [thrice], 30 [twice], 37 [four times], 38, 47, 56, 60, 71, 75, 76, 77 [thrice], 82 [twice], 84, 89, and 90). Of the 49 Coptic examples are the four quotations (logia 5 [the Berlin *Kephalaia* 163,26–29], 23 [ibid. 285,24–25] and 44 [the Dublin *Kephalaia* 416,12–16 and 417,25–29]), whereas 45 are allusions. It is a bit peculiar, though, that no quotations are found in the *Psalm-Book*, since it presents nearly three and a half times more parallels (37) to the *Gospel of Thomas* than the two books of the *Kephalaia* from Berlin and Dublin (eleven).[84] Yet, the *Psalm-Book* often shows multiple attestations within the same logion (i.e. 3, 19, 28, 30, 37, 77, and 82), which only happens three times in the two texts of the *Kephalaia* (i.e. logia 13, 23 and 44).

In the Biblia Manichaica Project, it has been possible to find 30 new parallels between the *Gospel of Thomas* and the Manichaean sources: One in Syriac (logion 13), twelve in Coptic (logia 13, 22, 28 [three parallels], 50, 71, 75, 77, 82 [two parallels], 89), and 17 in Iranian languages (logia 1, 3 [four parallels], 14, 19, 22, 23, 24, 28, 71 [two parallels], 98, 99, 111 [two parallels]). Lastly, eleven previously cited parallels are not included in the list, since they are unconvincing.[85]

---

[84] An explanation of the lack of quotations in the *Psalm-Book* could relate to its genre ('psalms'), since prose texts like the *Gospel of Thomas* were rewritten to fit the poetic genre of the *Psalm-Book*; then, perhaps, also rewritten from a quotation into an allusion.

[85] One Manichaean parallel to logion 4 (i.e. Alexander of Lycopolis, *Against Mani's Doctrines* 2,24; cf. Doresse 1959, 128); four parallels to logion 10 (i.e. Berlin *Kephalaia* 5,3; 102,32 ff.; *Psalm-Book* II 11,6 ff.; 49,6; cf. Ménard 1975, 95; Blatz 1987, 100 n. 17); two to logion 11 (i.e., first, the Berlin *Kephalaia* 54,23–55,7; cf. Blatz 1987, 100 n. 18; Klimkeit 1991, 156; Helderman 1999, 485; and, second, the Turfanfragment M2; cf. Blatz 1987, 100 n. 18; Klimkeit 1991, 156); two to logion 37 (i.e. *Psalm-Book* II 19,26–28; 59,2–9; cf. Doresse 1959, 170; Helderman 1999, 485); one to logion 69 (i.e. *Psalm-Book* II 172,15 ff.; cf. Blatz 1987, 108 n. 73); and, finally, one to logion 76 (i.e. *Psalm-Book* II 52,31; cf. Ménard 1975, 177).

3 Manichaean Quotations of the *Gospel of Thomas*

The six quotations of the *Gospel of Thomas* are important, since they provide a smoking gun regarding a secure Manichaean use of it.[86] Two logia (5 and 17) represent one single quotation in the Manichaean sources, whereas two other logia (23 and 44) represent a double quotation. If we take a closer look at the first quotation, it compares logion 5 with the Berlin *Kephalaia*. In the *Gospel of Thomas*, Jesus says:

> Know what is before your (sg.) face and what is hidden from you will be revealed to you.[87]
>
> 33,11–13

In the Berlin *Kephalaia*, Jesus tells his disciples:

> Know what is before your (pl.) face and what is hidden from you will be revealed to you.[88]
>
> 163,28–29

The main difference between the two is the use of the singular pronoun in logion 5 and the plural in the Berlin *Kephalaia*, probably because Jesus here is adressing the group of disciples.[89] Nevertheless, the Manichaean saying qualifies as a quotation.

The second quotation compares logion 17 with the Parthian fragment M789. However, before moving on to the Manichaean parallel, we need to be aware that logion 17 itself presents a quotation from Paul ("What eyes did not see and what ears did not hear"; 1 Cor 2:9)[90] in the following words of Jesus:

---

86 In the Biblia Manichaica Project, a quotation is defined in the following way: "The Manichaean text is a recitation of the Bible text. For a Manichaean saying to qualify as a Bible quotation there must be strong agreement in wording between them, although the Manichaean text needs not be an exact reproduction of the Bible text. In addition, the appearance of a quotation formula heightens the likelihood of a Manichaean saying being a Bible quotation" (Pedersen, Falkenberg, Larsen, and Leurini 2017, xlii).

87 ⲥⲟⲩⲱⲛ ⲡⲉⲧⲙ̄ⲡⲙ̄ⲧⲟ ⲙ̄ⲡⲉⲕϩⲟ ⲉⲃⲟⲗ ⲁⲩⲱ ⲡⲉⲑⲏⲡ ⲉⲣⲟⲕ ϥⲛⲁϭⲱⲗⲡ ⲉⲃⲟⲗ ⲛⲁⲕ (text from Layton 1989, 54).

88 ⲙ̄ⲙⲉ ⲁⲡⲉⲧϣⲟⲟⲡ ⲙ̄ⲡⲙ̄ⲧⲟ ⲁⲃⲁⲗ ⲙ[ⲡ]ⲉⲧⲛ̄ϩⲟ ⲁⲩⲱ ⲡⲉⲧϩⲏⲡ ⲁⲣⲱⲧⲛⲉ ⲛⲁϭⲱⲗⲡ ⲛⲏⲧⲛ̄ ⲁⲃⲁⲗ (text from Polotsky and Böhlig 1940, 163; here, including the corrections by Funk 2002, 74–75).

89 The original use of the singular is confirmed in the Greek text of the *Gospel of Thomas* (P. Oxy. 654,27–29).

90 All translations of the New Testament writings from Greek text in Nestle-Aland (28. ed.).

> I will give you what eyes did not see and what ears did not hear and what hands did not touch.[91]
>
> 36,5–8

Here, the main difference between Paul and logion 17 is the addition of "I will give you" and "what hands did not touch." Exactly these two additions are found in the Manichaean fragment in Parthian:

> I will give you what corporeal eyes did not see, ears did not hear and hands did not grasp.[92]
>
> M789/R/4–7

There are only minor differences between logion 17 and the Parthian text, i.e. the addition of "corporeal" to "eyes" and the use of "grasp" instead of "touch," where the latter two, semantically, come very close to one another.

The third quotation is a Manichaean double quotation, where logion 23 is compared to both the Berlin *Kephalaia* and the Parthian fragment M763. In logion 23, Jesus says:

> I will choose you, one out of a thousand and two out of ten thousand.[93]
>
> 38,1–2

In the parallel from the Berlin *Kephalaia*, Mani says:

> I have [chosen] you, one [among a thousand], two among ten thousand.[94]
>
> 285,24–25

Main differences here are that the use of Future tense in logion 23 ("I will choose") is changed to Perfect tense in the Berlin *Kephalaia* ("I have [chosen]"), and also that the wording is transferred from a saying of Jesus to a saying of Mani, which also happens in the fourth quotation below. The other quotation of logion 23 in the Parthian fragment is somehow enlarged when an anonymous person says to Manichaean adherents:

---

91 ϯⲛⲁϯ ⲛⲏⲧⲛ̄ ⲙ̄ⲡⲉⲧⲉ ⲙ̄ⲡⲉ ⲃⲁⲗ ⲛⲁⲩ ⲉⲣⲟϥ ⲁⲩⲱ ⲡⲉⲧⲉ ⲙ̄ⲡⲉ ⲙⲁⲁϫⲉ ⲥⲟⲧⲙⲉϥ ⲁⲩⲱ ⲡⲉⲧⲉ ⲙ̄ⲡⲉ ϭⲓϫ ϭⲙ̄ϭⲱⲙϥ (text from Layton 1989, 60).

92 Translation from Pedersen, Falkenberg, Larsen, and Leurini 2020, 376.

93 ϯⲛⲁⲥⲉⲧⲡ̄ ⲑⲏⲛⲉ ⲟⲩⲁ ⲉⲃⲟⲗ ϩⲛ̄ ϣⲟ ⲁⲩⲱ ⲥⲛⲁⲩ ⲉⲃⲟⲗ ϩⲛ̄ ⲧⲃⲁ (text from Layton 1989, 64).

94 ⲁⲓ̣[.] . ⲧ̣ . ⲑⲏⲛ[ⲉ] ⲟⲩϩ̣ [ϩⲛ̄ϣⲟ] ⲥⲛⲉⲩ ϩⲛ̄ⲟⲩⲧⲃⲁ (text from Funk 2002, 87; including the tentative restoration ⲁⲓ̣[ⲥⲁ]ⲧ[ⲡ̄]ⲑⲏⲛ[ⲉ] by Nagel 2008, 278).

> Selected and chosen you are from among many, one among thousand and two among ten thousand.[95]
>
> M763/R/ii/24–28

Except for the added words, "and chosen … from among many," also the Parthian text makes a convincing quotation. The reason for this addition probably owes to the Manichaeans' fondness of mixing two (or more) Jesus logia with each other; here, it seems as if the quotation of logion 23 has been combined with Matt 22:14 ("many are called, but few chosen").

In the Manichaean sources, the fourth quotation is double attested too, namely logion 44 in comparison with two sections in the Dublin *Kephalaia*. Logion 44 goes as follows:

> Jesus said, "Whoever blasphemes against the father will be forgiven, and whoever blasphemes against the son will be forgiven, but whoever blasphemes against the holy spirit will not be forgiven either on earth or in heaven".[96]
>
> 40,26–31

This saying is in itself enlarging a saying from the synoptic gospels in the New Testament, where only the son and the holy spirit are mentioned.[97] The quotation in the Dublin *Kephalaia* comes remarkably close to the *Gospel of Thomas*:

> Jesus said, "Whoever blasphemes against [the father will] be [forgiven]; whoever blasphemes against the son will be forgiven; [whoever] blasphemes against the holy spirit will not be for[given] on earth or in the heavens".[98]
>
> 416,12–15

---

95 Translation from Pedersen, Falkenberg, Larsen, and Leurini 2020, 380.

96 ⲡⲉϫⲉ ⲓ̅ⲥ̅ ⲡⲉⲧⲁϫⲉⲟⲩⲁ ⲁⲡⲉⲓⲱⲧ ⲥⲉⲛⲁⲕⲱ ⲉⲃⲟⲗ ⲛⲁϥ ⲁⲩⲱ ⲡⲉⲧⲁϫⲉⲟⲩⲁ ⲉⲡϣⲏⲣⲉ ⲥⲉⲛⲁⲕⲱ ⲉⲃⲟⲗ ⲛⲁϥ ⲡⲉⲧⲁϫⲉⲟⲩⲁ ⲇⲉ ⲁⲡⲡ̅ⲛ̅ⲁ̅ ⲉⲧⲟⲩⲁⲁⲃ ⲥⲉⲛⲁⲕⲱ ⲁⲛ ⲉⲃⲟⲗ ⲛⲁϥ ⲟⲩⲧⲉ ϩⲙ̅ⲡⲕⲁϩ ⲟⲩⲧⲉ ϩⲛ̅ⲧⲡⲉ (text from Layton 1989, 70).

97 Cf. Matt 12:31–32 ("son of man" and "holy spirit") par Mark 3:28–29 ("sons of men" and "holy spirit"); Luke 12:10 ("son of man" and "holy spirit"). The third part with "the father" is only found in the *Gospel of Thomas*.

98 ⲁⲓ̅ⲏ̅ⲥ̅ ϫⲟⲟⲥ ϫⲉ ⲡⲉⲧⲁϫⲓⲟⲩⲁ ⲁ[ⲡⲓⲱⲧ] ⲥⲉ[ⲛⲁⲕⲱ ⲛ]ⲉϥ ⲁⲃⲁⲗ ⲡⲉⲧⲁϫⲓⲟⲩⲁ ⲁⲡϣⲏⲣⲉ ⲥⲉⲛⲁⲕⲱ ⲛ[ⲉϥ ⲁⲃⲁⲗ ⲡⲉⲧ]ⲁϫⲓⲟⲩⲁ ⲛ̅ⲧⲁϥ ⲁⲡⲡ̅ⲛ̅ⲁ̅ ⲉⲧⲟⲩⲁⲃⲉ ⲥⲉⲛⲁⲕ[ⲱ ⲛⲉϥ ⲁⲃⲁ]ⲗ ⲉⲛ ϩⲓϫⲙ̅ⲡⲕⲁϩ ⲟⲩⲧⲉ ϩⲛ̅ⲙ̅ⲡⲏⲟⲩⲉ (text from Funk 2002, 80).

The only and minor difference seems to be that "heaven" occurs in the singular in logion 44 and in the plural in the Dublin *Kephalaia*. The second quotation is found on the next page in the Dublin *Kephalaia* (417,25–28) and it is almost identical with the first quotation; so, no need to quote the same saying again. However, the main difference is that the saying there is put in the mouth of Mani. Again, we have an example of the transfer of Jesus logia to the teaching of Mani, indicating that Mani was viewed as a new Christ figure.[99] It is, however, noteworthy that the author of the Dublin *Kephalaia* makes little attempt to conceal this fact. On the contrary, the idea seems to have been that 'what Jesus said, Mani also says', even explicitly within two pages of the same text.

4 Manichaean Allusions to the *Gospel of Thomas*

Let us also have a closer look at some of the many Manichaean allusions to the *Gospel of Thomas*.[100] We begin with the famous logion 1, where Jesus says, "The one who finds the interpretation of these words will not taste death" (32,12–14).[101] The promise not to taste death is an expression that originates from the New Testament (Matt 16:28; John 8:52; Heb 2:9) and is found in the *Psalm-Book* too:

> Grace surrounds this name Jesus. You (are a spring, O Jesus).[102] Blessed is the one who will find you, fortunate is the one, who will come to know

---

99   "Very widespread is the transfer of stories, expressions, titles, etc. from Jesus and his life to Mani and his life … Thus, there was probably a conscious religious attempt to shape the image of Mani after Jesus, which goes beyond a mere reuse of stylistic features linked to holy men" (Pedersen, Falkenberg, Larsen, and Leurini 2020, xiv).

100 In the Biblia Manichaica Project, an allusion is defined in the following way: "The Manichaean text must contain one recognizable and explicit word from the Bible text; that is, one word clearly related to a specific Bible passage. However, that word cannot stand alone. At least one second word (a metaphor, synonym, or the like) in the Manichaean text must refer to the Bible text too, establishing a similar vocabulary on one and the same semantic level. Additionally, if the Manichaean text shares genre with the Bible text (e.g. a 'psalm' or 'letter') the probability of the Manichaean saying to be a Bible allusion increases. We also operate with the possibility of a Manichaean text depending on a parabiblical text that, again, can be said to depend on the Bible" (Pedersen, Falkenberg, Larsen, and Leurini 2017, xliii).

101 ⲡⲉⲧⲁϩⲉ ⲉⲑⲉⲣⲙⲏⲛⲉⲓⲁ ⲛ̄ⲛⲉⲉⲓϣⲁϫⲉ ϥⲛⲁϫⲓ ϯⲡⲉ ⲁⲛ ⲙ̄ⲡⲙⲟⲩ (text from Layton 1989, 52).

102 "You" is an abbreviation of the refrain in the psalm.

you. You (are a spring, O Jesus). For the one who will come to know you will not taste death.[103]

II 185,20–23

Here, the Jesus figure, and not his words, is at centre stage. The passage fits as an allusion, since the New Testament sayings do not associate 'not taste death' with 'find' or 'know'. Logion 1 does not combine 'not taste death' with 'know', but logion 19 does, where this passage of the *Psalm-Book* is listed too. Jesus is in logion 13 also associated with a 'spring', from which his adherents can drink and even get drunk from it. This notion of 'drinking', or 'drunkenness', is presented in two ways: Either the disciple experiences 'drunkenness' in a positive manner, i.e. as being overwhelmed by divine teaching as Thomas does in logion 13, which is alluded to in the Berlin *Kephalaia* (90,18–19) and the *Psalm-Book* (II 201,27–27). Or, as logion 28 attests, 'drunkeness' is also understood negatively, which is found in other parallels from the *Psalm-Book* (II 56,15–16; 172,28–29).

Knowing Jesus and his teaching is important in both the *Gospel of Thomas* and Manichaeism. Comparable to the Gospel of John, the *Gospel of Thomas* tends to present a so-called 'high' christology, as is the case in logion 77, where Jesus says:

> I am the light that is above them all, I am everything, everything came out of me, and everything reached towards me.[104]
>
> 46,22–26

An identical kind of christology is found in the *Psalm-Book*:

> I am in everything, I bear the skies, I am the foundation, I support the earths, I am the light that shines, that gives joy to souls, I am the life of the world.[105]
>
> II 54,25–28

---

103 ⲡⲓⲣⲉⲛ ϫⲉ ⲓⲏ̄ⲥ ⲉⲣⲉ ⲟⲩⲭⲁⲣⲓⲥ ⲕⲱⲧⲉ ⲁⲣⲁϥ ⲛ̄ⲧⲕ ⲛⲉⲓ̈ⲉⲧϥ̄ ⲙ̄ⲡⲉⲧⲛⲁϭⲛ̄ⲧⲕ ⲟⲩⲛⲁϥϫⲁⲓ̈ ⲡⲉ ⲡⲉⲧⲛⲁⲥⲛⲟⲩⲱⲛⲕ ⲛ̄ⲧⲕ ⲡⲉⲧⲛⲁⲥⲛⲟⲩⲱⲛⲕ ⲅⲁⲣ ϥⲁϫⲓ ϯⲡⲉ ⲉⲛ ⲙ̄ⲡⲙⲟⲩ (text from Allberry 1938, 185).

104 ⲁⲛⲟⲕ ⲡⲉ ⲡⲟⲩⲟⲉⲓⲛ ⲡⲁⲉⲓ ⲉⲧϩⲓϫⲱⲟⲩ ⲧⲏⲣⲟⲩ ⲁⲛⲟⲕ ⲡⲉ ⲡⲧⲏⲣϥ ⲛ̄ⲧⲁ ⲡⲧⲏⲣϥ ⲉⲓ ⲉⲃⲟⲗ ⲛ̄ϩⲏⲧ ⲁⲩⲱ ⲛ̄ⲧⲁ ⲡⲧⲏⲣϥ ⲡⲱϩ ϣⲁⲣⲟⲉⲓ (text from Layton 1989, 82).

105 ϯϩⲛ̄ⲡⲧⲏⲣϥ ϯⲃⲓ ϩⲁⲙⲡⲏⲩⲉ ϯⲟ ⲛ̄ⲥⲛ̄ⲧⲉ ϯⲧⲱⲱⲛ ϩⲁⲛⲕⲁϩ ⲁⲛⲁⲕ ⲡⲉ ⲡⲟⲩⲁⲓ̈ⲛⲉ ⲉⲧⲡⲣⲓ̈ⲉ ⲉⲧϯⲣⲉϣⲉ ⲛ̄ⲙ̄ⲯⲩⲭⲁⲩⲉ ⲁⲛⲁⲕ ⲡⲉ ⲡⲱⲛϩ̄ ⲙ̄ⲡⲕⲟⲥⲙⲟⲥ (text and translation: Allberry 1938, 54).

A similarly all-pervading Christ figure is found elsewhere in the *Psalm-Book* (II 120,25–28). In the Gospel of John, Christ is the object of preaching, whereas the synoptic gospels presents the kingdom as the primary preaching object. In a like manner, the *Gospel of Thomas* switches between, or even combines, finding Christ with finding the kingdom. In relation to that, logion 3 elaborates on the infamous saying from the gospels, "the kingdom of God is inside of/among you (ἐντὸς ὑμῶν)" (Luke 17:21). The *Gospel of Thomas* 3 even presents the possibility of both an inner and outer kingdom, when Jesus says, "the kingdom is inside of you and outside of you" (32,25–26).[106] Again, a parallel is retrieved in the *Psalm-Book*: "As for the kingdom of heaven, Behold, it is within us, Behold, it is outside us" (II 160,20–21).[107] In logion 22, the ability to align the inside with the outside, and the above with the below, even serves as a condition to enter the kingdom, which also may be mirrored in a rather fragmentary text from Kellis (P. Kellis Copt. 34,9–15). In connection with the spatiality of the Christ figure, one Manichaean text from the *Psalm-Book* even alludes to the *Gospel of Thomas* as many as four times:

> You are a marvel to tell, you are within, you are without, you are above, you are below; he who is near and far away, he who is hidden and revealed, he who is silent and even speaks too.[108]
>
> II 155,33–38

The concepts of "within/without" may allude to logion 3. Christ as "above/below" to logion 77. All of these four ("within/without" and "above/below") to logion 22. The saying that "he who is near and far away" alludes to logion 82, of which another allusion is found in the *Psalm-Book* (II 39,23–24).

In the synoptic gospels, 'children' are presented as having an advantage when it comes to attaining divine knowledge and entering the heavenly kingdom.[109] Such a prominent role of children is found in the *Gospel of Thomas* and Manichaeism too. In logion 4, Jesus says:

---

106 ⲧⲙⲛ̄ⲧⲉⲣⲟ ⲥⲙ̄ⲡⲉⲧⲛ̄ϩⲟⲩⲛ ⲁⲩⲱ ⲥⲙ̄ⲧⲛ̄ⲃⲁⲗ (text from Layton 1989, 52).
107 ⲧⲙⲛ̄ⲧⲣ̄ⲣⲟ ⲛ̄ⲙ̄ⲡⲏⲩⲉ ⲉⲓⲥⲧⲉ ⲙ̄ⲡⲛ̄ϩ[ⲟⲩ]ⲛ ⲉⲓⲥⲧⲉ ⲙ̄ⲡ[ⲛ]ⲃ[ⲁⲗ] (text from Allberry 1938, 160).
108 ⲛ̄ⲧⲕ ⲟⲩϣⲡⲏⲣⲉ ⲁⲥⲉϫⲉ ⲕⲛ̄ϩⲟⲩⲛ ⲕⲛ̄ⲃⲁⲗ· ⲕⲛ̄ⲧⲡⲉ ⲕⲛ̄ⲡⲓⲧⲛ̄ ⲡⲉⲧϩⲏⲛ ⲉⲧⲟⲩⲏⲩ ⲡⲉⲧϩⲏⲡ ⲉⲧϭⲟⲁⲗⲡ ⲁⲃⲁⲗ ⲡⲉⲧⲕⲁⲣⲁⲓⲧ ⲉⲧⲥⲉϫⲉ ⲁⲛ (text and translation [modified] from Allberry 1938, 155).
109 Cf. Matt 11:25 (par Luke 10:21); Matt 18:1–5 (par Mark 9:33–37; Luke 9:46–48); Matt 19:13–15 (par Mark 10:13–16; Luke 18:15–17).

> The old man should not, in his days, hesitate to ask a little son, being seven days young, about the place of life, and he will live.[110]
>
> 33,5–10

A similar saying is found in the *Psalm-Book*:

> The little children instruct the grey-heared old men; those who are six years old instruct those who are sixty years old.[111]
>
> II 192,2–3

Of course, we are not dealing with a social context involving actual 'children'. It is more likely that they function as role models, as is the case here in logion 4, but also in logia 21 and 37. In logion 37, we hear that the disciples must behave *like* little children, when they disrobe themselves and tread on their clothing. Such a scene is replayed four times in the *Psalm-Book* (II 64,23–24; 76,9–15; 99,26–30; 164,30).

Among scholars who work with the *Gospel of Thomas*, our final Manichaean allusion is well known. In logion 19, Jesus explains his disciples: "For you have there the five unmoved trees in paradise summer and winter" (36,21–23).[112] The parallel in the *Psalm-Book* goes: "For [five] trees, which are in paradise [...] in summer and winter" (II 161,17–18).[113] In the *Gospel of Thomas*, the meaning of the saying is unclear, except that we know of two trees in the biblical creation account.[114] In Manichaeism, we do find lots of trees, also five of them, especially in Chapter 2 (*On the Parable of the Tree*) of the Berlin *Kephalaia* (16,32–23,13), where we hear of 'the five trees of life' and 'the five trees of death'. Since the trees here are located "in paradise," we can be sure that the Manichaean text concerns 'the five trees of life'. However, the most popular use of 'trees' among

---

110   ⲡⲉϫⲉ ⲓ̅ⲥ̅ ϥⲛⲁϫⲛⲁⲩ ⲁⲛ ⲛ̅ϭⲓ ⲡⲣⲱⲙⲉ ⲛ̅ϩⲗⲗⲟ ϩⲛ̅ ⲛⲉϥϩⲟⲟⲩ ⲉϫⲛⲉ ⲟⲩⲕⲟⲩⲉⲓ ⲛ̅ϣⲏⲣⲉ ϣⲏⲙ ⲉϥϩⲛ̅ ⲥⲁϣϥ̅ ⲛ̅ϩⲟⲟⲩ ⲉⲧⲃⲉ ⲡⲧⲟⲡⲟⲥ ⲙ̅ⲡⲱⲛϩ (text from Layton 1989, 54).

111   ⲛⲛⲓϩⲗⲗⲁⲓ̈ ⲛⲁ ⲛⲓⲥⲕⲓⲙ ⲛⲓⲕⲟⲩⲓ̈ ⲛ̅ⲁⲗⲟⲩ ⲛⲉⲧϯ ⲥⲃⲱ ⲛⲉⲩ ⲛⲁ ϯⲥⲟⲉ ⲛ̅ⲣⲁⲙⲡⲉ ⲛⲉⲧϯ ⲥⲃⲱ ⲛ̅ⲛⲁ ϯⲥⲉ ⲛ̅ⲣⲁⲙⲡⲉ (text from Richter 1998, 68; translation [modified] from Allberry 1938, 192).

112   ⲟⲩⲛ̅ⲧⲏⲧⲛ̅ ⲅⲁⲣ ⲙ̅ⲙⲁⲩ ⲛ̅ϯⲟⲩ ⲛ̅ϣⲏⲛ ϩⲛ̅ ⲡⲁⲣⲁⲇⲓⲥⲟⲥ ⲉⲩⲕⲓⲙ ⲁⲛ ⲛ̅ϣⲱⲙ ⲙ̅ⲡⲣⲱ (text from Layton 1989, 60).

113   [ϯⲟⲩ] ⲅⲁⲣ ⲛ̅ϣⲏⲛ ⲛⲉⲧϩⲛ̅ⲡⲡⲁⲣⲁⲇⲓⲥ[ⲟⲥ . . .]. ⲇⲉ ϩⲛ̅ⲡϣⲱⲙ ⲁⲩⲱ ⲙⲛ̅(ⲧ)ⲡⲣⲱ (text from Allberry 1938, 161).

114   In Genesis, we hear about "the tree of life" (2:9; 3:22) and "the tree of knowledge" (2:9, 16; 3:3, 6, 11, 17). For further studies in "the five trees" in the *Gospel of Thomas*, cf. Gathercole 2013, 293–296 (Manichaean parallels, pp. 294–295); Crégheur 2015, 430–451 (Manichaean parallels, pp. 443–444).

Manichaeans is their speculation on 'the good and the bad tree' (Matt 7:17–20), which also forms the largest entry in *The New Testament Gospels in Manichaean Tradition*, covering some 17 pages.[115]

5 Part II: A Manichaean Reading of the *Gospel of Thomas* 49–50

The number of the above quotations and allusions proves, beyond reasonable doubt, that Manichaeans used the *Gospel of Thomas*.[116] Therefore, Manichaeans probably also read the Coptic version of the *Gospel of Thomas* 49–50, to which we now turn.[117] Of the two logia, only logion 50 has an entry in the appendix of the *Gospel of Thomas* in *The New Testament Gospels in Manichaean Tradition* (see below). What makes exactly these two logia interesting is the fact that they address the 'elect', which in Manichaeism is well-known nomenclature for the superior adherents, in comparison to the hierarchically inferior 'hearers'. Thus, from a Manichaean viewpoint, the two logia concern persons of the higher order of the religion. Moreover, it is clear that the logia discuss eschatology, especially the first logion. The second logion adds the subjects of protology and its meaning in the present, when the elect are asked questions concerning their origin and identity. When read together, logia 49 and 50 deal with beginning, present, and end, i.e. what we could characterise as 'salvation history'. Thus, the current hypothesis is that the two logia may produce a more plausible interpretation when read in light of Manichaean salvation history, since scholars hitherto have had certain exegetical problems when interpreting this passage. It goes like this:

---

115 Cf. Pedersen, Falkenberg, Larsen, and Leurini 2020, 46–62.
116 By the sheer amount of numbers, critical opinions on whether Manichaeans ever used the *Gospel of Thomas* should be laid in the grave; contra Coyle 2009, 123–138.
117 Still, we do not know much else about its readers, even if our earliest mentions of the *Gospel of Thomas*, until the 5th century, are found in a large variety of Patristic writers, such as Origen, Augustine, Eusebius, Didymus the Blind, Jerome, Ambrose, Philip of Side, and Pseudo-Athanasius (cf. the lists in Attridge 1989, 103–107; Gathercole 2014, 35–40). What we do know is that they viewed the *Gospel of Thomas* as heretical. However, Hippolytus of Rome (3rd century) informs us about an actual readership in the sect of the Naassenes (*Refutatio* 5.7.20–21). A little more than a century later, Cyril of Jerusalem also tells us about Manichaeans readers in Palestine (see the Introduction); still, owing to the large amount of the Coptic-Manichaean parallels to the *Gospel of Thomas*, a Manichaean readership finds even more solid ground in Egypt.

(49) Jesus said, "Blessed are the single ones and elect,[118] for you (pl.) will find the kingdom; since you are from it, you will go there again." (50) Jesus said, "When they say to you, 'Where are you from?'—say,

'We came from the light, the place where only the light is from; it sto[od] and appeared in their image'.

When they say to you, 'Is it you?'—say,

'We are its children' and 'We are the elect of the living father'.

When they ask you, 'What is the sign of your father within you?'—say to them,

'It is movement and rest'."[119]

41,28–42,7

The peculiarity of the passage concerns, i.a., the understanding of 'the double movement' in logion 49; first down to earth ("you are from it [= the kingdom]") and then up to heaven once more ("you will go there again"), indicating the pre-existence of the elect.[120] On the one hand, this is hardly a biblical concept of the earliest Christ-believers, because only the Christ figure originates in heaven, comes down to earth, and returns to the divine realm (e.g. John 16:28). On the other hand, the concept of the pre-existent souls of Christians became widespread in post-biblical times, especially in the thought of Origen of Alexandria (3rd century) and onwards. Therefore, it is quite possible that such a double scheme is a later addition to the *Gospel of Thomas*. Nevertheless,

---

118 Lit. "Blessed are the single ones and (those) who are elect" (cf. next note for Coptic text). In early research on the *Gospel of Thomas*, it has been suggested that logion 49 was influenced by Manichaeism: "Hier scheint verbreitetes Einsiedlertum und Manichäismus vorausgesetzt" (Leipoldt 1958, 488 n. 71). Apparently, not only a Manichaean but also a monastic context may be indicated here ("Einsiedlertum [= anchorite monasticism]"). The noun ⲙⲟⲛⲁⲭⲟⲥ ("single one") equals μοναχός ("monk") and is only attested from the 4th century onwards, so the Coptic text of the *Gospel of Thomas* may in fact have a monastic connection too; cf. Falkenberg 2021. Not only the text of the *Gospel of Thomas*, but also the rest of the texts from the Nag Hammadi codices may have been copied in codices produced by Pachomian monks, thus also an indication of a monastic readership; cf. Lundhaug and Jenott 2013, 263–268.

119 ⲡⲉϫⲉ ⲓ̅ⲥ̅ ϫⲉ ϩⲉⲛⲙⲁⲕⲁⲣⲓⲟⲥ ⲛⲉ ⲛⲙⲟⲛⲁⲭⲟⲥ ⲁⲩⲱ ⲉⲧⲥⲟⲧⲡ ϫⲉ ⲧⲉⲧⲛⲁϩⲉ ⲁⲧⲙⲛ̅ⲧⲉⲣⲟ ϫⲉ ⲛ̅ⲧⲱⲧⲛ̅ ϩⲛ̅ⲉⲃⲟⲗ ⲛ̅ϩⲏⲧⲥ̅ ⲡⲁⲗⲓⲛ ⲉⲧⲉⲧⲛⲁⲃⲱⲕ ⲉⲙⲁⲩ (50) ⲡⲉϫⲉ ⲓ̅ⲥ̅ ϫⲉ ⲉⲩϣⲁⲛϫⲟⲟⲥ ⲛⲏⲧⲛ̅ ϫⲉ ⲛ̅ⲧⲁⲧⲉⲧⲛ̅ϣⲱⲡⲉ ⲉⲃⲟⲗ ⲧⲱⲛ ϫⲟⲟⲥ ⲛⲁⲩ ϫⲉ ⲛ̅ⲧⲁⲛⲉⲓ ⲉⲃⲟⲗ ϩⲙ̅ ⲡⲟⲩⲟⲉⲓⲛ ⲡⲙⲁ ⲉⲛⲧⲁ ⲡⲟⲩⲟⲉⲓⲛ ϣⲱⲡⲉ ⲙ̅ⲙⲁⲩ ⲉⲃⲟⲗ ϩⲓⲧⲟⲟⲧϥ̅ ⲟⲩⲁⲁⲧϥ̅ ⲁϥⲱϩ[ⲉ ⲉⲣⲁⲧϥ̅] ⲁⲩⲱ ⲁϥⲟⲩⲱⲛϩ ⲉ[ⲃ]ⲟⲗ ϩⲛ̅ ⲧⲟⲩϩⲓⲕⲱⲛ ⲉⲩϣⲁϫⲟⲟⲥ ⲛⲏⲧⲛ̅ ϫⲉ ⲛ̅ⲧⲱⲧⲛ̅ ⲡⲉ ϫⲟⲟⲥ ϫⲉ ⲁⲛⲟⲛ ⲛⲉϥϣⲏⲣⲉ ⲁⲩⲱ ⲁⲛⲟⲛ ⲛ̅ⲥⲱⲧⲡ ⲙ̅ⲡⲉⲓⲱⲧ ⲉⲧⲟⲛϩ ⲉⲩϣⲁⲛϫⲛⲉ ⲑⲏⲩⲧⲛ̅ ϫⲉ ⲟⲩ ⲡⲉ ⲡⲙⲁⲉⲓⲛ ⲙ̅ⲡⲉⲧⲛ̅ⲉⲓⲱⲧ ⲉⲧϩⲛ̅ ⲑⲏⲩⲧⲛ̅ ϫⲟⲟⲥ ⲉⲣⲟⲟⲩ ϫⲉ ⲟⲩⲕⲓⲙ ⲡⲉ ⲙⲛ̅ ⲟⲩⲁⲛⲁⲡⲁⲩⲥⲓⲥ (text from Layton 1989, 72).

120 Cf. Gathercole 2015, 405. In addition, this is the only place in the *Gospel of Thomas* that attests that double movement.

Manichaeans could easily interpret this double movement as part of their own salvation myth. They identified themselves with the First Man's armour of *light*, which originated in the Light Realm (i.e. the heavenly world), when he came down to battle the archons of the Dark Realm (i.e. the physical world), but as an outcome of this primeval war, the light substance of his armour was scattered throughout the world and mixed with physical matter. In the final days, all that light captured in the Dark Realm is to be untangled from its mixture with matter in order to ascend back to its first home in the Light Realm. Essentially, this double movement of the light equals the destiny of the saved Manichaeans. Although logion 49 does not mention light, this is the main theme in the following logion, where it characterises the elect's place of origin ("We came from the light") and their identity ("We are its [= the light's] children").[121]

6   To Whom Does the "Image" Belong?—A Manichaean Answer

In logion 50, the first exegetical problem concerns the elect's answer to the question on their place of origin, "We came from the light, the place where only the light is from; it sto[od] and appeared in their image."[122] Scholars wonder about the identity of the antecedent of the possessive pronoun "in *their* image," where the only available person in the plural is the interrogators, which hardly fits the context.[123] Therefore, we are encouraged to find alternative persons or entities in the external context; in our case, the Manichaean context. Furthermore, likely candidates must be evaluated positively, since it is the divine "light" that "appeared in their image." To a Manichaean reader, the first part of the

---

121   In Manichaeism, adherents can be addressed as "sons (or children)" and "sons (or children) of the living race"; cf. Pedersen and Larsen 2013, 204–207. The longer expression is especially relevant here, since the designation as "children" is immediately followed by the sentence, "We are the elect *of the living* father" (cf. also John 6:57).

122   Another issue that scholars earlier have disagreed over is the question of the genre of logion 50 or, to be more precise, the identity of those who pose questions to the elect. A 'mission dialogue' has been suggested, either of an affirmative or polemical nature, when the elect seek out potential adherents or are confronted by critics; another suggestion is the genre of an 'ascent dialogue', either *pre* or *post mortem*, where archons demand certain signs or answers in order to permit the elect to ascend up through the heavens and return to the divine realm (cf., e.g., Gathercole 2013, 406–407). However, the main function of the dialogue is most likely to set the scene by posing questions that provide an opportunity to present central doctrines related to the identity formation of the elect (Manichaean or not).

123   Cf. Gathercole 2015, 408.

sentence concerns the Light Realm ("the place where only the light is from"), where the elect ultimately have originated ("We come from the light"); at the end of the sentence, it seems as if the light is hypostasised and acts ("it sto[od] and appeared"); finally, the light comes forth "in their (pl.) image (sg.) (ⲦⲞⲨⲈⲓⲔⲰⲚ)." In Manichaeism, such a divine image is at work at two stages which rely on the anthropogonies in Genesis (1:26–28; 2:7). The first stage involves a myth entitled 'the seduction of the archons', where we hear that

> the (Third) Messenger then revealed his male and female images (ܐܕ̈ܝܐ) and became visible to all the archons, the children of Darkness, both male and female. At the appearance of the Messenger, who was attractive in his forms, all of the archons became excited with desire, the males for the female likeness (ܕܕܡܘܬܐ) and the females for the male likeness.[124]
>
> THEODORE BAR KONAI, *Liber Scholiorum* 316,11–16

Afterwards, because all archons became aroused, they spontaneously aborted and ejaculated their light, and thus is liberated much of the light substance stolen from the First Man in the primeval war. The second stage continues immediately after, in the myth on 'the creation of Adam and Eve', where the archons became so terrified by the loss of light that they cunningly planned to retain the remaining light through the creation of humankind; therefore, they copied the Third Messenger's image as model for the human body. Since the image had similarity with the light souls, the archons hoped that their creation would deceive the souls to believe that they belonged to the body. So, in Manichaean myth, the Third Messenger first entailed his image to trick the archons to liberate the stolen light substance, and the archons then reused a copy of his divine image to create the first human beings to get back that light.

Returning to logion 50, we may ask how this myth on the image of the Third Messenger helps us find the meaning of the enigmatic notion of "their image"? The plural pronoun could be taken to refer to the Third Messenger's androgynous image as it is found in the *Liber Scholiorum* above, i.e. "their (= his male and female) image"; but the Manichaean sources consistently describe the

---

124 Text from Scher 1912, 316; translation (modified) from Reeves 2011, 150. In this text, Syriac ܐܕ̈ܝܐ (in Reeves, translated as "form") seems to correspond to εἰκών in Gen LXX 1:26–27, even though the word used in Gen Peshitta 1:26–27 is ܨܠܡ. However, ܕܡܘܬܐ (in Reeves, translated as "image") in Gen Peshitta 1:26 and here corresponds to ὁμοίωσις in Gen LXX 1:26. Cf. Pedersen, Falkenberg, Larsen, and Leurini 2017, 8 n. 1.

image of the Third Messenger in the singular, "*his* image."¹²⁵ Then, maybe it could refer to the first human beings, i.e. "their (Adam's and Eve's) image." However, to find a plausible solution we would need a *verbatim* parallel to "their image" in the Manichaean sources. The following two sayings from Chapter 64 (*On Adam*) of the Berlin *Kephalaia* (157,1–158,23) may settle the case:

> So, the *seal* of the whole world is stamped on Adam. Since even heaven and earth moved for his sake, disturbance and commotion happened, by the cause of him, between the good ones and the evil ones. The good ones drew him to life because of *their image* and *their form* set upon him, whereas the evil ones drew him to death so that they will exercise authority by him, steal the kingdom, and humiliate the whole world by him.¹²⁶
>
> 157,25–32

> So that there will be a great protection for them (= the archons) by the image of the exalted one (= the Third Messenger) set upon him (= Adam), since the ones above will spare him because of *their seal* and *their form* ....¹²⁷
>
> 158,19–21

In the context of these two paragraphs, "the good ones" and "the ones above" are not named, but they clearly are divine beings, probably representing all entities from the Light Realm. They are the ones who provide the generic Adam figure with "life" and salvation by setting upon him "their image (ⲧⲟⲩϩⲓⲕⲱⲛ)" and "their form," and "their seal" as well. These three markers all seem to be understood as identical to the image of the Third Messenger, who is even mentioned in the second paragraph ("the image of the exalted one"). Owing to its divine origin from the Light Realm and all its inhabitants, this image cannot cause

---

125 For multiple examples, cf. Pedersen, Falkenberg, Larsen, and Leurini 2017, 7–19. Once in the Greek sources and once in the Syriac sources, the Manichaeans present the First Man as the bearer of the divine image, and not the Third Messenger; cf. ibid., 7 n. 1. This alternative is actually more in accordance with the biblical text of Gen 1:26–27.

126 ⲉⲡⲉⲓⲇⲏ ⲡⲧⲁⲃⲉϥ ⲙ̄ⲡⲕⲟⲥⲙⲟⲥ ⲧⲏⲣϥ̄ ⲧⲁⲃⲉ ϩⲛ̄ ⲁⲇⲁⲙ ⲉⲧⲃⲉ ⲡⲉⲓ̈ ⲣⲱ ⲁ ⲧⲡⲉ ⲙⲛ̄ ⲡⲕⲁϩ ⲕⲓⲙ ⲉⲧⲃⲏⲧϥ̄ ⲁⲩϣⲧⲁⲣⲧⲣ̄ ⲙⲛ̄ ⲟⲩⲧⲁⲣⲁⲭⲏ ϣⲱⲡⲉ ⲛ̄ⲧⲉϥⲁⲗⲟϭⲉ ⲟⲩⲧⲉ ⲛⲉⲧⲁⲛⲓⲧ ⲙⲛ̄ ⲛⲉⲧϩⲁⲩ ⲛⲉⲧⲁⲛⲓⲧ ⲙⲉⲛ ⟨ⲛ⟩ⲉⲩⲥⲱⲕ ⲙ̄ⲙⲁϥ ⲁⲡⲱⲛϩ ⲉⲧⲃⲉ ⲧⲟⲩϩⲓⲕⲱⲛ ⲙⲛ̄ ⲧⲟⲩⲙⲟⲣⲫⲏ ⲉⲧⲕⲁⲁⲧ ⲁⲭⲱϥ ⲛⲉⲧ[ϩ]ⲁⲩ ϩⲱⲟⲩϥ ⲛⲉⲩⲥⲱⲕ ⲙ̄ⲙⲁⲩ ⲁⲡⲙⲟⲩ ⲡⲉ ϫⲉⲩⲛⲁⲣⲉϩⲟⲩ[ⲥ]ⲓⲁ ⲛ̄ϩⲏⲧϥ̄ ⲛ̄ⲥⲉϫⲓⲟⲩⲱ ⲛ̄ⲧⲙⲛ̄ⲧⲣ̄ⲣⲟ ⲛ̄ⲥⲉⲑⲃⲃⲓⲟ ⲛ̄ϩⲏⲧϥ̄ [ⲙ̄]ⲡⲕⲟⲥⲙⲟⲥ ⲧⲏⲣϥ̄ (text from Polotsky and Böhlig 1940, 157).

127 ϫⲉ ⲉⲣⲉ ⲟⲩⲛⲁϭ ⲙ̄ⲡⲁⲧⲣⲱⲛⲓⲁ ⲛⲁϣⲱⲡⲉ ⲛⲉⲩ ϩⲛ̄ ⲧϩⲓⲕⲱⲛ ⲙ̄ⲡ(ⲡ)ⲉⲧϫⲁⲥⲉ ⲉⲧⲕⲁⲁⲧ ⲁⲭⲱϥ ϫⲉ ⲉⲣⲉ ⲛⲁⲧⲡⲉ ⲛⲁϯⲥⲟ ⲁⲣⲁϥ ⲉⲧⲃⲉ ⲡⲟⲩⲧⲁⲃⲉϥ ⲙⲛ̄ [ⲧ]ⲟⲩⲙⲟⲣⲫ[ⲏ] (text from Polotsky and Böhlig 1940, 158).

evil but only protection for every worldly creature, even the archons ("the evil ones"). Thus, we are now able to qualify the plural pronoun in logion 50, since it would seem, at least to a Manichaean reader, to refer to *all* divine beings in the Light Realm (i.e. "the place where only the light is from"). Therefore, "their image (ⲧⲟⲩϩⲓⲕⲱⲛ)" is the same as the "image" of all "the good ones/ the ones above," as just confirmed in the Berlin *Kephalaia*.

7 How Can "Movement" Signify God?—A Manichaean Answer

The second exegetical problem concerns the last part of logion 50, which has puzzled scholars for a long time, namely the third question, "What is the sign of your father within you?"—and its answer, "It is movement and rest." In antiquity, "rest" could easily be affiliated to the godhead (and is an esteemed quality of the heavenly realm too), whereas "the sign of your father (= God)" can hardly be said to be "movement (ⲟⲩⲕⲓⲙ = κίνησις)." To solve this problem, many scholars have consulted contemporary philosophical traditions, especially Platonism.[128]

In Manichaean myth, the cosmological war is transferred to an anthropological war that still took place within each Manichaean in the present; in other words, the movement of the physical world (macrocosmos) was transferred into every Manichaean (microcosmos) as the movement, or emotion, of his or her soul.[129] Such a view hardly applied to current philosophy, which also was noticed by the Egyptian philosopher Alexander of Lycopolis. In the late 3rd century, when Manichaeans arrived in northern Africa, he seemingly met some of them and, on that basis, countered Mani's worldview in a treatise against his teachings:

---

128   Cf., e.g., Gathercole 2014, 409–410; Miroshnikov 2018, 155–158.
129   In fact, we have already touched upon the concept of movement in our above study on the "image" in the Berlin *Kephalaia*: "Since even heaven and earth moved (ⲕⲓⲙ) for his (= Adam's) sake, disturbance and commotion happened, by the cause (ⲗⲁⲓϭⲉ = αἰτία) of him, between the good ones and the evil ones" (157,26–28). Here, cosmological locomotion ("heaven and earth moved" and "disturbance and commotion") was no longer caused by the primordial war primarily, but a new war was now commenced between the Light Realm and the Dark Realm, namely an anthropological war that took place "by the cause of him (= Adam)." As we also saw above, when the archons created Adam and Eve, they used a copy of the Third Messenger's image, which the light beings substituted for their own ("their image/ form/ seal") in order to enable the human light souls to escape the clutches of the archons.

He (= Mani) laid down as principles 'God' and 'matter', God being good and matter evil, the measure of God's good far surpassing that of matter's evil. He does *not* speak of matter as Plato, namely as that which becomes all things when it assumes quality and shape ... *nor* as Aristotle, namely as the element in relation to which form and privation occur. No, Mani means something besides these points, for he labels matter as that which is within each existing thing as random movement (ἄτακτον κίνησιν).[130]

Against Mani's Opinions 4,24–5,8

As a school teacher of Platonism, Alexander did not see Manichaean myth as philosophical at all and therefore polemicised, at length, against Mani's notion of "matter" as "random movement" (ibid., e.g., 9,16–14,17). Here, Mani's concept of "random movement" clearly had a cosmological component, i.e. evil matter, but in Manichaeism also a psychological component, i.e. lust and desire.[131] Again, macrocosmos aligns with microcosmos. However, even if "random movement" was a negative qualification of matter, it did not mean that movement in itself was qualified negatively in Manichaean salvation history. It may be quite the opposite, if the movement no longer was 'random' but instead 'focused' on liberating light from earth to heaven.

Now, if we go through logion 50 again, there appears a clear line of thought in harmony with Manichaean salvation history. First, the place of origin of the elect is stated ("We came from the light"), a location where unmixed light exists ("the place where only the light is from"). That light is even hypostasised ("it sto[od] and appeared") and refers to all divine beings, who provide salvation by bringing forth the divine image ("their image") to the first human beings in primordial time and to the elect in the present. Then these elect are asked if they are that unmixed light ("Is it you?"). They are not exactly the unmixed light, since they exist in the physical world, but at least they are offspring of that light ("We are its children"). As offspring they also have a parent ("We are the elect of the living father"), which points to the "father" as identical with "the place where only the light is from." From a Manichaean point of view, the "children" and "elect" in logion 50 represent the mixed and imprisoned light in

---

130 Text from Brinkmann 1895, 4–5; translation (modified) from van der Horst and Mansfeld 1974, 52–53. In an analysis of this pericope, Johannes van Oort concludes, regarding the work of Alexander, that "what he describes as being Mani's tenets turns out to be highly accurate" (van Oort 2013, 277–278).
131 As suggested by Johannes van Oort (1987, 144–145).

the physical world, awaiting to be untangled from matter and reintegrated into the heavenly place of unmixed light, where the Manichaean godhead, "the living father," resides.

Now, when the elect is asked, "What is the sign of your father within you?"— it means in the Manichaean context: What is it that characterises the light substance, which, on the one hand, is trapped within the body of the elect and which, on the other hand, ultimately derives from the divine father? The enigmatic answer, "It is movement and rest," is not a hard nut to crack in that Manichaean context. From a semiotic point of view, the signifier ("the sign") is not identical with the one signified ("your father within you").[132] But then again, the divine father is to be identified as light.[133] If the father is the pure light in heaven, then his children are his light mixed with matter on earth; the former characterises heavenly existence as "rest," the latter characterises earthly existence as "movement," owing to the Manichaean's inner light and its infiltration with matter. Since these two kinds of light ultimately originates from the same source, they can both be said to represent God.

Consequently, in conformity with Manichaean myth, the character ("the sign") of the divine light indeed is twofold: (1) Precisely "movement" can be said to characterise the worldly light substance, ever since it *came down* as the light armour of the First Man, was trapped by the archons, mixed with physical matter, and then imprisoned in the bodies of humankind. Even in the present time of the Manichaean, the light substance was in a state of movement, not "random" but focused "movement," especially regarding Manichaean soteriology, where the practising elect through rituals helped the light substance untangle from its mixture with matter in order to *go back* to the Light Realm. So, when "the sign of the living father" is "movement" it refers to all his divine light imprisoned in the physical world, awaiting its ascent back home. (2) When "the

---

132   The Manichaean theology is of a pantheistic nature, where the godhead, to some extent, shares destiny with his own light substance, also the light previously stolen by the archons and now trapped in the physical world. The divinity of both the free and captured light is a well-known Manichaean concept. The captured light can be seen as a multiplicity of souls and as a single entity often called the Living Soul, which occasionally is identified with the suffering Jesus (*Jesus patibilis*).

133   This can be confirmed in the first Psalm of Thomas from the *Psalm-Book* (II 203,3–5), where the godhead is called upon in the *incipit*: "[My father, the] happy light. The happy light, [my] glorious one. My father, the happy light. The happy and blessed light ([ⲡⲁⲓⲱⲧ ⲡ]ⲟⲩⲁⲓⲛⲉ ⲉⲧⲧⲁⲗⲏⲗ· ⲡⲟⲩⲁⲓⲛⲉ ⲉⲧⲧⲁⲗⲏⲗ [ⲡⲡⲁ]ⲡⲉⲁⲩ· ⲡⲁⲓⲱⲧ ⲡⲟⲩⲁⲓⲛⲉ ⲉⲧⲧⲁⲗⲏⲗ· ⲡⲟⲩⲁⲓⲛⲉ [ⲉⲧ]ⲧⲁⲗⲏⲗ ⲉⲧⲥⲙⲁⲙⲁⲁⲧ)" (text from Allberry 1938, 203). Here, the Manichaean God ("My father") is "the happy light" in the Light Realm. Its structural counterpart could be, by implication, 'the unhappy light', which would be the same as the divine light mixed with evil matter in the earthly world.

sign of the living father" is "rest" it refers to all unbound light substance in the heavenly world, the ultimate resting place for all Manichaeans at the end of days.

Therefore, in a Manichaean context, when logion 49 says, "you (= the elect) will find the kingdom (= the Light Realm); since you are from it, you will go there again," Manichaean salvation history is activated in its description of the double movement of the mixed and imprisoned light, which equals all Manichaean "children" of light on their way to salvation. The only allusion to the present passage that we have from the appendix of the *Gospel of Thomas* in *The New Testament Gospels in Manichaean Tradition* seems fitting to quote here, even if the manuscript of the Berlin *Kephalaia* at this point is rather damaged:

> ... while you (sg.) will go to this [great land] of rest together [with the] children of the living ones, [and you will] enter in glory ....[134]
> 195,18–19

To be clear, in the present analysis, I do not suggest that Manichaeans *composed* logia 49 and 50, which seems very unlikely, but I am suggesting two other things. First, I ask my reader to keep an open mind concerning the above Manichaean reading that may provide, in relation to earlier suggestions, a better explanation of the two exegetical problems in logion 50. Second, if such a reading appears plausible, can we, by all means, exclude the possibility that Manichaeans, during the course of textual transmission, made small redactions in the *Gospel of Thomas* to highlight wording of specific Manichaean affiliation? A quick glance at the Greek text (3th century) in comparison with the Coptic version (4th–5th century) confirms that the *Gospel of Thomas* was a fluid text, which surely was redacted over time (cf., e.g., logia 30 and 36). Furthermore, if we take into consideration that Manichaeism existed for nearly a century in Egypt before the Nag Hammadi codices were produced, this allows time for a Manichaean redactor to make (minor) changes in the text.[135]

---

[134] [.] . ⲁⲓ̈ ⲉⲕⲁⲃⲱⲕ ⲁϯⲭ[ⲱⲣⲁ] ⲉ[ⲧⲁⲓ] ⲛⲧⲉ ⲙⲡⲧⲁⲛ ⲙ[ⲛ ⲛ]ϣⲏⲣⲉ ⲛ̄ⲛⲉⲧⲁⲛϩ` [ⲛ̄ⲕⲉⲓ] ⲁϩⲟⲩⲛ ϩⲛ̄ ⲟⲩⲉⲁⲩ (text and translation [modified] from Pedersen, Falkenberg, Larsen, and Leurini 2020, 386; cf. also Polotsky and Böhlig 1940, 195).

[135] Falkenberg 2018, 264.

8   Conclusions

Since the middle of the 4th century, we have confirmation of a Manichaean readership pertaining to the *Gospel of Thomas*, as it seems to be indicated by Cyril of Jerusalem in his *Catechesis* (4,36; 6,31). Such a claim can be supported by the reference work *The New Testament Gospels in Manichaean Tradition*, which, in an appendix, lists the Manichaean use of the *Gospel of Thomas* and detects 73 parallels of that text in Manichaean sources. Furthermore, the argument of a Manichaean readership is strengthened by the fact that six of these parallels are quotations.

Since more than two thirds of the parallels are found in Coptic-Manichaean texts, we have tried to analyse logia 49 and 50 in the Coptic version of the *Gospel of Thomas* from a Manichaean perspective. It turns out that such an experiment may have provided at least two new answers to old exegetical problems in the text of logion 50. First, we came up with a new suggestion regarding the identity of those who reveal "their" heavenly "image." Second, the enigmatic saying that "the sign" of God, which exists in the body of each believer, is "movement and rest," also found an explanation when read in light of Manichaean salvation history. The godhead can be signified by "movement," when referring to the fallen light within the Manichaeans. And God is signified by "rest," when referring to that inner light as consubstantial with the godhead and the unfallen light of its original home in the heavenly world. Even though we cannot be sure if any Manichaean redaction ever took place in logia 49 and 50, the text most likely to have been supplied by a Manichaean redactor is precisely these two expressions, namely "their image" and the sign of God as "movement" in logion 50.

Bibliography

Allberry, Charles Robert Cecil
1938. *A Manichaean Psalm-Book. Part II*. Manichaean Manuscripts in the Chester Beatty Library II. Stuttgart: W. Kohlhammer.

Attridge, Harold A.
1989. "The Greek Fragments [of the *Gospel of Thomas*]." In: B. Layton, ed., *Nag Hammadi Codex II,2–7 together with XIII,2*, Brit. Lib. Or.4926(1), and P. Oxy. 1, 654, 655 with contributions from many scholars. Volume One: Gospel According to Thomas, Gospel According to Philip, Hypostasis of the Archons, and Indexes*. NHS 20. Leiden: E.J. Brill, 95–128.

Barns, J.W.B., G.M. Browne, and J.C. Shelton, eds.
1981. *Nag Hammadi Codices: Greek and Coptic Papyri from the Cartonnage of the Covers.* NHS 16, Leiden: E.J. Brill.

Blatz, Beate
1987. "Das koptische Thomasevangelium." In: E. Hennecke and W. Schneemelcher, eds., *Neutestamentliche Apokryphen in deutscher Übersetzung. I. Evangelien* (5. Auflage). Tübingen: Mohr Siebeck, 93–113.

Brinkmann, Augustus, ed.
1895. *Alexandri Lycopolitani Contra Manichaei Opiniones Disputatio*, Leipzig: B.G. Teubner.

Coyle, J. Kevin
2009. *Manichaeism and Its Legacy.* NHMS 69. Leiden and Boston: Brill.

Crégheur, Eric
2015. "Le motif des cinq arbres dans l'*Évangile selon Thomas* (log. 19) et la littérature ancienne." In: ZAC 19, 430–451.

Drijvers, Han J.W.
1989. "Thomasakten." In: E. Hennecke and W. Schneemelcher, eds., *Neutestamentliche Apokryphen in deutscher Übersetzung. II. Apostolisches, Apokalypsen und Verwandtes* (5. Auflage). Tübingen: Mohr Siebeck, 289–367.

Falkenberg, René
2018. "What Has Nag Hammadi to Do with Medinet Madi? The Case of *Eugnostos* and Manichaeism." In: H. Lundhaug and L. Jenott, eds., *The Nag Hammadi Codices and Late-Antique Egypt.* STAC 110. Tübingen: Mohr Siebeck, 261–286.
2021. "The 'Single Ones' in the *Gospel of Thomas*: A Monastic Perspective." In: H. Lundhaug & C.H. Bull, eds., *The Nag Hammadi Codices as Monastic Books.* STAC. Tübingen: Mohr Siebeck. Forthcoming.

Funk, Wolf-Peter
2002. "'Einer aus Tausend, zwei aus zehntausend': Zitate aus dem Thomas-Evangelium in den koptischen Manichaica." In: H.-G. Bethge, S. Emmel, K.L. King, and I. Schletterer, eds., *For the Children, Perfect Instruction: Studies in Honour of Hans-Martin Schenke on the occasion of the Berliner Arbeitskreis für koptisch-gnostische Schriften's Thirtieth Year.* NHMS 54. Leiden and Boston: Brill, 67–94.

2018. *Kephalaia. I, Zweite Hälfte, Lieferung 17/18*. Manichäische Handschriften der staatlichen Museen zu Berlin. Stuttgart: W. Kohlhammer.

Gärtner, Bertil

1961. *The Theology of the Gospel of Thomas* (translated by Eric J. Sharpe). London: Collins [first published 1960].

Gardner, Iain, Jason BeDuhn, and Paul C. Dilley

2018. *The Chapters of the Wisdom of My Lord Mani. Part III: Pages 343–442 (Chapters 321–347)*. Edited and translated. Manichaean Manuscripts in the Chester Beatty Library: The Kephalaia Codex. NHMS 92. Leiden and Boston: Brill.

Gathercole, Simon

2014. *The Gospel of Thomas: Introduction and Commentary*. TENT 11. Leiden and Boston: Brill.

Hammerschmidt, Ernst

1962. "Das Thomasevangelium und die Manichäer." In: *OrChr* 46, 120–123.

Helderman, Jan

1999. "Manichäische Züge im Thomasevangelium." In: S. Emmel, M. Krause, S.G. Richter, and S. Schaten, eds., *Ägypten und Nubien in spätantiker und christlicher Zeit: Akten des 6. Internationalen Koptologenkongresses Münster, 20.–26. Juli 1996. 2: Schrifttum, Sprache und Gedankenwelt*. Wiesbaden: Reichert Verlag, 483–494.

van der Horst, Pieter Willem, and Jaap Mansfeld

1974. *An Alexandrian Platonist Against Dualism: Alexander of Lycopolis' Treatise 'Critique of the Doctrines of Manichaeus'. Translated, with an Introduction and Notes*. Leiden: E.J. Brill.

Klimkeit, Hans-Joachim

1991. "Die Kenntnis apokrypher Evangelien in Zentral- und Ostasien." In: A. Van Tongerloo and S. Giversen, eds., *Manichaica Selecta: Studies Presented to Professor Julien Ries on the Occasion of his Seventieth Birthday*. Manichaean Studies 1. Louvain: Brepols, 149–175.

Layton, Bentley

1989. "The Gospel According to Thomas [Critical Edition]." In: B. Layton, ed., *Nag Hammadi Codex II,2–7 together with XIII,2*, Brit. Lib. Or.4926(1), and P. Oxy. 1, 654, 655 with contributions from many scholars. Volume One: Gospel According to Thomas, Gospel*

According to Philip, Hypostasis of the Archons, and Indexes. NHS 20. Leiden, New York, Copenhagen, and Cologne: Brill, 52–92.

Leipoldt, Johannes
1958. "Ein neues Evangelium? Das koptische Thomasevangelium übersetzt und besprochen." In: *ThLZ* 83, 481–496.

Leurini, Claudia
2018. *Hymns in Honour of the Hierarchy and Community, Installation Hymns and Hymns in Honour of Church Leaders and Patrons: Middle Persian and Parthian Hymns in the Berlin Turfan Collection*. Berliner Turfantexte 40. Turnhout: Brepols.

Lundhaug, Hugo, and Lance Jenott
2015. *The Monastic Origin of the Nag Hammadi Codices*. STAC 97. Tübingen: Mohr Siebeck.

Ménard, Jacques-É.
1975. *L'Évangile selon Thomas*. NHS 5. Leiden: Brill.

Mirecki, Paul
1991. "Manichaean Psalm 278 and the *Gospel of Thomas* 37." In: A. Van Tongerloo and S. Giversen, eds., *Manichaica Selecta: Studies Presented to Professor Julien Ries on the Occasion of his Seventieth Birthday*. Manichaean Studies 1. Louvain: Brepols, 243–262.

Miroshnikov, Ivan
2018. *The Gospel of Thomas and Plato: A Study of the Impact of Platonism on the "Fifth Gospel"*. NHMS 93. Leiden and Boston: Brill.

Müller, Friedrich Wilhelm Karl
1904. *Handschriften-Reste in Estrangelo-Schrift aus Turfan, Chinesisch-Turkistan*. II. APAW, Anhang 2. Berlin: Verlag der Königlichen Preussischen Akademie der Wissenschaften.

Nagel, Peter
2008. "Synoptische Evangelientradition im *Thomasevangelium* und im Manichäismus." In: J. Frey, E.E. Popkes, and J. Schröter, eds., *Das Thomasevangelium: Entstehung—Rezeption—Theologie*. BZNW 157. Berlin and New York: De Gruyter, 272–293.
2010. "Apokryphe Jesusworte in der koptischen Überlieferung." In: J. Frey and J. Schröter, eds., *Jesus in apokryphen Evangelienüberlieferungen: Beiträge zu außerkanonischen*

Jesus-Überlieferungen aus verschiedenen Sprach- und Kulturtraditionen. WUNT 254. Tübingen: Mohr Siebeck, 495–526.

van Oort, Johannes

1987. "Augustine and Mani on concupiscentia sexualis." In: J. van Oort and J. den Boeft, eds., *Augustiniana Traiectina: Communications présentées au Colloque International d'Utrecht, 13–14 novembre 1986.* Paris: Études augustiniennes, 137–152.

2013. "Alexander of Lycopolis, Manichaeism and Neoplatonism." In: K. Corrigan, T. Rasimus, D.M. Burns, L. Jenott, and Z. Mazur, eds., *Gnosticism, Platonism and the Late Ancient World: Essays in Honour of John D. Turner.* NHMS 82. Leiden and Boston: Brill, 275–283.

Otero, Aurelio de Santos

1989. "Der Pseudo-Titus-Brief." In: E. Hennecke W. Schneemelcher, eds., *Neutestamentliche Apokryphen in deutscher Übersetzung. II. Apostolisches, Apokalypsen und Verwandtes* (5. Auflage). Tübingen: Mohr Siebeck, 50–70.

Pedersen, Nils Arne, René Falkenberg, John Møller Larsen, and Claudia Leurini

2017. *The Old Testament in Manichaean Tradition: The Sources in Syriac, Greek, Coptic, Middle Persian, Parthian, Sogdian, New Persian, and Arabic. With an Appendix on General References to the Bible.* CFM Biblia Manichaica I. Turnhout: Brepols.

2020. *The New Testament Gospels in Manichaean Tradition: The Sources in Syriac, Greek, Coptic, Middle Persian, Parthian, Sogdian, Bactrian, New Persian, and Arabic. With Appendices on the Gospel of Thomas and Diatessaron.* CFM Biblia Manichaica II. Turnhout: Brepols.

Pedersen, Nils Arne, and John Møller Larsen

2013. *Manichaean Texts in Syriac: First Editions, New Editions, and Studies. With contributions by Zsuzsanna Gulácsi and Myriam Krutzsch.* CFM Series Syriaca 1. Turnhout: Brepols.

Polotsky, Hans Jakob, and Alexander Böhlig

1940. *Kephalaia. 1. Hälfte, Lieferung 1–10, mit einem Beitrag von Hugo Ibscher.* Manichäische Handschriften der staatlichen Museen zu Berlin. Stuttgart: W. Kohlhammer.

Puech, Henri-Charles

1978a. "Un *logion* de Jésus sur bandelette funéraire". In: Puech, H.-C., *En quête de la Gnose. II. Sur l'Évangile selon Thomas.* Paris: Gallimard, 59–62 [first published 1955].

1978b. "Explication de l'Évangile selon Thomas et recherches sur les Paroles de Jésus qui y sont réunies (Collège de France, 1956–1960)." In: H.-C. Puech, *En quête de la*

Gnose. II. Sur l'Évangile selon Thomas. Paris: Gallimard, 65–91 [first published 1956–1960].

1978c. "Une collection de paroles de Jésus récemment retrouvée: l'Évangile selon Thomas." In: H.-C. Puech, *En quête de la Gnose. II. Sur l'Évangile selon Thomas.* Paris: Gallimard, 33–57 [first published in 1957].

1978d. "Doctrines ésotériques et thèmes gnostiques dans l'Évangile selon Thomas (Collège de France, 1960–1972)." In: H.-C. Puech, *En quête de la Gnose. II. Sur l'Évangile selon Thomas.* Paris: Gallimard, 93–284 [first published 1960–1972].

1979. "Saint Paul chez les manichéens d'Asie Centrale." In: H.-C. Puech, *Sur le Manichéisme et autres essais.* Paris: Flammarion, 153–167 [first published 1960].

Puech, Henri-Charles, and Beate Blatz

1987. "Andere gnostische Evangelien und verwandte Literatur." In: E. Hennecke and W. Schneemelcher, eds., *Neutestamentliche Apokryphen in deutscher Übersetzung. I. Evangelien* (5. Auflage). Tübingen: Mohr Siebeck, 285–329.

Quispel, Gilles

2008. "The Muslim Jesus." In: J. van Oort, ed., *Gnostica, Judaica, Catholica: Collected Essays of Gilles Quispel.* NHMS 55. Leiden and Boston: Brill, 627–662.

Reeves, John C.

2011. *Prolegomena to a History of Islamicate Manichaeism.* Comparative Islamic Studies. London and Oakville: Equinox Publishing.

Richter, Siegfried G.

1998. *Psalm Book. II,2. Die Herakleides-Psalmen.* CFM Series Coptica 1. Turnhout: Brepols.

Scher, Addai

1912. *Theodorus bar Kōnī: Liber scholiorum. Pars posterior.* CSCO Scriptores Syri II 66. Leipzig: Harrassowitz.

Sundermann, Werner

1981. *Mitteliranische manichäische Texte kirchengeschichtlichen Inhalts mit einem Appendix von Nicholas Sims-Williams.* Berliner Turfantexte 11. Berlin: Akademie Verlag.

Wurst, Gregor

1996. "A Dialogue between the Saviour and the Soul (Manichaean Psalm Book, Part I, No. 136)." In: *BSAC* 35, 149–160.

7
"For only our lord the Paraclete is competent to praise you as you deserve" (P.Kellis I Gr. 63): Identifying a Roman-Egyptian Patron of the Manichaeans in Kellis

Mattias Brand

Abstract

Relatively newly published papyri from ancient Kellis (modern Ismant el-Kharab in the Dakhleh Oasis) enable us to identify a Roman-Egyptian patron of the local Manichaeans. Prosopographical connections reveal not only his name, Pausanias son of Valerius, but also his prominent role as the strategos of the Great Oasis. This chapter places Pausanias in the context of other Manichaean patronage relationships, like those between the elect and the catechumens. The similarities between the fundraising letters of the elect and a Greek letter praising Pausanias, including marked religious rhetoric and observable asymmetrical relationship between author and recipients, raises the question of Pausanias's religious affiliation. Specifically, the Greek letter's statement that "only our lord the Paraclete is competent to praise you as you deserve", seems to imply that Pausanias was familiar with Manichaean terminology. Would he have identified as Manichaean catechumen? If so, would it be warranted to connect the Kellis evidence for patronage with Manichaean hagiographical narratives about converting wealthy and powerful patrons as a strategy for the propagation of the Manichaean church? Rather than harmonizing these different types of accounts, I propose to reflect on their situatedness—as well as how the context and desires of present-day scholars shape our interpretation of the ancient sources.

1   Introduction

The discovery of authentic Manichaean liturgical documents as well as associated letters and business accounts at ancient Kellis (modern Ismant el-Kharab in the Dakhleh Oasis) offers a unique and novel insight into the everyday lives of Manichaean catechumens in fourth-century Egypt. As new finds, they challenge previous reconstructions of the Manichaean way of life and supplement our knowledge of the practical application of the Manichaean religion within the day-to-day structures of Roman Egypt. The documentary letters in Greek and Coptic provide us with enough information to reconstruct Manichaean families over several generations, showing their social interactions and business ties with other villagers. The letters reveal an economically active community that was in touch with the Egyptian Nile valley, as well as the Roman world at large. Locating the Manichaeans of Kellis within a dense regional network that included members of the Roman military and administrative elite fundamentally alters our perspective on the postulated "sectarian" and "persecuted" nature of Manichaeism in Late Antiquity.[1]

This chapter will look into the patronage relationships of Manichaeans in Kellis. After a brief examination of Manichaean dependency relationships, I will argue that it is possible to identify a Roman-Egyptian patron of the local Manichaean community in the early fourth century: Pausanias son of Valerius.[2] This identification is built on a careful sifting through of the papyrological record, with particular focus on potential prosopographical connections between Greek and Coptic documents. As we will see, this patron donated land to individuals in Kellis belonging to Manichaean circles, but it remains unclear whether he himself belonged to their community. The linchpin is a Greek letter addressing the patron in religious terminology, saying, "only our lord the Paraclete is competent to praise you as you deserve" (P.Kellis I Gr. 63). Such marked Manichaean language suggests that Pausanias had more profound knowledge of Manichaean doctrine than other papyri revealed. While newly published Greek texts contain further information about his social position, they do not shed light on the question whether he himself was a Manichaean catechumen. Beyond the specific historical and papyrological work,

---

[1] This chapter is an elaborated version of an interpretation made in M. Brand, *The Manichaeans of Kellis: Religion, Community, and Everyday Life* (Leiden University PhD dissertation, 2019). I would like to thank J. van Oort, C. Uehlinger, the anonymous reviewer, and J. Swank for their feedback. The Greek and Coptic texts in this chapter are cited from the editions and translations (listed at the end of the chapter). Important recent reflections on the Manichaean community at Kellis are found in I. Gardner, "Once More on Mani's Epistles and Manichaean Letter-Writing," *Journal of Ancient Christianity* 17, no. 2 (2013): 291–314; I. Gardner, "P.Kellis 82 and an Unnoticed Record of the Manichaean Daily Prayers," *Zeitschrift für Papyrologie und Epigraphik* 211 (2019): 89–91.

[2] More information about the social and economic surroundings of the Oasis can be found in R.S. Bagnall et al., eds., *An Oasis City* (New York: Institute for the Study of the Ancient World, New York University Press, 2015)—reviewed in M. Brand, "Religious Diversity in the Egyptian Desert: New Findings from the Dakhleh Oasis," *Entangled Religions* 4 (2017): 17–39— and O.E. Kaper, "The Western Oases," in *The Oxford Handbook of Roman Egypt*, ed. C. Riggs (Oxford: Oxford University Press, 2012), 717–735.

this chapter aims to raise the methodological question whether we can use Pausanias's position in Kellis to confirm the existence of a Manichaean missionary method of converting wealthy and powerful patrons for the propagation of the Manichaean church.

2 Manichaeans seeking Patronage

Patronage in the Roman world included a wide variety of relationships and interactions, like those between a landlord and a tenant, or a senator and a farmer. It has been defined as "an enduring, reciprocal relationship of exchange between individuals of unequal status that contains more than one point of common interest and is entered into voluntarily by both parties".[3] Andrew Wallace-Hadrill stressed three key ingredients of patronage, namely: (1) a reciprocal exchange of services; (2) the personal nature of the relationship; (3) the asymmetrical or unequal status fueling the interaction.[4] The exact interplay of these three features varied from case to case, since there was a plurality of settings in which inequalities in wealth, status and power could be translated into mutually supportive social relations.

Manichaean patronage relationships have to be located within the changing social and economic circumstances of the later Roman Empire. Due to the increasing complexity and fragmentation of society, individuals and families could call upon an increasing number of would-be patrons, including urban and rural councilors, emerging bishops, ascetics, military leaders, former magistrates, as well as the provincial governor and his staff. The plurality of patrons led to shifting allegiances and the negotiation of services, placing more agency in the hands of the clients. Prominent elite figures like the fourth-century rhetor Libanius of Antioch complained about this situation as indicating the decay of well-structured society. In his opinion, it should have been the rural landlord who "assumes the role of the protector, monopolizing the dual functions of a patron, as a provider of protection and resources and as a broker controlling access to the outside world."[5] In reality, rural landowners had to face an increasing complex landscape of power relations, not simply hierarchically

---

3 C. Grey, "Concerning Rural Matters," in *The Oxford Handbook of Late Antiquity*, ed. S.F. Johnson (Oxford: Oxford University Press, 2012), 15 citing all the relevant literature.
4 A. Wallace-Hadrill, "Introduction," in *Patronage in Ancient Society*, ed. A. Wallace-Hadrill (London: Routledge, 1989), 3.
5 G. Woolf, "Patronage of the Rural Poor in the Roman World," in *Patronage in Ancient Society*, ed. A. Wallace-Hadrill (London: Routledge, 1989), 162; Libanius, *Oration* 47.19, 22.

structured according to status or prestige, but rather organized locally. Seeking patronage relationships with powerful figures was in the hands of villagers or townspeople. It pragmatically provided them with access to local knowledge and money, rather than with empire-wide connections. As Giovanni Ruffini observed about the inhabitants of late antique Aphrodito:

> When they need legal guarantees that someone will not disappear, they do not obsess over status or rank. Power does not need status or rank, but it does need money. Put most simply, the men and women of Aphrodito care about pragmatics, about who has enough money to give a good guarantee. When they face theft or vandalism, they are less interested in the letter of the law than in who has the local knowledge to help them solve their problems. When they face murder, they just want to know where the bones are buried. When they do think about going to law, they work on the sidelines first, in the shadows of the court, to find informal solutions through the help of friends.[6]

The local focus of most patronage relationships, as well as their personal nature, are exemplified in the early life trajectory of Augustine (354–400 CE). Augustine was financially supported by Romanianus in his education and part of his career, eventually even converting him to Manichaeism (and later maybe to Nicaean Christianity).[7] In Rome, other wealthy Manichaeans hosted Augustine, although a direct relationship with Constantius, the initiator of a Manichaean monastic experiment, cannot be proven.[8] Augustine was by no means unique in his dense network of relationships. Legal sources intimate that other upper class Manichaeans received support from members of the Roman elite. Fourth and fifth-century legislation forbade Manichaeans to serve an imperial office—suggesting that they did—and outlawed any type of protection by their colleagues in the imperial forces.[9] The need for powerful friends

---

6 G.R. Ruffini, *Life in an Egyptian Village in Late Antiquity: Aphrodito before and after the Islamic Conquest* (Cambridge: Cambridge University Press, 2018), 209.
7 See the references in J. van Oort, "Manichaean Women in Augustine's Life and Works," in *Mani and Augustine* (Leiden: Brill, 2020), 427.
8 Augustine described Constantius's monastic experiment in *De moribus ecclesiae catholicae et de moribus Manichaeorum* 20.74, but does not name his host in *Conf.* 5.10.18–19. The usage friendship-language (*amicitia*) in the latter passage points to a patronage relationship. Cf. J. BeDuhn, *Augustine's Manichaean Dilemma 1: Conversion and Apostasy, 373–388 C.E.* (Philadelphia: University of Pennsylvania Press, 2010), 143–144.
9 Prohibition to serve in the imperial service in 445 CE (the so-called Novel of Valentinian). Under Justinian, there were specific penalties for officers who failed to denounce their

was made explicit in Libanius request to Priscianus, the proconsul of Palestina, to protect the Manichaeans so they could be "free from anxiety".[10] Around the same time, Athanasius accused Sebastianus, the prefect of Egypt and a Roman military general, of secretly supporting Manichaeans and torturing Nicaean Christians. Others reported that the Manichaeans could live freely during the reign of Emperor Anastasius (r. 491–518 CE) because his mother actively supported and protected them.[11] While some of these stories may have been slanderous efforts to discredit other Christian groups, they correlate to Roman legal measures focusing on the patronage relationships that enabled Manichaeans to gather under the radar in private villas (CTh xvi.5.7 and xvi.7.3 with a full suppression of domestic meeting places in CTh xvi.5.11).[12] It is through the support of wealthy patrons, and their network connections, that Manichaeism could spread throughout the Roman Empire, and establish a foothold in the city of Rome.[13]

Authentic Manichaean sources also narrate about the patronage of kings, and the support of military and political elite. Throughout hagiographical narratives, Mani and the earliest generations of Manichaeans are depicted as converting the Sasanian and Roman elites, like queen Zenobia of Palmyra, the Tūrān Shāh, and vassal king Baat of Armenia.[14] A Coptic Manichaean text of

---

Manichaean colleagues (527 CE, CJ I.5.16). The rhetorical nature of the complaints about 'Manichaeans' and the portrayal of persecution of Manichaeans in the *Liber Pontificalis* is discussed by S. Cohen, "Schism and the Polemic of Heresy: Manichaeism and the Representation of Papal Authority in the *Liber Pontificalis*," *Journal of Late Antiquity* 8, no. 1 (2015): 195–230.

10 Libanius, *Epistle* 1253, translation and citation in I. Gardner, and S.N.C. Lieu, ed. *Manichaean Texts from the Roman Empire* (Cambridge: Cambridge University Press, 2004), 125.

11 Athanasius, *History of the Arians*, 59 and 61. Theodorus Lector, *Historia ecclesiastica*, IV. Discussed in R. Matsangou, "Real and Imagined Manichaeans in Greek Patristic Anti-Manichaica (4th–6th Centuries)," in *Manichaeism East and West*, ed. S.N.C. Lieu (Turnhout: Brepols, 2017), 166.

12 On the post-Constantinian marginalization of heterodox groups in the domestic sphere, see Harry O. Maier, "Heresy, Households, and the Disciplining of Diversity," in *A People's History to Christianity. Late Ancient Christianity*, ed. V. Burrus (Minneapolis: Fortress Press, 2005), 213–233. All this is discussed in depth in the forthcoming dissertation of R. Matsangou. Cf. P. Beskow, "The Theodosian Laws against Manichaeism," in *Manichaean Studies. Proceedings of the First International Conference on Manichaeism*, ed. P. Bryder (Lund: Plus Ultra, 1988), 1–11; K. Bowes, *Private Worship, Public Values and Religious Change in Late Antiquity* (Cambridge: Cambridge University Press, 2008), 92–98.

13 Fifty years ago, Peter Brown already stressed the connection between the demise of Manichaeism and their (in)ability to connect to late antique patronage relationships. P. Brown, "The Diffusion of Manichaeism in the Roman Empire," *Journal of Roman Studies* 59, no. 1 (1969): 99.

14 The texts are translated in H.-J. Klimkeit, *Gnosis on the Silk Road. Gnostic Texts from Central*

historical nature explicitly refers to the "patronage" (βοήθεια) of King Amaro (of Edessa?), describing him as a "great patron" (πάτρων).[15] These stories have been taken to indicate a specific Manichaean missionary method of converting elite figures in order to receive their patronage. As Werner Sundermann stated: "The second [Manichaean missionary] method was to turn first to the ruler of a territory or to members of its ruling class, in order to win them over or get their permission to conduct a mission among their subjects."[16] However, reports about Mani's own example of winning over the Persian King Shapur, who subsequently granted him access to the entire Sassanian Empire, have recently been described as "heavily mythologized". In fact, Iain Gardner warns that "any idea of imperial patronage or time spent in the entourage or at court should be subject to critical scepticism."[17] Similar skepticism should be applied to other hagiographical patronage stories, especially when the Manichaean disciples are portrayed as following in Mani's footsteps. The asserted Manichaean missionary method of winning over important patrons was a literary strategy, and, therefore, has to face extensive critical scrutiny before it can be used to confirm or supplement the representation of Manichaean patronage relationships in Roman legal sources.

The most well-known patronage relationships of Manichaeans, those between wealthy auditors and elect, were less focused on strategic dissemination of the Manichaean church, but rather driven by the pragmatics of local resource management. Since Manichaean elect were not supposed to sustain themselves due to their ascetic lifestyle, they depended on auditors (catechumens in Greek and Coptic Manichaean sources) for their everyday needs. Within the Manichaean religious ideology, catechumens were the supporters *par excellence*. They were called upon to provide the ascetic elect with alms-gifts of food, shelter, or clothing. In fact, catechumens were such an important

---

Asia (San Francisco, CA: HarperSanFrancisco, 1993), 201–211. The identification of Nafshā's sister as the famous queen Zenobia is tentative, and the text's statement that the queen "received the truth" is open for multiple interpretations. On Mani's journey to Armenia, see I. Gardner, "Did Mani Travel to Armenia?," *Iran and the Caucasus* 22 (2018): 341–352.

15 N.A. Pedersen, "A Manichaean Historical Text," *Zeitschrift für Papyrologie und Epigraphik* 119 (1997): 199; F. de Blois, "Who Is King Amaro?," *Arabian Archaeology and Epigraphy* 6, no. 3 (1995): 196–198.

16 W. Sundermann, "Manicheism IV. Missionary Activity and Technique," in *Encyclopædia Iranica online* A short overview of the missionary history is found in S.N.C. Lieu, *Manichaeism in the Later Roman Empire and Medieval China*, 2nd edition ed. (Tübingen Mohr Siebeck, 1992), 86–120.

17 I. Gardner, *The Founder of Manichaeism* (Cambridge: Cambridge University Press, 2020), 58.

facet of Manichaean life that the *Kephalaia* states that a "place wherein there are no catechumens does not have the holy church resting there" (1 Keph. 87, 218.8–10). The mutual dependency between catechumens and elect in an asymmetrical relationship led, therefore, to a description of the duty of catechumens as "the patronage of the church" ([т]ⲡⲁⲧⲣⲱⲛⲓⲁ ⲛⲧⲉⲕⲕⲗⲏⲥⲓⲁ 1 Keph. 91 233.24).[18]

Patronage language is also used in one of the Manichaean letters from Kellis, where the recipients were described as "helpers," "worthy patrons," and "firm unbending pillars" (ⲛ̄ⲃⲟⲏⲑⲟⲥ ϩⲓ ⲡⲁⲧⲣⲟⲛ ⲉⲩⲣ̄ϣⲉⲩ· ϩⲓ ⲥⲧⲩⲗⲟⲥ ⲉⲩⲧⲁϫⲣⲁⲓ̈ⲧ P.Kellis v Copt. 31.16–18). Together with P.Kellis v Copt. 32, this Coptic fundraising letter attests to the local patronage ties between catechumens and elect. In both letters, the author skillfully combined the language of daughterhood with the social asymmetry of patronage structures. He introduced himself as an anonymous "father" (ⲓⲱⲧ) writing to his "daughter(s)" (ϣⲉⲣⲉ) for financial or material support:[19]

> My loved daughters, who are greatly revered by me: the members of the holy Church, the daughters of the Light Mind, they who also are numbered with the children of God; the favoured, blessed, God-loving souls; my *shona* children. It is I, your father who is in Egypt, who writes to you: in the Lord, greetings!.
>
> P.Kellis v Copt. 31.1–9

And,

> To our loved daughter: the daughter of the holy church, the catechumen of the faith; the good tree whose fruit never withers, which is your love that emits radiance every day. She who has acquired for herself her riches and stored them in the treasuries that are in the heights, where moths shall not find a way, nor shall thieves dig through to them to steal; which

---

18 For more references to the Greek use of the term, see S. Daris, *Il Lessico Latino Nel Greco D'egitto*, 2 ed. (Barcelona: Institut de Teologia Fonamental, Seminari de Papirologia, 1991), 88.

19 The Coptic texts are found in the edition. Gardner, *Coptic Documentary Texts from Kellis 1* (Oxford: Oxbow Books, 1999), 209–211 and 214–215. Fourth-century Christian parallels for the usage of the paternal title mostly derive from monastic environments. See also the frequent use of the honorific title "apa" in monastic sources. S.J. Clackson, *Coptic and Greek Texts Relating to the Hermopolite Monastery of Apa Apollo* (Oxford: Griffith Institute, Ashmolean Museum, 2000), 8, 29.

(storehouses) are the sun and the moon. She whose deeds resemble her name, our daughter, Eirene. It is I, your father who writes to you: in God, greetings!.

P.Kellis v Copt. 32.1–17

In both of these address formulas, the author incorporated extensive honorific designations like "good tree whose fruit never withers" into the framework of a father-daughter relationship. The daughter(s) are characterized with elaborate Manichaean designators that indicate their status as catechumens, a position made explicit in P.Kellis v Copt. 32 where Eirene—a personal name meaning "peace"—is called a "catechumen of the faith".

The combination of patronage language and kinship metaphors creates a paradoxical situation, as the "daughters" were the patrons and the "father" was the dependent, contrary to what one might expect. In most ancient letters, clients or petitioners used politeness strategies and extensive honorific phrases to address their patron. In this case, the "fathers" used polite and flattering language to frame their requests for material support. In one of the letters, the fundraising purpose is expressed through the allusion to a biblical parable and the Manichaean image of the sun and the moon as storehouses. P.Kellis v Copt. 32 alludes to a New Testament parable about investing treasures in heaven, where moths and thieves cannot reach it (Matt 6.19–20, the parallels with Mt. 24:42–44 and 1 Thess 5.2).[20] This image featured frequently in Manichaean scripture, where it connected the almsgiving of pious catechumens to the released Light particles of the Living Soul that were stored on the sun and the moon (for example in 2 PsB. 151.4–152.9).[21] In this letter, the parable is reworked into a directive for Eirene to commit herself to her almsgiving. The explicit reference to the sun and the moon as storehouses of spiritual riches ingeniously creates a connection between the kinship language, the Manichaean ideology of giving, and the peace (*eirene*) brought about by these gifts.

---

20 M. Franzmann, "An 'Heretical' Use of the New Testament: A Manichaean Adaptation of Matt 6:19–20 in P. Kell. Copt 32," in *The New Testament Interpreted*, ed. B.C. Lategan and C. Breytenbach (Leiden: Brill, 2006), 153–162.

21 M. Franzmann, "The Treasure of the Manichaean Spiritual Life," in *'In Search of Truth': Augustine, Manichaeism and Other Gnosticism*, ed. J.A. van den Berg, et al. (Leiden: Brill, 2011), 235–243. To which we can now add the parallel citation of Jesus in 1 Keph. 149, 362.27. The same theme is used in Iranian texts from the Zoroastrian tradition. A. Hintze, "Treasure in Heaven. A Theme in Comparative Religion," in *Irano-Judaica VI. Studies Relating to Jewish Contacts with Persian Culture Throughout the Ages*, ed. S. Shaked and A. Netzer (Jerusalem: Ben-Zvi Institute, 2008), 9–36.

3 The Patronage of a Former Strategos?

The Kellis papyri do not only add novel insights to the everyday dynamics between elect and catechumens, they also offer insights into the social network of Manichaeans in the Dakhleh Oasis. Specifically, I contend that the earliest generations of Manichaeans at Kellis had the support of a former magistrate. Newly published Greek documents identify Pausanias son of Valerius as the *strategos* of the Great Oasis between 326 and 333 CE. As the *strategos* was one of the most powerful figures of the regional government, in charge of the daily administration of one of the districts (*nomoi*), his support must have improved social, economic, and religious circumstances of the Manichaean families in the oasis.[22] The following paragraphs will unpack the papyrological identification of Pausanias son of Valerius, and the next section will explore the implications of this identification for our knowledge of the Manichaean community at Kellis.

Pausanias, the son of Valerius had strong ties to local Manichaeans. His name appears in a Greek legal contract from 333 CE, recording the gift of a plot of land in the eastern part of the village of Kellis to Aurelius Psais, son of Pamour (P.Kellis I Gr. 38 a and b). The plot of land was located adjacent to other land belonging to Pausanias, and it may have been just north of House 3 in Kellis.[23] The recipient, Aurelius Psais, son of Pamour is one of the prominent figures in the Greek and Coptic documentary papyri from House 3. The various papyri shed light on his family relationships and business transactions, especially through the correspondence of his sons Psais, Pamour and Pegosh (Pekysis in Greek).[24] Their Manichaean affiliation is visible in some of the personal letters (particularly P.Kellis I Gr. 71 and P.Kellis VII Copt. 64–72), and it is confirmed by the many fragments of Manichaean psalms and Mani's *Epistles* that were found throughout the house.[25] The Greek contract provides two

---

22   On the role of the *strategos* in Late Antiquity, see A. Jördens, "Government, Taxation, and Law," in *The Oxford Handbook of Roman Egypt*, ed. C. Riggs (Oxford: Oxford University Press, 2012), 58–59; J. Rowlandson, "Administration and Law: Graeco-Roman," in *A Companion to Ancient Egypt*, ed. A.B. Lloyd (Chichester: Wiley-Blackwell, 2010), 237–254.

23   K.A. Worp, *Greek Papyri from Kellis 1* (Oxford: Oxbow Books, 1995), 109.

24   In Worp's reconstruction of the family tree, he is marked as Psais II, the husband of Tapollos and father of Psais, Pamour, Pegosh and Tagoshe. Worp, *Greek Papyri*, 51.

25   Establishing a relationship between the individuals known from the papyri and the liturgical documents is notoriously difficult, as there are multiple ways in which papyri can end up together in one find location. I contend that the usage of Manichaean terminology in some of the personal letters points to a scribal context in which Manichaean liturgical

further details to the interaction. First, it designates Pausanias as a former magistrate of Mothis (the largest town in the oasis), and second, it hints at a deeper familiarity between Psais and Pausanias. The phrase used for the donation of the plot of land, namely 'irrevocable gift' (χάρις ἀναφαίρετος), is otherwise used in interactions between family members or in the "quasi-sale" of property to a minor.[26] The lack of payment, the asymmetrical social standing of the parties involved, and the almost personal nature of the gift suggest that this interaction was not a one-off, but rather took place within an enduring, reciprocal relationship of exchange between individuals of unequal status. This interpretation is strengthened by a contract of *parachoresis* in which Pausanias son of Valerius handed over a plot of land (or even a house) in the eastern part of Kellis to a certain "Aurelius P—", whose full name is no longer legible (P.Kellis I Gr. 4). The contract's date in 331 CE would allow for the identification of the same Aurelius Psais son of Pamour, but his father Aurelius Pamour is another possibility.[27] In both cases, it is clear that long-term relations existed between Pausanias and the inhabitants of House 3. It is also tempting to ask whether the familial background of the 'irrevocable gift' intimates a shared religious affiliation between Psais and Pausanias.

A more specific description of Pausanias's social position is found in another Greek document derived from Hibis. In this petition (P.Gascou 69), he is addressed as the strategos and *riparius* of the Great Oasis, a jurisdiction encompassing the entire Dakhleh and Khargeh Oases, presumably between 326 and 333 CE.[28] On the basis of his function, Pausanias was called on to mediate between a brother and sister in a conflict about the inheritance from their father, who belonged to the class of former magistrates living in the Khargeh Oasis. Other documents also attest to Pausanias's important role in the Oases. In 337 CE, Pausanias son of Valerius paid for the transportation of the president of the local town council, (P.Gascou 71) and some of his business transactions are traceable in his correspondence with Gena the carpenter, who addresses him

---

      texts were known. Letter P.Kellis V Copt. 19, addressed to a contemporary of Psais, Pamour, and Pegosh, also evidences the local copying of Manichaean psalms.

26   R.S. Bagnall and D.D. Obbink, eds., *Colombia Papyri X* (Atlanta: Scholars Press, 1996), 107 in the commentary on P.Col. X. 274. Cf. H.F. Teigen, *Limbs of the Light Mind: The Social World of a Manichaean Community in Fourth-Century Egypt* (Bergen University PhD Dissertation, 2018), 237.

27   Worp, *Greek Papyri*, 19–20.

28   Worp suggests that Optatus in P.Gascou 70 was the precursor of Pausanias. K.A. Worp, "Miscellaneous New Greek Papyri from Kellis," in *Mélanges Jean Gascou*, ed. J.L. Fournet and A. Papaconstantinou (Paris: Association des Amis du Centre d'Histoire et Civilisation de Byzance, 2016), 447.

TABLE 7.1 List of documents associated with Pausanias

Document	Description and find location
P.Kellis I Gr. 4	Contract of cession. Parcel given to Aurelius P– (House 2, 331 CE)
P.Kellis I Gr. 5–6	Correspondence with Gena (House 2)
P.Kellis I Gr. 38ab	Grant of a plot of land to Psais (House 3)
P.Kellis I Gr. 63	Manichaean letter addressed to Pausanias and Pisistratos (House 3)
P.Gascou 69 and 71	Petition to Pausanias the *strategos* and a tax receipt from 337 CE (D/8)

as "my master", "your nobility", and "your goodness" (P.Kellis I Gr. 5 from Gena, P.Kellis I Gr.6 addressing Gena). All of these texts attest to Pausanias's central position in a wider network of individuals depending on him (see table 7.1).

Was this influential individual more than a friendly and powerful ally? The "irrevocable gift" to Psais already indicated a more profound connection, one that I understand as a patronage relationship. Similar religious patronage relationships are attested in Kellis, for example in an inscription for Isis-Demeter by a former magistrate (who is described as *"prostates"*, a patron or leader of an association), and a graffito mentioning a letter to (or from) the "leadership" (*prostasia*) of an association.[29] The reciprocal relationships behind these inscriptions are difficult to reconstruct. Presumably, the patron paid for the association's expenses, including the inscription, and he received honor and support in exchange. In the case of Pausanias, it might be possible to define the interaction in more detail. A Greek personal letter found in House 3 (P.Kellis I Gr. 63) suggests that he may have shared a Manichaean affiliation with Psais and other villagers.

P.Kellis I Gr. 63 is an undated Greek papyrus letter addressing Pausanias and another recipient named Pisistratos in laudatory style as "my lords sons who are most longed-for and most beloved by us". The anonymous author praises them for their piety and gifts with exceptional Manichaean phrases to make his gratefulness known. He writes that he has "benefitted also from the fruits of the soul of the pious …" and therefore "shall set going every praise towards your

---

29   K.A. Worp and C.A. Hope, "Dedication Inscriptions from the Main Temple," in *Dakhleh Oasis Project: Preliminary Reports on the 1994–1995 to 1998–1999 Field Seasons*, ed. C.A. Hope and G.E. Bowen (Oxford: Oxbow Books, 2002), 325. The graffito in House 4 was found in a context with third-century depictions of Isis and Serapis. C.A. Hope et al., "Report on the 2010 Season of Excavations at Ismant El-Kharab, Dakhleh Oasis," *Bulletin of the Australian Centre for Egyptology* 21 (2010): 42.

most luminous soul". Specifically highlighting the Manichaean background, he adds that "only our lord the Paraclete is competent to praise you as you deserve and to compensate you at the appropriate moment."[30] As is well-known, the title "Paraclete" derives from a gospel passage in which Jesus promised his disciples a supernatural advocate (παράκλητος, John 14.16), whom Manichaeans identified with Mani, or Mani's supernatural twin.[31] References to "the Paraclete" are strictly limited to papyrus letters with a marked Manichaean background (P.Kellis I Gr. 63, P.Kellis V Copt. 19, P.Harr. 107). It stands to reason then, to assume that both Pausanias and Pisistratos were associated with the Manichaean community, and appreciated the prospect of the Paraclete's compensation for their piety.

The use of Manichaean language, and the purpose of letter P.Kellis I Gr. 63 suggest that Pausanias and Pisistratos were supporters—maybe even catechumens—of the Manichaean community. Elsewhere, I have argued that P.Kellis I Gr. 63 is not a letter of recommendation, as the editor suggested, but rather a fundraising letter like the abovementioned Coptic letters P.Kellis V Copt. 31 and 32.[32] Other scholarship supports this interpretation. Specifically, Jean-Daniel Dubois has argued that the letter's reference to "fruits of the soul of the pious …" points to almsgiving, since "fruits" (καρπος) is used in Manichaean literature for almsgifts to the elect (see the parallels in P.Kellis V Copt. 53, 42.24). At Kellis, the author of the letter to Eirene described her shining exemplary behavior as a tree bearing "fruit" (P.Kellis V Copt. 32.4–5).[33] Just as Eirene and the anonymous daughters of P.Kellis V Copt. 31, Pausanias and Pisistratos may have been praised for their almsgiving. The letter does not elaborate about the gifts, but mentions "indications of your sympathy", a "basket" and "objects destined for the lord–ryllos" as charitable gifts that the author(s) received (P.Kellis I

---

30 κ[α]ὶ νῦν ἀπολαύομεν πνευματικῶν ὀλίγων καρπῶν, ἀπολαύ[ο]μεν δ[ὲ] πάλιν καὶ τῶν ψυχικῶν τῆς εὐσεβοῦς... φορᾶς δηλονότι· καὶ ἀμφοτέρ[ω]ν πεπλησμ[έ]νοι πᾶσαν εὐλογίαν σπ[ε]υσόμεθα πρὸς τὴν φωτινοτάτη[ν] ὑμῶν ψυχὴν καθ' ὅσον ἡμῖν ἐ[στι] δυνα[τὸν‥]. Μόνος γὰρ ὁ δ[ε]σπότης ἡμῶν [ὁ] π[α]ρ[άκ]λητος |ἱκανὸς/ ἐπαξίως ὑμᾶς εὐλογῆσα[ι] κ[α]ὶ τ[ῷ] δέοντι καιρῷ ἀνταμείψα[σ]θαι. P.Kellis I Gr. 63.20–30.

31 This identification is made in the citation from the *Living Gospel* in CMC, 69, but also in CMC 17, 36, 63, and 70. J. van Oort, "The Paraclete Mani as the Apostle of Jesus Christ and the Origins of a New Church," in *The Apostolic Age in Patristic Thought*, ed. A. Hilhorst (Leiden: Brill, 2004), 139–157.

32 The interpretation as a recommendation letter is built on the gratitude expressed by the letter's author for having received "indications of your sympathy and the welcome letter of yours". Worp, *Greek Papyri*, 169. Cf. Brand, *The Manichaeans of Kellis*, 207.

33 On the metaphoric language of trees and bearing fruit, see J.K. Coyle, "Good Tree, Bad Tree: The Matthean/Lukan Paradigm in Manichaeism and Its Opponents," in *Manichaeism and Its Legacy*, J.K. Coyle (Leiden: Brill, 2019), 65–88.

Gr. 63.34). Additionally, Dubois proposes to reconstruct payment of "pocket money" (πεκουλιον, P.Kellis I Gr. 63.35) as one of the good deeds for which gratitude is expressed.[34] The parallels with the Coptic fundraising letters of the elect are, thus, threefold: (1) an anonymous author (2) praises the addressees with extensive flattering and religious language, (3) while asking, or thanking, for material or financial support.

As P.Kellis I Gr. 63 offers no contextual information, and Pausanias's other letters contain no trace of a religious identification, further insights into Pausanias's role can only come from prosopographical connections to the other Kellis papyri. Who was, for example, the Pisistratus mentioned alongside Pausanias? Could we use his name to further secure the identification of Pausanias as the former strategos, and learn more about his connection to the Manichaeans? Some finds are promising. One of the ostraca from the West Church at Kellis contains a message from a Pausanias to "his colleague" Kome, mentioning "our (?) son Pisistratus" (O.Kellis 85).[35] It is unknown whether any of these names referred to the individuals associated with House 2 and 3, but Kome is a name that appears more often in the Kellis documents. He acts as an intermediary agent in another ostracon from the West Church (O.Kellis 112, cf. O.Kellis 60.1, 85.1, 119.3 and 131.1) and a tenant called Kome features prominently in the Kellis Agricultural Account Book. In the latter, Kome is connected to a monk Timotheos. It is tantalizing to associate this monk with a Manichaean monastery, but the evidence for this specific religious identification is flimsy. Both the monk and his monastery may have belonged to non-Manichaean Christian traditions.[36] If any of these connections could be verified, we would be able to place two wealthy individuals, Kome and Pausanias, in direct relationship to Christians and/or Manichaeans in the oasis.

---

34 J.D. Dubois, "Greek and Coptic Documents from Kellis: A Contribution to the History of a Manichaean Community," *Journal of Coptic Studies* 15 (2013): 25, who considers Pausanias and Pisistratos the authors of the letter.

35 K.A. Worp, ed. *Greek Ostraka from Kellis* (Oxford: Oxbow Books, 2004), 84.

36 Timotheos the monk may have been the son of Kome, brother of Nos (KAB 1079–1080, 1199, 1360, 1557 etc.). The existence of—and connection to—a Manichaean monastery is build on the phrase "topos Mani" in the KAB. Bagnall even suggested that the connection to tenant Kome explains why the "topos" owned orchard land. R.S. Bagnall, ed. *Kellis Agricultural Account Book* (Oxford: Oxbow Books, 1997), 68, 69, and 82. Cf. the more detailed argument in Teigen, *Limbs of the Light Mind*, 238–239. Since the existence of a Manichaean monastery is unprecedented within the Roman Empire, I consider it more likely that Timotheos was a "Christian" monk (associated with the monastery mentioned in P.Kellis II Gr. 12, P.Kellis V Copt 12 and maybe P.Kellis VII 123) and that "topos Mani" refers to a field or "place" of another tenant. Brand, *Manichaeans of Kellis*, 243–246.

Alternative prosopographical connections are equally difficult to establish. A Pausanias features in O.Kell. 137, where Pchoirus is acting on his behalf. The Nestorius mentioned in this ostracon is otherwise only known from a letter by Pegosh (P.Kellis I Gr. 72), offering a potential connection to the Manichaean community. Pisistratos's name appears in O.Kellis 58, as "Philosarapis son of Pisistratus" and without additional information in O.Kellis 287, which may bear a Christian staurogram.[37] If one of these individuals was the second recipient of P.Kellis I Gr. 63, it would add significant information to the social and religious networks at Kellis. Further potential prosopographical connections involve Pausanias's father, Valerius. His name appears in a Greek document from 355 CE concerning a female slave, who is set free because of Valerius's "exceptional Christianity, under Zeus, Earth and Sun" (P.Kellis I Gr. 48.4–5).[38] Although this unusual combination of formulas may shed light on his religious identification, the date of the document seems too late to inform us about the father of a strategos in the 330s. Another (?) Valerius appears in P.Kellis I Gr. 64, a letter concerning transportation costs, addressed to Philammon. This Philammon might have been associated with the Manichaean community, but it is difficult to discern between multiple figures with the same name.[39] Many of these prosopographical observations, thus, remain speculative, as none of these texts provide patronyms or additional information that would enable us to identify Pausanias the son of Valerius or Pisistratos with certainty.

4 Implications for the Manichaean community at Kellis

As the papyrological record allows for the reconstruction of some of the most important social interactions in the village, it is no surprise to find patronage relationships. Just as most of their neighbors, Manichaeans in Kellis were in need of connections to wealth and power. Outstanding in this case is the possibility to discuss the Manichaean affiliation of the patron himself. If the Pausanias in P.Kellis I Gr. 63 is to be identified with the former strategos of the oases, it becomes likely that he not only knew about the Manichaean affiliation of the people he supported, but was actually part of their religious community.

There are two wider implications for the nature of the Manichaean community at Kellis. First, it strengthens earlier hypotheses about when the Mani-

---

37 Worp, *Greek Ostraka from Kellis*, 175.
38 On this a-typical situation and vocabulary, see Worp, *Greek Papryi*, 140–143.
39 Worp, *Greek Papyri*, 171; I. Gardner, A. Alcock, and W.-P. Funk, ed. *Coptic Documentary Texts from Kellis. Volume* 2 (Oxford: Oxbow Books, 2014), 118–119.

chaeans reached the oasis. Second, it raises questions about previous characterizations of the community as a being "persecuted" or "sectarian". In the earliest editions of the Kellis papyri, Iain Gardner has suggested that Manichaeism came to the oasis in the first decades of the fourth century, even though the majority of the texts dated after 350 CE. Letter P.Kellis I Gr. 63 (alongside other Greek Manichaean liturgical texts) was included as one of the indications of an earlier stratum that was superseded by a strong Coptic tradition.[40] The identification of Pausanias as the strategos from the early 330s now solidifies this early date, as Gardner states: "if the Manichaean mission succeeded in gaining the support and enthusiasm of leading members of oasis society at this time, it was probably just early enough in terms of the broader advance of Christianity in Egypt for the community to establish itself in the locality."[41]

The early introduction of the Manichaean community in the oasis has also been associated with the Diocletian persecutions at the end of the third century. Is it possible that the Manichaeans fled to the remoteness of Kellis? To what extent were they hiding in the oasis, concealing their religious practices?[42] The identification of a powerful patron in the early decades of the fourth century bolsters such questions: patrons like Pausanias may have created a safe haven in the Dakhleh Oasis. Despite the *possibility* of such reconstructions, I highly doubt their *plausibility*. First, scholars of Roman legal history now agree that it is unlikely that the laws in collections like the Theodosian Code (CTh) presented empire-wide regulations.[43] Outbursts of anti-Manichaean behavior were local affairs that cannot be tied directly to the diffusion of Manichaeism through the Roman Empire. Second, even though documentary papyri from Kellis report about situations characterized by economic, social, and even religious difficulties, there is no trace of systematic religious persecution.[44] Rather, the texts mostly attest to peaceful relationships

---

40 Gardner, *Coptic Documentary Texts from Kellis 1*, 8–11; I. Gardner, ed. *Kellis Literary Texts. Volume 2* (Oxford: Oxbow Books, 2007), 5; I. Gardner "'He Has Gone to the Monastery …'." In *Studia Manichaica: IV. Internationaler Kongreß Zum Manichäismus, Berlin, 14.–18. Juli 1997*, ed. R.E. Emmerick, W. Sundermann and P. Zieme (Berlin: Akademie Verlag, 2000), 248.

41 Gardner, *Founder of Manichaeism*, 101–102.

42 S.N.C. Lieu, "The Self-Identity of the Manichaeans in the Roman East," *Mediterranean Archeology* 11 (1998): 207 states: "the rescript of Diocletian might have the effect of driving Manichaeans in Upper Egypt to seek shelter in remote oases like that of Dakhleh."

43 J.F. Matthews, *Laying Down the Law. A Study of the Theodosian Code* (New Haven: Yale University Press, 2000).

44 With the exception of P.Kellis V Copt. 37.13–20, in which Ammon reports about a situation in the Nile valley. Elsewhere, I have argued that the interpretation of the Kellis community as being "persecuted" is based on fragile evidence, potentially influenced by a strongly

with Roman officials. The names of known Manichaeans appear throughout legal appeals to the Roman administrative and military elite (P.Kellis I Gr.20, 21, 24, P.Kellis V Copt. 20.40–42), indicating a lack of fear. As the example of Pausanias shows, local representatives of the Roman administration were nearby, as were members of the Roman military.[45] As some of the Manichaeans in Kellis belonged to a well-to-do social segment of society, these ties would have belonged to their ordinary day-to-day life (e.g. P.Kellis I Gr. 72 about the financial constraints of a public office). Any characterization of the Manichaean community in Kellis as "persecuted" or "sectarian", therefore fails to convey some of the most prominent new insights from papyri: the Manichaeans of Kellis lived local lives, traveled frequently between the oasis and the Nile valley, and engaged actively in the social and economic networks of the region.

5 Conclusion

I would like to conclude with a final methodological reflection on the relationship between the painstaking papyrological identification of Pausanias as a Roman-Egyptian patron of the Manichaeans in Kellis and the reconstructions of patronage relationships based on hagiographical, legal, and heresiological sources. Is Pausanias's prominent role in the oasis another indication of a Manichaean missionary method of converting powerful and wealthy patrons in order to gain access to large parts of society? While it is tantalizing to think about similarities and potential connections, I would resist a harmonization of the different strands of data into a single narrative about Manichaean missionary methods. Instead, I would like to highlight three—more methodologically sound—approaches to Manichaean patronage relationships.

First, the hagiographical narratives about the healing and conversion the sister of the queen of Palmyra (as reported in Iranian and Coptic sources) are of another nature than the Kellis papyri. Where literary sources tend to highlight "late antique melodramas", the papyri belong to the realm of the "not-

---

religious insider discourse of suffering and persecution. M. Brand, "In the Footsteps of the Apostles of Light: Persecution and the Manichaean Discourse of Suffering," in *Heirs of Roman Persecution: Studies on a Christian and Para-Christian Discourse in Late Antiquity*, ed. E. Fournier and W. Mayer (London: Routledge, 2019), 112–134.

45 P.Gascou 67 mentions an honorably discharged veteran living in a house where a wooden tablet with Manichaean psalms was found (House 4). While it is impossible to relate the tablet and the veteran in time, they were culturally and geographically close. The Roman army is otherwise attested in the archaeological remains of fortresses in the oases, and the references in the KAB to a military unit stationed in Dakhleh (KAB 793, 1263, 1407).

so-exciting everyday nuisances" and routines.⁴⁶ The former require extensive rhetorical analysis, for example by examining how Mani's life in the *Cologne Mani Codex* served as a behavioral model for the elect. Specifically, it includes a foreshadowing of missionary success in Mani's cry "[how] will the world, its princes or its teachings, receive me when it comes to hearing these secrets and to accepting these hard precepts? How shall I (speak) before the kings ... and ... of the world, and the leaders of religions?" (CMC 103–104).⁴⁷ Subsequent stories with court scenes and royal conversions answered this call, portraying the Manichaean mission before princes, kings, and religious leaders as a tremendous success.

The rhetoric in Manichaean narratives about royal conversion correlates with some of the dreams and fears of ancient Christian leaders, who urged rural landowners and other patrons to use their power to support Christian communities. Augustine, for example, wrote about the landlord as a *paterfamilias* with the authority to encourage all his dependents to remain (or become) Christians, while Maximus, the bishop of Turin, urged landowners in his sermons to end peasant's sacrifices on their land.⁴⁸ These fourth and fifth-century concerns hardly constitute an equivalent to *cuius regio, eius religio*, but they remind us that late antique Christians and Manichaeans imagined patronage relationships as affecting religious choice. To what extent patrons influenced rural religious affiliation in Egypt is difficult to grasp, especially since the most prominent difference between narrated Manichaean patronage and Pausanias's reconstructed role in Kellis lies in the absence of indications for a missionary aim. The author of P.Kellis I Gr. 63 only thanked Pausanias and Pisistratos for their material and financial support, never even connecting their patronage to the Manichaean scribal activities that become so visible in the let-

---

46 M. Kahlos, "Christianisation and Late Antique Patronage: Conflicts and Everyday Nuisances." In *Reconceiving Religious Conflict: New Views from the Formative Centuries of Christianity*, edited by W. Mayer and C.L. de Wet (London: Routledge, 2018), 182.

47 Translation by J.M and S.N.C. Lieu. In 1 Keph. 76, 183.26–32, this theme is developed in the request of the disciples to receive two Manis: one for the community and one to go to court. The literary nature of the CMC's "prophet" going to the court of the kings was already highlighted in A.F. de Jong, "The *Cologne Mani Codex* and the Life of Zarathushtra," in *Jews, Christians and Zoroastrians. Religious Dynamics in a Sasanian Context*, ed. G. Herman (Piscataway, NJ: Gorgias Press, 2014), 141–147. On the connection between the CMC and court scenes in the Dublin *Kephalaia*, see P. Dilley, "Mani's Wisdom at the Court of the Persian Kings: The Genre and Context of the Chester Beatty Kephalaia," in *Mani at the Court of the Persian Kings*, ed. I. Gardner, J.D. BeDuhn, and P. Dilley (Leiden: Brill, 2014), 18–19 and 32–47.

48 Augustine, *City of God*, 19.16. Maximus, *Sermons*, 42.1, 106.2, 107.1, 108. Discussed in Kahlos, "Christianisation and Late Antique Patronage", 186.

ters from the next generation of Manichaeans in Kellis (e.g. P.Kellis V Copt. 19). Pausanias's religious story remains untold.

Rather than speculating about postulated missionary aims and methods behind Pausanias's patronage, we should take into account Giovanni Ruffini's observation that late antique villages were "organized solely by the push and pull of the day to day".[49] Access to a wealthy patron served many pragmatic purposes other than missionary success. Evoking this mundane perspective to late antique village relationships does not trivialize the role of religious considerations within the lives of these individuals, but it situates religious "groupness" within the practicalities of daily life. Without localized insights, we run the risk of putting Late Antiquity in a wholly "other" category, characterized as "an exotic territory, populated by wild monks and excitable virgins and dominated by the clash of religions, mentalities and lifestyles".[50] As Thomas Hunt reminds us:

> The particular ways of describing late antique society show clearly the ways that scholarship is shaped by its social and cultural context." … "[The study of Late Antiquity] is always structured by ideological commitments. Not least of these is the commitment to integrate 'religion' as a central component of the lives of people in the late antique past."[51]

A second approach to Pausanias's patronage role and Manichaean narratives of royal conversion could therefore include a full reflection on modern ideological commitments in the study of Late Antiquity, as well as its implications for the study of Manichaeism. Where and how has previous scholarship perceived similarity and coherence in Manichaean sources from widely different areas and periods without questioning its own comparative approach?[52] Hunt's

---

49 Ruffini, *Life in an Egyptian Village*, 27, 110.
50 A. Cameron, *The Mediterranean World in Late Antiquity AD 395–600* (London: Routledge, 1993), 6.
51 T.E. Hunt, "Religion in Late Antiquity—Late Antiquity in Religion," in *A Companion to Religion in Late Antiquity*, ed. J. Lössl and N. Baker-Brian (Malden, MA: John Wiley & Sons, 2018), 20.
52 With the publication of new textual sources bridging the eastern and western wing of the Manichaean world, we should be able to reflect more fully on the methodological questions raised by R. Lim, "Unity and Diversity among Western Manichaeans: A Reconsideration of Mani's *Sancta Ecclesia*," *Revue des études augustiniennes* 35 (1989): 232. First steps have been taken in Gardner, *Founder of Manichaeism* and J.D. BeDuhn, "Parallels between Coptic and Iranian Kephalaia: Goundesh and the King of Touran," In *Mani at the Court of the Persian Kings*, ed. I. Gardner, J.D. BeDuhn and P. Dilley (Leiden: Brill, 2015), 52–74.

observation can act as a warning not to underestimate how the context and desires of present-day scholars (including the desire to understand the rise and fall of ancient religions) may influence our willingness to see connections between various ancient sources.

Foregoing reflection on evidence for the patronage relationships of Manichaeans has highlighted their one-sided nature. The hagiographical narratives of royal conversions contain Manichaean perspectives, while Roman legal sources only give a normative outsider view on the support structures of individual Manichaeans and their communities. We do not know how actual patrons perceived the relationship. Unfortunately, the documentary evidence is not better. We are otherwise (almost) uninformed about Eirene and the anonymous recipients of P.Kellis V Copt. 31. Would they have recognized themselves in the pious descriptions and honorific phrases used for them by the elect? Eirene, to whom we have one other reference in the Kellis letters,[53] was probably an active businesswoman, but she is reduced to the stereotypical role of daughter and catechumen in P.Kellis V Copt. 32; She is the quintessential "good tree", a supporter of the elect. A third approach would therefore focus on the pragmatics and inherent tension of patronage relationships, highlighting the different expectations and varied outcomes of local interactions between patrons and their clients. Pausanias was approached in marked religious language, just like Eirene and other catechumens, but the papyri never reveal how he himself conceptualized his relationship with the Manichaeans. Instead, the text intimates mundane everyday interactions, like the donation of land to a local family, mediation in a family quarrel about inheritance, and financial responsibility for administrative tasks in the oasis. Undoubtedly, Pausanias could also have be called upon in case of conflict, as Psais's father Pamour appealed the governor of Egypt after having suffered theft (P.Kellis I Gr. 20), and called upon another local magistrate in a case of violence (P.Kellis I Gr. 21). The presence of other members of the managerial class, not to mention the prominent landowner Faustianos, suggest that local families had multiple access routes to wealth and power. The absence of further specific insights in how Psais's family benefited from the invaluable support of Pausanias only stems from the selective and incomplete historical preservation of the papyrus recordings their interactions.

Armed with the extant records of daily life in Kellis, one cannot but recognize how profoundly Manichaean lives were integrated in the social structures

---

53 Letter P.Kellis VII Copt. 105 includes Eirene as a proper name, but does not reveal more about her identity, beyond the fact that Psais (maybe Psais III) greeted her.

and rhythms of late antique Egypt. The identification of Pausanias as a patron of the Manichaeans—regardless all the associated questions—is a valuable addition to our knowledge of Manichaeism in practice. For this insight into the everyday social and religious dynamics of ancient Kellis, we have to thank the excavators of Ismant el-Kharab, Colin Hope and Gillian Bowen, and the papyrologists Klaas Worp and Iain Gardner.

Abbreviations and Translations

CMC The Greek biography of Mani, known as the *Cologne Mani Codex*. Published in L. Koenen, and C. Römer, ed. *Der Kölner Mani-Kodex (Über das werden seines Leibes), Kritische Edition Aufgrund der von A. Henrichs und L. Koenen besorgten Erstedition*. Opladen: Westdeutscher Verlag, 1988.

KAB The Kellis Agricultural Account Book followed by the specific line. Published in R.S. Bagnall, ed. *Kellis Agricultural Account Book*. Oxford: Oxbow Books, 1997.

1 Keph. The Berlin *Kephalaia*, also known as the "Kephalaia of the Teacher". Manuscript pages 1–295 are translated in I. Gardner, ed. *The Kephalaia of the Teacher*. Leiden: Brill, 1995. Pages 291–440 are published and translated by W.-P. Funk, ed. *Kephalaia 1. Zweite Hälfte. Lieferung 13/14*. Stuttgart: Kohlhammer Verlag, 1999; W.-P. Funk, ed. *Kephalaia 1. Zweite Hälfte. Lieferung 15/16*. Stuttgart: Kohlhammer Verlag, 2000; W.-P. Funk, ed. *Kephalaia 1. Zweite Hälfte. Lieferung 17/18*. Stuttgart: Kohlhammer Verlag, 2018. The Dublin *Kephalaia*, known as the "Kephalaia of the Wisdom my Lord Mani" was for a long time only published in facsimile editions. A recent project has led to the publication of a first volume with a critical edition and English translation. I. Gardner, J.D. BeDuhn, and P. Dilley. *The Chapters of the Wisdom of my Lord Mani*. Leiden: Brill, 2018. Mostly cited with a chapter number followed by the specific manuscript pages.

2 PsB. The Manichaean Psalmbook, English tr. by C.R.C. Allberry, ed. *A Manichaean Psalm-Book. Part II*. Stuttgart: Kohlhammer Verlag, 1938.

The Kellis texts are cited according to the digital checklist of papyri. John F. Oates and William H. Willis, *Checklist of Greek, Latin, Demotic and Coptic Papyri, Ostraca and Tablets*, http://papyri.info/docs/checklist. In chronological order, the critical editions and translations were published in:

K.A. Worp, ed. *Greek Papyri from Kellis 1*. Oxford: Oxbow Books, 1995.
I. Gardner, ed. *Kellis Literary Texts. Volume 1*. Oxford: Oxbow Books, 1996.

I. Gardner, A. Alcock, and W.-P. Funk, ed. *Coptic Documentary Texts from Kellis. Volume 1.* Oxford: Oxbow Books, 1999.

I. Gardner, ed. *Kellis Literary Texts. Volume 2.* Oxford: Oxbow Books, 2007.

I. Gardner, A. Alcock, and W.-P. Funk, ed. *Coptic Documentary Texts from Kellis. Volume 2.* Oxford: Oxbow Books, 2014.

The P.Gascou texts have been published in K.A. Worp, "Miscellaneous New Greek Papyri from Kellis." In *Mélanges Jean Gascou*, edited by J.L. Fournet and A. Papaconstantinou, 435–483. Paris: Association des Amis du Centre d'Histoire et Civilisation de Byzance, 2016.

Many other Manichaean texts have been translated in I. Gardner, and S.N.C. Lieu, ed. *Manichaean Texts from the Roman Empire*, Cambridge: Cambridge University Press, 2004.

Secondary Literature

Bagnall, R.S., N. Aravecchia, R. Cribiore, P. Davoli, O.E. Kaper, and S. McFadden, eds. *An Oasis City.* New York: Institute for the Study of the Ancient World, New York University Press, 2015.

Bagnall, R.S., and D.D. Obbink, eds. *Colombia Papyri X.* Atlanta: Scholars Press, 1996.

BeDuhn, J.D. *Augustine's Manichaean Dilemma 1: Conversion and Apostasy, 373–388 C.E.* Philadelphia: University of Pennsylvania Press, 2010.

BeDuhn, J.D. "Parallels between Coptic and Iranian Kephalaia: Goundesh and the King of Touran." In *Mani at the Court of the Persian Kings*, edited by I. Gardner, J.D. BeDuhn and P. Dilley, 52–74. Leiden: Brill, 2015.

Beskow, P. "The Theodosian Laws against Manichaeism." In *Manichaean Studies. Proceedings of the First International Conference on Manichaeism*, edited by P. Bryder, 1–11. Lund: Plus Ultra, 1988.

Blois, F. de. "Who Is King Amaro?". *Arabian Archaeology and Epigraphy* 6, no. 3 (1995): 196–198.

Bowes, K. *Private Worship, Public Values and Religious Change in Late Antiquity.* Cambridge: Cambridge University Press, 2008.

Brand, M. "Religious Diversity in the Egyptian Desert: New Findings from the Dakhleh Oasis." *Entangled Religions* 4 (2017): 17–39.

Brand, M. *The Manichaeans of Kellis: Religion, Community, and Everyday Life.* Leiden University PhD dissertation 2019.

Brand, M. "In the Footsteps of the Apostles of Light: Persecution and the Manichaean Discourse of Suffering." In *Heirs of Roman Persecution: Studies on a Christian and Para-Christian Discourse in Late Antiquity*, edited by E. Fournier and W. Mayer, 112–134. London: Routledge, 2019.

Brown, P. "The Diffusion of Manichaeism in the Roman Empire." *Journal of Roman Studies* 59, no. 1 (1969): 92–103.

Cameron, A. *The Mediterranean World in Late Antiquity AD 395–600*. London: Routledge, 1993.

Clackson, S.J. *Coptic and Greek Texts Relating to the Hermopolite Monastery of Apa Apollo*. Oxford: Griffith Institute, Ashmolean Museum, 2000.

Cohen, S. "Schism and the Polemic of Heresy: Manichaeism and the Representation of Papal Authority in the *Liber Pontificalis*." *Journal of Late Antiquity* 8, no. 1 (2015): 195–230.

Coyle, J.K. "Good Tree, Bad Tree: The Matthean/Lukan Paradigm in Manichaeism and Its Opponents." In *Manichaeism and Its Legacy*, J.K. Coyle, 65–88. Leiden: Brill, 2009.

Daris, S. *Il lessico Latino nel Greco d'egitto*. 2nd ed., Barcelona: Institut de Teologia Fonamental, Seminari de Papirologia, 1991.

Dilley, P. "Mani's Wisdom at the Court of the Persian Kings: The Genre and Context of the Chester Beatty Kephalaia." In *Mani at the Court of the Persian Kings*, edited by I. Gardner, J.D. BeDuhn, and P. Dilley, 15–51. Leiden: Brill, 2014.

Dubois, J.D. "Greek and Coptic Documents from Kellis: A Contribution to the History of a Manichaean Community." *Journal of Coptic studies* 15 (2013): 21–28.

Franzmann, M. "An 'Heretical' Use of the New Testament: A Manichaean Adaptation of Matt 6:19–20 in P. Kell. Copt 32." In *The New Testament Interpreted*, edited by B.C. Lategan and C. Breytenbach, 153–162. Leiden: Brill, 2006.

Franzmann, M. "The Treasure of the Manichaean Spiritual Life." In *'In Search of Truth': Augustine, Manichaeism and Other Gnosticism. Studies for Johannes van Oort at Sixty*, edited by J.A. van den Berg, A. Kotzé, T. Nicklas and M. Scopello, 235–243. Leiden: Brill, 2011 (repr. 2017).

Gardner, I. "'He Has Gone to the Monastery …'." In *Studia Manichaica: IV. Internationaler Kongreß zum Manichäismus, Berlin, 14.–18. Juli 1997*, edited by R.E. Emmerick, W. Sundermann and P. Zieme, 247–257. Berlin: Akademie Verlag.

Gardner, I. "Once More on Mani's Epistles and Manichaean Letter-Writing." *Journal of Ancient Christianity* 17, no. 2 (2013): 291–314.

Gardner, I. "Did Mani Travel to Armenia?" *Iran and the Caucasus* 22 (2018): 341–352.

Gardner, I. "P.Kellis 82 and an Unnoticed Record of the Manichaean Daily Prayers." *Zeitschrift für Papyrologie und Epigraphik* 211 (2019): 89–91.

Gardner, I. *The Founder of Manichaeism*. Cambridge: Cambridge University Press, 2020.

Grey, C. "Concerning Rural Matters." In *The Oxford Handbook of Late Antiquity*, edited by S.F. Johnson, 625–666. Oxford: Oxford University Press, 2012.

Hintze, A. "Treasure in Heaven. A Theme in Comparative Religion." In *Irano-Judaica VI. Studies Relating to Jewish Contacts with Persian Culture Throughout the Ages*, edited by S. Shaked and A. Netzer, 9–36. Jerusalem: Ben-Zvi Institute, 2008.

Hope, C.A., D. Jones, L. Falvey, J. Petkov, H. Whitehouse, and K.A. Worp. "Report on the

2010 Season of Excavations at Ismant El-Kharab, Dakhleh Oasis." *Bulletin of the Australian Centre for Egyptology* 21 (2010): 21–54.
Hunt, T.E. "Religion in Late Antiquity—Late Antiquity in Religion." In *A Companion to Religion in Late Antiquity*, edited by J. Lössl and N. Baker-Brian, 9–30. Malden, MA: John Wiley & Sons, 2018.
Jördens, A. "Government, Taxation, and Law." In *The Oxford Handbook of Roman Egypt*, edited by C. Riggs, 56–67. Oxford: Oxford University Press, 2012.
Jong, A.F. de. "The *Cologne Mani Codex* and the Life of Zarathushtra." In *Jews, Christians and Zoroastrians. Religious Dynamics in a Sasanian Context*, edited by G. Herman, 129–147. Piscataway, NJ: Gorgias Press, 2014.
Kahlos, M. "Christianisation and Late Antique Patronage: Conflicts and Everyday Nuisances." In *Reconceiving Religious Conflict: New Views from the Formative Centuries of Christianity*, edited by W. Mayer and C.L. de Wet, 182–207. London: Routledge, 2018.
Kaper, O.E. "The Western Oases." In *The Oxford Handbook of Roman Egypt*, edited by C. Riggs, 717–735. Oxford: Oxford University Press, 2012.
Klimkeit, H.-J. *Gnosis on the Silk Road. Gnostic Texts from Central Asia*. San Francisco, CA: HarperSanFrancisco, 1993.
Lieu, S.N.C. *Manichaeism in the Later Roman Empire and Medieval China*. 2nd ed., Tübingen: Mohr Siebeck, 1992.
Lieu, S.N.C. "The Self-Identity of the Manichaeans in the Roman East." *Mediterranean Archeology* 11 (1998): 205–227.
Maier, H.O. "Heresy, Households, and the Disciplining of Diversity." In *A People's History to Christianity. Late Ancient Christianity*, edited by V. Burrus, 213–233. Minneapolis: Fortress Press, 2005.
Matsangou, R. "Real and Imagined Manichaeans in Greek Patristic Anti-Manichaica (4th–6th Centuries)." In *Manichaeism East and West*, edited by S.N.C. Lieu, 159–170. Turnhout: Brepols, 2017.
Matthews, J.F. *Laying Down the Law. A Study of the Theodosian Code*. New Haven: Yale University Press, 2000.
Oort, J. van. "The Paraclete Mani as the Apostle of Jesus Christ and the Origins of a New Church." In *The Apostolic Age in Patristic Thought*, edited by A. Hilhorst, 139–157. Leiden: Brill, 2004.
Oort, J. van. "Manichaean Women in Augustine's Life and Works." In *Mani and Augustine*, J. van Oort, 418–432. Leiden: Brill, 2020.
Oort, J. van. *Mani and Augustine. Collected Essays on Mani, Manichaeism and Augustine*. Leiden: Brill, 2020.
Pedersen, N.A. "A Manichaean Historical Text." *Zeitschrift für Papyrologie und Epigraphik* 119 (1997): 193–201.
Rowlandson, J. "Administration and Law: Graeco-Roman." In *A Companion to Ancient Egypt*, edited by A.B. Lloyd, 237–254. Chichester: Wiley-Blackwell, 2010.

Ruffini, G.R. *Life in an Egyptian Village in Late Antiquity: Aphrodito before and after the Islamic Conquest*. Cambridge: Cambridge University Press, 2018.

Sundermann, W. "Manicheism IV. Missionary Activity and Technique." In *Encyclopædia Iranica online*.

Teigen, H.F. *Limbs of the Light Mind: The Social World of a Manichaean Community in Fourth-Century Egypt*. Bergen University PhD Dissertation, 2018.

Wallace-Hadrill, A. "Introduction." In *Patronage in Ancient Society*, edited by A. Wallace-Hadrill, 1–13. London: Routledge, 1989.

Woolf, G. "Patronage of the Rural Poor in the Roman World." In *Patronage in Ancient Society*, edited by A. Wallace-Hadrill, 152–170. London: Routledge, 1989.

Worp, K.A. *Greek Ostraka from Kellis*. Oxford: Oxbow Books, 2004.

Worp, K.A. "Miscellaneous New Greek Papyri from Kellis." In *Mélanges Jean Gascou*, edited by J.L. Fournet and A. Papaconstantinou, 435–483. Paris: Association des Amis du Centre d'Histoire et Civilisation de Byzance, 2016.

Worp, K.A. and C.A. Hope. "Dedication Inscriptions from the Main Temple." In *Dakhleh Oasis Project: Preliminary Reports on the 1994–1995 to 1998–1999 Field Seasons*, edited by C.A. Hope and G.E. Bowen, 323–331. Oxford: Oxbow Books, 2002.

8

Les *Acta Archelai* et ses principaux personnages : Notes historiques et lexicales

Madeleine Scopello

Résumé

Nous montrons dans la première partie de cette étude sur les *Acta Archelai*, composés par Hégémonius en grec vers 345 et conservés dans une version latine datant d'environ 365, que la ville de Carchara/Carrhes (l'ancienne Harran) où l'auteur situe une *disputatio* entre Mani et l'évêque de la ville Archélaüs n'est pas chrétienne comme il voudrait le faire croire. Carrhes est en effet restée fidèle pendant de longs siècles à la foi païenne et au culte de la divinité lunaire Sin, et le christianisme peina à s'y enraciner. Il n'y eut d'ailleurs pas d'évêque à Carrhes avant 361. Dans l'intrigue nouée par Hégémonius, Mani avait projeté de se rendre à Carrhes pour entrer en contact avec l'homme le plus puissant de la ville, Marcellus, présenté comme un chrétien exemplaire, dans l'espoir de gagner ensuite à la religion des Deux Principes la région tout entière. Notre analyse fait apparaître que l'illustre Marcellus n'est vraisemblablement pas un chrétien, mais un haut fonctionnaire provincial, sans doute païen. La vision christianisée de la ville ne correspond donc aucunement à sa réelle situation historique, religieuse et sociale : c'est une réinterprétation artificielle opérée par Hégémonius pour les besoins de sa controverse. Dans la seconde partie de ce travail nous analysons les caractères de trois principaux personnages des *Acta Archelai*, Marcellus, Archélaüs et Mani et leurs interactions à travers une étude lexicale qui met en évidence les traits de leurs caractères. Le langage d'Hégémonius est d'une extrême précision, chaque terme est choisi avec soin pour illustrer les thèmes et motifs qu'il entend développer. Cela transparaît à travers la traduction latine des *Acta Archelai*, effectuée par un traducteur expérimenté.

Les *Acta Archelai*, composés en grec vers 345[1] par un certain Hégémonius,[2] constituent la première réfutation chrétienne d'ampleur contre le mani-

---

[1] Des extraits de la rédaction grecque sont parvenus grâce à Épiphane de Salamine qui les utilisa dans son hérésie 66 du *Panarion* contre les manichéens, rédigée en 376. La première citation connue des *Acta Archelai* remonte à 348 et est faite par Cyrille de Jérusalem dans sa *Sixième catéchèse baptismale*.

[2] Cf. *Acta Archelai* LXVIII, § 5 : « *Ego Hegemonius scripsi disputationem istam exceptam ad des-*

chéisme. Intégralement conservés sous une version latine effectuée vers 365,[3] ils se présentent comme le compte rendu de deux *disputationes* entre Mani et l'évêque Archélaüs qui auraient eu lieu, la première dans la ville de Carchara (Carrhes), la seconde dans un village des environs.[4] La venue de Mani dans cette ville de Mésopotamie romaine avait été motivée par son vif désir d'entrer en contact avec son personnage le plus en vue, le *vir notus* Marcellus, présenté comme un fervent chrétien ; sa renommée, due essentiellement à ses actes de miséricorde lors d'une opération de rachat de captifs, était parvenue jusqu'à Mani qui se cachait à ce moment-là dans un *castellum*[5] situé sur le *limes* pour fuir la vengeance du roi perse[6] : s'il parvenait à convertir Marcellus à la doctrine des Deux Principes, la région tout entière l'aurait suivi. Mani décide d'écrire à

---

cribendum volentibus » ; cf. Héraclien de Chalcédoine cité par Photius, *Bibliothèque* 85. Hégémonius est par ailleurs inconnu. Voir Madeleine Scopello, « Hégémonius, les *Acta Archelai* et l'histoire de la controverse anti-manichéenne en Occident », dans Ronald E. Emmerick, Werner Sundermann, Peter Zieme éd., *Studia Manichaica. IV. Internationaler Kongress zum Manichäismus*, Berlin, 14-18 Juli 1997, Berlin, Akademie Verlag, 2000, p. 528-545 ; Ead., « Un témoin de la controverse religieuse entre chrétiens et manichéens aux frontières de l'Iran : les *Acta Archelai* », dans Cristelle Jullien éd., *Controverses des chrétiens dans l'Iran sassanide*, Studia Iranica, Cahier 36 (Chrétiens en terre d'Iran, vol. II), Paris, Association pour l'avancement des études iraniennes, 2008, p. 147-168. Johannes van Oort, « Hegemonius », dans *Religion Past and Present* (RPP), Brill On Line (print edition : Hans Dieter Betz et al. éd., 2000, réimprimé 2008).

3 Charles Beeson éd., Hegemonius, *Acta Archelai*, Die Griechischen Christlichen Schriftsteller 16, Leipzig, J.C. Hinrichs'sche Buchhandlung, 1906. Beeson utilise des manuscrits allant du VIe au XIIe siècle, dont le ms. Traube (Monacensis) retrouvé en 1903 : Ludwig Traube, « Acta Archelai. Vorbemerkung zu einer neuen Ausgabe », *Sitzungsberichte der Königlichen Bayerischen Akademie der Wissenschaften zu München*, Phil.-hist. Klasse, 1903, p. 533-549.

4 Le titre de la version latine ne mentionne toutefois que la première dispute : « Le véritable trésor ou dispute tenue dans la ville de Carchara en Mésopotamie par l'évêque Archélaüs contre Mani, en présence des juges Manippus, Aegialeüs, Claudius et Cléobulos ». Cela a été noté par Kevin Coyle, « A Clash of Portraits : Contrasts between Archelaus and Mani in the Acta Archelai », dans Id., *Manichaeism and its Legacy*, NHMS 69, Leiden, Brill, 2009, p. 37-47, voir p. 38.

5 Il s'agit du *Castellum Arabionis*, mentionné dans *Acta Archelai* VI, § 4 et LXV, § 7. Le *Castellum Arabionis* est attesté dans les papyrus de l'administration romaine retrouvés à Doura Europos, relatifs à la XXe *Cohors Palmyrenorum*, sous les abréviations *Castel Arab, Castel ar, castelo ara*. Voir Fabrizio Pennacchietti, « Il posto dei Cipri », *Mesopotamia* XXI (1986), p. 85-95, et Id., « Gli *Acta Archelai* e il viaggio di Mani nel Bêt Arbâyê », *Rivista di storia e letteratura religiosa* 24 (1988), p. 503-514.

6 Cf. *Acta Archelai* LXIV, § 8. Archélaüs, dans la vie (fictive) de Mani qu'Hégémonius raconte aux chapitres LXII-LXVI précise que le roi recherchait Mani, qui s'était enfui de prison, l'accusant d'avoir tué son fils par ses mauvais soins médicaux. Sur la construction hérésiologique de cette *Vita Mani*, voir Madeleine Scopello, « Vérités et contre-vérités dans les *Acta Archelai* », *Apocrypha* 6 (1995), p. 203-234.

Marcellus, sollicitant une invitation afin de lui expliquer de vive voix sa doctrine et confie la lettre à son disciple Turbon. Celui-ci parvient à Carchara après cinq jours d'un voyage périlleux. Hégémonius précise que ces évènements ont eu lieu sous le consulat de Probus (276-282),[7] donc quelques années avant la mort de Mani (276/277).

L'intérêt des *Acta Archelai* réside dans le fait qu'ils fournissent, outre un contenu doctrinal et exégétique de valeur – la confrontation entre l'évêque et Mani est fondée sur l'interprétation de passages bibliques – des éléments factuels d'ordre historique, géographique et social. Précisons d'abord la situation réelle de la ville de Carrhes à l'époque où sont censés se dérouler les événements mais aussi au moment où Hégémonius compose son ouvrage, ce qui nous conduit à remettre en cause la présentation des faits opérée par Hégémonius ainsi que les fonctions des deux principaux personnages de la ville, Marcellus et Archélaüs qui se partagent avec Mani la scène des *Acta Archelai*.

1 Carrhes la païenne

Le contexte culturel et religieux de la ville est notoirement païen depuis la plus haute antiquité.[8] Sise à une quarantaine de km d'Édesse, Carrhes,[9] l'ancienne Harran, fut un nœud commercial de première importance au croisement de pistes caravanières, dont la réputation était liée à la présence du temple consacré à la divinité lunaire Sin,[10] déjà signalée par une tablette de Mari. La ville qui fut successivement akkadienne, babylonienne et assyrienne, fut intégrée à l'empire perse au VIe siècle av. J.-C. Mentionnée dans la Bible comme lieu de séjour d'Abraham (Genèse 11, 31), Harran était célèbre comme lieu d'échanges

---

7   *Acta Archelai* XXXI, § 8.
8   Nous renvoyons à Madeleine Scopello, « Autour de Carrhes : quelques témoignages chrétiens entre souvenirs bibliques et *realia* », *Semitica et Classica* 12 (2019), p. 129-143. Nous résumons ici les principaux acquis de cette étude.
9   Winfrid Cramer, « Harran », dans *Reallexikon für Antike und Christentum*, tome 13, Stuttgart, Hiersemann Verlag, 1986, col. 634-665 ; Karlheinz Kessler, « Harran », dans *Brill's New Pauly*, volume 5, Leiden, Brill, 2004, col. 1152. Henri Leclercq, « Carrhes », dans *Dictionnaire d'Archéologie chrétienne et de Liturgie* (DACL), tome II, 2, Paris, Letouzey et Ané, 1910, col. 2189-2190. Seton Lloyd, William Brice, « Harran », *Anatolian Studies* 1 (1951), p. 77-112. David Storm Rice, « Medieval Harran. Studies on its Topography and Monuments, I », *Anatolian Studies* 2 (1952), p. 36-84.
10   L'impact du culte lunaire sur l'histoire religieuse de Carrhes, depuis les origines à l'Islam, a été étudié par Tamara M. Green, *The City of the Moon God. Religious Traditions of Harran*, RGRW 114, Leiden, Brill, 1992.

de marchandises précieuses (Ézéchiel 27, 23). On se limitera à rappeler qu'elle devint une colonie macédonienne sous Alexandre le Grand.

À l'époque romaine,[11] par sa situation frontalière et son importance stratégique et commerciale, la ville constitua un enjeu majeur entre Perses et Romains qui la conquirent à tour de rôle.[12] *Colonia Aurelia* sous Marc-Aurèle et *Colonia Antoniniana* sous Commode, Carrhes devint colonie romaine et *Metropolis Mesopotamiae* en 214. Aux IIIe et IVe siècles, qui nous intéressent plus particulièrement ici, la ville fut marquée par plusieurs événements. Caracalla y fut assassiné le 8 avril 217, lorsqu'il se rendait au temple de la divinité lunaire pour y consulter les oracles.[13] En 238, sous le règne de Maximinus, Ardashir Ier s'empara de Carrhes et de Nisibe, mais en 243 les Sassanides furent vaincus à Resaina par Gordien III qui reconquit la Mésopotamie et l'Osrhoène et prit possession de quelques villes dont celle de Carrhes. En 260 Shabur Ier assiégea la ville, et l'empereur Valérien fut capturé entre Carrhes et Édesse. Quatre ans après, le roi de Palmyre Odénath, allié des Romains, parvint à reconquérir Carrhes et Nisibe. En 297, la campagne de Galère contre les Sassanides fut marquée par une victoire de Narseh à Carrhes mais les événements évoluèrent en faveur des Romains qui rétablirent la frontière au-delà du Tigre. Malgré la détérioration progressive de la situation, la région resta aux mains de Rome jusqu'en 359, lorsque Shabur II pénétra en Mésopotamie ; Carrhes, mal protégée par ses remparts, fut évacuée par les Romains qui mirent le feu aux champs cultivés aux alentours et déplacèrent en lieu sûr ses habitants.[14] En 363 Julien lança une nouvelle campagne contre les Perses où l'empereur trouva la mort en juin de la même année. Ainsi que le note Ammien Marcellin,[15] Julien était parvenu à Carrhes à marches forcées, il s'y était arrêté quelques jours et avait sacrifié « selon le rite du pays » au temple de la Lune, « objet de culte dans ces régions » ; Ammien ne spécifie toutefois pas si ce temple se situait dans la ville

---

11   Sur la ville grecque et romaine, voir Arnold Hugh Martin Jones, *The Cities of the Eastern Provinces*, Oxford, Clarendon Press, 1937, p. 217-222 (2e édition revue par Michael Avi-Yonah, 1971).
12   Carrhes a particulièrement marqué l'imaginaire romain à cause de la défaite de l'armée de Crassus, tué par les Parthes dans les environs de la ville, en 53 av. J.-C. Cf. Ammien Marcellin, *Histoires* XXIII, 3, 1 : « *Carras, antiquum oppidum, Crassorum et Romani exercitus aerumnis insigne* ». Voir Giusto Traina, *Carrhes, 9 juin 53 avant J.-C. Anatomie d'une défaite*, Paris, Les Belles Lettres, 2011.
13   Cet assassinat fut commandité par son frère selon Spartianus, *Vie de Caracalla* 6, 3. Hérodien, *Histoire des empereurs romains* précise que ce temple était « assez éloigné de la ville pour que le trajet fût presque un voyage ».
14   Ammien Marcellin, *Histoires* XVIII, 7, 3.
15   Ammien Marcellin, *Histoires* XXIII, 3, 1.

même; dans le même contexte, il souligne l'importance de Carrhes comme nœud routier: « de là divergent deux routes royales qui mènent en Perse, celle de gauche par l'Adjabène et le Tigre, celle de droite par l'Assyrie et l'Euphrate » (*Histoires*, XXIII, 3, 1).

Même après la conversion constantinienne et encore pendant plusieurs siècles, Carrhes resta un foyer très actif de paganisme.[16] Cela est mis en évidence aussi bien par des auteurs grecs et romains qui attestent la vivacité du culte lunaire que par la littérature chrétienne de langue syriaque[17] et par des écrivains ecclésiastiques, notamment Théodoret de Cyr et Sozomène. Ces deux derniers auteurs ont mis en opposition spéculaire Carrhes la païenne et Édesse la chrétienne.[18]

En effet à Carrhes le christianisme s'installa difficilement et lentement. Le premier évêque de la ville fut le moine Barses[19] qui fut transféré au siège épiscopal d'Édesse en 361 sur ordre de Constance II.[20] Lui succédèrent Vitus, qui assista au concile de Constantinople en 381, et Protogène[21] mais, encore à la fin du IVe siècle, les chrétiens à Carrhes se comptaient sur les doigts de la main. Selon Théodoret,[22] Julien, lors de sa campagne contre les Perses, préféra faire une étape à Carrhes, cité fidèle à l'Ancienne foi, plutôt qu'à Édesse. Quant au culte lunaire pratiqué dans la ville, il se maintint même après la conquête de Carrhes, en 639, par l'armée musulmane conduite par 'Iyadh ibn Ghanam.[23]

---

16   Carrhes fut une ville refuge pour les philosophes néoplatoniciens: voir Michel Tardieu, *Les paysages reliques. Routes et haltes syriennes d'Isidore à Simplicius*, Louvain/Paris, Peeters, 1990.
17   Cf. par exemple, *Doctrine d'Addai* 50; Éphrem de Nisibe, *Hymnes pascales* 31-34; Isaac d'Antioche, *Homélie* XI.
18   Voir Hendrik Jan Willem Drijvers, *Cults and Beliefs in Edessa*, ÉPRO 82, Leiden, Brill, 1980, chapitre VII (« Edessan Religion, Paganism in the Roman Empire, and Early Christianity »), p. 175-196 et Id., « The Persistence of Pagan Cults and Practices in Christian Syria », dans Nina Garsoian, Thomas F. Mathews, Robert W. Thomson éd., *East of Byzantium: Syria and Armenia in the Formative Period*, Washington D.C., Dumbarton Oaks, 1982, p. 35-45. Voir aussi Judah Benzion Segal, *Edessa, the Blessed City*, Oxford, Clarendon Press, 1970.
19   Éphrem (*Carmina Nisibena* XXX, 8) appelle Carrhes « fille de Barses » pour signifier que celui-ci fut son premier évêque.
20   *Chronique d'Édesse* 24.
21   Pour la mention de Vitus et Protogène, cf. Sozomène, *Histoire ecclésiastique* VI, 33. Selon Théodoret de Cyr, *Histoire ecclésiastique* V, 4, 6, Eulogios installa Protogène comme évêque de Carrhes.
22   Théodoret de Cyr, *Histoire ecclésiastique* III, 26.
23   Il ne faut pas oublier la présence des Sabéens à Carrhes, attestée par l'historiographie musulmane: voir Jan Hjärpe, *Analyse critique des traditions arabes sur les Sabéens harraniens*, Uppsala, Skriv Service AB, 1972, et Michel Tardieu, « Ṣābiens coraniques et "ṣābiens" de Ḥarrān », *Journal Asiatique* 274 (1986), p. 1-44.

Compte tenu du contexte païen de Carrhes, il nous est permis de douter fortement de l'image christianisée de la ville que fournit Hégémonius et qui relève, selon nous, non pas de l'observation de la réalité historique – tant à celle du moment où il écrit son œuvre en grec, vers 354, que celle où il situe les événements (sous le consulat de Probus) – mais d'un gauchissement volontaire qui le porte à présenter Carrhes comme un foyer actif de christianisme. Hégémonius revisite la situation religieuse et sociale de la ville et revêt Carrhes la païenne d'habits chrétiens: il place, en effet, un évêque (Archélaüs), dans la ville et décrit l'homme qui tient dans ses mains les destinées de Carrhes (Marcellus), comme un fervent chrétien. Il faut donc que nous revisitions les deux personnages principaux des *Acta Archelai* qui interagissent avec Mani par un examen critique de leurs fonctions et de leurs rôles.

2   Marcellus, un haut fonctionnaire païen

Marcellus est un personnage clé dans les *Acta Archelai*, comme le montre tout d'abord l'*enkômium*[24] qui ouvre les *Acta Archelai* (I, § 1-3).[25] Bien que nous ayons déjà examiné la figure de Marcellus dans des travaux antérieurs,[26] dans la présente étude nous allons plus loin et apportons de nouveaux éléments. Hégémonius pare Marcellus de toutes les vertus chrétiennes et relate les actes de miséricorde qu'il accomplit à l'égard des survivants (environs 5300) d'un raid opéré dans la campagne environnante par les soldats de la garnison romaine de Carrhes contre un groupe de 7700 personnes.[27] Non seulement Marcellus paie

---

24   Voir Laurent Pernot, *La rhétorique de l'éloge dans le monde gréco-romain*, vol. 1-2, Paris, Institut d'Études Augustiniennes, 1995; Id., *La rhétorique dans l'Antiquité*, Paris, Librairie Générale Française, 2000. Voir aussi Georg A. Kennedy, *The Art of Rhetoric in the Roman World, 300 B.C.–A.D. 300*, Princeton, Princeton University Press, 1972.

25   Nous traitons de cet éloge dans notre commentaire à paraître des *Acta Archelai* et nous nous limitons ici à fournir notre traduction de ce passage (*Acta Archelai* I, § 2-3): « 2. Dans cette ville vivait un homme appelé Marcellus. Sa conduite, sa culture et sa naissance, ainsi que sa sagesse et la pureté de ses mœurs, l'avaient rendu fort célèbre. Il était également riche en biens et, par-dessus tout, il craignait Dieu avec une piété profonde, écoutant toujours avec révérence tout ce qui était dit au sujet du Christ: il n'y avait vraiment point de vertu qui manquât à cet homme. 3. C'est pourquoi sa cité tout entière le tenait en grande estime et lui, en retour, la gratifiait souvent de nombreuses libéralités: il donnait aux pauvres, il réconfortait les malheureux, il secourait les opprimés. Nous n'en dirons pas plus, de peur que nos maigres propos n'ôtent aux vertus de cet homme plutôt qu'ils ne les expriment comme il conviendrait. Venons-en donc à la tâche que nous nous sommes fixée. »

26   Nous renvoyons à la note 2.

27   *Acta Archelai* I, § 4: *qui ibi castra servabant*. L'épisode de la capture d'un groupe de 7700

une généreuse rançon pour racheter les captifs mais les héberge sur ses terres, les nourrit et leur prodigue des soins, leur fournissant même un *viaticum* pour regagner leur pays, une fois rétablis. C'est d'ailleurs le retentissement extraordinaire qu'eut cet épisode dans la région qui décida Mani, qui se trouvait dans une forteresse sur le *limes*, le *Castellum Arabionis*, à entrer en contact avec Marcellus.[28]

Mais Marcellus est-il vraiment chrétien comme l'affirme Hégémonius et ses actes de miséricorde relèvent-ils de la seule charité privée ? Nous ne le pensons pas. Des remarques éparses dans les premiers chapitres des *Acta Archelai* font apparaître que les tâches de Marcellus sont celles d'un fonctionnaire provincial de l'Empire ; or à l'époque où se déroulent les faits ces fonctionnaires sont païens, d'autant plus dans une ville fidèle au paganisme comme Carrhes, et il en va de même à l'époque où Hégémonius écrit sa *disputatio*.

Hégémonius mentionne les *largitiones* que Marcellus offrait périodiquement à la ville, tout en revêtant cela d'un langage chrétien.[29] Or les *largitiones* (distributions d'argent, de denrées alimentaires, organisation de spectacles ou de jeux) faisaient partie des obligations d'un haut fonctionnaire provincial. En outre, Hégémonius emploie le terme de *thesaurus* pour désigner la réserve où Marcellus puise l'argent pour payer la rançon des captifs : ce terme est technique et indique le dépôt où étaient gardées les *sacrae largitiones* dans les plus importantes villes provinciales.[30] Plus encore, il est dit que Marcellus avait ins-

---

personnes sorties hors les murs pour une prière collective afin d'obtenir la pluie pour leurs récoltes et de la tuerie de 1300 d'entre eux est narré avec abondance de détails (*Acta Archelai* I, § 4 – II, § 8).

28 *Acta Archelai* IV, §1; cf. aussi *ibid.*, III, § 5: « Le retentissement de cette action ajouta immensément aux autres actions charitables de Marcellus. À travers toute cette région, le bruit de la piété de Marcellus se répandit avec une telle ampleur que de gens en grand nombre provenant de différentes villes brûlaient du désir de voir et de connaître cet homme, surtout ceux qui n'avaient jamais eu auparavant à supporter l'indigence. »

29 *Acta Archelai* I, § 2 : *ipse (Marcellus) civitatem suam frequenter largitionibus remunerabatur, pauperibus tribuens, adflictos relevans, tribulatis auxilium ferens*.

30 Cf. Henry Thédenat, « Largitio », dans *Dictionnaire des antiquités grecques et romaines* (DAGR), tome 3/2, Paris, Hachette, 1904, col. 949-950. Arnold Hugh Martin Jones, *The Cities of the Eastern Roman Provinces, op. cit.*, p. 426-429. L'administration financière de l'Empire créa, au IVe siècle, un fonctionnaire nommé *comes sacrarum largitionum*, regroupant sur lui les fonctions du ramassage, puis de la distribution de l'argent : cf. *Notitia Dignitatum* et *Code de Justinien* 7, 62, 21 ; *Code théodosien* 1, 6, 132. Voir aussi Roland Delmaire, *Largesses sacrées et res privata. L'aerarium impérial et son administration du IVe au VIe siècle*, Collection de l'École française de Rome 121, Paris/Rome, De Boccard/L'Erma di Bretschneider, 1989.

tallé des relais dans la région. Nous avons montré dans des travaux publiés[31] que ces relais, désignés par Hégémonius avec une terminologie technique (*hospitia, diversoria, mansiones*),[32] sont des étapes le long du *cursus publicus*[33] et que leur installation à des distances fixées fait aussi partie des obligations d'un haut fonctionnaire provincial ou du gouverneur de la région. Nous ne pouvons toutefois pas aller jusqu'à envisager que Marcellus avait les fonctions d'un gouverneur provincial car son nom ne se retrouve pas parmi ceux des gouverneurs romains en Mésopotamie qui d'ailleurs ne résidaient pas à Carrhes. Néanmoins, son rôle dans l'établissement des relais ajoute une pièce significative à notre interprétation d'un Marcellus fonctionnaire publique. Hégémonius précise aussi que Marcellus avait doté ces relais de surveillants (*servatores hospitiorum*).[34] Cette information est exacte du point de vue administratif, en effet les relais du *cursus publicus* étaient mis sous la responsabilité de surveillants, eux-mêmes fonctionnaires de l'Empire, nommés par l'autorité publique qui avait installé les relais. C'est donc une indication supplémentaire des responsabilités officielles de Marcellus. Ces surveillants avaient l'obligation de vérifier l'identité des voyageurs avant de les accueillir en examinant leur laissez-passer officiel (*evectio*) pour savoir s'ils avaient le droit d'utiliser le *cursus publicus* : nous trouvons une allusion à cette vérification dans les *Acta*, lorsque les surveillants de l'*hospitium* où Turbon fait une halte lui demandent de déclarer son identité.[35] Ayant traité ailleurs dans le détail de l'organisation du *cursus publicus*, limitons-nous ici à préciser que, bien que les normes de son fonctionnement aient été complètement édictées dans le Code théodosien,[36] il était

---

31 Cf. Madeleine Scopello, « Autour de Carrhes : quelques témoignages chrétiens entre souvenirs bibliques et *realia* », *art. cit.*, notamment p. 141-142.
32 *Acta Archelai* IV, § 4-5.
33 Le terme *cursus velox*, est mentionné dans les *Acta Archelai* IV, 4 (*veloci etenim usus est cursu*). Il diffère du *cursus tabularius*, plus lent.
34 *Acta Archelai* IV, § 4.
35 *Acta Archelai* IV, § 4 : « (*Turbo*) *si quando enim ad vesperam velut peregrinans ad hospitium pervenisset, quae quodam hospitalissilus Marcellus instruxerat, cum a servatoribus hospitiorum interrogaretur unde et quis vel a quo missus esset, aiebat...*). À cause de son *ignotum nomen*, les surveillants chassent Turbon à coups de pied, sans même lui donner à boire (IV, § 5), l'ayant très probablement pris par un espion perse s'infiltrant en territoire romain. Turbon aurait péri s'il n'avait pas révélé qu'il se rendait chez Marcellus. Il nous paraît hautement improbable que Turbon ait pu emprunter le *cursus publicus*, destiné à des fonctionnaires de l'État et à des voyageurs haut placés ; néanmoins cela montre qu'Hégémonius connaissait bien le maillage routier de Mésopotamie.
36 *Code théodosien* 8, 5, 1. Voir Gustave Humbert, « *Cursus publicus* », dans *Dictionnaire des antiquités grecques et romaines, op. cit.*, tome 2, 1887, p. 1655. Hans-Christian Schneider, *Altstrassenforschung*, Darmstadt, Wissenschaftliche Buchgesellschaft, 1982. Pascal Stof-

déjà opérationnel au moins depuis l'époque de Pline l'Ancien[37] et la terminologie technique avait déjà été fixée. L'ensemble des informations que nous avons réunies au sujet de Marcellus le désignent comme un haut fonctionnaire en poste à Carrhes. Compte tenu du contexte historique et social de cette ville, tant à la fin du IIIe siècle qu'au moment où Hégémonius écrit, Marcellus n'est vraisemblablement pas un chrétien mais un païen. Nous estimons que l'auteur des *Acta Archelai* a christianisé, pour les besoins de sa réfutation contre Mani, le personnage de Marcellus, en le moulant sur un modèle de haut fonctionnaire de l'Empire.

3   Un évêque à Carrhes ?

Tout comme le personnage de Marcellus est une reconstruction d'Hégémonius qui ne résiste pas à la réalité historique, celui d'Archélaüs évêque de Carrhes est également problématique. Interrogeons-nous d'abord sur la réelle présence d'un évêque dans la ville au temps des événements décrits par Hégémonius. Rien n'est moins sûr. D'une part, les listes épiscopales ne mentionnent pas un évêque de Carrhes portant le nom d'Archélaüs[38] ; d'autre part, comme nous l'avons déjà rappelé, le premier évêque de la ville, le moine Barses, ne monta sur le siège épiscopal qu'en 361, donc une quinzaine d'années après la composition en grec des *Acta Archelai*.

3.1   *Le témoignage de la pèlerine Égérie*
Pour préciser la situation du christianisme à Carrhes, nous avons fait appel à un écrit datant d'une quarantaine d'années après la composition des *Acta Archelai* : il s'agit de l'*Itinerarium ad loca sancta* d'Égérie.[39] Dans son journal de

---

fel, *Über die Staatspost, die Ochsengespanne und die requirierten Ochsengespanne: Eine Darstellung des römischen Postwesens auf Grund der Gesetze des Codex Theodosianus und des Codex Iustinianus*, Bern, P. Lang, 1994. Voir également Denys Gorce, *Les voyages, l'hospitalité et le port des lettres dans le monde chrétien des IVe et Ve siècles*, Wépion sur Meuse/Paris, Monastère du Mont-Vierge/Librairie Auguste Picard, 1925.

37   Pline, *Histoire naturelle* VI, 96. 102 ; XII, 64-65.
38   Une liste des évêques de Carrhes est présentée par Raymond Janin, « Carrae », dans *Dictionnaire d'histoire et de géographie ecclésiastique* (*DHGE*), tome 11, Paris, Letouzey et Ané, 1949, col. 1123-1124.
39   Égérie, *Journal de voyage (Itinéraire)*, Introduction, texte critique, traduction, notes et cartes par Pierre Maraval, suivi par Valerius du Bierzo, *Lettre sur la Bse Égérie*, Introduction, texte et traduction par Manuel C. Díaz y Díaz, Sources chrétiennes 296, Paris, Cerf, 2017 (réimpression de la première édition revue et corrigée). Nous citons la traduction de Pierre Maraval.

voyage, cette moniale d'origine galicienne décrit avec précision et vivacité son pèlerinage aux lieux saints qui se déroula de 380 à 384 et la conduisit de Jérusalem à l'Égypte, à la Palestine et à la Mésopotamie. Égérie porte aussi une attention soutenue aux *realia*, ce qui fait de son journal, écrit au terme du voyage lorsqu'elle parvint à Constantinople, un témoignage historique très significatif.

Égérie se rend en Mésopotamie (*ad Mesopotamiam Syriae*) « après trois années pleines » depuis son arrivée à Jérusalem ; après trois jours passés à Édesse, elle arrive à Carrhes le 9 des calendes de mai (*Journal* 20, 5), ce qui correspond au 23 avril de l'année 384,[40] et y passe également trois jours. Elle désire visiter les lieux, aux environs de la ville, où séjourna Abraham, les ermitages des moines et le tombeau du martyre Elpidius (chapitres 20-21). Dès son arrivée, Égérie se rend, comme il est son habitude dans tous les lieux qu'elle visite, chez l'évêque de la ville[41] :

> Lorsque je suis arrivée là, à Charra, je suis allée aussitôt à l'église qui se trouve à l'intérieur de cette ville. J'ai vu aussi sur le champ l'évêque de ce lieu, un vrai saint, un homme de Dieu, lui aussi moine et confesseur, qui a daigné nous montrer là tous les lieux que nous désirions voir.
>
> *Journal* 20, 2

Égérie ne donne aucun détail sur cette église, mais décrit l'évêque comme un « moine et confesseur » ; bien qu'elle ne donne pas son nom, il doit s'agir de Protogène, évêque de Carrhes à partir de 381. À son sujet, Théodoret de Cyr avait rappelé les très grandes difficultés qu'il rencontra pour diffuser la foi chrétienne dans cette ville :

> Protogène fut mis dans un champ inculte, tout rempli d'épines, et où il y avait beaucoup à travailler. C'est ainsi que je parle de la ville de Carrhes, ou il y avait encore quantité de païens, et où il fut ordonné évêque. Cela n'arriva, comme je le viens de dire que depuis que la paix eut été rendue à l'Église.
>
> *Histoire ecclésiastique* IV, 18, 14

Pour ce qui est du titre d'évêque qu'utilise Égérie au sujet de celui de Carrhes, il est utile de rappeler la remarque que Sozomène fait au sujet de Barses et de

---

40   Discussion dans Pierre Maraval, *Égérie, Journal de voyage, op. cit.*, p. 31-32. Voir aussi Paul Devos, « La date du voyage d'Égérie », *Analecta Bollandiana* 85 (1967), p. 165-194.
41   Il en va de même à son arrivée à Séleucie d'Isaurie : « Arrivée là, je suis allée chez l'évêque, un véritable saint, un ancien moine » (*Journal* 23, 1).

l'évêque d'Édesse, Eulogios : « L'un comme l'autre furent ordonnés évêques, mais non pour une église particulière, car il s'agissait plutôt d'un titre honorifique qui leur avait été conféré à cause de la pureté de leur vie, et ils avaient été ordonnés dans leur propre monastère » (*Histoire ecclésiastique* VI, 34, 1). En effet, Égérie désigne l'évêque comme « *monachum et confessorem* » (*Journal* 20, 2) ; le terme *confessor*,[42] qui indique celui qui confesse le Christ dans la persécution ou qui est jeté en prison sans devenir martyr,[43] est attribué à des évêques qui ont eu un comportement irréprochable pendant les persécutions ou qui ont fermement défendu l'orthodoxie[44] : c'est le cas de Protogène qui avait été exilé en Égypte, à Antinoé, avec Eulogios[45] sur ordre de l'empereur pro-arien Valens (364-378). Quant au terme *monachus*, les évêques de Mésopotamie étaient souvent issus des monastères, nombreux dans la région. C'est sous le guide savant de l'évêque anonyme de Carrhes qu'Égérie et le groupe qui l'accompagne visitent les ermitages des environs (*Journal* 20, § 5-7 ; 21, § 3). Cet évêque, toutefois, ne devait avoir qu'une poignée de fidèles, comme le constate Égérie avec sa franchise habituelle :

> Dans cette ville, en dehors d'un petit nombre de clercs et de saints moines, s'il en est du moins qui résident en ville, je n'ai trouvé absolument aucun chrétien : ce sont tous des païens ! (*penitus nullum christianum inveni, sed totum gentes sunt*).
>
> *Journal* 20, § 8

La situation de Carrhes est donc, encore à la fin du IVe siècle, environ quarante-cinq ans après la rédaction grecque des *Acta Archelai*, bien différente par rapport à celle de la proche Édesse, fortement christianisée, qu'Égérie avait visitée auparavant (*Journal* 19, § 2-19).

Compte tenu de l'ensemble de ces informations, que ce soient celles fournies par Égérie, par Théodoret de Cyr ou par Sozomène, la présence d'un évêque à Carrhes à la fin du IIIe siècle est fortement douteuse tout comme à l'époque où Hégémonius écrivit les *Acta Archelai*. Nous pourrions, au mieux,

---

42   Voir Albert Blaise, *Dictionnaire latin-français des auteurs chrétiens*, Turnhout, Brepols, 1954, 195a pour d'autres références.
43   Cf. Tertullien, *De corona* 11 et 2.
44   Par exemple, Jérôme, *Épître* 15, 2 : *Aegyptios confessores*.
45   Théodoret de Cyr, *Histoire ecclésiastique* V, 4 : « Eulogios (évêque d'Édesse) avait généreusement défendu la doctrine des Apôtres, et avait été relégué avec Protogène dans la ville d'Antinoüs. Barsès ce prélat si admirable était mort. Il (Eulogios) sacra encore Protogène compagnon des combats d'Eulogios, évêque de Carrhes, et le laissa dans cette ville comme

envisager qu'Archélaüs était un évêque sans siège épiscopal, ou un moine à la tête d'un petit groupe de fidèles.

Pour quelle raison Hégémonius, qui avait certainement une bonne connaissance de la géographie de la région et de Carrhes, ville de garnison, a-t-il tracé une telle image de la ville? Il a peut-être voulu faire de Carrhes une autre Édesse, en lui donnant des couleurs chrétiennes et allant jusqu'à lui attribuer un évêque pour y placer une controverse entre celui-ci et Mani, dans le cadre des conflits religieux qui étaient fréquents en Mésopotamie.

Dans sa reconstruction christianisée de la ville, Hégémonius se trahit néanmoins de temps à autre: la *disputatio* est présidée par quatre juges *religione gentiles*. Mentionnés dans le titre conservé de la version latine des *Acta Archelai*, ce qui est déjà significatif, ils sont issus de l'élite païenne de Carrhes et c'est bien cette élite qui remplit l'immense demeure de Marcellus pour assister à la joute d'Archélaüs et Mani:

> XIV, § 5. Cependant, Marcellus, dans sa grande sagesse, avait écarté toute volonté de querelle et, ayant invité les notables de la ville, il avait pris la décision d'entendre aussi bien l'un que l'autre. Parmi ces notables, il choisit des juges, de religion païenne, au nombre de quatre. Voici leurs noms: Manippus, très savant dans l'art de la grammaire et de l'enseignement rhétorique; Aegialeüs, très illustre professeur de médecine et fort érudit dans les lettres; Claudius et Cléobulos, deux frères, éminents orateurs. 6. Une assemblée imposante fut donc réunie, si bien que la maison de Marcellus, pourtant immense, était remplie par tous ceux que l'on avait fait venir pour écouter le débat.

Où sont donc les chrétiens?

4 Les portraits des protagonistes des *Acta Archelai* brossés par Hégémonius

4.1 *Mani, ses projets, sa lettre à Marcellus*

Venons-en maintenant à considérer le portrait psychologique de Mani tel qu'il est brossé par Hégémonius. Dès le début du traité on constate un parti pris d'Hégémonius à l'égard du prophète de Babylone; l'hérésiologue s'emploie à

---

un sage médecin, pour guérir les maladies spirituelles de ses habitants». Cf. Sozomène, *Histoire ecclésiastique* VI, 33.

insinuer le doute dans le lecteur pour le discréditer en le présentant habilement sous un mauvais jour.[46]

Au fil du texte, le portrait psychologique de Mani, soutenu par un portrait vestimentaire, s'enrichit de nouvelles touches et d'une série de thèmes et motifs jusqu'à la magistrale pièce finale dans laquelle Hégémonius fournit un compte rendu mi réel, mi imaginaire de la vie de Mani où s'entrecroisent, ainsi que nous l'avions montré dans un article publié, vérités et contre-vérités.[47] Nous allons examiner, dans la présente étude, un certain nombre de passages des *Acta Archelai* et les commenter en nous appuyant sur notre traduction personnelle, accompagnée de notes de commentaire, destinée au *Corpus Fontium Manichaeorum*.[48] Dans cette traduction nous avons prêté une attention particulière au lexique déployé dans les *Acta Archelai*. Certes, tels qu'ils nous sont parvenus, les *Acta Archelai* sont une traduction latine d'un texte grec qui n'a pas été conservé à l'exception de quelques extraits utilisés par Épiphane de Salamine dans la notice 66 contre les manichéens du *Panarion*,[49] rédigée en 376. Ainsi, notre analyse lexicale ne peut se fonder que sur la traduction latine des *Acta Archelai* que nous considérons comme une œuvre à part entière[50] et qui, en tant que telle, mérite d'être l'objet d'une telle recherche. Nous avons pu constater que celui qui a transposé du grec au latin les *Acta Archelai* était un traducteur expérimenté, particulièrement cultivé, qui a souvent eu recours à un langage nourri d'échos de la littérature gréco-latine, notamment dans les parties descriptives de l'œuvre, et a sans doute su rendre dans sa traduction la technicité de l'original grec.

Mais venons-en aux passages que nous allons examiner et dont l'on fournira un commentaire accompagné de notations lexicales.

---

46   Notre regretté collègue et ami Kevin Coyle a consacré une étude importante au portrait de Mani dans les *Acta Archelai*, et une autre à ceux d'Archélaüs et Mani. Nous lui rendons hommage avec notre étude. Voir Kevin Coyle, « Hesitant and Ignorant : The Portrayal of Mani in the *Acts of Archelaus* », dans Id., *Manichaeism and its Legacy, op. cit.*, p. 25-36, et l'article que nous avons déjà mentionné, « A Clash of Portraits : Contrasts between Archelaus and Mani in the *Acta Archelai* », *art. cit.*

47   Madeleine Scopello, « Vérités et contre-vérités dans les *Acta Archelai* », *art. cit.*

48   Dans la *Series Latina*, sous la direction de Johannes van Oort. Une nouvelle traduction anglaise a été publié par Marc Vermes, *Acta Archelai*, Manichaean Studies IV, Louvain, Brepols, 2001.

49   Voir Calogero Riggi, *Epifanio contro Mani, Revisione critica, traduzione italiana e commento storico del Panarion di Epifanio Haer. LXVI*, Rome, Pontificium Institutum Altioris Latinitatis, 1967.

50   Parmi les études théoriques sur la traduction, on rappellera l'essai de Walter Benjamin, *La tâche du traducteur*, traduction française, Paris, Payot, 2011. Voir aussi Umberto Eco, *Dire quasi la stessa cosa : esperienze di traduzione*, Milan, Bompiani, 2003.

4.2 Le plan de Mani pour rencontrer Marcellus (Acta Archelai IV, § 1-3)

Les tout premiers éléments du portrait psychologique de Mani apparaissent lorsque Hégémonius prête à Mani l'intention de rentrer en contact avec Marcellus :

> IV, § 1. Comme on parlait donc très souvent de Marcellus en divers lieux, l'admiration qui lui était portée s'étendit au-delà même du fleuve Stranga, dans le pays des Perses où demeurait un certain Mani. Celui-ci, ayant eu vent de la réputation de cet homme hors du commun, remuait nombre de pensées dans son esprit (*plurimum ipse secum volvebat*) sur le moyen de l'enserrer dans les filets de sa doctrine (*quemadmodum eum doctrinae suae posset laqueis inretire*), espérant que Marcellus puisse devenir un défenseur de ses opinions. 2. Mani, en effet, présumait qu'il pourrait s'emparer de la province tout entière (*praesumebat enim universam se posse occupare provinciam*), s'il parvenait d'abord à s'assujettir un tel homme (*si prius talem virum sibimet subdere potuisset*).

Dans ces lignes Hégémonius présente Mani en train d'échafauder un plan pour diffuser sa doctrine en Mésopotamie, en se servant de Marcellus : plan stratégique, qui découle d'une réflexion intense et retorse (*plurimum ipse secum volvebat*) de la part de Mani pour réussir à enserrer Marcellus dans les filets de sa doctrine (*quemadmodum eum doctrinae suae posset laqueis inretire*). Hégémonius mobilise ici le champ sémantique de la ruse et introduit l'image des filets de chasse ou de pêche (*laquei*) pour mettre en évidence les astuces de Mani. Examinons le lexique de ce passage.

La première expression qui attire notre attention est «*secum volvere*» (IV, §1), qui, outre sa signification de «méditer»,[51] signifie également «rouler dans son esprit, remuer des pensées dans son cœur». Dans ce second sens, on retrouve cette expression chez Salluste, dans le *De coniuratione Catilinae* 32, 1 (*Ibi multa ipse secum volvens*),[52] dans une dense atmosphère de complot qu'indiquent plusieurs termes, et dans le *De bello jugurthino* 113,1 (*Haec Maurus secum ipse diu volvens*),[53] dans un contexte de préparation d'une opération militaire.

La deuxième formule qui mérite un commentaire est «*quemadmodum eum doctrinae suae posset laqueis inretire*» (IV, §1). Hégémonius se sert ici d'une

---

51 Sénèque, *Lettre à Lucilius* 24,15. Des expressions similaires se retrouvent également chez Tacite et chez bien d'autres auteurs classiques.
52 Salluste, *De coniuratione Catilinae* 32, 1-2.
53 Salluste, *De bello jugurthino* 113, 1.

image fondée sur une observation du réel – celle des pièges, des lacets et des traquenards posés par les chasseurs ou les pêcheurs – qui, dans son sens métaphorique, a eu un certain succès à la fois dans la littérature grecque et romaine, les *biblica*, les manuscrits esséniens, la patristique et aussi dans la gnose et le manichéisme,[54] pour ne citer que quelques domaines. Le latin *laqueus* traduit généralement le grec παγίς. Dérivé de πήγνυμι dont la signification originelle est « tout ce qui enserre, qui retient ou qui fixe solidement », il désigne le lacet, les rets ou le filet.[55] La métaphore des filets qu'utilise Hégémonius lui a été vraisemblablement inspirée par la Première Épître à Timothée 3, 7 (παγίδα τοῦ διαβόλου), dans un contexte concernant les responsables de l'Église, ou par la Deuxième Épître à Timothée 2, 26 (ἐκ τῆς τοῦ διαβόλου παγίδος)[56], dans une mise en garde contre l'empiété, où le terme « filet » est associé au diable – une expression probablement issue de celle des « filets de Bélial » attestée dans la littérature essénienne, notamment dans les Hymnes.[57] Même si Hégémonius n'établit pas ici directement le lien entre Mani et le Malin, il le fera ultérieurement dans sa réfutation, au chapitre XL,[58] proclamant que Satan est le père de Mani, une filiation usuelle concernant ceux qu'on considérait hérétiques.

---

54   Voir Madeleine Scopello, « Pièges et filets dans les écrits gnostiques de Nag Hammadi et la littérature manichéenne du Fayoum », dans Aram Mardirossian, Agnès Ouzounian, Constantin Zuckerman éd., *Mélanges en l'honneur de Jean-Pierre Mahé*, « Travaux et mémoires » 18, Paris, ACHCByz, 2014, p. 573-594. Dans cet article nous avons fourni un aperçu des différentes littératures ayant prêté à l'image des filets une attention particulière, avant d'examiner de plus près les domaines de la gnose et du manichéisme.

55   Voir Johannes Schneider, « παγίς », dans Gerhard Kittel, Gerhard Friedrich éd., *Theologisches Wörterbuch zum Neuen Testament* (traduction italienne : Gerhard Kittel, Gerhard Friedrich éd., *Grande lessico del Nuovo Testamento*, a cura di Felice Montagnini, Giuseppe Scarpat, Omero Soffritti, Bologna, Paideia, 1974, vol. IX, col. 97-103). Henri Lesêtre, « Filet », dans Fulcran Vigouroux éd., *Dictionnaire de la Bible*, tome II, Paris, Letouzey et Ané, 1899, col. 2245-2249.

56   On trouve également le terme παγίς dans l'Épître aux Romains 11, 9, dans un contexte différent. Dans tous ces exemples, ce terme a une valeur métaphorique ; sa seule autre utilisation dans le Nouveau Testament, mais au sens concret, se trouve dans Luc 21, 35.

57   Voir Madeleine Scopello, « Pièges et filets dans les écrits gnostiques de Nag Hammadi et la littérature manichéenne du Fayoum », *art. cit.*, p. 593-595 pour les références esséniennes. Concernant Augustine et par exemple *l'Epistula fundamenti* de Mani, voir Johannes van Oort, « Augustine's Criticism of Manichaeism. The Case of *Confessiones* 3,10 and Its Implications », dans Johannes van Oort, *Mani and Augustine: Collected Essays on Mani, Manichaeism and Augustine*, NHMS 97, Leiden, Brill, 2020, p. 245-262, notamment p. 253. Et comparer également son vaste « Index of Terms and Concepts », s.v. 'snare(s)'.

58   Acta Archelai XL (XXXVI) « Même si tu accomplis des signes et des prodiges, même si tu ressuscites les morts, même si tu nous amènes Paul en personne, tu es maudit, Satan ! (...) 2. Tu es le vase de l'Antichrist, non pas un vase de prix, mais un vase abject et hon-

En poursuivant l'analyse de ce passage on notera qu'au § 2 du chapitre IV le registre change et assume une coloration militaire dans l'expression (Mani) «*praesumebat enim universam se posse occupare provinciam*». Le verbe *occupare* («se rendre maître de; prendre une possession exclusive de») est employé pour désigner l'occupation *manu militari* d'une ville.[59] Ce lexique militaire se poursuit avec la formule «*si prius talem virum sibimet subdere potuisset*», *subdere* («soumettre, assujettir à») étant utilisé dans les mêmes contextes.

Penchons-nous maintenant sur la suite du § 2 et le § 3 de ce même chapitre IV:

> IV, § 2. L'esprit inquiet, il hésitait entre deux partis (*in quo duplici cogitatione animus aestuabat*): valait-il mieux se rendre personnellement chez Marcellus ou essayer de l'atteindre, dans un premier temps, par lettre (*utrumnam ipse ad eum pergeret an litteris eum primo temptaret adoriri*)? Il craignait en effet qu'une démarche intempestive et précipitée (*ne improviso et subito ingressu*) pût lui causer quelque tort. 3. Finalement, il adopta la solution la plus astucieuse (*ad ultimum versutioribus consiliis parens*) et décida d'écrire. Il fit venir un de ses disciples, un dénommé ⟨Adda⟩ Turbon qui avait été instruit par Adda; lui ayant remis la lettre, il lui ordonna de se mettre en route et de la porter à Marcellus.

Hégémonius décrit ici l'hésitation de Mani sur les méthodes à adopter pour entrer en contact avec Marcellus: fallait-il se rendre directement sur place ou plutôt lui écrire? Le vocabulaire du passage rend tout d'abord l'atmosphère d'un Mani échafaudant le meilleur plan dans son repaire sur le *limes* par l'expression *in quo duplici cogitatione*. L'adjectif *duplex* peut signifier simplement «deux» mais au sens figuré il exprime l'idée de duplicité. Horace l'utilise pour mettre en exergue la ruse et la fourberie bien connues d'Ulysse[60] mais l'usage concerne aussi le langage amoureux de la duplicité de l'amante.[61] Quant au verbe *aestuare* – qui comporte une idée d'excès[62] –, il faut en rap-

---

teux que l'Antichrist, tel un barbare ou un tyran, envoya d'abord en reconnaissance (...) 4. (...) Qui es-tu donc, toi, qui n'as même pas obtenu au sort, de Satan ton père, un rang convenable? (...) 8. Faut-il, peut-être, que tu te multiplies comme l'ivraie, jusqu'à ce que ton puissant père ne vienne en personne, ressuscitant les morts, poursuivant quasiment jusqu'à la géhenne tous ceux qui auront refusé de se conformer à sa volonté, lui qui en effraye tant par ce superbe mépris dont il se pare?».

59 Cf. par exemple, Tite Live, *Ab urbe condita* 26, 7.
60 Horace, *Odes* 1, 6, 7.
61 Ovide, *Amores* 1, 12, 27: «*Vos ego sensi duplices*».
62 Voir Alfred Ernout, Antoine Meillet, *Dictionnaire étymologique de la langue latine*, Paris, Paris, Klinsieck, 4ᵉ édition, 2001, 13a.

peler les deux significations, d'une part «s'agiter», «bouillonner», d'autre part «être brûlant»; l'une et l'autre s'appliquent au feu et à son effervescence mais aussi aux flots de la mer. Au sens figuré, *aestuare* exprime le fait de bouillonner sous l'emprise d'une passion. On retrouvera ce verbe ultérieurement, concernant non pas Mani mais Archélaüs. Mani craint les conséquences d'une démarche intempestive et précipitée (*ne improviso et subito ingressu*): l'astuce s'accompagne de la prudence avisée; Mani est décrit aux couleurs d'un personnage retors dont l'archétype littéraire est le héros d'Ithaque.

Au §3 est à nouveau mobilisé le lexique de la ruse et de l'astuce – déjà rendu par la *duplici cogitatione* de Mani, et auparavant, au §1, par le motif du *laqueus* – dans l'expression «*ad ultimus versutioribus consiliis parens, scribere decrevit*». Le terme *versutia* rêvet la signification de ruse, fourberie, malice ou artifice,[63] et a une palette de synonymes dont les principaux sont *astutia, calliditas, ars, dolus*. Quant à l'adjectif *versutus*, (synonymes: *callidus, subdulus, dolosus, fallax*), il indique celui «qui sait se retourner, qui est fécond en expédients». Un excellent exemple sur la signification de *versutus*, éclairé par ses synonymes, est fourni par Cicéron dans le *De natura deorum* 3, 10, 25[64]: «*Et Chrysippus tibi acute dicere uidebatur, homo sine dubio uersutus et callidus – uersutos eos appello, quorum celeriter mens uersatur, callidos autem, quorum tamquam manus opere, sic animus usu concalluit*». L'adjectif *versutus* est en outre employé en des contextes militaires où cette disposition de l'esprit est fondamentale pour piéger l'adversaire; on peut retenir à cet égard un passage du *Brutus* 178 de Cicéron: «*in capiendo adversario versutus*» (habile à prendre l'adversaire au dépourvu), ou encore un texte de Tite Live, dans le *Ab urbe condita* XLII, 42, 47, 7. Le choix de l'adjectif *versutus* dans ce passage des *Acta Archelai* est particulièrement adapté pour cerner la démarche de Mani qui échafaude ses plans en vrai tacticien. Il est enfin à noter que le terme *versutia* a eu une certaine fortune dans la patristique qui l'a utilisé pour cerner la *versutia haereticorum*.[65] Quant à l'équivalent grec de *versutus*, il correspond à εὐτράπηλος qui, outre le sens de «versatile»,[66] possède celui de «sachant se retourner, fourbe».[67] Une fois la décision prise d'écrire à Marcellus, Mani opte pour la prudence et confie sa lettre à son disciple Turbon qui entreprend le voyage vers Carrhes et l'apporte à Marcellus.

---

63 Voir le lemme «*Versutus/versutia*» dans Alfred Ernout, Antoine Meillet, *Dictionnaire étymologique de la langue latine, op. cit.*, 725b–726a.
64 Cicéron emploie aussi le superlatif *versutissimus* dans le *De officiis* 1, 109.
65 Tertullien, *De resurrectione* 63.
66 Élien, *Histoires variées* 5, 13.
67 Pindare, *Pythiques* 1, 92.

4.3 La lettre de Mani à Marcellus (V, §1-6)

La lettre écrite par Mani dont on apprend le contenu au moment où Marcellus la reçoit et la lit, est un biais indirect pour mettre une nouvelle fois en évidence le caractère de Mani dans l'optique du thème de la ruse. Nous n'examinerons pas dans le détail cette lettre, qui a fait l'objet d'une étude importante de Iain Gardner.[68] Rappelons néanmoins les différents points de sa doctrine qu'aborde Mani: les Deux Principes; la nécessité de ne pas mélanger les contraires; la parabole de l'arbre; la contestation de l'incarnation du Christ dans le ventre d'une femme, le tout étayé par l'interprétation de quelques citations néotestamentaires. Quant à l'ouverture de la lettre, elle est très proche de celle de l'*Épître du fondement* de Mani citée par Augustin dans le *Contra Epistulam fundamenti*, ce qui montre qu'Hégémonius avait dû se servir d'un document manichéen de première main qu'il avait inséré dans sa narration. Nous nous limiterons ici à quelques observations concernant la formule qui conclut la lettre (*Acta Archelai* V, §6): «Je ne tends de pièges à personne (*non enim laqueum alicui inicio*) comme le font la plupart des insensés» où l'on reconnaîtra une citation de la Première Épître aux Corinthiens 7, 35 («Je dis cela dans votre propre intérêt, ce n'est pas pour vous prendre au piège»)[69]; cette formule fait pendant à celle que Mani avait écrit au début de sa missive: «*Manichaeus apostolus Iesu Christi (...) et dextera lucis conservet te a praesenti saeculo malo et a ruinis eius et laqueis maligni. Amen*» (V, §1).[70] Si le traducteur latin des *Acta Archelai* a conservé le terme *laqueus* aux deux endroits, on observera qu'en revanche, dans le texte grec transmis par le *Panarion* le terme attesté dans l'ouverture de la lettre est παγίς (66, 6, 1)[71] tandis que dans la formule conclusive (66, 6, 9) il y a le terme βρόχος, tout comme dans la lettre paulinienne; ce terme est d'ailleurs un hapax dans le Nouveau Testament.

5 Les traits de caractère de Marcellus et d'Archélaüs

Après l'analyse de ces premiers éléments du caractère de Mani, que l'on reprendra en suivant l'ordre des chapitres des *Acta Archelai*, comparons main-

---

68   Iain Gardner, «Mani's Letter to Marcellus: Fact and Fiction in the *Acta Archelai* Revisited», dans Jason BeDuhn, Paul Mirecki éd., *The Christian Encounter with Manichaeism in the Acts of Archelaus*, NHMS 61, Leiden, Brill, 2007, p. 33-48.
69   Épitre aux Corinthiens 7, 35: οὐχ ἵνα βρόχον ὑμῖν ἐπιβάλω.
70   *Acta Archelai* V, §6: «*non enim laqueum alicui inicio*»; Épiphane, *Panarion* 66, 6, 9: οὐδὲ γὰρ βρόχον τινὶ ἐπιβάλλω.
71   Καὶ παγίδων τοῦ πονηροῦ.

tenant les traits de caractère de Marcellus et d'Archélaüs tels qu'on peut les préciser en examinant les quelques épisodes où ils apparaissent ensemble : le rachat des captifs ; la réception de la lettre de Mani ; leurs réactions à l'exposé sur la doctrine de Mani fait par Turbon, et ensuite au moment de l'arrivée de Mani à Carrhes. Ces traits de caractère ne vont pas se démentir dans la suite de l'œuvre. Archélaüs et Marcellus ont des caractères opposés : l'un est passionnel, l'autre est rationnel ; l'un ne sait pas comment réagir lors du rachat des captifs, l'autre trouve immédiatement une solution ; l'un ne veut pas entendre parler de Mani, l'autre décide de le faire venir à Carrhes : en effet, Marcellus préfère organiser une confrontation publique entre Mani et Archélaüs plutôt que laisser ce dernier défier Mani dans un face-à-face.

5.1 L'épisode du rachat des captifs (Acta Archelai I, § 4-6)

Ce passage, qui fait suite à l'*enkômium* de Marcellus dans les toutes premières lignes des *Acta Archelai*, offre une bonne description des caractères d'Archélaüs et de Marcellus, en les mettant en net contraste :

> I, § 4. Un jour, une foule de sept-mille sept-cents captifs fut présentée à l'évêque Archélaüs par les soldats qui défendaient cette place. Celui-ci fut saisi d'une grande inquiétude (*non mediocris eum sollicitudo constrinxerat*), car les soldats réclamaient de l'or pour le rachat des prisonniers. Incapable de cacher ses sentiments (*quique cum dissimulare non posset*), l'évêque était en proie à une violente agitation, en raison de sa piété et de sa crainte de Dieu (*pro religione et timore dei vehementer aestuabat*). Pour finir, il se rendit en toute hâte chez Marcellus (*et tandem a Marcellum properans*) pour lui soumettre l'affaire.

Devant la demande de rançon faite par les soldats, Archélaüs est saisi d'une grande inquiétude (*sollicitudo*) : ce terme se charge ici d'une connotation biblique : la Vulgate l'utilise dans II Macchabées 15, 18-19 : « *erat enim pro uxoribus et filiis itemque pro fratribus et cognatis minor sollicitudo* (LXX : φόβος) *maximus vero et primus pro sanctitate timor erat templi sed et eos qui in civitati erant non minima sollicitudo* (LXX : ἀγώνια) *habebat pro his qui congressi erant* ». Dans les Actes des Apôtres 24, 25, en revanche, l'inquiétude que saisit le gouverneur Felix est rendue en grec par ἐμφόβος que la Vulgate traduit par *timefactus*.[72] On retrouve le terme *sollicitudo* chez Cyprien dans l'*Epître* 57, 5 et dans l'*Epistula ad*

---

[72] Pour *timefactus* en latin classique, voir Lucrèce, *De rerum natura* 2,44 ; Cicéron, *De officiis* 2,24.

catholicos 20, 55 d'Augustin (*propter christianam sollicitudinem*). Chez Cassien, *sollicitudo* est un quasi synonyme de *cura* : *tanta sollicitudine curaque* (*Institutions cénobitiques* 4, 19, 3). On notera qu'à la fin de l'exposé de Turbon (*Acta Archelai* XIV, 1), il est question de la *cura pro populo* qu'Archélaüs, tel un berger pour ses brebis devant les traquenards des loups, éprouve pour sa communauté qui pourrait être séduite par la doctrine de Mani. On reviendra sur ce passage ultérieurement.

Archélaüs est aussi « incapable de cacher ses sentiments (*quique cum dissimulare non posset*) ». Le terme *dissimulare*[73] n'a pas ici la valeur péjorative de cacher ou de masquer volontairement sa pensée ou ses intentions véritables, mais indique simplement le fait de ne pas laisser paraître ce que l'on pense, ce que l'on éprouve. Or l'incapacité de cacher ses émotions n'est pas une qualité dans le monde gréco-romain, mais un aveu de faiblesse ; on ne rappellera qu'un exemple tiré de la *Lettre à Atticus* de Cicéron V, 1, 4 : « je souffris, ne laissant rien paraître de ma peine » (*dissimulare dolens*),[74] où l'on décèle une influence stoïcienne.

La description des émotions d'Archélaüs procède en crescendo : « l'évêque était en proie à une violente agitation (*vehementer aestuabat*), en raison de sa piété et de sa crainte de Dieu (*pro religione et timore dei*). Ayant déjà fourni quelques notes sur la signification d'*aestuare* dans notre analyse du passage des *Acta Archelai* IV, § 2, on se contentera d'ajouter que le substantif *aestus* possède également un sens moral de « bouillonnement de l'âme, trouble, fureur »,[75] et qu'il est utilisé pour indiquer le bouillonnement des passions ou l'agitation violente : on peut rappeler un passage de Virgile, *Énéide*, Chant 8, 19 : «*quae Laomedontius heros cuncta videns, magno curarum fluctuat aestu* (le héros, né de Laomédon, hésite, plongé dans un océan de soucis) » – *cura* et *sollicitudo* recouvrent la même idée – ou encore un extrait de Salluste, *Jugurtha* 93, 2 : «*quae cum multos dies noctesque aestum agitaret* (comme il remuait ses pensées dans l'agitation) ». Par ailleurs et dans un autre contexte, une expression de Cassien est particulièrement intéressante à cet égard car on y trouve, comme dans ce passage des *Acta Archelai*, le substantif *sollicitudo* et le verbe *aestuare* : *inter has sollicitudines, graviter aestuabat* » (*Institutions cénobitiques* 8, 3).

---

73 Cf. Felix Gaffiot, *Dictionnaire Latin-Français*, Paris, Hachette, 1934, 543c–544a.
74 Cicéron, *Lettre à Atticus* V, 1, 4 : *Magnum itaque me ipsum commoverat, sic absurde et aspere verbis vultusque responderat* (« mon émotion fut extrême devant une réponse aussi aigre et déplacée. Le ton et la physionomie étaient à l'avenant. Néanmoins, je ne laissai rien paraître de ma peine »).
75 Voir Alfred Ernout, Antoine Meillet, *Dictionnaire étymologique de la langue latine, op. cit.*, 13a.

C'est cette violente agitation qui pousse Archélaüs à se rendre en toute hâte (*properans*) chez Marcellus pour lui soumettre l'affaire. Archélaüs est donc incapable de résoudre personnellement la situation difficile qu'est le paiement d'une rançon de captifs ; il perd son sang-froid, à la différence d'autres évêques, cités dans la littérature patristique, qui mènent adroitement la négociation avec les demandeurs de rançon, organisent une collecte ou vendent les ustensiles précieux de leur église.[76] Mais y-avait-il une église à Carrhes ? S'il n'y avait, dans le meilleur des cas, qu'une poignée de chrétiens, les moyens financiers devaient être insuffisants pour organiser une collecte. Force est de constater que le récit d'Hégémonius contient des éléments anachroniques.

Examinons maintenant la réaction de Marcellus lorsque l'évêque arrive chez lui pour lui faire part de la demande de rançon par les soldats de la garnison.

> I, § 5. Or, dès que le très pieux Marcellus eut entendu cela, il rentre dans sa maison sans perdre un seul instant (*nihil omnino moratus, ingreditur domum*) pour y préparer la rançon des captifs, en réunissant la somme réclamée par ceux qui les avaient faits prisonniers, si grande qu'elle pût être. Aussitôt (*et continuo*), ayant ouvert les réserves où il conservait l'argent, il répartit parmi les soldats le prix de sa piété, sans calcul ni distinction, de sorte qu'on eût dit un don plutôt qu'une rançon.

La rapidité de décision et l'efficacité de Marcellus dans une situation d'émergence comme celle d'un rachat de captifs sont très bien rendues dans la traduction latine par l'expression *nihil moratus* et, dans la phrase successive, par l'adverbe *continuo*. Sa gestion de cette crise, habituelle en zone de frontière, est décisive. Il ouvre ses réserves d'argent (*thesauri*) et distribue la rançon parmi les soldats. Marcellus a d'ailleurs l'habitude des actions concrètes, du fait de sa charge publique : nous avons déjà mentionné, dans la première partie de cette étude, l'installation de relais le long du *cursus publicus* et *les liberalitates* qu'il effectue pour sa cité.

---

76 Voir, pour des épisodes de rançons gérés par des évêques, Samuel N.C. Lieu « Fact and Fiction in the Acta Archelai », dans Peter Bryder éd., *Manichaean Studies, Proceedings of the First International Conference on Manichaeism, August 5-9, 1987*, Lund Studies in African and Asian Religions, vol. I, Lund, Plus Ultra, 1988, p. 69-88, spécialement p. 80-81 ; voir aussi Id., « Captives, Refugees and Exiles. A Study of Cross-Frontier Civilian Movements and Contacts between Rome and Persia from Valerian to Jovian », dans Philip Freeman, David Kennedy éd., *The Defence of the Roman and Byzantine East*, vol. 2, BAR International Series 297, Oxford, BAR, 1986, p. 475-508.

5.2 La réception de la lettre de Mani (Acta Archelai v, § 1-6)

Comparons maintenant les réactions de Marcellus et d'Archélaüs à la réception de la lettre de Mani, apportée en mains propres à Marcellus par Turbon : l'évêque se trouvait en effet, à ce moment-là, dans la maison de Marcellus.

> VI, § 1. Ayant lu cette lettre, Marcellus manifestait à son porteur la plus obligeante hospitalité. Archélaüs en revanche, qui n'avait guère apprécié le contenu de la lettre, grinçait des dents comme un lion en cage (*velut leo conclusus dentibus infrendebat*) et réclamait qu'on lui livrât l'auteur de la missive (*auctorem epistulae sibi desirans dari*). Marcellus le persuadait de se calmer (*quem Marcellus suadebat quiescere*), en l'assurant qu'il se chargerait lui-même de faire venir Mani. Marcellus décida donc de répondre par une lettre à celle qu'il avait reçue.

Ce passage fournit des éléments supplémentaires sur le portrait psychologique des deux personnages. De Marcellus on met en exergue son hospitalité prévenante envers l'envoyé de Mani, Turbon – le thème de l'hospitalité de Marcellus a déjà été développé par Hégémonius dans le récit du rachat des captifs –, sa prompte décision d'inviter Mani afin qu'il puisse exposer de vive voix sa doctrine, et surtout sa capacité de calmer la fureur d'Archélaüs (*Marcellus suadebat quiescere*). Ce dernier, en effet, réagit à la lecture de la lettre de Mani *velut leo conclusus dentibus infrendebat et auctorem epistulae sibi desirans dari*. Le naturel impétueux d'Archélaüs, qu'Hégémonius avait déjà mis en évidence dans les lignes précédentes, est maintenant renforcé par une comparaison animalière assez banale ; nous avons identifié des parallèles littéraires pour l'utilisation de ce lexique, en nous limitant à la langue latine du traducteur, et en donnons ici quelques exemples. Le terme *infrendere* (grincer des dents) est, par exemple, appliqué au lion chez Silius Italicus et Stace.[77] Quant à *conclusus*, Plaute l'emploie au sujet d'une bête sauvage.[78] On peut aussi remarquer que, lorsqu'Archélaüs exige qu'on lui livre (*dari*) Mani, la forme verbale *dari* évoque le langage du cirque où les chrétiens sont livrés aux fauves.

Rappelons ici en parallèle le texte grec fourni par Épiphane dans le *Panarion* 66, 7, 1-3. On ne peut savoir si, dans cette occurrence comme dans d'autres, Épiphane amplifie le texte d'origine des *Acta Archelai* ou s'il transcrit fidèlement ce passage à partir de l'œuvre d'Hégémonius, mais il nous paraît pouvoir distinguer sa touche personnelle :

---

[77] Cf. par exemple, Silius Italicus, *Punica* 2, 688 : *murmure anhelo infrendens leo, laceros inter spatiatur acervos*. Cf. aussi, *ibid.*, 12, 636 ; 15, 522 ; 17, 222. Stace, *Thébaïde* 2, 477 et 5, 663.
[78] Cf. Plaute, *Rudens* 610 : *concludo in vincla bestiam nequissimam*.

À la lecture de cette lettre, le très illustre Marcellus, homme vraiment pieux et éclairé, fut stupéfait et déconcerté (ἐθαύμαζε καὶ ἐξεπλήτετο). Le jour même où la lettre de Mani était parvenue à ce serviteur de Dieu, l'évêque de la ville Archélaüs se trouvait chez lui par le plus pur des hasards. 2. Ayant appris les faits et lu la lettre, Archélaüs avait commencé à grincer des dents comme un lion rugissant (ἔβρυχε τοὺς ὀδόντας ὡς λέων ὠρυόμενος) et, pris de zèle à l'égard de Dieu, il tentait de s'élancer pour attaquer (ὁρμῆσαι) Mani jusque dans sa demeure et de mettre hors d'état de nuire (χειρώσασθαι) un tel homme, un étranger venant des barbares, qui s'était lancé dans l'extermination des fils des hommes. 3. Mais le prudent Marcellus suppliait l'évêque de se calmer et incitait Turbon à mener à terme son voyage en retournant au *Castellum Arabionis* chez Mani, qui sûrement l'attendait. Cette forteresse se trouve entre la Perse et la Mésopotamie, c'est pourquoi Turbon se refusa à y retourner. Marcellus n'insista pas, et envoya l'un de ses courriers, après avoir écrit la lettre suivante.

La stupéfaction et la perplexité de Marcellus décrites par Épiphane contrastent avec son impassibilité mentionnée dans la version latine des *Acta Archelai* qui se borne à évoquer un certain étonnement de la part de Marcellus seulement lorsque Mani arrive dans la ville, habillé à la mode perse (XIV, § 3).[79] Quant à Archélaüs, il est tout de même très surprenant qu'il soit comparé à un « lion rugissant » (ὡς λέων ὠρυόμενος), expression qui renvoie très probablement à la Première Épître de Pierre 5, 8[80] où le lion est identifié au diable. On note aussi que, selon le texte d'Épiphane, Archélaüs voudrait se rendre chez Mani, ce dont il n'est pas question dans le texte latin, et on remarque également la présence de deux verbes appartenant au lexique de la guerre et de la lutte contre un adversaire, ὁρμῆσαι et χειρώσασθαι, qui rendent bien le caractère belliqueux d'Archélaüs. Rien de chrétien dans ses sentiments, cette terminologie impliquant une violence physique. En outre, Épiphane a recours dans ce passage au thème de Mani comme « Perse barbare » que la version latine des *Acta Archelai* exploite en revanche, avec davantage d'ampleur, au chapitre XXXIX, § 5 et § 7.[81]

---

79   Voir notre commentaire ci-après.
80   Première Épître de Pierre 5, 8 : « Humilité et fermeté dans la foi. Soyez sobres ! Veillez ! Votre adversaire, le diable, comme un lion rugissant, rode, cherchant qui dévorer » (ὁ ἀντίδικος ὑμῶν διάβολος ὡς λέων ὠρυόμενος περιπατεῖ ζητῶν [τινα] καταπιεῖν). Ce terme est un hapax dans le Nouveau Testament.
81   *Acta Archelai* XXXIX, § 5: *Persa barbare non Graecorum linguae, non Aegyptiorum, non Romanorum, non ullius alterius linguae scientiam habere potuisti*; § 7: *O barbare sacerdos*

Quant au fait que Marcellus incite l'évêque à se calmer, cela recoupe exactement la version latine.

Le caractère fougueux d'Archélaüs contraste singulièrement avec le portrait idéal de l'épiscope tel qu'il est tracé dans les Épîtres pastorales et la littérature patristique dans lesquelles, parmi les qualités qu'on exige de lui, on signale l'importance du calme et de la pondération dont il doit faire preuve dans la gestion de la communauté. On a déjà noté auparavant qu'Archélaüs n'a pas été capable de gérer le rachat des captifs; maintenant, son attitude face à une menace qu'il pressent doctrinale – celle de Mani et de sa doctrine des Deux Principes – est colérique et irréfléchie, et animée par le désir de recourir à la violence physique.

Les textes fondateurs sur les qualités de l'épiscope ne sont que deux dans le Nouveau Testament. Rappelons les versets de la Première Épître à Timothée 3, 1-2: «Si quelqu'un aspire à la charge d'évêque, il désire une œuvre excellente. Il faut donc que l'évêque soit irréprochable, mari d'une seule femme, sobre, modéré, réglé dans sa conduite, hospitalier, propre à l'enseignement. Il faut qu'il ne soit ni adonné au vin, ni violent, mais indulgent, pacifique, désintéressé.»[82] L'Épître à Tite 1, 7-9 reprend la même thématique, avec un développement concernant l'enseignement de la vraie doctrine – un point qui ne pas sans intérêt pour le profil d'Archélaüs, défenseur de la doctrine de la Grande Église contre celle de Mani: «Car il faut que l'épiscope soit irréprochable, comme économe de Dieu; qu'il ne soit ni arrogant ni colérique ni adonné au vin, ni violent, ni porté à un gain honteux; mais qu'il soit hospitalier, ami des gens de bien, modéré, juste, saint, tempérant, attaché à l'enseignement sûr, conforme à la doctrine, afin d'être en mesure à la fois d'exhorter dans la saine doctrine et de confondre les contradicteurs.»[83] Ces deux passages ont été peu commentés à l'époque patristique, avec quelques exceptions néanmoins, notamment l'*Homélie* x *sur Timothée* de Jean Chry-

---

Mithrae et conlusor. Voir également *ibid.*, LXVI, §1: *Turbae volebant Manen comprehensum tradere potestati barbarum, qui erant vicini ultra Strangam fluvium*. Nous avons traité du thème du Perse barbare dans Madeleine Scopello, «*Persica adversaria nobis gens*: controverse et propagande anti-manichéennes d'après les *Acta Archelai*», *Comptes rendus de l'Académie des Inscriptions et Belles-Lettres* (2008/2), p. 929-950.

82 Traduction par Louis Segond, *La Sainte Bible*, Nouvelle édition de Genève 1979, Genève, Société biblique de Genève, 35ᵉ édition, Genève, 2012.
83 Nous reprenons en partie la traduction d'André Lemaire pour ce passage de Tite 1, 9: voir André Lemaire, *Les ministères aux origines de l'Église. Naissance de la triple hiérarchie: évêques, presbytres et diacres*, Paris, Cerf, 1971, notamment p. 124-136 sur l'Épître à Tite et la Première Épître à Timothée.

sostome. En revanche, la littérature patristique a amplement repris en des récits de caractère historique le thème de la pondération et du calme qui conviennent aux responsables de communautés dans l'exercice de leur mission.

5.3 Les réactions d'Archélaüs à l'exposé de Turbon (Acta Archelai XIV, § 1)

Ayant refusé de retourner chez Mani pour lui apporter la réponse de Marcellus l'invitant à venir lui expliquer sa doctrine de vive voix (*Acta Archelai* VI, § 2), « Turbon ne quittait plus la maison de Marcellus et ne cessait de s'entretenir avec Archélaüs (…) Tous les deux examinaient attentivement les doctrines de Mani, désireux de savoir qui il était, d'où il venait et quel était son message » (VI, § 5). Turbon se lance alors dans un exposé très clair (*dilucide enarravit*) de la foi de Mani qui couvre les chapitres VII-XIII des *Acta Archelai*. Aucune animosité d'Archélaüs ne se dégage des conversations avec Turbon, l'évêque ne répercutant pas sa hargne envers Mani sur son disciple – peut-être envisageait-il déjà de faire passer Turbon dans le camp de la grande Église, chose qui finit par se vérifier, selon les dires d'Hégémonius qui, au chapitre XLIII, § 4, mentionne que Turbon fut ordonné diacre par Archélaüs.[84] Mais c'est en revanche lorsque Turbon achève son long exposé que le courroux d'Archélaüs se manifeste avec une nouvelle poussée de violence.

> XIV, § 1. Lorsque Turbon eut terminé de parler, Archélaüs s'enflammait violemment (*vehementer accendebatur*); Marcellus, pour sa part, demeurait impassible (*vero non movebatur*), attendant que Dieu vienne au secours de sa propre vérité, car Archélaüs avait souci du peuple, comme le berger pour ses brebis lorsque les loups préparent leurs traquenards (*Archelaus autem erat cura pro populo, tamquam pastori pro ovibus, cum luporum parantur insidiae*).

Dans ce passage également Hégémonius souligne le caractère emporté d'Archélaüs (*vehementer accendebatur*) en le mettant en contraste avec l'impassibilité de Marcellus (*vero non movebatur*). La terminologie est quasiment identique à celle utilisée au chapitre I, § 4 lorsque Hégémonius décrivait la violente agitation de l'évêque face au problème du rachat des captifs (*pro religione et timore dei vehementer aestuabat*). Au lieu du verbe *aestuo*, c'est un synonyme

---

84 *Acta Archelai* XLIII, § 4 : « Quant au serviteur Turbon, Marcellus le confia à Archélaüs et, une fois que ce dernier l'eut ordonné diacre, Turbon habita dans la maison de Marcellus ».

qui est employé, *accendo*, qui, outre un sens physique, a aussi un sens moral.[85] Quant à l'expression *non movebatur*, nous la traduisons en lui donnant son sens d'«être impassible» voire d'«être indifférent».[86]

Dans ce passage Hégémonius a recours à une comparaison tirée du monde animal, celle du loup et de ses traquenards (*insidiae*), pour désigner les dangers auxquels Archélaüs doit faire face pour protéger sa communauté de l'enseignement de Mani. On trouve dans la littérature patristique d'autres exemples où un maître hérétique est comparé à un loup, notamment chez Tertullien qui l'applique à Marcion. Il est aussi à noter que le terme *insidiae* se situe dans le sillage du registre sémantique de la ruse et des pièges adopté précédemment par Hégémonius.

6 Mani se rend à Carrhes: les réactions de Marcellus et d'Archélaüs

Changeons maintenant de focale et analysons l'arrivée de Mani à Carrhes (*Acta Archelai* XIV, § 3). Mani, en effet, ayant reçu la lettre de réponse de Marcellus apportée par un de ses jeunes esclaves, Calixte, se réjouit de l'invitation et «se mit en route sans tarder. Néanmoins, soupçonnant de fâcheux contretemps à cause du retard de Turbon, après avoir pris des précautions pour son itinéraire, il se rendit chez Marcellus.»

6.1 Un portrait vestimentaire

Cette fois-ci c'est un portrait vestimentaire et physique de Mani qu'offre Hégémonius, mais tracé d'une façon qui n'est pas du tout innocente et qui est faite pour mettre en mauvaise lumière le personnage. Mani fait sensation, étant habillé à la mode des Perses:

> XIV, § 2. Le même jour exactement, Mani s'en vint, amenant avec lui des jeunes hommes et des vierges qu'il avait choisis, vingt-deux en tout. Il chercha d'abord Turbon à la porte de Marcellus et, ne l'ayant point trouvé, il entra pour saluer Marcellus. 3. À la vue de Mani, Marcellus fut avant tout étonné par son accoutrement (*quo ille viso, admiratus est primo habitus indumenta*). Mani chaussait, en effet, une sorte de souliers appelés communément à triple semelle (*habebat enim calciamenti genus, quod trisolium vulgo appellari solet*); il était revêtu d'un manteau aux teintes

---

85 Voir Alfred Ernout, Antoine Meillet, *Dictionnaire étymologique de la langue latine, op. cit.*, au lemme (*cando*) *accendo*, 92a.
86 Cf. Felix Gaffiot, *Dictionnaire Latin-Français, op. cit.*, 998a.

nuancées, pour ainsi dire d'une couleur azurée (*pallium autem varium, tamquam aërina specie*); dans sa main il tenait un bâton très solide en bois d'ébène (*in manu vero validissimum baculum tenebat ex ligno ebelino*). Il portait aussi un livre babylonien sous son bras gauche (*Babylonium vero librum portabat sub sinistra ala*); ses jambes étaient recouvertes de braies de couleur différente, l'une rouge, l'autre d'un vert tendre comme le poireau (*crura etiam bracis obtexerat colore diverso, quarum una rufa, alia velut prasini coloris erat*). Il ressemblait, dans son aspect, à un vieux magicien perse et à un chef de guerre (*vultus vero ut senis Persae artificis et bellorum ducis videbatur*).

Nous allons analyser d'abord les diverses pièces de l'habillement de Mani dans l'ordre où Hégémonius les présente, et considérerons ensuite comment Marcellus et Archélaüs réagissent à la vue de Mani. Notons d'emblée que ce portrait haut en couleurs est fondé sur une connaissance précise qu'Hégémonius a de la façon de s'habiller des Perses dont il reprend certains éléments qui visent à mettre en évidence plus encore que l'exotisme du personnage, le fait qu'il s'agit d'un étranger, d'un barbare et qui plus est, d'un représentant de l'ennemi le plus craint de l'Empire romain.[87]

6.1.1   Les souliers à triple semelle (*trisolium*)

Le premier élément vestimentaire est constitué par les souliers que porte Mani (*habebat enim calciamenti genus, quod trisolium vulgo appellari solet*). *Solea* (dérivée de *solum*, partie plate et inférieure d'un tout; plante du pied; base, fondement) a trois significations: une sorte de sandale, consistant dans une semelle placée sous la plante du pied; un soulier d'osier ou une plaque de fer placée sous le sabot d'une bête de somme; le poisson du même nom.[88] Les termes *mono-solis, bi-solis, trisolium* (*genus calciamenti*) existent également. Le latin *solea* traduit le grec σανδάλιον,[89] sandale ou semelle en bois ou en cuir; ce talon formant un bloc de bois posé sous les sandales servait à protéger les pieds de la chaleur et pouvait avoir une hauteur variée. Les cavaliers perses portaient

---

87 Nous avions déjà fourni quelques éléments sur l'habillement de Mani du chapitre XIV dans Madeleine Scopello, «*Persica adversaria nobis gens*: controverse et propagande antimanichéennes d'après les *Acta Archelai*», art. cit., p. 929-950, mais nous les développons dans la présente étude.

88 Alfred Ernout, Antoine Meillet, *Dictionnaire étymologique de la langue latine*, op. cit., p. 634a.

89 Henry George Liddell, Robert Scott, *A Greek-English Lexicon*, Oxford, Clarendon Press, 1968, 1582b: σανδάλιον (surtout au pluriel): Hérodote, *Histoires* 2, 91; σανδάλον: Eupolis comique, 295.

d'ailleurs des chaussures à talon qu'ils accrochaient à l'étrier, ce qui leur assurait une grande stabilité et jouait un rôle important dans leurs performances. Néanmoins l'usage de sandales à plate-forme, souvent en liège, était diffusé aussi parmi les acteurs, tant en milieu perse que dans le monde gréco-romain, et la hauteur du talon servait à indiquer le statut social du personnage qu'ils incarnaient. La comparaison de Mani à un « mime raffiné » qu'Hégémonius fait au chapitre XL des *Acta Archelai* est peut-être en lien avec la remarque sur les souliers à triple semelle qu'il porte.[90]

6.1.2 Le manteau

Hégémonius s'arrête ensuite sur la qualité et les couleurs du tissu du manteau de Mani « aux teintes nuancées, pour ainsi dire d'une couleur azurée (*pallium autem varium, tamquam aërina specie*) ». L'adjectif *aerinus* rend aussi bien la couleur que la consistance aérienne du tissu.[91] Cette description évoque celle qu'Ammien Marcellin consacre au costume perse dans le passage ethnographique des *Histoires* XXIII, 6 sur les coutumes et les traditions des Perses et leurs différences par rapport à celles des Romains.[92] Dans les *Histoires* XXIII, 6, 84 on lit :

> La plupart d'entre eux se couvrent si complètement le corps de vêtements aux couleurs claires, éclatantes et bigarrées (*lumine colorum fulgentibus vario*), que, de la tête aux pieds, il n'est aucune partie de leur corps que l'on puisse voir à découvert, en dépit des plis et des crevés qu'ils laissent, sans les coudre, flotter aux souffles des vents.[93]

---

90 *Acta Archelai* XL, §7 : « Mais que devrais-je dire de plus ? 7 O prêtre barbare et acolyte de Mithra, tu honores Mithra, soleil qui illumine les lieux des mystères et, comme tu le penses, porteur de connaissance. Voilà à quoi tu joueras en ces lieux-là et, tel un mime raffiné, tu accompliras les mystères (*hoc est quod apud eos ludes, et tamquam elegantem mimum perages mysteria*). »

91 *De cultu feminarum* I, 8 *Aerina specie* : pour *aerinus*, cf. Tertullien, *La toilette des femmes*, Introduction, texte critique, traduction et commentaire par Marie Turcan, Sources Chrétiennes 71, 1973, p. 76-79, et son excellente note sur les couleurs.

92 Sur ce passage ethnographique, voir Olivier Devillers, « Fonction de l'excursus sur le Perse chez Ammien Marcellin (XXIII, 6) », *Vita Latina* 165 (2002), p. 5-68. Wijdene Bousleh, *L'image de la Perse et des Perses au IVᵉ siècle chez Ammien Marcellin : tradition romaine et tradition arabo-persane. Regards croisés*, Thèse de doctorat soutenue le 5 janvier 2016 à l'Université de Strasbourg.

93 *Histoires* XXIII, 6, 84. Nous citons la traduction de Jacques Fontaine (texte traduit et établi), Ammien Marcellin, *Histoires*, tome IV, 1, Collection des Universités de France, Paris, Les Belles Lettres, 2002, p. 123. Voir aussi Ammien Marcellin, *Histoires* XIV, 6, 9, sur la mode romaine influencée par l'Orient : « D'autres mettent leur point d'honneur (...) dans

Dans les mots d'Hégémonius on décèle également un motif hérésiologique qui vise le côté à la fois théâtral, multicolore et luxueux des étoffes de prix dont se couvrent les hérétiques.

6.1.3 Le bâton et le livre

Après la description des souliers et du manteau, il est question du solide bâton en bois d'ébène (*validissimum baculum tenebat ex ligno ebelino*) que Mani tient dans sa main (la droite); il s'agit vraisemblablement d'un bâton de voyageur. Quant au livre babylonien qu'il porte sous son bras gauche, l'adjectif choisi indique que ce *liber* était écrit en langue chaldéenne: on remarque ici la présence d'un motif polémique qu'Hégémonius reprendra dans les *Acta Archelai* XL, § 5 lorsqu'il s'adresse à Mani par l'expression «Perse barbare» pour lui signifier son mépris en affirmant qu'il n'avait appris aucune langue et n'était en mesure d'en comprendre aucune excepté la langue chaldéenne, parlée par peu de gens.[94] Le thème de l'infériorité linguistique et intellectuelle des barbares par rapport aux Grecs est courant dans la littérature grecque depuis Démosthène[95] et implique que le barbare ne possède pas le *logos* car il ne sait pas s'exprimer correctement. Par ce thème Hégémonius démantèle également la prétention de Mani d'être le Paraclet[96] – ce qu'aucun hérétique n'avait osé faire.[97]

---

        la somptueuse parure de leur vêtement; ils transpirent sous le poids des manteaux qu'ils enfilent à leur cou et attachent à leur gorge: ces manteaux étant sensibles au moindre souffle en raison de la minceur extrême du tissu, ils les déploient par des mouvements rapides, surtout de la main gauche, afin d'en faire chatoyer en transparence les franges plus longues ainsi que leur tunique» (Édouard Galletier, texte établi et traduit avec la collaboration de Jacques Fontaine, Ammien Marcellin, *Histoires*, tome I, Collection des Universités de France, Paris, Les Belles Lettres, 2002, p. 74).

[94] *Acta Archelai* XL, § 5: «Ô Perse barbare, tu n'as pas été capable d'apprendre la langue des Grecs, ni celle des Égyptiens, ni celle des Romains, mais la seule langue des Chaldéens qui est pratiquée par très peu de gens. Tu n'es pas en mesure de comprendre quelqu'un qui s'exprime en une autre langue que celle-là».

[95] Démosthène, *Olynthiaca* III, 24.

[96] *Acta Archelai* XL, § 6: «Il n'en va pas ainsi pour l'Esprit saint, mais lui qui connaît toutes les langues les a distribuées sans partage à tous (...) que dit en effet l'Écriture? Que tout un chacun entendait parler les apôtres dans sa propre langue, par l'entremise de l'esprit Paraclet.»

[97] *Acta Archelai* XLII, § 1-2: «Et moi – dit Archélaüs – je dis bienheureux Marcion, le Valentinien, Basilide et les autres hérétiques, si je les compare à cet individu (...) Personne parmi eux n'a eu l'audace de se déclarer Dieu, Christ ou Paraclet, à l'instar de cet homme qui disserte parfois sur les éons ou le soleil et sur la façon dont ils sont faits, comme s'il leur était supérieur.»

6.1.4 Les braies

Hégémonius fait porter à Mani des braies de couleur différente; le latin *bracae* traduit le grec ἀναξυρίδες. Il s'agit de larges braies aux couleurs vives,[98] parfois bicolores,[99] que les Perses portaient habituellement.[100] Représentées dans l'art parthe et sassanide,[101] les anaxyrides[102] étaient considérées par les Grecs comme un élément distinctif de la tenue du guerrier perse[103] et firent l'objet dans la littérature grecque et latine des commentaires sarcastiques.[104] Les braies portées par Mani sont l'une *rufa*, l'autre *velut prasini coloris*. Le terme latin *prasinus* est calqué sur le grec πράσινος, le poireau; ce terme botanique désigne la couleur d'une étoffe chez Pétrone,[105] et chez Tertullien[106] elle fait référence à la tenue des auriges.

C'est vraisemblablement la remarque sur les larges braies que sont les anaxyrides qui a suggéré à Hégémonius la digression sur Mani-*artifex*, car les mages perses les portent aussi, comme le montre une peinture retrouvée dans le Mithraeum de Doura Europos. Joseph Bidez et Franz Cumont[107] ont commenté cette image et ont identifié les deux personnages qui y sont repré-

---

98 Cf. par exemple, Xénophon, *Anabase* I, 5, 8, 7: ποικίλας ἀναξυρίδες (pantalons bariolés).

99 Élien, *Histoires* IX, 3, dans un chapitre consacré au luxe d'Alexandre, décrit les robes pourpre et jaune de ses Mélophores et celles des archers comme «mi-parties couleur de feu et d'une autre couleur tirant sur le rouge».

100 Voir Henri Seyrig, «Armes et coutumes iraniens de Palmyre», *Syria* 18 (1937), p. 4-31; les anaxyrides apparaissent dans les scènes représentées sur le sarcophage d'Alexandre: voir Volkmar von Graeve, *Der Alexandersarkophag und seine Werkstatt*, Berlin, 1970, p. 95. Les anaxyrides étaient non seulement portées par les Perses mais aussi par les Scythes et les Saces.

101 Le relief de Bishapour constitue un témoignage intéressant pour l'habillement de Shabour II et de sa suite.

102 Rolf Michael Schneider, *Bunte Barbaren. Orientalen Statuen aus farbigem Marmor in der römischen Repräsentationskunst*, Worms, Werner, 1986, p. 95-98.

103 Voir pour les représentations des guerriers perses sur les vases grecs, Anne Bovon, «La représentation des guerriers perses et la notion de Barbare dans la première moitié du Vᵉ siècle», *Bulletin de correspondance hellénique* 87 (1963), p. 579-602. Selon Hérodote (*Histoires* VII, 61), «les Perses avaient sur la tête des bonnets de feutre mou qu'on appelle des tiares; autour du corps, des tuniques à manches, de couleurs variées et des (cuirasses) formées d'écailles de fer, qui avaient l'apparence d'écailles de poisson; aux jambes, des anaxyrides» (traduction par Philippe-Ernest Legrand, Hérodote, *Histoires*, tome VII, Collection des Universités de France, Paris, Les Belles Lettres, 2003, p. 95).

104 Les ἀναξυρίδες sont aussi appelées trivialement «sacs» (θύλακοι): Euripide, *Les cyclopes* 182; Aristophane, *Les guêpes* 1087.

105 Pétrone, *Satyricon* 64, 4.

106 Tertullien, *De spectaculis* IX, 5.

107 Joseph Bidez, Franz Cumont, *Les mages hellénisés. Zoroastre, Ostanès et Hystaspe d'après la tradition grecque*, vol. I, Paris, Les Belles Lettres, 1938 (2ᵉ tirage, 1973).

sentés à Zoroastre et Ostanès. Assis sur une chaire, outre les braies bouffantes, ils tiennent, ainsi que le précisent les deux savants, «de la main droite la baguette d'ébène des thaumaturges et de la gauche un *volumen* où sont consignées leurs révélations». Bidez et Cumont n'avaient manqué de souligner la parenté entre cette peinture et la description de Mani faite dans les *Acta Archelai*[108] sans toutefois fournir un commentaire sur les pièces vestimentaires des deux personnages. Par ailleurs, le «solide bâton en bois d'ébène» décrit dans l'œuvre d'Hégémonius nous paraît bien différent de la fine baguette des thaumaturges.

Hégémonius conclut sa description en remarquant que Mani «ressemblait, dans son aspect, à un vieux magicien perse et à un chef de guerre» (*vultus vero ut senis Persae artificis et bellorum ducis videbatur*). Le terme *artifex* peut signifier «expert en arts magiques».[109] Dans ce cas, le traducteur des *Acta Archelai* devait probablement rendre le grec μάγος ou γόης; le thème de Mani magicien apparaît par ailleurs au chapitre XL des *Acta Archelai*, mais l'argument est tourné en ridicule car Hégémonius présente Mani comme un magicien de bas niveau,[110] semblable aux magiciens égyptiens Jannès et Jambrès qui s'opposèrent à Moïse.[111] Quant à la ressemblance avec un *dux bellorum*, l'habillement évoqué précédemment est aussi, du moins pour les souliers à semelle haute, les tissus et les braies, celui des guerriers perses. Jugeant ainsi Mani à l'aune du pouvoir religieux des mages et de la puissance militaire perse, Hégémonius fait siens deux stéréotypes de l'ennemi le plus craint des Romains. Si le premier *topos* qui associe la Perse à une terre de magie relève plutôt de l'imaginaire, le second reflète en revanche la crainte réelle du redoutable guerrier perse. Les mots employés par l'édit de Dioclétien[112] contre les manichéens

---

108 *Ibid.*, p. 39 et note 2; planche I.
109 Cf. Augustin, *De civitate Dei* 21, 6: *magicae artes earumque artifices extiterunt*. Le contexte porte sur les œuvres magiques des démons. Cette signification est toutefois peu fréquente.
110 *Acta Archelai* XL, §2: «Tu es un réceptacle de l'Antichrist, non pas un réceptacle de prix mais un abject et honteux réceptacle.» §4-5: «Qui es-tu donc, qui n'as même pas obtenu au sort de Satan ton père un rang convenable? Voyons, quel mort réveilles-tu, quelle hémorragie arrêtes-tu, avec quelle boue redonnes-tu la vue aux yeux de l'aveugle, après les avoir oints? Quand restaures-tu, de quelques pains, une foule affamée? Où marches-tu sur les eaux?»
111 *Acta Archelai* XL, 8: «Il n'ira pas plus avant "car sa folie deviendra manifeste pour tous" comme il advint pour Jannès et Mambrès» (cf. Deuxième Épître à Timothée 3, 8). Cf. aussi *Acta Archelai* LII, 6. On notera la forme «Mambrès» au lieu de «Jambrès».
112 Sur cet édit et ceux qui vont suivre, voir Samuel N.C. Lieu, *Manichaeism in Mesopotamia & the Roman East*, RGRW 118, Leiden, Brill, 1994, chapitre III («The State, the Church and Manichaeism»), p. 121-150. Valerio Massimo Minale, *Legislazione imperiale e manicheismo da Diocleziano a Costantino. Genesi di un'eresia*, Naples, Jovene Editore, 2013.

résonnent en toile de fond: les manichéens, que l'édit définit par la formule d'*adversaria nobis gens*, sont condamnés comme *maleficii*.[113]

Disons un mot sur les réactions de Marcellus et d'Archélaüs à la vue de Mani ainsi habillé. Pour une fois l'impassible Marcellus montre quelque étonnement: *quo ille viso, admiratus est primo habitus indumenta* (XIV, § 3). Cette brève remarque reflète le jugement négatif que le monde gréco-romain, partisan d'une grande sobriété dans la toilette, porte sur les habitudes vestimentaires des Perses.

Dès l'arrivée de Mani, Marcellus fait immédiatement avertir Archélaüs afin qu'il se rende chez lui:

> XIV, § 4. Marcellus fit donc aussitôt chercher Archélaüs; ce dernier, arrivé plus vite que la parole (*qui cum verbo citius adfuisset*),[114] avait hâte, en son for intérieur, d'attaquer Mani (*invehi in eum animo urgebatur*), non seulement pour l'effet que celui-ci avait produit par un accoutrement si singulier (*ex ipso habitu ac specie eius*), mais surtout parce que, tout à fait en privé, il avait réexaminé en lui-même ce dont il avait pris connaissance par le récit de Turbon (*et maxime quidem quod et quae Turbone referente cognoverat, secretius factum apud semet ipsum retractaverat*). Archélaüs était ainsi arrivé scrupuleusement préparé (*et diligenter praeparatus advenerat*). 5. Cependant, Marcellus, dans sa grande sagesse (*prudentissimus*), avait écarté toute volonté de querelle (*omni contentionum studio sublato*) et, ayant invité les notables de la ville, il avait pris la décision d'entendre aussi bien l'un que l'autre.

Encore une fois Archélaüs, fidèle à lui-même, montre son caractère fougueux illustré par le dicton « arriver plus vite que la parole ». Son envie d'en découdre avec Mani (*invehi in eum animo urgebatur*) est rendue par la forme verbale *invehi* (*in aliquem*) au passif réfléchi, dont la signification est « attaquer quelqu'un par la parole », et qui trouve maint exemple dans le langage des orateurs.[115] Hégémonius précise que les raisons de s'en prendre à Mani vont au-delà de l'aversion provoquée par sa tenue vestimentaire perçue comme délibé-

---

113　L'accusation de pratiquer la sorcellerie, et d'utiliser des φαρμακά est par exemple adressée à Julie d'Antioche, propagandiste du manichéisme à Gaza, par Marc le Diacre (*Vie de Porphyre* 86). Voir Madeleine Scopello, « Julie, manichéenne d'Antioche (d'après Marc le Diacre, *Vita Porphyri* 85-91) », *Antiquité tardive* 5 (1997), p. 187-209, notamment p. 202-203.
114　Il s'agit d'un dicton.
115　Cf. Felix Gaffiot, *Dictionnaire Latin-Français*, *op. cit.*, 851c–852a: voir par exemple, Cicéron, *De oratore* 2, 304; *Orator ad Brutum* 3, 2.

rément provocatrice, et découlent également de la réflexion solitaire (*secretius*) qu'Archélaüs a menée sur la doctrine de Mani, une fois instruit par l'exposé de Turbon. On notera encore, au § 5, la fonction pacificatrice et organisationnelle de Marcellus, déjà relevée dans les passages que nous avons examinés précédemment, qui est ici qualifié de *prudentissimus*: très avisé, plein de sagesse, de discernement. Son souhait est d'éviter toute *contentio*,[116] c'est-à dire toute querelle ou tout conflit: c'est pourquoi il met en place une confrontation publique devant des juges

7 Conclusion

En conclusion, l'analyse lexicale des passages que nous avons considérés nous a fourni une matière significative pour approfondir les caractères des trois personnages majeurs des *Acta Archelai* – dans l'ordre de parution de la narration: Marcellus, Archélaüs et Mani – et de saisir également leurs interactions. Le langage d'Hégémonius est d'une extrême précision, chaque terme est choisi avec soin pour illustrer les thèmes et motifs qu'il entend développer. Cela transparaît à travers la traduction latine des *Acta Archelai*, effectuée par un traducteur expérimenté qui a saisi en profondeur le sens de l'œuvre d'Hégémonius. C'est sur cette traduction, qui constitue à son tour une œuvre à part entière, que s'est construite notre recherche.

Mais avant de cerner le caractère des personnages, il fallait examiner la scène où ils se situent: la ville de Carchara/Carrhes. Notre recherche a montré qu'Hégémonius a volontairement modifié l'image de cette ville mésopotamienne, connue pour sa fidélité au paganisme, en lui donnant des couleurs chrétiennes qui ne résistent pas à l'analyse historique – ce qui a déteint sur la façon dont Hégémonius a présenté les personnages. Marcellus, que nous estimons être un haut fonctionnaire provincial de l'empire, n'était certainement pas chrétien, compte tenu de l'époque où se déroulent les faits mais aussi de celle où Hégémonius a composé son œuvre. Quant à la présence d'un évêque à Carrhes, on peut la mettre en doute si l'on tient compte des témoignages des voyageurs et des écrivains ecclésiastiques.

Nous n'avons donné que quelques exemples de cette narration qui associe des éléments factuels, dont certains sont habilement biaisés, et de doctrine. Une lecture lexicale de la suite du texte des *Acta Archelai*, presque exclusive-

---

116   Cf. Felix Gaffiot, *Dictionnaire Latin-Français, op. cit.*, 415c–416a: voir par exemple Cicéron, *Pro a Cluentio habito oratio ad iudices* 44; *Catilina* 4, 13.

ment composée par le débat doctrinal entre Mani et Archélaüs, fournit tout aussi bien une matière digne d'attention, le décryptage du vocabulaire hérésiologique pouvant conduire à préciser ultérieurement la palette de rapports entre «Manichaeism and Early Christianity».

9
Snakes in the Garden and Tares in the Wheat Field: Ephrem of Nisibis' Polemic of Lineage against the Manichaeans

Robert Morehouse

Abstract

This chapter explores Ephrem of Nisibis' use of a polemic of lineage in his heresiological works against Manichaeism. It focuses on Ephrem's efforts to symbolically read Mani into the biblical narrative of salvation history by connecting him to the work of the Evil One. Ephrem portrays the ministry of Mani as founded in the work of forebears, especially Marcion and Bar Daysan, whose true pedigree can be traced back to the serpent in the garden, and thus to Satan himself. Ephrem tells his audience that these opponents are the true heirs of the Evil one and thus of the serpent in the garden (Genesis 3) and the tares in the field (Matthew 13), carefully weaving them into a tapestry depicting arch-heretics and their satanic heritage.

Introduction

In his prose and metrical writings against heresies, Ephrem of Nisibis (d. 373) portrays himself as entrenched in a battle for the safety of his congregation against a number of heretical influences. Among orthodoxy's foes whom Ephrem addresses by name are Arians, Jews, Valentinians, Marcionites, Bar Daysanites, and Manichaeans. He summarizes these groups well in the twenty-second of his *Hymns against Heresies*:

> Because Marcion added fraud
> the church rejected and expelled him;
> Valentinus, because he deviated;
> and, likewise, the 'Potter' [because he] polluted.
> Bar Dayṣān enhanced his fraud.
> Mani went completely mad.
> A bundle of thorns and tares!
> May the good one in his love turn them

from wandering to within his pasture.
Blessed is he who cares about the evil ones.

Valentinus stole a flock
from the church and called it by his name.
The Quqite gave one his own name.
The crafty Bar Dayṣān stole one.
And they [each] made it like a flock that is inside.
Marcion had abandoned his sheep;
Mani fell upon and captured them from him,
one rabid man was biting another rabid man.

They [each] called a flock by their own names.
Blessed is the one who threw them out of his house.
Since they erred and went astray the Arians,
and the Aetians, since they were subtle,
and the Paulinians, since they were perverse,
and the Sabellians, since they were cunning,
and the Photinians, since they were fraudulent,
and the Borborians, since they were defiled
and the Qathari, since they were purified,
and the Audians, since they were ensnared,
and the Messalians, since they were lavish.
May the Good One will turn them to his fold.[1]

My purpose here is to focus on Ephrem's treatment of the Manichaeans. By the nature of Ephrem's approach to the matter—much like that of his contemporaries—we will need to wrestle a bit with his treatment of several of these other groups because Ephrem treats them and their ministries as inextricably linked. In particular, Ephrem often groups the Manichaeans with Marcionites and Bar Daysanites. He sees some of the teachings of these three groups as coming from the same roots. For this reason, Marcionites and Bar Daysanites will appear more often than other heretical groups in our discussion of Ephrem's treatment of Manichaeism.

I will focus here on a particular aspect of Ephrem's polemic against Manichaeans. This is Ephrem's argument against their religious authority. A com-

---

1 Edmund Beck, *Des heiligen Ephraem der Syrers Hymnen contra Haereses* (Louvain: L. Durbecq, 1957). All translations are my own, save where stated otherwise.

mon claim for any teacher in Late Antiquity is that they are the heir of an ancient tradition. Mani was no different. He claimed an ancient heritage for his teaching. However, Ephrem will not concede that Mani's teachings are descended from a long unbroken tradition. Instead, he portrays Mani—along with Marcion and Bar Daysan—as belonging to a tradition marked not by consistency and integrity, but by deception and opportunism.

Ephrem's work is carried out within the imperial church. Born sometime in the first decade of the fourth century, he comes into adulthood and begins his ministry in a world where Christianity is tolerated, if not favored. Likewise, at very least, the majority of his ministerial work is conducted in the wake of the Council of Nicea (325). As Sidney Griffith has shown, a significant feature of Ephrem's work is that he communicates Nicene orthodoxy in a Syriac idiom.[2] Indeed a great deal of Ephrem's polemic can be understood as his attempt to clearly demarcate his understanding of orthodoxy, its supporters and its opponents, for his community.

Conversely, during this same time frame, Manichaeism was squarely on the wrong side of both the Roman and the Persian empires. The persecution of Manichaeans in the Persian Empire began with the execution of Mani in 276 by Bahram I (273–276) and the Zoroastrian priest Kartir, and it spread, fueled by Zoroastrian zeal, to include [mainstream] Christians, Jews and Buddhists. Bahram II's reign (276–293) brought a return to religious tolerance in Persia that would persist until persecutions were renewed under Shapur II (r. 309–379).[3] While Manichaean missionaries had certainly already been active within the Eastern provinces of the Roman Empire for decades, Manichaeism was marked for persecution by Diocletian not long after its immigration into North Africa.[4]

---

2 Sidney H. Griffith, "'Faith Seeking Understanding' in the Thought of Ephraem the Syrian," in *Faith Seeking Understanding: Learning and the Catholic Tradition*, ed. George C. Berthold (Manchester, New Hampshire: Saint Anselm College Press, 1991), 35–55.

3 See Samuel Lieu, *Manichaeism in Mesopotamia and the Roman East* (Leiden: Brill, 1994), 80f.

4 See Samuel Lieu's discussion of Diocletian's response to Manichaeism in his *Manichaeism in the Later Roman Empire and Medieval China: A Historical Survey* (Manchester: Manchester University Press, 1985), 91–95. On Alexandrian Christian responses see Iain Gardner and Samuel Lieu, *Manichaean Texts from the Roman Empire* (Cambridge: Cambridge University Press, 2004), 114–116. On the arrival of the Manichaeans in the region see Lieu's *Manichaeism in Mesopotamia and the Roman East*, 61–105; cf. Peter Brown, "The Diffusion of Manichaeism in the Roman Empire." *Journal of Roman Studies* 59, no. 1/2 (1969): 92–103. See also Lieu's more recent "The Diffusion, Persecution and Transformation of Manichaeism in Late Antiquity and pre-Modern China," in *Conversion in Late Antiquity: Christianity, Islam, and Beyond: Papers from the Andrew W. Mellon Foundation Sawyer Seminar, University of Oxford 2009–2010*, edited by Arietta Papaconstantinou and Daniel L. Schwartz (London: Routledge, 2016), 124–140.

It would benefit, however, from the growing religious tolerance of the fourth century. The tensions between the great Roman and Persian empires during that same century seems to have exacerbated suspicions of expatriate communities in each realm.[5]

The Roman northern Mesopotamian cities of Nisibis and Edessa housed a diverse spectrum of Christian communities, and tensions over religious identity and allegiance. Religious communities that identified their own doctrines with the names of Marcion or Bar Daysan or Mani or Palut, among others, were associated with the Christian tradition and with the title "Christian."[6] For over half a century, Ephrem called Nisibis home, and he spent roughly the last ten years of his life in Edessa. Edessa was a cosmopolitan, border, trade city with diverse populations and broad geographical connections, and a diverse Christian population.[7] While much less is known about Nisibis than Edessa, we have

---

5   For a good introduction to the persecutions of Christians within Persia, see Sebastian Brock and Susan Ashbrook Harvey, *Holy Women of the Syrian Orient* (Berkeley: University of California, 1987), 63–67. See also, Sebastian Brock, "Christians in the Sasanian Empire: A Case of Divided Loyalties," in *Religion and National Identity*, ed. Stuart Mews, Studies in Church History, vol. 18 (Oxford: B. Blackwell, 1982), 1–19. One must also now consider Kyle Smith's rereading of these stories. Smith makes a compelling case that the texts traditionally employed to reconstruct the history of Christians in fourth-century Persia are not reliable sources of that history as much as they are sources for understanding later Roman, Christian, and Persian memories or tellings of that period. See his *Constantine and the Captive Christians of Persia: Martyrdom and Religious Identity in Late Antiquity*, The Transformation of Classical Heritage 57 (Oakland, California: University of California Press, 2016). See also David Bundy, "Bishop Vologese and the Persian Siege of Nisibis in 359 C.E.: A Study in Ephrem's *Mēmrē on Nicomedia*." *Encounter* 63 (2000): 53–65.

6   It was not a teaching of any of these groups to go by a name other than "Christian." However, Ephrem's accusation against even his own "Palutian" community suggests that—by Ephrem's own time—it was a commonplace to refer to one's own group by something more than "Christian" to be clear about one's association. This was a central thesis of Walter Bauer's work on early Edessan Christianity in his *Orthodoxy and Heresy in Earliest Christianity*, 2nd ed., trans. and ed. by Robert A. Kraft, Gerhard Krodel, et. al. (Mifflintown, PA: Sigler, 1971). For a fuller discussion of this topic see Sidney Griffith's "The Marks of the 'True Church' according to Ephraem's Hymns against Heresies," in *After Bardaisan: Studies on Continuity and Change in Syriac Christianity in Honour of Professor Han J.W. Drijvers*, ed. G.J. Reinink and A.C. Klugkist (Leuven: Peeters, 1999), 125–140. See also Jason BeDuhn and Paul Mirecki, "Placing the Acts of Archelaus," in *Frontiers of Faith*, ed. Jason BeDuhn and Paul Mirecki (Leiden: Brill, 2007), 2. More recently, see Flavia Ruani, "Les controverses avec les manichéens et le développement de l'hérésiologie syriaque," in *Les controverses religieuses en syriaque*, edited by Flavia Ruani (Études syriaques 13) (Paris: Geuthner, 2016), 67, 71.

7   See Annette Yoshiko Reed, "Beyond the Land of Nod: Syriac Images of Asia and the Historiography of 'The West'" *History of Religions* 49, no. 1 (2009): 48–87. It is my assertion that what Reed says of Edessa also applies to Nisibis, even though less evidence to this effect survives. The standard surveys of Edessa are J.B. Segal's *Edessa: The Blessed City* (Piscataway, NJ:

good reason to believe it to have been a similarly cosmopolitan city, with a similar panorama of Christian expression.[8] Within this Northern Mesopotamian context, the title Christian was highly contested by a number of communities.[9] At very least, Christians who might also be recognized as Marcionites, Bar Daysanites, and certainly Manichaeans were active in the region.[10]

Ephrem comes into his ministerial work with key structures already in place. Rome is pro-Christian, even if the version of Christian theology that has the empire's approval changes with nearly every emperor from Constantine to Theodosius.[11] Rome is also anti-Manichaean. Zoroastrian zeal and anti-Roman sentiment have left Persia both anti-Manichaean and anti-Christian. Living his entire life within the eastern border of the Roman Empire, Ephrem was

---

Gorgias, 2005) and Steven Ross, *Roman Edessa: Politics and Culture on the Eastern Fringes of the Roman Empire, 114–242CE* (London: Routledge, 2001).

[8] Paul Russell provides an excellent overview of the current state of information on Nisibis in his "Nisibis as the Background to the Life of Ephrem the Syrian," *Hugoye: Journal of Syriac Studies* 8, no. 2 (July 2005), http://www.bethmardutho.org/index.php/hugoye/volume-index/416.html (accessed September 10, 2019). For a discussion of Ephrem's treatment of the city in his *Hymns on Nicomedia*, see David Bundy, "Vision for the City: Nisibis in Ephraem's Hymns on Nicomedia," in *Religions of Late Antiquity in Practice*, edited by Richard Valantasis (Princeton: Princeton University Press, 2000), 189–206. See also his "Bishop Vologese and the Persian Siege of Nisibis in 359 C.E.: A Study in Ephrem's *Mēmrē on Nicomedia*," *Encounter* 63 (2000): 53–65.

[9] While there is not enough evidence to confirm Walter Bauer's proposal that the proto-orthodox Christians of Edessa went by many other titles because "Christian" had been taken by another community, it cannot be denied that the title "Christian" was contested, that it did not simply refer to a single group. We know this to be the case on the Persian side of the border as well. The "Ka'bah of Zoroaster" inscription at Naqsh-i Rustam (near Persepolis) bears the names "Nazareans" (N'CL'Y, Nāzrāy, from ܢܨܪܝܐ), who BeDuhn and Mirecki suggest are Syriac-speaking "Nazareans" who adhere to a form of Christianity that did not pass through the environment of the Hellenistic cities of the west; "Christians" (KLSTYD'N, Kristādān, from Χριστιανοι, through ܟܪܣܛܝܢܐ), whose Greek name implies a western connection; "Purifiers/Baptists" (MKTKY, Maktaky, as Syriac ܡܟܬܟܝ); and "interpreters/ heretics" (ZNDKY, Zandaky), who BeDuhn and Mirecki suggest are the Manichaeans. See their "Placing the Acts of Archelaus," 2–3. See also Joel Walker's discussion of the history of the interpretation of this inscription in his *The Legend of Mar Qardagh* (Berkley: University of California Press, 2006), 110.

[10] Mani, who wrote in Syriac, penned letters specifically to a community of his followers in Edessa. See Lieu, *Manichaeism*, 75. On Manichaean Syriac, see Nils Arne Pedersen, "Syriac Texts in Manichaean Script: New Evidence," in *Mani in Dublin: Selected Papers from the Seventh International Conference of the International Association of Manichaean Studies in the Chester Beatty Library, Dublin, 8–12 September 2009*, edited by Siegfried G. Richter, Charles Horton, and Klaus Ohlhafer (Leiden: Brill, 2015), 284–288.

[11] On the significance of these shifting allegiances in the Syriac Christian environment, see Sebastian Brock, "Eusebius and Syriac Christianity," in *Eusebius, Christianity, and Judaism*,

keenly aware of these religio-political realities. However, Walter Bauer, and others, have shown that Northern Mesopotamia was not a place where orthodoxy was enforced with a heavy hand. Indeed, evidence suggests a much more cosmopolitan context in Edessa and Nisibis, the cities Ephrem called home.

The nature of Ephrem's poetic thought and expression results in allusions to and echoes of his polemics throughout his broader corpus. However, the bulk of his polemical work is found in two collections. The first are his *Prose Refutations* (PR), which consist of a dozen polemical works directed chiefly against the likes of Marcion, Bar Daysan, and Mani.[12] We have these treatises all together in a single manuscript from the sixth century.[13] The second set of texts are commonly known as the *Hymns against Heresies* (*HcH*).[14] These exist in a number

---

ed. Harold Attridge and Gohei Hata (Detroit: Wayne State University Press, 1991), 212–234 and Sidney Griffith, "Ephraem, the Deacon of Edessa, and the Church of the Empire" in DIAKONIA: *Studies in Honor of Robert T. Meyer*, ed. Thomas Halton and Joseph P. Willman (Washington: The Catholic University of America Press, 1986): 22–52.

12   These texts have been published by Charles Wand Mitchell, completed by A.A. Bevan and Francis Crawford Burkitt. *S. Ephrem's Prose Refutations of Mani, Marcion and Bardaisan*, vol 2. (London: Williams and Norgate, 1921). Translations of this text are modified from Mitchell, unless otherwise noted.

13   BL Add. 14574 and 14623, which are actually two portions of the same original manuscript. For the story of this manuscript see the Preface (no pagination) to the first volume of Mitchell's *S. Ephraim's Prose Refutations of Mani, Marcion, and Bardaisan: Transcribed from the Palimpsest B.M. 14623*, vol. 1 (Oxford: Williams and Norgate, 1912). Ute Possekel (*Evidence of Greek Philosophical Concepts in the Writings of Ephrem the Syrian* (Louvain: Secrétariat du CSCO, 1999), 10, n.55) notes the difficulties with the text and that her own efforts to improve Mitchell's reading through the use of ultraviolet light proved unfruitful. In a recent article connected with the 8th meeting of the IAMS at SOAS, Ursala Sims-Williams discusses this manuscript and the methods used to get at Ephrem's text; "Some Syriac Manichaean Treasures in the British Library," British Library, last modified September, 23, 2013, https://britishlibrary.typepad.co.uk/asian-and-african/2013/09/some-syriac-manichean-treasures-in-the-british-library.html. References to the *Prose Refutations* (PR) begin with the volume indicated by an upper case Roman numeral (I or II), they are then followed by an Arabic numeral and a lower case Roman numeral. The Arabic numeral indicates the page of the relevant Syriac text and the lower case Roman numeral the page number where the corresponding English text can be located within that same volume.

14   Text and Translation published in two volumes by Edmund Beck. For the text, see *Des heiligen Ephraem des Syrers Hymnen contra haereses* [Textus], vol. 1, 2 vol. (Louvain: Secretariat du Corpus Scriptorum Christianorum Orientalium, 1957). For Beck's translation, see *Des heiligen Ephraem des Syrers Hymnen contra haereses* [Versio], vol. 2, 2 vol. (Louvain: Secrétariat du Corpus Scriptorum Christianorum Orientalium, 1957). For a French translation, see Flavia Ruani, *Hymnes contre les hérésies*, Bibliothèque de l'Orient chrétien 4 (Paris: Les Belles Lettres, 2018); cf. Flavia Ruani, "Le manichéisme vu par Éphrem le Syrien: analyse d'une refutation doctrinal," 2 vols (PhD diss., École Pratique des Hautes Études, Paris

of manuscripts all likely dating to the sixth century.[15] The authenticity of both collections are generally accepted by scholars.[16]

An ardent defender of Nicene Orthodoxy, Ephrem sees theological authority as resting in the true [Nicene] church. Disregard for the authority of the church, in Ephrem's mind, is itself heresy, and it breeds false teaching. For him, a failure to recognize the import of the continuity of the church's doctrines and its authority plays a significant role in the breakdown of the theological method. There are four main manifestations of this breakdown that Ephrem claims to have witnessed in his opponents' communities: failure to maintain the title "Christian";[17] to venerate the whole of the scriptures, both the Old and the New Testaments; to maintain the sacraments; and to respect apostolic succession and the ordination of the church. Each of these offenses is a sign that a teacher is not operating within the authority of the true church. Likewise, they are evidence that a community has not properly placed itself under the authority, nor within the tradition, of the teachings of the true church.

When speaking of these false teachers and their communities, Ephrem groups them into two general categories. The first are those who teach false doctrines within the Christian tradition. Those in this group bear the marks of the true church, but still teach false doctrines. These he terms "insider" adversaries. This group consists of the likes of Arius, and the Aetians. While these errant teachers are certainly a significant concern for Ephrem, and do feature within the texts we are primarily concerned with in this study, they are not our focus.[18]

/ Sapienza Università di Roma, 2012). Except where noted otherwise, all English translations of this text are my own.

15 Vat. sir. 111, the only manuscript with the entire collection of the *HcH*; and BL Add. 12176, BL Add. 14574, and Add. 1741, which all have only portions of the *HcH* collection. For a thorough discussion of these manuscripts as well as other editions and translations, see Ruani, *Hymnes*, XXIV–XXV.

16 See the two previous notes. Also see Blake Hartung, "The Authorship and Dating of the Syriac Corpus attributed to Ephrem of Nisibis: A Reassessment," *Zeitschrift für Antikes Christentum* 22, no. 2 (2018): 296–321.

17 There is no evidence that Marcion, Bar Daysan, or Mani were directing their disciples to call themselves anything other than "Christian." However, it does appear that by Ephrem's day many Christian groups were using other identifiers to distinguish their communities, or at least idiosyncrasies in their teachings or practices, one from another.

18 For a fuller discussion of Ephrem's treatment of these adversaries, which occurs more extensively in his *Hymns on Faith*, see Jeffrey Wickes, *St. Ephrem the Syrian: The Hymns on Faith*, Fathers of the Church 130 (Washington, DC: Catholic University of America Press, 2015), and *Bible and Poetry in Late Antique Mesopotamia: Ephrem's* Hymns on Faith, Christianity in Late Antiquity 5 (Oakland: University of California Press, 2019). See also Paul Russell, *St. Ephraem the Syrian and St. Gregory the Theologian Confront the Arians*, Mōrān

The second category is for the "outsider" adversaries. This cohort is made up of those promoting false religious teachings outside of the Church. These are characters who violate one or more of these marks of the true Church. Some were never ordained within a line of apostolic succession. Some do not accept both testaments of the scriptures as authoritative, or have otherwise decided that they have authority to pick and choose portions of the scriptures as they see fit. Most of these entertain the use of appellations other than that of Christ for their own community, and many of these—at least according to Ephrem— have adopted practices that are outside of the sacraments of the Church. Bar Daysan, Mani, and their followers fall squarely within the "outsider adversary" camp. They bear none of the marks of the true church. Ephrem instead portrays them as upstarts whose only real heritage is deception and innovation.

1   Ephrem's Polemic of Lineage

In Ephrem's polemics against Bar Daysan and Mani he casts his opponents as polar opposites of genuine Christian leaders who derive their authority from their ordination, in apostolic succession leading back to Christ. In addition, he counters existing images of his adversaries as Christian teachers, philosophers, prophets, and even the Paraclete. Instead of being a part of the heritage of the true church, Ephrem contrasts their claims to authority with his own proclamation of the true nature of the heritage of these false teachers. First he suggests that these heretics are simply fighting amongst themselves, trying to outdo one another, each stealing from the other to try to make the most of his own mission. Then Ephrem posits the serpent in the garden and Satan himself as the appropriate predecessors and mentors of these heretics. Ultimately, Ephrem sketches caricatures of Bar Daysan and Mani that clearly place them on the side of error in the essential battle between truth and error, between Christ and Satan, between orthodox and heterodox Christians.

Ephrem's rhetorical style embraces this sort of polarity, often for the sake of association and disassociation.[19] He wants his audience to associate positively

---

'Eth'ō 5 (Kottayam, India: St. Ephrem Ecumenical Research Institute, 1994); Christina Shepardson, *Anti-Judaism and Christian Orthodoxy: Ephrem's Hymns in Fourth Century Syria* (Washington: The Catholic University of America Press, 2008); and Emanuel Fiano, "The Trinitarian Controversy in Fourth Century Edessa," *Le Muséon* 128 (2015): 85–125.

19   Philip J. Botha's work on Ephrem's rhetoric is foundational. For example, see his "Antithesis and Argument in the Hymns of Ephrem the Syrian." *Hervormde Teologiese Studies* 44 (1988): 581–595; and his "The Structure and Function of Paradox in the Hymns of Ephrem

with certain poles of the antitheses within his symbolism and to disassociate with those he casts as negative. Simply put, he wants them to feel drawn closer to his orthodox community and its thinking and to repel the heterodox fray.[20] In his polemic of lineage this feature of his rhetoric is overt. When dealing with the heritage of Bar Daysan and Mani, Ephrem is dealing with the founders of communities that are still active and identifiable.[21]

Ephrem follows heresiological norms in the construction of lineages of heterodox teachers as a means of branding his opponents. Irenaeus used lineages to shame opponents.[22] In Irenaeus' work, Simon Magus, rather than Marcion or Satan, was the first of the line. Ephrem's contemporary, Cyril of Jerusalem used a similar tactic to attack heretics, including Manichaeans;[23] so too Didymus the Blind.[24] Hegemonius, writing the earliest extant Christian anti-Manichaean work, employed this motif specifically against Mani.[25]

---

the Syrian." *Ekklesiastikos Pharos*, N.S. 73, no. 2 (1991): 50–62. See too Kees den Biesen, *Simple and Bold: Ephrem's Art of Symbolic Thought*, Gorgias Dissertations 26, Early Christian Studies 6 (Piscataway, NJ: Gorgias, 2006). More recently, see Andrew Hayes' *Icons of the Heavenly Merchant: Ephrem and Pseudo-Ephrem in the Madrashe in Praise of Abraham of Qidun* (Piscataway: Gorgias, 2016).

20 For background to this heresiological approach, see Alain Le Boulluec, *La notion d'hérésie dans la littérature grecque IIe–IIIe siècles*, vol. 1, *De Justin à Irénée*; vol. 2, *Clément d'Alexandrie et Origène* (Paris: Études Augustiniennes, 1985).

21 In several passages Ephrem remarks in allusion about the practices of his opponents, suggesting that his audience is familiar enough with his opponents that they will recognize these subtleties. Likewise, Ephrem employs clever puns not simply on the names of his opponents (See Sidney Griffith, "The Thorn among the Tares: Mani and Manichaeism in the Works of St. Ephrem the Syrian," *Studia Patristica* 35 (2001): 412) but also with key terms within Manichaean teaching. Examples of his remarks regarding his opponents' practices are outside the scope of the present enterprise. Examples related to their teaching are noted throughout the present paper. For a fuller discussion of these issues see my "Bar Dayṣān," 98–137.

22 *Adversus Haereses* 3.

23 *Catechesis* 16. 10; PG 33.931.

24 *De Trinitate Liber* 3.42; PG 39.989.

25 *Acta Archelai* 62.1–65.9. Eszter Spät suggests that creating such genealogies and seeing them as analogous to Satan's first sin is a commonplace in early heresiography. Spät adds that the *Acta* account is unique in positing that Mani began his career as a heretic when he stole a book of one Scythianus and edited it for his own purposes. However, Spät says nothing of making Satan and the serpent in the garden part of the lineage, nor does she address Ephrem. Eszter Spät, "The 'Teachers' of Mani in the *Acta Archelai* and Simon Magus," *Vigiliae Christianae* 58 (2004): 1–23. For the English text of the *Acts*, see Mark Vermes, *Hegemonius, Acta Archelai* (Turnhout: Brepols, 2001); for the Greek: Charles Henry Beeson, *Acta Disputationis Archelai* (Leipzig: J.C. Hinrichs'sche Buchhandlung, 1906).

Ephrem casts Bar Daysan, Mani, and their disciples as heretics. He associates them with one another to discredit the bunch as a whole, and he associates them with other more famous heretics in order to indicate that their faults ought to be obvious. As part of his understanding and communicating religious truths through types and symbols, Ephrem illustrates the deeper, spiritual truths involved in this discussion. Ephrem offers a spiritual exegesis of the heritage of his opponents. He incorporates what appear to him to be real aspects of lineage into his symbolic, polemical rhetoric. He associates his opponents with the side of error through its types. Sidney Griffith has called this Ephrem's "typology of error."[26]

As Ephrem sees the world, all heretics belong to the side of error. They share this with the serpent in paradise, who turned Eve and Adam from the truth. They also share it with Satan, the original member of that realm, and the force behind all error. This typology of error must be understood, however, as the antithesis to Ephrem's typology of truth. These are the only options in Ephrem's world: truth or error, orthodoxy or heresy, Christ or Satan. Just as his typological treatment of true teachers and his treatment of apostolic succession, the apostolic lineage draws on types of Christ, the true one. Similarly, his polemic of lineage associates his adversaries as types of Satan, innovation, and deception. His polemic of lineage against Bar Daysan and Mani consistently follows this paradigm. Ephrem repeatedly associates his opponents with error and ascribes to them its characteristics.

2 Apparent Associations and their Symbolic Value

For Ephrem, symbolism and poetry are preferred vehicles for theological communication,[27] and these symbols point toward realities, either apparent or hidden. Within his formative and polemical compositions Ephrem is intertwining mysteries and apparent realities into his symbolic idiom, generating a coherent typological system. Thus, in reading his remarks on Bar Daysan and Mani we find references to details about their lives, teachings, and practices as Ephrem understood them. The significance of those details is magnified as he incorporates them into his symbolic framework. This section explores how Ephrem employs these associations in his own polemical use of symbols of lineage, or pedigree.

---

26   "Thorn," 402.
27   The most comprehensive study of symbolic thought in Ephrem is den Biesen, *Simple*. In particular, his first chapter (7–46) situates the now broadly held view that Ephrem's symbolism and poetry are essential to and dynamic within his writing and theology.

Some of his references to links between his adversaries seem to be more observation than accusation. One example is his linking them through a vehicle that each used to spread their teaching. Both Bar Daysan and Mani were composers of *madrāšê*.[28] Ephrem may even have believed that Mani learned the composition of *madrāšê* from Bar Daysan's school. The use of *madrāšê* is very dear to Ephrem.[29] This is the literary form he prefers for his theological discourse and part of his polemical mission is actually to displace his opponents' *madrāšê* with his own.[30]

One of Ephrem's more direct statements about the relationship between Bar Daysan and Mani is that Bar Daysan was Mani's master or teacher (ܪܒܗ).[31] While ideological connections had sparked many other late antique authors to suggest that there was a strong link between the two communities, none of

---

28   See *HcH* I.17; LIII.5–6 and LV.5–6 for Ephrem's reference to the use of this form by Bar Daysan, and *HcH* I.16 for his reference to Mani's use of it. See also Sidney H. Griffith, "St. Ephrem, Bar Daysān and the Clash of *Madrāshê* in Aram: Readings in St. Ephrem's Hymni contra Haereses," *The Harp* 21 (2006): 447–472.

29   On just how dear this form of composition was to Ephrem, see Griffith, "St. Ephrem;" cf. Joseph Amar, *A Metrical Homily on Holy Mar Ephrem by Jacob of Sarug: Critical Edition of the Syriac Text, Translation and Introduction* (Turnhout: Brepols, 1995); and Kathleen McVey, "Were the Earliest *Madrāšē* Songs or Recitations?" in *After Bardaisan: Studies on Change and Continuity in Syriac Christianity: A Festschrift in Honor of Professor Han J.W. Drijvers*, ed. G.J. Reinink and A.C. Klugkist (Louvain: Peeters, 1999), 185–199; and most recently Wickes, *Bible*, 14–23.

30   "St. Ephrem," 460–463. The depth of the importance of a poetic even lyrical nature of the idiom for theological discourse in early northern Mesopotamian Christianity is furthered by two other factors. First, Drijvers has argued that the thirty-eighth of the *Odes of Solomon* is the earliest anti-Manichaean text. See Drijvers, "Die Oden Salomos und die Polemik mit den Markioniten im syrischen Christentum," in *Symposium Syriacum 1976*, Orientalia Christiana Analecta, 205 (Rome: Pont. Institutum Studiorum Orientalium, 1978), 39–55. Second, there is a hint in Ephrem's *madrāšê against Heresies* 40.14 that Marcionites were also using songs to advance their thought. The *madrāšâ*, which focuses on the antithesis between Moses' account of creation and Marcion's interpretation, ends with:

   He (Marcion) sang in catena (ܒܩܠܐ, which also invokes Cana) at the wedding feast, renowned tunes about the creator.
   He changed the catena so that you hear the silence of
   that new lyre (Mani) who composed,
   and exchanged the proper strings so that when we would sing
   we might empty (ܢܣܠܐ or "sing" ܢܫܠܐ) full vessels.
   Blessed is the learned one who sings with the lyre
   of the true one who sent him.

   This juxtaposition of Marcion and Mani as sharing in their dualistic cosmogony echoes throughout this *madrāšâ*. See stanza's 2 and 4.

31   For the flexibility of the meaning of this term, see Robert Payne Smith, *Thesaurus Syriacus*, vol. 1 (Oxford: Clarendon, 1879), 3783f. Hereafter *ThSyr*.

those authors ever suggested that Mani was actually a student in Bar Daysan's school.[32] Nor is Ephrem making such an assertion. He begins his *Second Discourse to Hypatius* with a discussion of what he understood to be internal contradictions in Mani's teaching. He interrupts this demonstration about the illogical nature of Mani's ideas regarding the binding of the soul within the body with a parallel attack on Bar Daysan: "Now on this matter Bar Daysan, that teacher of Mani, is found to speak subtly."[33] This statement introduces a brief discussion of Bar Daysan's teaching concerning the composite nature of the soul.

The remark about Bar Daysan's role as master itself, however, is made in passing, as an anecdotal fact. Ephrem's own words suggest that the inclusion of Bar Daysan was a mere tangent. After his explanation of Bar Daysan's error regarding the soul, Ephrem continues, "However, it is not the filth of Bardaisan we have come to stir up now; for the decay of Mani is enough."[34] The inclusion of Bar Daysan at this point in a discourse devoted to disproving Mani is a matter of showing doctrinal precedence and of creating an association between the two for his audience.

Ephrem again indicates the precedent set for Mani by Bar Daysan in his *Fourth Discourse to Hypatius*. He says in one place, "Because Mani was unable to find another way out, he entered, though unwillingly, by the door which Bar Daysan opened;"[35] and later, "Since Mani saw then that he was not able to find a river crossing at another spot, he was forced to come and cross from where Bar Daysan had crossed."[36] These two quotations imply a hint of reluctance on Mani's part, a relationship of expedience more than anything else.[37] Ephrem's portrayal of their association here should dispel the thought that any master-disciple relationship might have been intended by Ephrem. Bar Daysan is Mani's teacher in that his teachings showed Mani the way forward in some

---

32   See Han Drijvers, "Mani und Bardaisan: Ein Beitrag zur Vorgeschichte des Manichäsmus," in *Mélanges d'histoire des religions offerts à Henri-Charles Puech*, 459–469 (Paris: Presses universitaires de France, 1974); idem, *Bardaisan of Edessa* (Assen: van Gorcum, 1966); Barbara Aland, "Mani und Bardesanes: Zur Entstehung des manichäischen Systems," in Albert Dietrich, ed. *Synkretismus im syrisch-persischen Kulturgebiet* (Göttingen: Vandenhoeck and Ruprecht, 1975), 123–143; See also Ilaria Ramelli, *Bardaisan of Edessa: A Reassessment of the Evidence and a New Interpretation* (Piscataway, NJ: Gorgias, 2009), esp. 53–54.
33   *PR* I, 8, xxxii. Translation adapted from Mitchell.
34   *PR* I, 9, xxxiii.
35   Adapted from Mitchell. *PR* I, 122; xc.
36   Ibid.
37   There is also a likely play on words in each instance here. Ephrem appears to be alluding to Bar Daysan's conceptions of how a soul enters and exits the world which were key points of contention for Ephrem with Bar Dayan as well as Mani's teaching.

difficult corners of heretical speculation. Mani is clothed in the garb of an opportunist more than that of a disciple.

Mani and Bar Daysan are not alone in Ephrem's polemic of association. Marcion figures in prominently. The second-century Christian teacher was an infamous heretic even by Ephrem's own time. Indeed, Bar Daysan himself was one of those who had written against him. Moreover, Marcion's significance within Edessa was such that he finds his way into the Chronicle of Edessa, as do Bar Daysan and Mani,[38] whom Marcion is often teamed with in Ephrem's polemics of association. The construction of this trio is based largely on Ephrem's perception of the similarities between the teachings of the three and the fact that they are all outsider adversaries whose influence Ephrem still needs to engage for the sake of his community.

Ephrem's first contention with their claims to religious authority is that they are 'outsiders.' Ephrem does not trust that any of these three has a legitimate claim to lead a congregation on account of proper ordination. He suggests they have either stolen their ordinations from the true church or they have simply fabricated their own. In his twenty-second *Hymn against Heresies* he says:

> Let them be questioned discerningly.
> From whom did they receive ordination?[39]
> If they received [it] from us and refused [it],
> this is sufficient for our truth.
> But if they ordained priests and were presumptuous,
> this is sufficient to rebuke [them].
> This is more than enough for their shame:
> that anyone is a priest if he is willing
> to lay his hand on his head.
>
> The exalted one inclined to Mount Sinai
> and laid his hand on Moses.
> Moses placed it on Aaron,
> and it stretched to John.

---

38 For the Syriac, see Ignacio Guidi, *Chronica Minora*, Scriptores Syri, Textus (Louvain: Secretariat du CSCO, 1903), 3; for the Latin translation, see Ignacio Guidi, *Chronica Minora*, Scriptores Syri, Versio (Louvain: Secretariat du CSCO, 1903), 4. See also Han J.W. Drijvers, "Marcionism in Syria: Principles, Problems, Polemics," *The Second Century* 6 (1987–1988): 153–172; and Witold Witakowski, "The Chronicles of Edessa," *Orientalia Suecana* 33–35 (1984–1986): 487–498.

39 The phrase ܐܝܕܐ ܩܒܠ literally means "receive the hand," and most likely refers to the imposition of the hand of ordination.

> Therefore, our Lord said to him,
> "It is righteousness that I be baptized by you,"[40]
> so that the order would not perish at him [John].
> Our Lord gave it to his apostles,
> and behold within our church is its succession.
> Blessed is the one who committed his order to us.[41]

These stanzas place the succession between Marcion, Bar Daysan and Mani alongside and in direct contrast to that of Ephrem's church. For Ephrem, there is only one true ordination, tied into apostolic succession and remaining within the true church. The appearance here of Christ's spiritual lineage serves to emphasize the antiquity and the continuity of the church's authority. A similar passage occurs in *Hymns against Heresies* XXIV where the priestly line in which Christ is the nexus is shown to originate in Eden with Adam. More importantly Marcion, Bar Daysan, and Mani are shown to have no place in this line of authority at all:

> He had brought the church of the nations
> and then ruined the temple of the nation.
> When he uprooted the temple of the nation,[42]
> a church was constructed there.
> Marcion did not minister in it,
> so that there had not been any memory of him until now.
> Neither did Arius enter it,
> nor Mani nor Bar Daysan.
> The prophets agree with the apostles.
> Blessed is He, the Lord of the orders!

> He handed down[43] from Adam to Noah,
> He extended from Noah to Abraham,
> and from Abraham to Moses,
> and from Moses to David,

40　Matthew 3:15.
41　*HcH* XXII.18–19.
42　For a discussion of the terms 'nation' and 'nations' applying to the Jews and the Gentiles respectively, see Robert Murray, *Symbols of Church and Kingdom* (1975. Reprint, Piscataway, NJ: Gorgias, 2004), 41–68. For notes on Ephrem's biblical, agrarian symbolism that may help to clarify his use of 'uprooted' (ܥܩܪ) here, see the final section of this paper.
43　ܫܠܡ indicates transmission, but it is also the root for the concept of succession, as in apostolic succession. *ThSyr*, 1, 1538 f.

and from David also to the captivity,
and from Babylon to our Savior.
The nation was scattered and cut off,
and all its transmissions ceased.
Now the hand of the apostles transmitted.
Blessed is the Lord of their transmissions.[44]

Yet again, Ephrem's mode in his polemic is to alienate the adversaries by contrasting their features with those of the true church. He is denying them any claim to authority based on apostolic succession through ordination. Any authority that they execute is not vested in them from the true church. Instead, they only have power because they have either stolen it or generated it themselves. As much is said by Ephrem about how they came about their congregations:

The crafty Bar Daysan stole one.
And they [each] made it like a flock that is inside.
Marcion had abandoned his sheep;
Mani fell upon and captured them from him,
One rabid man was biting another rabid man.
They [each] called a flock by their own names.
Blessed is the one who threw them out of his house.[45]

Ephrem represents this troika as competing, even thieving shepherds. Ephrem is trying to exploit connections between these groups. In doing this, he unites their works for two primary purposes. First, when any one of them is found guilty of faulty teaching, the others are equally shamed through their association.[46] Second, their disputes with one another become the defining element of their tradition. Thus, Ephrem links them through their contrast as well as their similarity. The polarity that Ephrem generates between their shared lineage and their incessant infighting and fabrication is intended to heighten the sense of chaos that Ephrem would like to attach to his audience's perception of these three. To build this tension, Ephrem comments on the similarities between

---

44 XXIV.21–22.
45 XXII.3. See Griffith, "Thorn," 417 for translation.
46 For the significance of the use of the polarity between shame and honor in Ephrem's polemics, see Phillipus J. Botha, "Social Values and Textual Strategy in Ephrem the Syrian's Sixth Hymn on the Fast," *Acta Patristica et Byzantina* 11 (2000): 22–32.

Marcion, Bar Daysan, and Mani; the discontinuities between the three; and the idea that discord is the constant that proves a shared tradition.

In his *Fifth Discourse to Hypatius* Ephrem shows that Bar Daysan and Mani share a heritage of critical syncretism: they take what they want from those who preceded them and they add to it as they see fit. In his discussion of the nature of God's relationship to space in the teachings of the three, Ephrem says, "But as for Mani and Marcion, the one before, the other after, with Bar Daysan in the middle, one inquiry is spread over against the three of them."[47] He addresses himself to Marcion first, on account of the fact that he came first. Bar Daysan, who came second, is shown to be a revisionist. From Marcion's teachings he "chose one and rejected another."[48] Finally, Mani, the most recent of the three, appears as a fabricator as he "yet again makes many things."[49] The image that Ephrem is casting of these three is not the perpetuation of a certain school of thinking from teacher to disciple. Instead, Marcion's ideas are picked over by Bar Daysan, whose innovation is then further developed by Mani. Ephrem presents a progression, however realistic, of adaptation and modification. He concludes his review of the developments of their thoughts in this section with the remark:

> So this proves concerning their teaching that it is the elaborate arrangement of men .... And as children who play on a wide staircase, when one sits on the lowest step, his companion, in order to anger him, sits on the middle step, and in order to resist both, another sits on the upper step, even such are the heralds of error.[50]

Here Ephrem portrays his opponents as childhood playmates who cannot resist the urge to try to outdo one another. He suggests that their actions are based in the response of each one to his predecessor's work rather than on true conviction regarding their own ministry.

Later in the same discourse, Ephrem more explicitly emphasizes the point that these three actually subjected their teachings to this competitive one-upmanship:

---

47 *PR* I, 134, xcvii.
48 *PR* I, 135, xcvii.
49 *PR* I, 136, xcvii.
50 *PR* I, 138–140, xcviii–ix. Following Mitchell's translation. See also *HcH* XLIX.1 where a similar progression is present.

And because Mani saw that before him his two elder brothers, namely Marcion and Bar Daysan, that one has said, 'below' and the other 'above' —because he saw that if he said 'below,' that had been said; and if he said 'above,' he saw that it was prior,[51] not knowing how he should represent the two entities which he introduced, when he saw that 'above' and 'below' [were] taken, he represented them one opposite the other on a level.[52]

For Ephrem, the teachings of his opponents are not based in revelation or in maintaining the continuity and integrity of the doctrines of the church, but in competition and contention. Reinforcing the theme of modification within the succession he is describing, Ephrem notes that Marcion "added deceit," Bar Daysan "embellished his deceit," and Mani "changed everything."[53]

Ephrem even defends against a potential counter-argument that these three did not come from a common lineage. He says:

> Let them be questioned about their ages,
> who is older than his friend?
> Might Mani seize the right of the first-born?
> Bar Daysan was prior to him
> and might Bar Daysan be declared the eldest?
> Younger is his age than the prior ones.
> Marcion, the prior thorn,
> the first-born of the thicket of sin,[54]
> the tare which was the first and germinated:
> May the upright one trample his growth![55]

This stanza implies that the disciples of Marcion, Bar Daysan, and Mani were prone to arguing for the authority of their traditions based on their antiquity. Ephrem argues that only one of them has the right to this claim. However, Marcion, who is acknowledged as the first among the trio, is not permitted to wear his status as a badge of honor. In this stanza, Ephrem subverts the perceived deference to antiquity. Being first is not actually to be coveted. Each of these

---

51 Mitchell has "not new" and adds "(lit. ancient)" here.
52 *PR* I, 140, xcix. Adapted from Mitchell.
53 *HcH* XXII.2.
54 See Irenaeus, *Adversus Haereses*, III.3.4 where he quotes Polycarp who, when asked by Marcion if he knows him, calls the latter "the first-born of Satan."
55 *HcH* XXII.17.

three wanted to claim their antiquity not in relation to one another, but as to who had the deepest, richest pedigree. However, by naming Marcion as the first-born, Ephrem prevents any of them from claiming ancient lines of inheritance.[56]

It is clear from Ephrem's inclusion of a specific example regarding Mani's own pedigree that Ephrem's arguments against the continuity and antiquity of his opponents' heritage are—at least in part—a reaction to their own claims. In Ephrem's *Against Mani* he opposes the Manichaean suggestion that Mani's philosophy could be found in more ancient times in the likes of Hermes and Plato, and moreover, in the teachings of Jesus.[57] Ephrem's response to this claim is logical. If the teachings of all of these thinkers agreed, Ephrem admits, the Manichaean claim would have merit. However, Ephrem notes that astrologers, Magians, geometers, and doctors, as well as the disciples of Plato and Jesus have faithfully maintained the teachings of their founders. Although these traditions have each been well maintained, they do not agree with one another. Therefore, they do not form any part of an ancient Manichaean tradition. Ephrem denies Mani's narrative concerning the antiquity of his traditions by pointing out that neither Hermes, Plato, nor their disciples were ever in agreement with each other, let alone with Jesus, or Mani himself.[58] He says:

> If they also with Hermes and Plato and Jesus and others from the beginning were proclaiming a refining in succession,[59] as Mani says, how is it their disciples are not proclaiming their teaching in Egypt and in Greece and in Judaea like that which Mani teaches? For how is what Jesus teaches like what Mani teaches?[60]

Rather than a faithful proponent of ancient tradition, Ephrem portrays Mani's claim to antiquity and his links to Christ in particular as a fraud. Indeed, Ephrem suggests Mani as a counter-type to Christ. In his twenty-second *madrāšâ against Heresies*, Ephrem singles out Mani saying:

---

56   For commentary on the use of the terms 'thorns' and 'tares' in Ephrem's polemic, see the section on biblical, agrarian symbolism below.
57   *PR* II, 208–212, xciii–c.
58   *PR* II, 211, xcix. On Mani's claims to the antiquity of his message, see Nicholas Baker-Brian, *Manichaeism: An Ancient Faith Rediscovered* (New York: T&T Clark, 2011), 27–28. There are many parallels between Ephrem's polemics against the dualists Mani and Marcion and those of Tertullian against Marcion. Much like Ephrem, Tertullian attests to Christians who are too focused on harmonizing their Christianity with Greek philosophy. See *De praescriptione haereticorum* 7.
59   Lit. "and are coming."
60   *PR* II, 209–210, xcix. Following Mitchell.

> May he (Mani) be called the Messiah of fraud.
> He breathes a spirit of falsehood into his prophets,
> and he broke his body for his disciples,
> and divided the earth for his heralds,
> in the name of our Lord, against our Lord!
> And when he judged that he was not being received; openly, among many
> he named himself an 'apostle,' the 'Paraclete,' who shot up (ܢܒܥ) yesterday.
> Blessed is the one who stayed and then caught him.[61]

A pretender to the role of Messiah, Mani is said to inspire his prophets. The phrase "spirit of falsehood" (ܪܘܚ ܫܘܩܪܐ) mocks the Manichaean claim that Mani was the Paraclete, or promised "spirit of truth" (ܪܘܚܐ ܕܫܪܪܐ) of John 15:26 and 16:13.[62] Likewise, the connection of "falsehood" to Mani's prophets ties this claim into the discussion of false prophets (ܢܒܝܐ ܕܓܠܐ) in Matthew 7:15–20. He "broke his body" as Jesus did at the Last Supper.[63] He sent out apostles, just as Jesus is said to have done.[64] Likewise, Ephrem suggests that it is only after Mani was not accepted as a messiah figure that he downgrades himself to apostle and Paraclete. The portrayal of Mani's actions as reactive in nature continues the theme that false teachers belong to a tradition of change and modification as opposed to one of continuity and consistency.

---

61 HcH XXII.14. The phrase "who sprung up just yesterday," appears in HcH XXIV.19 as well. Ephrem claims that Mani proclaimed his status as the Paraclete after 300 years had passed since Pentecost; PR II, 209; xcviii–ix. It is clear that Ephrem is trying to emphasize his perception of this claim as an obvious anachronism. The verb ܢܒܥ is used again of the impetus for Marcion's teaching about the origin of the world in Ephrem's *Third Discourse to Hypatius* (PR I, 70, l. 6).

62 For the Peshitta, I have used the Comprehensive Aramaic Lexicon's online edition at http://cal.huc.edu/.

63 Matthew 26:26 and parallels, including 1 Corinthians 11:24. Ephrem may also be making an allusion to Mani's purported violent death by flaying. See HcH 1.18. For a discussion of the state of our knowledge about the accounts of Mani's 'Last Days,' their place within polemics against Manichaeism, and the potential veracity of their core features, see Iain Gardner, "Mani's Last Days," in *Mani at the Court of the Persian Kings: Studies on the Chester Beatty Kephalaia Codex* (Leiden: Brill, 2014), 159–205.

64 Luke 9:1f., 22:35–38, and Matthew 28:18–20. Mani taught his followers to spread his message throughout the world. There are several accounts of early Manichaean missionary efforts, and also of the reactions of the Church and government officials within the Roman Empire to this new faith. Mani's sending out his own apostles is recounted in the Cologne Mani Codex (CMC). See e.g. Gardner and Lieu, *Manichaean Texts from the Roman Empire* (Cambridge: Cambridge University Press, 2004), 5, 77.

With the concept of the truth (orthodoxy) of the true one (Christ) residing with the true ones (Nicene Orthodox Christians) in the true church as his starting point, each reference Ephrem makes to a teacher as deceptive, fraudulent, or misleading is intended to automatically initiate a reaction of disavowal within Ephrem's audience.[65] Through such repetition, Ephrem is attempting to etch these word associations into the minds of his congregants, driving a mental wedge between their orthodoxy and the teaching of these opponents. Are they to be members of the true church of the true one, Christ, or are they to join the side of the "sons of error" who serve the master of error, Satan?

3   Combating Satan's Legacy

While the focus so far has been on Ephrem's remarks about Bar Daysan and Mani as heroes of their own upstart, broken, and corrupt traditions, Ephrem does introduce another champion: Satan—the patriarch of the legacy of error, which does not bolster authority, but tears it down. Marcion, Bar Daysan and Mani have not fallen out of the picture, they are recast in this dramatic symbolism as Satan's pawns in this ancient battle between truth and error. In this section we first look at Satan as the instigator of the deeds of the enemies of the church in Ephrem's heresiography. It is evident that the lineage of error and the lineage of Satan are one and the same. Furthermore, Ephrem constructs a familial structure wherein Satan is the patriarch of the family of error, in which the heterodox trio are sons together.

4   Satan as Catalyst for Error

In his *Hymns against Heresies*, Ephrem suggests that Satan is working vicariously through Marcion, Bar Daysan and Mani, guiding their deceitful actions:

> Indeed how zealous the Evil one has become in the body of Bar Daysan! With his mouth he cut off the hope he was pronouncing to his sect.

---

65   For Ephrem's dichotomous depiction of religious history between the poles of truth and error, see Griffith, "Thorn," 402. Philip Botha emphasizes Ephrem's use of certain language to create polarities to encourage his audience to have a personal sense of antithesis toward a particular pole in Ephrem's antitheses, "Christology and Apology." *Hervormde Teologiese Studies* 45, no. 1 (1989): 21; see also "The Textual Strategy of Ephrem the Syrian's Hymn Contra Haereses I," *Acta Patristica et Byzantina* 15 (2004): 80.

He drew his tongue and denied his own resurrection.
But he (the Evil one) drove Marcion rabid and he maddened him,
And he (Marcion) attacked his maker and insulted his creator.
With Mani (ܒܡܢܝ) as with his own clothes (ܒܡܐܢܘ) he (the Evil one)
dressed himself up and spoke through him.[66]

In this stanza Ephrem portrays the Evil one using Bar Daysan's body as his agent. The irony in this is that it is through Bar Daysan's body that the Evil one directs Bar Daysan to deny bodily resurrection.[67] Satan also tampers with Marcion's mind leading him to publish blasphemous things about the God of creation.[68] Embodying himself in Mani, Satan speaks through him.[69] In all, Ephrem condemns Satan as the kernel for the fallacies of each of these adversaries.

Later in the same *madrāšâ against Heresies* Ephrem speaks further of Satan's operative role in the propagation of error. In this instance, Satan does not maneuver within his hosts, but rather gives them the appropriate tools with which to wage war on the truth:

---

66 *HcH* I.9.
67 Ephrem was convinced that Bar Daysan did not believe in the resurrection of the body. See *Carmina Nisibina* in *Des heiligen Ephrem des Syrers Carmina Nisibina*, Corpus Scriptorum Christianorum Orientalium, vols. 92–93/102–103 (Louvain: Secrétariat du CSCO, 1961–1963), especially XLVI and LI; see also Drijvers, *Bardaisan*, 152–153. Ramelli (*Bardaisan*, 217–231) argues that Ephrem misunderstood Bar Daysan's conception of the resurrection of the body, which she suggests has a spiritual more than physical focus and is thus akin to that of Origen and Gregory of Nyssa. Ute Possekel has drawn strong lines of comparison between Origen and Bar Daysan concerning their thoughts on the role of astral bodies in regards to determining events. See her "Bardaisan and Origen on Fate and the Power of the Stars," *Journal of Early Christian Studies* 20 (2012), 515–541.
68 Elsewhere Ephrem more specifically refers to Marcion's "stranger." There are many examples, but the most explicit is perhaps *HcH* XLVIII.1: "Marcion, who authored, 'the stranger,' he declared estranged (or excommunicated)."
69 Ephrem mocks Mani's claim that his inspiration was given to him by his divine twin, Greek σύζυγος, particularly highlighted in the *CMC*. Ephrem is making a pun off of Mani's name. The evil one is 'in Mani' (ܒܡܢܝ) just as one might be "in their own clothes" (ܒܡܐܢܘ). This mockery is based in Ephrem's use of the term *manâ* (ܡܐܢܐ), which can mean, 'instrument,' 'vessel,' or 'garment.' What is particularly interesting about this pun is that Ephrem utilizes the image of the heretics being mere garb for Satan in his own acts of deception, whether it is dealing with Mani or not. Perhaps Ephrem simply found a coincidence ripe for the exploitation when applying this trope to Mani. For further discussion of this particular play on Mani's name, see Griffith, "Thorn," 412. It is also worthwhile to consider Andrew Palmer's article "'A Lyre without a Voice:' The Poetics and Politics of Ephrem the Syrian," which deals with the positive imagery of biblical heroes and even Ephrem as a lyre played by Christ. See *ARAM* 5 (1993): 371–399. In *HcH* XL Ephrem contrasts the lyre of Moses to that of Marcion and Mani.

> He arms them all with every evil;
> Marcion with blasphemy, Bar Daysan with error;
> the dregs which are left over are emptied into Mani.[70]

In this stanza, Marcion and Bar Daysan are being outfitted by Satan.

The imagery of Satan utilizing and empowering these opponents of the church is similar to Ephrem's interpretation of the relationship between Satan and the serpent in the garden. The serpent is merely the medium that God permitted Satan to utilize in carrying out his testing of Adam and Eve.[71] In Ephrem's *Commentary on Genesis*, Satan speaks through the serpent in such a way that Eve does not even recognize him. She even denies that it was Satan who deceived her.[72] In this way Ephrem's adversaries are like serpents being assumed by Satan in his effort to deceive and corrupt. The serpent, Satan's original dupe, is their ancient ancestor, the first in a primal lineage of error.

5   The Ancient Family of Error

In his first *madrāšâ* written against the enemies of the true church, Ephrem associates Marcion, Bar Daysan, and Mani with the serpent explicitly:

> And the sons of the serpent begin to creep in the earth
> so that they might lead astray the ignorant and lead away captive the innocent
> head of the race like the former serpent.
> He saw Eve in the time of ignorance.
> He pacified her and she trusted; he counseled her and she rejoiced;
> he sprang upon her and she repented; and he struck her and she mourned.[73]

---

70   *HcH* I.12.
71   *CGen* II.32. Sebastian Brock (*Hymns on Paradise* (Crestwood: St. Vladimir's Seminary Press, 1990), 226) refers to the *Wisdom of Solomon* 2.24 for further insight into Satan as the "secret instigator."
72   *CGen*, II.16, 18. This also relates very closely to the portion of the tale of Job where Satan asks for permission to try Job's faith. See Ephrem's *Hymns on Paradise*, XII.11. For how the *Commentary on Genesis* is likely intended as a refutation of Bar Daysan, Marcion and Mani, see Edward G. Matthews Jr. and Joseph P. Amar, *St. Ephrem the Syrian: Selected Prose Works*, ed. Kathleen McVey (Washington: Catholic University of America Press, 1994), 61–62, and 64.
73   *HcH* I.13.

In Ephrem's symbolic interpretation of the careers of this trio, these outsider adversaries are tied directly into the initial act of deception. In their lineage is that deceit which brought about the first sin. This is their family. They are 'sons of error'[74]—sons of the original author of error, of Satan himself.

In his *Third Discourse to Hypatius* Ephrem addresses Satan's ancestral role in the lineage of our troika. First, he alludes to the nature of the relationship between the three as cancers which pervert the teaching(s) of one another and then spread their new aberrations. Ephrem's caricature of his adversaries is one of infestation and mutation. In the following passage, however, Ephrem names the originator of the consistently deviant behavior of these "sons of error." It is their father, Satan. Ephrem says:

> And see how they are like, one to the other, perverse (ܚܕܬܐ) cancers (ܣܪܛܢܐ),[75] since each of them distorts (ܗܦܟ) and metastasizes, not in order to draw nearer to the scripture, but in order to turn away (ܣܛܐ) from it. And doubtless, Satan (ܣܛܢܐ) their father, swift is his distorting (ܗܦܟ), because he is a native of error. Since they are foreigners among foreigners (the most foreign), they blaspheme endlessly.[76]

---

74 Cf. *HcH* XIV.7; they are called 'sons of fraud' in the following stanza (8).

75 Ephrem seems to be aware of either Tertullian's use of the imagery of a spreading cancer, or a common or intermediary source exists, for Tertullian says in his section against Aristotelian dialectic: *Hinc illae fabulae et genealogiae interminabiles et quaestiones infructuosae et sermones serpentes uelut cancer* ... [From here (that dialectic art) those endless fables and genealogies and fruitless questions and conversations are creeping like a cancer]. Both *sartanê* (ܣܪܛܢܐ) and *cancer* can be translated either as a crab or as the disease cancer. Each term was used for the sign in the zodiac. Indeed, each instance could be read as referring to the crawling of a crab. Interestingly, *sartanê* has excellent potential for mocking the name of Satan, ܣܛܢܐ, and Tertullian's participle *serpentes* can also be the *nomen agentis* meaning 'serpents.' For Ephrem's play on the names of his opponents, see Griffith ("Thorn," 412–413) where he discusses how Ephrem plays on the names of the adversaries in *HcH* 11.1 as well. Tertullian *De praescriptione haereticorum* 7; S.L. Greenslade, *Early Latin Theology* (Philadelphia: Westminster, 1956), 35.

76 *PR* I, 70. Ephrem notes the link between Satan's relationship to the adversaries and their inclination toward infighting in *4Hyp* where he calls Mani and Bar Daysan serpents saying, "For it is right for us to lift ourselves from between the two serpents in order that they might fight with one another." (*PR* I, 122, xc). The nature of the relationship is not clear. However, Ephrem's interest in conveying an image of conflict between the communities is certain. Note that Mitchell misread parts of this passage. He has:
> And see how like the perverse crabs are to one another each one of whom takes a devious course and goes forth, not to come to the Scriptures, but to turn aside from the Scriptures! And, perhaps, Satan, their father, took a somewhat devious course, because he is a native in Error—that is because they are foreigners from foreigners, who do not blaspheme at all.

This quote emerges in the *Third Discourse to Hypatius* amidst a discussion of the initial incident that caused the darkness and the light, good and evil, or matter and soul to intermingle.[77] Satan is also portrayed as an indigenous resident in the realm of error. On account of the fact that he is their father, by birthright Marcion, Bar Daysan, and Mani are also citizens within that realm. In this territory their ancestry could not be more illustrious. They are descended not only from the original medium of deception, the serpent, but they are indeed heirs of the one who secretly worked through him and them, Satan.

6   Ephrem's Biblical, Agrarian Symbolism of Error

Throughout Ephrem's polemic against Bar Daysan and Mani runs a symbolic theme of agrarian society. Ephrem talks about thorn bushes and tares, sheepfolds and pastures, wolves, and springs. The use of this natural imagery in his polemic of lineage is the focus of this section. Let us begin with a quote we have looked at already in this paper, one that is clearly dealing with the heritage of our duo:

> Let them be questioned about their ages,
> who is older than his friend?
> Might Mani seize the right of the first-born?
> Bar Daysan was prior to him
> And might Bar Daysan be declared the eldest?
> Younger is his age than the prior ones.
> Marcion, the prior thorn,
> the first-born of the thicket of sin,[78]
> the tare which was the first and germinated:
> May the upright one trample his growth![79]

As noted above, Ephrem's point in this stanza is to rob these heretics of their

---

[77]   The section immediately preceding this quotation, in which Ephrem was apparently laying out his perception of the positions of Marcion, Bar Daysan, and Mani regarding the cause of the initial encounter between their respective dualist principles, is ridden with lacunae. On Bar Daysan's cosmology according to Ephrem, see Drijvers, *Bardaisan*, 130–143. For a summary of Manichaean cosmogony and cosmology, see Johannes van Oort, "Manichaeism," In *Religion, Past and Present*, ed. Hans Dieter Betz, et al. vol. VIII (Leiden: Brill, 2010), 25–30 and Baker-Brian, *Manichaeism*, 110–118.
[78]   See note 54 above.
[79]   *HcH* XXII.17.

ability to claim that any one of their lineages is ancient. To do this Marcion is declared the first, suggesting that their heritage begins with him in the second century. Likewise, his being the "first" also implies that these others came along in succession.

Agrarian imagery also appears when Ephrem explicitly qualifies just how Marcion is primogenitor. Specifically, he is the first thorn "of the thicket of sin." Alternately, he is also named the first weed to sprout. In these images we begin to see something of Ephrem's biblical-agricultural symbolism of lineage or pedigree. The uses of the terms "thorn" (ܟܘܒܐ) and "tare" (ܙܝܙܢܐ) function here as allusions to the parable of the sower and that of the tares in the thirteenth chapter of the Gospel of Matthew.[80]

In the parable of the sower (Matthew 13:3–23), a farmer casts seeds in such a fashion that they fall on various surfaces. Some of the seed will grow well, in good soil, with little or no disturbance; some will fall on rock and not grow at all; some will grow but will be choked out by thorns (ܟܘܒܐ) that grow along with it. In this allusion, Ephrem is inserting these false teachers as the thorns that choke the young plants and suffocate orthodoxy.

In the parable of the tares (Matthew 13:24–30, 36–43), a landowner sows wheat in a field only to have his servants tell him later that someone else has come along and sown tares (ܙܝܙܢܐ). The final course of action ordered by the master is to allow the weeds to remain among the wheat and only separate it out once the wheat has had a chance to grow, rather than any action that might cause some of the wheat to fail to grow.

Jesus' own interpretation of the tares parable in Matthew 13.37b–39a reflects its formative role in Ephrem's symbolic thought here. Jesus says:

> He who sows the good seed is the Son of man. The field is the world; the good seed are the sons of the kingdom; the tares are the sons of the evil one; and the enemy is the one who sowed them.[81]

For Ephrem, the wheat that are "sons of the kingdom" are members of the true church, while the tares, those "sons of the evil one," are the adherents of false religious traditions. The tares' status as sons of the evil one reinforces the links between these heterodox teachers and Satan that were discussed in the previous section. Ephrem's use of this imagery places Bar Daysan and Mani

---

80 Cf. Matthew 13:3–23 and 24–30, 36–43 respectively and their parallels.
81 Translated from the Syriac Gospel according to Matthew, British Foreign Bible Society edition, accessed through the Comprehensive Aramaic Lexicon site at cal.huc.edu.

as shoots that have grown within the thorny thicket of Marcion. When reading Ephrem, references to thorns and tares must conjure up images from the parables in Matthew 13. Moreover, Jesus' explanation of the latter parable in Matthew 13:37–43 is a rubric for Ephrem's use of the terms 'tares' and 'thorns' within his polemic. This reading of Ephrem is reflected in the first stanza of the twenty-third of his *Hymns against Heresies*:

> The apostles were the twelve
> plowmen of the whole world.
> And there was not a place nor a region
> that was called by their names
> until the tares appeared,
> after the plowmen departed.
> And the tares called the wheat
> by their (the tares') own names.
> On the day of the harvest they will be uprooted.
> Blessed is the one whose harvest has come about!

Ephrem assumes Jesus' antitheses into his own typology.

To further understand the force of the polarizing nature of these remarks for Ephrem's community, one must consider his parallel use of biblical-agricultural imagery to highlight the continuity and strength of his own tradition. Much as he uses the symbols of a briar patch and sprouting weeds to describe his opponents, Ephrem speaks of Christ as the vine of truth of John 15. Ephrem joins other early Christians in interpreting this passage of scripture along communal lines. Commenting on a passage from the hymns *On the Crucifixion* (V.9) Robert Murray says, "the whole image once again emphasizes the vital continuity, through grafting, of the new shoot (Christ) and its abundant growth (the church) with the former vine [Judaism]..."[82] Indeed, Ephrem's use of agricultural imagery is pervasive. He sees each person metaphorically as having a particular horticultural pedigree. Unlike his dualist opponents however, this pedigree is not essential, but associative. It has not to do with whether one is evil or good by nature, but whether or not one belongs to the true one or the evil one.[83] Ephrem's symbolic idiom is universal. Every reference to a branch,

---

[82] *Symbols*, 102. Insertions in parentheses are from Murray's commentary; that in brackets is mine.

[83] See my "Bar Dayṣān" (98–137) for Ephrem's engagement with Matthew 7:15–20 (and its parallels) and 12:33–37 in response to the actions and words of his adversaries, and his interpretation of those passages over against his opponents. There Ephrem's terminology

root, tree, fruit, bitterness, sweetness, vine, grape, fig, thorn, tare, thicket, etc. must be recognized as part of this biblical, agricultural typology. Each of these is either on the side of Christ, the true vine and the vineyard of truth, or of the evil one, the thorn and the thicket.[84]

For Ephrem, the antithesis of the vine and the thicket juxtaposes two alternative models of heritage and tradition. Just as Marcion was the first of a thicket of sin, Christ is the first shoot of the vineyard of truth.[85] The latter is grafted into the vineyard of Israel which has despaired and will otherwise die. Thus, the vine of the Jews was rejected, and through Christ a fresh vine was grafted in, the Gentile church. In contrast, the traditions of Mani and Bar Daysan are those of a thicket attempting to choke out the truth as it grows of tares which have "sprung up," crowding the true wheat.[86]

Ephrem employs the imagery of a sprouting weed to show a lack of heritage in his opponents. As opposed to the church which was grafted into a deep tradition, Marcion simply "sprang up" (ܕܢܚ). Similar language is also used of Mani:

> And when he judged that he was not being received (as a Messiah himself); openly, among many
> he named himself an 'apostle,' the 'Paraclete,' who shot up (ܕܢܚ) yesterday.
> Blessed is the one who stayed and then caught him.[87]

Here, Ephrem portrays Mani's claim to be an apostle and a Paraclete as Mani's attempt to graft himself into the vine of Christ. However, Ephrem's suggestion

---

expands into trees, their roots, their fruit, and whether that fruit is bitter or sweet. This biblical, agrarian imagery is simply another layer of symbolism in Ephrem's polemic. That it already resonates with antithetical interpretations makes it particularly appealing for Ephrem's polemical aims.

84 See Murray's entire chapter, "The vineyard, the Grape and the Tree of Life," in *Symbols* (95–130) in order to get a broader perspective on the role of some of this agricultural imagery in early Syriac Christian literature.
85 John 15.
86 In Ephrem's *Hymns against Julian* we find the term 'tare' used in an association with pagans (1.4). The reference to thorns is present as well (11.10) where it is said of Julian: "the thorns, the people of his kindred, and the brambles, his kindred." In the same stanza, Julian is also said to be a direct threat to the orthodox church; he might "cover them up with the thorny tangle of his paganism." For an English translation, see Judith M. Lieu, "Translation," in *The Emperor Julian: Panegyric and Polemic*, ed. Samuel N.C. Lieu (Liverpool: Liverpool University Press, 1986) 112.
87 *HcH* XXII.14.

that Mani "shot up just yesterday" argues that Mani's claim is anachronistic and invalid.[88] Mani is a furtive weed, planted after the fact. He, like Marcion, has no true roots of which to speak.

Similar agricultural imagery is also used in associations of heretics with the evil one and his agency within them:

> He (the Evil one) gave to Bar Daysan a storehouse of tares.
> He (Bar Daysan) covered and suffocated wheat with his thorns and tares.
> He (the Evil one) girded him (Bar Daysan) with a bundle of tares.
> Naked wolves he (the Evil one) gave to Marcion
> The clothes of lambs he (Marcion) stole so that on the outside he might cover them.
> As for Mani, he is like a wild boar always stirring up its mud.[89]

Again Satan endows Marcion and Bar Daysan with tools fit for participants in a subversive mission against the church while Mani, on the other hand, is engulfed in filth. Ephrem is securing for Bar Daysan a place as the sower of the tares (heterodox believers) that will crowd the wheat (orthodox believers) of the true church and will not be able to be sorted out until later. This is yet another place where it seems as though Ephrem is revealing that there are those in his congregation whom he views as Marcionites, Bar Daysanites and Manichaeans. Bar Daysan is also cast as the sower of thorn bushes which will try to choke out the faith of orthodox believers. The fact that Ephrem is suggesting that Bar Daysan is both the origin of weeds which will crowd in the church and thorns that will attack is enhanced by the remark that the Evil one will also bundle him up in tares, presumably to hide the thorns.[90]

Accusations of hiding one's true vicious intent behind a less ominous façade are common in polemical discourse. Ephrem slots Marcion as the agent who dressed wolves with sheep's clothing. The term I have translated as "naked" (ܥܪܛܠܐ) here could also be read as "apostles." The play on words is fully intended. Ephrem is suggesting that Marcion's emissaries are wolves in sheep's

---

88 Recall that the introduction of the Paraclete (John 15:26–27) comes on the heels of Jesus' explanation of the vine and the branches in John 15:1–17. See note 54 above.
89 *HcH* 1.10. There is likely a reference to 2 Peter 2:22 in the final line here, where, referring to false prophets and teachers it says "but it has happened to them according to the true verb: 'the dog returns to its vomit and the pig to its rolling in the mud.'"
90 Similar imagery appears in XXII.2, where Ephrem calls Mani "a sheaf of thorns and tares."

clothing. His apostles are naked wolves, ready to don their ovine disguises.[91] This image is strong enough on its own. Its connotations are very meaningful for Ephrem's context; his opponents appear to be safe, but what lies beneath is deadly.

This image alludes to Matthew 7:15 where false prophets are referred to by Jesus as "wolves in sheep's clothing." Particularly significant about this reference, however, is that to Mani—and to Marcion as well[92]—Luke 6:43–45 (Matthew 7:16–20 is its parallel) was a very important exegetical proof text for dualism.[93] For Ephrem, among the implications of the phrase "wolves in sheep's clothing" is a demonstration of the faulty exegesis of this gospel pericope by his opponents. In keeping with Ephrem's symbolic polemic, the power of this association does not stop with its vulgar negative connotations, nor with its exegetical allusion. Ephrem is also drawing an analogy between wolves in sheep's clothing and Satan in heretics' bodies.

The association of Mani with dregs, filth and waste in so many of the passages we have examined is further evidence that he is the one adversary Ephrem is most concerned with discrediting. This is seen in a similar line found in his *Fifth Discourse to Hypatius* which reads:

> And because this is the teaching which comes from the party of Marcion and Valentinus and Bar Daysan and he (i.e. Mani) is the last of all, that is to say, the dregs, lower than that above him, so this one (Mani) is more abominable than those before him.[94]

Ephrem again uses the imagery of filth, dregs, or muck portraying Mani's teachings as sediment that is muddying the waters of the spring of the true Christian

---

91 The double entendre here is utilized by Ephrem in a similar way in the seventy-fourth of his *Hymns on Faith*, where it is a true apostle who is naked and being clothed in the warmth of the spirit. See Wickes, *St. Ephrem*, 352. The image of one's true essence being covered over by an alternate exterior is common in Ephrem's symbolic thought, whether formative or polemical. One can find it dealing with the garment of words by which humans know God, but not fully; the robes of glory upon the initial human couple in Paradise; the body of Jesus; the serpent which Satan wore; wolves in sheep's clothing; and so on. See Sebastian Brock, *The Luminous Eye: The Spiritual World Vision of Saint Ephrem the Syrian* (Kalamazoo: Cistercian Publications, 1992), 86, 88, 95; Murray, *Symbols*, 80.

92 Notably, Tertullian begins his *Adversus Marcionem* (2) by addressing the Marcionite interpretation of this pericope.

93 It is also worth noting that though a tale of a wolf in sheep's clothing does appear in later editions of *Aesop's Fables*, no evidence exists for its presence in that collection by the time of Ephrem.

94 *PR* I, 125, xcii. Following Mitchell.

faith.⁹⁵ This agrarian imagery of the spring or watering hole is central to the pastoral symbolism of his theology. Indeed Ephrem sees the aim of his teaching as a means to clear the sediment from the well of Christian doctrine.⁹⁶ He envisions the troika as disturbed silt that is polluting the church. Furthering the imagery of filth, Ephrem describes Marcion and Bar Daysan alongside Mani in their efforts to muddy the pool of truth in the church. Ephrem's final *Hymn against Heresies* captures well how his use of these types is directly connected to his vision of his heresiographical ministry:

> Truly also in all the mouths of the church is the straining
> of my pool (ܪܡܬܐ) from that mud and filth
> of the house of the rabid Marcion; and my clearing from the dregs
> and the ungodliness of the house of Mani; and my purifying from the dirt
> of the wiles of Bar Daysan, and from the stink
> of the stinking Jews.⁹⁷
>
> Your horn exalts your Lord, believing church!⁹⁸
> For there is not in you the book of that rabid Marcion,

---

95 Ephrem's referring to Mani in particular as filth, sewage, muck, dregs, etc. is undoubtedly motivated by the cosmological and ritual language of matter in Manichaeism. See *CMC* 84.6 where the reference is to human refuse; throughout the *Kephalaia* are references to waste that settles to the ground or is swept into the abyss in the working out of cosmic salvation (see Sarah Clackson, et. al., *Dictionary of Manichaean Texts*, vol. 1 (Turnhout: Brepols, 1998), 132); for the data on the use of similar terms in Persian texts, see Nicholas Sims-Williams and Desmond Durkin-Meisterernst, *Dictionary of Manichaean Texts*, vol. 3, part 1 (Turnhout: Brepols, 2004), 208. See Morehouse, "Bar Dayṣān," 169–170.

96 The concept of a clear pool calls to mind Sebastian Brock's discussion of the image of the 'luminous eye' in his work by the same title (*Luminous*, 71f.). ܥܝܢܐ ܢܗܝܪܐ, the Syriac for 'luminous eye,' can also be read 'clear well.' Ephrem is often found playing on this phrase intending one or both of these images.

97 This inclusion of the Jews as a tagline at the end of a polemical statement against Marcion, Bar Daysan and Mani occurs in a few places. For example, see the conclusion of the *Fifth Discourse to Hypatius* (*PR* I, 185, cxix). See Morehouse, "Bar Dayṣān," 173–176. However, it is not nearly as common as when Ephrem is addressing neo-Arians. For more on the role that the Jews play in Ephrem's polemic against the Arians, see Shepardson, *Anti-Judaism* and "'Exchanging Reed for Reed:' Mapping Contemporary Heretics onto Biblical Jews in Ephrem's *Hymns on Faith*." *Hugoye* 5, no. 1 (January 2002). http://www.bethmardutho.org/index.php/hugoye/volume-index/137.html (accessed April 24, 2013).

98 For Ephrem's use of 'horn' (ܩܪܢܐ) to indicate the church's teaching, see *HcH* XXV.4; Murray, *Symbols*, 174. Murray also notes the potential for the contemporary use of the trumpet (or *shofar*) in the liturgy of the Syriac-speaking church, *ibid.*, n.6.

> nor even a book of that raving Mani,
> nor the Book of Mysteries, the thorns of Bar Daysan.[99]
> Two covenants of the king and the son of the king
> are set down in your Ark.[100]
>
> Let not, my Lord, the labors of your pastor be cheated,
> so that I have not troubled your sheep, except what was appropriate.
> I have kept the wolves from it and built, as far as I could,
> enclosures (ܣܝܓ̈ܐ)[101] of *madrāšê* for the lambs of your pasture.[102]

Ephrem is a composer of orthodox *madrāšê* against the compositions of Marcion, Bar Daysan, and Mani. Sidney Griffith demonstrates well that this is indeed a conscious illustration and motivation in Ephrem's psyche.[103] His use of the imagery of the shepherd protecting his flock from wolves alludes once again to Matthew 7:15.[104] The extent of the function of this pericope in Ephrem's polemics may be further emphasized by the fact that it bookends both the collection of his *Hymns against Heresies* and his *Discourses*

---

99 This claim that the true church does not contain a specific book of Bar Daysan is particularly interesting. It is also mentioned in *HcH* I.14, where Ephrem also mentions a *Book of Thunder* and a *Book of Hosts*. Is it possible that not all of Bar Daysan's writings were understood to be objectionable by Ephrem? That Ephrem explicitly rejects any of Bar Daysan's writings does further intrigue the reader in light of the similarities between the *BLC* and Ephrem's polemic, which I discuss in "Bar Dayṣān," 55–66. Ute Possekel explores Bar Daysan's legacy in early Christianity, including Ephrem, in her "Bardaisan's Influence in Late Antique Christianity," *Hugoye* 21 (2018): 81–125. For discussion of the *Book of Mysteries*, see Drijvers, *Bardaisan*, 163; Ramelli, *Bardaisan*, 59 and 224n393, where she suggests that the role of "mysteries" (ܐܪ̈ܙܐ) in the title may reflect a symbolic nature of this text, perhaps further linking Ephrem to Bar Daysan. Mani also seems to have written a work by this name, polemicizing against Bar Daysan's homonymous composition. See Michel Tardieu, *Manichaeism*, trans. M.B, DeBevoise (Urbana, Il: University of Illinois Press, 2008), 38. For a discussion of this work from the Manichaean perspective, see Baker-Brian, *Manichaeism*, 84–85.

100 A connection between the Ark of the Covenant, right teaching, and Scripture is also established in *Hymns on Paradise*, VI.1; Brock, 108 f.

101 Interestingly, in his *Second Discourse to Hypatius* Ephrem accuses the Manichaean god of being inept because it did not prepare defenses for itself when it ought to have known the dark was coming against it. Among the metaphors that he uses for this type of protective wall, he suggests a hedge for his vineyard and an enclosure for his flock. Ephrem is using the very images with which he discusses defending his own proto-orthodox community to attack weakness in his opponent's mythology. See *PR* I, xlv; 292.

102 *HcH* LVI, 8–10.

103 See his "St. Ephrem."

104 See the discussion of Ephrem's utilization of this allusion in my "Bar Dayṣān," 90–94.

to Hypatius.[105] Heir to and subject under the apostolic authority of the true church, he beseeches Jesus to join him in his efforts. In his twenty-second *Hymn against Heresies*, Ephrem uses language of Jesus, the good one, as a good shepherd guiding his wayward flock toward reconciliation:

> May the good one in his love turn them
> from wandering to within his pasture.
> Blessed is he who cares about the evil ones.[106]

Ephrem quite expectedly sees himself as doing "the Lord's work." He certainly wants his audience to distinguish his work from that of his opponents. And his teaching from those of Bar Daysan and Mani.

7   Conclusion

When Ephrem refers to Bar Daysan as Mani's master he has an ideological lineage in mind. Moreover, Ephrem uses the links he can show between Marcion, Bar Daysan and Mani to develop the idea of a succession of error. It is certainly the idea that is more significant than the reality for Ephrem as well. Much else could be said about what actual historical links there might be between each of these teachers and their disciples,[107] but Ephrem's work is not one of

---

105   *HcH* I.10 and LVI.10, as well as the closing remarks in both the first and the final *Discourses to Hypatius* at very least allude to Matthew 7:15–20.
106   *HcH* XXII.2.
107   While it is highly unlikely that any of these three ever met in person, there are real connections between their works. Marcion's influence on subsequent generations cannot be underestimated. Indeed, we know from Eusebius (*Hist. Eccl. 4.30.1–3*) that Bar Daysan wrote against Marcion. From Hippolytus (*Haer. 7.31*) we know that a Marcionite, Prepon, wrote against Bar Daysan. For a further discussion of the differences between the Bar Daysan preserved in sources, see T. Jansma, *Natuur, lot en vrijheid: Bardesanes, de filosoof der Arameeërs en zijn images* [Nature, fate and freedom: Bardaisan, the philosopher of the Aramaeans and his "images"] (Wageningen: Veenman, 1969), who concludes that it is nearly impossible to tease out the real Bar Daysan from the variety of accounts we possess. For a more positivist approach to the potential reconstruction of Bar Daysan's own views, and with an eye toward rehabilitating his reputation, see Ilaria Ramelli's *Bardaisan of Edessa*. Conversely, Mani, or at very least his early disciples, used Marcion's work. Samuel Lieu tells us that Adda used Marcion's *Antitheses* and even wrote his own work based on it (*Manichaeism in the Later Roman Empire*, 38–40). Richard Lim suggests that this work was the *Modion* (*Public Disputation, Power, and Social Order in Late Antiquity* (Berkeley: University of California Press, 1995), 238 f.), but Jacob Albert van den Berg contends that it is instead Adimantus' *Disputationes* (*Biblical Argument in Manichaean Missionary*

history, but of theology, not as much of the concrete as of the typological. In Ephrem's telling, Mani borrowed from and added to the erroneous teachings of Bar Daysan who had done the same with Marcion's. Having established this progressive relationship, Ephrem ventures to reveal the progenitors of their legacy, tying them to the most despicable of characters—Satan and the serpent in the garden. Indeed, Ephrem posits a legacy for them that stretches from the work of Satan inside the serpent down to his own time. By showing their roots to be in the deceptive works of Satan, Ephrem discredits his opponents' claims to true teaching or revelation. Thus, Ephrem's positing of Mani's dependence on Bar Daysan is part of a much larger project to show that Mani's teachings and practices are not the faithful representation of ancient antecedents. He is not the disseminator of some aged tradition. On the contrary, his pronouncements are either corruptions of previous teachings or complete fabrications, which are not brought to him by a divine emissary as he claimed, but rather by Satan himself.

In this way he directly opposes the legacy of Mani and that of Marcion and Bar Daysan to that which Ephrem himself has in his church. Within this antithesis, Ephrem portrays his church's legacy as rooted in God's revelation to Adam and passed down by the laying on of hands all the way to John the Baptist's baptism of the Christ. It is Christ's commissioning of the apostles, which passed on this unbroken succession to the church Ephrem himself participates in. This is the chief assurance of spiritual authority for Ephrem, and he assures his audience that that authority rests in their church alone.

More to the point, especially in the *Prose Refutations and the Hymns against Heresies*, Ephrem assures his audience that his opponents' churches bear no genuine religious authority. Ephrem was not simply looking to marginalize these three outsider adversaries, but to demonstrate their belonging to an altogether other 'church,' that of error. Their marks are not those of solidarity, but of disjunction. They are the tares and thorns that ruin the harvest; the muck that pollutes the pure spring of truth; and the wolves in sheep's clothing

---

Practice: The Case of Adimantus and Augustine (Leiden: Brill, 2009), 140–141, 150–160). His argument is based in part on the connections between the names Addas, Adda(i), and Adimantus (19–21). Cf. Nicholas Baker-Brian, "'… *quaedam disputationes Adimanti*' (Retr. I.xxii.1): Reading the Manichaean Biblical Discourse in Augustine's *Contra Adimantum*," *Augustinian Studies* 34 (2003): 184. The suggested links between Bar Daysan and Mani are as unlikely as those between Marcion and Bar Daysan. Moreover, a number of later Arabic sources tell us that Mani wrote against Bar Daysan. See Ramelli, 53–54. Cf. Drijvers, 202–203. Indeed, the earliest known claim that Mani owes anything to Bar Daysan is in fact Ephrem's.

mingling with the flock. Their champion is not Christ, but Satan. They are not the redeemed sons of Adam, but the cursed children of the serpent.

Acknowledgements

This paper is based on the third chapter of my doctoral dissertation "Bar Dayṣān and Mani in Ephraem the Syrian's Heresiography" (PhD diss., The Catholic University of America, 2013).

Bibliography

Aland, Barabara. "Mani und Bardesanes: Zur Entstehung des manichäischen Systems." In *Synkretismus im syrisch-persischen Kulturgebiet*, ed. A. Dietrich, 122–143. Abhandlungen der Akademie der Wissenschaft in Göttingen 96. Göttingen: Vandenhoeck and Ruprecht, 1975.

Amar, Joseph P. *A Metrical Homily on Holy Mar Ephrem by Jacob of Sarug: Critical Edition of the Syriac Text, Translation and Introduction*. Turnhout: Brepols, 1995.

Baker-Brian, Nicholas. "'*quaedam disputationes Adimanti*' (Retr. I.xxii.1): Reading the Manichaean Biblical Discourse in Augustine's *Contra Adimantum*." *Augustinian Studies* 34 (2003): 175–196.

Baker-Brian, Nicholas. *Manichaeism: An Ancient Faith Rediscovered*. New York: T&T Clark, 2011.

Bauer, Walter. *Orthodoxy and Heresy in Earliest Christianity*. Translated and edited by Robert A. Kraft and G. Krodel. Philadelphia: Fortress Press, 1971.

Beck, Edmund. *Des heiligen Ephraem des Syrers Carmina Nisibina*. Louvain: Secrétariat du CSCO, 1961–1963.

Beck, Edmund. *Des heiligen Ephraem des Syrers Hymnen contra haereses* [*Textus*], vol. 1, 2 vol. Louvain: Secretariat du Corpus Scriptorum Christianorum Orientalium, 1957.

Beck, Edmund. Ed., *Des heiligen Ephraem des Syrers Hymnen contra haereses* [*Versio*], vol. 2, 2 vol. Louvain: Secretariat du Corpus Scriptorum Christianorum Orientalium, 1957.

BeDuhn, Jason, and Mirecki, Paul. "Placing the *Acts of Archelaus*." In *Frontiers of Faith*, edited by Jason BeDuhn and Paul Mirecki, 1–22. Leiden: Brill, 2007.

Beeson, Charles Henry. *Acta Disputationis Archelai*. Leipzig: J.C. Hinrichs'sche Buchhandlung, 1906.

Berg, Jacob Albert van den. *Biblical Argument in Manichaean Missionary Practice: The Case of Adimantus and Augustine*. Leiden: Brill, 2009.

Biesen, Kees den. *Simple and Bold: Ephrem's Art of Symbolic Thought*. Piscataway, NJ: Gorgias, 2006.

Botha, Phillipus, J. "Antithesis and Argument in the Hymns of Ephrem the Syrian." *Hervormde Teologiese Studies* 44 (1988): 581–595.

Botha, Phillipus, J. "Christology and Apology." *Hervormde Teologiese Studies* 45, no. 1 (1989): 19–29.

Botha, Phillipus, J. "Social Values and Textual Strategy in Ephrem the Syrian's Sixth Hymn on the Fast." *Acta Patristica et Byzantina* 11 (2000): 22–32.

Botha, Phillipus, J. "The Structure and Function of Paradox in the Hymns of Ephrem the Syrian." *Ekklesiastikos Pharos, N.S.* 73, no. 2 (1991): 50–62.

Botha, Phillipus, J. "The Textual Strategy of Ephrem the Syrian's Hymn Contra Haereses I," *Acta Patristica et Byzantina* 15 (2004): 57–75.

Brock, Sebastian P. "Christians in the Sasanian Empire: A Case of Divided Loyalties." In *Religion and National Identity*, edited by Stuart Mews, 1–19. Studies in Church History, vol. 18. Oxford: B. Blackwell, 1982.

Brock, Sebastian P. "Eusebius and Syriac Christianity." In *Eusebius, Christianity, and Judaism*, edited by Harold Attridge and Gohei Hata, 212–234. Detroit: Wayne State University Press, 1991.

Brock, Sebastian P. *The Luminous Eye: The Spiritual World Vision of Saint Ephrem the Syrian*. Kalamazoo: Cistercian Publications, 1992.

Brock, Sebastian P., and Susan Ashbrook Harvey. *Holy Women of the Syrian Orient*. Berkeley: University of California, 1987.

Brown, Peter. "The Diffusion of Manichaeism in the Roman Empire." *Journal of Roman Studies* 59, no. 1/2 (1969): 92–103.

Bundy, David. "Bishop Vologese and the Persian Siege of Nisibis in 359 C.E.: A Study in Ephrem's *Mēmrē on Nicomedia*." *Encounter* 63 (2000): 53–65.

Bundy, David. "Vision for the City: Nisibis in Ephraem's Hymns on Nicomedia." In *Religions of Late Antiquity in Practice*, edited by Richard Valantasis, 189–206. Princeton: Princeton University Press, 2000.

Clackson, Sarah, Erica Hunter, Samuel N.C. Lieu, and Mark Vermes. *Dictionary of Manichaean Texts*. Vol. 1. Corpus Fontium Manichaeorum, Subsidia II. Turnhout: Brepols, 1998.

Drijvers, Han J.W. *Bardaisan of Edessa*. Assen: van Gorcum, 1966.

Drijvers, Han J.W. "Die Oden Salomos und die Polemik mit den Markioniten im syrischen Christentum." In *Symposium Syriacum 1976 célébré du 13 au 17 septembre 1976 au Centre Culturel 'Les Fontaines' de Chantilly (France), Communications*, 39–55. Roma: Pontificium Institutum Orientalium Studiorum, 1978.

Drijvers, Han J.W. "Mani und Bardaisan: Ein Beitrag zur Vorgeschichte des Manichäismus." In *Mélanges d'histoire des religions offerts à Henri-Charles Puech*, 459–469. Paris: Presses universitaires de France, 1974.

Drijvers, Han J.W. "Marcionism in Syria: Principles, Problems, Polemics." *The Second Century* 6 (1987–1988): 153–172.

Fiano, Emanuel. "The Trinitarian Controversy in Fourth Century Edessa." *Le Muséon* 128 (2015): 85–125.

Gardner, Iain. "Mani's Last Days." In *Mani at the Court of the Persian Kings: Studies on the Chester Beatty Kephalaia Codex*, edited by Iain Gardner, Jason BeDuhn, and Paul Dilley, 159–205. Nag Hammadi and Manichaean Studies 87. Leiden: Brill, 2014.

Gardner, Iain, and Samuel Lieu. *Manichaean Texts from the Roman Empire*. Cambridge: Cambridge University Press, 2004.

Greenslade, S.L. *Early Latin Theology*. Philadelphia: Westminster, 1956.

Griffith, Sidney H. "'Faith Seeking Understanding' in the Thought of Ephraem the Syrian." In *Faith Seeking Understanding: Learning and the Catholic Tradition*, edited by George C. Berthold, 35–55. Manchester, NH: Saint Anselm College Press, 1991.

Griffith, Sidney H. "Ephraem, the Deacon of Edessa, and the Church of the Empire." In *DIAKONIA: Studies in Honor of Robert T. Meyer*, edited by T.P. Halton and J.P. Willman, 22–52. Washington: Catholic University of America Press, 1986.

Griffith, Sidney H. "The Marks of the 'True Church' according to Ephraem's *Hymns against Heresies*." In *After Bardaisan: Studies on Change and Continuity in Syriac Christianity: A Festschrift in Honor of Professor Han J.W. Drijvers*, edited by G.J. Reinink and A.C. Klugkist, 125–140. Louvain: Peeters, 1999.

Griffith, Sidney H. "St. Ephraem, Bar Daysān and the Clash of *Madrāshê* in Aram: Readings in St. Ephraem's Hymni contra Haereses." *The Harp* 21 (2006): 447–472.

Griffith, Sidney H. "The Thorn among the Tares: Mani and Manichaeism in the Works of St. Ephrem the Syrian." *Studia Patristica* 35 (2001): 403–435.

Guidi, Ignacio. *Chronica Minora*. Scriptores Syri, Textus. Louvain: Secretariat du CSCO, 1903.

Guidi, Ignacio. *Chronica Minora*. Scriptores Syri, Versio. Louvain: Secretariat du CSCO, 1903.

Hartung, Blake. "The Authorship and Dating of the Syriac Corpus attributed to Ephrem of Nisibis: A Reassessment." *Zeitschrift für Antikes Christentum* 22, no. 2 (2018): 296–321.

Hayes, Andrew. *Icons of the Heavenly Merchant: Ephrem and Pseudo-Ephrem in the Madrashe in Praise of Abraham of Qidun*. Piscataway: Gorgias, 2016.

Jansma, T. *Natuur, lot en vrijheid: Bardesanes, de filosoof der Arameeërs en zijn images* [Nature, fate and freedom: Bardaisan, the philosopher of the Aramaeans and his "images"]. Wageningen: Veenman, 1969.

Lieu, Judith M. "Translation [of *Hymns against Julian*]." In *The Emperor Julian: Panegyric and Polemic*, edited by Samuel N.C. Lieu, 105–128. Liverpool: Liverpool University Press, 1986.

Lieu, Samuel. "The Diffusion, Persecution and Transformation of Manichaeism in Late Antiquity and pre-Modern China." In *Conversion in Late Antiquity: Christianity, Islam, and Beyond: Papers from the Andrew W. Mellon Foundation Sawyer Seminar, University of Oxford 2009–2010*, edited by Arietta Papaconstantinou and Daniel L. Schwartz, 124–140. London: Routledge, 2016.

Lieu, Samuel. *Manichaeism in Mesopotamia and the Roman East*. Leiden: Brill, 1994.

Lieu, Samuel. *Manichaeism in the Later Roman Empire and Medieval China, a Historical Survey*. Manchester: Manchester University Press, 1985.

Lim, Richard. *Public Disputation, Power, and Social Order in Late Antiquity*. Berkeley: University of California Press, 1995.

Le Boulluec, Alain. *La notion d'hérésie dans la littérature grecque, IIe–IIIe siècles*. Vol. 1, *De Justin à Irénée*. Paris: Études Augustiniennes, 1985.

Le Boulluec, Alain. *La notion d'hérésie dans la littérature grecque, IIe–IIIe siècles*. Vol. 2, *Clément d'Alexandrie et Origène*. Paris: Études Augustiniennes, 1985.

Matthews, Edward G. Jr. and Joseph Amar. *St. Ephrem the Syrian: Selected Prose Works*, edited by Kathleen McVey. Washington: Catholic University of America Press, 1994.

McVey, Kathleen E. "Were the Earliest *Madrāšē* Songs or Recitations?" In *After Bardaisan: Studies on Change and Continuity in Syriac Christianity: A Festschrift in Honor of Professor Han J.W. Drijvers*, edited by G.J. Reinink and A.C. Klugkist, 185–199. Louvain: Peeters, 1999.

Mitchell, Charles Wand. *S. Ephrem's Prose Refutations of Mani, Marcion and Bar Daisan*. Vol. 1. London: Williams and Norgate, 1912.

Mitchell, Charles Wand, completed by A.A. Bevan and Francis Crawford Burkitt. *S. Ephrem's Prose Refutations of Mani, Marcion and Bar Daisan*. Vol 2. London: Williams and Norgate, 1921.

Morehouse, Robert. "Bar Dayṣān and Mani in Ephraem the Syrian's Heresiography." PhD diss., The Catholic University of America, 2013.

Murray, Robert. *Symbols of Church and Kingdom*. 1975. Reprint: Piscataway, NJ: Gorgias, 2004.

Oort, Johannes van. "Manichaeism." In *Religion, Past and Present*, edited by Hans Dieter Betz, Don S. Browning, Bernd Janowski, and Eberhard Jüngel, vol. VIII, 25–30. Leiden: Brill, 2010.

Palmer, Andrew. "'A Lyre without a Voice:' The Poetics and Politics of Ephrem the Syrian." *ARAM* 5 (1993): 371–399

Pedersen, Nils Arne. "Syriac Texts in Manichaean Script: New Evidence." In *Mani in Dublin: Selected Papers from the Seventh International Conference of the International Association of Manichaean Studies in the Chester Beatty Library, Dublin, 8–12 September 2009*, edited by Siegfried G. Richter, Charles Horton, and Klaus Ohlhafer, 284–288. Leiden: Brill, 2015.

Possekel, Ute. "Bardaisan and Origen on Fate and the Power of the Stars." *Journal of Early Christian Studies* 20 (2012): 515–541.

Possekel, Ute. "Bardaisan's Influence on Late Antique Christianity." *Hugoye* 21, no. 1 (2018): 81–125.

Possekel, Ute. *Evidence of Greek Philosophical Concepts in the Writings of Ephrem the Syrian*. Louvain: Secrétariat du CSCO, 1999.

Ramelli, Ilaria. *Bardaisan of Edessa: A Reassessment of the Evidence and a New Interpretation*. Piscataway, NJ: Gorgias, 2009.

Reed, Annette Yoshiko. "Beyond the Land of Nod: Syriac Images of Asia and the Historiography of 'The West.'" *History of Religions* 49, no. 1 (2009): 48–87.

Ross, Stephen K. *Roman Edessa: Politics and Culture on the Eastern Fringes of the Roman Empire, 114–242 C.E.* London: Routledge, 2001.

Ruani, Flavia. *Hymnes contre les hérésies*. Bibliothèque de l'Orient Chrétien 4. Paris: Les Belles Lettres, 2018.

Ruani, Flavia. "Le manichéisme vu par Éphrem le Syrien: analyse d'une refutation doctrinal." 2 vols. PhD diss., École Pratique des Hautes Études, Paris / Sapienza, Università di Roma, 2012.

Ruani, Flavia. "Les controverses avec les manichéens et le développement de l'hérésiologie syriaque." in *Les controverses religueses en syriaque*. Edited by Flavia Ruani. Études syriaques 13. Paris: Geuthner, 2016.

Russell, Paul. "Nisibis as the Background to the Life of Ephrem the Syrian." *Hugoye* 8, no. 2 (July 2005). http://www.bethmardutho.org/index.php/hugoye/volume-index/416.html (accessed April 24, 2013).

Russell, Paul. *St. Ephraem the Syrian and St. Gregory the Theologian Confront the Arians*. Mōrān 'Eth'ō 5. Kottayam, India: St. Ephrem Ecumenical Research Institute, 1994.

Shepardson, Christine, *Anti-Judaism and Christian Orthodoxy: Ephrem's Hymns in Fourth Century Syria*. Washington: The Catholic University of America Press, 2008.

Shepardson, Christine, "'Exchanging Reed for Reed:' Mapping Contemporary Heretics onto Biblical Jews in Ephrem's *Hymns on Faith*." *Hugoye* 5, no. 1 (January 2002). http://www.bethmardutho.org/index.php/hugoye/volume-index/137.html (accessed April 24, 2013).

Sims-Williams, Nicholas, and Desmond Durkin-Meisterernst. *Dictionary of Manichaean Texts*. Vol. 3, Part 1. Corpus Fontium Manichaeorum, Subsidia III. Turnhout: Brepols, 2004.

Sims-Williams, Ursala. "Some Syriac Manichaean Treasures in the British Library." British Library. Last modified September, 23, 2013. https://britishlibrary.typepad.co.uk/asian-and-african/2013/09/some-syriac-manichean-treasures-in-the-british-library.html (accessed April 1, 2018).

Smith, Kyle. *Constantine and the Captive Christians of Persia: Martyrdom and Religious*

Identity in Late Antiquity. The Transformation of Classical Heritage 57. Oakland, California: University of California Press, 2016.

Smith, Robert Payne. *Thesaurus Syriacus*. Vol. 1. Oxford: Clarendon, 1879.

Spät, Eszter. "The 'Teachers' of Mani in the *Acta Archelai* and Simon Magus." *Vigiliae Christianae* 58 (2004): 1–23.

Tardieu, Michel. *Manichaeism*. Translated by M.B. DeBevoise. Urbana, Il: University of Illinois Press, 2008.

Vermes, Mark, trans. *Acta Archelai [The Acts of Archelaus]*. Louvain: Brepols, 2001.

Walker, Joel. *The Legend of Mar Qardagh*. The Transformation of the Classical Heritage 40. Berkley: University of California Press, 2006.

Wickes, Jeffrey. *Bible and Poetry in Late Antique Mesopotamia: Ephrem's Hymns on Faith*. Berkley: University of California Press, 2019.

Wickes, Jeffrey, trans. *St. Ephrem the Syrian: The Hymns on Faith*. Fathers of the Church 130. Washington, DC: Catholic University of America Press, 2015.

Witakowski, Witold. "The Chronicles of Edessa." *Orientalia Suecana* 33–35 (1984–1986): 487–498.

10

Manichaeism in John Chrysostom's Heresiology

Chris L. de Wet

Abstract

This chapter examines John Chrysostom's (ca. 349–407 CE) statements about Manichaeism. The study enquires regarding the extent of his knowledge of Manichaean beliefs and practices, and whether he possibly had contact with Manichaeans. The study is not so much interested in determining how accurately or inaccurately Chrysostom understands and characterises Manichaeism, although at some points the analysis does venture into some of these issues. In the first instance, Chrysostom's views about Manichaean theology and—especially—Christology are delineated. Proceeding from the negative evaluation of the material cosmos in Manichaeism, the study then analyses Chrysostom's critique of Manichaean views of the body, especially as it relates to freedom of choice. His accusations of Manichaean practices, namely starving as salvation, and the accusation of castration, are also examined. Finally, Chrysostom's response to the Manichaean rejection of a corporeal resurrection is analysed, after which some conclusions are drawn.

1   Introduction[1]

John Chrysostom (ca. 349–407 CE), the prolific preacher who later became the bishop of Constantinople in the early fifth century CE,[2] was probably no

---

[1] A version of this study was presented as a paper at a conference with the theme, "Manichaeism and Early Christianity," organised by Prof. Johannes van Oort, 23–25 March 2019, University of Pretoria. I especially thank Johannes van Oort, Nils Arne Pedersen, Michel Tardieu, Iain Gardner, and Jason BeDuhn for their comments on the paper and our discussions about Manichaeism, more generally, during the conference. An abbreviated version of this study was published as: Chris L. de Wet, "John Chrysostom on Manichaeism," *HTS Theological Studies* 75.1 (2019): 1–6.

[2] General studies on Chrysostom's life include: Chrysostomus Baur, *John Chrysostom and His Time*, trans. M. Gonzaga, 2 vols. (Vaduz: Büchervertriebsanstalt, 1988); John N.D. Kelly, *Golden Mouth: The Story of John Chrysostom—Ascetic, Preacher, Bishop* (Ithaca, NY: Cornell University Press, 1998); Wendy Mayer and Pauline Allen, *John Chrysostom* (London: Routledge, 1999); Rudolf Brändle, *John Chrysostom: Bishop–Reformer–Martyr*, trans. John Cawte and Silke Trzcionka, Early Christian Studies 8 (Strathfield: St. Paul's, 2004).

stranger to Manichaeism. "Chrysostomus erhebt sich gegen die Manichäer, weil sie ihm zeitlich nicht so ferne stehen," writes a nineteenth-century translator and commentator of Chrysostom's homilies.[3] Having been born and raised in Syrian Antioch most of his life, he regularly rebukes Manichaeans in his homilies and treatises.[4] Besides Chrysostom, we know of several other historical sources attesting to the presence of persons adhering to the Manichaean faith Antioch.[5] The purpose of this study is to examine Chrysostom's claims on the nature of Manichaeism and the practices of Manichaeans.[6] The study is not so much interested in determining how accurately or inaccurately Chrysostom understands and characterises Manichaeism, although at some points the analysis will venture into some of these issues. It is commonly known that the polemics of late antique Christian heresiology was least concerned with accurate and fair descriptions and judgements of non-orthodox opponents.

I will pose two questions: first, what did Chrysostom profess to know about Manichaeism and what should we make of these Chrysostomic references to Manichaeism? Second, what is signified in the way Chrysostom speaks about Manichaeans, and all those with whom they are grouped? Thus, I should clarify that I am more interested in Chrysostom's construction of Manichaeism— how he constructs the movement, and to what ends. The study, inevitably, also enquires about the nature and form of Chrysostom's heresiography, which exhibits a slightly different form compared to other well-known Eastern heresiologists.

---

3 Joseph Schwertschlager, trans., *Des heiligen Kirchenlehrers Johannes Chrysostomus: Commentar zum Galaterbrief, aus dem Griechischen übersetzt und mit kurzen Erläuterungen versehen*, Ausgewählte Schriften des heiligen Chrysostomus, Erzbischof von Constantinopel und Kirchenlehrer 7, ed. Valentin Thalhofer (Kempten: Kösel, 1882), 27.

4 Some initial comments on Manichaeism in Chrysostom's thought and rhetoric are made by Maria G. Mara, "Aspetti della polemica antimanichea di Giovanni Crisostomo," in *Atti dell'undicesimo simposio Paolino: Paolo tra Tarso e Antiochia. Archeologia/storia/religione*, ed. Luigi Padovese (Rome: Pontificia Università Antonianum, 2008), 195–199 and Wichard von Heyden, *Doketismus und Inkarnation: Die Entstehung zweier gegensätzlicher Modelle von Christologie* (Tübingen: Francke, 2014).

5 Samuel N.C. Lieu, *Manichaeism in Mesopotamia and the Roman East*, Religions in the Graeco-Roman World 118 (Leiden: Brill, 2015), 26–131; David Woods, "Strategius and the 'Manichaeans,'" *Classical Quarterly* 51.1 (2001): 255–264; Peter Brown, "The Diffusion of Manichaeism in the Roman Empire," *Journal of Roman Studies* 59 (1969): 92–103.

6 All translations from John Chrysostom's works are my own unless otherwise indicated. References to critical editions of Greek texts are provided in parentheses. It should be noted that for Chrysostom's homilies on the Pauline Epistles, I use the critical edition of Frederick Field, ed., *Ioannis Chrysostomi interpretatio omnium epistularum Paulinarum*, 7 vols. (Oxford: J.H. Parker, 1854–1862).

2 John Chrysostom's Knowledge about Manichaeism

Interestingly enough, Chrysostom does not have one single treatise devoted to the refutation of Manichaeism per se. We do possess an exegetical homily on Matthew 26:39 (with a parallel in Luke 22:42), with the title: "On the passage 'Father if it be possible let this cup pass from me, nevertheless not as I will but as you will': and against Marcionites and Manichaeans: also, that we ought not to rush into danger, but to prefer the will of God before every other will." (CPG 4369).[7] Besides this homily, we find only short and scattered, yet in some cases descriptive, references to Mani and Manichaeism throughout the mammoth Chrysostomic corpus.

What knowledge about Manichaeism does Chrysostom exhibit? His refutation of Manichaean teaching is based on two key premises: first, he attacks Manichaean theology, especially their views of God and Christ. Secondly, he criticizes what he perceives as Manichaean cosmic and corporeal pessimism. This is especially evident in his homilies on Genesis and other references to the creation narrative, in which he needs to prove that the material cosmos and corporeality is not inherently evil. Chrysostom is, broadly speaking, aware of the complex Manichaean pantheon and Manichaean dualism, and how it differs from other, apparently similar, views.[8] In reference to 2 Corinthians 4:4 and its notion of the "god of this age" (ὁ θεὸς τοῦ αἰῶνος τούτου), Chrysostom states:

> But who is the "god of this age"? Those that are diseased with Marcion's ideas declare that this is said referring to the Creator, the just only, but not good. For they say that there is a certain God, just but not good. But the Manichaeans say that the devil is meant here, wanting to introduce, from this passage, another creator of the world besides the true One, quite senselessly.[9]

Although Chrysostom often groups Marcionism and Manichaeism (and Valentinianism, actually) together, he shows here that he has some idea of the

---

7 The original Greek title reads: ΕΙΣ ΤΟ: Πάτερ, εἰ δυνατόν ἐστι, παρελθέτω ἀπ' ἐμοῦ τὸ ποτήριον τοῦτο· πλὴν οὐχ ὡς ἐγὼ θέλω, ἀλλ' ὡς σύ· καὶ κατὰ Μαρκιωνιστῶν καὶ Μανιχαίων· καὶ ὅτι οὐ χρὴ ἐπιπηδᾶν τοῖς κινδύνοις, ἀλλὰ παντὸς θελήματος προτιμᾶν τὸ τοῦ Θεοῦ θέλημα. The shorter Latin title reads: *In illud: Pater, si possible est, transeat hic calix.*
8 Mara, "Aspetti della polemica antimanichea," 195–196.
9 *Hom. 2 Cor.* 8.2 (Field 3.101): Τί δέ ἐστιν, Ὁ Θεὸς τοῦ αἰῶνος τούτου; Οἱ μὲν τὰ Μαρκίωνος νοσοῦντες, λέγουσι περὶ τοῦ Δημιουργοῦ τοῦ δικαίου μόνον, καὶ οὐκ ἀγαθοῦ, ταῦτα εἰρῆσθαι· λέγουσι γὰρ εἶναί τινα Θεὸν δίκαιον, καὶ οὐκ ἀγαθόν. Μανιχαῖοι δέ φασι τὸν διάβολον ἐνταῦθα λέγεσθαι, ἐκ τούτου δημιουργὸν τῆς κτίσεως ἕτερον ἐπεισαγαγεῖν παρὰ τὸν ὄντα βουλόμενοι, σφόδρα ἀνοήτως.

theological differences between these movements.[10] Furthermore, when we look at other Manichaean–'orthodox' Christian exchanges, especially between Augustine and Faustus, we know that this text was often used as a proof-text for Manichaean dualism.[11] Chrysostom is therefore knowledgeable of what we might call the economy of proof-texting among different alternative Christian groups, and he prepares his audience accordingly. He is also acutely aware of the Manichaean usual disdain for the Old Testament.[12] Let us consider more closely some of the topics to which Chrysostom responds in his anti-Manichaean rhetoric.

2.1 Christology

A great deal of Chrysostom's theological polemic against Manichaeism is reserved for refuting Manichaean Christology. The first issue relates to the incarnation of Christ. The most detailed description of the docetic tendencies in Manichaeism and similar movements is found in Chrysostom's homily against Marcionism and Manichaeism, in which he states:

> If then after all these things [in the Gospel accounts] have occurred, the evil mouth of the devil, speaking through Marcion of Pontus, and Valentinus, and Manichaeus of Persia, and many more heretics, has attempted to subvert the doctrine of the incarnation and has asserted a satanic utterance saying that He did not become flesh, nor was clothed with it, but that this was mere semblance [δόκησις], and an illusion [φαντασία], a piece of acting and pretence [σκηνὴ καὶ ὑπόκρισις], despite the suffering, the death, the burial, the thirst, crying aloud against this teaching.[13]

---

10   Mara, "Aspetti della polemica antimanichea," 197.
11   See esp. the discussion of Stephan Verosta, *Johannes Chrysostomus: Staatsphilosoph und Geschichtstheologe* (Graz: Verlag Styria, 1960), 225–226; see also, more generally, Jason D. BeDuhn, "A War of Words: Intertextuality and the Struggle over the Legacy of Christ in the *Acta Archelai*," in *Frontiers of Faith: The Christian Encounter with Manichaeism in the Acts of Archelaus*, ed. Jason D. BeDuhn and Paul Mirecki, Nag Hammadi and Manichaean Studies 61 (Leiden: Brill, 2007), 95.
12   *Hab. eun. spir.* 4, 5 (PG 51.284.52–55, 285.24–32); see, more generally, A. Böhlig, *Die Bibel bei den Manichäern und verwandte Studien.* Herausgegeben von Peter Nagel [und] Siegfried G. Richter. Nag Hammadi and Manichaean Studies 80. (Leiden: Brill, 2013), *passim* and, more specifically, Nils Arne Pedersen, René Falkenberg, John Møller Larsen, Claudia Leurini, *Biblia Manichaica I, The Old Testament in Manichaean Tradition. The Sources in Syriac, Greek, Coptic, Middle Persian, Sogdian, New Persian, and Arabic.* Corpus Fontium Manichaeorum. Biblia Manichaica I. (Turnhout: Brepols, 2017), *passim*.
13   *Pater, si poss.* 4 (PG 51.37.61–38.6): Εἰ οὖν τούτων ἁπάντων γενομένων τὸ πονηρὸν τοῦ διαβόλου στόμα διὰ Μαρκίωνος τοῦ Ποντικοῦ καὶ Οὐαλεντίνου, καὶ Μανιχαίου τοῦ Πέρσου, καὶ ἑτέρων

We again observe the pattern of comparing doctrines between Marcionites, Manichaeans, and Valentinians, this time highlighting their similarities in terms of docetism, with Chrysostom using the technical terms signified by it (e.g. δόκησις φαντασία).[14] We know that the issue of docetic Christology in Manichaeism is a complex matter,[15] but Chrysostom does not hesitate to generalise all the Christologies of Manichaeism and the other groups he mentions under the banner of δόκησις, as was common in early Christian polemical discourse.[16]

Moreover, Chrysostom devoted a significant amount of attention to the problem of volition and freedom of choice, both that of Christ and of humanity, in Manichaean thought, which is also evident in Augustine.[17] The idea that there is one divine will because there is only one divine Person is somewhat common among groups with a docetic Christology.[18] This issue about freedom of will is a major theme in Chrysostom's homily against the Marcionites and Manichaeans. In response to his Manichaean opponents, Chrysostom believed that "Christ is one divine Person possessing two natures and two wills, of which the one nature and will are divine, while the other nature and will belong to him as true man. Each nature and will has its own proper activities."[19] With refer-

---

πλειόνων αἱρέσεων ἐπεχείρησεν ἀνατρέψαι τὸν περὶ τῆς οἰκονομίας λόγον, καὶ ἤχησε σατανικήν τινα ἠχὴν λέγων, ὅτι οὐδὲ ἐσαρκώθη, οὐδὲ σάρκα περιεβάλετο, ἀλλὰ δόκησις τοῦτο ἦν καὶ φαντασία, καὶ σκηνὴ καὶ ὑπόκρισις, καίτοι τῶν παθῶν βοώντων, τοῦ θανάτου, τοῦ τάφου, τῆς πείνης. See also Chrysostom, *Ex. Ps.* 110.2 (PG 55.267.52–58).

14 On the phenomenon of Docetism in early Christianity more generally, see several essays in Joseph Verheyden et al., eds., *Docetism in the Early Church: The Quest for an Elusive Phenomenon*, Wissenschaftliche Untersuchungen zum Neuen Testament 402 (Tübingen: Mohr Siebeck, 2018). On the development of early Christian Christological discourse related to Docetism, see Wichard von Heyden, *Doketismus und Inkarnation: Die Entstehung zweier gegensätzlicher Modelle von Christologie* (Tübingen: Francke, 2014).

15 Majella Franzmann, *Jesus in the Manichaean Writings* (London: T&T Clark, 2003), 77–78.

16 Lieu, *Manichaeism in Mesopotamia*, 162–163, 204, 222, has shown a similar tendency with other Eastern Christian authors.

17 Kenneth M. Wilson, *Augustine's Conversion from Traditional Free Choice to "Non-Free Free Will": A Comprehensive Methodology*, Studien und Texte zu Antike und Christentum 111 (Tübingen: Mohr Siebeck, 2018), 293–298; Jason D. BeDuhn, *Augustine's Manichaean Dilemma, Volume 1: Conversion and Apostasy, 373–388 C.E.*, Divinations: Rereading Late Ancient Religion (Philadelphia: University of Pennsylvania Press, 2013), 284–285.

18 Paul W. Harkins, trans., *St. John Chrysostom: On the Incomprehensible Nature of God*, The Fathers of the Church 72 (Washington, D.C.: Catholic University of America Press, 1984), 106.

19 Harkins, *On the Incomprehensible Nature of God*, 206; see also Raymond J. Laird, *Mindset, Moral Choice and Sin in the Anthropology of John Chrysostom*, Early Christian Studies 15 (Strathfield: St. Paul's, 2012), 87–88.

ence again to Christ's prayer in Matthew 26, but in a different homily on this occasion, Chrysostom states:

> Furthermore, if the words of Christ's prayer are the words of God, there is another absurdity involved. For the words not only reveal a struggle but they point to two wills [θελήματα] opposed to each other: one, the Son's, and the other, the Father's. Christ's words: "Not as I will but as you will" (Matt. 26:39) are the words of one who is making this clear. But those heretics [i.e. followers of Mani, Marcion, and Paul of Samosata] never conceded this. When we constantly quote the text: "The Father and I are one" (John 10:30) in connection with his power, they keep saying that this was said in connection with the will because they maintain that the will of the Father and of the Son is one.[20]

The problem of Matthew 26:39, on the tension between the will of the Father and that of Christ, constantly props up in Chrysostom's anti-Manichaean discourse. Chrysostom goes to great lengths, then, not only to distinguish between the various divine wills, but also to show that Christ suffered the crucifixion without any external compulsion. He did it of his own accord. The cross is not the cosmic struggle, as it is depicted in some Manichaean sources.[21]

2.2 Cosmology and the Body

The next polemical premise against the Manichaeans is their view of the cosmos and the body, which Chrysostom understands as being absolutely pessimistic. In one of his homilies on Genesis, he states: "Even if Mani accosts you saying matter pre-existed, or Marcion, or Valentinus, or pagans, tell them directly: 'In the beginning God made heaven and earth' (Gen. 1:1)."[22] This is

---

20   *Consubst. (Contr. Anom.)* 7.503–511 (SC 396.154): χωρὶς γὰρ τούτων καὶ ἕτερον ἄτοπον ἔσται, ἂν τοῦ Θεοῦ τὰ ῥήματα ᾖ. Οὔτε γὰρ ἀγωνίαν μόνον ἐμφαίνει τὰ ῥήματα, ἀλλὰ καὶ δύο θελήματα, ἓν μὲν Υἱοῦ, ἓν δὲ Πατρός, ἐναντία ἀλλήλοις· τὸ γὰρ εἰπεῖν, Οὐχ ὡς ἐγὼ θέλω, ἀλλ' ὡς σύ, τοῦτό ἐστιν ἐμφαίνοντος. Τοῦτο δὲ οὐδὲ ἐκεῖνοί ποτε συνεχώρησαν, ἀλλ' ἡμῶν ἀεὶ λεγόντων τό, Ἐγὼ καὶ ὁ Πατὴρ ἕν ἐσμεν, ἐπὶ τῆς δυνάμεως, ἐκεῖνοι ἐπὶ τῆς θελήσεως τοῦτο εἰρῆσθαί φασι, λέγοντες Πατρὸς καὶ Υἱοῦ μίαν εἶναι βούλησιν. Trans. Harkins, *On the Incomprehensible Nature of God*, 206. See also Chrysostom, *In fac. ei rest.* 9 (PG 51.379.20–37).

21   Franzmann, *Jesus in the Manichaean Writings*, 86–87, 97.

22   *Hom. Gen.* 2.3 (PG 53.29.55–30.2): Κἂν γὰρ Μανιχαῖος προσέλθῃ λέγων τὴν ὕλην προϋπάρχειν, κἂν Μαρκίων, κἂν Οὐαλεντῖνος, κἂν Ἑλλήνων παῖδες, λέγε πρὸς αὐτούς· Ἐν ἀρχῇ ἐποίησεν ὁ Θεὸς τὸν οὐρανὸν καὶ τὴν γῆν. Trans. Robert C. Hill, trans., *St. John Chrysostom: Homilies on Genesis 1–17*, The Fathers of the Church 74 (Washington, DC: Catholic University of America Press, 1999), 37.

a very interesting occurrence in Chrysostom's thought. Here, and in some other instances,[23] he prescribes what almost looks like a mantra or magical formula—the instinctive repetition of Gen. 1:1—against the Manichaeans. In his forty-ninth homily on Matthew, Chrysostom reinterprets the miracle of the multiplication of the fish and the loaves of bread (Matt. 14) as a creation story, in which Christ demonstrates, on the one hand, the creative power of God, and on the other, the fact that his creation is good and beneficial. Chrysostom states:

> And why does he not create them [i.e. the fish and the loaves] from nothing? Stopping the mouth of Marcion, and the Manichaeans, who alienate His creation from Him, and teaching by His very works, that surely all the visible things are His works and creatures, and demonstrating that it is He who provides the fruits, who said at the beginning, "Let the earth sprout vegetation" (Gen. 1:11), and "Let the waters bring forth moving creatures with living souls" (Gen. 1:20). For this is not at all an inferior work compared to the other. For although those were made out of things that do not exist, yet they were still from the water. And it was no greater feat to produce fruits out of the earth, and moving living things out of the water, than out of five loaves to make so many; and in reference to the fishes, again, which was a sign that He was the ruler both of the earth and of the sea.[24]

The fact that Christ creates by means of multiplication, rather than creating *ex nihilo* (which God has done previously), is evidence that the divine Christ, the good Creator God, is ruler over his creation. Once again Chrysostom here brings together views of Marcionism and Manichaeism.

In another instance, in his treatise *On the Providence of God*, Chrysostom states: "The Greeks, admiring it [i.e. creation] more than is appropriate, and

---

23 In the Chrysostomic corpus, we have a series of 67 *homilies* on Genesis, and another Lenten series of 7 homilies, referred to as *sermons* in order to distinguish them from the longer series. In both of these series on Genesis, Chrysostom warns his audience about the Manichaean view of creation and ὕλη.

24 *Hom. Matt.* 49.2 (PG 58:498.32–44): Καὶ διατί οὐ ποιεῖ ἐκ μὴ ὄντων; Ἐμφράττων τὸ Μαρκίωνος καὶ Μανιχαίου στόμα, τῶν τὴν κτίσιν ἀλλοτριούντων αὐτοῦ, καὶ διὰ τῶν ἔργων αὐτῶν παιδεύων, ὅτι καὶ τὰ ὁρώμενα ἅπαντα αὐτοῦ ἔργα καὶ κτίσματά εἰσι, καὶ δεικνὺς, ὅτι αὐτός ἐστιν ὁ τοὺς καρποὺς διδοὺς, ὁ εἰπὼν ἐξ ἀρχῆς· Βλαστησάτω ἡ γῆ βοτάνην χόρτου· καὶ, Ἐξαγαγέτω τὰ ὕδατα ἑρπετὰ ψυχῶν ζωσῶν. Οὐδὲ γὰρ ἔλαττον τοῦτο ἐκείνου. Εἰ γὰρ καὶ ἐξ οὐκ ὄντων ἐκεῖνα, ἀλλ' ὅμως ἐξ ὕδατος· οὐκ ἔλαττον δὲ τοῦ ἀπὸ γῆς δεῖξαι καρπὸν καὶ ἀπὸ ὑδάτων ἑρπετὰ ἔμψυχα, τὸ ἀπὸ ἄρτων πέντε ποιῆσαι ἄρτους τοσούτους, καὶ ἀπὸ ἰχθύων πάλιν· ὃ σημῆτις γῆς καὶ τῆς θαλάττης αὐτὸν κρατεῖν.

exceeding proper measure, considered it to be divine. On the other hand, among the Manichaeans and other heretics, some said that it was not the work of a benevolent god."[25] In this source, he shows the differences between Greek philosophical views of the cosmos, and that of Manichaeism. The notion of the divine cosmos is common among Stoic philosophers like Chrysippus and Cleanthes.[26] An important pattern becomes evident in this regard, namely that Chrysostom uses comparison between different religious groups and their views to exhibit certain ideological excesses in the views of his opponents—while the Manichaeans devalue the cosmos, the Greeks provide too much value to it. We will return to this strategy of excessive or deficient elements in Chrysostom's polemic momentarily.

Directly related to Manichaean cosmic pessimism is, according to Chrysostom, their perceived corporeal pessimism. Chrysostom is aware of the Manichaean belief of the dispersion of the divine light substance in the world, especially in certain foods.[27] He accuses the Manichaeans of "introducing the substance [οὐσίαν] of God into dogs and apes and all sorts of animals."[28] This apparent tension between corporeal pessimism and the substantial presence of the divine in the world does not seem to bother Chrysostom. He vilifies Manichaeans as persons who not only hate the body, but as actively warring against it through rigorous ascetic practices in which fasting borders on starvation and sexual abstinence mirrors castration.

2.3 Fasting
In regard to fasting, Chrysostom perceives Manichaean dietary regulations not as a case of cosmic appreciation (which is perhaps closer to what Manichaean

---

25 *Scand.* 4.11–12 (SC 79.88): Ἑλλήνων μὲν γὰρ παῖδες ὑπὲρ τὸ δέον αὐτὴν θαυμάσαντες καὶ τὸ μέτρον ὑπερεκβάντες, θεὸν εἶναι αὐτὴν ἐνόμισαν. Μανιχαῖοι δὲ καὶ ἕτεροι πάλιν αἱρετικοί, οἱ μὲν οὐκ ἀγαθοῦ θεοῦ ἔργον ἔφησαν αὐτὴν εἶναι.

26 See e.g. Ricardo Salles, "Chrysippus on Conflagration and the Indestructibility of the Cosmos," in *God and Cosmos in Stoicism*, ed. Ricardo Salles (Oxford: Oxford University Press, 2009), 118–134; Johan C. Thom, *Cleanthes' Hymn to Zeus: Text, Translation, and Commentary*, Studien und Texte zu Antike und Christentum 33 (Tübingen: Mohr Siebeck, 2005), 70–79; and several essays in Barbara Neymeyr, Jochen Schmidt, and Bernhard Zimmermann, eds., *Stoizismus in der europäischen Philosophie, Literatur, Kunst und Politik: Eine Kulturgeschichte von der Antike bis zur Moderne* (Berlin: De Gruyter, 2008).

27 Johannes van Oort, 'God, Memory and Beauty: A 'Manichaean' Analysis of Augustine's Confessions, Book 10,1–38', in: *idem* (ed.), *Augustine and Manichaean Christianity. Selected Papers from the First South African Conference on Augustine of Hippo, University of Pretoria, 24–26 April 2012*. Nag Hammadi and Manichaean Studies 83 (Leiden: Brill. 2013), 155–175.

28 *Diem nat.* 6 (PG 49.359.38–41): εἰς κύνας καὶ πιθήκους καὶ θηρία παντοδαπὰ τὴν οὐσίαν εἰσάγοντες τοῦ Θεοῦ. See also *Diem. Nat.* 6 (PG 49.360.7–12).

writings attest), but rather as disdain and animosity towards to cosmos. In another homily on Matthew, he draws an interesting distinction between mainstream Christian monastic values and the values of Manichaean monks with regards to fasting and food, stating:

> Therefore they [i.e. Christian monks] say, "Glory be to You, O Lord, glory be to You, O Holy One, glory be to You, O King, that You have given us food to delight us." For we ought to give thanks not only for the greater things, but also for the lesser things. And they do also give thanks for these lesser things, bringing the heresy of the Manichaeans in disrepute, and many of those who profess our current life to be evil. For it is not that you should hold them [i.e. Christian monks] in suspicion, by their high self-discipline and contempt for the stomach, as abhorring [βδελυττομένων] the food, like the aforementioned heretics, who almost starve themselves to death [ἀπαγχονιζόντων]. They teach you by their prayer that they abstain not from an abhorrence of God's creatures, but as practicing self-discipline [φιλοσοφίαν ἀσκοῦντες].[29]

Rather than using the usual terms for fasting, such as νηστεύειν ("to fast") and ἀπέχειν ("to abstain"), he uses the word ἀπαγχονίζειν ("to starve"), as hyperbole, to describe Manichaean fasting. It should be remembered in this instance that Chrysostom mostly speaks to urban audiences, among whom he was promoting a more moderate and popular form of asceticism.[30] The preacher understands (or perhaps, misunderstands) Manichaean fasting, then, not as being motivated from self-discipline (he uses the term φιλοσοφία, here), but because of their abhorrence of edible material.

---

29 *Hom. Matt.* 55.6 (PG 58.547.51–548.1): Διὸ λέγουσι· Δόξα σοι, Κύριε, δόξα σοι, Ἅγιε, δόξα σοι, Βασιλεῦ, ὅτι ἔδωκας ἡμῖν βρώματα εἰς εὐφροσύνην. Οὐδὲ γὰρ ὑπὲρ τῶν μεγάλων μόνον, ἀλλὰ καὶ ὑπὲρ τῶν μικρῶν δεῖ εὐχαριστεῖν. Εὐχαριστοῦσι δὲ καὶ ὑπὲρ τούτων, καταισχύνοντες τὴν Μανιχαίων αἵρεσιν, καὶ ὅσοι τὴν παροῦσαν ζωὴν πονηρὰν εἶναι λέγουσιν. Ἵνα γὰρ μὴ, διὰ τὴν ἄκραν φιλοσοφίαν καὶ τὴν ὑπεροψίαν τῆς γαστρός, ὑποπτεύσῃς περὶ αὐτῶν ὡς τὰ σῖτα βδελυττομένων, οἷον περὶ ἐκείνων τῶν ἀπαγχονιζόντων ἑαυτούς, διὰ τῆς εὐχῆς σε παιδεύουσιν, ὅτι οὐ βδελυττόμενοι τὰ κτίσματα τοῦ Θεοῦ, τῶν πλειόνων ἀπέχονται, ἀλλ' ἢ φιλοσοφίαν ἀσκοῦντες.

30 See Jan R. Stenger, *Johannes Chrysostomos und die Christianisierung der Polis*, Studien und Texte zu Antike und Christentum 115 (Tübingen: Mohr Siebeck, 2019), 49–54; Chris L. de Wet, "The Preacher's Diet: Gluttony, Regimen, and Psycho-Somatic Health in the Thought of John Chrysostom," in *Revisioning John Chrysostom: New Approaches, New Perspectives*, ed. Chris L. de Wet and Wendy Mayer, Critical Approaches to Early Christianity 1 (Leiden: Brill, 2019), 410–463.

Chrysostom is perhaps only halfway correct. Scholars like BeDuhn[31] and Van Oort[32] have shown that the dietary and fasting practices of the Manichaean elect were not so much motivated from a perspective of corporeal pessimism or even corporeal mortification, which is actually closer to Chrysostom's own view of fasting.[33] Nor was their fasting motivated from an attitude of animosity towards the food itself. Beduhn states:

> Far from Manichaean discipline aiming to replace consumption, it had its own end in consumption .... By fasts, the Elect both prepare their bodies for the meal and, after the meal, process the ingested food toward salvation rather than redispersing it. Fasting produces "angels" from the food, who ascend to heaven. Manichaean disciplines should be described not as mortification, but as vivification.[34]

Van Oort similarly explains that Manichaeans considered food "beautiful and splendid and bright because of their light substance."[35] This is not how Chrysostom perceived it. He saw the Manichaeans as rigorous ascetics, basically starving themselves, because of their hate of foodstuffs, the body, and matter more generally.

2.4 Castration?

Not only do the Manichaeans starve themselves, in Chrysostom's view, but they are also guilty of corporeal mutilation and even, possibly, castration. A most interesting reference occurs in the fifth homily of Chrysostom's commentary on Galatians. While discussing Galatians 3:12, in which the Apostle Paul shares his wish that those promoting circumcision among Gentile Christians, have the knife slip and castrate themselves, Chrysostom states:

> If they wish, let them not only be circumcised, but mutilated [περικοπτέσθωσαν]. Where then are those who dare to castrate [ἀποκόπτειν] themselves, since they draw down the curse, and scandalise the workmanship

---

[31] Jason D. BeDuhn, *The Manichaean Body: In Discipline and Ritual* (Baltimore: Johns Hopkins University Press, 2000), 213–215.
[32] van Oort, "God, Memory and Beauty."
[33] de Wet, "Preacher's Diet," 432–446; Teresa M. Shaw, *The Burden of the Flesh: Fasting and Sexuality in Early Christianity* (Minneapolis, MN: Fortress, 1998), 131–139.
[34] BeDuhn, *Manichaean Body*, 214.
[35] van Oort, "God, Memory and Beauty," 165; revised, updated and with a new Postcript also in: idem, *Mani and Augustine. Collected Essays on Mani, Manichaeism and Augustine*. Nag Hammadi and Manichaean Studies 97. (Leiden: Brill, 2020), 295.

of God, and take part [συμπράττοντες] with the Manichaeans? For the latter call the body treacherous [ἐπίβουλον], and from evil matter [ὕλης τῆς πονηρᾶς]; and the former by their deeds provide a pretext to these miserable doctrines, cutting off the member [ἀποκόπτουσι τὸ μέλος] as being hostile and treacherous. Ought they not much more to gouge out the eyes, for it is through the eyes that desire enters the soul? But in truth neither the eye nor any other part of us is to blame, but the depraved will [ἡ πονηρὰ προαίρεσις] only. But if you will not allow this, why do you not cut out the tongue for blasphemy, the hands for theft, the feet for their evil courses and, as to say, the whole body?[36]

This text is somewhat ambiguous on various levels. Chrysostom does not directly say that the Manichaeans castrate themselves. He rather implies that those persons who castrate themselves, even those who practice circumcision, provide a pretext for Manichaean corporeal pessimism. It is not clear whether Chrysostom means that Christians who castrate themselves join Manichaeans in the practice of castration or simply in the view that the body is evil and treacherous. Chrysostom's use of the term συμπράσσειν might imply an instance of someone joining together in the practice of another, but it remains somewhat ambiguous. It could simply be another case of invective hyperbole for the sexual abstinence practiced by Manichaeans, as with the equation of fasting and starvation.

There is indeed evidence for the practice of self-castration among early Syrian Christian communities. In Bardaisan's *Book of the Laws of the Countries* there is a reference to King Abgar of Edessa, who apparently outlawed castration.[37] Some slightly later sources, like the Canon of Rabbula 55, reads: "No one

---

36 *Comm. Gal.* 5.3 (Field 4.83): Εἰ βούλονται, μὴ περιτεμνέσθωσαν μόνον, ἀλλὰ καὶ περικοπτέσθωσαν. Ποῦ τοίνυν εἰσὶν οἱ τολμῶντες ἀποκόπτειν ἑαυτούς, καὶ τὴν ἀρὰν ἐπισπώμενοι, καὶ τὴν τοῦ Θεοῦ δημιουργίαν διαβάλλοντες, καὶ τοῖς Μανιχαίοις συμπράττοντες· Ἐκεῖνοι μὲν γάρ φασι τὸ σῶμα ἐπίβουλον εἶναι καὶ ὕλης τῆς πονηρᾶς· οὗτοι δὲ διὰ τῶν ἔργων τοῖς χαλεποῖς δόγμασι τούτοις διδόασιν ἀφορμήν· ὡς γὰρ ἐχθρὸν καὶ ἐπίβουλον ἀποκόπτουσι τὸ μέλος. Οὐκοῦν πολλῷ μᾶλλον τοὺς ὀφθαλμοὺς πηρῶσαι ἐχρῆν· διὰ γὰρ τῶν ὀφθαλμῶν εἰς τὴν ψυχὴν κάτεισιν ἡ ἐπιθυμία. Ἀλλὰ οὔτε ὀφθαλμὸς οὔτε τι ἄλλο μέλος αἴτιον, ἀλλ' ἡ πονηρὰ προαίρεσις μόνον. Εἰ δὲ οὐκ ἀνέχῃ, διὰ τί μὴ καὶ γλῶτταν διὰ τὴν βλασφημίαν, καὶ χεῖρας διὰ τὴν ἁρπαγὴν, καὶ πόδας διὰ τοὺς ἐπὶ πονηρίαν δρόμους, καὶ πᾶν, ὡς εἰπεῖν, τὸ σῶμα κατακόπτεις;

37 Han J.W. Drijvers, ed., *The Book of the Laws of Countries: Dialogue on Fate of Bardaisan of Edessa* (Piscataway, NJ: Gorgias, 2006), 59; see also Irfan Shahîd, *Rome and the Arabs: A Prolegomenon to the Study of Byzantium and the Arabs* (Washington, D.C.: Dumbarton Oaks Research Library and Collection, 1984), 99; Daniel F. Caner, "The Practice and Prohibition of Self-Castration in Early Christianity," *Vigiliae Christianae* 51.4 (1997): 396–415; Susan Tuchel, *Kastration im Mittelalter*, Studia Humaniora 30 (Düsseldorf: Droste, 1998), 289.

from among the sons of the church, those who call upon themselves the name of Christ, shall dare to castrate himself."[38] A Syriac letter from the Collection of Severus of Antioch makes a similar prohibition. Many of the references to self-castration in Roman Syria and Mesopotamia should also be read within the context of the cult of Atargatis, or Dea Syria, in which self-castration was a feature.[39] Overall, castration was a very prominent discourse in this area. I could not find any fourth- or early fifth-century references to Manichaean castration. There are some scattered references to a certain radical Manichaean ascetic from the early Islamic period, known as Meṣallyāne, but he seems to be an exception, and other Manichaeans rejected his behaviour. It should not, however, surprise us if there were Manichaeans in Syria and Mesopotamia who practiced, along with some Christian monks, self-castration.[40] But the issue remains uncertain. The fact that Manichaeans, especially the Elect, were against harming any living creature might count against the occurrence of castration among conservative Manichaeans.[41]

What is not uncertain is that for Chrysostom, whether one actually mutilates the body through starvation or castration is beyond the point—the fact that the Manichaeans harbour such an abhorrence, in his view, toward the body is not very different from practicing such extreme forms of corporeal discipline. Even if Manichaeans did not castrate themselves, Chrysostom would say, they might as well do it. Chrysostom even accuses the Manichaeans for performing exegetical corporeal mutilation, in that they mutilate the Pauline corpus of scripture:

> And despite many heretics having attempted to cut him [Paul] into pieces, yet still, even though dismembered, he displays a mighty strength. For both Marcion and Manichaeus certainly use him, but only after cutting him into pieces. But still even so they are refuted by the several body parts.

---

38 Robert R. Phenix and Cornelia B. Horn, eds., *The Rabbula Corpus: Comprising the Life of Rabbula, His Correspondence, a Homily Delivered in Constantinople, Canons, and Hymns*, Writings from the Greco-Roman World 17 (Atlanta, GA: SBL Press, 2017), 113.

39 Jacob B. Lollar, "A Sanctifying Myth: The Syriac *History of John* in Its Social, Literary, and Theological Context" (Ph.D Dissertation, Florida State University, 2018), 75–106. I want to express my gratitude to Jacob Lollar for sharing his Ph.D. dissertation with me, and for pointing out some of these important sources relating to castration in late antique Syria.

40 Chris L. de Wet, *Preaching Bondage: John Chrysostom and the Discourse of Slavery in Early Christianity* (Oakland: University of California Press, 2015), 263–264.

41 Gábor Kósa, "The Manichaean Attitude to Natural Phenomena as Reflected in the Berlin *Kephalaia*," *Open Theology* 1 (2015): 255–268; Jason D. BeDuhn, *Augustine's Manichaean Dilemma, Volume 2: Making a "Catholic" Self, 388–401 C.E.*, Divinations: Rereading Late Ancient Religion (Philadelphia: University of Pennsylvania Press, 2013), 78–81.

For even a hand alone of this champion being found among them utterly defeats them; and a foot alone, left among others, pursues and wears them out.[42]

For Chrysostom, the Manichaean disdain for the physical body is mirrored in their misuse of the scriptural body. Manichaean exegesis is likened to scriptural mutilation, a form of invective often also applied against Jewish and Rabbinic expositions of scripture.[43] Even a dismembered and mutilated Paul, however, overcomes the heretics.

It is important to note, however, that Chrysostom's invective against Manichaean ascetic rigorism (including their perceived corporeal and exegetical mutilation) takes shape in the context of discussions about the responsibilities and limits of human freedom of choice, or προαίρεσις. In another reference about castration and Manichaeism, in Homily 49 on Matthew, Chrysostom makes this explicit:

> For such a person [i.e. who castrates himself] dares to do the work of murderers [ἀνδροφόνων], and giving pretext to those who slander God's creation, he opens the mouths of the Manichaeans, and is guilty of the same unlawful acts as those who mutilate themselves among the Greeks [i.e. the cult of Atargatis]. For to cut off [ἀποκόπτειν] body parts has been a demonic act and a satanic plot from the beginning, with the purpose of bringing the work of God into disrepute, so that they may mar this living creature. In so doing, they reckon everything not to the freedom of choice [προαιρέσει], but to the nature [φύσει] of our members, so that the majority of the members may sin in security, as being inculpable. So, they doubly harm this living being, both by mutilating the members, and by impeding the importance of the freedom of choice with regards to good deeds.[44]

---

42 *Hom. 2 Cor.* 21.4 (Field 3.223): Καίτοι γε πολλοὶ κατατέμνειν αὐτὸν ἐπεχείρησαν αἱρετικοί· ἀλλ' ὅμως κατὰ μέλος ὢν πολλὴν ἐπιδείκνυται τὴν ἰσχύν. Κέχρηται μὲν γὰρ αὐτῷ καὶ Μαρκίων καὶ Μανιχαῖος, ἀλλὰ κατατέμνοντες· ἀλλ' ὅμως καὶ οὕτως ἐλέγχονται ἀπὸ τῶν μελῶν. Καὶ γὰρ καὶ χεὶρ μόνη τοῦ ἀριστέως τούτου παρ' αὐτοῖς οὖσα, κατ' ἄκρας αὐτοὺς ἐλαύνει· καὶ ποὺς μόνος παρ' ἑτέροις διώκει καὶ καταβάλλει.

43 Susanna Drake, *Slandering the Jew: Sexuality and Difference in Early Christian Texts*, Divinations: Rereading Late Ancient Religion (Philadelphia: University of Pennsylvania Press, 2013), 38–58.

44 *Hom. Matt.* 62.3 (PG 58.599.53–600.7): Καὶ γὰρ τὰ τῶν ἀνδροφόνων ὁ τοιοῦτος τολμᾷ, καὶ τοῖς τοῦ Θεοῦ διαβάλλουσι τὴν δημιουργίαν δίδωσιν ἀφορμὴν, καὶ τῶν Μανιχαίων ἀνοίγει τὰ στόματα, καὶ τοῖς παρ' Ἕλλησιν ἀκρωτηριαζομένοις τὰ αὐτὰ παρανομεῖ. Τὸ γὰρ ἀποκόπτειν τὰ μέλη,

While there is much debate about the specifics and ideological varieties, Manichaeism may have generally held the opinion that although human beings have freedom of choice, the departure of the soul from the divine and the inherently evil nature of materiality, and also the influence and compulsion of evil beings on human subjects, limited the responsibility of each individual's freedom of moral choice.[45] In many mainstream Christian–Manichaean exchanges, the debate was on the role of φύσις versus προαίρεσις. In reference to Jesus's virtue teaching, Chrysostom comments:

> Do you see how again he calls us to the natural virtues [τὰ φυσικὰ κατορθώματα], demonstrating that by freedom of choice [προαιρέσεως] it is possible to attain them, and so silences the wicked madness of the Manichaeans? For if nature [ἡ φύσις] is something evil, why does he deduce from it [sc. nature] his models of temperance [τῆς φιλοσοφίας τὰ παραδείγματα]?[46]

Chrysostom also positions himself against Manichaean teachings on the grace and call of God.[47] In commenting on John 6:44, which reads, "No one can come to me unless the Father who sent me draws them," he states:

> The Manichaeans pounce on these words, saying that nothing lies in our own power. Yet the expression proves that we are masters of our mindset [κυρίους ὄντας τῆς γνώμης]. "For if a person comes to Him," says someone, "what need is there for drawing near?" But the words do not negate our free will but show that we greatly need support. And he does not imply that the one who comes is unwilling, but someone who enjoys much assistance.[48]

δαιμονικῆς ἐνεργείας καὶ σατανικῆς ἐπιβουλῆς ἐξ ἀρχῆς γέγονεν ἔργον· ἵνα τοῦ Θεοῦ τὸ ἔργον διαβάλλωσιν· ἵνα τὸ ζῶον τοῦτο λυμήνωνται· ἵνα μὴ τῇ προαιρέσει, ἀλλὰ τῇ τῶν μελῶν φύσει τὸ πᾶν λογισάμενοι, οὕτως ἀδεῶς ἁμαρτάνωσιν αὐτῶν οἱ πολλοί, ἅτε ἀνεύθυνοι ὄντες· καὶ διπλῆ παραβλάψωσι τὸ ζῶον τοῦτο, καὶ τῷ τὰ μέλη πηροῦν, καὶ τῷ τῆς προαιρέσεως τὴν ὑπὲρ τῶν ἀγαθῶν προθυμίαν κωλύειν. See also Laird, *Mindset, Moral Choice and Sin*, 110–111, on προαίρεσις.

45   Brian Stock, *Augustine's Inner Dialogue: The Philosophical Soliloquy in Late Antiquity* (Cambridge: Cambridge University Press, 2010), 151–153.
46   *Hom. Matt.* 58.3 (PG 58.569.8–12): Εἶδες πῶς πάλιν ἡμᾶς πρὸς τὰ φυσικὰ κατορθώματα ἐκκαλεῖται, δεικνὺς ὅτι ἐκ προαιρέσεως ταῦτα κατορθοῦν δυνατόν, καὶ τὴν πονηρὰν Μανιχαίων ἐπιστομίζει λύτταν; Εἰ γὰρ πονηρὸν ἡ φύσις, τίνος ἕνεκεν ἐκεῖθεν τῆς φιλοσοφίας τὰ παραδείγματα ἕλκει;
47   BeDuhn, *Augustine's Manichaean Dilemma*, Volume 2, 294–295.
48   *Hom. Jo.* 46.1 (PG 59.257.58–258.18): Τούτῳ ἐπιπηδῶσι Μανιχαῖοι λέγοντες, ὅτι οὐδὲν ἐφ' ἡμῖν κεῖται· ὅπερ μάλιστα βεβαιοῖ κυρίους ὄντας τῆς γνώμης. Εἰ γάρ τις ἔρχεται πρὸς αὐτὸν, φησί, τί

For Chrysostom, it is not an evil nature that leads human subjects into evil and wicked behaviour, but a corrupt mindset (γνώμη).[49] Thus, the body, which is part of the inherently good nature of God's creation, cannot be forced to goodness by means of corporeal mutilation. The state and action of προαίρεσις and γνώμη remain central and fundamental in human moral behaviour, yet φύσις is not inherently corrupt.

2.5 The Resurrection of the Body

All of the above discussions about the body and self-responsibility lead us to a final and major dispute between Chrysostom and the Manichaeans, namely the issue about the resurrection of the body.[50] Manichaeans rejected the resurrection of the physical body, and rather opted for a type of psychic transmigration or metempsychosis, in which the pure soul, free from the bonds of matter, will ascend to the realm of light.[51] In his seventh homily *Against the Anomeans*, Chrysostom writes: "Do you not still hear, even today, that Marcion, Manichaeus, Valentinus, and many others denied the plan of redemption in the flesh?"[52] Again, Chrysostom groups the different heresies according to their similarities with regards to the resurrection of the body. In his thirty-ninth homily on 1 Corinthians, commenting on 1 Cor. 15:18, he states: "Where are those wicked mouths of the Manichaeans now, who say that by 'resurrection' here he [Paul] means the liberation from sin?"[53] He knows that the Manichaeans only believe in a non-physical resurrection from sin. His most elaborate defence of the physical resurrection is found in his seventh sermon on Genesis, in which Chrysostom discusses the narrative of the robber on the cross, who Christ admits to Paradise (as per Luke 23:43):

δεῖ τῆς ἕλξεως; "Ὁ καὶ αὐτὸ οὐ τὸ ἐφ' ἡμῖν ἀναιρεῖ, ἀλλὰ μᾶλλον ἐμφαίνει ἡμᾶς βοηθείας δεομένους, ὅτι δείκνυσιν ἐνταῦθα, οὐ τὸν τυχόντα ἐρχόμενον, ἀλλὰ τὸν πολλῆς ἀπολαύοντα συμμαχίας.

49 I follow Laird, *Mindset, Moral Choice and Sin*, in his study on γνώμη in Chrysostom by translating the word as "mindset".
50 Mara, "Aspetti della polemica antimanichea," 197–198.
51 Cristos Theodorou, "The Concept of Body and the Body of Christ in the Manichaean Coptic Psalm-Book," in *Mani in Dublin: Selected Papers from the Seventh International Conference of the International Association of Manichaean Studies in the Chester Beatty Library, Dublin, 8–12 September 2009*, ed. Siegfried G. Richter, Charles Horton, and Klaus Ohlhafer, Nag Hammadi and Manichaean Studies 88 (Leiden: Brill, 2015), 338–358.
52 *Consubst. (Contr. Anom.)* 7.170–172 (SC 396.126): Οὐκ ἀκούεις ἔτι καὶ νῦν Μαρκίωνος ἀρνουμένου τὴν οἰκονομίαν, καὶ Μανιχαίου, καὶ Οὐαλεντίνου, καὶ πολλῶν ἑτέρων; Trans. Harkins, *On the Incomprehensible Nature of God*, 192. See also Chrysostom, *Ex. Ps.* 110.1 (PG 55.264.60–265.4).
53 *Hom. 1 Cor.* 39.2 (Field 2.490): Ποῦ νῦν εἰσι τὰ πονηρὰ τῶν Μανιχαίων στόματα, τῶν λεγόντων ἀνάστασιν αὐτὸν ἐνταῦθα λέγειν τῆς ἁμαρτίας τὴν ἀπαλλαγήν;

At this point pay attention: an issue arises that is not a chance one, namely the Manichees, stupid and rabid dogs, presenting an appearance of mildness but having on the inside savage fury of dogs, wolves in sheep's clothing. Lest you look to appearances, however, examine instead the wild beast hidden within. These people, then, seize upon this passage to claim that Christ said, "Amen, amen, I say to you, this day you will be with me in paradise," so reward of good things has already been made, and resurrection in unnecessary; if the brigand was awarded good things that very day whereas his body has not yet risen even today, there will be no resurrection of the body in future.[54]

In the broader argument Chrysostom provides in the sermon, the first response is to say that Paradise (παράδεισος), here, does not refer to the kingdom of heaven (he states that some Manichaeans profess this interpretation of the verse). Chrysostom reminds his readers that Adam's garden, the παράδεισος, was not heaven. This stands in contrast to the notion of the New Paradise of Life in Manichaean thought,[55] which was one of the three paths a soul could take after death. The robber therefore did not get to heaven and was not the recipient of the eschatological blessings of heaven. He only reaches paradise, at this stage, which is almost like a halfway house between this life and heaven. Secondly, and following the thought of Diodore of Tarsus and Theodore of Mopsuestia, both exegetes who gave preference to literal rather than allegorical readings of scripture, Chrysostom emphasizes, especially in his thirteenth homily on Genesis, the belief that Paradise is a physical place on earth, and not an ethereal heavenly place.[56] So, Paradise is part of the material realm, which supports Chrysostom's case for a bodily resurrection. The focus on the lit-

---

54 Serm. Gen. 7.4 (SC 433.332): Καὶ γὰρ οἱ Μανιχαῖοι, οἱ κύνες, οἱ ἐννεοὶ καὶ λυττῶντες, τὸ σχῆμα μὲν ἐπιδείκνυνται ἐπιεικείας, τὴν χαλεπὴν δὲ ἔνδον ἔχουσι τῶν κυνῶν μανίαν, καὶ κατακρύπτουσι τῇ δορᾷ τοῦ προβάτου τὸν λύκον. Ἀλλὰ μὴ τὸ φαινόμενον ἴδῃς, ἀλλὰ τὸ ἔνδον κεκρυμμένον θηρίον ἐξέτασον. Οὗτοι τοίνυν ἐπιλαβόμενοι τοῦ χωρίου τούτου φασίν· Εἶπεν ὁ Χριστός· Ἀμὴν, ἀμὴν λέγω σοι, σήμερον μετ' ἐμοῦ ἔσῃ ἐν τῷ παραδείσῳ· οὐκοῦν ἀντίδοσις ἤδη γέγονε τῶν ἀγαθῶν, καὶ περιττὴ ἡ ἀνάστασις. Εἰ γὰρ ἐν ἐκείνῃ τῇ ἡμέρᾳ ἀπέλαβεν ὁ λῃστὴς τὰ ἀγαθά, τὸ δὲ σῶμα αὐτοῦ οὐκ ἀνέστη οὐδέπω καὶ τήμερον, οὐκ ἔσται σωμάτων λοιπὸν ἀνάστασις. Trans. Robert C. Hill, trans., *St. John Chrysostom: Eight Sermons on the Book of Genesis* (Brookline, MA: Holy Cross Orthodox Press, 2004), 123.

55 Johannes van Oort, 'Manichaean Eschatology: A Sketch of Gnostic-Christian thinking about the Last Things', *Journal of Early Christian History* 7, 1 (2017) 108–120. Also in *idem*, *Mani and Augustine* (n. 35), 111–121.

56 Hanneke Reuling, *After Eden: Church Fathers and Rabbis on Genesis 3:16–21*, Jewish and Christian Perspectives 10 (Leiden: Brill, 2006), 139.

eral interpretation of Scripture serves in Chrysostom's interest when he refutes Manichaean understandings of paradise as heaven and the denial of the resurrection.

3 Manichaeism and Chrysostom's Heresiology

Having examined Chrysostom's views about Manichaeism, let us now proceed to the second question stated in this study: what is signified in the way Chrysostom speaks about Manichaeans, and all those with whom they are grouped? This is essentially a question about the nature of Chrysostom's heresiography and the place, function, and construction of Manichaeism in this heresiological structure. What has been delineated so far in the analysis regarding Chrysostom's polemical construction of Manichaeism? First, we have seen that Chrysostom rarely discusses Manichaeism in isolation—he usually groups Manichaeans with other opponents like the Marcionites, Valentinians, followers of Paul of Samosata, and some forms of Greek philosophy, most likely Platonism and Stoicism (or in other contexts, with the cult of Atargatis). Second, Chrysostom usually discusses the different heretical groups under one major point of contention, for instance, their view of creation, incarnation, resurrection, and so on. Furthermore, with some exceptions, Chrysostom is often more concerned with pointing out the *similarity* between these heretical groups, albeit on a rather low level of abstraction. When he is concerned with pointing out *difference*, he usually isolates one or two of the heretical groups, and highlights the differences between the particular heresy or heresies, and his brand of Orthodox or Nicene Christianity. Therefore, although we see many similarities between Chrysostom and other heresiographers like Epiphanius and Theodoret, for instance, Chrysostom is not exactly a cataloguer of heresy. His mode and structure of heresiological classification is somewhat different. Chrysostom appears to be more interested in *homogenizing* various heretical groups, including the Manichaeans.

Why does Chrysostom exhibit such a homogeneous classification of heresies? The main explanation is probably related to his overall understanding of the nature of heresy. More than anything, Chrysostom views heresy as a disease of the soul, a psychic illness. In several cases, when referring to Manichaeism, for instance, Chrysostom speaks of those who are "diseased" with Manichaeism—he uses variants of νοσεῖν.[57] Similar medical rhetoric is

---

57 See e.g. *Hom. 2 Cor.* 8.2 (Field 3.101); *Contr. Anom.* 11.76–79 (SC 396.294); *Hab. eun. spir.*

also evident in Epiphanius's *Panarion*, which is a medicine chest (for Epiphanius heresy is like a poison),[58] and Theodoret's *Cures for Greek Maladies*.[59] Augustine, too, uses medical discourse against heresy.[60] Medical encyclopedism was popular in late antiquity, as we see in the case of Oribasius.[61] From a late antique Christian perspective, some heresiographies are somewhat akin to psychic medical encyclopaedias. This is especially the case with the *Panarion*.

Chrysostom, however, is not an encyclopaedist of heresies. More than anything, Chrysostom considers himself to be a medical philosopher, and a physician of the soul. In his one homily explicitly directed against the Marcionites and Manichaeans, he states:

> For in this way the doctor also cuts open the ulcer, not as attacking the diseased body, but fighting against the disease and the wound. Today, then, let us grant them [the heretics] a little reprieve, that they may recover from their distress, and not resist the therapy by being constantly rebuked. Doctors also act in this way: after the knife they apply bandages and medicine, and allow a few days to pass while they contrive of things to ease the pain. Following their example, and devising a way for them to benefit from my argument, let me today start a question concerning doctrine ...[62]

(PG 51.284.50–55); *Exp. Ps.* 109.2 (PG 55.267.53–55); *Hom. Matt.* 17.7 (PG 57.247.50–53), 26.6 (PG 57.341.42–45).

58 Frank Williams, ed. and trans., *The Panarion of Epiphanius of Salamis: Book 1: (Sects 1–46)*, Nag Hammadi and Manichaean Studies 63 (Leiden: Brill, 2009).

59 Thomas P. Halton, trans., *Theodoret of Cyrus: A Cure for Pagan Maladies*, Ancient Christian Writers 67 (New York: Paulist, 2013).

60 C.f. e.g. van Oort, *Mani and Augustine* (n. 35), 141 and 357–358 for Manichaeism as a 'pestis' and a 'pestilentissima haeresis'; also *ibidem*, 209 for Augustine's biographer Possidius speaking of the 'Manichaeorum pestilentia'.

61 Mark Grant, trans., *Dieting for an Emperor: A Translation of Books 1 and 4 of Oribasius' Medical Compilations with an Introduction and Commentary* (Leiden: Brill, 1997).

62 *Pater, si poss.* 1 (PG 51.31.8–19): Ἐπεὶ καὶ ἰατρὸς τέμνει τὸ ἕλκος, οὐ τῷ νοσοῦντι σώματι πολεμῶν, ἀλλὰ τῇ νόσῳ καὶ τῷ τραύματι μαχόμενος. Φέρε δὴ, σήμερον μικρὸν ἐνδῶμεν αὐτοῖς, ὥστε αὐτοὺς ἀπὸ τῆς ὀδύνης ἀναπνεῦσαι, καὶ μὴ συνεχῶς πληττομένους ἀποσκιρτῆσαι τῆς θεραπείας. Οὕτω καὶ ἰατροὶ ποιοῦσι· μετὰ τὰς τομὰς ἐμπλάστρους ἐπιτιθέασι καὶ φάρμακα, καὶ διαλιμπάνουσιν ἡμέρας, τὰ παραμυθούμενα τὴν ὀδύνην ἐπινοοῦντες. Τούτους δὴ καὶ ἡμεῖς μιμούμενοι σήμερον ἐπινοοῦντες, ὥστε καρπώσασθαι τὴν ἀπὸ τῆς ἡμετέρας διαλέξεως ὠφέλειαν, καὶ τὸν περὶ δογμάτων κινήσωμεν λόγον ...

The language of heresy as disease is more than metaphorical language, as scholars like L. Michael White,[63] Wendy Mayer,[64] and myself,[65] have shown. The soul, in Chrysostom's thought, was inextricably intertwined with the body. Heresy, therefore, disrupted the health of the soul, which greatly affect the mind and the body. Chrysostom meticulously fashions his pathology of heresy on the same principles used by ancient doctors, like Galen of Pergamum, to classify physical disease. In Galen's thought—and Galen was indeed highly influential in the East, and in Chrysostom's own medical thought[66]—disease was the result of an imbalance of the four humours, blood, yellow bile, black bile, and phlegm. Chrysostom structures heresy in similar terms. He explains:

> One person says that there is no resurrection; and another looks for none of the things to come; another says there is a different God; another that He has His origin from Mary. And look, specifically, how they have all gone astray from a lack of moderation [ἀμετρίας], some by excess [πλεονάσαντες], others by deficiency [ἐλαττώσαντες]. So, for example, the first heresy of all was that of Marcion; this heresy introduced a different God, who has no existence. Look at the excess. After this, there is the heresy of Sabellius, saying that the Son and the Spirit and the Father are One. Next the heresy of Marcellus and Photinus, professing the same things. Moreover, we have the heresy of Paul of Samosata, who says that He had His origin from Mary. Afterwards that of the Manichaeans, for this is the most recent of all. After these the heresy of Arius. And there are others as well.[67]

---

63   L. Michael White, "Moral Pathology: Passions, Progress, and Protreptic in Clement of Alexandria," in *Passions and Moral Progress in Greco-Roman Thought*, ed. John T. Fitzgerald, Routledge Monographs in Classical Studies (London: Routledge, 2008), 284–321.
64   Wendy Mayer, "Medicine in Transition: Christian Adaptation in the Later Fourth-Century East," in *Shifting Genres in Late Antiquity*, ed. Geoffrey Greatrex and Hugh Elton (Farnham: Ashgate, 2015), 11–26; "The Persistence in Late Antiquity of Medico-Philosophical Psychic Therapy," *Journal of Late Antiquity* 8.2 (2015): 337–351.
65   de Wet, "Preacher's Diet."
66   Mayer, "Medicine in Transition," 11–16.
67   *Hom. Heb* 8. (Field 7.109–110): Ὁ μὲν λέγει μὴ εἶναι ἀνάστασιν, ὁ δὲ οὐδὲν τῶν μελλόντων προσδοκᾷ, ἄλλος ἕτερον λέγει Θεόν, ἄλλος ἀπὸ Μαρίας αὐτὸν ἔχειν τὴν ἀρχήν. Καὶ θέα εὐθέως πῶς ἐξ ἀμετρίας πάντες ἐξέπεσον, οἱ μὲν πλεονάσαντες, οἱ δὲ ἐλαττώσαντες. Οἷον, πρώτη μὲν πάντων αἵρεσις ἡ Μαρκίωνος· ἐκείνη ἕτερον Θεὸν ἐπεισήγαγε τὸν οὐκ ὄντα. Ἰδοὺ τὸ πλέον· Μετ' ἐκείνην ἡ Σαβελλίου, τὸν Υἱὸν καὶ τὸν Πατέρα καὶ τὸ Πνεῦμα ἓν πρόσωπον εἶναι λέγουσα. Εἶτα ἡ Μαρκέλλου καὶ Φωτεινοῦ, καὶ αὕτη τὰ αὐτὰ πρεσβεύουσα. Εἶτα ἡ Παύλου τοῦ Σαμοσατέως, ἐκ Μαρίας λέγουσα τὴν ἀρχὴν αὐτὸν ἐσχηκέναι. Εἶτα ἡ Μανιχαίων· αὕτη γὰρ πασῶν νεωτέρα. Μετ' ἐκείνας, ἡ Ἀρείου. Εἰσὶ δὲ καὶ ἕτεραι.

Heresy is therefore one disease that manifests itself in various forms, depending on the nature of the philosophical or doctrinal point of excess or deficiency. Even two groups that appear to oppose one another most, namely the Jews and the Manichaeans, are not so different to Chrysostom, who states:

> The Manichaeans and those who are sick with their disease seem to accept the Christ who was foretold but they dishonor the prophets and patriarchs who foretold him. On the other hand, we see that the Jews accept and revere those who foretold Christ, I mean the prophets and the lawgiver, but they dishonor him whom they foretold.[68]

The Jews are excessively bound to the Jewish scriptures, while the Manichaeans have this as a deficiency. So while Chrysostom shows the differences between various heretical and opposing religious groups, there are simply different manifestations of the same imbalance. Pathic excess and deficiency was a common invective strategy in late ancient Christian discourse. Moral vice, too, was defined in terms of excess and deficiency—being prone to some pathic excess or deficit was a sign that a person or group could not exercise one of the most important virtues of late ancient society, namely self-control and moderation, or σωφροσύνη. Lacking σωφροσύνη and being prone to excess or deficiency also meant that one was in an unmasculine and effeminate state. It was believed that women were physically more prone to excess than men due to the moist and spongy structure of their bodily composition. Women's bodies had to expand and stretch in order to accommodate the excess of tissue associated with pregnancy. However, deficiency in something like courage or reason was also seen as effeminate and even slavish. When Chrysostom declares that the Manichaeans are prone to ideological excess, it is also, then, a strategy to effeminize them. According to Chrysostom, Manichaeans are, in fact, even worse than the most sexually deviant persons of society:

> Even prostitutes [πόρνοι] and effeminate men [μαλακοί] shut the mouths of the Manichaeans, who say that evil is immoveable, siding with the devil, and weakening the hands of those who would desire to be earnest, and overturning everything in life.[69]

---

68   *Contr. Anom.* 11.76–82 (SC 396.295): Μανιχαῖοι μὲν γὰρ καὶ οἱ τὰ αὐτὰ νοσοῦντες ἐκείνοις τὸν μὲν κηρυττόμενον δοκοῦσι δέχεσθαι Χριστόν, τοὺς δὲ κηρύττοντας αὐτὸν ἀτιμάζουσι προφήτας καὶ πατριάρχας· Ἰουδαῖοι δὲ πάλιν ἀπεναντίας τοὺς μὲν κηρύττοντας αὐτὸν δοκοῦσι δέχεσθαι καὶ θεραπεύειν, προφήτας λέγω καὶ τὸν νομοθέτην αὐτῶν, τὸν δὲ κηρυττόμενον ὑπ' αὐτῶν ἀτιμάζουσιν. Trans. Harkins, *On the Incomprehensible Nature of God*, 274.

69   *Hom. Matt.* 26.5 (PG 57.340.15–19): Καὶ πόρνοι καὶ μαλακοὶ τὰ Μανιχαίων ἐμφράττουσι

As Susanna Drake has shown, Chrysostom often calls his opponents πόρνοι and μαλακοί. This is a strategy to sexually shame those opponents.[70] For Chrysostom, at least and acknowledge that the wickedness of the flesh can be overcome. He probably has in mind some of the famous stories of the late antique East of actors and prostitutes who have converted and turned their back on their former lives. Thus, Manichaeans, like all heretics and Jews, are diseased, effeminate, and servile due to the imbalance and excesses of their belief systems. In this way, Chrysostom's classification of Manichaeism often coincides with other "heretical" groups, and he constructs his version of Manichaeism in conjunction with other opposing religious groups. This observation relates to the recent work of Todd Berzon on the practice of religious classification in late antiquity.[71] While Berzon demonstrates how religious and heresiological classifications in late antiquity often functioned as a type of ethnography, in this case we see how religious and heretical classification works on the basis of medico-moral pathology.

Finally, by homogenizing the various heresies, Chrysostom also establishes the shared origins of all heresy, namely the devil. A good example of this type of rhetoric is found in his interpretation of 1 Tim. 4:1–3:[72]

> As those who have the faith are docked on a steadfast anchor, so those who lapse from the faith cannot stand anywhere, but after many wanderings [πλανηθέντες πλάνους] to and fro, they are finally carried into the very pit of perdition. And this he [Paul] had demonstrated before, saying, that some had already suffered shipwreck regarding the faith, and now he says, "Now the Spirit expressly says that in later times some will renounce the faith, giving heed to deceiving spirits [πνεύμασι πλάνοις]" (1 Tim. 4:1). This refers to the Manichaeans, the Encratites, and the Marcionites, and their whole gang [ἐργαστηρίου], that they should depart from the faith in the last days. Do you see that this departure from the faith is the cause of

---

στόματα, οἳ τὴν κακίαν ἀκίνητον εἶναί φασι, τῷ διαβόλῳ τελούμενοι, καὶ τὰς τῶν σπουδάζειν βουλομένων χεῖρας ἐκλύοντες, καὶ τὴν ζωὴν ἅπασαν ἀνατρέποντες.

70 Drake, *Slandering the Jew*, 78–98; see also Chris L. de Wet, "John Chrysostom on Homoeroticism," *Neotestamentica* 48.1 (2014): 187–218.

71 Todd S. Berzon, *Classifying Christians: Ethnography, Heresiology, and the Limits of Knowledge in Late Antiquity* (Oakland: University of California Press, 2016).

72 This text reads: "Now the Spirit expressly says that in later times some will renounce the faith by paying attention to deceitful spirits and teachings of demons, through the hypocrisy of liars whose consciences are seared with a hot iron. They forbid marriage and demand abstinence from foods, which God created to be received with thanksgiving by those who believe and know the truth" (NRSV).

all the wickedness that follows? But what is mean by "expressly"? Simply, clearly, and beyond a doubt. Do not be surprised, he says, if some having departed from the faith still adhere to the practices of Judaism. There will be a time when even those who have shared in the faith will lapse into a more grievous error, not only with respect to food, but to marriages, and other similar things, introducing the most destructive notions. This does not refer to the Jews, for "in the later times" and "renounce the faith", is not applicable to them, but to the Manichaeans, and their founders. And he rightly calls them "deceitful spirits", for they were driven to action by those spirits, having spoken these things.[73]

Chrysostom's heresiology is intertwined with his demonology. He believes that there is one same voice behind all heretics, namely the devil, and by homogenizing the different heresies, he also justifies his argument that when Scripture speaks against heresy, it speaks against them all, even those like the Manichaeans, who did not exist at the time when Scripture was being written.[74] When speaking of the "gang" of heresies, Chrysostom uses the word ἐργαστήριον. This word has connotations relating to a factory or workshop, which might refer, negatively, to the fabrication of heretical teachings. The word also served as a euphemism for a brothel.[75] Manichaeism is therefore part of the same

---

73   *Hom. 1 Tim.* 12.1 (Field 6.92–93): "Ὥσπερ οἱ τῆς πίστεως ἐχόμενοι ἐπ' ἀσφαλοῦς τῆς ἀγκύρας ὁρμίζονται, οὕτως οἱ ταύτης ἐκπεσόντες οὐδαμοῦ στῆναι δύνανται, ἀλλὰ πολλοὺς ἄνω καὶ κάτω πλανηθέντες πλάνους, τὸ τελευταῖον εἰς αὐτὰ τῆς ἀπωλείας φέρονται τὰ βάραθρα. Καὶ τοῦτο ἤδη μὲν ἐδήλωσεν εἰπών, ὅτι ἐναυάγησάν τινες περὶ τὴν πίστιν· καὶ νῦν δέ φησι· "Τὸ δὲ Πνεῦμα ῥητῶς λέγει, ὅτι ἐν ὑστέροις καιροῖς ἀποστήσονταί τινες τῆς πίστεως, προσέχοντες πνεύμασι πλάνοις." Περὶ Μανιχαίων, καὶ Ἐγκρατιτῶν, καὶ Μαρκιωνιστῶν, καὶ παντὸς αὐτῶν τοῦ ἐργαστηρίου τοῦ τοιούτου ταῦτα φησιν, "ὅτι ἐν ὑστέροις καιροῖς ἀποστήσονταί τινες τῆς πίστεως." Ὁρᾷς ὅτι πάντων αἴτιον τῶν μετὰ ταῦτα κακῶν τὸ τῆς πίστεως ἀποστῆναι; Τί δέ ἐστι, "ῥητῶς"; Φανερῶς, σαφῶς, ὡμολογουμένως, ὡς μὴ ἀμφιβάλλειν. Μὴ θαυμάσῃς, φησίν, εἰ νῦν ἀπὸ τῆς πίστεώς τινες ἀποστάντες ἔτι Ἰουδαΐζουσιν· ἔσται καιρὸς ὅτε χαλεπώτερον αὐτοὶ οἱ τῆς πίστεως μετεσχηκότες τοῦτο ἐργάσονται, οὐ μέχρι βρωμάτων, ἀλλὰ καὶ μέχρι γάμων, καὶ πάντων τῶν τοιούτων τὴν ὀλέθριον συμβουλὴν εἰσάγοντες. Οὐ περὶ Ἰουδαίων λέγει ταῦτα· πῶς γὰρ τὸ, "ἐν ὑστέροις καιροῖς," καὶ τὸ, "ἀποστήσονταί τινες τῆς πίστεως," ἔχει χώραν; ἀλλὰ περὶ Μανιχαίων, καὶ τῶν ἀρχηγετῶν τούτων. Πνεύματα δὲ πλάνης ἐκάλεσεν αὐτοὺς, εἰκότως· ὑπὸ γὰρ ἐκείνων ἐνεργούμενοι, ταῦτα ἐφθέγξαντο.

74   Virginia Burrus, *The Making of a Heretic: Gender, Authority, and the Priscillianist Controversy*, Transformation of the Classical Heritage 24 (Berkeley: University of California Press, 1995), 47–78, demonstrates a similar type of rhetoric and power dynamic in the context of the Priscillianist controversy; see also Dayna S. Kalleres, *City of Demons: Violence, Ritual, and Christian Power in Late Antiquity* (Oakland: University of California Press, 2015), 74–75, 276n101.

75   Marguerite Johnson and Terry Ryan, *Sexuality in Greek and Roman Society and Literature: A Sourcebook* (London: Routledge, 2005), 88.

heretical *Geist*, originating from the deceitful spirits that lead people astray (πνεύμασι πλάνοις), which has been there since the devil's beginning. For Chrysostom, the true founders (ἀρχηγέται) of Manichaeism are the deceitful spirits to which 1 Tim. 4:1 refers. We witness here a type of "damnation history", so to speak.

4 Conclusion

We may conclude, then, that Chrysostom possessed not an insignificant measure of knowledge about Manichaean dualism, and even seems to comment on their habitus. He states that Manichaeans appear pious, mild, and meek, and even wear a mask of (true) Christian identity. He says: "For even Manichaeans, and all the heresies, have assumed this mask [of being Christian], so in order to deceive the more simple-minded ones."[76] He certainly does not display the type of detailed and nuanced insider knowledge we find in Augustine,[77] but it is possible that Chrysostom had dealings with Manichaeans, especially while in Antioch, and possibly debated with Manichaean intellectuals. It is also possible that, especially while in Antioch, there may have been Manichaeans in his audience. In his homily against the Manichaeans and Marcionites, he explicitly states that there is a possibility that these heretics might be in his audience. This latter point is further supported by the fact that Chrysostom is acutely aware of the economy of scriptural proof-texting between Orthodox Christians and Manichaeans one finds in other authors, like Augustine. He even provides mantra-like responses to his audience for when they might find themselves in a "Manichaean encounter."

Chrysostom also has knowledge about Manichaean ascetic practices, albeit biased, such as fasting, the sacred meal, and sexual abstinence. He goes to great lengths, as we have seen, to discern between Christian and Manichaean ascetic practices. This could quite plausibly mean that the differences between Christian monks and the Manichaean Elect were *not* so apparent as some may think. Manichaeism was very much at home in Christian Syria. In their nascent stages, both ascetic groups may have been influenced by the same literary traditions, such as those of Tatian, Marcion, Bardaisan, and Thomasine literary tradition. Even if Chrysostom's statements about Manichaean fasting

---

76   *Hom. Heb.* 8.4 (Field 7.109): ἐπεὶ καὶ Μανιχαῖοι καὶ πᾶσαι αἱρέσεις τοῦτο ὑπέδυσαν τὸ προσωπεῖον, πρὸς τὸ οὕτως ἀπατᾶν τοὺς ἀφελεστέρους.
77   See e.g. van Oort, *Mani and Augustine* (n.35), *passim*.

as starvation are not hyperbole, we have similar accounts about Syrian Christian monks who also practiced rigorous fasting that bordered on starvation.[78] Even if Manichaeans did practice castration, so did some 'orthodox' Christian monks. Thus, while literary sources like those of Chrysostom aim to highlight difference and distinction between these groups, the historical-cultural realities may have been less apparent. This is probably also why Chrysostom's homogenized heresiology was so convenient, since by ideologically grouping the various heretics together and labelling them as the "other", he also hoped to discern and fashion the identity of his own group, not as diseased or effeminate, but as healthy and masculine, as moderate and, dare we say, "normal".

Bibliography

Editions of Chrysostom's Works

Ad eos qui scandalizati sunt (*Scand.*). In A.-M. Malingrey, *Jean Chrysostome: Sur la providence de Dieu*. SC 79. Paris: Éditions du Cerf, 1961.

Contra Anomoeos homilia II (*Contr. Anom.*). In A.-M. Malingrey, *Jean Chrysostome: Sur l'égalité du Père et du Fils: Contre les Anoméens homélies VII–XII*. SC 396. Paris: Éditions du Cerf, 1994.

De consubstantiali (*contra Anomoeos homilia 7*) (*Consubst.*). In A.-M. Malingrey, *Jean Chrysostome: Sur l'égalité du Père et du Fils: Contre les Anoméens homélies VII–XII*. SC 396. Paris: Éditions du Cerf, 1994.

Expositiones in Psalmos (*Ex. Ps.*). In PG 55.39–498.

In diem natalem (*Diem nat.*). In PG 49.351–362.

In epistulam ad Galatas commentarius (*Comm. Gal.*). In Field 4.1–103.

In epistulam ad Hebraeos homiliae (*Hom. Heb.*). In Field 7.1–384.

In epistulam I ad Corinthios homiliae (*Hom. 1 Cor.*). In Field 2.1–555.

In epistulam I ad Timotheum homiliae (*Hom. 1 Tim.*). In Field 6.1–161.

In epistulam II ad Corinthios homiliae (*Hom. 2 Cor.*). In Field 3.1–316.

In Genesim homiliae (*Hom. Gen.*). In PG 53.21–385, 54.385–580.

In Genesim sermons (*Serm. Gen.*). In L. Brottier. *Jean Chrysostome: Sermons sur la Genèse*. SC 433. Paris: Éditions du Cerf, 1998.

In illud: Habentes eundem spiritum (*Hab. eun. spir.*). In PG 51.187–208.

In illud: In faciem ei restiti (*In fac. ei rest.*). In PG 51.371–388.

In illud: Pater, si possibile est, transeat hic calix (*Pater si poss.*). In PG 51.31–40.

In Joannem homiliae (*Hom. Jo.*). PG 59.23–482.

In Matthaeum homiliae (*Hom. Matt.*). PG 57.13–472, 58.471–794.

---

78 de Wet, "Preacher's Diet."

Modern Sources

Baur, Chrysostomus. *John Chrysostom and His Time*. Translated by M. Gonzaga. 2 vols. Vaduz: Büchervertriebsanstalt, 1988.

BeDuhn, Jason D. "A War of Words: Intertextuality and the Struggle over the Legacy of Christ in the *Acta Archelai*." Pages 77–102 in *Frontiers of Faith: The Christian Encounter with Manichaeism in the Acts of Archelaus*. Edited by Jason D. BeDuhn and Paul Mirecki. Nag Hammadi and Manichaean Studies 61. Leiden: Brill, 2007.

BeDuhn, Jason D. *Augustine's Manichaean Dilemma, Volume 1: Conversion and Apostasy, 373–388 C.E.* Divinations: Rereading Late Ancient Religion. Philadelphia: University of Pennsylvania Press, 2013.

BeDuhn, Jason D. *Augustine's Manichaean Dilemma, Volume 2: Making a "Catholic" Self, 388–401 C.E.* Divinations: Rereading Late Ancient Religion. Philadelphia: University of Pennsylvania Press, 2013.

BeDuhn, Jason D. *The Manichaean Body: In Discipline and Ritual*. Baltimore: Johns Hopkins University Press, 2000.

Berzon, Todd S. *Classifying Christians: Ethnography, Heresiology, and the Limits of Knowledge in Late Antiquity*. Oakland: University of California Press, 2016.

A. Böhlig, *Die Bibel bei den Manichäern und verwandte Studien*. Herausgegeben von Peter Nagel [und] Siegfried G. Richter. Nag Hammadi and Manichaean Studies 80. (Leiden: Brill, 2013).

Brändle, Rudolf. *John Chrysostom: Bishop–Reformer–Martyr*. Translated by John Cawte and Silke Trzcionka. Early Christian Studies 8. Strathfield: St. Paul's, 2004.

Brown, Peter. "The Diffusion of Manichaeism in the Roman Empire." *Journal of Roman Studies* 59 (1969): 92–103.

Burrus, Virginia. *The Making of a Heretic: Gender, Authority, and the Priscillianist Controversy*. Transformation of the Classical Heritage 24. Berkeley: University of California Press, 1995.

Caner, Daniel F. "The Practice and Prohibition of Self-Castration in Early Christianity." *Vigiliae Christianae* 51.4 (1997): 396–415.

Drake, Susanna. *Slandering the Jew: Sexuality and Difference in Early Christian Texts*. Divinations: Rereading Late Ancient Religion. Philadelphia: University of Pennsylvania Press, 2013.

Drijvers, Han J.W., ed. *The Book of the Laws of Countries: Dialogue on Fate of Bardaisan of Edessa*. Piscataway, NJ: Gorgias, 2006.

Field, Frederick, ed. *Ioannis Chrysostomi interpretatio omnium epistularum Paulinarum*. 7 vols. Oxford: J.H. Parker, 1854–1862.

Franzmann, Majella. *Jesus in the Manichaean Writings*. London: T&T Clark, 2003.

Grant, Mark, trans. *Dieting for an Emperor: A Translation of Books 1 and 4 of Oribasius' Medical Compilations with an Introduction and Commentary*. Leiden: Brill, 1997.

Halton, Thomas P., trans. *Theodoret of Cyrus: A Cure for Pagan Maladies*. Ancient Christian Writers 67. New York: Paulist, 2013.

Harkins, Paul W., trans. *St. John Chrysostom: On the Incomprehensible Nature of God*. The Fathers of the Church 72. Washington, D.C.: Catholic University of America Press, 1984.

Heyden, Wichard von. *Doketismus und Inkarnation: Die Entstehung zweier gegensätzlicher Modelle von Christologie*. Tübingen: Francke, 2014.

Hill, Robert C., trans. *St. John Chrysostom: Eight Sermons on the Book of Genesis*. Brookline, MA: Holy Cross Orthodox Press, 2004.

Hill, Robert C., trans. *St. John Chrysostom: Homilies on Genesis 1–17*. The Fathers of the Church 74. Washington, DC: Catholic University of America Press, 1999.

Johnson, Marguerite, and Terry Ryan. *Sexuality in Greek and Roman Society and Literature: A Sourcebook*. London: Routledge, 2005.

Kalleres, Dayna S. *City of Demons: Violence, Ritual, and Christian Power in Late Antiquity*. Oakland: University of California Press, 2015.

Kelly, John N.D. *Golden Mouth: The Story of John Chrysostom—Ascetic, Preacher, Bishop*. Ithaca, NY: Cornell University Press, 1998.

Kósa, Gábor. "The Manichaean Attitude to Natural Phenomena as Reflected in the Berlin *Kephalaia*." *Open Theology* 1 (2015): 255–268.

Laird, Raymond J. *Mindset, Moral Choice and Sin in the Anthropology of John Chrysostom*. Early Christian Studies 15. Strathfield: St. Paul's, 2012.

Lieu, Samuel N.C. *Manichaeism in Mesopotamia and the Roman East*. Religions in the Graeco-Roman World 118. Leiden: Brill, 2015.

Lollar, Jacob B. "A Sanctifying Myth: The Syriac *History of John* in Its Social, Literary, and Theological Context." Ph.D Dissertation, Florida State University, 2018.

Mara, Maria G. "Aspetti della polemica antimanichea di Giovanni Crisostomo." Pages 195–199 in *Atti dell'undicesimo simposio Paolino: Paolo tra Tarso e Antiochia. Archeologia/storia/religione*. Edited by Luigi Padovese. Rome: Pontificia Università Antonianum, 2008.

Mayer, Wendy. "Medicine in Transition: Christian Adaptation in the Later Fourth-Century East." Pages 11–26 in *Shifting Genres in Late Antiquity*. Edited by Geoffrey Greatrex and Hugh Elton. Farnham: Ashgate, 2015.

Mayer, Wendy. "The Persistence in Late Antiquity of Medico-Philosophical Psychic Therapy." *Journal of Late Antiquity* 8.2 (2015): 337–351.

Mayer, Wendy, and Pauline Allen. *John Chrysostom*. London: Routledge, 1999.

Migne, Jacques-Paul, ed. *Patrologiae cursus completus: Series graeca*. 162 vols. Paris, 1857–1886.

Neymeyr, Barbara, Jochen Schmidt, and Bernhard Zimmermann, eds. *Stoizismus in der europäischen Philosophie, Literatur, Kunst und Politik: Eine Kulturgeschichte von der Antike bis zur Moderne*. Berlin: De Gruyter, 2008.

Oort, Johannes van. 'God, Memory and Beauty: A 'Manichaean' Analysis of Augustine's *Confessions*, Book 10,1–38', in: *idem* (ed.), *Augustine and Manichaean Christianity. Selected Papers from the First South African Conference on Augustine of Hippo, University of Pretoria, 24–26 April 2012*. Nag Hammadi and Manichaean Studies 83 (Leiden: Brill. 2013), 155–175.

Oort, Johannes van. 'Manichaean Eschatology: A Sketch of Gnostic-Christian thinking about the Last Things', *Journal of Early Christian History* 7, 1 (2017) 108–120.

Oort, Johannes van. *Mani and Augustine. Collected Essays on Mani, Manichaeism and Augustine*. Nag Hammadi and Manichaean Studies 97. Leiden: Brill, 2020.

Pedersen, Nils Arne, René Falkenberg, John Møller Larsen, Claudia Leurini, *Biblia Manichaica I, The Old Testament in Manichaean Tradition. The Sources in Syriac, Greek, Coptic, Middle Persian, Sogdian, New Persian, and Arabic*. Corpus Fontium Manichaeorum. Biblia Manichaica I. (Turnhout: Brepols, 2017).

Phenix, Robert R., and Cornelia B. Horn, eds. *The Rabbula Corpus: Comprising the Life of Rabbula, His Correspondence, a Homily Delivered in Constantinople, Canons, and Hymns*. Writings from the Greco-Roman World 17. Atlanta, GA: SBL Press, 2017.

Reuling, Hanneke. *After Eden: Church Fathers and Rabbis on Genesis 3:16–21*. Jewish and Christian Perspectives 10. Leiden: Brill, 2006.

Salles, Ricardo. "Chrysippus on Conflagration and the Indestructibility of the Cosmos." Pages 118–134 in *God and Cosmos in Stoicism*. Edited by Ricardo Salles. Oxford: Oxford University Press, 2009.

Schwertschlager, Joseph, trans. *Des heiligen Kirchenlehrers Johannes Chrysostomus: Commentar zum Galaterbrief, aus dem Griechischen übersetzt und mit kurzen Erläuterungen versehen*. Ausgewählte Schriften des heiligen Chrysostomus, Erzbischof von Constantinopel und Kirchenlehrer 7. Edited by Valentin Thalhofer. Kempten: Kösel, 1882.

Shahîd, Irfan. *Rome and the Arabs: A Prolegomenon to the Study of Byzantium and the Arabs*. Washington, D.C.: Dumbarton Oaks Research Library and Collection, 1984.

Shaw, Teresa M. *The Burden of the Flesh: Fasting and Sexuality in Early Christianity*. Minneapolis, MN: Fortress, 1998.

Stenger, Jan R. *Johannes Chrysostomos und die Christianisierung der Polis*. Studien und Texte zu Antike und Christentum 115. Tübingen: Mohr Siebeck, 2019.

Stock, Brian. *Augustine's Inner Dialogue: The Philosophical Soliloquy in Late Antiquity*. Cambridge: Cambridge University Press, 2010.

Theodorou, Cristos. "The Concept of Body and the Body of Christ in the Manichaean Coptic Psalm-Book." Pages 338–358 in *Mani in Dublin: Selected Papers from the Seventh International Conference of the International Association of Manichaean Studies in the Chester Beatty Library, Dublin, 8–12 September 2009*. Edited by Siegfried G. Richter, Charles Horton, and Klaus Ohlhafer. Nag Hammadi and Manichaean Studies 88. Leiden: Brill, 2015.

Thom, Johan C. *Cleanthes' Hymn to Zeus: Text, Translation, and Commentary*. Studien und Texte zu Antike und Christentum 33. Tübingen: Mohr Siebeck, 2005.

Tuchel, Susan. *Kastration im Mittelalter*. Studia Humaniora 30. Düsseldorf: Droste, 1998.

Verheyden, Joseph, Reimund Bieringer, Jens Schröter, and Ines Jäger, eds. *Docetism in the Early Church: The Quest for an Elusive Phenomenon*. Wissenschaftliche Untersuchungen zum Neuen Testament 402. Tübingen: Mohr Siebeck, 2018.

Verosta, Stephan. *Johannes Chrysostomus: Staatsphilosoph und Geschichtstheologe*. Graz: Verlag Styria, 1960.

de Wet, Chris L. "John Chrysostom on Homoeroticism." *Neotestamentica* 48.1 (2014): 187–218.

de Wet, Chris L. "John Chrysostom on Manichaeism." *HTS Theological Studies* 75.1 (2019): 1–6.

de Wet, Chris L. *Preaching Bondage: John Chrysostom and the Discourse of Slavery in Early Christianity*. Oakland: University of California Press, 2015.

de Wet, Chris L. "The Preacher's Diet: Gluttony, Regimen, and Psycho-Somatic Health in the Thought of John Chrysostom." Pages 410–463 in *Revisioning John Chrysostom: New Approaches, New Perspectives*. Edited by Chris L. de Wet and Wendy Mayer. Critical Approaches to Early Christianity 1. Leiden: Brill, 2019.

White, L. Michael. "Moral Pathology: Passions, Progress, and Protreptic in Clement of Alexandria." Pages 284–321 in *Passions and Moral Progress in Greco-Roman Thought*. Edited by John T. Fitzgerald. Routledge Monographs in Classical Studies. London: Routledge, 2008.

Williams, Frank, ed. & trans. *The Panarion of Epiphanius of Salamis: Book I: (Sects 1–46)*. Nag Hammadi and Manichaean Studies 63. Leiden: Brill, 2009.

Wilson, Kenneth M. *Augustine's Conversion from Traditional Free Choice to "Non-Free Free Will": A Comprehensive Methodology*. Studien und Texte zu Antike und Christentum 111. Tübingen: Mohr Siebeck, 2018.

Woods, David. "Strategius and the 'Manichaeans.'" *Classical Quarterly* 51.1 (2001): 255–264.

11

Augustine's *De pulchro et apto* and its Manichaean Context

Johannes van Oort

Abstract

We only know Augustine's youth work *De pulchro et apto* from his famous *Confessiones*. There he slightly lifts the veil that hangs over its contents. The present essay examines the possible subject matter of *De pulchro et apto* within the context of Augustine's former Manichaeism. Apart from the *Confessiones*, other writings of the Catholic Church Father seem to shed light on his former Manichaean work. But most important to unravel the topics of Augustine's first writing appear to be some genuine Manichaean sources. My search for the contents of *De pulchro et apto* in the context of 'Manichaeism and Early Christianity' ends up with twelve conclusions.

Introduction

The contents of the work of Augustine's youth, *De pulchro et apto*, is largely shrouded in mysteries. Everything we know about it is related by Augustine some twenty years later in *conf.* 4,20–27. The passage is too long to be cited here in its entirety and analyzed in every detail. I do, however, briefly mention the most important opinions that have been put forward about the work. In 1966 Takeshi Katô published the (in our context) most cited study 'Melodia interior. Sur le traité *De pulchro et apto*'.[1] He refers to Manichaean sources from Egyptian Medinet Madi for Augustine's speaking of 'beauty' and some other aspects, but—although the evidence in his article is evocative rather than conclusive— one cannot agree with later criticism that none of the texts he puts forward proves direct or indirect influence from Manichaean sources.[2] In the course of

---

1 Takeshi Katô, 'Melodia interior. Sur le traité *De pulchro et apto*', REA 12 (1966) 229–240.
2 J.-M. Fontanier, 'Sur le traité d' Augustin *De pulchro et apto*: convenance, beauté et adaptation', RSPT 73 (1989) 413–421: 'T. Katô affirme l' influence, directe ou indirecte, des écrits manichéens sur le traité du jeune Augustin. Malheureusement aucun élément textuel précis dans les fragments de Médinêt Mâdî mis en avant par l' auteur, ne vient corroborer une telle hypothèse' (413).

my chapter I will return to some of the texts that he cites, but often in a different way. Ten years after Katô, Donald A. Cress again reviewed several possible sources, but his article does not designate any of them as decisive.[3] Cress' main conclusion is that Augustine's work does not actually have 'beauty' as its main theme, but 'love'.[4] The already cited article by Jean-Michel Fontanier delved deeper into a number of possible philosophical and rhetorical influences (Plato's [?] *Hippias Maior*; more likely Stoic coloured texts from Cicero).[5] However, he comes—quite rightly—to no firm conclusion and winds up by pointing to parallels in Augustine's later works.[6] Virtually the same goes for Fontanier's recent lemma 'Pulchro et apto (De –)' in the *Augustinus-Lexikon*, which mainly repeats his 1989 article.[7] In the meantime Kyung Burchill-Limb has offered some reflections from antique philosophy and rhetoric;[8] her main conclusion is that—in Augustine's whole oeuvre—'the idea of *amare pulchrum* itself never changed'.[9] Apart from the just mentioned lexicon article by Fontanier, the most recent discussion of *De pulchro et apto* of which I am aware is by Jason David BeDuhn.[10] Some relevant comments in the more general works about Augustine and his *Confessiones* will be mentioned later.

In addition to the scholarly opinions made so far, I would like to contribute a number of observations which emphasize the Manichaean context of the work. As we shall see, the contents of *De pulchro et apto* have been placed within the reflective framework of the later Catholic bishop in the *Confessiones*. Nevertheless, it will become evident that both its title and many facets of its contents are first and foremost understandable from within Manichaean texts and Manichaean patterns of thought.

---

3   D.A. Cress, 'Hierius & St. Augustine's Account of the lost 'De Pulchro et Apto': Confessions IV,13–15', AS 7 (1976) 153–163.
4   Cress, 'Augustine's Account', 162: 'Augustine's first treatise dwelt only incidentally on beauty, in spite of its title. Primarily, it must have been a treatise on love'.
5   Fontanier, 'Sur le traité d' Augustin', 414–418.
6   Fontanier, 'Sur le traité d' Augustin', 418–421.
7   J.-M. Fontanier, 'Pulchro et apto (De –)', AL IV, Fasc. 7–8, Basel: Schwabe 2018, 1004–1007.
8   K.-Y. Burchill-Limb, '"Philokalia" in Augustine's *De pulchro et apto*', Aug(L) 53 (2003) 69–75.
9   Burchill-Limb, '"Philokalia"', 74.
10 J.D. BeDuhn, *Augustine's Manichaean Dilemma*, 1: *Conversion and Apostasy, 373–388 C.E.*, Philadelphia: University of Pennsylvania Press 2010, 98–102.

1 The Manichaean Work's Literary Form and Dedication to Hierius

First of all, I remark that the writing dates from Augustine's Manichaean period. He says this more or less emphatically at the start of his memoir about *De pulchro et apto* in *conf.* 4,20:

> Haec *tunc* non noueram et amabam pulchra inferiora et ibam in profundum et dicebam amicis meis: 'Num amamus aliquid nisi pulchrum? Quid est ergo pulchrum? Et quid est pulchritudo? Quid est quod nos allicit et conciliat rebus, quas amamus? Nisi enim esset in eis decus et species, nullo modo nos ad se mouerent.'[11]

> *At that time*[12] I did not know[13] this.[14] And I loved beautiful things of lower degree and I was going down into the depth;[15] and I said to my friends: 'Do we love anything but the beautiful? What, then, is a beautiful object? And what is beauty? What is it that attracts us and wins over to the things we love? For unless there were *decus* and *species* in them, they would in no way move us towards them.'

Later I will return to the words *decus* and *species*; here I emphasize that his discussion is being held with *Manichaean* friends.

On the basis of the just quoted questions it is also worth noting that in all probability Augustine's first work—just like his early works from Cassiciacum, the *Soliloquia*[16] and several of his later writings—was written in the form of a dialogue, a well-known literary form not only in rhetorical-philosophical circles but certainly also among the Manichaeans.[17] One may see confirmation

---

11 *Conf.* 4,20 (CCL 27,50).
12 I.e. about 380–381, still during his Manichaean years.
13 Also this 'non noueram' (in opposition to Mani's and the Manichaeans' claim of possessing and proclaiming the 'truth') is very typical of Augustine's critical view of his Manichaean period; cf. e.g. *conf.* 3,12: '... quia non noueram malum non esse nisi priuationem boni ...' *ibidem*: 'Et non noueram deum esse spiritum ...'; 3,13: 'Et non noueram iustitiam ueram interiorem ...'; 4,3: 'Non enim amare te noueram, qui nisi fulgores corporeos cogitare non noueram'; 5,8: '... ista uero quia non nouerat [sc. Manichaeus]'; 5,19: 'Et quoniam cum de deo meo cogitare uellem, cogitare nisi moles corporum non noueram ...'; etc.
14 Sc. all that has been said in the preceding paragraphs about the *true* love of things in God.
15 Cf. '*ima*' in *conf.* 4,27; with regard to the Manichaeans and their opinions also e.g. *conf.* 3,11: '... quibus gradibus deductus in *profunda inferi* ...'.
16 Some researchers consider this work as belonging to the Cassiciacum dialogues as well.
17 See e.g. several psalms in *A Manichaean Psalm-Book*, Part II, edited [and translated] by C.R.C. Allberry, Stuttgart: Kohlhammer 1938 and also various Parthian hymns.

of this dialogical character in Augustine's words towards the end of *conf.* 4,23: '... and that "beautiful and harmonious" ... was a topic my mind enjoyed turning over and reflecting upon'.

The last quoted words are part of the following full sentence:

> Et tamen pulchrum illud atque aptum, unde ad eum scripseram, libenter animo uersabam ob os contemplationis meae et nullo conlaudatore mirabar.[18]

> And yet that 'beautiful and harmonious' about which I had written to him, I gladly let it turn over in my mind before the mouth of my contemplation, and I admired it without anyone praising it with me.

The (fairly literal translated) full sentence raises a number of interesting issues. The phrase *'unde ad eum scripseram'* refers to a certain Hierius. Apart from his mention in two subscriptions in manuscripts of Ps.-Quintilian,[19] we know nothing about this Hierius except what Augustine reports here and in *conf.* 4,21: he was an orator in Rome (*Romanae urbis oratorem*), originally a Syrian who first learned good Greek and then in Latin had become an admirable orator (... *Syro, docto prius graecae facundiae, post in latina etiam dictor mirabilis* ...), a man also well versed in philosophical issues (... *scientissimus rerum ad studium sapientiae pertinentium* ...). Considering that he was so much praised by Augustine's friends and also admired by the Manichaean Augustine himself, one might wonder: was he also a Manichaean? His great linguistic knowledge (so characteristic of the Manichaeans) could further indicate this; as perhaps his familiarity with philosophical issues.[20] Moreover, he was a Syrian: it is not only a known fact that Mani came from the Syro-Mesopotamian world and composed nearly all his works in Syriac, but also that his message (like that of other 'gnostic' movements) was first and very successfully spread in the Syriac speaking areas.

The words *'nullo conlaudatore mirabar'* have given rise to curious translations and similar reflections. A well known rendering such as 'Although no one

---

18   *Conf.* 4,23 (CCL 27,52).
19   Cf. e.g. PLRE 1,431 and also J.J. O'Donnell, *Augustine*, Confessions, II: *Commentary on Books 1–7*, Oxford: Clarendon Press 1992, 250–251.
20   As was already the case with Mani himself. Cf. e.g. *conf.* 5,8. One may also compare, for instance, the Manichaeans in the school of Alexander of Lycopolis. See also below, p. 284–285 and n. 146.

else admired the book, I thought very well of it myself'[21] gives the impression that Augustine would have been spiritually isolated and not understood by anyone. However, this seems to be contradicted by his initially reported and rather strong emphasis on his circle of friends. In my view, *'nullo conlaudatore'* (*conlaudator*, sg.) will specifically refer to the aforementioned Hierius, of which Augustine just told in *conf.* 4,23 that he did not know whether the highly acclaimed *rhetor* would approve of his writing. I therefore propose the following paraphrased rendering of this part of the last full sentence of *conf.* 4,23, which does not accidentally start with '*et tamen*':

> And yet [despite the fact that Hierius' judgement about my book was unknown to me] ... I admired it, even without co-praiser.

There may have been a special reason for Augustine's concern that his writing would please Hierius. In *conf.* 4,23 he also reveals: 'It mattered a great deal to me to make my discourse (*sermo*) and my studies (*studia*) known to that man. If he approved of them, I would have been vastly enflamed; but if he disapproved, my heart, vain (*uanum*) and lacking your solidity (*soliditas*), would be wounded'. *Sermo* can mean 'discourse' and indicate the subject of a discussion. But (again with e.g. Cicero's use) it can also mean 'manner of speaking', 'style'. Could it be that Augustine had a distinct style in mind, i.e. not only a dialogical manner of speaking, but a dialogical *monologue* such as we firstly know from his *Soliloquia*? The just quoted '*animo uersabam ob os contemplationis meae*' do not only seem to indicate the work's dialogical character, but especially its being a monologue.[22] Its additional qualifications as being 'vain'[23] and 'lacking your solidity'[24] without a doubt refer to its Manichaean character.

The words '*os contemplationis meae*' are also noticeable. I literally translated as 'the *mouth* of my contemplation'. The imagery may have classical roots, although James O'Donnell in his well-known commentary does not provide a better example than '*ante os*' in Cicero's *Rep.* 3,15.[25] He also mentions John Gibb's and William Montgomery's comment in their widespread edition of the *Confessiones*: 'An elaborate variation, in the manner of the late rhetoric, on the

---

21 H. Chadwick, *Saint Augustine*, Confessions. *Translated with an Introduction and Notes*, Oxford: Oxford University Press 1991 (several reprints), 67.
22 One may also compare 'Et ista consideratio scaturriuit in animo meo ex intimo corde meo' in *conf.* 4,20 (CCL 27,51). See further below.
23 Cf. e.g. *conf.* 4,12: 'uanum phantasma'.
24 Cf. e.g. the just in *conf.* 4,23 mentioned 'solidity of [God's] truth' (*soliditas ueritatis*) in contrast to the repeated Manichaean claim (see e.g. *conf.* 3,10) of heralding 'the truth'.
25 O'Donnell, *Augustine*, Confessions, II: *Commentary on Books 1–7*, 254.

phrase "ob oculos mentis".²⁶ It might be for that reason that most English translations render as 'the *eye* of my mind', or rather similar expressions such as 'a contemplative *eye*', or even 'surveyed'.²⁷

One may wonder whether this is all one can reasonably say of the curious expression. Notable in Augustine's *Confessiones* are the metaphors that appear in the grammatical form of the appositional genitive.²⁸ These include turns of phrase such as '*aures cordis*'²⁹ (*conf.* 1,5); '*aure cordis*'³⁰ (*conf.* 4,10); '*in aure cordis*' (*conf.* 4,16); '*de manu linguae meae*' (*conf.* 5,1); '*foribus oculorum*' (*conf.* 6,13), etc.; and also '*os contemplationis*'. These expressions are not found in the Scriptures, not even in the so abundantly metaphorical Psalms which deeply influenced Augustine's masterpiece.³¹ As regards the mouth (*os*), we find metaphorical speech in the *Confessiones* such as '*oris intus animae meae*' (*conf.* 1,21); '*ore cordis*' (*conf.* 9,23); '*in ore cogitationis*' (*conf.* 10,22); '*manus oris mei*' (*conf.* 11,12). The phrase '*os contemplationis meae*' in our passage most closely matches '*in ore cogitationis*' in *conf.* 10,22. There it runs (in context):

> Forte ergo sicut de uentre cibus ruminando, sic ista de memoria recordando proferuntur. Cur igitur *in ore cogitationis* non sentitur a disputante, hoc est a reminiscente, laetitiae dulcedo uel amaritudo maestitiae?³²

> Perhaps then, even as food is in ruminating brought up from the stomach, so by recollection these (sc. the *perturbationes animi*) are brought up from the memory. But then, why does not the person speaking, that is recollecting, perceive *in the mouth of his contemplation* the sweetness of joy or the bitterness of sorrow?

---

26   *The Confessions of Augustine*. Edited by J. Gibb and W. Montgomery, Cambridge: At the University Press 1927, 100.
27   Cf. e.g. E.B. Pusey's translation (1838), printed for instance as a volume of Everyman's Library: *The Confessions of St. Augustine*, London-New York: J.M. Dent-E.P. Dutton 1907 (repr. 1949), 66: 'surveyed'; M. Boulding, transl. *The Confessions* (WSA I/1), Hyde Park, NY: New City Press 1997, 107: 'a contemplative eye'; C.J.-B. Hammond, ed. and transl., *Augustine, Confessions, Books 1–8* (LCL), Cambridge, Mass. & London: Harvard University Press 2014, 171: 'my mind's eye'. Cf. e.g. the still leading French translation by E. Tréhorel and G. Bouissou in *BA* 13, 449: 'le regard de ma contemplation'.
28   M.R. Arts, *The Syntax of the Confessions of Saint Augustine*, Washington, D.C.: The Catholic University of America 1927, 16–17.
29   Not mentioned by Arts.
30   *Idem*.
31   Cf. e.g. G.N. Knauer, *Psalmenzitate in Augustins Konfessionen*, Göttingen: Vandenhoeck & Ruprecht 1955.
32   *Conf.* 10,22 (*CCL* 27,166).

Quite the same phrase is also found in *Contra Faustum*:

> quod enim utile audieris, uelut ab intestino memoriae tamquam ad *os cogitationis* recordandi dulcedine reuocare quid est aliud quam spiritaliter quodam modo ruminare?[33]

> For what else is it to recall something useful (i.e. some word of wisdom) you have heard—as if from the stomach of memory so to say to *the mouth of contemplation*, because of the sweetness of recalling—but somehow to spiritually ruminate?

The figure of speech with 'mouth' is closely linked here with alimentary language. As we will see in the case of *De pulchro et apto*, this would not be coincidental given the likely 'alimentary' content of (part of) this work. Anyway, '*os contemplationis*', just as the closely related '*os cogitationis*', seems to be best translated as 'the *mouth* of my contemplation'.

There might be another reason for the literal rendering of '*os*' with 'mouth'. I mention this reason for the sake of completeness and also from the awareness that Augustine in the *Confessiones* quite often converses ingeniously with his Manichaean (or ex-Manichaean) readers.[34] In *De moribus Manichaeorum* we read in his discussion of the three Manichaean seals (*tria signacula*) that, according to the Manichaeans, the seal of the mouth (*signaculum oris*) relates to much more than just nutrients:

> Sed cum os, inquit, nomino, omnes sensus qui sunt in capite intelligi uolo ... .[35]

---

33 C. Faust. 6,7 (CSEL 25,295).
34 Cf. e.g. J. van Oort, 'Augustine's Criticism of Manichaeism: The Case of *Confessions* 3,10 and Its Implications' (1995), revised and updated in idem, *Mani and Augustine: Collected Essays on Mani, Manichaeism and Augustine*, Leiden-Boston: Brill 2020, 245–262; and various other chapters in this collection. See also several studies by A.M. Kotzé, e.g. 'A Protreptic to a Liminal Manichaean at the Centre of Augustine's *Confessiones* 4', in J. van Oort (ed.), *Augustine and Manichaean Christianity. Selected Papers from the First South African Conference on Augustine of Hippo, University of Pretoria, 24–26 April 2012*, Leiden-Boston: Brill 2013, 107–135 and, for two other early works of Augustine, Th. Fuhrer, 'Re-coding Manichaean Imagery: the Dramatic Setting of Augustine's *De ordine*', ibidem, 51–71 and J. Lössl, 'Augustine on "True Religion": Reflections on Manichaeism in *De vera religione*', ibid. 137–153.
35 Mor. 2,19 (CSEL 90,104–105).

> But, he [the Manichaean] says,[36] when I mention the mouth, I want (you) to understand all the senses that are found in the head ... .

It could also be that Augustine in our passage from *conf*. 4,23, when reflecting on his Manichaean treatise, deliberately uses this metaphor of the 'mouth' in such a broad Manichaean sense.

2 The Manichaean Work's Speaking of 'Beauty' and 'Harmony' and Focus on the 'Corporeal'

There are other and even more important elements in Augustine's report which seem to refer to typical Manichaean traits. No doubt the young rhetorician made use of his knowledge of main philosophical themes from the Platonic and Stoic tradition such as acquired through his studying of e.g. Cicero. But we appear to encounter a typical Manichaean basic principle in his exposition on *De pulchro et apto* when he writes that he focused on the forms of *material things* (*per formas corporeas*, *conf*. 4,24), in which search he (typical of a rhetor in his dialectic activity and—as we have seen—typical of his later works in dialogue form) 'determined and distinguished' (*definiebam et distinguebam*). According to him, the beauty (*pulchrum*) is 'that which is so in itself' (*quod per se ipsum*) and the harmonious or fitting (*aptum*) 'that which is graceful because it corresponds to some other thing' (*quod ad aliquid adcommodatum deceret*). All this does not just remind of 'Stoic-Ciceronian vocabulary',[37] but particularly parallels a discussion of Augustine in his book against Mani's *Epistula fundamenti* about the border between the land of light and the land of darkness.[38] The starting point there is a passage in Mani's *Epistula* stating that

> iuxta unam uero partem ac latus illius inlustris ac sanctae terrae erat tenebrarum terra profunda et inmensa magnitudine.[39]

---

36 'It is replied'; 'you say'.
37 Thus Fontanier, 'Pulchro et apto (De –)', 1005: 'le caractère stoïco-cicéronien du vocabulaire'. Cf. Fontanier, 'Sur le traité d'Augustin', 416 f., in both instances with reference to M. Testard, *Saint Augustin et Cicéron*, I: *Cicéron dans la formation et dans l'œuvre de saint Augustin*, Paris: Études Augustiniennes 1958, e.g. 60 ff.
38 *C. ep. Man.* 26,28–27,29 (CSEL 25, 225–227).
39 *C. ep. Man.* 25,28 (CSEL 25,224).

near to one section and side of that bright and holy land there was the land of darkness with its deep and immense size.

In his polemical discussion of this word of Mani's with the directly addressed Manichaeans, Augustine repeatedly points to a generally accepted principle, namely that when a straight side is touched by a straight side, there is harmony (*concordia*) and that such a circumstance is most beautiful (*speciosius*) and most fit (*conuenientius*).[40] In the continuation of his argument, this discourse about 'beauty' (*pulchra*; *pulchritudinem*; *pulchrius*; *pulchritudinem*; *pulchritudinem*; *pulchritudinem*; *speciem*; *pulchrum*; *decus*) and 'harmony' (*congruerent*; *concordius*; *concordabat*; *congruebat*) constantly returns.[41] Also, Augustine's remark in *conf.* 4,24 that he focused his mind on 'lines and colours and swollen magnitudes' will only be understood in the context of his Manichaean thinking and concrete representations: without a doubt the 'swollen magnitudes' (*tumentes magnitudines*) are the *corporeal* depictions of both the kingdom or land of the light and its counterpart, the kingdom or land of darkness.[42]

Yet it may be even more interesting to see how the—according to the work's title—apparently main theme of *De pulchro et apto* seems to return in what Augustine reports in *De moribus Manichaeorum*. In that work he explains in detail which criteria the Manichaeans say their food must meet, namely good colour, pleasant smell and sweet taste.[43] But, so he wonders in the continuation of his strict-logical (and often sarcastic) reasoning, are the sensual indices of eyes, nose and palate sufficient to determine the presence of a part of God?[44] He then remarks:

---

40 *C. ep. Man.* 26,28 (*CSEL* 25,226).
41 *C. ep. Man.* 26,28–27,29 (*CSEL* 25, 226–227).
42 Cf. e.g. *conf.* 4,26: '... et imaginabar formas corporeas ...' and '... a mea uanitate fingebantur ex corpore ...' (*CCL* 27,53) and, moreover, his introductory words to the just referenced discussion in *c. ep. Man.* 26,28–27,29, immediately after the just given quotation from Mani's *Epistula fundamenti*: 'Quid expectamus amplius? tenemus enim, quod iuxta latus erat. quomodo libet iam fingite *figuras* et qualibet *liniamenta* describite, *moles* certe inmensa terrae tenebrarum aut recto latere adiungenatur terrae lucis aut curuo aut tortuoso ...' (*c. ep. Man.* 26,28; *CSEL* 25,225).
43 E.g. *mor.* 2,39 (*CSEL* 90,123): 'Primo enim quaero, unde doceatis in frumentis et legumine et oleribus et floribus et pomis inesse istam nescio quam partem dei. Ex ipso coloris nitore, inquiunt, et odoris iucunditate et saporis suauitate manifestum est ...'.
44 *Mor.* 2,43 (*CSEL* 90,127): 'Quid igitur restat, nisi ut dicere desinatis habere uos idoneos indices oculos, nares, palatum, quibus diuinae partis praesentiam in corporibus approbetis?' I note that several mss. instead of '*indices*' read '*iudices*'; the best reading, however, seems to be '*indices*': cf. '*indicia*' later in the same chapter.

His autem remotis, unde docebitis non modo maiorem dei partem in stirpibus esse quam in carnibus, sed omnino esse aliquid eius in stirpibus? An pulchritudo uos mouet, non quae in suauitate coloris est, sed quae in partium congruentia? Utinam hoc esset. Quando enim corporibus animantium, in quorum forma paria paribus membra respondeant, auderetis distorta ligna conferre? Sed si corporalium sensuum testimoniis delectamini, quod necesse est his qui uim essentiae mente uidere non possunt, quomodo probatis per moram temporis et per obtritiones quasdam fugere de corporibus substantiam boni, nisi quia inde discedit deus, ut asseritis, et de loco in locum migrat? Plenum est dementiae.[45]

But, without these (indices), how can you teach not only that there is a greater part of God in plants than in flesh, but even that there is anything of God in plants at all? Does their *beauty* move you, not that which is in the sweetness of colour but in the *harmony* of their parts? Would that this were so! For then you will be so bold as to compare distorted wood with the bodies of living beings in whose shape equal members correspond to each other! But since you take delight in the testimony of the bodily senses, which is necessary for those who cannot see the power of being[46] with their mind, how do you prove that the substance of the good escapes from bodies in the course of time, and by some kind of attrition, except because God goes out from there, as you claim, and migrates from place to place? This is complete madness.

In the preceding paragraphs Augustine has extensively argued that the sensual manner in which the Manichaeans determine how much light element, i.e. how much of God will be present in the different kinds of food, leads to many illogicalities and even absurdities. But would it not be better to use one's mind (*mens*) to determine God's presence in food, i.e. by observing its beauty (*pulchritudo*) and harmony (*harmony*)? '*Utinam hoc esset*: Would that be the case!' However, the Manichaeans in their complete madness[47] do not use their mind, but stick to the *bodily* senses of their eyes, nose and palate, which by no means lead to true knowledge of God's real nature.

---

45 *Ibidem.*
46 I.e. the nature or essence, i.e. substance of God. Note Augustine's interesting remark on terminology in *mor.* 2,2: 'essence' (derived from *esse*) is a new term for 'substance'; the ancients did not have these terms but used 'nature' instead of 'essence' and 'substance'.
47 *Dementia*: the usual wordplay on Mani and his teachings.

It seems that Augustine here again reminds both himself and his (directly addressed Manichaean and also other) readers of his former writing *De pulcho et apto*. If so, this is yet another possible indication of the alimentary content of (part of) his youth writing. One could imagine that the *auditor* Augustine—both in thinking about his own food and in collecting suitable nutriments for the *electi* entrusted to him—has come to these conclusions, and that he himself, when discussing the indicators of God's presence in the food with his friends, laid stress on its beauty which is in the harmony of its parts. In *De moribus* however he also indicates a possible absurdity even of this way of selecting food: 'For *then* you will be so bold as to compare *distorted* wood with the bodies of living beings in whose shape equal members correspond to each other!' Without a doubt 'wood' is synonymous with 'tree' here,[48] whereas the Manichaeans' high esteem for trees is indicated by Augustine in, for instance, *mor.* 2,55: trees have a rational soul.[49] Such a high esteem, even in the case of *distorted* wood, easily leads to the said absurdity. Either way, the Manichaeans in Augustine's *mor.* 2 act and think 'in complete madness'.

Apparently Manichaean issues on 'beauty' and 'harmony' such as these are already c. 380–381 discussed with Manichaean friends[50] and they are explained with (only) *corporeal*, i.e., physical examples.

3   'Not Able to See My Spirit': Not Able to Attain the True Gnosis

It is in this context that Augustine then remarks:

> et, quia non poteram ea uidere in animo, putabam me non posse uidere animum. Et cum in uirtute pacem amarem, in uitiositate autem odissem discordiam, in illa unitatem, in ista quandam diuisionem notabam, inque illa unitate mens rationalis et natura ueritatis ac summi boni mihi esse uidebatur, in ista uero diuisione inrationalis uitae nescio quam substantiam, et naturam summi mali, quae non solum esset substantia, sed omnino uita esset et tamen abs te non esset, deus meus, ex quo sunt omnia, miser opinabar. Et illam monadem appellabam tamquam sine

---

48 See e.g. *mor.* 2,59 (CSEL 90,141): '... arboribus ... in ligno ...'.
49 *Mor.* 2,55 (CSEL 90,138): 'Anima namque illa quam rationalem inesse arboribus arbitramini ...'.
50 As perhaps later, in their company, with Faustus; cf. e.g. *conf.* 5,12 (CCL 27,63): 'Et eum in omnibus difficilioribus et subtilioribus quaestionibus [i.e., apart from the astronomical / astrological questions mentioned earlier] talem inueniebam'.

ullo sexu mentem, hanc uero dyadem, iram in facinoribus, libidinem in flagitiis, nesciens quid loquerer. Non enim noueram neque didiceram nec ullam substantiam malum esse nec ipsam mentem nostram summum atque incommutabile bonum.[51]

And, not being able to see these in my spirit, I thought I could not see my spirit. And whereas in virtue I loved the peace, and in viciousness I hated the discord, in the former I distinguished unity, but in the latter a kind of division. And in that unity I conceived the rational soul and the nature of truth and of the highest good to consist. But in this division there was I know not what substance of irrational life and the nature of the supreme evil, which—I, miserable, opined—was not only a substance, but full life, and yet it was not from You, my God, from whom are all things. And the one I called 'monad', as a mind without sex, the other 'dyad', anger in criminal acts, lust in shameful deeds, not knowing what I was talking about. For I did not know nor had I learnt that evil is not a substance, nor that our mind is not the supreme and unchangeable good.

'These' (*ea*) in the beginning of the text refers to the aforementioned 'lines and colours and swollen magnitudes'. Elsewhere, I have argued that these terms are most likely an additional proof that Augustine seems to have been familiar with Mani's *Icon* or *Ārdahang*.[52] Here he states that—in his search for the nature of the spirit (*natura animi*)—he could not see his spirit, i.e. in real Manichaean parlance, most likely based upon Mani's *Epistula fundamenti*: that he could not obtain the true *gnosis*,[53] simply because he could not see 'lines, colours and swollen magnitudes' in his spirit (*in animo*). As argued in the just mentioned essay, these 'lines, colours and swollen magnitudes' probably refer to the lines, colours and vast quantities of the Manichaean two kingdoms as depicted in Mani's *Icon*. In other words, as a Manichaean, Augustine was only able to think corporeal, physical (i.e. light or darkness) substance, but no *in*corporeal reality, no spiritual entities.

---

51 *Conf.* 4,24 (CCL 27,52–53).
52 See 'What Did Augustine See? Augustine and Mani's *Picture Book*', *Aug(L)* 70 (2020) (forthcoming).
53 In the prooemium of his *Epistula fundamenti*, Mani stated (*c. Fel.* 1,16; CSEL 25,819): 'pietas uero spiritus sancti intima pectoris uestri adaperiat, *ut ipsis oculis uideatis uestras animas*: Indeed, may the grace of the Holy Spirit open up the depths of your heart *so that you may see your souls with your own eyes*'. Seeing the soul with one's own eyes is a typical Manichaean expression for having received the gnosis. It is already reported in the *Cologne Mani Codex*: Mani recognised in his Syzygos or Double his soul, i.e. his real Self: 'I recognised him, and understood that I am he from whom I was separated' (*CMC* 24,10–12).

4 Virtue and Vice, Unity and Division

The subsequent words of the long quote *conf.* 4,24 seem to demonstrate the Manichaean orientation of his *De pulchro et apto* as well. Augustine relates that he argued that in 'virtue' he loved the peace but in 'viciousness' hated the 'discord'; also, that in virtue he noted its 'unity' but in vice 'a kind of division'. What he further says about the division (*diuisio*) of the vice (*uitiositas*) without a doubt refers to Manichaean ideas: the said division was seen as being caused by some 'substance' (*substantia*) of 'irrational life' (*uita inrationalis*) and the 'nature' (*natura*) of 'the supreme evil' (*summum malum*). This evil he also considered not only a substance (*substantia*), but full life (*omnino uita*), even life not stemming from God. All of this is entirely in accordance with the Manichaean descriptions of the kingdom of darkness, its internal division and irrational life as it is so often mentioned by Augustine in his works.[54] Completely consistent with Neoplatonic thinking, Augustine would later claim that evil is not a substance, but the lack of good (*privatio boni*; cf. Plotinus' *stérēsis tou agathou*); in accordance with the Manichaean way of thinking, he here says that evil is not only a 'substance' but also 'life'. In the Manichaean texts one finds repeatedly stated that this life of evil is 'irrational' and therefore divisive; also, that it is *independent* of the Good.[55] Augustine, in his first writing, is still entirely a Manichaean dualist.

5 Monad and Dyad

'And the one I called "monad", as a mind without sex, the other "dyad", anger in criminal acts, lust in shameful deeds'. The distinction of 'monad' and 'dyad' was especially well known from Pythagoreanism and also Platonism. However, here the distinction is fully interpreted within a Manichaean framework.

In regard to the Monad, it is emphasized that it is a mind without sex. In his *Commentary on the Dream of Scipio*, Augustine's contemporary (and possibly African compatriot) Macrobius reports that the Monad is 'both male and female';[56] however, this is not the same as '*without* sex'. Rather, the concept of a

---

54 Such as, e.g., in many passages in *c. Faust.*, *haer.* 46 and *mor.* 2,14 ff.
55 E.g. Coptic Manichaean *Psalm-Book* (ed. Allberry), 9 ff.; *Kephalaia* (ed. and transl. by H.J. Polotsky-A. Böhlig-W.-P. Funk, Stuttgart: Kohlhammer 1940–2018), 3 ff.; specifically on its inner division and divisiveness e.g. *Kephalaia* 128,5–8.
56 Macrobius, *Somnium Scipionis* 1,6,7 (ed. & transl. W.H. Stahl, New York: Columbia University Press 1990): 'unum autem, quod Monas, id est unitas, dicitur, et mas idem et femina est'. Cf. e.g. the Greek *arsenothēlon* in other sources on Pythagorean opinions.

'*mens sine ullo sexu*' is consistent with the Manichaeans' speaking of the highest Deity as being sexless: the (traditionally so called) 'Father' of Greatness lives surrounded by 'his' countless aeons, which aeons he does not generate but 'calls forth'.[57] Moreover, the Arabic writer al-Biruni tells that in Mani's *Thesaurus* it was stated that '… in the region of delight [i.e., the Land of Light] there is neither male nor female: sexual organs are lacking'.[58]

Most interesting is what is said in regard to the Dyad. It is the other entity, not a unit (*unitas*) such as the Monad, but a division (*divisio*). A few sentences earlier in *conf.* 4,24, Augustine has remarked that in virtue (*uirtus*) he loved the peace and noted the unity (*unitas*), but in vice (*uitiositas*) hated the discord and noticed a kind of division (*diuisio*). Here he tells in more detail what this *uitiositas* causing *diuisio* meant to him: it is 'anger in criminal acts, lust in shameful deeds'. In Augustine's defining understanding, criminal acts (*facinores*; *facinora*) are acts against the life or property of other people; shameful deeds (*flagitia*) the acts against the nature and morals of men. For example, the famous pear theft is described in *conf.* 6,12 as being a crime (*facinus*);[59] *flagitia* are indicated, for example, in the well-known opening sentence of *conf.* 3: 'Veni Carthaginem, et circumstrepebat me undique sartago *flagitiosorum* amorum'.[60] About the same time as he wrote his *Confessiones*, Augustine makes the distinction between the two kinds of acts very clear in *De doctrina christiana*: 'Quod autem agit indomita cupiditas ad corrumpendum animum et corpus suum, *flagitium* vocatur; quod autem agit ut alteri noceat, *facinus* dicitur: But what unsubdued lust does towards corrupting one's own soul and body, is called *vice*; but what it does to injure another is called *crime*'.[61] As in several of Augustine's other works, in classical Latin the two terms are also often linked, for instance in his favourite authors such as Cicero and Sallustius.[62]

---

57 Cf. e.g. Theodore bar Kōnai's Syriac quotes from Mani's own writings in his *Liber scholiorum* XI (ed. Scher, CSCO 66, 313–314), in the translation of J.C. Reeves (*Prolegomena to a History of Islamicate Manichaeism*, Sheffield-Bristol: Equinox 2011, 147): 'He says that the Father of Greatness evoked the Mother of Life, and the Mother of Life evoked the Primal Man, and the Primal Man evoked his five sons …'. Etc.

58 See the translated quote from Biruni in Reeves, *Prolegomena*, 110.

59 Cf. *conf.* 6,11.

60 Elsewhere in his immense oeuvre, Augustine sometimes distinguishes these *flagitia* in acts *contra naturam* and acts *contra mores hominum*. Recently I have argued that the *flagitia* of *conf.* 3,1 are likely to have been of a homoerotic character; cf. 'Sin and Concupiscence' in T. Toom (ed.), *The Cambridge Companion to Augustine's 'Confessions'*, Cambridge: CUP 2020, 92–106.

61 *Doctr. chr.* 3,16.

62 See e.g. O'Donnell, *Augustine*, Confessions, II: *Commentary on Books 1–7*, 191.

6 Augustine's Manichaean Dyad: Anger and Lust

But what about the statement of Augustine that he sees the Dyad in anger or wrath (*ira*) and in lust (*libido*)? Anger is leading to crimes of violence, lust to sins of passion. I have not been able to find this combination as emphatically stated like some sort of technical terms in the classical sources; nor in the biblical ones. However, one finds the distinctive combination of 'anger'/'wrath' and 'lust' in several Manichaean sources, always as typical features of the kingdom of darkness and the behaviour of the persons under its influence. Concerning the self-divided realm of darkness, it reads in the Coptic *Kephalaia* that from this kingdom through the 'conduits' (*lihme*), the demonic waste is poured down and exerts its influence on human behaviour:

> The waste too, and the **lust** (*epithymía*) and the evil-doing and the **anger** (*blke*) that will be greater in the powers of heaven, shall be poured to the ground through their various conduits (*lihme*). They shall be discharged upon mankind and the other remaining animals.
>
> When what is heavenly will wash the waste and the stench and the poison down on the creations of the flesh below, in their turn the creations shall be greater in **lust** (*epithymía*) and **anger** (*blke*) and evil-doing against each other through the action of their fathers (i.e. the evil archons) who are on high.[63]

This passage speaks of all 'creatures' (thus including humankind), but in many other places the 'anger' and 'lust' (whether or not associated with a just mentioned vice such as *kakía*, evil-doing) only refer to the behaviour of humans. Elsewhere in the *Kephalaia*, for example, it reads in a sort of self-reflection of the Manichaean believer on his inner struggle between good and bad:

> There are also times when I shall be troubled. My doctrines are confused. Gloom increases with them, and grief and **anger** (*blke*) and envy and **lust** (*epithymía*). I am troubled, struggling with all my might that I would subdue them ...
>
> Understand this: The soul that assumes the body when the Light Mind will come to it, shall be purified by the power of wisdom and obedience, and it is cleansed and made a new man.[64] There is no trouble in (the

---

63 *Kephalaia* 121,30–31.
64 Cf. Paul and Pauline theology in e.g. Rom. 6–7; Eph. 4,22–23; cf. 2 Cor. 4,16; Col. 3,9.

soul), nor confusion nor disturbance. However, when a disturbance will rise for him and he will be troubled, this disturbance shall go in to him in ..., first through his birth-signs and his difficult stars that ... they turn over him and stir him and trouble him with **lust** (*epithymía*) and **anger** (*blke*) and depression and grief, as he wills. Also, as he wills, the powers of heaven shall trouble him through their roots,[65] to which he is attached. (...) Again, trouble and confusion and **anger** (*blke*) will increase in him, and **lust** (*epithymía*) multiplies upon him together with depression and grief; because of the nourishment of the bread he has eaten and the water he has drunk, which are full of bothersome parts, a vengeful counsel (*enthymèsis*). They shall enter his body, mixed in with these foods, even become joined in with the wicked parts of the body; and the sin (*nabe*) which is in it [sc. the body] changes into **anger** (*blke*) and **lust** (*epithymía*) and depression and grief, these wicked thoughts of the body.[66]

I will come back to some interesting expressions in this long passage shortly. First, however, I mention a few other passages in which anger/wrath and lust/(sexual) desire form a remarkable pair. In the Coptic Manichaean Psalms it runs:

> He whom grief has killed, he on whom **anger** (*blke*) has leapt:
> He for whom **lust** (*hèdoné*) has soiled the whiteness of his clothes:[67]

Elsewhere in the same *Psalms of the Bêma*:

> He that is **angry** (*boolk*), sins; he that causes **wrath** (*blke*) is a murderer[68]

> The **wanton** (or **wantonness**: *dzrdzir*) ... of wickedness, do thou rule over them: the ...
>   and that of foul **lust** (*hèdoné*);
>   .... and do thou
>   ...... **wrath** (*blke*) and envy and sadness; .... [69]

---

65 In all likelihood, the 'roots' are closely related to the 'conduits' (*lihme*) in the previous quotation. Cf. e.g. A. Böhlig, *Die Gnosis*, III, *Der Manichäismus*, Zürich-München: Artemis Verlag 1980, 332 n. 72.
66 *Kephalaia* 214,4–5 and 215,1–22 (improved).
67 *Psalm-Book* 45,17–18.
68 *Psalm-Book* 39,25.
69 *Psalm-Book* 7,26–28.

In the *Psalmoi Sarakōtōn* ('Psalms of the Wanderers'), Jesus is speaking to the soul:

> Give not room to **wrath** (*blke*). My soul, and [thou shalt live].
> Subdue **desire** (*epithymía*). My soul, and [thou shalt live].[70]

Lust (often with a sexual connotation) and desire (idem) are time and again mentioned in other texts. I quote only a few. In a 'Psalm to Jesus' it runs:

> Come, my Saviour Jesus, do not forsake me.
> Jesus, thee have I loved, I have given my soul ...
> armour; I have not given it rather to the foul **lusts** (*hèdoné*)
> of the world. Jesus, do not forsake me.[71]

In some other psalms of the same collection:

> The **lust** (*hèdoné*) of the sweetness that is bitter I have not tasted. .
> ... the **fire** (*sete*) of eating and drinking, I have not suffered them to [lord it over me.
> The gifts of Matter (*hylè*) I have cast away: thy sweet
> yoke I have received in purity.[72]

> The bitter darts of **lust** (*hèdoné*), the murderers of souls,
> thou hast not tasted, thou, o holy Son
> undefiled.[73]

> They pass their whole life, given over to eating and drinking
> and **lust** (*hèdoné*) ....[74]

Elsewhere in the *Psalmoi Sarakōtōn*, the lust (*hèdoné*) and desire (*epithymía*) are reported to be related to or even identical with the 'fire' (*sete*) of the body:

> Its (i.e., the body's) **fire** (*sete*), its **lust** (*hèdoné*), they trick me daily.[75]

---

70 *Psalm-Book* 183,5–6.
71 *Psalm-Book* 51,4–7.
72 *Psalm-Book* 55,27–31.
73 *Psalm-Book* 64,25–27.
74 *Psalm-Book* 81,31–82,1.
75 *Psalm-Book* 152,17.

He that conquers the **fire** (*sete*) shall be the sun by day; he that conquers
desire (*epithymía*) shall be the moon by night.
The sun and the moon in the sky, they conquer these two, the heat
and the cold, the summer and the winter.
The holy Church will conquer them also, the **fire** (*sete*) and
the **lust** (*hèdoné*), the lion-faced dragon.[76]

7 Anger, Lust and the Nourishment

I notice that in these texts anger and lust are not only connected with the body (which according to the Manichaeans consists of evil substance), but that some texts also explicitly associate these vices with the nourishment that enters the body. A just quoted Psalm to Jesus speaks of 'the fire of eating and drinking' in direct combination with lust; another Psalm also links 'eating and drinking' to 'lust'; the long quotation from the *Kephalaia* tells that anger and lust in the believer are caused because of 'the bread he has eaten and the water he has drunk, which are full of bothersome parts, a vengeful counsel (*enthymēsis*)'.[77] Anger and lust, so this *Kephalaion* 86 continues, 'even become joined in with the wicked parts of the body and the sin (*nabe*[78]) that is in the body changes[79] into anger (*blke*) and lust (*epithymía*) ...'. Lust is also often associated with fire (*tsete mn thèdoné*): both are elements of darkness; both can rule in the body when it is not ruled by the Light Mind.

Reading Augustine's report on *De pulchro et apto* in light of these texts, one gets the impression that its part dealing with the Dyad has been a kind of philosophical-ethical treatise on human behaviour: 'anger in criminal acts, lust in shameful deeds'. These 'anger'/'wrath' (*ira*) and 'lust' (*libido*) seem to find their striking equivalents in the 'anger'/'wrath' (*blke*) and 'lust' (*epithymía*) of the Coptic Manichaean texts.

It is quite possible that Augustine has also addressed the deeper causes of anger and lust in *De pulchro et apto*; thus he may also have discussed the importance of how nourishment relates to them.

---

76 *Psalm-Book* 156,9–22.
77 *Kephalaia* 215,17–18. In many Coptic and other Manichaean texts, this *enthymèsis* is specifically mentioned as 'the *enthymèsis of death*' and closely associated with Āz, the female demon preeminent representative of (and often identical with) evil matter.
78 More or less equivalent to Āz and reminiscent of the Jewish rabbinical concept of יצר הרע (*yeṣer hara'*). Cf. e.g. my 'Was Julian Right? A Re-Evaluation of Augustine's and Mani's Doctrines of Sexual Concupiscence and the Transmission of Sin', now in *Mani and Augustine* (n. 34), 384–410.
79 Or: 'exceeds'.

8 Once Again: A Fully Manichaean Treatise

In addition to the indications mentioned above, I would like to point out a number of other Manichaean characteristics for *De pulchro et apto*.

At the end of *conf.* 4,24, Augustine reports: 'For I did not know nor had I learnt that evil is not a substance, nor that our mind is not the supreme and unchangeable good'. Both notions (evil a substance; our *mens* part of the supreme and unchangeable Good, i.e. God) are fully Manichaean.

In *conf.* 4,25 Augustine tells that once he did not know that his 'reasoning mind' (*mens rationalis*) 'needs to be enlightened (*inlustrandam esse*) by light from outside itself, in order to participate in the truth, because it is not itself the nature of truth'.[80] Apart from the obviously Manichaean principle of the consubstantiality of God and the soul or mind, Augustine as a Manichaean also certainly knew about the principle of the *illuminatio* or *illustratio*: in innumerable texts Mani is described as the *phōstèr*, the one who brings the illumination, i.e. the *gnosis*.[81] Augustine himself relates that those who heard the readings from Mani's *Epistula fundamenti* were called 'inluminati';[82] also, that in Mani's (?) epistle to his 'daughter' Menoch he wishes that 'God may enlighten (*illustret*)' her mind.[83]

The same Manichaean principle of the consubstantiality of God and the soul or mind is rejected in *conf.* 4,26; here Augustine also repeats that, in his Manichaean arrogance, he imagined *corporeal* shapes (*formas corporeas*) of the divine spiritual world.[84]

All this indicates that his mindset in *De pulchro et apto* still was entirely Manichaean, as is also confirmed in the statement that in his wandering he 'wandered on and on into things which have no existence either in You or in me or in the body' because they were 'corporeal *fictions*'.[85]

---

80 *Conf.* 4,25 (CCL 27,53): '... nesciente alio lumine illam inlustrandam esse, ut sit particeps ueritatis, quia non est ipsa natura ueritatis ...'.
81 For instance, time and again it runs in the *Kephalaia*: 'Once again the enlightener (*phōstèr*) speaks: ...'.
82 *C. ep. Man.* 5,6 (CSEL 25,197): 'ipa [sc. epistula] enim nobis illo tempore miseris quando lecta est, inluminati dicebamur a uobis'.
83 *C. Iul. op. imp.* 3,172 (CSEL 85,473): '... ipseque [sc. uerus deus] tuam mentem illustret ...'.
84 *Conf.* 4,26 (CCL 27,53): 'Sed ego conabar ad te et repellebar abs te, ut saperem mortem, quoniam superbis resistis. Quid autem superbius, quam ut assererem mira dementia me id esse naturaliter, quod tu es? (...) et resistebas uentosae ceruici meae et imaginabar formas corporeas ...'.
85 *Ibidem*: '... et ambulando ambulabam in ea, quae non sunt neque in te neque in me neque in corpore neque mihi creabantur a ueritate tua, sed a mea uanitate fingebantur ex corpore ...'.

In *conf.* 4,27 it sounds again that he was concerned with 'corporeal[86] fictions' (*corporalia figmenta*) in his youth work when he was reflecting on 'pulchrum' and 'aptum'.[87]

9 A Strikingly 'Manichaean' Finale?

The last part of the separate section Augustine devotes to *De pulchro et apto* deserves some special attention. One gets the impression that, in *conf.* 4,27, the man who has in the meantime become a Nicene-Catholic bishop once again opens the registers of his language virtuosity in striking images and expressions particularly intended for his (ex-)Manichaean readers.[88] Let us first look at the passage in its entirety:

> Et eram aetate annorum fortasse uiginti sex aut septem, cum illa uolumina scripsi, uoluens apud me corporalia figmenta obstrepentia cordis mei auribus, quas intendebam, dulcis ueritas, in interiorem melodiam tuam, cogitans de pulchro et apto et stare cupiens et audire te et gaudio gaudere propter uocem sponsi, et non poteram, quia uocibus erroris mei rapiebar foras et pondere superbiae meae in ima decidebam. Non enim dabas auditui meo gaudium et laetitiam, aut exultabant ossa, quae humiliata non erant.[89]

> And I was perhaps twenty-six or twenty-seven years of age when I wrote those volumes, turning over in myself corporeal fictions that clamoured to the ears of my heart. These I directed, o sweet Truth, to your interior melody, reflecting on the beautiful and the harmonious and longing to stay and hear You and to rejoice with joy at the voice of the Bridegroom (John 3:29), and I could not; for by the voices of my own errors I was snatched away to external things, and by the weight of my own pride I tumbled into the depths. For You did not grant joy and gladness to my hearing, nor did my bones exult which were not humbled (Ps. 50:10).

---

86 I.e., once again: material, physical as opposed to spiritual.
87 *Conf.* 4,27 (CCL 27,53–54): '… cum illa uolumina scripsi, uoluens apud me corporalia figmenta …'.
88 As this is the case in my opinion in e.g. *conf.* 3,10; cf. 'Augustine's Criticism of Manichaeism: The Case of *Confessions* 3,10' (above, n. 34).
89 *Conf.* 4,27 (CCL 27,53–54).

The (two or three) *libri* from the beginning (*conf.* 3,20) are here referred to as *uolumina*: they may have been (fairly) extensive works. The words '*uoluens apud me*' are closely related to '*animo uersabam*' in *conf.* 3,23: they reinforce the impression that the literary form of the work was a dialogical *monologue*. The question whether '*uoluens*' subtly indicates that the books were written on scrolls and did not have the 'modern' form of a codex may remain open here.[90] As noted earlier, the expression '*corporalia figmenta*' refers to the Manichaean '*phantasmata*' and the adjective '*corporalia*' indicates its absolute imperfectness in comparison to '*spiritualia*'. But why does Augustine speak of 'the ears of my heart'? The phrase '*aures cordis mei*' also occurs in *conf.* 1,5 and reminds of Manichaeans' parlance: they liked to mention parts of the body[91] while texts such as their Coptic *Psalmbook* are full of metaphors like 'the eyes of my heart';[92] 'the eyes of my soul';[93] the 'eye of my soul';[94] 'the eye of plenty';[95] 'the eye of malice';[96] or 'these hands of pity'[97] and 'the ears of the (unhearing) soul'.[98] I already mentioned the special occurrence of metaphors in the grammatical form of the appositional genitive;[99] now I add that many of them pertain to body parts. One may wonder whether Augustine in many such telling metaphors in his *Confessiones*[100] has not been influenced by Manichaean poetry. In any case, the striking idiom 'the ears of my heart' here in *conf.* 4,27 makes this impression.

Yet there seems to be more to be noted in our passage. God is addressed as 'o sweet Truth'. As Augustine specifically reports in *conf.* 3,10 and as many Manichaean texts confirm, the Manichaeans claimed to make known 'the truth';[101] moreover, they described God as 'the Father of Truth' and also Christ

---

90 Cf. e.g. both Faustus and Ambrose still reading 'uolumina' (*conf.* 5,11 and 6,3), but 'codices' for the younger Alypius (*conf.* 6,16) and Augustine (e.g. *conf.* 6,18; 8,13.29.30).
91 Cf. e.g. T. Säve-Söderbergh, *Studies in the Coptic Manichaean Psalm-Book*, Uppsala etc.: Almquist & Wiksells 1949, 98–105 on 'the enumerations of the senses and limbs'; Säve-Söderbergh draws particular attention to Mandaean parallels.
92 *Psalm-Book* 89,6.
93 *Psalm-Book* 86,24.
94 *Psalm-Book* 101,23.
95 *Psalm-Book* 163,10.
96 *Psalm-Book* 171,20.
97 *Psalm-Book* 16,31–32.
98 *Psalm-Book* 194,26.
99 Above, p. 258.
100 See, apart from the instances mentioned on pp. 258–259, e.g. '*oculus carnis mei*' in *conf.* 3,11; '*manus linguae meae*' in *conf.* 5,1; '*manus cordis*' and '*facies recordationis meae*' in *conf.* 10,12.
101 Cf. e.g. *Psalm-Book* 14,14; 43,8; etc.; *Kephalaia* 5,31.32; 7,5; etc.

as, for instance, 'the Right Hand of Truth'.[102] Of course, many biblical texts for such speaking of '(the) truth' may be invoked, but perhaps nowhere else in Augustine's world it was more common than among the Manichaeans. The same seems to apply to 'sweet': it is well known from a biblical text such as Ps. 33 (34):9 which resounds in 1 Pet. 2:3, but conceivably nowhere else in religious speech in Augustine's environment will it have been heard as often and as articulated as among the Manichaeans. From the almost innumerable examples in their texts which have come down to us so far, I quote only three instances, i.e. two from 'Psalms to Jesus' and also the refrain of one of the *Psalmoi Sarakōtōn*:

> In a **sweet** voice he [my Saviour] answered me saying, O blessed and
>   righteous (*díkaios*)
> man, come forth, be not afraid,
> I am thy guide in every place.[103]

> The joy, my Lord, of thy **sweet** cry has made me forget
> life (*bíos*); the **sweetness** of thy voice has made me remember my city
>   (*pólis*).[104]

> Taste and know that the Lord is **sweet** (*halc*).
> Christ is the word or Truth (*mèe*): he that hears it shall live.[105]

As a next case in point I may mention Augustine's speaking of

> ... et stare cupiens et audire te et gaudio gaudere propter vocem sponsi, et non poteram, quia vocibus erroris mei rapiebar foras et pondere superbiae meae in ima decidebam.

Here (with some modification[106]) a large part of Joh. 3:29 is quoted: '*Qui habet sponsam, sponsus est: amicus autem sponsi, qui stat, et audit eum, gaudio gaudet propter vocem sponsi. Hoc ergo gaudium meum impletum est*'. The same Bible

---

102   Cf. 'Manichaean Imagery of Christ as God's Hand' (2018), now in *Mani and Augustine* (n. 34), 89–110.
103   *Psalm-Book* 50, 18–20.
104   *Psalm-Book* 53, 27–28.
105   *Psalm-Book* 158, 18–19. Cf. e.g. the commentary by A. Villey, *Psaumes des errants. Écrits manichéennes du Fayyūm*, Paris: Cerf 1994, 327–329.
106   Cf. L. Verheijen's note '*et gaudio ... sponsi* Ioh. 3, 29' in CCL 27, 54, his asterisk meaning that 'Les scribes n'ont pas commis ici une fausse transcription de leur modèle, mais adapté le

text plays a role in *conf.* 11,10[107] and *conf.* 13,14.[108] In all these cases, a strong mystical feature in Augustine's *Confessiones* becomes apparent. But why is here—and in fact quite unexpected—the image of the Bridegroom evoked and is the emphasis on his voice? The Manichaean sources are full of statements about the Bridegroom, his calling voice, and the believer who waits to hear this voice and to rejoice. I quote only a very few of these texts:

> Light your lamps (*lampás*) and ....
> and **keep watch** on the day of the Bêma for the **Bridegroom**
> of **joy** (...)[109]
>
> Let me be worthy of thy **bridechambers** [that are full
> of] Light.
> Jesus Christ, receive me into thy **bridechambers**, [thou my]
> Saviour. (...)
> Purify me, my **bridegroom**, o Saviour, with thy waters
> ......that are full of grace (*cháris*). (...)
> .... shines like the sun, I have lighted it, o
> **bridegroom**, with the excellent oil of purity ..
> ... maiden, I **making music** (*psállein*) unto thee, my Saviour ... (...)
> ...... Christ, take me into thy **bridechambers**.
> .... grace (*cháris*) and the garlands of victory. Lo,
> ..... **joy**, as they **make music** (*psállein*) with them; let me **rejoice**
> in all the **bridechambers**, and do thou give me the crown of
> the holy ones.[110]

---

texte des *Confessions* à leur propre Psautier' (CCL 27, LXXXI). In my quote here (and in the two next notes) I follow as closely as possible M. Skutella in the latest edition by H. Jürgens and W. Schaub: *S. Avrelii Avgvstini Confessionvm libri XIII*, Stuttgart-Leipzig: Teubner 1996, 73, although in my view also 'stare' and 'audire' are reminiscent of Joh. 3:29.

107 *Conf.* 11,10: 'quia et per creaturam mutabilem cum admonemur, ad veritatem stabilem ducimur, ubi vere discimus, cum stamus et audimus eum et gaudio gaudemus propter vocem sponsi, reddentes nos, unde sumus'.

108 *Conf.* 13,14: 'illi enim suspirat sponsi amicus, habens iam spiritus primitias penes eum, sed adhuc in semet ipso ingemescens, adoptionem expectans, redemptionem corporis sui. illi suspirat—membrum est enim sponsae—et illi zelat—amicus est enim sponsi— illi zelat, non sibi ...'.

109 *Psalm-Book* 37,30–33 (= *Psalm of the Bêma* 237).

110 *Psalm-Book* 79,17–80,22 (= *Psalm to Jesus* 263).

O first-born [take me in unto thee.]
I have become a holy **bride** in the **bridechambers**
of Light that are at rest, I have received the gifts of the victory.¹¹¹

Take me in to thy **bridechambers** that I may **chant** with
them that **sing** to thee. Christ [guide me: my Saviour, do not forget
   me.]¹¹²

Lo, the] wise virgins, they do put oil into their lamps.
      We weave [a royal garland and give it to all the holy ones.]
Lo, the **Bridegroom** has come: where is the **Bride** who is like
him?   We weave.
The **Bride** is the Church, the **Bridegroom** is the Mind (*nous*)
of Light.   We weave.
The **Bride** is the soul, the **Bridegroom** is Jesus.
My brethren, let us purify ourselves from all pollutions,
for (*gár*) [we know not] the hour when the **Bridegroom** shall **summon**
   us.¹¹³

The image of the Bridegroom is often inspired by Mt. 25 and so it appears countless times in Manichaean texts.¹¹⁴ But the influence of a passage such as Mt. 25:1–13 (perhaps via Tatian's Diatessaron?) is not always evident and it is also often the Father (and not Jesus or Christ) who is invoked as the Bridegroom.¹¹⁵ What may be underlined is that—in addition to the 'Psalms to Jesus' and the 'Psalms of the Wanderers'—the image is also prominent in the 'Psalms of the Bêma'. Was it perhaps during the annual Bêma festival—attended and

---

111 *Psalm-Book* 81,12–14 (= *Psalm to Jesus* 264).
112 *Psalm-Book* 117,29–30 (= *Psalm to Christ*).
113 *Psalm-Book* 154,1–9 (= *Psalmoi Sarakōtōn*).
114 It is also present in the newly edited Dublin *Kephalaia*: see *The Chapters of the Wisdom of My Lord Mani*, Part III: *Pages 343–442 (Chapters 321–347)*. Edited and translated by I. Gardner, J. BeDuhn and P.C. Dilley (*NHMS* 92), Leiden-Boston: Brill 2018, 438, with right reference not only to Mt. 25:1 ff. but also to Ev.Thom. log. 75.
115 E.g. *Psalms of Heracleides*, *Psalm-Book* (ed. Allberry) 199,1–2.14–15.23–24:
     '[The Land of] Light, the house of the **Father**, the **bridechamber** (*numphōn*) of all the
        Aeons.   Tell the news.'
     'I [the *presbeutés*] was sent, the **Father** rejoicing, he being in the **bridechamber** (*numphōn*) of the Land of Light, that I might tell the news.'
     'I was sent, the **bridechamber** (*numphōn*) rejoicing, the Land of Light, the house of
        the **Father**.   Lo, this is the new of the skies.'

celebrated by all 'Hearers' and thus also by *auditor* Augustine[116]—that he was introduced to these and similar songs about the Bridegroom? It will be no coincidence that now, in the description of his Manichaean *De pulchro et apto*, he uses—for the first time in the *Confessiones* and quite unexpectedly—the orthodox-Christian (and solely biblical) image of the Bridegroom as an essential reminiscence of his first writing. In all likelihood, it contained mystical tones: in actual fact it was 'a first attempt at an intellectual ascent to God',[117] as particularly expressed at the beginning of *conf.* 4,26:

> Sed ego conabar ad te et repellebar abs te, ut saperem mortem, quoniam superbis resistis.[118]

> But I tried to reach You and was pushed back by You to taste death, for You resist the proud.

Finally, Augustine once again emphasizes in *conf.* 4,27 that his work was thoroughly Manichaean: 'by the voices of my own errors I was snatched away to external (i.e. corporeal, physical) things, and by the weight of my own pride (*superbia*) I tumbled into the depths (*ima*)'. 'Pride', 'being pride' and 'the proud' are often keywords in the *Confessiones* that indicate the Manichaeans and their behaviour;[119] *ima* (pl., the depths) here resounds '*in profundum*' of *conf.* 4,20 and seems to indicate also here the Manichaeans and their teachings.

10 One again: 'Pulchrum' and 'Aptum'; 'Decus' and 'Species'; 'Monad' and 'Dyad'

In my observations so far I deliberately left a number of issues open. After the Manichaean contents, purpose and some characteristics of Augustine's *De pulchro et apto* have been delineated, some remaining subjects may receive a proper discussion from within a now more clearly established Manichaean frame of reference.

---

116   E.g. *c. ep. Man.* 8,9 (CSEL 25,203): 'hoc enim *nobis* erat in illa bematis celebritate gratissimum, quod pro pascha frequentabatur, quoniam uehementius desider*abamus* illum diem festum subtracto alio, qui solebat esse dulcissimus'.

117   O'Donnell, *Augustine*, Confessions, II: *Commentary on Books 1–7*, 247. Cf. e.g. *conf.* 4,26 (quoted above, n. 84).

118   *Conf.* 4,26 (CCL 27,53–54).

119   Apart from the just given quote from *conf.* 4,26 (based on 1 Pet. 5:5 and Jas. 4:6), cf. e.g. *conf.* 3,10.

As regards 'aptum', most has been said already in §2. Although in the first writing of a young rhetor one certainly should not exclude other parallels and influences,[120] I hold that in young Augustine's case the most essential impetus came from Manichaean sources. Based on this finding, I conclude the best translation of 'aptum' is 'harmony'.

Essentially, the same can be said about 'pulchrum'. Undoubtedly it has been a designation of God and the divine world since Plato, and without a doubt this designation had an essential place in Neoplatonism[121] and many popular philosophical currents. And albeit that in Augustine's reflection on his first writing Neoplatonic views resound,[122] the work was written long before his Milanese discovery of Plotinus and (in all likelihood) Porphyry. Thus, for his speaking of God and the divine world as being 'Beauty' and 'beautiful', the parallels from the Manichaean sources are most compelling. In his aforementioned article, Katô has reproduced a whole range of passages from the (then known) Manichaean writings from Medinet Madi. Perhaps the nearly complete lack of clarifying context in his article caused his quotations not to convince everyone. They need not all be repeated here, nor supplemented from countless other Manichaean sources. I only mention a few texts, principally from the Manichaean *Psalmbook* and especially from the psalms genres most quoted before:

> Let us not hide our sickness from him [the great Physician, i.e. Mani]
>   and leave the cancer in our members (*mélos*),
> the **fair** (*saiè*) and mighty image (*eikōn*) of the New Man, so that it
>   destroys it.[123]

> Draw now the veil (*ouèlon*) of thy secrets until I see
> the **beauty** (*saïe*) of the joyous Image (*eikōn*) of my Mother, the holy
>   Maiden, who will ferry me until she brings me to my city (*pólis*).[124]

---

120 Such as especially those from rhetorical-philosophical works; cf. e.g. Fontanier, 'Sur le traité d'Augustin' (n. 2).
121 Of course I think above all of Plotinus' treatise 'On Beauty' (*Enn*. I,6) which—as is generally assumed—was well known to Augustine.
122 E.g. *conf.* 4,24 (CCL 27,53): 'Non enim noueram neque didiceram nec ullam substantiam malum esse nec ipsam mentem nostram summum atque incommutabile bonum'.
123 *Psalm-Book* 46,16–17 (= *Psalm of the Bema* 241).
124 *Psalm-Book* 84,30–32 (= *Psalm to Jesus* 267).

Who has changed for thee
thy **fair** (*houten*) **beauty** (*mntsaïe*)?[125]

'I will [give] my body (*sōma*) to death for thy body (*sōma*) and give my
    fair (*houten*)
beauty (*saïe*) for thy **beauty** (*saïe*).'[126]

Fair (*nece-*) is the ship, the sailor being aboard it: **fair** (*nece-*) is the
    Church (*ekklèsía*), the Mind (*nous*) steering it.
Fair (*nece-*) is the dove that has found a holy pool: Jesus is
    .... in the heart of his faithful (*pistós*).[127]

Play with thy lute (*kithára*), play with thy lute (*kithára*); that we may
    play to these pious ones.
God, God, God, **fair** (*nece-*) is God, God, God, God, my God, God.
Jesus, the Maiden (*parthénos*), the Mind (*nous*),—**fair** (*necō≈*) are they
    to love within: the Father, the Son, the holy Spirit,—**fair** (*necō≈*) are
    they to look at without.
My brethren, let us make festival and sing to our Saviour that has rescued us from the deceit (*apátè*).
Let us therefore get ourselves a heart that tires not of singing (...)[128]

Thou art a mighty Light: Jesus, enlighten me.
First-born of the Father.   **Beauty** (*saïe*) of the **fair** (*houten*) One.[129]

Fair (*nece-*) .... God, he singing hymns (*hymneúein*).
Fair (*nece-*) is an Intelligence (*nous*) collected if it has received the
    love (*agápè*) of God.   **Fair** (*nece-*).
Fair (*nece-*) is a Reason of Light which Faith has reached.
Fair (*nece-*) is a perfect Thought which Perfection...
Fair (*nece-*) is a good Counsel that has given place to endurance
    (*hypomoné*).

---

125 *Psalm-Book* 146,45–46 (= *Psalmoi Sarakōtōn*).
126 *Psalm-Book* 148,29.30 (= *Psalmoi Sarakōtōn*).
127 *Psalm-Book* 161,5–8 (= *Psalmoi Sarakōtōn*).
128 *Psalm-Book* 164,9–18 (= *Psalmoi Sarakōtōn*).
129 *Psalm-Book* 166,23–24.32 (= *Psalmoi Sarakōtōn*). It may be remarked that, in the last case,
     E.B. Smagina ('Some Word with Unknown Meaning in Coptic Manichaean Texts', *Enchoria* 17 (1990) 111–122 [120–121]) reads *mñthouten* ('of the image') instead of *m̂pihouten* ('of the fair one').

Fair (*nece-*) is a blessed Intention that has been flavoured with
   Wisdom (*sophía*).   Fair (*nece-*).
Fair (*nece-*) is a holy soul that has taken unto her the holy Spirit.
Fair (*nece-*) are the five virgins in whose lamps (*lampás*) oil was
   found.   Fair (*nece-*).
Fair (*nece-*) is the ship laden with treasure (*chrèma*), the sailor being
   aboard it.   Fair (*nece-*).
Fair (*nece-*) are the birds ascending . . . .
   before them.   [Fair (*nece-*).]
Fair (*nece-*) are the sheep gathered, their . . . .
Fair (*nece-*) are we also together . . . .
Though we see not the Saviour (*Sōtèr*) let us worship his . . . .
May he abide with us and we abide with him
   from everlasting to everlasting.
Glory and honour to Jesus, the King of the holy ones. (...)[130]

These quotations from the 'Psalms to Jesus', the 'Bèma Psalms' and—in particular—the 'Psalms of the Wanderers' may suffice to demonstrate how often Manichaean texts spoke about God and the divine world in terms of 'beauty' and 'beautiful'. Besides, not only in these texts which Augustine may have known in some Latin form,[131] but also in a writing by Mani himself such as the *Thesaurus* we find these terms in abundance.[132]

Does this mean, then, that Augustine's *De pulchro et apto* was 'a treatise of aesthetics'? Peter Brown calls it that in his famous biography[133] and—as far as I

---

130   *Psalm-Book* 174,11–31 (= *Psalmoi Sarakōtōn*).
131   Cf. e.g. *conf.* 3,14 (CCL 27,34): '... et cantabam carmina ...', sc. Manichaean songs in Latin; *conf.* 5,11 (CCL 27,62) on Faustus: 'Et quia legerat aliquas Tullianas orationes et paucissimos Senecae libros et nonnulla poetarum *et suae sectae si qua uolumina latine atque composite conscripta erant* ...'; *conf.* 5,12 (CCL 27,63): 'Libri quippe eorum [sc. of the Manichaeans] pleni sunt longissimis fabulis de caelo et de sideribus et sole et luna: quae mihi eum, quod utique cupiebam, conlatis numerorum rationibus, quas alibi ego legeram, utrum potius ita essent, ut *Manichaei libris* continebantur ...; 5,13 (*ibidem*): 'Refracto itaque studio, quod intenderam in *Manichaei litteras* ...'; etc. One may also compare, for instance, *c. Sec.* 3 (CSEL 25,909): '... innumerabilibus locis de *libris Manichaei* recitabo ...' and *mor.* 2, 25 (CSEL 90,110): 'Non hoc sonant *libri Manichaei* ...'. All these sources must have been available to Augustine and others in *Latin* translation.
132   Cf. the long quotation from its seventh book in Augustine's *nat. b.* 44 (CSEL 25,881–884): 'tunc beatus ille pater, qui *lucidas* naues habet diuersoria (...) itaque inuisibili suo nutu illas suas uirtutes, quae in *clarissima* hac naui habentur ...'; etc.
133   P. Brown, *Augustine of Hippo. A Biography. A New Edition with an Epilogue*, Berkeley and Los Angeles: University of California Press 2000, 41 and 56.

can see—this is a still prevailing general opinion, another one being that it is a 'philosophical' writing.[134] I venture to challenge this scholarly consensus, however; or at least to make some modifying comments. Indeed, Augustine starts the account of his first writing with the questions: 'Do we love anything but the beautiful? What, then, is a beautiful object? And what is beauty?' However, this is in a context where is first said: 'I loved these beautiful things of lower degree and I was going down into the depth'; and immediately afterwards: 'And I took notice (litt.: I turned my mind [to it]: *adimaduertebam*) and saw that in bodies (i.e. in material objects) there was ...' (*conf.* 3,20). In other words, the emphasis here is on the fact that Augustine (being a Manichaean and so descending 'into the depth') focuses only on 'corporeal' objects. This is not about 'high' aesthetics, but about a Manichaean who considers with his friends that they 'love nothing but the beautiful', i.e. 'those things' (*rebus*) in which the Light element (sc. God) 'attracts' (*allicit*) them and 'wins over' (*conciliat*) to love them (*amamus*; cf. the previous *amabam*). Earlier I spoke of the likely 'alimentary' background of *De pulchro et apto*; here one may see another confirmation of this conjecture in the essential motive for his writing, namely the reflection on the observation of Light elements (i.e., in essence: God) in 'corporeal' objects.

In regard to these objects, it then reads: 'For unless there were *decus* and *species* in them, they would in no way move us towards them.' 'Decus' has a whole range of meanings in the *Confessiones* (and also elsewhere in Augustine's works); to name just a few: it may denote 'glory', 'splendour' or 'grace';[135] but also translations such as 'beautiful' and 'fair' seem appropriate.[136] In all of these instances there is a certain overlap with 'species' and when both words occur together, synonyms in the translation will be appropriate. The very first meaning of 'species' (cf. *specere*: to look at, behold, see) is: a 'view', a 'look'; hence it also denotes: 'form', 'appearance', 'beautiful form', 'beauty'. In Augustine's *Confessiones* (and elsewhere) the word is quite common and entails this whole spectrum of meanings.[137] Also, in some cases it seems best translated as 'beautiful to see', even as 'attractiveness'.[138] But what do 'decus' and 'species' mean

---

134 Cf. e.g. P. Courcelle, *Recherches sur les Confessions de saint Augustin*, Paris: De Boccard 1950¹, 60: '... son premier essai philosophique'.
135 *Conf.* 10,8 (CCL 27,159): 'Quid autem amo, cum te amo? Non speciem corporis nec decus temporis ...'.
136 E.g. in *conf.* 12,31 (CCL 27,232): 'Non enim adhuc informes sunt [sc. aquae] et inuisae, quas ita decora specie fluere cernimus'.
137 Cf. e.g. *conf.* 2,1 (CCL 27,18): '... et contabuit species mea ...'; *conf.* 2,12 (CCL 27,23): 'non saltem ut est quaedam defectiua species et umbratica uitiis fallentibus'; *conf.* 3,17 (CCL 27,37): '... cum saepe se aliter habet species facti ...'; etc.
138 E.g. *conf.* 2,10 (CCL 27,22): 'Etenim species est pulchris corporibus ...'. Cf. e.g. BA 13,346:

in Augustine's *De pulchro et apto* (or, in any case, in the retrospective report on the contents of his work)?

The sequel of his report provides a first answer:

> Et animaduertebam et uidebam in ipsis corporibus aliud esse quasi totum et ideo *pulchrum*, aliud autem, quod ideo *deceret*, quoniam *apte* accommodaretur alicui, sicut pars corporis ad uniuersum suum aut calciamentum ad pedem et similia. Et ista consideratio scaturriuit in animo meo ex intimo corde meo, et scripsi libros 'De Pulchro et Apto' ... .[139]

> And I observed and perceived that in bodies themselves there is one thing as a kind of a whole and for that reason *beautiful*, and another which for that reason is *beautiful* because it is *harmoniously* fitting to some other thing, such as a part of the (human) body to its whole, or a shoe to a foot[140] and like instances. And this consideration gushed up into my mind from my inmost heart, and I wrote books 'On the beautiful and the harmonious' ... .

This further explanation clarifies a bit more about the true meaning of 'decus' and 'species', although I think the best translation is 'beautiful' in both cases. Fortunately, a completely different passage in Augustine's oeuvre not only sheds a surprising light on our whole passage *conf.* 4,20, but also clearly indicates in which way its keywords 'pulchrum', 'aptum', 'decus' and 'species' may (or even should) be interpreted from within a Manichaean context. In his anti-Manichaean work *De natura boni* it runs in a polemical passage on the kingdom of darkness and its rulers (*principes*):

> nisi autem etiam qualiscumque *pulchritudo* ibi fuisset, nec amarent coniugia sua, nec partium *congruentia* corpora eorum constarent: quod ubi non fuerit, non possunt ea fieri quae ibi facta esse delirant. et nisi *pax* aliqua ibi esset, principi suo non obedirent. nisi *modus* ibi esset, nihil aliud agerent, quam comederent, aut biberent, aut saeuirent, aut quodlibet aliud sine aliqua satietate:[141] quamquam nec ipsi qui hoc agebant, *formis*

'C'est un fait qu'il y a un aspect attrayant dans les beaux objets ...'.
139   *Conf.* 4,20 (CCL 27,51).
140   These two examples seem to be *topoi* in rhetorical-philosophical literature; see for instance for the second one Cicero, *fin.* 3,46.
141   I suppose the best reading—with codex S(angallensis)—is *societate* and translate accordingly. On the meaning of *societas* as '(ordered) society' one may compare e.g. *ciu.* 15,8.

suis determinati essent, nisi *modus* ibi esset: nunc uero talia dicunt eos egisse, ut in omnibus actionibus suis *modos* sibi *congruos* habuisse negare non possint. si autem *species* ibi non fuisset, nulla ibi *qualitas* naturalis subsisteret. si nullus *ordo* ibi fuisset, non alii dominarentur, alii subderentur, non in suis elementis *congruenter* uiuerent, non denique suis locis haberent membra *disposita*, ut illa omnia, quae uana isti fabulantur, agere possint.[142]

But unless there had been some sort of *beauty* there, they (sc. the rulers of the kingdom of darkness) would not have loved their spouses, nor would their bodies have been steady by the *suitability* of their parts. If this *suitability* did not exist there, the things could not have happened there which in their madness they say happened there. And unless some *peace* had been there, they would not have obeyed their Prince. Unless *measure* had been there, they would have done nothing else than eat or drink, or rage, or whatever they might have done, without any *society*: although not even those who did these things would have had determinate *forms*, unless *measure* had been there. But now they (the Manichaeans) say that they (the rulers of darkness) did such things, they cannot deny that in all their actions they have had *measures suitable* to themselves. But if *attractiveness of form* had not been there, no natural *quality* would have there subsisted. If there had been no *order* there, some would not have ruled, others been ruled; they would not have lived *harmoniously* in their elements; and, finally, they would not have members *arranged* in their places, so that they could do all those things that they (sc. the Manichaeans) vainly fable.

These sentences constitute a digression in Augustine's account of the Manichaeans' opinions on the nature of good and evil. The digression is, as it were, a separate entity that can be extracted 'en bloc' from an argument in which a number of Manichaean views are discussed, all these opinions being introduced in a striking manner by 'dicunt' ('they say'), which seems to refer to direct Manichaean sources. In between, Augustine unexpectedly gives his comment, as just indicated. He points out various inconsistencies in the Manichaean teaching about the kingdom of darkness: '*Nisi autem etiam ...*'. It is as if in this digression we hear a correcting view Augustine once already expressed in *De pulchro et apto*. In any case, that supposed love, steadiness, obeisance, soci-

---

[142] *Nat. b.* 41 (CSEL 25,875–876).

ety, forms etc. in the kingdom of darkness would not have been there without some sort of *pulchritudo, congruentia, pax, modus, species* and *ordo*. The most appropriate translation of *species* here seems to be 'attractiveness of form' or 'attractive/beautiful appearance'.

I also propose this last mentioned rendering on the basis of the noteworthy fact that Mani, in his *Thesaurus*, speaks emphatically about *species*. Augustine transmits a long passage from its Book 7 in which 'the blessed Father' (...) 'transforms his powers (*uirtutes*)' and 'makes them to show themselves to the hostile powers (*potestates*)' in the 'attractive appearance' (*species*) of naked boys or bright virgins. By means of these 'most beautiful appearances' (*speciebus pulcherrimis*) they seduce the opposite sex.[143] Besides, *species* also occurs in Mani's (?) *Epistula ad Menoch*, here also in the sense of 'appearance'.[144]

Based on the above, it may be concluded that in Augustine's account of *De pulchro at apto*, '*pulchrum*' is best translated as 'beautiful', '*aptum*' as 'harmonious', '*decus*' as 'splendour' and '*species*' as 'attractiveness of form'. It may also have become evident that close synonyms of these words can be used as well, provided that the (anti-) Manichaean context of the words is considered.

Finally, some additional remarks on 'Monad' and 'Dyad'. Earlier, I have pointed to their likely origin as *philosophical* terms and tried to establish their meaning in *De pulchro et apto*. Here, after having indicated how some key terms in the work seem to have their true and full significance in Manichaean sources and even in Mani's own writings, I add that also the terms 'Monad' and 'Dyad' may have been used by Mani himself. The self-styled 'apostle of the true God, in the land of Babylon'[145] appears to have been aware of several Hellenistic philosoph-

---

143 *Nat. b.* 44 (CSEL 25,881–884), e.g. 'tunc beatus ille pater, qui lucidas naues habet diuersoria et habitacula secundum magnitudines, pro insita sibi clementia fert opem, qua exuitur et liberatur ab inpiis retinaculis et angustiis atque angoribus suae uitalis substantiae. (...) quae [sc. *potestates*] quoniam ex utroque sexu masculorum ac feminarum consistunt, ideo praedictas uirtutes partim *specie* puerorum inuestium parere iubet generi aduerso feminarum, partim uirginum lucidarum forma generi contrario masculorum, sciens eas omnes hostiles potestates propter ingenitam sibi letalem et spurcissimam concupiscentiam facillime capi atque iisdem *speciebus pulcherrimis*, quae adparent, mancipari hocque modo dissolui. (...) Itaque cum ratio poposcerit, ut masculis adpareant eaedem sanctae uirtutes, illico etiam suam effigiem uirginum *pulcherrimarum* habitu demonstrant. rursus cum ad feminas uentum fuerit, postponentes *species* uirginum puerorum inuestium *speciem* ostendunt.'

144 *C. Iul. imp.* 3,172.187 (CSEL 85,473.487): '... ex quo genere animarum emanaueris, quod est confusum omnibus corporibus et saporibus et *speciebus* variis cohaeret'; '... et post factum memoria sola eius operis, non ipsa *species* manet'.

145 Thus in his *Shābuhragān* according to the Muslim writer Al-Bīrūnī; cf. e.g. A. Adam, *Texte zum Manichäismus*, Berlin: Walter de Gruyter 1969², 6: '... meiner selbst, des Mani, des

ical views.[146] A key concept such as 'Hylè' seems to have been derived directly from Greek sources and even occurs untranslated and countless times in his own writings and those of his followers. In the Manichaean texts available so far, neither the word 'Monad' nor 'Dyad' appear (although of course the concepts do!); however, Hegemonius' *Acta Archelai*[147] and, in its wake, Epiphanius in his *Panarion* mention Pythagoras as one of Mani's authorities.[148] It may very well be that young Augustine knew the terms (and its associated dualism) not only from his early rhetorical-philosophical studies,[149] but also directly from one or more Manichaean sources, perhaps even from one of Mani's own writings. Using these terms, he presented himself not only as a philosophically trained young rhetor, but also as a true Manichaean.

Conclusions and Final Remarks

At the end of this rather long exposition, my main conclusions are as follows:

(1) Augustine's first writing was a thoroughly Manichaean work and therefore the reason for writing and what we know about its contents deserve to be understood first and foremost in this context;

(2) the likely 'title' of the (two or three) books '*de pulchro et apto*' (*conf.* 4,20.26) is best translated as 'On the beautiful and the harmonious';

(3) the work was not so much a treatise on beauty (i.e. '*de pulchritudine*') and so a purely theoretical 'work of aesthetics', but rather a philosophical and theological[150] work with a practical focus initially inspired by Augustine's *auditor*-ship;

Gesandten des wahren Gottes, in das Land Babel' and Reeves, *Prolegomena* (n. 57), 103: '... by me, Mānī, the apostle of the God of truth to Babylonia'.

146 Cf. e.g. A. Böhlig, 'Denkformen hellenistischer Philosophie im Manichäismus', *Perspektiven der Philosophie. Neues Jahrbuch 1986*, 12 (1986) 11–39.

147 Hegemonius, *Acta Archelai* 62,3 (ed. C.H. Beeson, Leipzig: J.C. Hinrichs 1906, 90): 'Hic ergo Scythianus dualitatem istam introducit contrariam sibi, quod ipse a Pythagora suscepit sicut et alli omnes huius dogmatis sectatores, qui omnes dualitatem defendunt ...'. As is well known, in Hegemonius' story Scythianus is presented as the direct forerunner (and even *alias*) of Mani.

148 Epiphanius, *Panarion haer.* 66,2,9 (ed. K. Holl, *Epiphanius*, III, *Panarion haer. 65–80, De fide*. 2. bearbeitete Auflage herausgegeben von J. Dummer, Berlin: Akademie Verlag 1985, 18).

149 Cf. e.g. A. Solignac, 'Doxographies et manuels dans la formation philosophique de saint Augustin', *RA* 1 (1958) 113–148.

150 Cf. e.g. P. Alfaric, *L'Évolution intellectuelle de saint Augustin*, I: *Du Manichéisme au Néoplatonisme*, Paris: Émile Nourry 1918, 222: 'une expression publique de sa foi religieuse'.

(4) what Augustine reports about the contents of his work is strikingly in line with passages from Mani's and other Manichaean writings as well as with passages in Augustine's own works in which he addresses the Manichaeans either directly or indirectly;

(5) in all likelihood, Augustine's work was written in the literary form of a dialogue, more specifically as a dialogical *monologue*;

(6) its dedication to a certain Hierius and what Augustine reports about this person gives rise to the assumption that this (otherwise virtually unknown) Hierius was also a Manichaean;

(7) the work's focus on the 'corporeal' as well as its speaking of 'virtue' and 'vice', 'unity' and 'division' and 'Monad' and 'Dyad' are best understood from within Manichaean texts;

(8) Augustine will have learned the terms and concepts 'Monad' and 'Dyad' not only through his rhetorical training and philosophical studies, but almost certainly also from the philosophically inspired writings of either Mani himself or his followers. In his first writing, these concepts are fully interpreted within a Manichaean framework;

(9) Augustine's illustrative speaking of the Dyad as being manifest in 'anger' and 'lust' is not only confirmed by many Manichaean texts, but also leads to the likely fact that (part of) his work was a practically oriented treatise on human behaviour;

(10) the fact that several Manichaean texts link the causes of 'anger' and 'lust' to nourishment may suggest that this aspect also had a place in Augustine's first writing, as seems to be confirmed by a passage from *mor.* 2,43 as well as the *impetus* to the work being the questions of Manichaean *auditores*;

(11) a comparison of the reported contents of *De pulchro et apto* with some passages in Augustine's anti-Manichaean works most likely indicates that 26- or 27-year-old Augustine reasoned not only on the basis of Manichaean beliefs, but also that he approached them critically and may have tried to rationally improve them;

(12) *De pulchro et apto* seems to prove that Augustine's equation of God and the divine world with the beautiful is a notion which he—even before his discovery of (Neo-)Platonism—learned and intimated among the Manichaeans.[151] Not least here—as well as in some previously identi-

---

The same in J.J. O'Meara, *The Young Augustine: An Introduction to the* Confessions *of St. Augustine* (1954), London-New York: Longman 1980, 97: 'a public expression of his Manichean faith'.

151 Cf. BeDuhn, '*Augustine's Manichaean Dilemma*, I' (n. 10), 99, with reference (327 n. 111) to

fied aspects of Augustine's mysticism—we may see a lasting influence that Gnostic Christian Manichaeism has exerted on mainstream Catholic Christianity.

In this chapter, of course, the last word about *De pulchro et apto* has not been said. In all likelihood, much more could have been observed in regard to its place in Augustine's philosophical, literary and spiritual development. For instance, did his speaking of '*pulchrum, pulchritudo, aptum, species, decus*', etc. in *De pulchro et apto* influence his later views and how? Was its literary form possibly a precursor to his later dialogical-monological works, even influencing his perhaps most famous masterpiece, the *Confessiones*? What about the fact that the work is described by its author as an attempt to ascend to God ('*Sed ego conabar ad te ...*')? What about its likely mystical aspects? Is there a link between this work and Augustine's possible vegetarian behaviour?[152] Why did he divide his work in two or three books?[153] Books, moreover, of which he states: 'We no longer possess them; they went astray from us, I do not know how'?[154]

These and other questions may remain for future research. Given the rapid development of Manichaeology and also in light of the growing interest in the anti-Manichaean works of Augustine, one may even wish that—sometime in the foreseeable future—a full monograph will be dedicated to *De pulchro et apto* and its importance in the personal development of—and likely influence on—the later Catholic church father Augustine.

Acknowledgements

I thank Jason BeDuhn, Nils Arne Pedersen and Edouard Iricinschi for their critical reading of this chapter.

K.E. Lee, *Augustine, Manichaeism, and the Good*, New York: Peter Lang 1999.

152 Cf. e.g. Possidius, *uita* 22 and also *conf.* 10,46.
153 The most plausible theories in this regard so far come from Alfaric and Solignac: see Alfaric, *Évolution* (n. 149), 223 n. 2 and Solignac, 'Le «De pulchro et apto»', BA 13, 670–673. But see also e.g. Cress, 'Augustine's Account' (n. 3), 155.
154 *Conf.* 4,20 (CCL 27,51): 'Nisi enim habemus eos, sed aberrauerunt a nobis nescio quo modo'.

12
Thing and Argument: On the Function of the Scenario in Augustine's *De beata vita*

Therese Fuhrer

Abstract

The Cassiciacum dialogues are directed to a readership that is capable of decoding the images and codes of the Manichaean religion. In this paper I focus on the scenery of *De beata vita*, staging Augustine's birthday on the Ides of November 386. Apart from the proem and its metaphor complex of seafaring and harbours, the dialogue is pervaded with a series of metaphors related to eating and drinking while the question of the happy life is equated with starving and thirsting. The aim of this approach is to show to what extent these metaphors and the real situation presented in the dialogue—the world of 'things'—can be understood as a statement vis-à-vis Manichaean dietary rules and hence also vis-à-vis Manichaean ontology and cosmology.

1 Preliminary Remarks: 'Things' and their Meaning in Augustine's Cassiciacum Dialogues

In this paper I look at the question of the function of 'things' as part of the dialogue scenario in the context of argumentation in Augustine's early dialogues. In 'thing theory' the term 'thing' denotes tangible and visible objects in our surroundings.[1] In the first instance these strike us only by their materiality, their thingness (a tree, a bird, a table), that surround us in our daily lives or in a given situation. In contrast to an object of contemplation—a picture, a book, an artefact to which we as contemplating subjects enter into a certain relation in order to interpret, read or understand—the thing is not transparent, it is unwieldy, in its material form it appears to us merely as matter.[2] However, in the process of dealing with things, they may be infused with meaning, acquiring connota-

---

[1] See Brown (2001); Knape (2019) 1–39.
[2] Cf. Hahn (2005): Starting with the materiality of things and their perception, the Thing Theory also includes the way in which we deal with things and in a third phase the meaning of things and/or things as carriers of meaning.

tions relating to ideas and concepts and thus becoming carriers of meaning: a plane tree may be seen as a reminiscence of Plato's *Phaidros*, a bird as a precursor of the spring, a table as a place for meals. Only then does the thing become an object of contemplation and interpretation.[3]

These considerations are relevant to my overall argument for the following reasons: Augustine's philosophical dialogues *Contra Academicos*, *De beata vita* and *De ordine* contain numerous scenic elements that are referred to more or less in passing in the course of the discussions. The texts place themselves in the tradition of the Ciceronian villa dialogues in which the rural setting is intended to highlight the spatial and mental distance to urban bustle. In *Contra Academicos* we find repeated references to the work of cultivation carried out on the estate of the villa, situated in Cassiciacum near Milan.[4] In *De ordine* the location where the first conversation takes place is a bedroom, in which a mouse can be heard scurrying and water running (*ord.* 1.5–7). One of the participants sings a psalm verse in the privy (1.22). Because of the bleak weather (*caelo tristi*) they decide to continue the conversation in the bathhouse and on the way there they observe two cocks fighting (1.25f.). In *De beata vita*, the frugal birthday meal in honour of Augustine is the scene of the first conversation (7–16). Augustine locates the dialogues in surroundings containing 'things' and as these are rural surroundings—not a schoolroom, a study, a library or colonnades as in the Ciceronian dialogues—these things have, at first sight, no direct connection to the subject of philosophical reflection. The connection has to be created by attributing to these everyday objects an importance that is relevant to the subject of the dialogue. This is most evident in *De ordine*, where the discussion partners regard even the bedroom, the night, the scurrying mouse, the running water, the privy and the fighting cocks as fulfilling a function in a comprehensive 'order'. The scene of the dialogues is read as it were a world text and is also semioticised and allegorised. The participants carry out a thoroughgoing thing-allegorisation.[5]

In my view we attain a further level of comprehension when we consider that the historical Augustine, the empirical author of the three dialogues men-

---

[3] This process can occur with every object. The best example is Pop Art in which everyday objects are exhibited and defamiliarised, transformed into objects of art that have a performative effect. Cf. Kuechler (2009).

[4] Cf. Fuhrer (1997) 13f.

[5] On the distinction between thing and word allegory cf. Mayer (1986–1994) col. 236; Teske (1995) 114; Fuhrer (2011/2017) 34 and n. 27. It corresponds to the distinction between *allegoria in verbis* and *allegoria in factis* in *trin.* 15.15; cf. *Gn. adv. Man.* 1.34; 2.3. See also Klockow (2006), esp. 110: The denoted object or matter in turn becomes a figure by referring to other objects or matters.

tioned above, wrote these texts in the year AD 386, more than ten years after he joined the Manichaean community and only a short time after his apostasy. The Manichaeans regarded the world of 'things' as a manifestation of cosmic events which are to be interpreted and treated as such. In previous studies, taking the example of *De ordine*, I have attempted to show that Augustine intends the scenery of this dialogue to be read in a decidedly anti-Manichaean, i.e. Platonic-Christian manner.[6] The Cassiciacum dialogues are directed to a readership that is capable of decoding these aspects, an audience that the author wishes to wean away from the Manichaean position and to convince of the rightness of his new Christian-Platonic position.[7]

Here I would like to focus on the scenery of the second of the Cassiciacum dialogues, *De beata vita*, staging Augustine's 32nd birthday on 13 November 386 and the following two days (*beata v.* 6).[8] I will attempt to read the dialogue *De beata vita*—so to say—with 'Manichaean spectacles'. The aim of this approach is to show the extent to which this text can be understood as an answer or a polemic speech against Manichaean teachings which the author and catechumen of the Catholic-Nicene church had espoused for more than nine years.

2 Proem and discussion of De beata vita

2.1 *The seafaring metaphors in the proem*

The proem opens with a complex of images consisting of 'sea—sea voyage and odyssey—harbour—mainland/home' that is applied explicitly to 'seekers', 'those studying philosophy' and the 'telos of eudaimonia',[9] into which an autobiographical sketch is inserted (§ 4).[10] The 'I' of the autobiography presents himself as a seeker who, motivated by "love of wisdom" (*amor sapientiae*), as

---

6   Fuhrer, Recoding (2013a); Fuhrer, Night and Days (2013b).
7   See Kotzé (2004).
8   The text of *De beata vita* is edited according to modern criteria: Fuhrer/Adam (2017); cf. Adam (2017). It has recently been studied by Weber (2004); Conybeare (2006); Kenyon (2018) 82–100.
9   § 1: *si ad philosophiae portum, e quo iam in beatae vitae regionem solumque proceditur* …; § 2: *igitur hominum, quos philosophia potest accipere, tria quasi navigantium genera mihi videor videre.* Cf. *Acad.* 1.1; 2.1; 3.3; *mor.* 74.
10 In metaphorical language the first-person-figure corresponds to the third group of seafarers (§ 2) who have set off the high seas and after long wanderings perceive "certain signs" (*quaedam signa*) and "remember their dear home" (*dulcissimae patriae … recordantur*), then hasten back, in order by means of further wanderings finally to attain the longed-for quiet life (*in optatissimam vitam quietamque*). See Pfligersdorffer (1987) 21–4; Doignon (1986) 134.

a consequence of his "naïve religiosity" (*superstitio puerilis*) at first strays from his course and then deviates again because of the Manichaeans (who are not explicitly named) who "believed that they should worship visible light as one of the highest divinities" (*quibus lux ista, quae oculis cernitur, inter summe divina colenda videretur*). He does not agree with them but believes that under their "veils something great is kept hidden that they will one day reveal" (*non adsentiebar, sed putabam eos magnum aliquid tegere illis involucris, quod essent aliquando aperturi*). Further obstacles are mentioned,[11] also Academic scepticism,[12] until finally the seeker finds his "pole star" (*septentrio*) and reliable nautical bearings in the form of the Bishop of Milan. He reads the works of Plotinus[13] and notices the affinities to Christian writings, but only a 'tempest' in the shape of health problems (*pectoris dolor*), compels him to give up his position as a rhetor and to steer the "wrecked, exhausted ship" into the calm harbour: a negative event thus acquires a positive function (*quae putatur adversa*).[14] However, even this harbour, i.e. Neoplatonic philosophy, is an enormous subject area and, as we see in the following section, it does not exclude the risk of straying from the right course (§ 5).[15]

The metaphor complex of seafaring and harbours is often used in classical philosophical literature[16] and can also be found in gnostic and Manichaean texts. It is of central importance in the Manichaean 'mythological system':[17] the sea is the terrestrial world; the ship's pilot is the Redeemer; the precious cargo, i.e. the soul, the light elements or light particles, are engaged in a struggle with

11 The concern for worldly status and honours (§ 4: *uxoris honorisque illecebra ... nonnullorum hominum existimatio*).
12 The Academic Sceptics are mentioned as a further obstacle because they force the seafarer in the midst of heavy seas to sail against the wind (§ 4: *diu gubernacula mea repugnantia omnibus ventis in mediis fluctibus Academici tenuerunt*).
13 On the transmission of the text (*Plotini* vs. *Platonis*) see Adam (2017) 199–203; Doignon (1977) 68 f.
14 § 4: *quid ergo restabat aliud, nisi ut immoranti mihi superfluis tempestas, quae putatur adversa, succurreret? itaque tantus me arripuit pectoris dolor, ut ilius professionis onus sustinere non valens, qua mihi velificabam fortasse ad Sirenas, abicerem omnia et optatae tranquillitati vel quassatam navem fessamque perducerem.*
15 § 5: *ergo vides, in qua philosophia quasi in portu navigem. sed etiam ipse late patet eiusque magnitudo, quamvis iam minus periculosum, non tamen penitus excludit errorem.* The seafarer does not know where on 'dry land' 'happiness' is to be found (§ 5: *nam cui parti terrae, quae profecto una beata est, me admoveam atque contingam, prorsus ignoro*), and Augustine asks Flavius Manlius Theodorus, the addressee to whom the text is dedicated, for support; cf. Solignac (1988) 51–4.
16 See Doignon (1986) 133 f.; Pfligersdorffer (1987) *passim*; Fuhrer (1997) 64 f.
17 On this, see Fuhrer, Moulding (2013c), esp. 533 and 535.

the powers of darkness which are attempting to steal the light soul. The harbour is the longed-for goal, the place of origin of the soul and hence the realm of light and redemption.[18]

If we try to read the proem of *De beata vita* according to the code of Manichaean pictorial language, it soon becomes clear that this cannot work: in the Manichaean system the ship with the light particles of the soul is attacked at sea by the elements of the evil powers whereas the Augustinian protagonist is either himself responsible for his straying or—as in the case of his illness[19]—this is seen as a manifestation of divine providence. The Manichaean conflict between the two principles, which will end in the harbour of redemption, is contrasted in the Augustinian text with the wandering of the seeker who, even when he has attained the harbour, still has to strive towards the goal of the *regio beatae vitae*. Augustine's proem can therefore—not only with its polemical reference to the worshippers of light as a God and to their promise of revelation (§ 4) but also with its recoding of Manichaean imagery—be regarded as an anti-Manichaean manifesto.

2.2 *The banquet and food metaphor and the question of the happy life*

In the transition from the proem to the conversation of *De beata vita* information about the dialogue's circumstances is provided: on his birthday on the Ides of November, 'Augustinus' asks those present to repair to the bathhouse after a light breakfast (§ 6).[20] The group consists of his mother, brother, pupils and cousins; the latter are described as uneducated but possessing sound common sense; his son Adeodatus is also present. This is certainly not a group of

---

18 See Arnold-Döben (1978) 63–70, who also produces further interpretations of the elements of the metaphor complex. The symbolism of the stormy sea-voyage of life is a commonplace in 'gnostic' writings; cf. Arnold-Döben (1986) 173–176: the sea is a metaphor for the terrestrial world, which for the Gnostics means danger; the pilot and the ship represent the work of redemption of the *Sotēr*, the ship that brings about rescue/redemption is the Gnostic community in which the faithful gather; understanding (*Nous*) is the pilot who saves human beings from earthly passions; the harbour represents the return to the light realm after the turbulence of earthly life and the future of the soul after death.

19 This development can also be read against the background of Manichaean pictorial language: sickness as an image of the sojourn of the Living Soul in the material world/the captivity of the light particles in the world; the Redeemer as doctor; fire, water, wind as remedies for the light particles that become part of the sun and the moon. See Arnold-Döben (1978) 97–107.

20 *Post tam tenue prandium, ut ab eo nihil ingeniorum impediretur.* Manichaeans were not allowed to bathe; cf. Lieu (1992) 174, with a reference to Aug. *mor.* 69 and 72.

intellectuals. On the assumption that we consist of 'body and soul' and that food belongs to the bodily sphere (§ 7), the teacher 'Augustinus' raises the following question for discussion: on this analogy, can "knowledge" (*scientia*) be described as "nourishment" (*alimenta*) for the soul? In both areas a distinction is made between "healthy and useful" (§ 8: *salubre atque utile*) and "dangerous and harmful" foods (*morbidum atque pestiferum*, sc. *genus alimentorum*). On this day the 'birthday boy' wishes to give his guests a "more delicious breakfast" (§ 9: *prandium paulo lautius*), i.e. a breakfast for the soul and the mind. However he wishes to wait with this (*quod autem hoc sit prandium, si esuritis, proferam*) and to prepare the group first, because if they are forced to eat the food they may resume or—like sick persons—vomit it out again.[21] Augustine then goes on to ask the old question about the definition of happiness. This becomes the central subject of the conversation at this Christianized 'symposium' which will be continued in the following two days.[22]

To summarise: the participants take their cue from the Stoic paradox that human beings may be either "happy" or "miserable" (*beatus* or *miser*), "wise" or "foolish" (*sapiens* or *stultus*), but point out that the Christian God is also concerned for the welfare of the foolish because even they can "have God" (*deum habere*), provided that they are seeking to know God and lead irreproachable lives.[23] At the end 'Augustinus' explains why he wishes the discussion to be regarded as a preparation: to awaken thirst for God, all forms of satiety (*fastidium*) must first be overcome (§ 35: *admonitio autem quaedam, quae nobiscum agit, ut deum recordemur, ut eum quaeramus, ut eum pulso omni fastidio sitiamus, de ipso ad nos fonte veritatis emanat*). Those who "thirst" (*sitientes*) in this way receive a "call" (*admonitio*) from God as the "source of wisdom" (*fons veritatis*) who in his "overflowing" (*emanat*) also manifests itself in the sphere of

---

21 § 9: *nam si vos invitos et fastidientes alere conabor, frustra operam insumam magisque vota facienda sunt, ut tales epulas potius quam illas corporis desideretis. quod eveniet, si sani animi vestri fuerint; aegri enim, sicut in morbis ipsius corporis videmus, cibos suos recusant et respuunt*. On the motif of *praeparatio*, cf. the following sentence in § 9: *omnes se vultu ipso et consentiente voce, quidquid praeparassem, iam sumere ac vorare velle dixerunt*.

22 Cf. Harwardt (1999); Weber (2004). On the Christian reception and transformation of the tradition of philosophical banquets and symposium literature see Smith (2003) 282 f.; König (2008). On *De beata vita* and its Platonic elements see Van der Meeren (in print) ch. VI.iii, against König (2008) 79 f. who thinks that Augustine rejects the "traditions of speculative and playful speech" of the sympotic dialogue; according to Van der Meeren the "food for the soul" metaphor is common to both Platonic and the Christian thought. Cf. also Conybeare (2006) 63–92: "Theology for Lunch".

23 On the metaphorical level this means: whoever is still hungry can get what he needs from his own cellar (§ 16: *quasi de suo cellario promendum*).

sense perception as the 'hidden sun' that sends its rays of light to human beings (*hoc interioribus luminibus nostris iubar sol ille secretus infundit*).[24]

The entire discussion is pervaded with a series of metaphors related to eating and to drinking. Again and again the longing for knowledge is equated with starving and thirsting, while the presentation of knowledge is compared to the serving of food and drink.[25] Augustine uses the old (also biblical) metaphors of *cibus et potus* again and again, also in his later writings, especially in his sermons.[26] What interests me here is the extent to which these metaphors and the real situation presented in the dialogue—the world of 'things'—can be understood as a statement vis-à-vis Manichaean dietary rules and hence also vis-à-vis Manichaean ontology and cosmology.

Food was centrally important in the texts of the Manichaeans. The aim of Manichaean religious practice is to purify and to liberate the light particles imprisoned in the corporeal world and thus to separate the conflicting powers of light and darkness.[27] God therefore—like evil—is immanent and omnipresent in nature. He is part of creation. The dietary rules for the *electi* are extremely strict. They were required to eat products containing a large proportion of light particles (as e.g. pumpkin fruit and vegetables). Any violation of this rule would lead to exclusion from the circle of the *electi*. It is expected that the elect will dutifully obey the strict rules, excreting the evil material from themselves and from the world and thus actively participating in the struggle of the realm of light against the evil principle. Meals were prepared not by the elect but by auditors because the preparing and cutting of natural products was seen as an act of violence which the elect were not allowed to perform, as their only task was to eliminate the particles of darkness. Criticisms of these practices were already widespread and polemics raged around this issue.[28]

According to the autobiographical narrative in the *Confessions*, the *auditor* Augustine, too, conceives of God as a 'particle' present in fruit that the *electus* can liberate within himself by eating and digesting it. With biting anti-Manichaean derision,[29] the author Augustine says that the *electi* whom he

---

24 On Augustine's use of the Platonic simile see Fuhrer (2018) 1705 f.; cf. *ord.* 1.20; *sol.* 1.23; *an. quant.* 25.
25 Cf. §§ 10; 13–17; 20; 23; 36; cf. 22.
26 See Zumkeller (1986–1994) 908–913.
27 On the organisation of Manichaean communities and their "alimentary rites" and "rationales", cf. BeDuhn (2000) 126–208; Hutter (2010) 26–32. Cf. Drecoll/Kudella (2011) 24 and 27 on the Manichaean "purification machinery".
28 Cf. Klein (1991), esp. 39 f.; 46; 202 f. Drecoll/Kudella (2011) 155 f. and 172–174.
29 On Augustine's polemics see Franzmann (2013) on "Manichaean practice with food alms";

served as an *auditor* were the creators of angels and gods because they could excrete the divine light particles in their food.[30]

The birthday meal in *De beata vita* is a frugal one, a fact that is stressed again and again.[31] The participants are anxious to practice moderation to keep their minds clear for thinking; other details play no part, neither the question of the dietary rules[32] nor of the persons preparing the meal.[33] The central question here and in the following conversations is that of the right measure and of deviation from it, and this is also a crucial criterion in the definition of what constitutes the happy or the good life. The *summus modus* and the *beata vita* are repeatedly referred to in connection with "fullness" (*plenitudo*) and "moderation" (*frugalitas*);[34] the *summus modus* is also "God's wisdom" (*sapientia Dei*) which is equated with the Son of God (§ 34). There is no 'more' here and no 'less' (§§ 32 f.). The opposite concepts to the above are *miseria* and *nequitia*, which is defined as non-Being (cf. §§ 8 and 30–3). Hence body and soul may be full or empty, knowing or ignorant, hungry or sated. In addition to the pairs of extremes, a state is defined in which human beings have not yet reached the highest level and therefore have 'not yet' attained happiness (§ 35: *nondum* occurs three times) but are still striving to do so and are living accordingly. At first diametrical opposites are invoked, which exclude a third or middle possibility. But soon afterwards precisely this mid-

---

Baker-Brian (2013) on "epideictic invective" in Aug. *mor.*; cf. Zumkeller (1986–1994) 910; Grote (2011), esp. 450 f.

30   *Conf.* 4.1: ... *seducebamur et seducebamus ... illac autem purgari nos ab istis sordibus expetentes, cum eis, qui appellarentur electi et sancti, afferremus escas, de quibus nobis in officinal aqualiculi sui fabricarent angelos et deos, per quos liberaremur*. The interpretation of this passage is disputed especially as to the question of the liturgical celebrations that the historical Augustine would have been able to participate in as an *auditor*. Cf. Fuhrer, Moulding (2013c), 540 f.; Van Oort (2008/2020) 448–51 (221–244).—See also Kotzé (2004) 112 on *conf.* 9.10: "it is interesting to note how Augustine combines in this passage also the culinary imagery used throughout the Confessions with Manichaean terminology. It is conceivable that the Manichaean doctrine surrounding food and eating and the eating ritual of their elect were subconsciously (or probably even deliberately) influencing Augustine's use of imagery here."

31   It is the usual mid-day *prandium* (cf. § 9), not a *cena*.

32   The only distinction made at the beginning is between useful and harmful kinds of food (§ 8). In § 14 "sweet foods" are mentioned as potentially harmful for a weak spleen. The image here relates to the discussion in *Contra Academicos*, which Licentius regards as the dessert, as he claims to be a sceptic.

33   In *Acad.* 2,13 the mother calls the group to the table, whether she prepared the meal herself is not stated. If servants or slaves were working in the household, this is not normally mentioned.

34   Which is, referring to Cicero, claimed to be the highest virtue (§ 31).

dle option is made available, which means that the seeker *does* after all have a possibility of 'more' or 'less'.[35]

Augustine is working here with the theory of the *privatio boni* which, in the *Confessiones*, he attributes to his knowledge of Platonic writings.[36] This is also fundamental to his idea of the nature of *malum* in *De ordine*, but there the idea is not developed further.[37] In the *De beata vita*, Platonic ontology is not explained but instead is illustrated using the example of the opposition between light and darkness (§ 29): darkness itself is not perceptible and consequently is not an autonomous substance but has to be explained in terms of the absence of light; analogously *stultitia* is defined as a "lack" (*egestas*) of wisdom (§§ 29 f.).[38] As it were below the level of the *plenitudo* of the *beata vita*, the possibility of 'more or less' in this area is conceded. Even in the case of eating, the right measure being aimed for may not be attained; but this is not an infringement of dietary rules, as there is no danger for status in the community, and above all failure to achieve the right measure, and hence the ideal state is not a violation of nature.[39] Just as darkness is understood as the absence or the reduction of light,[40] unhappiness or 'folly' means that individuals have fallen short of the ideal of the highest measure[41]—which is God—but nevertheless they can always freely and of their own volition turn to and approach him again. The *stultus* is not on the level on which—like the wise person—he 'has God' but God continues to provide him, like all others, in particular with spiritual nourishment (§ 17: *alius est enim, qui omnibus cum omnes tum maximas tales epulas praebere non cessat*).[42] This notion of God as a 'food-supplier' would be

---

35   On this cf. Harwardt (1999).
36   *Conf*. 3.12; 7.18.
37   See Fuhrer, Recoding (2013a) 55.
38   See in particular § 30: *egestas autem stultitia est egestatisque nomen*. Cf. also *ord*. 2.10: *adducor, ut dicam neminem posse videre tenebras. quamobrem si menti hoc est intellegere, quod sensui videre, et licet quisque oculis apertis sanis purisque sit, videre tamen tenebras non potest, non absurde dicitur intellegi non posse stultitiam; nam nullas alias mentis tenebras nominamus*. See Torchia (1994); Conybeare (2006) 84; Fuhrer, Recoding (2013a) 67–96; Fuhrer, Night and Days (2013b) 4.
39   Cf., in contrast, the polemics against the strict Manichaean rules of food abstinence in *mor*. 2.29–30.
40   § 29: *tale est enim ac si locum aliquem, qui lumine careat, dicamus habere tenebras, quod nihil aliud est quam lumen non habere*.
41   Cf. in particular § 29: *quamquam nescio quomodo dicamus: 'habet egestatem' aut 'habet stultitiam'*.
42   This figure recurs in *De ordine* with the example of the wise person who is "with God" and the "fool" who is "not with" but also "not without" God (2.4 f.; 2.19 f.). Cf. the biblical notion of God as provider of spiritual nourishment in *sol*. 1.3 (referring to John 6:35): *deus, qui*

diametrically opposed to the Manichaean hierarchy according to which this God would assume the role of an *auditor* serving an *electus*.[43] All the individual needs to do is to (wish to) accept the meal. God's action, analogously to the Platonic sun simile, is compared to that of the sun (§ 35), but he *is* not the visible light (§ 4).

Whereas Manichaean dualistic ontology regards Good and Evil as intermingled but as separable thanks to the efforts of individuals—for example by complying with the dietary rules—the Christian-Neoplatonic philosophy sees only the Good as existing. It does not need to be released by means of purification, it is in a state of perfection and pure plenitude above everything, allowing everyone to participate in the Good, which is metaphorically understood as nourishment. The act of eating both in the literal sense and in the sense of sharing a meal and engaging in philosophical communication as part of a community are understood as an effort to achieve the right measure. The philosophical dialogue becomes a tangible demonstration—even in things themselves—of this specifically Neoplatonic ontology.[44] All participants are involved and although their intellectual qualities may differ considerably there is no social hierarchy. Success and failure in the striving for the right measure both have their place in the scaled status of goodness. The surroundings, the things in them and what the actors can do with them can therefore be interpreted as anti-Manichaean.

3   Summary

For Manichaean as well as for Platonic Nicene-Christian individuals, the goal is a similar one: knowledge or *gnosis*, which is described in the imagery common to both philosophies as the appearance of light or as illumination. Motifs and images are certainly comparable: foolishness versus wisdom, plenitude versus emptiness, light versus darkness—these are similar or identical. Yet there is a crucial difference in the attribution of meaning and the evaluation of the deficient state before knowledge is attained. For the Neoplatonist and the Christian, the binary differences between foolish and wise, weak and strong, good

---

nobis das panem vitae. deus, per quem sitimus potum, quo hausto numquam sitiamus. On the strategy of "dévalorisation des thèses manichéennes" in the initial prayer of *Sololoquia* see Doignon (1987).

43 Cf. e.g. *mor*. 2.36: *hinc est quod mendicanti homini, qui Manichaeus non sit, panem vel aliquid frugum vel aquam ipsam, quae omnibus vilis est, dare prohibetis, ne membrum dei, quod his rebus admixtum est, suis peccatis sordidatum a reditu impediat.*

44 See Kenyon (2018), esp. 94–96 on this "Platonic pedagogy in *De beata vita*".

and evil/bad, light and darkness are not decisive. On the contrary, this mode of thinking opens up the possibility of recognising in deficiency an attempt to achieve the Good, in error a chance of success, in foolishness a path to wisdom, in deficiency a possibility of plenitude, and in darkness a hope of light.[45]

I would argue that numerous arguments favour a reading of the early dialogues on the premise that the author is expecting a Manichaean readership, that he encodes the literary dialogues and the surroundings in a Manichaean style but also infuses these codes with new meaning, recoding the motifs and pictorial imagery in accordance with Platonic-Christian ontology and theology and transforming them into a metaphorical arrangement based on Platonic ontology. To the idea of the immanence of good and evil powers in the world of things, he opposes a world view in which every 'thing'—as it is created by God—contains traces of the good that point back to God.[46]

4 Bibliography

Primary Sources

Augustinus, *Confessiones*, rec. M. Skutella (ed.), corr. H. Jürgens/W. Schaub, Bibliotheca scriptorum Graecorum et Romanorum Teubneriana 1106 (Stuttgart 1996).

Augustinus, *Contra Academicos, De beata vita, De ordine*, rec. T. Fuhrer and S. Adam, Bibliotheca scriptorum Graecorum et Romanorum Teubneriana 2022 (Berlin/Boston 2017).

Augustinus, *De moribus ecclesiae catholicae et de moribus Manichaeorum libri duo*, rec. J.B. Bauer, Corpus Scriptorum Ecclesiasticorum Latinorum 90 (Wien 1992) 3–156.

Secondary Sources

Adam (2017): Simone Adam, *Augustinus, De beata vita. Textkritische Edition, Übersetzung und Einleitung* (Diss. München).

Arnold-Döben (1978): Victoria Arnold-Döben, *Die Bildersprache des Manichäismus* (Köln).

Arnold-Döben (1986): Victoria Arnold-Döben, *Die Bildersprache der Gnosis* (Köln).

Baker-Brian (2013): Nicholas Baker-Brian, 'Between Testimony and Rumour: Strategies of Invective in Augustine's *De moribus manichaeorum*', in A.J. Quiroga Puertas (ed.),

---

45 See Fuhrer, Recoding (2013a) 68.

46 This article has benefited greatly from my stay as a visitor at the Maimonides Centre for Advanced Studies at the University of Hamburg in the summer of 2019; I am deeply grateful to my hosts and fellows for their friendly and professional support and for stimulating discussions. I would also like to thank Paul Knight for translating this article from German.

The Purpose of Rhetoric in Late Antiquity. From Performance to Exegesis (Tübingen) 31–53.

BeDuhn (2010): Jason D. BeDuhn, *Augustine's Manichaean Dilemma*, vol. 1: *Conversion and Apostasy, 373–388 C.E.* (Philadelphia).

Brown (2001): Bill Brown, 'Staining Theory', *Critical Inquiry* 28, 1–22.

Colditz (1992): Iris Colditz, 'Befreiung des Lichts. Religiöse Speisevorschriften: Essen und Trinken bei den Manichäern', *Mahfel. Nachrichten aus dem nicht-arabischen West- und Mittelasien* 23/24, 16–17.

Conybeare (2006): Catherine Conybeare, *The Irrational Augustine* (Oxford).

Doignon (1977): Jean Doignon, 'Notes de critique textuelle sur le *De beata vita* de saint Augustin', *REAug* 23, 63–82.

Doignon (1986): Jean Doignon, *Oeuvres de saint Augustin 4, 1: Dialogues philosophiques: De beata vita—La vie heureuse*. Introduction, texte critique, traduction, notes et tables par J.D., Bibliothèque Augustinienne (Paris).

Doignon (1987): Jean Doignon, 'La prière liminaire des *Soliloquia* dans la ligne philosophique des Dialogues de Cassiciacum', in J. den Boeft/J. van Oort (eds.), *Augustiniana Traiectina. Communications présentées au Colloque International d'Utrecht, 13–14 novembre 1986* (Paris) 85–105.

Drecoll/Kudella (2011): Volker H. Drecoll/Mirjam Kudella, *Augustin und der Manichäismus* (Tübingen).

Franzmann (2013): Majella Franzmann, 'Augustine and Manichaean Almsgiving: Understanding a Universal Religion with Exclusivist Practices', in J. van Oort (ed.), *Augustine and Manichaean Christianity. Selected Papers from the First South African Conference on Augustine of Hippo*, University of Pretoria 24–26 April 2012, NHMS 83 (Leiden/Boston) 37–49.

Fuhrer (1997): Therese Fuhrer, *Augustin 'Contra Academicos' (vel 'De Academicis') Bücher 2 und 3, Einleitung und Kommentar* (Berlin/New York).

Fuhrer (2011/2017): Therese Fuhrer, 'Allegorical Reading and Writing in Augustine's *Confessions*', in J.A. van den Berg et al. (eds.), *'In Search of Truth': Augustine, Manichaeism and other Gnosticism: Studies for Johannes van Oort at Sixty*, NHMS 74 (Leiden/Boston) 25–45.

Fuhrer (2013a): Therese Fuhrer, 'Recoding Manichaean Imagery: the Dramatic Setting of Augustine's *De Ordine*', in J. van Oort (ed.), *Augustine and Manichaean Christianity. Selected Papers from the First South African Conference on Augustine of Hippo*, University of Pretoria 24–26 April 2012 (Leiden/Boston) 51–71.

Fuhrer (2013b): Therese Fuhrer, 'Night and Days in Cassiciacum: The Anti-Manichaean Theodicy of Augustine's *De Ordine*', HTS *Teleogiese Studies/Theological Studies* 69,1, 1–7.

Fuhrer (2013c): Therese Fuhrer, 'Augustine's Moulding of the Manichaean Idea of God in the *Confessions*', *VChr* 67, 531–547.

Fuhrer (2018): Therese Fuhrer, 'Augustinus von Hippo (§144)', in C. Riedweg et al. (eds.), *Grundriss der Geschichte der Philosophie* („Der neue Ueberweg'). *Die Philosophie der Antike*, vol. 5.3: *Philosophie der Kaiserzeit und der Spätantike* (Basel) 1672–1750 and 1828–1853.

Grote (2011/2017): Andreas E.J. Grote, '*Optimi viri sanctissimique*: Augustins Konzept einer Synthese von Askese und Pastoral in *De moribus* 1,65–80. Eine Replik auf manichäische Polemik', in J.A. van den Berg et al. (eds.), '*In Search of Truth*': *Augustine, Manichaeism and other Gnosticism: Studies for Johannes van Oort at Sixty*, NHMS 74 (Leiden/Boston) 441–461.

Hahn (2005): Hans Peter Hahn, *Materielle Kultur: Eine Einführung* (Berlin).

Harwardt (1999): Sabine Harwardt, 'Die Glücksfrage in der Stoa in Augustins *De beata vita*: Übernahme und Anwendung stoischer Argumentationsmuster', in T. Fuhrer/ M. Erler (eds.), *Zur Rezeption der hellenistischen Philosophie in der Spätantike* (Stuttgart) 151–171.

Hutter (2010): Manfred Hutter, 'Manichäismus', RAC 24, 6–48.

Kenyon (2018): Erik Kenyon, *Augustine and the Dialogue* (Cambridge).

Klein (1991): Wassilios W. Klein, *Die Argumentation in den griechisch-christlichen Antimanichaica* (Wiesbaden).

Klockow (2006): Reinhard Klockow, '*Confessiones* 13: Versuch einer Orientierung in einer 'unwegsamen Lektüre'', in N. Fischer/D. Hattrup (eds.), *Schöpfung, Zeit und Ewigkeit. Augustinus: Confessions 11–13* (Paderborn etc.) 107–139.

Knape (2019): Joachim Knape, *Die Dinge. Ihr Bild, ihr Design, ihre Rhetorik* (Wiesbaden).

König (2008): Jason König, 'Sympotic dialogue in the first to fifth centuries CE', in S. Goldhill (ed.), *The End of Dialogue in Antiquity* (Cambridge) 85–113.

Kotzé (2004): Annemaré Kotzé, *Augustine's* Confessions: *Communicative Purpose and Audience* (Leiden/Boston).

Kuechler (2009): Susanne Kuechler, 'Was Dinge tun. Eine anthropologische Kritik medialer Dingtheorie', in K. Ferus/D. Rubel (eds.), *Die Tücke des Objekts* (Berlin) 230–249.

Lieu (1992): Samuel N.C. Lieu, *Manichaeism in the Later Roman Empire and Medieval China* (Tübingen).

Mayer (1986–1994): Cornelius Mayer, 'Allegoria', *Augustinus-Lexikon* 1, coll. 234–239.

Pfligersdorffer (1987): Georg Pfligersdorffer, 'Bemerkungen zu den Proömien von Augustins *Contra Academicos* I und *De beata vita*', in K. Forstner/M. Fussl (eds.), *Augustino praeceptori. Gesammelte Aufsätze zu Augustinus. Zum 1600 Jahre Jubiläum der Taufe Augustins (387–1987)* (Salzburg) 33–58.

Smith (2003): Dennis E. Smith, *From Symposium to Eucharist. The Banquet in the Early Christian World* (Minneapolis).

Solignac (1988): Aimé Solignac, 'Il circolo neoplatonico milanese al tempo della conversione di Agostino', in M. Sordi (ed), *Agostino a Milano: il battesimo: Agostino nelle terre di Ambrogio* (Palermo) 43–56.

Teske (1995): Roland J. Teske, 'Criteria for Figurative Interpretation in St Augustine', in D.W.H. Arnold/T. Bright (eds.), *De doctrina christiana, A Classic of Western Culture* (Notre Dame/London) 109–122.

Torchia (1994): Joseph Torchia, 'The Significance of Privation Language in St Augustine's Analysis of the Happy Life', *Augustinus* 39, 533–549.

Van der Meeren (in print): Sophie Van der Meeren, *Entrer en philosophie: la fonction psychagogique des Dialogues de Cassiciacum* (Paris).

Van Oort (2008/2020): Johannes van Oort, 'The Young Augustine's Knowledge of Manichaeism: An Analysis of the *Confessiones* and Some Other Relevant Texts', *VChr* 62, 441–466 (Revised and updated in Van Oort, *Mani and Augustine*, 221–244).

Van Oort (2020): Johannes van Oort, *Mani and Augustine. Collected Essays on Mani, Manichaeism and Augustine* (Leiden-Boston).

Weber (2004): Dorothea Weber, 'Augustinus' Geburtstagsfeier in *De beata vita*', *WHB* 46, 12–25.

Zumkeller (1986–1994): Adolar Zumkeller, 'Cibus—potus', *Augustinus-Lexikon* 1, coll. 908–913.

13
Augustine, Faustus, and the Jews

Jason David BeDuhn

Abstract

Taking Paula Fredriksen's *Augustine and the Jews* as representative of deeply entrenched assumptions regarding Manichaean hostile attitudes towards Judaism, the present study compares Augustine's and Faustus's treatment of the Jews within the *Contra Faustum*, and finds in Faustus a complex and nuanced set of attitudes towards Jews and Judaism which—contrary to Fredriksen—are more benign and favourable than Augustine's. To the degree that Faustus strikes anti-Jewish notes, they derive from developments peculiar to western Manichaeism, in an environment where issues of biblical canon hardened Manichaean opposition to the Old Testament, which—rather than Jews—is the true target of Faustus's polemic. By contrast, Mani and early Manichaeism show greater continuity with Jewish traditions, albeit in a sectarian Jewish-Christian form that apparently had marginalized Moses and Torah. Traces of this earlier position vis-à-vis Jewish traditions still can be found in Faustus.

This study aims to challenge deeply entrenched assumptions regarding Manichaean attitudes towards Judaism.[1] Those assumptions ascribe to Manichaeans *tout court* an anti-Jewish, if not anti-Semitic orientation. As evidence of such an orientation, scholars typically point to Manichaean criticisms of the Jewish scriptures, for example the latter's characterizations of God, its account of creation, and the conduct of its heroes. This critical tradition culminated in Faustus of Milev, whose *Chapters on True Christianity* offers a thorough argument against Christian adoption of the Jewish scriptures as the Old Testament. As part of that argument, Faustus engages in some familiar tropes of the Christian *adversus Iudaeos* discourse; yet these have tended to be read as manifestations of an essential anti-Jewish position of Manichaeism, and revealing

---

1   The present work started as a paper delivered at the 2017 meeting of the North American Patristics Society in Chicago, and was developed further for the 2019 symposium in Pretoria, from which the present volume derives. I wish to express my gratitude to Johannes van Oort for organizing the symposium, as well as for his critical encouragement of my research over the course of the last twenty-five years.

fundamental anti-Jewish beliefs held by Faustus as a Manichaean, rather than as a tactical rhetorical deployment of a long-established discursive tradition of the Christians Faustus addresses. A decade ago, Paula Fredriksen upheld this long-established anti-Jewish reading of Faustus in her book, *Augustine and the Jews*.[2] Taking this work of scholarship as representative of habits of interpretation that require re-examination, the present study compares Augustine's and Faustus's treatment of the Jews within the contrived dialogue of the *Contra Faustum*, and finds in Faustus a complex and nuanced set of attitudes towards Jews and Judaism, more benign and favorable than Augustine's.

Paula Fredriksen sees in Augustine of Hippo's "doctrine of Jewish witness"[3] a "Christian defense of Jews and Judaism."[4] She sets out to demonstrate her thesis of Augustine as a defender of Jews and Judaism in part through a contrast to an anti-Jewish position she ascribes to Faustus, the Manichaean bishop of North Africa.[5] Indeed, she credits Faustus for being the catalyst that caused Augustine to pull together disparate parts of his thinking into a defense of Jews and Judaism. Fredriksen's book is full of insights and discoveries, and serves as an important corrective to many previous interpretations. My argument with Fredriksen focuses specifically on the dichotomy she draws between Augustine and Faustus on their respective views of Jews and Judaism. I contend that in doing full justice to the nuances of Augustine's position, Fredriksen has done grave injustice to Faustus's, and while there are clear dichotomies between Augustine and Faustus, one cannot be drawn between a pro-Jewish Augustine and an anti-Jewish Faustus.

Both Faustus and Augustine say all sorts of negative things about Jews and Judaism rooted in the *adversus Iudaeos* tradition that permeates Christian patristic literature.[6] Yet Fredriksen finds a positive turn in Augustine's view that the Jews did and do serve a positive role in the history of salvation, albeit

---

[2] Paula Fredriksen, *Augustine and the Jews: A Christian Defense of Jews and Judaism* (New Haven: Yale University Press, 2010).

[3] As provocatively paraphrased by Fredriksen, this doctrine holds that Jews are "wandering book slaves who witness to Christian truth" (2010, 320). See Enar. in Ps. 56.9: "The Jew carries the book from which the Christian takes his faith. They have become our librarians, like slaves who carry books behind their masters; the slaves gain no profit by their carrying, but the masters profit by their reading." This sums up a position developed earlier in C. Faust. 12.

[4] This is where the benefit comes, according to Fredriksen's analysis: involuntarily providing witness to Christian truth, they are protected from annihilation.

[5] The authority of a Manichaean bishop extended over a sizable region, more analogous to a Christian archbishop than to someone with the limited domain of a bishop.

[6] From Faustus, e.g., circumcision is "shameful" (*pudendam*) and the precepts of the Law are "degrading" (*turpium*, C. Faust. 6.1); nonetheless, in most specifics he describes the Law as merely superfluous and unnecessary (*superuacuus, inutilis*, etc., C. Faust. 6.1).

one from which they themselves will not benefit. But Faustus, too, has positive things to say about Jews and Judaism, which Fredriksen omits. In fact, Faustus praises the faithfulness of Jews to their religion, and uses it as a stick with which to beat catholic Christians who would seize ownership of Jewish scriptures while utterly neglecting to follow its commandments. To balance Fredriksen's work on behalf of Augustine, we need to bring out the positive aspects of Faustus's rhetoric related to Jews and Judaism, and conclude by assessing which of these two late antique religious leaders reach a position with more benign implications for the Jewish people and the Jewish religious tradition.

Fredriksen astutely analyzes the common debt Augustine and Faustus had to the established *adversus Iudaeos* tradition of Christian rhetoric, and how this rhetoric had been deployed over the centuries not in direct debate with Jews, but as part of intra-Christian polemic, with "Jews" serving as a convenient, largely imagined Other.[7] "In this one realm, catholics and Manichees seemed curiously agreed."[8]

> What made Faustus so dangerous was the way that he built his case by appealing to so many of the anti-Jewish attitudes and traditions of interpretation that the Manichees held in common with Augustine's own church.[9] ... much of his critique of Jews and Judaism simply echoed what generations of more orthodox North Africans had already heard in their own churches.[10] ... On dangerous display throughout the *Capitula* ... was Faustus' ... mastery of the various interlocking themes and arguments well known to North African catholics, especially through preaching: the polemics *adversus Iudaeos* of their own tradition. Thanks to Faustus' inge-

---

7   See Fredriksen 2010, 424 n.12 for references to secondary scholarship on the *adversus Iudaeos* literature of early Christianity. Fredriksen points out how much the "Jews" of Christian polemic are rhetorical constructs, imagined rather than observed, such as when the practice of sacrifices is discussed centuries after the practice had ceased (226 ff.). This is true of Faustus as well.

8   Fredriksen 2010, 211. She continues: "Both churches decried the carnality of Jewish practices. *Both churches condemned the obtuseness of Jewish biblical interpretation.* And both churches held that the Jewish cult of animal sacrifices in Jerusalem linked Jewish worship to idolatry." The italicized sentence is in error; Manichaeans agreed with Jews on a literal interpretation of scriptures against the allegorical fashions of the catholic tradition. They attacked the Old Testament on its literal meaning, not on Jewish misconstrual of that meaning. See Jason BeDuhn, "Manichaean Biblical Interpretation," in P. Blowers and P. Martens, eds., *The Oxford Handbook of Early Christian Biblical Interpretation* (Oxford: Oxford University Press, 2019), 399–414.

9   Fredriksen 2010, 223.

10 Fredriksen 2010, 232.

nuity, these familiar, biblically based critiques ricocheted off of their original targets back onto the church that had launched them.[11]

Fredriksen credits Faustus's deployment of this tradition with forcing Augustine to take a different tack in his response.[12]

> Challenged by a thoughtful Manichaean missionary on the unseemly Jewishness of the scriptures and doctrines of catholic Christianity, Augustine answered with a brilliant and novel defense. He reimagined the relationship of God and Israel, and thus he reimagined as well the relationship of his church, past and present, to the Jews.[13]

Since Faustus was decrying catholic Christianity as "semi-Christianity" because of its continuity with both Jewish and pagan religious attitudes and practices, and anchored his attack on catholic retention of the Old Testament, Augustine had no choice but to defend the Old Testament as integral to Christian identity.

Much of what Fredriksen credits as Augustine's defense of "Jews and Judaism," then, is collateral to his defense of the Old Testament. Jews have value—have a right to exist, and to exist as Jews—Augustine holds, only as receivers and transmitters of the Old Testament. In other words, they exist for the sake of this text, and for the benefit this text has for Christians alone. This "Witness Doctrine" of Augustine is most succinctly outlined in Book 18 of *City of God*:

> By the evidence of their own scriptures they bear witness for us that we have not fabricated the prophecies about Christ .... It follows that when the Jews do not believe in our scriptures, their scriptures are fulfilled in them, while they read them with blind eyes .... It is in order to give this testimony which, in spite of themselves, they supply for our benefit by their possession and preservation of those books that they are themselves dispersed among all nations, wherever the Christian church spreads .... Hence the prophecy in the Book of Psalms: 'Slay them not, lest they forget your law; scatter them by your might.'
> City of God 18.46

---

11 Fredriksen 2010, 240.
12 For Augustine, "the general utility of this older catholic tradition [of *adversus Iudaeos* tropes], for this specific project [against Faustus], had been compromised: The astute Faustus had co-opted too much of it in his *Capitula*" (Fredriksen 2010, 262).
13 Fredriksen 2010, 211.

Augustine's "Witness Doctrine" thus entails the following elements:

1. Jews and Jewish scriptures exist for the benefit of Christians, as a source of a proof of Christianity through prior prophecy.
2. Jews do not themselves benefit from their scriptures, because they are blind to their meaning, and their own scriptures prophesize their blind obstinance.
3. Jews are dispersed and exiled to benefit Christians.
4. Jews must be preserved alive and in their ignorance of the truth to play the role they have to benefit Christians.

Fredriksen argues that this doctrine necessarily entails some positive concessions about Jews and Judaism, in order to validate catholic Christian continuity and connectedness with the Jewish tradition against Faustus's critique.

1 Augustine's Two Breakthroughs

Fredriksen identifies two interrelated breakthroughs in Augustine's thinking in his *Contra Faustum*. First, Augustine made an exegetical breakthrough that recognized the value of the historicity of the events described in the biblical text. Whereas before he was indifferent to whether the events actually happened or not, and found their meaning solely as revealed words, he now embraced the idea that the events as events could serve just as well as signs that could be allegorically or typologically interpreted. "The lives of these men as well as their words were prophetic" (Faustus 4.2; cf. 13.15, 22.24).[14] This breakthrough is essential for his defense of the Old Testament in *Contra Faustum*, where in defending against Faustus's criticism of the behavior of the patriarchs and prophets, he does not resort to allegory, but acknowledges the behavior as real, giving a historical defense of its significance.

The hermeneutical basis of this tactic of defense was first worked out in *De doctrina christiana*: "We must pay careful attention to the conduct appropriate to different places, times, and persons, lest we make rash imputations of wickedness" (Doctr. chr. 3.12,20). Even if there is a figurative significance in the stories of Old Testament heroes, we must accept that they really did behave in the ways they are described (Doctr. chr. 3.23,33), and examine these behaviors either as negative moral lessons or search out their pious motive despite appearances (e.g., polygamy but with a procreative rather than lust-based motive). Augustine still insists on a primarily typological reading of the

---

14 See Fredriksen 2010, 244–245.

Old Testament: *Christum igitur sonant haec omnia*: (The Bible) everywhere speaks of Christ (C. Faust. 22.94; cf. C. Faust. 12.4, 12.7). Nevertheless, the scriptures *facta narrantur*: narrate (actual) things done (C. Faust. 12.7).

Fredriksen contends that this new mode of reading led to the second breakthrough in Augustine's affirmation of the validity of the Law in its own time, and the morality of the patriarchs and prophets in their own culture.[15] Whereas the earlier Christian *adversus Iudaeos* tradition had tended to disparage Jews as in error right from the start, carnally minded, and wrongfully trying to put into literal practice a Law that was always meant to be understood symbolically,[16] Augustine argued that they were right to put the Law into practice, and that observance of the Law served a valid spiritual purpose in the era before Christ. So much so that Jesus and the first generation of Christians continued to observe the Law to signal its past value in contrast to pagan practices.

This point is brought out especially in Augustine's *Epistle 82* to Jerome:[17] "At that time, the [Christian] Jews were not to be kept from those rites as if they were wicked, and the Gentiles were not to be forced to those rites as if they were necessary" (Ep. 82.2,9). "They are not bad, because they were commanded by God as appropriate to those times and purposes" (Ep. 82.2,14). It is noteworthy that at Ep. 82.2,17 Augustine refers Jerome to the argument he made in Contra Faustum 19.17. Augustine affirms in Fredriksen's words "not only that the Law itself was good, but also ... that *the Jewish understanding of the Law as enacted by Israel and as described in the Bible was also good*."[18] "This simple assertion was revolutionary," Fredriksen continues. "It stood centuries of traditional anti-Jewish polemic, both orthodox and heterodox, on its head."[19]

Leaving aside the question of just how revolutionary Augustine truly is here,[20] what Fredriksen misses with regard to Faustus is the degree to which the Manichaean leader had already anticipated both of these breakthroughs in

---

15   Fredriksen 2010, 242.
16   "The Jews' 'literal-mindedness' in observing the Law had long provided critics with absolute proof of Israel's turpitude ... Instead of understanding the Law 'spiritually,' Jews had understood 'carnally' and thus remained enmeshed in the fleshly 'works of the Law'" (Fredriksen 2010, 244).
17   Fredriksen 2010, 299.
18   Fredriksen 2010, 243.
19   Fredriksen 2010, 244.
20   Justin Martyr already had suggested that Jews were meant to actually observe the Law, as a kind of punitive training, and Tyconius had argued for the typological value of actual historical deeds and practices commanded and reported in the Old Testament, so Augustine is not as unique and revolutionary as he may appear in Fredriksen's characterization (see Fredriksen 2010, 247).

his *Capitula*. First, Faustus like other Manichaeans already agreed with Jews on the literal meaning of the biblical text, while Augustine had inherited a catholic Christian appropriation of the biblical texts that relied on a rejection of that literal sense as immoral, absurd, and "carnal"—all adjectives that can be equally applied to those who read the text in that literal way. Augustine himself had learned the Manichaean literal reading of the Old Testament as a means of critiquing it, and then later had welcomed the discovery of allegorical interpretation as the catholic solution to those critiques. But it was not a solution that would be accepted by Manichaeans or meet their critique. So now he found himself rolling up his sleeves to attempt a defense of even the literal meaning of the biblical text, in order to meet Manichaeans on their own exegetical terms.

Second, Faustus makes a sustained argument that the core of religion is in *practice*, rather than belief. Commitment to a particular religion entails enactment of its precepts and living the life its teachings dictate.[21] Faustus does not have the built-in disparagement of physical observances that drove a great deal of the Christian *adversus Iudaeos* rhetoric. Religions that fail to demand concrete results in human conduct, or are unable to successfully motivate people to good actions, do not merit consideration, Faustus contends. By that standard, he thinks Jews have done well, and have lived up to the obligations placed upon them by their god. In fact, he takes Jews as his prime example of defining religion by its precepts, and assessing its practitioners by their faithful observance of those precepts (C. Faust. 4.1); they "carefully obey Moses" and are "very zealous" (C. Faust. 16.6). So even if their god is a false one, Faustus asserts, Jews themselves have conducted themselves earnestly and honestly and are fully entitled to all the promises that god made as to their rewards for obedience. Indeed, they "did not believe in Christ on account of their attachment to Moses" (C. Faust. 16.7), and Faustus contends that they had every right to accuse Christ of coming to destroy the Law, given his open disregard for it (C. Faust. 17.2).

In other words, for Faustus Jews have not only understood the scripture they have received correctly, that is, literally; they also have dutifully lived the life enjoined by it, which has validity for them as long as they remain Jews. As a Manichaean, Faustus disavows any claim on the Jewish scripture as well as any judgment on the continuing validity of the practices it commands. It is

---

21 See Jason BeDuhn, "A Religion of Deeds: Scepticism in the Doctrinally Liberal Manichaeism of Faustus and Augustine," in J. BeDuhn (ed.), *New Light on Manichaeism: Papers from the Sixth International Congress of Manichaeism* (Leiden: Brill, 2009), 1–28; Jason BeDuhn, *Augustine's Manichaean Dilemma, 1: Conversion and Apostasy, 373–388 C.E.* (Philadelphia: University of Pennsylvania Press, 2010), 113–117.

catholic Christians, who are at one and the same time both semi-Christians and semi-Jews, that Faustus condemns. For while making a big pretense of belief, and insisting upon their ownership of the Old Testament, they have failed to carry out its commands. Therefore, they are hypocrites, much worse than Jews (C. Faust. 6.1; 16.2–8). Just as Augustine found it necessary to meet Faustus on the ground of literal exegesis of scripture, then, he may have considered it essential to take Faustus's own emphasis on religious practice as the basis for mounting a defense of the Old Testament and the practices it commands.

2 Fredriksen on the "Mark of Cain"

Fredriksen cautions that "our own sympathies trick us into identifying with Augustine and his arguments, indeed into seeing him, in this one exceptional instance, as something of a religious liberal."[22] She continues:

> He is not that, of course, nor could he ever be. Nonetheless, I think we can still admire him for the exceptional, original, creative, even daring … thinker that he was. And his theology of Judaism in particular showcases all of these admirable qualities.[23]

This assessment, however, depends on the very trick Fredriksen cautions against. Reiterating the concessions Augustine makes to Jews and Judaism as the protases of his arguments, she consistently elides the negative apodoses of his doctrine of Jewish witness. Having worked through this doctrine, she lifts only the positive parts of it for her summaries of Augustine's achievement. Such selective emphasis may have its place, were it not achieved by the reverse treatment of Augustine's opponent, Faustus, whose thinking on Judaism has its own positive aspects Fredriksen ignores. The one-sided bias of Fredriksen's argument is particularly egregious in her analysis of Augustine's understanding of the "mark of Cain."[24]

---

22   Fredriksen 2010, 373–374.
23   Fredriksen 2010, 374.
24   On this subject, one should compare Lisa Anne Unterseher, "The Mark of Cain and the Jews: Augustine's Theology of Jews and Judaism" (Ph.D. diss., Southern Methodist University, 2000), subsequently published as, *The Mark of Cain and the Jews* (Gorgias, 2009). Unterseher's interpretation of the "mark of Cain" in Augustine in part develops ideas Fredriksen had introduced in "Excaecati Occulta Justitia Dei: Augustine on Jews and Judaism," *Journal of Early Christian Studies* 3 (1995) 299–324, which in turn presage Fredriksen's more expansive treatment in her 2010 book.

Fredriksen wishes to credit Augustine with the positive aspects of his application of the Cain story to the Jews: the protection afforded them, and to their continued observance of the Law, by their association with the "mark" God puts upon Cain. In this way, Fredriksen maintains, Augustine defends Jews from the threat of being exterminated due to Christian hostility towards them. Ironically, Augustine receives credit for protecting Jews from a threat that only his religious community poses to them. It had never occurred to any other community, including Faustus's Manichaean one, to even consider slaughtering the Jews. Fredriksen does not remark on this peculiarity of the issue. But, more seriously, Fredriksen fails to note that Augustine himself is responsible for fully developing an identification of the Jews with the fratricidal Cain: "Abel, the younger brother, is killed by the elder brother; Christ, the head of the younger people, is killed by the elder people of the Jews" (C. Faust. 12.9). "Thus from the sacred scriptures does God's voice accuse the Jews" (Faustus 12.10), who are to be identified with "this murderer" Cain (C. Faust. 12.11). In this, as in so many things, Augustine appears to take his cue from Ambrose, who in *De Cain et Abel* 1.2.5 says: "In Cain we perceive the parricidal people of the Jews, who are stained with the blood of their Lord ... and ... brother." Augustine, following Ambrose, connects the Cain and Abel story to the *adversus Iudaeos* polemic of Jews as Christ killers. In other words, he exacerbates the issue, builds up and emphasizes Jewish guilt more than any previous commentator on the Cain story, before offering his protective concession that they not be killed as a consequence. By ignoring Augustine's own role in expanding and developing the identification of the Jews with the fratricidal Cain, Fredriksen removes his positive concessions to the Jews from their much more negative context. "It should be clear that, in point of fact, the mark of Cain can *not* be interpreted as a predominantly positive sign," Johannes van Oort counters, going on to contend that "here, as in all other texts in which [Augustine] mentions the sign of Cain, this divine protection is *for the benefit of the Church*."[25]

Fredriksen acknowledges that the "mark of Cain" subjects Jews to exile and blame, as well as a role of servitude to the Church; but it also guarantees their persistence, and protection from being slain.[26] Fredriksen is correct that Augustine equates the "mark" they bear as analogs of Cain with observance of the Law, which is fruitless (C. Faust. 12.11). These observances, then, have no efficacy whatsoever for the Jews; they serve only as a "mark" upon them. Yet,

---

25 J. van Oort, "Iudaei," *Augustinus-Lexikon*, Band III, Fasc. 5/6 (Basel: Schwabe Verlag 2008), 781–792 at 785; cf. idem, "Augustinus en de Joden: een inleidend overzicht," *Verbum et Ecclesia* 30 (2009) 349–364.

26 Fredriksen 2010, 265.

in a backhanded way, that very "mark" benefits them, since it signals a prohibition on killing them, as it did for Cain. "The impious race of the carnal Jews will never die a bodily death," Augustine argues. "Whosoever would destroy them in this way will unloose a vengeance seven-fold, that is, he will bear away from them the seven-fold vengeance which I have wrapped around the Jewish people [to protect them] on account of their guilt in murdering Christ" (C. Faust. 12.12, Fredriksen's translation).[27]

But Fredriksen's misunderstanding of Augustine's meaning here is signaled by the bracketed "to protect them" that she adds to her translation, which in effect reverses Augustine's meaning.[28] The problem for Fredriksen, as for other modern researchers,[29] appears to involve reading an understanding of the original Genesis story into Augustine's handling of it. But it is a mistake to assume that Augustine understands the Genesis story in the same way as a modern expert reading, informed by knowledge of the original Hebrew and the work of academic biblical studies. Augustine had neither of these at his disposal, and his only access to Cain's story came by way of the Latin text he used. His interpretation of the passage, therefore, takes its start from the wording *omnis qui occiderit Cain, septem vindictas exsolvet*. While *exsolvere* could be read in light of the original story to mean "unleash (upon oneself)," that is not the verb's primary meaning, which is simply "undo, loose, release," and even "put an end to, do away with." From what Augustine goes on to say in his interpretation of this verse, it seems clear that he is relying on those more common meanings. The Latin biblical passage is not explicit is stating where the *septem vindictae* go when they are released; it creates an ambiguity by stating only that they will be released. Accordingly, Augustine expresses concern only for the fact that Jews—as those symbolized by Cain—are released from the *septem vindictae*, not for the ultimate resting place of them on anyone else.

Augustine makes clear his understanding of *exsolvere* when, immediately after quoting the verse, he adds, *id est, auferet ab eis septem vindictas*. Augustine, therefore understands *exsolvere* by *auferre*, which means "take away, remove, do away with, dispel." Again, the word choice keeps the focus on the removal of the curse from Jews, not on its transference to another. Some modern trans-

---

27 "Quicumque enim eos ita perdiderit, septem vindictas exsolvet; id est, auferet ab eis septem vindictas, quibus alligati sunt propter reatum occisi Christi."
28 Fredriksen 2010, 271.
29 E.g., E. Bammel, "Die Zeugen des Christentums," in H. Frohnhofen (ed.), *Christlicher Antijudaismus und jüdischer Antipaganismus* (Hamburg: Steinmann and Steinmann, 1990), 170–183 at 176.

lators and commentators[30] (likely influenced by the original Cain story) have apparently misread the following *ab eis* as the ablative of personal agent, so that the *vindictae* are carried away and suffered "by those" who kill Cain/Jews, like a contagion clinging to them. But such a reading would require the passive future *auferetur ab eis*, rather than the active future used by Augustine, *auferet ab eis* (in which the subject of *auferre* is understood to be the *quicumque* "whoever" of the previous clause). In the latter case, the preposition *ab* has its usual sense "from" and *eis* refers not to those taking away the *vindictae*, but the Jews who previously suffered under them. For Augustine, then, if one dispels the *septem vindictae*, one removes them "from them" i.e., the Jews. The agents of the action completely disappear from Augustine's consideration. He is not concerned with what happens to them, but only with what happens to the Jews, namely, their release from a continuing existence that is meant as a punishment.

Unlike the biblical story of Cain, in which the sevenfold curse arises only when and if someone undertakes to attack Cain, for Augustine the sevenfold curse exists already on Cain/Jews. In fact, Augustine conflates the mark with the sevenfold vengeance. By killing Jews, he says, one risks *auferet ab eis septem vindictas, quibus alligati sunt propter reatum occisi Christi*, "removing from them (Jews) seven curses which have been wrapped around them (Jews) on account of their guilt in murdering Christ." Augustine understands the *vindictae* primarily as a punishment already inflicted on the Jews, rather than as something that arises to punish those who kill Jews. To kill them is to free them of this punishment. He explains its sevenfold nature as a reference to the entirety of history through which they are supposed to suffer it.[31]

The sevenfold vengeance does not have for Augustine the purpose of protecting the Jews, therefore. The mark of Cain (which Augustine equates with the sevenfold vengeance) has been placed on the Jews "on account of their guilt in murdering Christ." Fredriksen has imported the idea that it is protective from the original passage in Genesis, not recognizing that Augustine does not follow it. This sevenfold vengeance is not "wrapped around" in a protective way, as Fredriksen translates it, but "tied" or "bound" (*alligati*) upon the Jews.

---

30 E.g., Teske 2007, 133.

31 "Thus, since the Jewish people has not perished in the whole of this time that passes under the number of seven days, the Christian faithful see well enough the subjection that the Jews merited when they killed the Lord for their proud kingdom" (C. Faust. 12.12: "ut hoc toto tempore quod septenario dierum numero volvitur, quia non interit gens Judaea, satis appareat fidelibus Christianis, quam subjectionem meruerint, qui superbo regno Dominum interfecerunt."; Teske 2007, 133).

Nowhere in his discussion in *Contra Faustum* does Augustine refer to the sevenfold vengeance as protective, or even address its effect on those who violate the mark by violent interaction with Jews, as Fredriksen's reading would demand. Rather, for Augustine, those who kill the Jews release them from a punishment they are meant to bear till the end of time, "unless," Augustine concedes, "any of them crosses over to Christ so that Cain"—i.e., their Jewishness—"may no longer be found" (C. Faust. 12.13).

Augustine's view, then, is much closer to the myth of the "wandering Jew," who is not to be released from his cursed life. In other words, Augustine has reversed the protective character of the sevenfold vengeance in the Genesis story, and read it as the burden of a curse that Cain is forced to carry as long as he lives, so that anyone who releases Cain (or Jews) from life, cuts short the punishment under which he (or they) live. Contrary to Fredriksen, Augustine himself shifts the significance of the "mark of Cain" from a mark of protection it has in the Genesis account to a "mark of shame" that it has come to mean in colloquial English. Fredriksen shifts it back to a protective sense, which is legitimate biblical exegesis, but not correctly attributed to Augustine.

The best that can be said of Augustine's reading and application of the "mark of Cain," therefore, is that it has the collateral effect of sparing Jews wholesale slaughter. But, of course, neither did Faustus advocate for such slaughter. As a Manichaean, Faustus opposed all violence against other living beings. The "mark" that Jews bear, namely circumcision, in Faustus's opinion, serves merely as an identity marker "so that, wherever on earth they might be, among whatever nations, they might still be recognized as his," i.e., by their god, "in the same way a shepherd or herdsman brands his animals so that no one may claim as their own what belongs to someone else" (C. Faust. 25.1). Moreover, unlike Augustine, for whom a Jew dying as a Jew is doomed to eternal damnation (despite the good they have involuntarily done for Christians), Faustus's Manichaeism taught that souls progress through multiple lifetimes, and a person who in this life is a Jew may in the next be a Manichaean. This long-term view stands behind Faustus's praise of the relative virtues Jews achieve through their faithful observance of the Law. Through its rules regarding what Faustus considers silly and inconsequential matters, the Law nonetheless provides the soul with training and disciplining that potentially advances it to the point where, either as a convert or in the next life, it is prepared to accept the true law of Mani.

3 The Character of Faustus's Views of the Old Testament and Jews

Fredriksen, unlike some predecessors in the field, is acutely aware of the rhetorical nature of Augustine's and Faustus's texts; not only do they not provide us with the true thoughts and feelings of these two late antique men, they also do not represent any sort of consistent, dogmatic positions. She readily admits that Augustine returns to familiar *adversus Iudaeos* rhetoric elsewhere, for example in his commentary on John.[32] The contrast between these two compositions provides "some measure of the force and the flexibility of Augustine's rhetoric and some appreciation for the way that different contexts and different audiences affect both what he says and how he says it." His rhetoric "illumines for us not Augustine's 'feelings' about or dealings with real Jews, but his construction and use of various kinds of 'Jews' in service to whatever teaching that, at a given moment, he wants to drive home."[33] It was only against Faustus that he had mounted an uncharacteristic defense of the Jewish heritage; his usual position is anti-Jewish.

The picture is not only different with Manichaean literature, however, but practically the opposite. Anti-Jewish rhetoric and argument is all but absent from Manichaean literature outside of the *Capitula* of Faustus, including the large bodies of primary Manichaean texts from Egypt and the Iranian world. Jews only find mention in very stereotyped remarks in accounts of the Passion of Christ inherited from earlier Christian tradition.[34] In short, there is no evidence of a developed and maintained *adversus Iudaeos* rhetorical tradition within Manichaeism, unless we are to include in that category the antithesis-style critiques of the Old Testament, originating with Marcion and adopted by the Manichaean missionary Adda for use in western Manichaeism.

Faustus regarded Adda ("Adimantus") as "the only teacher since our blessed father Manichaeus worthy of our study" (C. Faust. 1.2). For both Adda and Faus-

---

[32] Fredriksen 2010, 304 ff. Cf. Johannes van Oort, "Jews and Judaism in Augustine's Sermones," in: Gert Partoens a.o., eds., *Ministerium Sermonis. Proceedings of the International Colloquium on St. Augustine's Sermones ad Populum*. Turnhout-Leuven, May 29–31 2008, Instrvmenta Patristica et Mediaevalia 53 (Turnhout: Brepols, 2009), 243–265.

[33] Fredriksen 2010, 307.

[34] See, e.g., in Coptic literature, 1Ke 12.21–13.10 (Iain Gardner, *The Kephalaia of the Teacher*, Nag Hammadi and Manichaean Studies 37 [Leiden: Brill, 1995], 18–19); in Iranian literature, Werner Sundermann, "Christliche Evangelientexte in der Überlieferung der iranisch-manichäischen Literatur," *Mitteilungen des Instituts für Orientforschung* 14 (1968) 386–405; Enrico Morano, "My kingdom is not of this world: Revisiting the Great Parthian Crucifixion Hymn," in N. Sims-Williams, ed., *Proceedings of the Third European Conference of Iranian Studies, Part 1: Old and Middle Iranian Studies* (Wiesbaden: Reichert, 1998), 131–145.

tus, as for Marcion before them, the primary target of critique was not Jews, but the Old Testament, whose god, commandments, and heroes displayed values considered to be antithetical to those of Jesus and Paul, Marcion and Mani. The point was to eject the Old Testament from scriptural standing within Christianity, not attack Jews. "Judaism" as the embodiment of the theology and values reflected in the Old Testament was simply a different religion, worshipping a different god, than "Christianity."

Marcion had introduced the benign corollary of this view, namely, that Jews had only their own god to answer to, and would be rewarded or punished by that god in accordance with how well or poorly they observed his commandments. Reworked in a Manichaean context, the position is somewhat less benign theologically, in that Manichaeans viewed those who followed any but the one true God to be doomed to destruction in the end, rather than just left to their own devices. Faustus, however, does not follow this negative corollary of the Manichaean view. Instead, he deploys rhetorically the fully benign Marcionite version, with scarcely any acknowledgement of the different theoretical consequences within Manichaean theology. He departs from Marcion only in pointing out that the god of the Old Testament "cannot provide what he has promised. He cannot even give these things to the synagogue, his proper wife, who obeys him in all things like a maidservant" (C. Faust. 15.1).

It is the last clause of the latter statement that brings out Faustus's distinctive pro-Jewish argument: in the course of demonstrating the hypocrisy of catholic "semi-Christianity," Faustus praises the Jews as faithful observers of Torah. This praise is a cornerstone of his consistent rhetorical strategy throughout the *Capitula*:

1. First, he draws on the *adversus Iudaeos* rhetorical tradition to ridicule and criticize the practices commanded in the Law;
2. then he concedes that nonetheless Jews at least show earnest devotion in obeying them;
3. finally he chides catholic Christians for wanting to appropriate the Law but being unwilling to observe it.

The "semi-Christians" are straddling the fence between Judaism and Christianity, and should just make up their minds once and for all which religion they will follow. As it stands, their claim to both traditions is hypocritical on both accounts (C. Faust. 15.1; 19.6; 32.3–4): until they obey the Law, they have no right to invoke the God of the circumcision (cf. C. Faust. 25.1), and until they reject the Law, they have no right to invoke the God of Jesus.

Faustus ridicules the church that claims the Old Testament without actually using it: "You sip so daintily from the Old Testament that your lips are scarcely wet" (C. Faust. 32.7). So, in being semi-Christians, they are also only semi-Jews

(C. Faust. 33.3). Faustus could argue cogently that his critiques of Jewish practices also were implicit in catholic practice: "You cannot blame me for rejecting the Old Testament, because you reject it as much as I do .... You deceitfully praise with your lips what you hate in your heart" (C. Faust. 6.1). If catholic Christians are not going to follow and make use of the Law, he argues, why lay claim to it and appropriate it from the Jews? "Christians have not adopted these observances, and no one keeps them; so if we will not take the inheritance, we should surrender the documents" (C. Faust. 4.1). Jews have every right to object to Christians claiming the Old Testament while disregarding its commandments (C. Faust. 10.1). "It would be an excess of forwardness to take the documents of others which pronounce me disinherited" (C. Faust. 4.1). "I conclude, therefore, that the promises [of the OT] do not belong to me. And mindful of the commandment, 'Thou shall not covet,' I gladly leave to the Jews their own property" (C. Faust. 10.1).

Faustus's *modus vivendi* with Judaism seems to owe a great deal to Marcionite rhetorical traditions, perhaps mediated through Adda. In the same way, Marcion understood Judaism and Christianity to offer two alternative religions, revealed by two different gods, each leading towards a certain future for its faithful. This "live and let live" attitude does not sit well in the Manichaean belief system, whose stark dualism left no room for worthy alternatives to the way of the God of Truth. It probably reflects an adaptation of Manichaean rhetoric made by Adda, who also adopted Marcionite antithetical analyses of the Old and New Testaments.

Yet Faustus and Adda have been read as representative of a Manichaean anti-Judaism that is fundamental to the faith; their rejection of the Old Testament has been taken to stem from a particular negation of Judaism that formed part of Mani's original teaching. It can be seen, for instance, in what is put into the mouth of Mani in the *Acts of Archelaus*. If that material derives from authentic writings of Mani, then it would offer evidence for this traditional reading of the Manichaean tradition. I have demonstrated elsewhere that the report of Diodorus (Acta Archelai 44–45), which focuses on antithetical contrasts of Old and New Testaments, has been taken from a Marcionite, not Manichaean source.[35] On the other hand, at one time I conjectured that an authentic let-

---

35   Jason BeDuhn, "Biblical Antitheses, Adda, and the *Acts of Archelaus*," in J. BeDuhn and P. Mirecki, eds., *Frontiers of Faith: The Christian Encounter with Manichaeism in the Acts of Archelaus*, Nag Hammadi and Manichaean Studies 61 (Leiden: Brill, 2007), 131–147. My conclusion is based on the fact that the New Testament citations in that discrete section of the text (the report by Diodorus) come completely from the Marcionite canon, i.e., the Gospel of Luke and the community letters of Paul. Mani knew the *Diatessaron*, and so

ter of Mani stands behind some of the material used in other sections of the work.[36] I now recognize some major problems with that hypothesis, namely (1) the manner in which the *Acts* has Mani speak of Old and New Testaments as literary sets, rather than old and new covenants in the Pauline sense, (2) the way in which it presents him addressing issues of canonicity that have no place in Mani's world, where the Bible never constituted a sacred scripture for his church, and (3) the way in which he is made to speak of gospels in the plural (e.g., Acta Archelai 15.8–14), when Manichaean sources appear to confirm Mani knew and used the *Diatessaron*. At the very least, Mani's words must have been touched up, "modernized" so to speak, to fit the fourth century world of the *Acts*. If, on the other hand, this material is lifted from writings of Adda, then we have to do with adaptation of Manichaean teachings to the specific conditions of the Roman west. It may be only in this setting that the inclusion of the Old Testament in the Christian canon became a *cause célèbre*, eliciting Manichaean appropriation of Marcionite antitheses and hardening the community's position against the Jewish scriptures.

It may be that traces of the prior, original Manichaean position on the Jewish scriptures can be found in Faustus, once one peels away the layer of Marcion-inspired antithetical critique. In *Contra Faustum* 22, Faustus seems to apply to the Old Testament the same narrative Manichaeism applies to all prior authentic revelations, namely, that it came originally from God, but was corrupted by its transmitters. "We are certainly not enemies or opponents of the Law and the prophets or of anyone at all," Faustus asserts (C. Faust. 22.1).[37] He goes on to distinguish the true, original Law from corrupting additions made to it as it was transmitted by the Jews.

> But by the Law I do not mean circumcision, nor the Sabbath and sacrifices and other Jewish things of this sort, but what is truly the Law, that is, 'You

---

would not be confined to Luke, and Adda used the larger catholic canon in formulating his antitheses.

36   Jason BeDuhn, "A War of Words: Intertextuality and the Struggle over the Legacy of Christ in the *Acta Archelai*," in J. BeDuhn and P. Mirecki, eds., *Frontiers of Faith: The Christian Encounter with Manichaeism in the Acts of Archelaus*, Nag Hammadi and Manichaean Studies 61 (Leiden: Brill, 2007), 77–102.

37   In the following quotes from this passage, I have made mostly cosmetic changes to the translation of Roland Teske, *Answer to Faustus, a Manichean*, The Works of Saint Augustine, a Translation for the 21st Century I/20 (Hyde Park: New City Press, 2007), 298–299. In a few cases indicated by the underlying Latin phrasing, I have translated differently than Teske.

shall not kill, you shall not commit adultery, you shall not swear falsely,' and the rest. For that Law was spread throughout the nations long ago, that is, from the time when the creation of this world was established. The Hebrew scribes intruded into and mixed with it (*Hebraeorum scriptores irruentes ... commiscuerunt*), like leprosy and mange, these abominable and shameful commandments of theirs, which refer to circumcision and sacrifices.

> C. FAUST. 22.2

Fausus thus reflects a critical analysis of the Law into authentic and inauthentic portions that had wider circulation in early Christianity. The rejection of sacrifices in Jewish-Christian sects such as the Ebionites (Epiphanius, Pan. 30.16.5) necessarily implies some qualification or critique of the Torah. In the Clementine Recognitions, Moses is said to have instituted sacrifice as a concession to habits of idolatry,[38] exactly as Faustus characterizes sacrifice as a form of *idolatria* (C. Faust. 6.1). More severely, the Elchasaites among whom Mani was raised rejected sacrifices as having never been instituted by the true Torah or fathers (Epiphanius, Pan. 19.3.6), related perhaps to the critical analysis of the Law into different sources seen in such sources as Ptolemy's *Letter to Flora*.[39] The Manichaean criticism of the Law, therefore, does not "touch the Law or the author of the Law, namely, God, but those who attach the name of God and of that Law to their wicked observances (*religionibus*)," that is the "Jewish precepts (*praecepta*)." This analysis evokes from Faustus the declaration that "we are enemies of Judaism, not of the Law," because one can "attribute to their scribes the crime of deforming it" (C. Faust. 22.2).

In contrast, Faustus cites favorably the Ten Commandments;[40] but adds that, "it is easy to prove that these were promulgated long ago among the gentiles by Enoch and Seth and other righteous men like them, who were given them by resplendent angels in order to restrain ferocity among human beings" (C. Faust. 19.3). Notice that he seems to be alluding to parabiblical sources, such as the Books of Enoch, rather than to Genesis; that he considers these commandments a kind of stopgap of basic morality rather than a source of salvation;

---

38 Clem. Rec. 1.37.2–4, 1.39.2, 1.48.5–6, 1.54.1, 1.64.1–2 (all part of the source 1.27–71).

39 I.e., its threefold division into (1) pure law, "which the savior did not come to abolish but to fulfill ... for it did not have perfection", (2) law interwoven with injustice, "which the savior abolished", and (3) symbolic and allegorical part, which "the savior changed ... from the perceptible, visible level to the spiritual, invisible one" (5.1–2).

40 Ptolemy's *Letter to Flora* 5.3 similarly identifies the 10 Commandments as the true law that needed to be perfected by Christ's fulfilment.

and that he attributes them not to God or Jesus, but to angels. Faustus contrasts these valid if limited commandments to "circumcision, and Sabbaths, and sacrifices, and the observances of the Hebrews" (C. Faust. 19.3), which he equates with Paul's "law of sin and death" (C. Faust. 19.2). But he also contrasts the Ten Commandments with the teachings of Jesus, which explicitly note their inadequacy, and had to "fulfill" them by raising them to a higher standard (C. Faust. 19.3). Faustus points out from Matthew 5 that when Jesus cites from the Ten Commandments, "he both confirms the old precepts and supplies their defects." But when Jesus cites from other parts of Jewish law outside the Ten Commandments (such as the commandments of eye-for-eye, loving friends and hating enemies, and divorce), he outright contradicts and rejects them.[41] "These precepts are evidently destroyed," Faustus concludes, "because they are the precepts of Moses; while the others are fulfilled because they are the precepts of the righteous men of antiquity" (C. Faust. 19.3). His whole presentation is strongly reminiscent of Ptolemy's discussion with Flora about the different categories of commandments, their respective sources, and their consequent differences in their abiding validity.

Whether this analysis and distinction of laws goes back to Mani or not, we cannot say; but it does reflect an ideological environment already present in Mani's time and place, where various Jewish, Christian, and Jewish-Christian sects speculated on the possible disparate origin of different parts of the Law, and attempted to distinguish the eternal parts of it from intruding laws of no lasting value or even evil inspiration.[42] Perhaps Faustus was informed on the nuances of Mani's views of Judaism, and his benign attitude toward the Jews, even while he is critical of Moses and the Torah beyond the Ten Commandments. But there can be little doubt that the battle over the status of the Old Testament in Christian faith raised the level of antagonistic rhetoric, first in Adda and then in Faustus.

Consequently, whenever Faustus discusses the issue of the Old Testament's status as scripture, he draws upon the heated anti-Jewish rhetoric of the *adver-*

---

41   Ptolemy also cites the lex talionis as the example of the type of law that Christ abolishes (5.4).
42   'Abd al-Jabbār reports that Mani asserted that sexual relations with women, slaughtering animals, and eating meat "had never been lawful" and "cursed anyone who declared it to be lawful," as well as disowning "any connection with Abraham, Moses, Aaron, Joshua, David, and anyone who deemed it proper to kill animals, to cause them pain, to eat meat, and the like," citing traditions of Jesus (Tathbīt dalā'il al-nubuwwa 114.15–115.2; see John C. Reeves, *Prolegomena to a History of Islamicate Manichaeism* [Sheffield: Equinox, 2011], 211).

sus Iudaeos tradition, in order to negatively characterize their supposed corruption of revelation with their own peculiar rites and customs, rendering the text unsuitable as scripture. The subject of the Jews is collateral to his attack on the Old Testament, just as the same subject is collateral to Augustine's defense of the Old Testament.

However, whenever Faustus turns to his attack from the Old Testament itself to the "semi-Christians" who call it scripture but fail to follow its precepts, his rhetoric changes dramatically. In these passages, he speaks highly of the Jews. Rather than praise "semi-Christians" for not implementing the "shameful," "superfluous," "idolatrous," or "useless" practices enjoined by the Old Testament (C. Faust. 6.1), he reprimands them for failing to follow through on commandments they believe to be from God. The Jews, on the other hand, as mistaken as they may be about the source of those commandments, at least show the courage of their convictions in faithfully adhering to them. Whatever Faustus had received from his predecessors on these subjects, he developed through his own emphasis on the value of deeds, and on evaluation of a person's faith by its effects on the person's conduct. He can see relative value in the earnestness of Jewish observance of the Law, even if the Law itself does not reflect Manichaean values and goals.

4   Implications

Much can be made of the fact that Augustine validates the Old Testament as scripture and affirms Jewish adherence to the Law in the pre-Christian past, whereas Faustus sees the Old Testament, as it has been transmitted as the foundation of Jewish practices, as invalid. Nevertheless, when it comes to the implications of their respective positions for actual Jews in the world around them, this contrast breaks down, and even reverses.

Augustine is unequivocal: Jews of his time continue to practice the Law in ignorance and even perversity; they carry the burden of their practices as a curse; their continued existence serves as an object lesson rather than a reward for their faithfulness; it serves only ironically to validate Christianity against the interests of Jews.

> The church recognizes that the Jewish people is cursed and reveals that, after Christ was killed, that people still carries out the work of earthly circumcision, the earthly Sabbath, the earthly unleavened bread, and the earthly Pasch. All these earthly works keep hidden the strength derived from understanding the grace of Christ, which is not given to the Jews

who continue in their impiety and unbelief. For it has been revealed in the New Testament.[43]

C. FAUST. 12.11

The Law was supposed to lead to Christ, and its only enduring value is in its reference to Christ,[44] not as a still valid mode of redemption. It is no longer good after the coming of Christ, whose grace is supposed to supersede it. "Earlier, the Jews had done these things rightly, but they were unfaithful in not distinguishing the period of the Old Testament form the period, once Christ appeared, of the New Testament" (C. Faust. 12.9).[45] Nonetheless, not only should Jews not be physically killed, they should not be "killed" as a people, in the sense of being forced to stop observing the practices that make them Jews (C. Faust. 12.13), for the latter observances are the "mark of Cain" that they carry as the burden of their wrongdoing,[46] and in that state they serve as independent if hostile witnesses to the pre-Christian text of the Old Testament as an essential cornerstone of the Christian proof from prophecy (C. Faust. 13.10, 15.11, 16.21).[47]

In short, Fredriksen's optimism to the contrary,[48] Augustine's breakthroughs do not mitigate his perpetuation of the supersessionism that lies at the very heart of orthodox Christianity. This supersessionist tradition, beginning in Justin Martyr, Tertullian, Melito of Sardis, etc., can be summed up in the words of Cyprian of Carthage, a contemporary of Mani: "The Jews, as foretold, have departed from God and lost his favor ... while the Christians have succeeded to their place" (Ad Quirinium 1.5). Augustine continues this tradition, explaining how Christ "left his mother the Synagogue, stuck as she was in a fleshly way to the old covenant, to cling to the church, his holy bride, so that in the peace of the new covenant they might be one flesh" (C. Faust. 12.8). Christianity is *Verus Israel*; Jews who have not become Christians are those branches broken off from the olive tree of Israel (C. Faust. 9.2). All that Augustine does against Faustus is defend the property that Christians have seized from Jews: the Old

---

43 Teske 2007, 132.
44 "The whole contents of the [Jewish] scriptures are either directly or indirectly about Christ" (C. Faust. 12.7). "The whole narrative of Genesis, in the most minute details, is a prophecy of Christ and the church" (C. Faust. 12.8).
45 "Now, however, if any Christian—even if he is a Jew—wishes to celebrate these observances once again, that would be like disturbing ashes already at rest; not like once again piously accompanying the body to its resting place, but rather like wickedly violating its tomb" (Ep. 82.2,16), it would be to "plunge into the Devil's pit" (Ep. 82.2,18).
46 Fredriksen 271–272.
47 Fredriksen 276–277.
48 Fredriksen 372 contends that Augustine departs from supersessionist ideas.

Testament. It is the value of that property, not its former proprietors, that concerns Augustine. His "defense of Judaism" applies only to the pre-Christian past. His "defense of Jews" only amounts to not cancelling out God's use of them as an object lesson, by cutting short their Jewish identity or their lives. None of this actually defends "Jews" or "Judaism" against anything that Faustus says against them, which indeed is precious little.

Faustus, of course, does not advocate for either the forced conversion or the death of Jews. Nor does he adopt, as Augustine does, any of the *Verus Israel* ideology that justifies appropriation of the Old Testament from the Jews and narrativizes them as a people rejected by God. The Law does not await fulfillment in Christ, for, Faustus notes, "the Law and the Prophets consider themselves already so faultlessly perfect, that they have no desire to be fulfilled. Their author and father condemns adding to them as much as taking away anything from them" (C. Faust. 17.2). Faustus therefore does not treat Judaism as a deviation and error by which God abandons Jews, but as a religion, founded like other false religions on a combination of misunderstanding divine revelation and being misled by evil forces. It stands on the same footing as paganism and catholic Christianity for Faustus (C. Faust. 19.2; 20.3). Jews are not bad Israelites who should have been superseded by the "semi-Christianity" of Augustine's church; they have lived true to their traditions and merit all the rewards their Law has promised to them. For Faustus, these rewards are mundane and transitory, and in that way do not amount to ultimate salvation (C. Faust. 10.1). But the road to salvation is a long process for the Manichaeans, and there is nothing preventing those who are Jews in this life finding their way in some future life. In fact, at least rhetorically, Faustus suggests that Jewish patriarchs and prophets may have already been saved by acts of God's grace, for their righteousness rather than for their faithfulness to the Law (C. Faust. 33.1). Nevertheless, Faustus's praise of the Jews as faithful practitioners of their Law, combined with his promotion of practice as the essence of religion, brings us logically to the implicit idea that Jews are being trained by their Law in a disciplined life that could be readily turned in the direction of the equally disciplined and rigorous Manichaean way of life. He lauds the moral commandments embedded in the Law, suggesting that they are fragments of true revelation, buried amid corrupting additions (C. Faust. 22.1–2). He is willing to entertain at least theoretically that the Jewish scriptures may serve to prepare Jews for true religion in the same way as pagan sacred literature may do so for Gentiles (C. Faust. 13.1).

In light of this analysis of Faustus's much more nuanced rhetoric about Jews and Judaism, we can spot the close correlation between the argument Faustus mounts and the approach Augustine takes in response, with its two breakthroughs identified by Fredriksen. In this way, we can affirm all the more her conclusion that "[T]he single most important factor contributing to his novel views on Jews and Judaism—the factor that gave his teaching its coherence, its scope, its power, and its sheer originality—was that Augustine had Faustus' *Capitula* to work against."[49] Faustus's *Capitula* "had great coherence, scope, power, and originality. It summoned the same from Augustine."[50] We once again find clear evidence that many of Augustine's key and unique moves as a thinker were prompted by his engagement with Manichaean interlocutors.[51] At times this engagement brought out Augustine's best, at other times his worst. But the Manichaeans can never be reduced historically to merely Augustine's foil as he might have wished, nor do they always represent the antithesis of his positions despite his efforts to so caricaturize them. We can understand Augustine better by detecting his tactics in dealing with a formidable Manichaean alternative. But to understand Manichaeism itself better requires freeing it from its use in Christian polemics, and seeing the tradition in its own distinct positions and relations to other religious communities, including that of the Jews.

49 Fredriksen 2010, 315.
50 Fredriksen 2010, 316.
51 See Johannes van Oort, "Manichaean Christians in Augustine's Life and Work," *Church History and Religious Culture* 90 (2010) 505–546; Jason BeDuhn, *Augustine's Manichaean Dilemma, 1: Conversion and Apostasy, 373–388 C.E.* (Philadelphia: University of Pennsylvania Press, 2010); idem, *Augustine's Manichaean Dilemma, 2: Making a "Catholic" Self, 388–401 C.E.* (Philadelphia: University of Pennsylvania Press, 2013).

14

Pelagius against the Manichaeans: Real Opponents or Clichéd Heresiology?

Nils Arne Pedersen

Abstract

In 1957 the Swedish scholar Torgny Bohlin argued that Pelagius primarily constructed his theology with the aim of opposing one theological enemy, Manichaeism, with its determinism and doctrine that human flesh was evil and sin belonged to nature. Subsequently, most scholars have repeated this hypothesis without re-examining the case. However, this paper argues that Bohlin's view of Manichaeism was only based on insufficient research literature and on the descriptions of Manichaeism as a deterministic system in Patristic sources. However, Manichaeism was, as we know from sources stemming from its own adherents, a religion centred on penance, judgment, and the possibility of eternal damnation, thus claiming that man is responsible for his own sin. The Patristic image of Manichaeism was a stylization and distortion which made it represent a consistent philosophical position, a denial of free will and confirmation of determinism. On this background all works of Pelagius either fully or partially preserved are scrutinized in the paper for explicit or implicit references to Manichaeism. It is shown that the terms "Manichaeus" and "Manichaeans" refer to stereotypes used by Pelagius to characterize his contemporary opponents within the Catholic Church.

It has often been claimed that Pelagius primarily constructed his theology with the aim of opposing one theological enemy, Manichaeism, with its determinism and doctrine that human flesh was evil and sin belonged to nature. As far as I can see, this claim goes back to the Swedish scholar Torgny Bohlin's monograph from 1957, *Die Theologie des Pelagius und ihre Genesis*. Bohlin understood Manichaeism as a deterministic doctrine in which the human being is regarded as a battleground for good and evil. Man has no will capable of choosing between good and evil, but is a passive bystander in the struggle between the good and evil will within him, with the good will in man being regarded as part of God.[1] Basing his arguments primarily on Pelagius' *Expositions of Thirteen*

---

[1] Cf. Bohlin 1957, 12: "So wie die Welt ist auch der Mensch selbst ein Kampfplatz für das Gute

Epistles of St Paul, Bohlin believed that Pelagius' theology had been formed as an antithesis to Manichaeism: "The Christian idea of creation which Pelagius tries to assert against Manichaeism forces him to replace its physical determinism with a doctrine of freedom which is still able to explain the origin of evil, though it avoids the Manichaean dualism. We will try to show the energy with which Pelagius carried out this task, an energy which made his whole opinion into an antithesis to the Manichaean idea that only the new man, the saved man can be described as God's creation."[2]

Even though scholars before Bohlin had said similar things,[3] his hypothesis was new. Subsequently, most scholars have, as far as I can see, simply followed Bohlin in this basic hypothesis, though without really re-examining the case. In 1966 Gerald Bonner entirely endorsed Bohlin's interpretation that Pelagius constructed "a theology to oppose his principal theological opponent: Manichaeism",[4] and he repeated this endorsement in 1992.[5] In 1968 Robert Evans praised Bohlin's monograph and stressed that the observation of the anti-Manichaean direction of Pelagius' thinking was due to Bohlin's work. Evans thought that one of the chief theological interests of Pelagius was and remained to combat Manichaean fatalism; but he also thought that Bohlin

---

und das Böse. Er hat also keinen Willen, der zwischen Gut und Böse wählen kann, sondern ist ohne Verantwortung, ein passiver Zuschauer bei dem Kampf des guten und des bösen Willens in seinem Inneren. Dabei wurde der gute Wille im Menschen als ein Teil Gottes aufgefasst."

2 Bohlin 1957, 14: "Der christliche Schöpfungsgedanke, den Pelagius gegen den Manichäismus geltend zu machen versucht, zwingt ihn dessen physischen Determinismus durch eine Freiheitslehre zu ersetzen, die unter Vermeidung des manichäischen Dualismus dennoch den Ursprung des Bösen erklären kann. Wir werden aufzuzeigen versuchen, mit welcher Kraft Pelagius diese Aufgabe durchführte, eine Kraft, die seine ganze Anschauung zu einer Antithese gegen den manichäischen Gedanken werden liess, dass nur der neue Mensch, der erlöste Mensch als Gottes Geschöpf bezeichnet werden kann." Cf. also Bohlin 1957, 16 (Pelagius' theology should be seen "gegen den Hintergrund des dunklen Determinismus des Manichäismus"), 17, 18, 22, 40, and *passim*.

3 Thus Bohlin 1957, 13 referred to de Plinval 1943, 151, 158, 217, whose scattered remarks about the Manichaeans as Pelagius' main adversaries are, however, not presented in the same dense and systematic way as in Bohlin. Bohlin 1957, 20 also referred to Harnack 1910, 201, who, however, wrote about the Pelagians' opposition to Manichaeism, not about Pelagius specifically (Harnack's footnote 1 refers to Julian of Eclanum). Finally, Bohlin 1957, 21 referred to Mausbach 1909, 399, i.e., to his short remark "der Widerpart des Manichäismus, der *pelagianische Irrtum*."—In Ferguson 1956, a monograph on Pelagius published a year before Bohlin, the Manichaeans are only mentioned occasionally in the context of Pelagius.

4 Bonner 1966, 353–355; quotation 353.

5 Bonner 1992, 34.

went "too far in attempting to organize the whole of Pelagius' theology around an anti-Manichaean polemic."[6] Brinley Roderick Rees, in his monograph *A Reluctant Heretic* from 1988, also adhered to Bohlin's view.[7] Earl Dale Lavender, in an unpublished dissertation from 1991, also followed Bohlin's lead, though he stressed that Pelagius' showdown with Manichaeism had a practical context, a different kind of asceticism.[8] In 1993 Theodore de Bruyn, in the introduction to his translation of Pelagius' *Commentary on Romans* (i.e., in the *Expositions of Thirteen Epistles of St Paul*), referred to Bohlin and stated that "Pelagius appears to have developed his theological tenets precisely to counter Manichaean (or virtually Manichaean) notions of creation, sin, redemption, and beatitude"; "Manichaean determinism was the foil for his sense of human freedom and responsibility".[9] The same acceptance of Bohlin's hypothesis was repeated in 1999 in a monograph by Sebastian Thier.[10] Finally, Mathijs Lamberigts has repeatedly confirmed Bohlin's interpretation, in 2000,[11] in 2003[12] and most recently in 2009 in his article on "Pelagius and Pelagians" in *The Oxford Handbook of Early Christian Studies*, where he wrote: "Mainly because he rejected Manichaean determinism, he emphasized the existence and value of human beings' free will. He considered Manichaeism as a threat to an authentic Chris-

---

6   Evans 1968, 21–22, 68–69, 86, 92, 97, 132 n. 87 (quotation), 159 n. 9. Besides Robert Evans' slight scepticism, I have also come across a stronger reservation in Gillian Evans (1981, 236), who thought that Pelagius did not give the Manichaean threat such a prominent place as Julian of Eclanum did later on. Evans suggested instead that the Apollinarists had been Pelagius' main enemy. Gisbert Greshake (1972) ignored the anti-Manichaean interpretation of Pelagius. Winrich Löhr 1999, in his treatment of Pelagius' *De natura*, sees anti-Manichaean arguments, but he does not identify Pelagius' opponents as Manichaeans; cf. below.

7   Rees 1988, 87; cf. also 14–15: Pelagius was "always on the alert for the smallest signs of a Manichean revival" and therefore accused both Augustine and Jerome "of neo-Manichaeism". In addition, see Rees 1988, 90.

8   Lavender 1991, 13, 71–75, 77, 79, 80, 85, 102, 125, 145–148, 156–157, 159, 162, 168.

9   De Bruyn 1993, 16. Cf. also de Bruyn 1993, 24.

10 Thier 1999, 2, 52–54.

11 Cf. Lamberigts 2000, 102.

12 Cf. Lamberigts 2003, 290–291: "Pelagius selbst wollte offenkundig ein Mann der Kirche sein. In seinen Kommentaren zu den Paulusbriefen profilierte er sich als ein rechtgläubiger Christ. Aufgrund dessen gab er sich als ein Gegner des Arianismus, des Manichäismus und der Positionen des Jovinian zu erkennen. Namentlich sein Protest gegen die zweite Strömung lässt erkennen, warum Pelagius solchen Nachdruck auf die Existenz eines freien Willens legte: Er betrachtete den manichäischen Determinismus als eine Gefahr für eine wahrhaft christliche Ethik, die seines Erachtens nur Bestand haben konnte, wenn Komponenten wie Freiheit und Verantwortlichkeit gesichert waren."

tian life, for its deterministic view would annihilate human freedom and thus ethical responsibility."[13]

Bohlin's monograph was certainly a great advance in Pelagian studies because it showed the coherence of Pelagius' ideas and took him seriously as a theologian instead of regarding him as a thinker who claimed creation's autonomy from God, as scholars had argued erroneously in the past. His hypothesis that the driving force of Pelagius' theology was anti-Manichaeism also deserves to be reconsidered, because this basic explanation of Pelagius' core intentions would be of great historical importance (if it were correct). However, Bohlin's view of Manichaeism was, even for its time, based on outdated or insufficient research literature and impaired by the methodological problem that he always accepted at its face value the descriptions of Manichaeism by its opponents like Augustine and Pelagius.

The only scholars on Manichaeism to whom Bohlin referred were in fact Georges de Plinval and my countryman Jens Nørregaard.[14] However, de Plinval's idea of Manichaeism was built entirely on the Church Fathers and Augustine's *Confessions*.[15] The chapter about Manichaeism in Nørregaard's habilitation thesis from 1920 about *Augustine's Religious Breakthrough* was a more serious attempt to describe North African Manichaeism including some consideration of the new Eastern sources. Nørregaard was also critical of Augustine's image of Manichaeism; but on one occasion in his description he repeated without criticism Augustine's description of his Manichaean past as a time when he understood himself as being passive and without responsibility for the outcome of the battle between good and evil in himself (cf., e.g., *Confessiones* v,x(18); viii,x(22); viii,x(24); ix,iv(10)).[16] Besides these scholars, Bohlin built his view of Manichaeism on its opponents. Thus Augustine's statement in the *Confessions* that as a Manichaean he believed he was innocent of any sin because an alien nature within him was sinning was simply accepted as "die Lehre der Manichäer" and consequently as the background against which Pelagius wrote.[17] There is no reflection in Bohlin about the polemical purpose

---

13 Lamberigts 2009, 264–265.
14 These are the only scholars (Nørregaard 1920 and de Plinval 1943) referred to in Bohlin 1957, 12–13.
15 Cf. de Plinval 1943, 108–109; 109 n. 2 de Plinval quoted from v,x(18), also crucial for Bohlin's view of Manichaeism.
16 Bohlin 1957, 12–18, 51 refers to Nørregaard 1920 in the footnotes.—The uncritical summary I refer to is Nørregaard 1920, 54. But unlike Bohlin, Nørregaard did not claim that this was Manichaean doctrine but only that this was what Augustine thought as a Manichaean.
17 Bohlin 1957, 12, 15; cf. Augustine, *Confessions* v,x(18), Verheijen 1981, 67,6–12: "Adhuc enim mihi videbatur non esse nos, qui peccamus, sed nescio quam aliam in nobis peccare natu-

of this statement, and no indication that it is Augustine's retrospective interpretation of his past. Pelagius' statements about Manichaeism are taken for granted in the same naïve way as correct information, which explains why Pelagius says something in opposition.[18]

However, it is not possible to reconcile this Patristic image of Manichaeism with the Manichaeism we know from the sources, that is a religion centred on penance, judgment, and the possibility of eternal damnation. It is not only the Coptic sources which stress that man is responsible for his own sin,[19] but also the Manichaean sources preserved in Latin, as demonstrated clearly by Ferdinand Christian Baur.[20] Human flesh was certainly evil according to the Manichaeans; but even though the soul was seen as part of God, it was still endowed with the power to choose between good and evil, provided that it was awakened from its slumber of oblivion first. It may be that by means of logic we could accept that the quasi-material way in which the Manichaeans describe the soul results in a kind of determinism; but this would not be a historical endeavour, since it would ignore the fact that the Manichaeans themselves did not make these deductions, and it would bring us close just to reproduce the Church Fathers' line of reasoning.

In this connection it is also worth remembering that in the prologue of his *Dialogus adversus Pelagianos*, Jerome put Pelagius in line with Origen, Manichaeus, Priscillian, Evagrius Ponticus, Jovinian and others, claiming that the dictum that man is capable of being sinless was based on the philosophical ideal of *apatheia* (cf. PL 23, 517–518). So Pelagius himself was lumped together

---

ram et delectabat superbiam meam extra culpam esse et, cum aliquid mali fecissem, non confiteri me fecisse, ut sanares animam meam, quoniam peccabat tibi, sed excusare me amabam et accusare nescio quid aliud, quod mecum esset et ego non essem." Translation by Chadwick 1991, 84: "I still thought that it is not we who sin, but some alien nature which sins in us. It flattered my pride to be free of blame and, when I had done something wrong, not to make myself confess to you that you might heal my soul; for it was sinning against you. I liked to excuse myself and to accuse some unidentifiable power which was with me and yet not I."

18 E.g. when Pelagius wrote in his *Libellus fidei* to Pope Innocent I that "just as they err who say with the Manichaeans that man is unable to avoid sin, so do they who with Jovinian claim that man cannot sin; for both groups remove free choice" ("et tam illos errare qui cum Manichæis dicunt hominem peccatum vitare non posse, quam illos qui cum Joviniano asserunt hominem non posse peccare; uterque enim tollit libertatem arbitrii." PL 45, 1718). This is taken by Bohlin (1957, 15) as a real "Lehre des Manichäismus" against which Pelagius claims free will. The same goes for Bohlin's use of Pelagius' anti-Manichaean polemics in the *Expositions of Thirteen Epistles of St Paul*.

19 Cf., e.g., *Kephalaia* Ch. 89 (Polotsky and Böhlig 1940, 221,18–223,16).

20 Cf. Baur 1831, 184–202.

with the Manichaeans, thus being a victim of the heresiological tradition of identifying positions based on some common feature detached from its context.[21] Why should Pelagius himself be different from this tradition, which was part of the culture he shared?

Against this background there are good reasons to investigate the statements about Manichaeism in Pelagius' oeuvre. Good questions would be whether these statements really are as important as Bohlin claimed; and if they are, what they reveal about Pelagius, and what he wanted to say. So I have examined the works of Pelagius which are either fully or partially preserved. Naturally, the most important of these are the passages which directly mention Manichaeus or Manichaeans, but there are also passages in which the unnamed adversaries might be Manichaeans.

It is well known that Pelagius originally came from the Roman province of Britannia. Some time in the last quarter of the 4th century he arrived in Rome, where he eventually became a celebrated Christian teacher. During his stay there he authored, according to Gennadius of Marseille's *De viris illustribus*, a work entitled *De fide trinitatis* attacking the Arians, and an exegetical work entitled *Liber eclogarum*. Only fragments are preserved of these two works, and they never mention the Manichaeans.[22] This is also the case with some fragments on Christology which probably belonged to an otherwise unknown treatise.[23] However, Pelagius' *Expositions of Thirteen Epistles of St Paul*, which he undoubtedly also wrote while he was still in Rome, are fully preserved, and in this work there are several references to Manichaeus and Manichaeans.[24]

In 410 when the Visigothic attack on the eternal city was imminent, Pelagius fled, firstly to North Africa and from there to Jerusalem. His disciple Caelestius also fled to North Africa, where he tried to be ordained as a presbyter in

---

21   Later on in the same prologue, Jerome also distinguished the heresy that man can be sinless from Manichaeism ("Manichæorum esse sententiæ hominum damnare naturam, et liberum auferre arbitrium, et adjutorium Dei tollere"), placing the true doctrine in the middle as the royal road, cf. PL 23, 520AB.

22   See Gennadius of Massilia, *De viris inlustribus* LXIII, Richardson 1896, 77. Cf. Martini 1938, 319–332 as regards *De fide trinitatis*; the fragments of *Liber eclogarum* are collected by J. Garnier in PL 48, 594–596.

23   Martini 1938, 324–326, 332–334. Evans 1968, 158–159 n. 6–7 argued that these fragments probably belonged not to *De fide trinitatis* but to an otherwise unknown treatise on Christology.—*Epistula ad Claudiam sororem de virginitate* (ed. Halm 1866) was probably also authored by Pelagius, and probably in Rome, cf. Evans 1968a; Duval 1990, 274–278. However, Manichaeus or the Manichaeans are not mentioned in it.

24   They were edited by Alexander Souter 1906; 1926. An English translation of the part commenting on Romans exists, as mentioned above, in de Bruyn 1993.

411. Instead he was accused of being a heretic, and was convicted in a trial in Carthage. This was the start of the Pelagian controversy, in which Augustine, Jerome and Pelagius himself would soon be involved.

Pelagius' *De natura* was probably only intended for his inner circle, but in 414 Augustine received a copy from Pelagius' disciples Timasius and James, and the following year he attacked it in his *De natura et gratia*, which contained quotations from it.[25] While most scholars have assumed that Pelagius wrote *De natura* after his flight (between 410 and 414), it has been argued by Yves-Marie Duval and Winrich Löhr that it was in fact written in Rome, before the flight, in the context of controversies over the fall of Adam, grace, and perhaps already the new watershed in Augustine's theology in his *Response to Simplician* and *Confessions*.[26] Whatever the truth of the matter, Manichaeans are not directly mentioned in the *De natura* fragments.

After his flight Pelagius authored the *Epistle to Demetrias*, which is also fully preserved but does not mention Manichaeism directly.[27] From the time of the controversy emanates his dialogue *De libero arbitrio*, in which he attacks Jerome. Several fragments are preserved, and Manichaeans are mentioned once.[28] His *Libellus fidei*, sent to the Roman Bishop Innocent I in 417, mentions Manichaeans twice.[29]

There are also a few other short letters from Pelagius which are unimportant in the present context. And there is a discussion of whether Pelagius was the author of an additional number of letters. In the 1930s and 40s de Plinval attributed a long list of 29 writings to Pelagius,[30] but instead Evans argued, in 1968, for a much shorter additional list consisting of four letters. But Pelagius' authorship has even been doubted for this list by Otto Wermelinger.[31]

---

25 *De natura et gratia* ed. Urba and Zycha 1913. Attempts to reconstruct Pelagius' *De natura* can be found by J. Garnier in PL 48, 599–606, and in Löhr 1999.

26 Cf. Duval 1990, esp. 272–283; Löhr 1999, 287–291.

27 Editions in PL 30, 15–45 and PL 33, 1099–1120. An English translation in Rees 1991, 29–70. Cf. also recently Greshake 2015.

28 Souter 1906, 29. Manichaeus or Manichaeans are not mentioned in the other fragments of Pelagius' *De libero arbitrio* (cf. Souter 1910; and fragments in Augustine, *De gratia Christi et de peccato originali*, ed. Urba and Zycha 1902a).

29 PL 45, 1716–1718.

30 Cf. de Plinval 1934; 1943; 1947. The list is followed and reproduced in Ferguson 1956, 186–187.

31 Evans 1968a, 10, 34–35 started with a list of certain writings and argued that four letters more from among de Plinval's list were also authored by Pelagius: *Epistula de virginitate*, *Epistula ad Celantiam*, *De vita christiana*, and *De divina lege*. Wermelinger 1989, 213 doubted this, though especially as regards *De vita christiana*, cf. Wermelinger 1989, 205–213. Nor are Manichaeus or Manichaeans mentioned in *De vita christiana* (ed. in PL 50,

Manichaeism is only mentioned in one of these four letters: the *Epistle to Celantia*.[32]

Pelagius made a great number of polemical remarks against his opponents in the *Expositions of Thirteen Epistles of St Paul*. In many instances he named the heretics: the Manichaeans,[33] Marcionists[34] (Marcionites), Arrians[35] (Arians), Novatians,[36] Macedonians,[37] and Apollinarists,[38] unless he preferred to mention the names of the heresiarchs: Manichaeus,[39] Marcion,[40] Arrius[41] (Arius), Novatus,[42] Apollinaris,[43] Fotinus[44] (Photinus), and Iovinianus[45] (Jovinian). Now it should be clear that this array of heretics is at least also Pelagius' way of demonstrating his own orthodoxy. As Evans wrote, "It is clear that as a theological writer Pelagius has no intention other than to think in and with the Catholic Church."[46] So this raises the question of whether Manichaeism really was a crucial adversary, or just one among many.

383–402), nor in *De divina lege* (ed. in PL 30, 105–116). The same goes for *Epistula de virginitate*, mentioned above in note 23.

32   Ed. Hartel 1894, 456,11–13. There is an English translation in Rees 1991, 127–144.
33   *In Rom* 1:2 (Souter 1926, 8,21); *In Rom* 6:19 (Souter 1926, 53,12); *In Rom* 7:7 (Souter 1926, 56,7); *In Rom* 8:7 (Souter 1926, 62,17); *In I Cor* 11:12 (Souter 1926, 189,5); *In II Cor* 3:7 (Souter 1926, 246,19); *In II Cor* 13:1 (Souter 1926, 302,13); *In Gal* 5:21 (Souter 1926, 336,15); *In Col* 1:16 (Souter 1926, 454,12); *In I Tim* 6:4 (Souter 1926, 499,17); *In I Tim* 6:16 (Souter 1926, 503,13). Together with the Apollinarists: *In I Cor* 15:45 (Souter 1926, 224,1–2).
34   *In Rom* 7:12 (Souter 1926, 57,22).
35   *In Rom* 8:34b (Souter 1926, 70,8); *In I Cor* 1:9 (Souter 1926, 130,19); *In I Cor* 8:6 (Souter 1926, 172,16); *In I Cor* 12:6 (Souter 1926, 196,2); *In I Cor* 15:28 (Souter 1926, 219,3); *In II Cor* 13:13 (Souter 1926, 305,5); *In Eph* 4:11 (Souter 1926, 364,14).
36   *In I Cor* 3:17 (Souter 1926, 144,19); *In II Cor* 12:21 (Souter 1926, 302,6); *In II Tim* 3:26 (Souter 1926, 517,8).
37   *In I Cor* 12:4 (Souter 1926, 195,21).
38   Together with the Manichaeans: *In I Cor* 15:45 (Souter 1926, 224,1–2).
39   Together with Fotinus (Photinus) and Arrius (Arius): *In Rom* 9:5 (Souter 1926, 73,7–8).
40   *In Eph* 3:9 (Souter 1926, 359,7; "contra Marcionem ... et ceteros haereticos").
41   *In II Cor* 12:4 (Souter 1926, 298,6); *In Phil* 2:5 (Souter 1926, 397,11); *In II Thess* 2:16 (Souter 1926, 447,2). Together with Apollinaris: *In I Cor* 2:8 (Souter 1926, 138,14); and together with Manichaeus and Fotinus (Photinus): *In Rom* 9:5 (Souter 1926, 73,7–8).
42   *In II Cor* 2:11 (Souter 1926, 241,13).
43   Together with Arrius (Arius): *In I Cor* 2:8 (Souter 1926, 138,14).
44   *In II Cor* 8:10 (Souter 1926, 275,20); and together with Manichaeus and Arrius (Arius): *In Rom* 9:5 (Souter 1926, 73,7–8).
45   *In I Cor* 3:8 (Souter 1926, 142,11); *In II Cor* 9:6 (Souter 1926, 281,12); *In I Thess* 2:3 (Souter 1926, 421,4).
46   Evans 1968, 92. Cf. also that Pelagius often polemises against unspecified heretics, e.g. *In II Cor* 4:6 (Souter 1926, 252,6–7 "contra omnes inimicos Veteris Testamenti"); *In Gal* 1:8 (Souter 1926, 308,12 "contra omnes hereticos"); *In I Tim* 4:1 (Souter 1926, 489,3 "Omnis haeretica doctrina").

These are the explicit remarks about Manichaeans from the *Expositions* (using de Bruyn's translation wherever it is available, or else my own):

1. *In Rom* 1:2. "Indeed, this entire passage contradicts the Manichaeans, for in it he states that already beforehand the Gospel was promised both through God's prophets and in the holy Scriptures; and that with regard to the flesh Christ was created from the line of David, that is, of the virgin Mary, just as Isaiah foretold it."[47]

2. *In Rom* 6:19. "[The fact is,] we presented our members to serve sin; it is not the case, as the Manichaeans say, that it was the nature of the body to have sin mixed in."[48]

3. *In Rom* 7:7. "[This contradicts] the Manichaeans. Because [if] they say: 'He is afraid of giving offence', [one should reply: 'If, therefore,] he was always afraid and never spoke against the law, [then] on what basis do you venture to say that he did not keep it?'"[49]

4. *In Rom* 8:7. "The flesh itself is not hostile to God, as the Manichaeans say, but the carnal mind is."[50]

5. *In Rom* 9:5. "Against Manichaeus, Photinus, and Arius, because he [is] from the Jews, [and according to the flesh [alone from them], [and] God blessed for ever."[51]

6. *In I Cor* 11:12. "This contradicts the Manichaeans who deny that the flesh is made by God."[52]

7. *In I Cor* 15:45. "It is to be noted that when he says 'two Adams', he shows that both of them are of the same nature: This contradicts the Mani-

---

[47] Translation from de Bruyn 1993, 59; Souter 1926, 8,20–24: "verum [tamen] totus hic locus contra Manichaeos facit, ubi dicit quod [et] ante evangelium sit promissum et per prophetas dei et in sanctis scripturis et quod Christus secundum carnem ex David stirpe, id est Maria virgine, sit creatus, secundum quod praedixerat Esaias."

[48] Translation from de Bruyn 1993, 99; Souter 1926, 53,11–13: "nos [sane] exhibuimus membra nostra servire peccato, non, sicut Manichaei dicunt naturam corporis insertum habere peccatum." Smith 1929, 26 compares the idea here with Augustine's *De lib. arb.*

[49] Translation from de Bruyn 1993, 101–102; Souter 1926, 56,8–11: "[Hoc facit] contra Manichaeos. quod [si] dixerint: 'timuit scandalum,' [respondendum est: 'si] semper [ergo] timuit et numquam contra legem locutus est, unde [ergo] vos audetis quod ille non fecit?'" Cf. here below about the possible connection with Augustine's *Contra Faustum*.

[50] Translation from de Bruyn 1993, 107; Souter 1926, 62,17–18: "Non ipsa caro, ut Manichaei dicunt, sed sensus carnalis inimicus est deo." Smith 1929, 26 compares the idea here with Augustine's *De lib. arb.*

[51] Translation from de Bruyn 1993, 115 (though revised by me since "Manichaeum" should not be translated here as "the Manichaean"); Souter 1926, 73, 7–9: "Contra Manichaeum, Fotinum, et Arrium, quia et ex Iudaeis [et] secundum carnem [est] [solam ex illis], [et] deus benedictus in saecula".

[52] Souter 1926, 189,5–6: "Contra Manicheos, qui negant carnem factam a deo."

chaeans and the Apollinarists who deny that a perfect man is received by God's Word."[53]

8. *In II Cor* 3:7. "This contradicts the Manichaeans, for the Apostle was never able to compare contraries, that is, to proclaim the servants of the New Covenant as greater than the glory of Moses, if nothing between them seemed to be common."[54]

9. *In II Cor* 13:1. "According to the law: This contradicts the Manichaeans."[55]

10. *In Gal* 5:21. "He says that hostilities and the rest are fleshly consequences which belong to the soul, not to the flesh, so that the Manichaeans should not ponder on accusing the substance of the flesh."[56]

11. *In Col* 1:16. "This contradicts the Manichaeans."[57]

12. *In I Tim* 6:4. "By abandonment of the understanding of truth they observe the ambiguities of the words, just as the Manichaeans who from words assign the contradiction of the Testaments."[58]

13. *In I Tim* 6:16. "This contradicts the Manichaeans who assert that the nature of evil is immortal and eternal."[59]

Now it is clear that heretics serve in this text as necessary counter-positions for demonstrating the true doctrine, so one could ask why these 13 passages about Manichaeans should be more important than all the other passages attacking various heresies. It is also different aspects of Manichaeism which are attacked: some passages concern Manichaean teaching about the separation of the Old and New Testament, stemming allegedly from the evil and good principles, respectively; others concern the Manichaean radical cosmological dualism with two eternal principles, and Manichaean docetic Christology is

---

53 Souter 1926, 223,19–224,3: "Notandum quod, cum duos Adam dicit, eiusdem naturae utrumque demonstrat: quod contra Manichaeos et Apollinaristas facit, qui negant a dei verbo perfectum hominem esse susceptum."

54 Souter 1926, 246,19–247,3: "Contra Manichaeos. numquam enim apostolus posset contraria comparare, id est, [maiorem] ministrorum novi testamenti quam Moysi gloriam praedicare, si nulla inter eos videretur esse communio."

55 Souter 1926, 302,13: "Secundum legem: contra Manichaeos." Paul argues by quoting Deut 19:15.

56 Souter 1926, 336,13–16: "Inimicitias et cetera sequenti[a] carnalia dicit, quae animae sunt, non carnis, ne Manichaei eum substantiam carnis accusare putarent."

57 Souter 1926, 454,12: "Contra Manichaeos." That is, that Paul says that dominions, principality, and powers were created in Christ.

58 Souter 1926, 499,16–18: "Relicto sensu veritatis ambiguitates verborum observant, sicut Manichaei, qui ex verbis diversitatem testamentorum adsignant." Pelagius is commenting on 'disputes about words' ("Et pugnas verborum") in the text.

59 Souter 1926, 503,13–14: "hoc contra Manichaeos, qui mali natura[m] adfirmant immortalem atque perpetuam."

criticised in No. 7. But the passages about anthropology, i.e. Nos. 2, 4, 6, 10, and also 13, are statements about the complex of themes which Bohlin regarded as Pelagius' central issue. Bohlin argued that the theme of creation and free will was crucial to Pelagius, and that Arians and Manichaeans therefore were the most basic opponents. The common work of Father and Son was essential to Pelagius' theology of creation, linking Creator and Saviour, hence the polemics against Arius, while his whole theology of the free will of the soul was in opposition to the Manichaeans.[60] As a result, some of the anti-Manichaean statements concern what was most important to Pelagius.

If this is correct, we can in fact expand the list if we assume that all similar polemics in the *Expositions* about sin being accidental instead of being nature or substance are also directed against the Manichaeans, even though they are not mentioned directly, as argued by previous scholars. Here are some good examples:[61]

14. *In Rom* 2:9: "The apostle threatens the soul with punishment because of heretics who say that only the flesh does wrong and deny that the soul can sin."[62]

---

60   Bohlin 1957, 10–15. Incidentally, Gisbert Greshake (1972, 53) thought that the heresies in Pelagius' *Expositions* could be classified in two groups: on the one hand, those which represented a dualistic, deterministic or particularistic tendency; and on the other hand those which denied the divinity or humanity of Christ. But this is not convincing, since Manichaeans and Marcionites as deniers of Christ's humanity fall into both categories.

61   Beside these examples, there are also other remarks not related to this anthropological-soteriological issue in which the opponent is not named but which may likewise be interpreted as being directed against the Manichaeans. Concerning the status of the Old Testament: *In Rom* 8:2, Souter 1926, 60,20–21: "Notandum quia gratiam legem appellat." De Bruyn 1993, 105 n. 1 assumes this to be directed against Marcionites and Manichaeans.— Similarly, *In IICor* 4:6, Souter 1926, 252,6–7 ("Hoc contra omnes inimicos Veteris Testamenti, quia a patre Christi sit datum") may be directed both against Marcionites and Manichaeans, cf. Bohlin 1957, 26.—The heretics denying the incarnation and death of Christ *In Rom* 1:16, Souter 1926, 12,6–12 must also include the Manichaeans, as rightly observed in de Bruyn 1993, 63 n. 24.—The heretics denying the resurrection of the flesh and Christ's incarnation *In IITim* 2:8, Souter 1926, 512,3–6 must also include the Manichaeans, and likewise with the deniers of the resurrection of the flesh *In IITim* 2:16, Souter 1926, 514,6–7.—When Pelagius at *In Eph* 3:9 assumes that *Qui omnia creavit* contradicts Marcion and other heretics, the Manichaeans may well be included (Souter 1926, 359,6–7: "Omnem creaturam, ut sensus contra Marcionem proficiat et ceteros haereticos.").

62   Translation from de Bruyn 1993, 71–72; Souter 1926, 22,5–7: "Animae poenam apostolus comminatur propter haereticos, qui solam carnem delinquere dicunt et animam negant posse peccare." This is rightly suggested as an anti-Manichaean remark in Bohlin 1957, 13; de Bruyn 1993, 72 n. 17.

15. *In Rom* 5:10: "We were enemies, then, in our actions, not by nature".[63]
16. *In Rom* 7:17: *"However, now I no longer do it.* Before it became a habit, therefore, I myself did it willingly. *But sin that lives in me.* It lives as a guest and as one thing in another, not as one single thing; in other words, as an accidental quality, not a natural one."[64]
17. *In Rom* 7:18: *"For I know that what is good does not live in me, that is, in my flesh.* He did not say: 'My flesh is not good.' *For it is near to me to wish.* The will is there, but not the deed, because carnal habit opposes the will."[65]
18. *In Rom* 8:3: "and in that same flesh he condemned sin, to show that the will was arraigned, not the nature, which God created in such a way that it [was able] not to sin[, if it so wished]."[66]
19. *In Rom* 8:8: *"Indeed, those who are in the flesh.* This proves that above he found fault not with the flesh, but with the works of the flesh, because those to whom he says this were no doubt living in the flesh."[67]

If we accept this line of argument, Bohlin was right that Pelagius put his central theological convictions forward in opposition to Manichaean teaching, at

---

63   Translation from de Bruyn 1993, 91–92; Souter 1926, 44,24–25: "inimici ergo actibus, non natura". This is suggested as an anti-Manichaean remark in de Bruyn 1993, 16 n. 102, however, de Bruyn (1993, 92 n. 17) also rightly refers to Rufinus' translation of Origen's *Commentary on Romans* IV,12, cf. *In Rom* 5:12,1–13 (Bammel 1997, 353–354), where the same idea is clearly present and the polemics are against Marcion and Valentinus.

64   Translation from de Bruyn 1993, 104; Souter 1926, 58,24–59,3: *"Nunc autem iam non ego illut operor.* Ante consuetudinem ergo libens ego ipse faciebam. *Sed quod habitat in me peccatum.* Habitat quasi hospes et quasi aliut in alio, non quasi unum, ut accidens scilicet, non naturale." This is suggested as an anti-Manichaean remark in de Bruyn 1993, 16 n. 102, 44; 94 n. 36. Smith 1929, 26 compares the idea here with a number of passages from Augustine's *De lib. arb.*

65   Translation from de Bruyn 1993, 104; Souter 1926, 59,3–6: *"Nam scio quoniam non [in]habitat in me, hoc est in carne mea, bonum.* Non dixit: 'Non est caro mea bona.' *Nam velle adiacet mihi.* Est voluntas, sed non est effectus, quia carnalis consuetudo voluntati resistit." This is suggested as an anti-Manichaean remark in de Bruyn 1993, 16 n. 102, 44; 94 n. 36.

66   Translation from de Bruyn 1993, 107; Souter 1926, 61,19–21: "et in eadem carne damnavit peccatum, ut ostenderet voluntatem esse in crimine, non naturam, quae talis a deo facta est, ut posset non peccare[, si vellet]." Souter's text "vellet" follows the Karlsruhe MS, while the Vatican fragment reads "velit" (cf. de Bruyn 1993, 32–34, 107 n. 10). But this is not of importance here, where the focus is on the opposition of will and nature. This is suggested as an anti-Manichaean remark in de Bruyn 1993, 16 n. 102. Smith 1929, 26 compares the idea here with a number of passages from Augustine's *De lib. arb.*

67   Translation from de Bruyn 1993, 108; Souter 1926, 62,22–24: *"Qui autem in carne sunt.* Hinc probatur quia superius non carnem sed opera accusaverit carnis, quia quibus hoc dicit, utique in carne vivebant." This is suggested as an anti-Manichaean remark in de Bruyn 1993, 16 n. 102, 45; 94 n. 36. Smith 1929, 26 compares the idea here with a number of passages from Augustine's *De lib. arb.*

least in his *Expositions of Thirteen Epistles of St Paul*, even though there are also arguments in previous scholarship for an anti-Manichaean context which are untenable.[68]

However, the Manichaean teachings are stereotyped, without life and concrete details, and to some extent not Manichaean teachings at all. Pelagius maintains that the Manichaeans rejected the Old Testament and the reality of Christ's incarnation and death, claiming that sin was nature, linked to the evil flesh and body, while the soul itself cannot sin. Nothing in these meagre comments suggests any first-hand knowledge of Manichaeism. We are missing a lot of details here which we would have found in Church Fathers like Hegemonius, Titus of Bostra and Augustine, who all really worked with Manichaean texts and who probably also had a real conflict with Manichaean congregations. Why are there no references to the central role of Mani, to the Manichaean congregations and their morality, or to the Manichaean mythology?

One explanation could be that Pelagius was consulting previous Catholic anti-Manichaeism. He did not know any Manichaeans, so most of his interest was centred on aspects of this literature which had a wider significance and which could be used against other groups than Manichaeans. Here we should remember that before Manichaeism came into existence it was already a tradition to depict heretics as determinists, a fact which Bohlin actually also stressed and which has been further stressed by Löhr.[69] Bohlin suggested dependence on anti-Manichaean arguments in Hilarius of Poitiers,[70] and it is

---

[68] Not all references in previous scholarship are convincing: The remark *In Rom* 1:8, Souter 1926, 10,9: "Natura deus omnium est, merito et voluntate paucorum" has nothing to do with anti-Manichaeism (against de Bruyn 1993, 61 n. 17).—De Bruyn 1993, 128 n. 25 claimed that the first part of the remark *In Rom* 11:22, Souter 1926, 90,8–10 should be directed against the Marcionites and the second part against the Manichaeans: "Contra eos qui alium deum iustum, alium adserunt bonum; et contra eos qui negant deum in peccantibus vindicare." However, it was probably not the Manichaeans whom Pelagius was thinking about. If it had been, this would be another Patristic distortion of Manichaeism. De Bruyn's references to Augustine, *C. Ep. Fund.* 39 and *De nat. boni* 31 are wholly misleading.—Pelagius' interpretation of *In Rom* 7:15, Souter 1926, 58,17–18: "et iam quasi inebriatus consuetudine peccatorum" is certainly expressing Pelagius' theology, but a counter-position is not mentioned here (mentioned in de Bruyn 1993, 16 n. 102).

[69] Bohlin 1957, 14; Löhr 1999, 282 makes precise references to anti-Manichaean authors like Serapion of Thmuis and Titus of Bostra, as well as the anti-Marcionite *Dialogue of Adamantius*, and the heritage from Origen's polemics against the Valentinians. Cf. also De Bruyn 1993, 16–17, who stresses that the assertion of human freedom and freedom of the will was already common in Christian authors of the 2nd and 3rd centuries. This was also the case for Origen, whose *Commentary on the Epistle to the Romans* Pelagius knew from the translation by Rufinus of Aquileia.

[70] Bohlin 1957, 58, 60.

also of interest that it has been argued both by means of philological comparison and in relation to content that one of the sources of Pelagius' *Expositions* and theology was Augustine's early writings, not least his anti-Manichaean works including his *De libero arbitrio*. However, Löhr has correctly pointed out that Augustine's position in *De libero arbitrio* already differed from Pelagius' position: both because free choice was not the highest good, and because Augustine assumed a weakening of mankind after the fall which leads to sin.[71] Some anti-Manichaean arguments in the *Expositions* may furthermore betray knowledge of Augustine's *Contra Faustum*: In No. 7 above, 1 Cor 15:45 is used against Manichaeans and Apollinarists. This may be inspired by Augustine's argument in *Contra Faustum* 11,3 (cf. also 2,4–5), although Pelagius' own Christological work may also have contributed anti-Apollinaristic arguments. And in No. 3 above, Pelagius also suggests that Manichaeans might argue that Paul, in Romans 7:7, denied that the law is sin because he was afraid of giving offence. De Bruyn has rightly compared this with *Contra Faustum* 19,1, but without elaborating.[72] What is remarkable, however, is Faustus' argument that when Jesus claimed to have come not to destroy the law but to fulfil it and the prophets (Matt 5:17), he might have said this to calm the anger of the Jews even though he in reality was not thinking about the law of the Hebrews. In the light of Pelagius' otherwise stereotypical knowledge of Manichaeism, his remark is probably not evidence of reading Faustus' original text or any first-hand encounter with Manichaeans in Rome. He is simply transferring Faustus' argument, which he knows from Augustine, from Matt 5:17 to Rom 7:7.

If we accept that the argument that sin is not substantial is, in a sense, anti-Manichaean, then anti-Manichaeism is also present in Pelagius' *De natura*. This was indeed claimed by Bohlin, Evans and Löhr.[73] The idea that sin is not nature but action is presented as anti-Manichaean in the *Expositions of Thirteen Epistles of St Paul*. In the fragments of *De natura* we find the same idea expressed several times, e.g. *De natura et gratia* XIX(21), "For this reason, I think we must

---

71 Smith 1918 had already demonstrated Pelagius' use of Augustine's *Expositio quarundam propositionum ex Epistula ad Romanos* and *Epistulae ad Romanos inchoata expositio* in the *Expositions*. Furthermore, Smith 1929 suggested the use of *De moribus ecclesiae catholicae*, *De moribus Manichaeorum*, *De libero arbitrio*, *De diversis quaestionibus lxxxiii*, *De Genesi adversus Manichaeos*, *De vera religione*, *De fide et symbolo*, *De continentia*, *De agone christiano*, *De diversis quaestionibus ad Simplicianum* I. Bohlin 1957, 46–57 presented additional arguments for using Augustine's *De libero arbitrio*. Löhr 1999, 291–292, cf. also 290 n. 139, stresses the differences between Pelagius' views and Augustine's in *De libero arbitrio*.
72 De Bruyn 1993, 102 n. 4: "On the Manichaean view of the law, cf. Aug. *Faust*. 19. 1, 9. 1 (CSEL 25: 496. 21–497. 16, 307. 18–28)."
73 Cf. Bohlin 1957, 18; Evans 1968, 86; Löhr 1999, 282–283.

investigate before all else" ... "what sin is. Is it a substance, or is it a word completely lacking substance which expresses not some thing, not an existence, not some body, but an act of wrongdoing?", and in a number of other instances.[74] However, it is not entirely clear whether Pelagius intended to say that his opponents were the Manichaeans: in the first part of the same fragment in *De natura et gratia* XIX(21), Pelagius says: "First of all" ... "we must debate the claim that nature is said to be weakened and changed by sin",[75] which seems to aim at a doctrine about the Fall of Adam[76] rather than Manichaeism. In another fragment, in *De natura et gratia* LIV(63), Pelagius wants to show that the same God made both human spirit and flesh, and both of them good, and this argument could actually be regarded as anti-Manichaean. In *De natura* Pelagius also quotes Augustine's anti-Manichaean treatise *De libero arbitrio*, which could also be understood in this context.[77] The arguments in *De natura* were certainly based on an anti-Manichaean tradition, but this does not necessarily mean that *De natura* claimed to be an anti-Manichaean text. At any rate, it seems to have been directed at some other group than the Manichaeans, since Pelagius' opponents argued that human beings had changed following Adam's fall.

When Pelagius lived in Rome, we know that there was also a Manichaean congregation in the city. De Bruyn referred to this fact in connection with Pelagius' anti-Manichaeism,[78] but we do not have to assume that Pelagius was in contact with Manichaeans while he was in Rome. The decline in numbers of the city's population had only just begun, and even though Augustine says that "the number of them secretly living in Rome was large" when talking about the Manichaeans (*Confessions* V,X(19)),[79] this would not necessarily mean that Pelagius ran into them since he would not have had the contacts

---

[74] *De natura et gratia* XIX(21): "unde ante omnia quaerendum puto," ... "quid sit peccatum: substantia aliqua an omnino substantia carens nomen, quo non res, non existential, non corpus aliquod, sed perperam facti actus exprimitur." Urba and Zycha 1913, 246,13–16. Translation by Teske 1997, 225. Cf., furthermore, *De natura et gratia* LIV(63); LVI(66); and the quotations from John Chrysostom LXIV(76).

[75] *De natura et gratia* XIX(21): "primo" ... "de eo disputandum est, quod per peccatum debilitate dicitur et inmutata natura." Urba and Zycha 1913, 246,12–13. Translation by Teske 1997, 225.

[76] Cf. Löhr 1999, 256–257.

[77] Cf. *De natura et gratia* LXVII(80). Even though Augustine in *De libero arbitrio* does not mention "Manichaeans" directly, he says on the first pages that it was the question of evil which in his youth pushed him towards the heretics (*De libero arbitrio* I,II,4,10; Green 1970, 213,3–5).

[78] De Bruyn 1993, 13–16, 24.

[79] Translation: Chadwick 1991, 85; Verheijen 1981, 68,34: "plures enim eos Roma occultat".

which Augustine had when he arrived.[80] And the Manichaeans would not have been interested in being easily identified because they were an illegal body. If many Manichaeans lived secretly there, this would presumably have been known publicly owing to constant rumours, and these rumours would have been strengthened by the imperial and episcopal initiatives to suppress them, leading to an atmosphere in which Manichaeism would often be suspected of being the secret motive of your opponents. So while the Manichaeans cannot really be regarded as the reason why Pelagius developed his own particular theological convictions, it seems fair to assume that stereotypical Manichaeism could have been the opponent against which he was writing.

In so far as Manichaeism is used as the dark background for presenting the central tenets of Pelagius' theology, man's ethical freedom as created in the image and similitude of God, it is, however, too reductionistic only to see all the anti-Manichaean remarks as tradition or conventional marks of orthodoxy. We must assume that there were real opponents against whom Pelagius advanced his own theology, but whom he (for some political reason) did not want to name directly. Instead, he apparently polemised against the Manichaeans and it was left to the readers themselves to draw the conclusion that a contemporary opponent in the Church was in fact identical to the Manichaeans.[81] Now we know that there must have been a discussion or controversy about traducianism in the Roman congregation at Pelagius' time, both from the inquiry of Caelestius in Carthage in 411, where he said that he heard the holy presbyter

---

80 TeSelle 1972, 87, Lavender 1991, 74–75, and de Bruyn 1992, 44–45 discuss whether it is possible to identify a certain "Constantius tractator", mentioned in *Praedestinatus* 1,88 as the first one who contradicted Pelagius and Caelestius (PL 53, 618B10–11), with the former Manichaean Constantius in Rome who was converted to Catholicism and is mentioned by Augustine in *De moribus* II, 20,74 and *Contra Faustum* v,5. *Praedestinatus* was probably written in Rome by Arnobius the Younger between 432 and 435 (cf. De Bruyn 1992, 40). De Bruyn has also reservations and he admits that Constantius was a common name. Of course, if one of Pelagius' and Caelestius' opponents in Rome was a convert from Manichaeism to Catholicism, we could assume that the anti-Manichaean remarks in the *Expositions* were a way of attacking him, in the same way as Augustine later on was smeared for his Manichaean past. But even if this was the case, it does not mean that Pelagius had met Manichaeans or had any first-hand knowledge about Manichaeism.

81 Evans 1968, 92 has a consideration which to a certain degree is similar to mine: "The third motif is closely related to the second. Pelagius wishes to formulate his conception of man in such a way as to make the Christian doctrine of man clearly distinguishable from Manichaean notions of man and so as to combat whatever influences and traces of Manichaeism are to be found within the Church."

Rufinus (who lived in Rome with the holy Pammachius) declare that there is no transmission of sin,[82] and from a passage in Pelagius' *Expositions* (*In Rom* 5:15), where he cites extensively a number of arguments "from those who oppose the transmission of sin" ("hi autem qui contra traducem peccati sunt") without openly disclosing his own position.[83] However, it is clear that Pelagius himself was one of the opposers of transmission of sin because he does not cite any arguments in favour of transmission of sin. Pelagius displays a "political" prudence, i.e., he is very careful not to polemise in an undisguised manner in highly controversial questions, just as he disguised his real opponents when he depicted them as Manichaeans. It is worth observing that one of the arguments advances the possibility that "if the soul does not exist by transmission, but the flesh alone, then only the flesh carries the transmission of sin and it alone deserves punishment" ("si anima non nest ex traduce, sed sola caro, ipsa tantum habet traducem peccati et ipsa sola poenam meretur").[84] This hypothetical argument makes the adherents of a doctrine about the transmission of sin resemble the Manichaeans, as they were presented by Pelagius in Nos. 2, 4, 6, 10, 14–19, where sin, evil, body, and flesh were woven together.[85] Naturally, this is heresiology or the drawing of malicious consequences.

Pelagius may also have had Augustine in mind when attacking the "Manichaeans". Perhaps the story in *De dono perseverentiae* XX,53 that Pelagius formerly, when he was still in Rome, reacted sharply when Augustine's prayer "da quod jubes et jube quod vis" was cited from the *Confessions* (X,XXIX(40); X,XXXI(45); X,XXXVII(60)) (cf. also *De gestis Pelagii* XXII(46)) should be seen in

---

82   Cf. Augustine, *De gratia Christi et de peccato originali* II, III,3, Urba and Zycha 1902a, 168,12–15. Whether this Rufinus was the same person as Rufinus the Syrian in Marius Mercator, *Commonitorium adversus Pelagianos et Caelestianos* (Schwartz 1924–1926, 5,36–39), the author of the treatise *Liber de fide* (cf. Miller 1964), and the presbyter Rufinus, whom Jerome, according to his *Ep.* 81,2, sent to Milan via Rome, is not crucial to my argument; on this cf., however, Altaner 1950; Refoulé 1963; Bonner 1970; and TeSelle 1972, who all assumed these identifications, while Dunphy 1992 argued that Rufinus the Syrian in Marius Mercator was a misunderstanding of Rufinus of Aquileia—but admitted (Dunphy 1992, 279–280) that it is difficult to conclude that Rufinus of Aquileia was the same as Caelestius' Rufinus since this Rufinus was a guest of Jerome's friend Pammachius, while Rufinus of Aquileia and Jerome were enemies.

83   Souter 1926, 46,25–47,13 (quotation 46,25–26); de Bruyn 1993, 94.

84   Souter 1926, 47,7–9; de Bruyn 1993, 94.

85   Cf. De Bruyn 1988, 38–39; de Bruyn 1993, 94 n. 36. However, de Bruyn still believed that Pelagius' real enemy was Manichaeism, which made him reject all ideas that no-one is sinless, including traducianism. Instead, I suggest that it was traducianists and all other groups claiming that man's state was fallen who were the real enemies.

this context. Pelagius may have seen this turning-point in Augustine's thinking as evidence of support for the same tendencies in Rome which he was opposing.

Since Pelagius' own theology was developed while he lived in Rome, the texts examined so far are the most important ones for my purpose. Now I wish to proceed to those texts by Pelagius which were written after leaving Rome to see if they confirm that references to Manichaeism were something Pelagius used when attacking people who were not Manichaeans.

The *Epistle to Demetrias* was written in Jerusalem in 413. Manichaeans are not directly mentioned, but in chapter 3,3 Pelagius opposes those who criticise God's work and assert that man ought to have been made so that he could do no evil at all.[86] It is doubtful whether this argument would have been advanced by Manichaeans. The idea that man ought to have been made so that he could not sin is rather a hypothetical viewpoint which is refuted philosophically, since only free choice allows virtue or vice, praise or blame.[87] But it is clear that this hypothetical viewpoint had to be associated with the Manichaeans whenever they were imagined as the deterministic opponents of freedom. Thus we also find it in anti-Manichaean literature, cf. Titus of Bostra, *Contra Manichaeos* II,4–8[88] or Augustine, *De continentia* 14–16. It is therefore possible (but not certain) that Pelagius was thinking of the Manichaeans in chapter 3,3.[89]

Other texts by Pelagius mention Manichaeans directly. Thus in his *De libero arbitrio*, which was written as a dialogue against Jerome, Pelagius discusses Galatians 5:17 and explains that Paul is only speaking of fleshly persons here, and that "flesh" signifies habit and not substance. In this connection he touches upon Romans 7:18, "non habitat in carne mea bonum": "unde et apostolus,— ut multi prudentium intellegunt, 'etsi in alterius persona' dicat, *non habitat in carne mea bonum*—, non ind⟨e⟩ agit ut naturam carnis malam esse demonstret,

---

86 *Epistle to Demetrias* 3,3: "Sed plerique impie, non minus quam imperite, cum super statu hominis quæritur (vereor dicere), quasi reprehendentes opus Domini, talem illum aiunt debuisse fieri, qui omnino facere non posset malum." (PL 30, 18B; PL 33, 1101A). Translation by Rees 1991, 38: "But most of those who, from lack of faith as much as of knowledge, deplore the status of man, are—I am ashamed to admit it—criticising the Lord's work and asserting that man ought to have been so made that he could do no evil at all," ...
87 This is commonplace, but cf., e.g., Pedersen 2004, 283, 286–287, 312.
88 Cf. Pedersen 2004, 24.
89 Orosius understood it as an accusation against 'us', i.e. the anti-Pelagianists, cf. *Liber apologeticus* 29,3 (Zangemeister 1882, 652,18–21): "inter haec ergo huiusmodi sensum in eadem epistula indigestis sermonibus eructasti, quod plerique nostrorum dicerent, Deum malam hominis condidisse naturam." (referring to the *Epistle to Demetrias*, cf. Zangemeister 1882, 652,5–6).

ne, ut tu putas, Manicheorum aplaudat errori, sed in consuetudine atque opere carnali habitare bonum negat, cumque ait:" (Galatians 5:17 is again quoted):[90] "for this reason the apostle also says, 'though in another person', as the majority of the wise understand, that 'nothing good dwells in my flesh',—not because he thinks that he should show that the nature of flesh is evil, not even, as you assume, to applaud the error of the Manichaeans, but he denies that good dwells in the fleshly habit and work, as he said:" ... This fragment supports the analysis that Pelagius continued anti-Manichaean arguments but was aiming at somebody else, in this case Jerome.

Pelagius' *Libellus fidei*, which he sent to the Roman Bishop Innocent I in 417, contains explicit references to various heretics (to Arius, Sabellius, Photinus, Apollinarius and Jovinian), but also one implicit reference and two explicit references to Manichaeism. The implicit reference is this: "We believe that the souls are given by God, and we say that they are made by him, while we anathematize those who say that the souls are almost a part of the divine substance; we also condemn the error of those who say that they sinned formerly or even have dwelled in the heavens before they were sent into bodies."[91] While the last clauses clearly condemn Origenism, the first anathematism here presumably aims at Manichaeism. Pelagius probably included it because in Diospolis he had been accused of believing the same as Caelestius, who had allegedly written as an interpretation of 2 Pet 1:4: "if the soul is not able to be without sin, then God too is subject to sin, since a part of him, namely, our soul, is subject to sin."[92] So the intention of this anathematism was probably apologetic, because of the accusations against Pelagius.

The first of the explicit references is as follows: "We curse also the blasphemy of those who say that any impossible thing is commanded to man by God, or that the commandments of God cannot be kept by single humans, but that by everybody in common they may, and both they who with Manichaeus con-

---

90   Souter 1906, 29. Manichaeus or Manichaeans are not mentioned in the other fragments of Pelagius' *De libero arbitrio* (cf. Souter 1910; and fragments in Augustine, *De gratia Christi et de peccato originali*, ed. Urba and Zycha 1902a).

91   "Animas a Deo dari credimus, quas ab ipso factas dicimus; anathematizantes eos qui animas quasi partem divinæ dicunt esse substantiæ. Eorum quoque condemnamus errorem, qui eas ante peccasse vel in cœlis conversatas fuisse dicunt, quam in corpora mitterentur." PL 45, 1718 (No. 9).

92   Augustine, *De gestis Pelagii* XVIII(42): "quoniam si anima non potest esse sine peccato, ergo et deus subiacet peccato, cuius pars, hoc est anima, peccato obnoxia est". Urba and Zycha 1902, 98,12–14. Translation by Teske 1997, 353. If this is a genuine quotation of Caelestius, it must be an anti-Manichaean deduction from his side which is maliciously cited as if it was Caelestius' own opinion.

demn first marriages, and with the Cataphrygians second marriages."[93] Clearly, the final passage refers not to Manichaeans or Cataphrygians (i.e., Montanists) as such, but to anyone who has the same viewpoints as these heretics. In reality, it is also a very imprecise description of the Manichaean view of marriage, for even though marriage and sexuality were seen as a sin and evil, they were only forbidden for the Manichaean elite, the so-called "electi" (i.e, "elect"), while they were allowed for the ordinary "laymen", the so-called "auditores" (i.e., "hearers"). So this passage is also stereotypical, although Evans has shown convincingly that the attacks on anyone who sides with Manichaeus and Cataphrygians are concealed attacks on Jerome, who in his *Adversus Iovinianum* seemingly attacked both marriage as such as well as second and third marriages, here influenced by Tertullian's writings from his Montanist phase.[94]

The second explicit reference to the Manichaeans is as follows: "We thus acknowledge the free choice, so that we say that we always are in need of God's help, and just as they err who say with the Manichaeans that man is unable to avoid sin, so do they who with Jovinian claim that man cannot sin; for both groups remove free choice."[95] The confession of God's daily help was what the pope required of Pelagius; otherwise Manichaeans and Jovinian served to fix the extremes between which Pelagius placed himself as the true middle. It is not correct that the historical Manichaeans said that man was unable to avoid sin, but presumably Pelagius was actually thinking of Jerome and Augustine. It is also worth observing that at Diospolis, Pelagius had condemned the aforementioned quotation of Caelestius, which said precisely that: "if the soul is not able to be without sin" (Augustine, *De gestis Pelagii* XVIII(42)).

There is also a reference to Manichaeus in *Epistula ad Celantiam* 28, although Wermelinger disputes Pelagius' authorship: "apostolicae doctrinae regula nec cum Ioviniano aequat continentiae opera nuptiarum nec cum Manichaeo coniugia condemnat."[96] This may be an attack on Jerome, since it is very similar to the first explicit reference in the *Libellus fidei*.

---

93   "Exsecramus etiam eorum blasphemiam, qui dicunt, impossibile aliquid homini a Deo præceptum esse, et mandata Dei non a singulis, sed ab omnibus in commune posse servari: vel qui primas nuptias cum Manichæo, vel secundas cum Cataphrygis damnant." PL 45, 1718 (No. 10).

94   Cf. Evans 1968, 26–42, esp. 41–42. Cf. Wermelinger 1975, 139, 141.

95   "Liberum sic confitemur arbitrium, ut dicamus nos semper Dei indigere auxilio; et tam illos errare qui cum Manichæis dicunt hominem peccatum vitare non posse, quam illos qui cum Ioviniano asserunt hominem non posse peccare; uterque enim tollit libertatem arbitrii. Nos vero dicimus, hominem semper et peccare, et non peccare posse; ut semper nos liberi confiteamur esse arbitrii." PL 45, 1718 (No. 13).

96   Ed. Hartel 1894, 456,11–13. The translation in Rees 1991, 141–142 ("The rule of apostolic doc-

In conclusion, it seems justified to claim that the terms "Manichaeus" and "Manichaeans" were stereotypes used by Pelagius to distance himself from his real opponents. Of course this heresiological game was played against the background that somewhere there existed an illegal body of heretics called Manichaeans. But this is not the same as saying that their existence explains why Pelagius developed his particular theology. There are at least two errors in much of the scholarship which followed in the footsteps of Bohlin. Firstly, it was wrongly assumed that when Pelagius apparently attacked "Manichaeans", he was really also attacking the historical Manichaeans, i.e., those religious groups which Augustine belonged to in his youth and whose texts we have found in deserts in modern times. Secondly, while it was correct that Pelagius was deeply influenced by preceding anti-Manichaean traditions, it was not understood that these traditions stylised and distorted Manichaeism to make it represent a consistent philosophical position, a denial of free will and confirmation of determinism. In order to interpret Pelagius' theology in its proper context, it will therefore be necessary to abandon heresiological fictions and accept that Pelagius' first enemies were to be found within his own Catholic congregation in Rome—not among the secret groups of real Manichaeans who at that time also dwelled in the eternal city.

Bibliography

Altaner, Berthold

1950. "Der Liber de fide (Migne, PL 21, 1123–1154 und PL 48, 451–488) ein Werk des Pelagianers Rufinus des 'Syrers'." *Theologische Quartalschrift* 130, 432–449.

Bammel, Caroline P. Hammond

1997. *Der Römerbriefkommentar des Origenes: Kritische Ausgabe der Übersetzung Rufins.* Buch 4–6 zum Druck vorbereitet und gesetzt von H.J. Frede und H. Stanjek. Vetus Latina 33. Freiburg: Verlag Herder.

Baur, Ferdinand Christian

1831. *Das Manichäische Religionssystem nach den Quellen neu untersucht und entwikelt.* Tübingen: Verlag von C.F. Osiander.

---

trine neither makes works of continence equal to those of marriage with Jovinian nor does it condemn marriage with the Manichaean") should be corrected since Manichaeus here is a name. Cf. Evans 1968a, 114; Wermelinger 1989, 213.

Bohlin, Torgny

1957. *Die Theologie des Pelagius und ihre Genesis.* Uppsala Universitets Årsskrift 1957:9. Acta Universitatis Upsaliensis. Uppsala: A.-B. Lundequitska Bokhandeln. Wiesbaden: Harrassowitz.

Bonner, Gerald

1966. "How Pelagian was Pelagius? An examination of the contentions of Torgny Bohlin," in: Cross, F.L. (ed.), *Studia Patristica* 9 (*Texte und Untersuchungen zur Geschichte der altchristlichen Literatur* 9). Berlin, Akademie Verlag, 350–358.

1970. "Rufinus of Syria and African Pelagianism." *Augustinian Studies* 1, 31–47.

1992. "Pelagianism and Augustine." *Augustinian Studies* 23, 33–51.

Bruyn, Theodore Sybren de

1988. "Pelagius's Interpretation of Rom. 5:12–21: Exegesis within the Limits of Polemic." *Toronto Journal of Theology* 4, 30–43.

1992. "Constantius the *Tractator*: Author of an Anonymous Commentary on the Pauline Epistles?" *The Journal of Theological Studies* NS 43, 38–54.

1993. *Pelagius's Commentary on St Paul's Epistle to the Romans: Translated with Introduction and Notes.* Oxford Early Christian Studies. Oxford: Clarendon Press.

Chadwick, Henry

1991. Saint Augustine *Confessions.* Translated with an Introduction. Oxford: Oxford University Press.

Dunphy, Walter

1992. "Marius Mercator on Rufinus the Syrian: Was Schwartz mistaken?" *Augustinianum* 32, 279–288.

Duval, Yves-Marie

1990. "La date du 'De natura' de Pélage: Les premiéres étapes de la controverse sur la nature de la grâce." *Revue des Études Augustiniennes* 36, 257–283.

Evans, Gillian R.

1981. "Neither a Pelagian nor a Manichee." *Vigiliae Christianae* 35, 232–244.

Evans, Robert F.

1968. *Pelagius: Inquiries and Reappraisals.* London: Adam & Charles Black.

1968a. *Four Letters of Pelagius.* London: Adam & Charles Black.

Ferguson, John
1956. *Pelagius: A Historical and Theological Study.* Cambridge: W. Heffer & Sons ltd.

Green, William M.
1970. "De libero arbitrio: Libri tres." *Sancti Aurelii Augustini Contra Academicos, De beata vita, De ordine, De magistro, De libero arbitrio* cura et studio W.M. Green, K.-D. Daur. Corpus Christianorum Series Latina XXIX. Turnhout: Brepols, 205–322.

Greshake, Gisbert
1972. *Gnade als konkrete Freiheit: Eine Untersuchung zur Gnadenlehre des Pelagius.* Mainz: Matthias- Grünewald-Verlag.
2015. Pelagius *Epistula ad Demetriadem, Brief an Demetrias. Lateinisch, Deutsch. Einleitung, Edition und Übersetzung von* Gisbert Greshake. Fontes Christiani 65. Freiburg: Herder.

Halm, Karl
1866. "Epistola S. Severi ad Claudiam sororem de virginitate." *Sulpicii Severi Libri qui supersunt* recensuit et commentario critico instruxit Carolus Halm. CSEL I. Vienna: Apud C. Geroldi Filium Bibliopolam Academiae, 224–250

Harnack, Adolf von
1910. *Lehrbuch der Dogmengeschichte.* III. 4. Auflage. Tübingen: J.C.B. Mohr.

Hartel, Wilhelm August von
1894. "Epistula II. Ad Celanciam." *S. Pontii Meropii Paulini Nolani Opera.* I. *Epistulae* ex recensione Guilelmi de Hartel. CSEL XXIV. Prague, Vienna, and Leipzig: F. Tempsky & G. Freytag, 436–459.

Lamberigts, Mathijs
2000. "Le mal et le péché. Pélage: La réhabilitation d'un hérétique." J. Pirotte and E. Louchez (eds.), *Deux mille ans d'histoire de l'Église: Bilan et perspectives historiographiques.* Revue d'histoire ecclésiastique XCV. Louvain-la-Neuve: Bibliothèque de l'Université, 97–111.
2003. "Der Pelagianismus: Von einer ethisch-religiösen Bewegung zur Ketzerei und wieder zurück." *Concilium: Internationale Zeitschrift für Theologie* 2003/3, 39–48.
2009. "Pelagius and Pelagians", in: Harvey, S.A. and Hunter, D.G. (eds.), *The Oxford Handbook of Early Christian Studies.* Oxford: Oxford University Press, 258–274.

Lavender, Earl Dale

1991. *The development of Pelagius' thought within a late fourth century ascetic movement in Rome*. A Dissertation Presented to the Faculty of the Graduate School of Saint Louis University in Partial Fulfillment of the Requirements for the Degree of Doctor of Philosophy. Copyright by Earl D. Lavender.

Löhr, Winrich A.

1999. "Pelagius' Schrift *De natura*: Rekonstruktion und Analyse." *Recherches augustiniennes* 31, 235–294.

Martini, P. Coelestinus

1938. "Quattuor fragmenta Pelagio restituenda." *Antonianum* XIII, 293–334.

Mausbach, Joseph

1909. *Die Ethik des heiligen Augustinus*. I: *Die sittliche Ordnung und ihre Grundlagen*. Freiburg: Herdersche Verlagshandlung.

Miller, Mary William

1964. Rufini Presbyteri *Liber De Fide: A Critical Text and Translation with Introduction and Commentary*. A Dissertation submitted to the Faculty of the Graduate School of Arts and Sciences of the Catholic University of America in partial fulfillment of the requirements for the degree of doctor of philosophy. Washington, D.C.: The Catholic University of America Press.

Nørregaard, Jens

1920. *Augustins religiøse Gennembrud: En kirkehistorisk Undersøgelse*. Copenhagen: V. Pios Boghandel– Povl Branner.

Pedersen, Nils Arne

2004. *Demonstrative Proof in Defence of God: A Study of Titus of Bostra's* Contra Manichaeos. *The Work's Sources, Aims and Relation to its Contemporary Theology*. NHMS 56. Leiden: Brill.

Plinval, Georges de

1934. "Recherches sur l'oeuvre littéraire de Pélage." *Revue de philologie, de littérature et d'histoire anciennes*, ser. 3, vol. 8, 9–42.

1943. *Pélage: Ses écrits, sa vie et sa réforme. Étude d'histoire littéraire et religieuse*. Lausanne, Genève, Neuchatel, Vevey, Montreux, Berne, and Bâe: Librairie Payot.

1947. *Essai sur le style et la langue de Pélage suivi du traité inédit* De induratione cordis pharaonis (*Texte communiqué par* Dom G. Morin). Collectanea friburgensia, Nouvelle série, Fasc. 31. Fribourg: Librairie de l'Université.

Polotsky, Hans Jakob; Böhlig, Alexander
1940. *Kephalaia*. 1. Hälfte, Lieferung 1–10, mit einem Beitrag von Hugo Ibscher. Manichäische Handschriften der staatlichen Museen zu Berlin. Stuttgart: W. Kohlhammer.

Rees, Brinley Roderick
1988. *Pelagius: A Reluctant Heretic*. Woodbridge: The Boydell Press.
1991. *The Letters of Pelagius and his Followers*. Woodbridge: The Boydell Press.

Refoulé, François
1963. "Duration du premier concile de Carthage contre les Pélagiens et du *Libellus fidei* de Rufin." *Revue d'Études Augustiniennes* 9, 41–49.

Richardson, Ernest Cushing (ed.)
1896. Hieronymus *Liber de viris inlustribus*. Gennadius *Liber de viris inlustribus*. Texte und Untersuchungen zur Geschichte der altchristlichen Literatur XIV,1. Leipzig: J.C. Hinrichs'sche Buchhandlung.

Schwartz, Edvard
1924–1926 *Concilium universale Ephesenum* edidit Edvardus Schwartz. Acta Conciliorum Oecumenicorum V,1. Berlin and Leipzig: De Gruyter.

Smith, Alfred J.
1918. "The Latin Sources of the Commentary of Pelagius on the Epistle of St Paul to the Romans. Part II." *The Journal of Theological Studies* 20, 55–65.
1929. "Pelagius and Augustine". *The Journal of Theological Studies* 31, 21–35.

Souter, Alexander
1906. *The Commentary of Pelagius on the Epistles of Paul: The Problem of its Restoration*. [from *Proceedings of the British Academy* 11]. London: Published for the British Academy by Henry Frowde, Oxford University Press.
1910. "Another New Fragment of Pelagius." *The Journal of Theological Studies* 12, 32–35.
1926. *Pelagius's Expositions of Thirteen Epistles of St Paul*. II: *Text and Apparatus Criticus*. Cambridge: Cambridge University Press.

TeSelle, Eugene
1972. "Rufinus the Syrian, Caelestius, Pelagius: Explorations in the Prehistory of the Pelagian Controversy." *Augustinian Studies* 3, 61–95.

Teske, Roland J.
1997. *Answer to the Pelagians: The Punishment and Forgiveness of Sins and the Baptism of Little Ones, The Spirit and Letter, Nature and Grace, The Perfection of Human Righteousness, The Deeds of Pelagius, The Grace of Christ and Original Sin, The Nature and Origin of the Soul*. Translated by Roland J. Teske. Edited by John E. Rotelle. The Works of Saint Augustine I, 23. New York: New City Press.

Thier, Sebastian
1999. *Kirche bei Pelagius*. Patristische Texte und Studien 50. Berlin & New York: Walter de Gruyter.

Urba, Karl F.; Zycha, Joseph
1902. "De gestis Pelagii." *Sancti Aureli Augustini De perfectione iustitiae hominis, De gestis Pelagii, De gratia Christi et de peccato originali libri duo, De nuptiis et concupiscentia ad Valerium comitem libri duo* recensuit Carolus F. Urba et Iosephus Zycha. CSEL XLII. Prague, Vienna and Leipzig: F. Tempsy & G. Freytag, 49–122.
1902a. "De gratia Christi et de peccato originali." *Sancti Aureli Augustini De perfectione iustitiae hominis, De gestis Pelagii, De gratia Christi et de peccato originali libri duo, De nuptiis et concupiscentia ad Valerium comitem libri duo* recensuit Carolus F. Urba et Iosephus Zycha. CSEL XLII. Prague, Vienna and Leipzig: F. Tempsy & G. Freytag, 123–206.
1913. "De natura et gratia." *Sancti Aureli Augustini Opera (sect. VIII pars I): De peccatorum meritis et remissione et de baptismo parvulorum ad Marcellinum libri tres, De spiritu et littera liber unus, De natura et gratia liber unus, De natura et origine animae libri quattuor, Contra duas epistulas Pelagianorum libri quattuor* ex recensione Caroli F. Urba et Iosephi Zycha. CSEL LX. Vienna and Leipzig: F. Tempsy & G. Freytag, 231–300.

Verheijen, Lucas
1981. Sancti Augustini *Confessionum* libri XIII. Edidit Lucas Verheijen. Corpus Christianorum, series latina; XXVII. Sancti Augustini Opera. Pars I, 1. Turnhout: Brepols.

Wermelinger, Otto
1975. *Rom und Pelagius: Die theologische Position der römischen Bischöfe im pelagianischen Streit in den Jahren 411–432*. Päpste und Papsttum 7. Stuttgart: Anton Hiersemann.
1989. "Neuere Forschungskontroversen um Augustinus und Pelagius." Cornelius Mayer & Karl Heinz Chelius (eds.), *Internationales Symposion über den Stand der Augustinus-Forschung vom 12. bis 16. April 1987 im Schloß Rauischholzhausen der Justus-Liebig-Universität Gießen*. Cassiacum XXXIX/1. "Res et Signa": Gießener Augustinus-Studien 1. Würzburg: Augustinus-Verlag, 189–217.

Zangemeister, Carl
1882. "Liber apologeticus." *Pauli Orosii Historiarum adversum paganos libri vii accedit eiusdem Liber apologeticus* recensuit et commentario critico instruxit Carolus Zangemeister. CSEL V. Vienna: Apud C. Geroldi Filium Bibliopolam Academiae, 601–664.

15

Evodius of Uzalis and the Development of Manichaeism in Roman North Africa

Aäron Vanspauwen

Abstract

This chapter examines part of the development of North African Manichaeism, with a specific focus on *Aduersus Manichaeos*, an anti-Manichaean treatise attributed to Evodius of Uzalis. Evodius, a friend of Augustine of Hippo, probably wrote *Aduersus Manichaeos* in the years 420–425. Thus, the treatise constitutes an important source on North African Manichaeism, written two decades after the major anti-Manichaean works of Augustine. A preliminary section discusses Evodius' sources. Unlike Augustine, he was not a former member of the Manichaean movement, and his *Aduersus Manichaeos* lacks the insiders' knowledge of Augustine's treatises. Nevertheless, it will be argued that Evodius had prepared himself thoroughly in order to write his anti-Manichaean treatise. The subsequent section offers an overview of *testimonia* on the Manichaean canon in the Latin world. These *testimonia* seem to suggest that—over time—the North African Manichaeans held one particular letter of Mani, the *Epistula fundamenti*, in high esteem. The concluding section briefly addresses the genre, status, contents and circulation of Mani's letter.

1   Introduction

Mani conceived his teachings as being universal, intended to bring the religions of earlier prophets to fulfilment. His prophetic self-awareness went hand in hand with his missionary intentions. Mani himself already preached his teachings outside the borders of the Sasanian Empire, and he would appoint missionaries to do the same. Because Mani's teachings did not contradict but rather fulfilled the essence of other religions, Manichaean missionaries were receptive of local religious traditions. In the Roman Empire, Manichaeism manifested itself as a dualistic Christian movement.

This paper focusses on a rather neglected anti-Manichaean work, namely the treatise *Aduersus Manichaeos* (also known as *De fide contra Manichaeos*) attributed to Evodius of Uzalis, a friend of Augustine.[1] Evodius was born in Thagaste (present-day Souk Ahras, Algeria) between 354 and 365, and ordained bishop of Uzalis (El Alia, Tunisia) at the end of the fourth century. The circumstances of his death are unknown. His latest known activities can be dated to 426.[2] The treatise *Aduersus Manichaeos* was probably written in the years 420–425.[3] Thus, it represents a source on Manichaeism in the third decade of the fifth century, two decades after Augustine's latest anti-Manichaean treatises *De natura boni* and *Contra Secundinum*. The paper will address three aspects of Evodius' *Aduersus Manichaeos* and its significance as a testimony on Latin Manichaeism. The first section treats the sources of Evodius, or the question to which extent he was familiar with Manichaeism when he wrote his anti-Manichaean treatise. The second section will offer an overview of *testimonia* to the development of the Manichaean canon in the Latin West. The third and final section focuses on Mani's *Epistula fundamenti*.

2   The sources of Evodius

For the preparation of his anti-Manichaean treatise, Evodius primarily relied on written sources.[4] Unlike Augustine, he was not a former member of the Manichaean Church, and hence he was not as intimately familiar with Manichaeism as Augustine was. Evodius does give the impression that—prior to writing the treatise—he had held discussions with the Manichaeans.[5] Confronted with the presence of Manichaeans in his diocese of Uzalis, he responded by writing his anti-Manichaean treatise. The addressees of his work are the Manichaeans, whom Evodius attempts to convert to Catholic Christianity. For many of his arguments, he was indebted to Augustine's works.

The range of Augustinian works Evodius seems to have known is impressive. Although he does not explicitly mention his friend Augustine as a source,

---

1   This paper is partly based on my doctoral dissertation "In Defence of Faith, against the Manichaeans. Critical Edition and Historical, Literary and Theological Study of the Treatise *Aduersus Manichaeos*, Attributed to Evodius of Uzalis" (KU Leuven, May 2019).
2   On the life of Evodius, see Féliers 1964, pp. 1–34; Mandouze et al. 1982, pp. 366–373.
3   The proposed dating of *Aduersus Manichaeos* relies on the following two assumptions: First, that it could be influenced by Augustine's treatise *Contra aduersarium legis et prophetarum* (419–420). Second, that Evodius wrote his anti-Manichaean treatise before his *Epistula ad Valentinum* (425–426). On this letter, see Duval 2003.
4   When referring to passages from *Aduersus Manichaeos*, I make use of chapter and line number of Vanspauwen 2018. Prior to this edition is Zycha 1892, pp. 951–975.
5   See, for example, *Adu. Man.* 20,1: *dictum est a quodam*: "it was said by someone".

his treatise *Aduersus Manichaeos* contains many reminiscences to Augustine's *De moribus ecclesiae catholicae* and *De moribus Manichaeorum, De uera religione, Contra Fortunatum, Contra epistulam quam uocant fundamenti, De agone christiano, Contra Faustum, Contra Felicem, De natura boni, Contra Secundinum,* and *Contra aduersarium legis et prophetarum*.[6] The similarities between *Aduersus Manichaeos* and the just mentioned Augustinian works suggest that Evodius had first studied these sources thoroughly before writing his own anti-Manichaean treatise. Nevertheless, Evodius knew more of Manichaeism than what can be found in Augustine's works. For example, he is the only Latin author who mentions the Manichaean doctrines of the "Third Messenger" (*tertius legatus*) and of Mani's "twin" (*geminus*). Since he could not have found these Manichaean teachings in Augustine's works, he must have consulted other sources as well.

Evodius probably had access to a Greek polemical (anti-Manichaean) text. His use of the term *ingenitus* in the description of the Manichaean principle of darkness resembles the Greek ἀγένητος ("unbegotten") rather than its usual meaning in Latin ("innate"). This use of ἀγένητος is attested in several Greek polemical texts, such as the *Acta Archelai*, Epiphanius' *Panarion* and Titus of Bostra's *Contra Manichaeos*.[7] It is possible that Evodius would have encountered the Manichaean notion of the "Third Messenger" in one of these works. The term appears in both the *Acta Archelai* and the *Panarion*.[8] A brief discussion on the circulation of Greek anti-Manichaica in the Latin world is in order.

In his *De haeresibus* (and in his epistolary correspondence with Quodvultdeus of Carthage, addressee of *De haeresibus*), Augustine refers to one of the sources he consulted, the heresiologist Epiphanius and his summary of heresies. However, scholars have pointed out that Augustine's source was not the *Panarion* itself, but rather the *Anacephaleoses*, which are summaries of the *Panarion*'s contents.[9] The fifth *Anacephaleosis* discusses the Manichaeans, but does not offer information on the third messenger.[10] Put differently, if one were to assume Evodius found the doctrine of the "Third Messenger" in the *Panarion*—for which we have no clear evidence—Evodius would have had the complete work in his possession, unlike Augustine. In the same corre-

---

6   I discuss Evodius' sources in greater detail in the fifth chapter of my doctoral dissertation "In Defence of Faith, Against the Manichaeans." For the sake of brevity, I will not compare parallel passages from *Adu. Man.* and its potential sources here.
7   See the overview in Clackson/Hunter/Lieu 1998, p. 28 and the comparative material in Poirier/Pettipiece 2017, pp. 143–144, n. 2.
8   Clackson/Hunter/Lieu 1998, p. 44.
9   See van Oort 2000, pp. 452–453.
10   Ps-Epiphanius, *Anacephaleosis* v; ed. Holl/Dummer 1985, p. 5, l. 10–15.

spondence with Quodvultdeus, Augustine also mentions the Latin heresiologist Filastrius of Brescia. His overview of heresies, the *Diuersarum hereseon liber*, does not appear to have influenced Evodius. What is interesting about Filastrius' anti-Manichaean section, however, is his testimony on the *Acta Archelai*.[11] Thus, at the very least, the *Acta Archelai* were known to Filastrius. Finally, Jerome, whom Augustine and Evodius knew, also mentions several anti-Manichaean Greek writers in his *De uiris illustribus*. These authors are "Archelaus" (of the *Acta Archelai*), Serapion of Thmuis, and Titus of Bostra.[12]

The previous paragraph offers some indications on the extent to which Greek anti-Manichaean writings were known in the Latin world. Such evidence proves that Evodius *could* have read one of these writings, but does not prove whether he did consult any of these works, and which he would have consulted specifically. Alternatively, Evodius may have discovered the Manichaean doctrines of the "Third Messenger" (and of Mani's "twin") in one of the Manichaean sources from which he cites. Finally, he could have also heard these terms from oral communication with or about Manichaeans, although this final claim is difficult to substantialize.

The author of *Aduersus Manichaeos* quotes from two of Mani's writings, namely the *Epistula fundamenti* and the *Thesaurus*. Before Evodius, Augustine had already cited from these works. Although Evodius is often indebted to Augustine's citations,[13] two indications suggest that he consulted both works himself. First, Evodius also cites passages which are not attested in Augustine's oeuvre. Second, he offers information on the two writings which Augustine did not provide. In particular, Evodius gives indications on the structure of both the *Epistula fundamenti* and the *Thesaurus*. As he is able to situate his citations within the whole of these works, he had probably consulted copies of both works in their entirety.[14]

---

11 Filastrius, *Diuersarum hereseon liber* LXI,4: *Qui ab Archelao sancto episcopo in disputatione superati, abiecti atque notati, manifestati sunt uniuersis in illo tempore*; ed. Heylen 1957, p. 243, l. 11–13.

12 Jerome, *De uiris illustribus* LXXII.XCIX.CII; ed. Richardson 1896, p. 40, l. 10–16; p. 47, l. 22–27; p. 48, l. 23–26.

13 Cf., for example, the citations of a part of Mt 12:33, a fragment of *Acts* attributed to Leucius, and a fragment of Mani's *Thesaurus* in *Adu. Man.* 5 and in Aug., *C. Fel.* 11,4–6 (ed. Zycha 1892, p. 831, l. 26–p. 833, l. 17).

14 For the *Ep. fund.*, see *Adu. Man.* 12, 13–15: *Dicit enim in fine ipsius epistulae, unde unum capitulum iam posuimus*: "For he says at the end of his epistle, of which we already put forward one chapter". For the *Thes.*, see *Adu. Man.* 5,11: *Nam sic in secundo* Thesauri *libro dicit*; *Adu. Man.* 13,5–6: *Hoc in primo libro* Thesauri *eorum scriptum est*; *Adu. Man.* 14,1–2: *Qualis interea turpitudo, quam in eodem* Thesauro *suo inter cetera turpia in septimo libro scribit*.

A fourth category of sources comprises the apocryphal *Acts* attributed to Leucius. Evodius is familiar with the *Acts of John* and the *Acts of Andrew*. In the 38th chapter of *Aduersus Manichaeos*, he summarizes two passages from the *Acts of Andrew*. His paraphrases of these passages mirror some of their original wording. It is possible that Evodius read the *Acts of Andrew* in their original Greek form.[15] For the citation from one of these *Acts* in the fifth chapter of his treatise, it would appear likely that he simply reproduces the citation he had found in Augustine's *Contra Felicem*.[16]

In sum: the treatise *Aduersus Manichaeos* was the result of Evodius' thorough study of available sources. He read many of Augustine's anti-Manichaean works and also consulted a Greek anti-Manichaean text, two of Mani's writings, and the apocryphal *Acts of John* and *Acts of Andrew*. On several occasions, Evodius gives information on Manichaeism which does not have parallels in Augustine's oeuvre. Given the range of sources Evodius consulted, he seems to be a more or less reliable witness regarding Manichaeism as it had spread in Roman North Africa.

3 A development of the Manichaean canon in the Latin West?

Lists of Manichaean writings are preserved in various regions and in various languages. Most scholars agree that seven works of Mani, all originally written in Syriac, constitute the core of the Manichaean canon. These works are, in more or less usual order: (1) the *Living Gospel*; (2) the *Treasury of Life* (*Thesaurus*); (3) the *Pragmateia*; (4) the *Book of Mysteries*; (5) the *Book of* (*the*) *Giants*; (6) a collection of *Epistles*; (7) Mani's *Psalms* and *Prayers*.[17] In eastern Manichaeism, the Middle Persian work *Šābuhragān* is often added, usually after the *Gospel*.[18] Finally, though not part of Mani's written works, the *Book of Pictures* or *Icon* is also attested in almost all regions where Manichaeism was diffused.[19] Local Manichaean communities also introduced innovations with regard to the canon. The Coptic *Kephalaia*, for example, lists the canon

---

15 A Latin summary of the *Acts of Andrew* by Gregory of Tours has been preserved. This summary derived from a Latin translation of the entire *Acts of Andrew*. It cannot be excluded that Evodius would have made use of a similar Latin version, even though he was likely able to read the *Acts of Andrew* in its Greek form. See Prieur 1989, p. 8.
16 Compare, *Adu. Man.* 5,5–9 and Aug., *C. Fel.* 11,6 (ed. Zycha 1892, p. 833, l. 13–17).
17 Tardieu 1980, pp. 45–67; van Oort 2002, pp. 732–734; Wurst 2005, pp. 242–243; Reeves 2011, pp. 90–94; Baker-Brian 2011, p. 67.
18 Reeves 2011, p. 98.
19 On Mani's *Book of Pictures*, see Gulácsi 2016.

of Mani's works as a pentateuch.[20] In Roman (Latin) North Africa, the Manichaean Felix appears to have had a (different) collection of five of Mani's works in his possession.[21] In this overview, the discussion on the Manichaean canon will primarily focus on Mani's primary works, even though the Manichaeans did not adhere exclusively to Mani's own works. For example, they accepted mainstream Christian scripture and wrote new texts themselves.

Sources on the Manichaean canon in the Latin world, predating Evodius' *Aduersus Manichaeos*, are an anti-Manichaean treatise attributed to Marius Victorinus and many of Augustine's works, in particular his *Confessiones* and his anti-Manichaean treatises. In *Ad Iustinum Manichaeum*, Ps-Marius Victorinus briefly refers to two Manichaean writings: the *Thesaurus* and the *Acts of Andrew*.[22] Evodius quotes from both works, yet he likely did not consult *Ad Iustinum Manichaeum* when preparing his anti-Manichaean treatise.

The extent to which Augustine had access to Manichaean scripture as a Manichaean Hearer has been the subject of some scholarly discussion.[23] In any case, the value of his testimony on the Manichaean canon cannot be overstated. In the *Confessiones*, he reports that the Manichaeans made use of many large books.[24] One of these books could be Mani's *Book of Pictures*, to which he would have referred with the words *phantasmata splendida*, among others.[25] He also states that he sang Manichaean songs,[26] and in his *Contra Faus-*

---

20 See Pettipiece 2009, pp. 45–46.209. See also Tardieu 1980, p. 66.
21 See Augustine, *C. Fel.* I,14: [*Felix dixit:*] ... *si adtuleris mihi scripturas Manichaei, quinque auctores, quos tibi dixi* ...: "[Felix said:] ... if you bring me the writings of Mani—the five authorities that I mentioned to you"; ed. Zycha 1892, p. 817, l. 17–18; trans. Teske 2006, p. 290.
22 *Ad Iustinum Manichaeum* I: *quod Manichaeus, et ut is Andreas actibus eloquitur, atque Thesauro reuelauit*; ed. *Patrologia Latina* 8, c. 999.
23 See, for example, Coyle 2011, pp. 49–50; van Oort 2008b, pp. 441–448.
24 See van Oort 2008b, p. 448, citing Aug., *Conf.* III,6,10: *et libris multis et ingentibus*; ed. Verheijen 1981, p. 31, l. 13–14.
25 Van Oort 2010, p. 510 refers to Aug., *Conf.* III,6,10: *Et apponebantur adhuc mihi in illis ferculis phantasmata splendida, quibus iam melius erat amare istum solem saltem istis oculis uerum quam illa falsa animo decepto per oculos*: "and all they set before me were dishes of glittering myths. It would have been more profitable to love the sun in the sky, which at least our eyes perceive truly, than those chimeras offered to a mind that had been led astray through its eyes"; ed. Verheijen 1981, p. 31, l. 19–22; trans. Boulding 1997, p. 81. Gulácsi (2016, pp. 51–52), however, is not convinced this term refers to Manichaean pictorial art. Recently, van Oort (2020) readdressed this question, and argued, rather convincingly, on the basis of the same passage from *Conf.*, that Mani's *Book of Pictures* was in use among the Manichaeans Augustine knew.
26 Aug., *Conf.* III,7,14: *et cantabam carmina*: "And I sang verses"; ed. Verheijen 1981, p. 34, l. 49; trans. van Oort 2013, p. 35, n. 106.

tum he—in all likelihood accurately—summarizes the account of one such songs, the "song of the lovers."[27] Augustine testifies that one of Mani's letters, the *Epistula fundamenti*, was being read during Manichaean gatherings.[28] He describes this letter as being very well known among the Manichaeans.[29] He also states that Mani's other letters began in a way similar to the *Epistula fundamenti*.[30] At the end of his treatise *De moribus Manichaeorum* he refers to another Manichaean letter, the so-called *Rule of Life*.[31] One allusion from *Contra Faustum* seems to suggest that Augustine could have been familiar with Mani's *Gospel*:

> But why do you not rather think of the great impudence with which you call those long and wicked myths of yours the gospel? What good news is announced in them, after all, where God is said to have been unable to look out for and care for his own kingdom against I know not what rebellious, opposing, and alien nature otherwise than by sending a part of his own nature into its hungry jaws to be devoured and polluted so that, after

---

27   Aug., *C. Faust.* xv,5: *annon recordaris amatorium canticum tuum, ubi describis maximum regnantem regem, sceptrigerum perennem, floreis coronis cinctum et facie rutilantem? quem si solum talem amares, erubescendum tibi esset; nam etiam uir unus floreis coronis cinctus pudicae coniugi displiceret*: "Or do you not recall your love song, in which you describe the sovereign king in his reign, the everlasting sceptre-bearer, girded with crowns of flowers and ruddy of face? If you loved one such lover, you ought to be ashamed. For a chaste wife would not be pleased by one husband girded with crowns of flowers"; ed. Zycha 1981, p. 425, l. 4–8; trans. Teske 2007, p. 189. See Lieu 1992, pp. 170–171; van Oort 2008b, p. 460.

28   Aug., *C. ep. fund.* 5: *ipsa enim nobis illo tempore miseris quando lecta est, illuminati dicebamur a uobis*: "When it was read to us poor wretches at that time, you said that we were enlightened"; ed. Zycha 1981, p. 197, l. 8–10; trans. Teske 2006, p. 236.

29   Aug., *C. ep. fund.* 25: *sed istas ipsas, de quibus nunc agitur, epistulae fundamenti, quae fere omnibus, qui apud uos illuminati uocantur solet esse notissima*: "But I mean the very words from the *Letter of the Foundation* which we are now discussing and which all of you who are called 'enlightened' know very well"; ed. Zycha 1981, p. 224, l. 21–28; trans. Teske 2006, p. 253.

30   Aug., *C. ep. fund.* 6: *certe si nihil interesse arbitratus est, cur non uarie in aliis epistolis apostolum Christi se nominat, in aliis, paracleti? sed Christi semper audiui, quotienscumque audiui, paracleti autem nec semel*: "For, if Paul thought that it made no difference, why does he not call himself in various ways an apostle of Christ in some letters and in others an apostle of the Paraclete? But I have always heard 'an apostle of Christ' as often as I heard it, but I have never heard 'an apostle of the Paraclete'"; ed. Zycha 1981, p. 199, l. 25–p. 200, l. 2; trans. Teske 2006, p. 239. Aug., *C. Faust.* xiii,4: *omnes tamen eius epistulae ita exordiuntur*: Manichaeus apostolus Iesu Christi: "Yet *all* his letters begin as follows: 'Mani, an apostle of Jesus Christ'"; ed. Zycha 1981, p. 381, l. 4–5; trans. Teske 2007, p. 160.

31   Cf. Lieu 1981, pp. 153–155. Van Oort 2010, p. 518.

such great labours and torments, it could not even be wholly purified? Is such bad news the gospel?[32]

In the same work Augustine also alludes to the contents of the *Epistula fundamenti* and the *Thesaurus*.[33] He would quote both works throughout his later anti-Manichaean works, such as *Contra epistulam fundamenti*, *Contra Felicem*, *De natura boni* and *Contra Secundinum*.

One testimony from Augustine's anti-Manichaean corpus deserving particular attention is Felix's pentateuch. This collection is mentioned in Augustine's *Contra Felicem*, i.e. in the minutes of a public debate between Augustine and the Manichaean 'doctor' Felix. Five works of Mani had been confiscated from Felix. Of these five works, only the first two are mentioned by name: the *Epistula fundamenti* and the *Thesaurus*.[34] If the order of works reflects the relative

---

[32] Aug., *C. Faust.* 11,6: *sed cur non potius cogitatis, quanta impudentia prolixas illas et impias fabulas uestras euangelium nominetis? quid enim illic boni annuntiatur, ubi dicitur deus aduersus rebellem nescio quam contrariam alienamque naturam non aliter regno suo potuisse prospicere atque consulere, nisi partem suae naturae in illius auidas fauces deuorandam mitteret, atque ita polluendam, ut post tantos labores atque cruciatus non posset saltem tota purgari? itane tam malus nuntius euangelium est?*; ed. Zycha, 1981, p. 260, l. 27–p. 261, l. 8; trans. Teske 2007, pp. 75–76.

[33] Augustine paraphrases a passage from the *Ep. fund.* (fr. 8, l. 1–2 in Stein 2002) in *C. Faust.* XXI,16 (ed. Zycha 1981, p. p. 589, l. 27–28); additionally, in the same work he frequently summarizes the Manichaean "seduction of the archons," which Augustine would later cite from the *Thes.*, and alludes to the terminology of a fragment of the *Thes.* which Evodius would cite later. For the seduction of the archons, see Augustine, *C. Faust.* XV,7 (ed. Zycha 1891, p. 431, l. 4–12); *C. Faust.* XX,6 (ibid., p. 540, l. 20–p. 541, l. 3); *C. Faust.* XX,8 (ibid., p. 543, l. 27–p. 544, l. 6); *C. Faust.* XXII,98 (ibid., p. 704, l. 19–22). For the terminology of the *Thes.*, see *C. Faust.* XVIII,7: *quippe quem dicitis, ne sua membra illius impetu capta et uastata conspiciat, uelum contra se posuisse*: "You of course say that he set a veil before his eyes so that he might not see his own members captured and devastated by the attack of that nation"; ed. Zycha 1891, p. 496, l. 6–7; trans. Teske 2007, p. 235; *C. Faust.* XXII,12: *quandoquidem deus eorum cum membra sua mersit in tenebras, uelum contra se posuit?*: "After all, when their God plunged his own members into the darkness, he set up a veil before his eyes"; ed. Zycha 1891, p. 600, l. 1–2; trans. Teske 2007, p. 303. Cf. Evodius, *Adu. Man.* 13,3–6: "*Velum contra se habet, qui dolorem eius temperet, ne corruptionem partis suae uideat. Hodie enim diuina quam commemorat substantia, subiacet genti tenebrarum, ut lutum figulo*". *Hoc in primo libro* Thesauri *eorum scriptum est*: "'he has a veil before himself, so he could soothe his pain, and so that he could not see the corruption of his own part. For today the divine substance which he mentions, is subject to the race of darkness like clay to a potter.' This is written in the first book of their *Treasure*".

[34] Aug., *C. Fel.* I,14: FEL. *dixit: Et ego, si adtuleris mihi scripturas Manichaei, quinque auctores, quos tibi dixi, quidquid me interrogaueris, probo tibi.* AUG. *dixit: De ipsis quinque auctoribus est ista epistula, cuius aperuimus principium et inuenimus ibi scriptum: Manichaeus apostolus Christi Iesu—et uideo, quia ipsum non mihi principium exponis, quia non probas, quo-*

importance of these works among the Manichaeans, then Felix's pentateuch is an interesting testimony to a development of the Manichaean canon. It would imply that the *Epistula fundamenti* was considered the most important work in North African Manichaeism. The second position of the *Thesaurus* corresponds to Manichaean canonical book lists elsewhere.

Evodius' *Aduersus Manichaeos* seems to corroborate the testimony of *Contra Felicem*. Evodius cites from two Manichaean writings, namely the *Epistula fundamenti* and the *Thesaurus*. Although he is aware that more works of Mani existed,[35] he does not name these works, nor does he cite from any of them. In the 36th chapter of his treatise, Evodius specifies the *Epistula fundamenti* as the "head" (*caput*) of all of Mani's stories.[36] This term could confirm the hypothesis that the *Epistula fundamenti* had become the most important Manichaean writing in Roman North Africa. The following section will address the contents and genre of the *Epistula fundamenti*.

First, however, it is necessary to consider another important *testimonium* on the Manichaean canon, sc. the *Decretum Gelasianum*. The *Decretum* is a sixth-century ecclesiastical document likely preserving fifth-century traditions. In its fifth section, it lists several 'forbidden' works. Some structure can be discerned in this list. For example, apocryphal *Acts* are grouped together, and the same also seems to be the case for Old Testament apocrypha. With regard to specifically Manichaean works, the list mentions "the book titled *Fundamentum*" and the *Thesaurus*.[37] Although the *Decretum Gelasianum* also lists a "Book of the giant Og," this book appears—together with the *Testament of Job* and the *Book of the Penitence of Adam*—among other Old Testament apocrypha and is thus likely a Jewish pseudepigraphical instead of the Manichaean *Book of Giants*.[38]

Felix's pentateuch, *Aduersus Manichaeos*, and the *Decretum Gelasianum* all three adduce Mani's *Epistula fundamenti* and *Thesaurus* as the two most important (or only known) Manichaean works. In comparison with the Manichaean canon of seven writings, or the range of works Augustine was familiar with, or compared to ecclesiastical documents from the Greek world,[39] this focus on

---

modo sit Manichaeus apostolus Iesu Christi. FEL. dixit: Si in ista non probo, in secundo probo. AUG. dixit: In quo secundo? FEL. dixit: In Thesauro; ed. Zycha 1892, p. 817, l. 17–27.

35   *Adu. Man.* 36,7: *uel in ceteris omnibus libris, in quibus* ...
36   *Adu. Man.* 36,4–6: *falsa omnia sunt quae Manichaeus dixit in* Epistula fundamenti, *quae caput est omnium uanarum fabularum*; "everything Mani says in his *Fundamental epistle*, the origin [lit. 'head'] of all their vain stories, is false".
37   *Decretum Gelasianum* v: *Liber qui appellatur Fundamentum, Liber qui appellatur Thesaurus*; ed. von Dobschütz 1912, p. 52, l. 284–285.
38   See also Lieu 1992, p. 118.
39   See Lieu 1983.

two texts is striking. At the very least, the sources demonstrate that the Latin church fathers were informed on the existence of only these two Manichaean writings. However, this focus could also suggest that the Manichaean canon had undergone a development in North Africa. In particular the first position of the *Epistula fundamenti* would be unique to North African Manichaeism.

4   The *Epistula fundamenti*

4.1   *Genre, content, and status*

Our initial question should be: What is the nature of the *Epistula fundamenti*?[40] A Manichaean work by this name is attested only in the Latin-speaking world, sc. in the anti-Manichaean works of Augustine and Evodius (and the *Decretum Gelasianum*). Hypotheses regarding this writing are many: it could be a handbook for initiates or a compendium of the Manichaean myth;[41] it could simply be one of Mani's authentic letters;[42] perhaps it could be identified with the written text that accompanied Mani's *Book of Pictures*.[43] Scholars have also attempted to identify the *Epistula fundamenti* with other Manichaean works, such as the *Kephalaia*[44] or Mani's *Gospel*.[45] Such identifications find support in parallels between the *Epistula fundamenti* and some of the aforementioned Manichaean works. An interesting complement to these hypotheses is that the *Epistula fundamenti* was not identical to, but did supplant Mani's *Gospel* in the Latin West.[46] This theory can be supported by the evidence in the Latin world and harmonizes with the hypotheses that the *Epistula fundamenti* was both a compendium of Manichaean teachings as well as an authentic letter of Mani. Alternative hypotheses hold that the *Epistula fundamenti* could have been a later epistolary redaction of one or more of Mani's works.[47]

---

40   Perhaps the most systematic attempt to formulate a response to this question had been undertaken in the unpublished doctoral dissertation Kaatz 2003, pp. 21–47.
41   Scopello 2001, pp. 216–217; Fox/Sheldon/Lieu 2010, p. 150.
42   This is the conclusion which Kaatz reached in his survey (Kaatz 2003, pp. 45–47). See also Gardner/Rasouli-Narimani 2017, pp. 83–84.
43   This hypothesis is suggested, for example, in van Oort 2008b, p. 450. Van Oort considers this possible identification an open question.
44   See Kaatz 2003, pp. 32–38 for a discussion (and rejection) of this hypothesis, and Scopello 2001, pp. 225–229 for several parallels between the two works.
45   Kaatz 2003, pp. 25–29; Gardner 2001, pp. 102–104.
46   This hypothesis has been addressed before by van Oort 2008b, p. 463, n. 101.
47   For example, Feldmann 1987, p. 34 suggests that the *Epistula fundamenti* contains elements which suggest it constituted a redaction of two originally separate letters.

Evodius and Augustine always refer to the work as a letter. As a consequence, Augustine could compare the *Epistula fundamenti* to other Manichaean letters. The letter has an addresser, namely Mani, and an addressee, Patticius (perhaps the same person as mentioned in Syriac as Patīg and in Arabic as Fatiq). The subject matter of the letter is the generation of Adam and Eve, though Mani also seems to have addressed the entirety of cosmic history, from the beginning to the end of time. In terms of writing style, the opening passage of the *Epistula fundamenti* displays parallels with a (possibly spurious) *Letter to Marcellus*, quoted in the *Acta Archelai*.[48] A passage from Augustine's *Contra Felicem* appears to describe a copy of the *Epistula fundamenti* in the form of a codex.[49]

The *Epistula fundamenti* was probably quite a long letter, perhaps comparable to Paul's Epistles to the Romans or Corinthians. The title *Epistula fundamenti* for one of Mani's letters appears to be unique for the Latin (North African) world. A (non-exhaustive) list of Mani's letters is preserved in Ibn al-Nadīm's *Fihrist*. Of these letters, the *Epistula fundamenti* might be identified with the *Long Epistle to Fatiq*.[50] Julian of Eclanum knew of a letter to "Patricius" (likely a misspelling of *Patticius*), which could be identified with the *Epistula fundamenti* as well.[51] If the letter to Patticius and the epistle to Fatiq are identical to the *Epistula fundamenti*, then it is remarkable that the African authors Augus-

---

48 Gardner 2007, pp. 41–42.
49 See Aug., *C. Fel.* I,1: *Et cum Augustinus episcopus epistulam Manichaei, quam Fundamenti appellant, protulisset, dixit: Si legero ex hoc codice, quem me uides ferre, epistulam Manichaei quam Fundamenti appellatis, potes agnoscere an ipsa sit? FEL. dixit: Agnosco. AUG. dixit: Accipe tu ipse et lege. Et cum accepisset codicem Felix, legit:* "And after Bishop Augustine had brought forth the letter of Mani known as *The Foundation*, he said: 'if I read from this book (*ex hoc codice*), which you see that I am carrying, the letter of Mani that you call *The Foundation*, can you recognize whether this is it?' Felix said: 'I recognize it.' Augustine said: 'Take it yourself and read.' And after Felix had taken the book, he read ..."; ed. Zycha 1892, p. 801, l. 10–16; trans. Teske 2006, p. 280. Two elements suggest that, at the very least in this case, the *Epistula fundamenti* encompasses an entire *codex*. First, Augustine is said to bring forth Mani's letter. Such phrasing implies that the *Epistula fundamenti* was identifiable as a physical object. Afterwards, Felix is also able to discern the letter from a certain distance: only after he identified it (see the use of *Agnosco*), he received the book from Augustine, so he could read from it. Second, Augustine employs an apposition, with the accusative *epistulam* [*Manichaei*] identifying the relative pronoun *quem* (which has, as its antecedent, *hoc codice*). The phrasing thus indicates that the letter is identical to the codex, and not part of the codex.
50 Al-Nadīm's list can be found, in translation, in Reeves 2011, pp. 115–119.
51 Harrison/BeDuhn 2001, p. 136, n. 38; Fox/Sheldon/Lieu 2010, p. 152; Gardner/Rasouli-Narimani 2017, p. 84.

tine and Evodius know the letter under the title *Epistula fundamenti*, yet Julian and Ibn al-Nadīm simply refer to it as a (long) epistle to Patticius/Fatiq.

The hypothesis that the *Epistula fundamenti* supplanted Mani's *Gospel* in the Latin Manichaean world is based on several observations. First, as mentioned before, the *Epistula fundamenti* is referred to as the first work in Felix's pentateuch and as the most important Manichaean text in *Aduersus Manichaeos*. In most Manichaean book lists, this first place is reserved for Mani's *Gospel*. Likewise, Augustine reports that the *Epistula fundamenti* was the most well-known of all of Mani's works. Second, the work seems to have performed a function similar to the *Gospel* during Manichaean gatherings, perhaps during the Bema feast. Its possible format as a single *codex* would be beneficial on these occasions. Usually, during these celebrations, Mani's *Gospel* was read to the community.[52] Although other texts could be read during the Bema festival as well (for example, some Bema psalms have been preserved), the *Epistula fundamenti* could at the very least have fulfilled the same role during Manichaean celebrations. In his *Contra epistulam fundamenti*, Augustine notes that the letter was read out loud during Manichaean gatherings, and was said to bring enlightenment to those who heard it.[53] The *Epistula fundamenti* seemingly fulfilled a (quasi-)liturgical function among the Manichaeans in North Africa. A similar development occurred in an eastern branch of Manichaeism with Mani's *Letter of the Seal*. According to Sogdian sources, this letter too was read during the Bema festival.[54]

In terms of content, the *Epistula fundamenti* contained several of the doctrines that were also part of Mani's *Gospel*. The Manichaean Felix described the *Epistula fundamenti* as containing "the beginning, the middle, and the end,"[55] a set of terms he also used to define Mani's teaching in general.[56] Similarly,

---

52   Tardieu 1980, p. 91; Baker-Brian 2011, p. 78.
53   Augustine, *C. ep. fund.* 5: *ipsa enim nobis illo tempore miseris quando lecta est, inluminati dicebamur a uobis*; ed. Zycha 1891, p. 197, l. 8–10. See van Oort 2013, pp. 79–80. Kaatz 2003, pp. 28–29.47 states explicitly that the *Ep. fund.* was read at the Bema festival, although he does not supply additional evidence in favour of this assumption.
54   See Gulácsi 2013, p. 248, n. 13. Reck 2009, pp. 225–226.
55   Hence Felix's description in Aug., *C. Fel.* II,1: *ista enim epistula Fundamenti est, quod et sanctitas tua bene scit, quod et ego dixi, quia ipsa continet initium, medium et finem*: "For there is the *Letter of the Foundation*, which Your Holiness knows well. I also said that it contains the beginning, the middle, and the end"; ed. Zycha 1892, p. 828, l. 23–25; trans. Teske 2006, p. 299.
56   Aug., *C. Fel.* I,9: *et quia uenit Manichaeus, et per suam praedicationem docuit nos initium, medium et finem; docuit nos de fabrica mundi, quare facta est et unde facta est, et qui fecerunt; docuit nos quare dies et quare nox; docuit nos de cursu solis et lunae*: "Because Mani came and by his preaching taught us about the beginning, the middle, and the end. He

Augustine described the *Epistula fundamenti* as containing almost everything the Manichaeans believed.[57] There are, in addition, several more specific similarities between preserved fragments of the *Gospel* and those of the *Epistula fundamenti*, although it must be admitted that the *Epistula fundamenti* has elements in common with other Manichaean texts too, such as the Coptic *Kephalaia* or a Coptic Manichaean psalm.[58] Preserved passages of the *Gospel* and the *Epistula fundamenti* demonstrate that the two works are clearly not identical.

Augustine's possible summary of Mani's *Gospel* (as discussed above) contains some details that parallel extant fragments of the *Epistula fundamenti*.[59] Additionally, Shahrahstānī, a twelfth-century Islamic author offers, some infor-

---

taught us about the making of the world, why it was made and whence it was made and who made it. He taught us why there is day and why there is night. He taught us about the course of the sun and the moon"; ed. Zycha 1892, p. 811, l. 12–16; trans. Teske 2006, p. 286.

57 Aug., *C. ep. fund.* 5: *Videamus igitur, quid me doceat Manichaeus, et potissimum illum consideremus librum, quem Fundamenti epistulam dicitis, ubi totum paene, quod creditis, continetur*: "Let us see, then, what Mani teaches me, and let us especially consider the book that you call *The Letter of the Foundation*, in which almost the whole of what you believe is contained"; ed. Zycha 1891, p. 197, l. 6–8; trans. Teske 2006, p. 236.

58 See Scopello 2001, pp. 225–229 and Lieu 1992, p. 170.

59 Compare the following citation from Augustine's *Contra Faustum* with preserved fragments of the *Epistula fundamenti*. Augustine, *C. Faust.* 11,662: *Sed cur non potius cogitatis, quanta impudentia prolixas illas et impias fabulas uestras euangelium nominetis? quid enim illic boni annuntiatur, ubi dicitur deus* **aduersus** *rebellem nescio quam contrariam alienamque naturam non aliter* **regno suo** *potuisse prospicere atque consulere,* **nisi** *partem suae naturae in illius auidas fauces deuorandam mitteret, atque ita polluendam, ut post tantos labores atque cruciatus* **non posset** *saltem* **tota** *purgari? itane tam malus nuntius euangelium est? certe omnes, qui graece uel tenuiter nouerunt, euangelium bonum nuntium aut bonam annuntiationem interpretantur. quomodo est autem iste bonus nuntius, quandoquidem ipse deus uobis uelo sibi opposito lugere nuntiatus est, donec sua membra ab illa* **uastatione** *et contaminatione reparentur atque purgentur? qui si aliquando luctum finierit, crudelis erit. quid enim de illo male meruit* **pars** *illa* **eius,** *quae* **in globo** *ligabitur? quae utique in aeternum lugenda est, quia in aeternum damnabitur. sed euasimus, quod istum nuntium quisquis diligenter aduerterit, non cogitur lugere, quia malus est, sed ridere, quia falsus est*; ed. Zycha 1891, p. 260, l. 27–p. 261, l. 18. Terms in bold also occur in extant fragments of the *Epistula fundamenti*. See *Ep. fund.*, fr. 3: *Lucis uero beatissimae pater sciens labem magnam ac* **uastitatem,** *quae ex tenebris surgeret,* **aduersus sua** *sancta impendere saeculae,* **nisi** *aliquod eximium ac praeclarum et uirtute potens numen opponat, quo superet simul ac destruat stirpem tenebrarum, qua extincta perpetua quies lucis incolis pararetur* (ed. Stein 2002, p. 68, l. 1–5); *Ep. fund.*, fr. 8,3: *Non igitur poterunt recipi in* **regna** *illa pacifica, sed configentur* **in** *praedicto horribili* **globo,** *cui etiam necesse est custodiam adhiberi. Vnde adhaerebunt his rebus animae eaedem, quas dilexerunt, reliciae* **in** *eodem tenebrarum* **globo** *suis meritis id sibi conquirentes* (ed. Stein 2002, p. 38, l. 9–12); Evodius, *Adu. Man.* 12,13–15: *Dicit enim in fine ipsius epistulae, unde unum capitulum iam posuimus, ipsam* **dei partem** *quae commixta est,* **non totam posse** *reuocari ad pristinam libertatem.*

mation about the contents of Mani's *Gospel* (and *Šhābuhragān*). His testimony contains two elements also attested in the *Epistula fundamenti*:

> Shahrahstānī, *Kitāb al-Milal wa al-Nihal*: "The sage Mănī in the first chapter of his *Jibilla* [*Gospel*] and in the beginning of the *Šhābuhragān* says that the Ruler of the World of Light is in all of His land: nothing is devoid of Him, and that He is both visible and concealed, and that He has no end apart from where His land ends at the land of His foe."[60]

The phrase "nothing is devoid of Him" is similar to the Latin *nullo indigente* of the *Epistula fundamenti*'s fragment 2.[61] The same fragment of the *Epistula fundamenti*, like Shahrahstānī's testimony, describes the kingdom of light and the kingdom of darkness, and refers to the border between the two kingdoms.[62]

To conclude, the extant evidence regarding both Mani's *Gospel* and his *Epistula fundamenti* indicates that the two works had some passages (or, at the very least, some phrases and concepts) in common. These similarities could further explain how this work may have supplanted the *Gospel* as the most important Manichaean text in the Latin West. Moreover, if the *Epistula fundamenti* would correspond in part to the contents of Mani's *Gospel*, then it might be possible that this Manichaean text would have been the source in which Evodius had discovered the notion of Mani's twin. A Greek fragment, which could belong to Mani's *Gospel*, contains the term σύζυγος.[63] Nevertheless, it should be noted that the term "twin" is also attested elsewhere.[64]

The prominence of the *Epistula fundamenti* in the Latin world appears to be an indication that Latin Manichaeism underwent some transformation at the turn from the fourth to the fifth century (or earlier). Whereas Augustine seems

---

60 See Reeves 2011, p. 97.

61 Cf. *Ep. fund.* 2,6: *nullo in regnis eius insignibus aut indigente*; ed. Stein 2002, pp. 22–24, l. 21–22. Fox/Sheldon/Lieu 2010, p. 9 translate this phrase as "in his splendid kingdoms [there is] no one who is poor." The verb *indigeo* can also mean "to be in want of," which seems to correspond with Reeves' translation "nothing is devoid of Him." The same fragment of the *Ep. fund.* also in *Adu. Man.* 11,2.

62 *Ep. fund.* 2,8: *iuxta unam uero partem ac latus illustris illius sanctae terrae erat tenebrarum terra profunda et immensa magnitudine, in qua habitabant ignea corpora, genera scilicet pestifera*: "Near the one section and side of that glorious and holy land, was situated the Land of Darkness, deep and of immeasurable extent; in it resided fiery bodies, pestilential beings"; ed. Stein 2002, p. 24, l. 24–26; trans. Fox/Sheldon/Lieu 2010, p. 9.

63 This fragment is preserved in the *Cologne Mani Codex*: ἐξαπέστειλεν ἐκεῖθεν σύζυγόν μου τὸν ἀσφαλέστατον: "he [God, the Father of Truth] sent from there my never-failing Syzygos"; ed. Koenen/Römer 1985, p. 136; trans. Fox/Sheldon/Lieu 2010, p. 3.

64 See, for example, Clackson/Hunter/Lieu 1998, p. 170.

to allude to Mani's *Gospel* and tells that he knew other letters of Mani's than the *Epistula fundamenti*, the situation seems to have changed afterwards. The *Epistula fundamenti* was singled out from Mani's letters and enjoyed a more authoritative status. Although our evidence is fragmentary and incomplete, there are no attestations of either Mani's *Gospel* or his other *Letters* in North Africa from the testimony of *Contra Felicem* onwards.

Finally, once again on the *Decretum Gelasianum*. The list refers to the *Epistula fundamenti* as a *Liber qui appellatur Fundamentum*. Two conclusions may be drawn from this reference, first on the form of the treatise (*liber*) and the second on its title (*fundamentum*). Above I suggested that the title *Epistula fundamenti* was an African innovation, whereas other authors knew the letter as a "letter to Patticius/Fatiq." The title as mentioned in the *Decretum Gelasianum* does not necessarily contradict this hypothesis, but is in accordance with the attestation that—after the Vandal invasion of North Africa—many Manichaean refugees fled to Italy.[65] These refugees would have brought their most important work, the *Epistula fundamenti*, with them. Secondly, the term *liber* might also reflect the material shape of the *Epistula fundamenti*, namely an independently circulating writing (possibly even as a *codex*), rather than its literary genre, an epistle. Alternatively, the term *liber* could indicate that its status as a handbook had become more significant than its origin as one of Mani's letters.

4.2   Circulation

The *Epistula fundamenti* circulated in several different copies in the Latin Manichaean world. First, Augustine stated that, when he was a Manichaean Hearer, the letter was being read during Manichaean gatherings or celebrations. When he paraphrases the Manichaean myth in *Contra Fortunatum*, his summary might have been based on a memory of these gatherings.[66] Second, when Augustine wrote his *Contra epistulam fundamenti*, he had an annotated copy of the letter in his possession.[67] Third, the *Epistula fundamenti* is reported

---

65   Cf. e.g. Lieu 1992, pp. 204–205; Schipper/van Oort 2000, p. 1.
66   See van Oort 2008a, pp. 118–121.
67   Aug., *Retr.* II,2: *Liber contra epistulam Manichaei quam uocant fundamenti principia eius sola redarguit; sed in ceteris illius partibus adnotationes ubi uidebatur adfixae sunt, quibus tota subuertitur et quibus commonerer, si quando contra totam scribere uacuisset*: "The book in answer to the letter of Mani known as *The Foundation* refutes only its beginnings. But, where it seemed appropriate, annotations were added to other parts of it that undermine the whole [letter] and that would serve as reminders if there were ever time to write

to be one of the works confiscated from the Manichaean Felix by civil authorities. During the debate with Felix, passages from this confiscated book were read. Fourth, Evodius quotes from the *Epistula fundamenti* on multiple occasions. Differences between his quotations and Augustine's suggest that Evodius had a copy of this writing in his possession. Fifth and finally, Julian of Eclanum quotes a brief passage from a letter to Patricius (or Patticius). This letter can probably be identified with the *Epistula fundamenti*, although the brief citation has no parallels in the works of Evodius or Augustine.

The aforementioned *testimonia* all concern Latin copies of the *Epistula fundamenti*. Put differently: When Augustine or Evodius cite from this letter, they cite from Latin translations which ultimately go back to Mani's Syriac original. The precise origins of the Latin *Epistula fundamenti* have not yet been subject to a separate study. One commonly held hypothesis assumes that Mani's writings reached the Latin world by means of a Greek intermediary translation.[68] However, discoveries from the Dakhleh oasis have demonstrated that Coptic-speaking Manichaeans in Egypt studied both Mani's Syriac as well as Latin.[69] It may well be possible that Manichaeans from the Latin world also studied Syriac in an attempt to translate Mani's writings directly into this language. A comparison between extant fragments of the Latin *Epistula fundamenti* may shed light on the manner in which the Manichaeans translated their authoritative texts.

Evodius cites from the *Epistula fundamenti* in five cases.[70] For three of these citations, (partial) parallels can be found in Augustine's works. Evodius' and Augustine's parallel citations display a strong uniformity. The textual variations mostly concern the use of synonyms or a slightly different choice of connectors. Two hypotheses could explain the textual variation in the extant fragments. First, the Latin fragments could descend from one authoritative Latin translation. In this case, the textual differences originated as errors in the textual transmission of Evodius' or Augustine's writings, or they can be attributed to the editorial activities of Augustine or Evodius. Second, and alternatively, the fragments of Augustine and Evodius may go back to independent translations

---

against all of it"; ed. Mutzenbecher 1984, p. 91, l. 3–6; trans. Teske 2010, p. 112. See also van Oort 2010, p. 513.

68 See, for example, Lieu 1992, p. 117.
69 Franzmann 2005; van den Berg 2010, pp. 41–42. Franzmann refers to the Kellis documents T. Kell. Syr./Copt. 1 and T. Kell. Syr./Copt. 2 (ed. Gardner *et. al.* 1996, pp. 115–126), whereas van den Berg cites from P. Kell. Copt. 20 (ed. Gardner/Alcock/Funk 1999, pp. 166–169).
70 *Adu. Man.* 5,15–29 (= *Ep. fund.*, fr. 8); *Adu. Man.* 7,1–2 (= *Ep. fund.*, fr. 9, l. 1); *Adu. Man.* 11,1–4 (= *Ep. fund.*, fr. 2, l. 21–24); *Adu. Man.* 11,4–8 (= *Ep. fund.*, fr. 3); *Adu. Man.* 28,5–7 (= *Ep. fund.*, fr. 7).

of the source text, either Syriac or Greek. My following observations, admittedly speculative, show how several textual variations in Latin may have their origins in the same Greek text.[71] In this regard the different concurrent Latin translations of the Greek New Testament (the *Vetus Latina*) constitute a corpus of comparative material.

Since Augustine's and Evodius' versions of the *Epistula fundamenti* are very similar, the Manichaean translator or (let us suppose) translators probably had a nearly identical model text in front of them, and tried to translate their model very faithfully, retaining the original syntax and word order as much as possible. Some of the variants in the fragments of the *Epistula fundamenti* may have originated as two different attempts to render the same Greek particle or connector into Latin. For example, the connectors *etiam* and *autem* in the same fragment[72] may be two different ways to translate a Greek particle such as δέ, which can express a contrast ("however," cf. *autem*), or introduce new information within a narrative ("furthermore," "also," cf. *etiam*).[73] Other, similar textual variations have parallels in Old Latin translations as well. One such example are the concurrent translations of the Greek καί by both *atque* and *et*.[74]

Another interesting variation consists of the participles *sciens* and *uidens* in the same fragment.[75] These participles may derive from a Greek participle of the verb εἶδον (inf. ἰδεῖν) ("to see"). The concepts of "seeing" and "knowing" are intertwined in this Greek verb (its perfect tense οἶδα/εἰδέναι means "to know"). The same variation (*sciens*—*uidens*) also occurs in the Old Latin translations of the New Testament. However, in these cases the Greek text itself may have read

---

71 Here we take into account only a hypothetical Greek *Vorlage*. Analysing the extant fragments of Latin Manichaean texts with a view to understanding their relationship to a possible Syriac *Vorlage* remains a scholarly desideratum.

72 *Adu. Man.* 11,2–3: *ita etiam fundata eiusdem splendidissima saecula*. Cf. Aug., *C. ep. fund.* 13: *ita autem fundata sunt eiusdem splendidissima regna*; ed. Zycha 1891, p. 209, l. 26–27.

73 Cf. the Old Latin translations of Lk 1:62: ἐνένευον δέ; ed. Nestle et al. 2012, p.182. This phrase is often translated as *adnuebant autem*, yet one Old Latin translation (*a*) has *adnuebant etiam* instead. See Jülicher 1938–1963, vol. 3, p. 12.

74 See 1 Pe 1:10: περὶ ἧς σωτηρίας ἐξεζήτησαν καὶ ἐξηραύνησαν; ed. Nestle et al. 2012, p. 697. In Old Latin translations, the connector καί has been translated as both *atque* and *et*. See Thiele 1956–1969, p. 78.

75 Aug., *C. Sec.* 20: *uidens magnam labem ac uastitatem aduersus sua sancta impendere saecula, nisi aliquod eximium ac praeclarum et uirtute potens numen opponeret*; ed. Zycha 1892, p. 935, l. 23–26. Cf., for example, Aug., *C. Fel.* 1,19: *Lucis uero beatissimae pater sciens labem magnam ac uastitatem, quae ex tenebris surgeret, aduersus sua sancta impendere saecula, nisi quod eximium ac praeclarum et uirtute potens numen opponat, quo superet simul ac destruat stirpem tenebrarum, qua exstincta perpetua quies lucis incolis pararetur*; ed. Zycha 1892, p. 824, l. 23–29.

either εἰδώς (*sciens*) or ἰδών (*uidens*).⁷⁶ It may be that the hypothetical Greek translation of the *Epistula fundamenti* circulated in at least two versions, or, if there was only one authoritative version, it may be that some Manichaean translators misread their Greek model.

It appears impossible to determine when these Latin versions originated. Augustine first alludes to the *Epistula fundamenti* in his *Contra Fortunatum* (392). During this debate, he probably referenced the text as he had heard or read it when he was a Manichaean Hearer in North Africa (373–382).⁷⁷ Hence, the only chronological information we have on the circulation of the *Epistula fundamenti* in North Africa, is that its oldest Latin translation would have been finished by the time Augustine joined the Manichaeans.

An alternative hypothesis deserves to be addressed here. Since Evodius was seemingly able to read Greek, he could have translated himself from a Greek exemplar of the *Epistula fundamenti*. If that should be the case, perhaps the similarities between Augustine's and Evodius' citations indicate that Evodius would have modelled his translations after the examples of Augustine. The differences would then indicate where Evodius wanted to correct Augustine's citations. Nevertheless, this hypothesis is not entirely satisfactory. It relies on the assumption that Evodius would have consulted a Greek rather than a Latin Manichaean source, and that such a Greek version of the *Epistula fundamenti* still circulated in North Africa. Not only does Evodius not give any such indication, the African Manichaeans' knowledge of Greek is also scarcely documented.

5 Conclusion

This paper has examined the development of Manichaeism in the Latin world, with particular attention to the information provided by Evodius' *Aduersus Manichaeos*. It was first necessary to address the question how well Evodius knew Manichaeism when he wrote his anti-Manichaean treatise. Since in all likelihood he was not as intimately familiar with Manichaeans as Augustine was, he seems to have primarily relied on studying Augustine's anti-Manichaean works as well as his own copies of Manichaean writings, (likely) one or

---

76 See, for example, Mk 12:15 (ed. Nestle et al. 2012, p. 154) and Mt 12:25 (ed. Nestle et al. 2012, p. 35), where the Greek manuscripts have either εἰδώς or ἰδών. Likewise, the Old Latin translations read either *sciens* or *uidens* in these passages. See Jülicher 1938–1963, vol. 2, p. 112 and ibid., vol. 1, p. 74 respectively.

77 See van Oort 2008a and the index in Decret/van Oort 2004.

even more Greek anti-Manichaean authors, and also the *Acts of John* and the *Acts of Andrew*. Having read these texts, Evodius would have been reasonably well informed about Manichaeism.

The Manichaean canon in North Africa seems to have undergone a certain development. One of Mani's letters received a more authoritative status and appears to have supplanted Mani's *Gospel* as the primary work. It might be possible that the Latin African community has first given the title *Epistula fundamenti* to this letter, which could have been known as the "(long) epistle to Patticius/Fatiq" elsewhere. The letter could have circulated as a single book. This pragmatic format would have allowed it to easily be carried around and read during Manichaean gatherings.

I also briefly examined the textual variation in fragments of the *Epistula fundamenti*. A comparison between Augustine's and Evodius' citations helped to clarify the manner in which the Manichaeans translated their texts. It is possible that the different versions of the *Epistula fundamenti* as reflected in the works of Evodius and Augustine go back to independent translations. The Manichaeans translated their models quite literally and faithfully. My comparison of several Latin fragments of the *Epistula fundamenti* with Old Latin translations of the Greek New Testament suggests (tentatively) that the Latin *Epistula fundamenti* could be translated from a Greek intermediary translation. This conclusion could imply that, when the Manichaeans settled in the Latin African world, they had brought a Greek version of this letter with them, which they translated and copied in a (very) careful manner.

Bibliography

Primary

Dobschütz, E. von (1912): *Das Decretum Gelasianum de libris recipiendis et non recipiendis*. Texte und Untersuchungen 38/4. Leipzig.

Gardner, I. et al. (eds.) (1996): *Kellis Literary Texts. Volume 1*. Dakhleh Oasis Project Monograph 4. Oxford.

Gardner, I. et al. (eds.) (1999): *Coptic Documentary Texts from Kellis. Volume 1*. Dakhleh Oasis Project Monograph 15. Oxford.

Heylen, F. (1957): "Filastrii episcopi Brixiensis diuersarum hereseon liber." In: *Eusebius Vercellensis, Filastrius Brixiensis, appendix ad Hegemonium, Isaac Iudaeus, archidiaconus Romanus, Fortunatianus Aquileiensis, Chromatius Aquileiensis*. CCSL 9. Turnhout, 207–324.

Holl, K./Dummer, J. (1985): *Epiphanius III. Panarion haer. 65–80, De fide*. Second edition. Berlin.

Jülicher, A. (1938–1963): *Itala. Das Neue Testament in altlateinischer Überlieferung*. 4 vols. Berlin.

Koenen, L./Römer, C. (1985): *Der Kölner Mani-Kodex. Abbildungen und diplomatischer Text*. Papyrologische Texte und Abhandlungen 35. Bonn.

Mutzenbecher, A. (1984): *Augustinus, Retractationum libri II*. CCSL 57. Turnhout.

Nestle, E. et al. (2012): *Novum Testamentum Graece*. 28th edition. Stuttgart.

Patrologia Latina 8 (1844). Paris.

Prieur, J.-M. (1989): *Acta Andreae*. CCSA 5–6. Turnhout.

Richardson, E.C. (1896): *Hieronymus liber de viris inlustribus, Gennadius liber de viris inlustribus*. Texte und Untersuchungen 14/1a. Leipzig, 1–56.

Stein, M. (2002): *Manichaica latina 2. Manichaei epistula fundamenti*. Papyrologica Coloniensia 27/2. Paderborn.

Thiele, W. (1956–1969): *Epistulae catholicae*. Vetus Latina Beuron 26/1. Freiburg.

Vanspauwen, A. (2018): "The anti-Manichaean Treatise *De fide contra Manichaeos*, Attributed to Evodius of Uzalis. Critical Edition and Translation." *Sacris Erudiri* 57, 7–116.

Verheijen, L. (1981): *Sancti Augustini confessionum libri XIII*. CCSL 27. Turnhout.

Zycha, J. (1891): *S. Aureli Augustini de utilitate credendi, de duabus animabus, contra Fortunatum, contra Adimantum, contra epistulam fundamenti, contra Faustum*. CSEL 25/1. Prague, Vienna, Leipzig.

Zycha, J. (1892): *S. Aureli Augustini contra Felicem, de natura boni, epistula Secundini, contra Secundinum, accedunt Euodii de fide contra Manichaeos et commonitorium Augustini quod fertur*. CSEL 25/2. Prague, Vienna, Leipzig.

Translations

Boulding, M. (1997): *The Confessions*. The Works of Saint Augustine I/1. Hyde Park, NY.

Teske, R. (2006): *The Manichaean Debate*. The Works of Saint Augustine I/19. Hyde Park, NY.

Teske, R. (2007): *Answer to Faustus, a Manichaean*. The Works of Saint Augustine I/20. Hyde Park, NY.

Teske, R. (2010): *Revisions*. The Works of Saint Augustine I/2. Hyde Park, NY.

Secondary

Baker-Brian, N.J. (2011): *Manichaeism. An Ancient Faith Rediscovered*. London.

Berg, J.A. van den (2010): *Biblical Argument in Manichaean Missionary Practice. The Case of Adimantus and Augustine*. NHMS 70. Leiden, Boston.

Clackson, S./Hunter, E./Lieu, S.N.C. (1998): *Dictionary of Manichaean Texts I. Texts from the Roman Empire (Texts in Syriac, Greek, Coptic and Latin)*. CFM, Subsidia II. Turnhout.

Coyle, J.K. (2001): "What did Augustine Know about Manichaeism When He Wrote

His Two Treatises *De moribus?*" In: Oort, J. van/Wermelinger, O./Wurst, G. (eds.), *Augustine and Manichaeism in the Latin West. Proceedings of the Fribourg-Utrecht Symposium of the IAMS*. NHMS 49. Leiden, Boston, 43–56.

Decret, F./Oort, J. van (2004): *Acta contra Fortunatum Manichaeum*. CFM, Series Latina II. Turnhout.

Duval, Y.-M. (2003): "Note sur la lettre d'Evodius à l'abbé Valentin d'Hadrumète (CPL 389)." *Revue des études augustiniennes* 49, 123–130.

Feldmann, E. (1987): *Die "Epistula Fundamenti" der nordafrikanischen Manichäer. Versuch einer Rekonstruktion*. Altenberge.

Féliers, J.-H. (1964): "Evodius d'Uzalis. Contribution à l'étude de l'église chrétienne d'Afrique du Nord au vème siècle" (unpublished doctoral dissertation, Université de Paris-Sorbonne, Paris).

Fox, G. (trans.)/Sheldon, J. (trans.)/ Lieu, S.N.C. (ed.) (2010): *Greek and Latin Sources on Manichaean Cosmogony and Ethics*. CFM, Subsidia VI. Turnhout.

Franzmann, M. (2005): "The Syriac-Coptic Bilinguals from Ismant el-Kharab (Roman Kellis). Translation Process and Manichaean Missionary Practice." In: Van Tongerloo, A./Cirillo, L. (eds.): *Il manicheismo. Nuove prospettive della ricerca*. Manichaean Studies 5. Turnhout, 115–122.

Gardner, I. (2001): "The Reconstruction of Mani's *Epistles* from Three Coptic Codices (Ismant el-Kharab and Medinet Madi)." In: Mirecki, P./BeDhun, J. (eds.): *The Light and the Darkness. Studies in Manichaeism and Its World*. NHMS 50. Leiden, Boston, 93–104.

Gardner, I. (2007): "Mani's Letter to Marcellus. Fact and Fiction in the *Acta Archelai* Revisited." In: BeDuhn, J./Mirecki, P. (eds.): *Frontiers of Faith. The Christian Encounter with Manichaeism in the Acts of Archelaus*. NHMS 61. Leiden, Boston, 33–48.

Gardner, I./Rasouli-Narimani, L. (2017): "Patīg and Pattikios in the Manichaean Sources." In: Lieu, S.N.C. et al. (eds.): *Manichaeism East and West*. CFM, Analecta Manichaica 1. Turnhout, 82–100.

Gulácsi, Z. (2013): "Chapter V: The Crystal Seal of '*Mani, the Apostle of Jesus Christ*' in the Bibliothèque nationale de France." In: Pedersen, N.A./Larsen, J.M. (eds.): *Manichaean Texts in Syriac: First Editions, New Editions, and Studies*. CFM, Series Syriaca I. Turnhout, 245–267.

Gulácsi, Z. (2016): *Mani's Pictures. The Didactic Images of the Manichaeans from Sasanian Mesopotamia to Uygur Central Asia and Tang-Ming China*. NHMS 90. Leiden, Boston.

Harrison, G./BeDuhn, J. (2001): "The Authenticity and Doctrine of (Ps.?) Mani's *Letter to Menoch*." In: Mirecki, P./BeDhun, J. (eds.): *The Light and the Darkness. Studies in Manichaeism and Its World*. NHMS 50. Leiden, Boston, 128–172.

Kaatz, K.W. (2003): "Augustine's *Contra Epistulam Fundamenti*. A Study of the *Epistula*

Fundamenti, Augustine's Knowledge of Manichaean Cosmogony and His Response to this *Epistula*, with Commentary" (unpublished doctoral dissertation, Department of Ancient History, Division of Humanities, Macquarie University, Sydney).

Kaatz, K.W. (2005): "What did Augustine Really Know about Manichaean Cosmogony?" In: van Tongerloo, A./Cirillo, L. (eds.): *Il manicheismo. Nuove prospettive della ricerca*. Manichaean Studies 5. Turnhout, 191–201.

Lieu, S.N.C. (1981): "Precept and Practice in Manichaean Monasticism." *Journal of Theological Studies* 32, 153–173.

Lieu, S.N.C. (1983): "An Early Byzantine Formula for the Renunciation of Manichaeism. The *Capita VI contra Manichaeos* of ⟨Zacharias of Mytilene⟩." *Jahrbuch für Antike Christentum* 26, 152–218.

Lieu, S.N.C. (1992): *Manichaeism in the Later Roman Empire and Medieval China*. Second edition. Wissenschaftliche Untersuchungen zum Neuen Testament 63. Tübingen.

Mandouze, A. et al. (1982): *Prosopographie de l'Afrique chrétienne (303–533)*. Prosopographie chrétienne du Bas-Empire 1. Paris.

Oort, J. van (2000): "Augustine on Heresy. Mani and Manichaeism in *De haeresibus*. An Analysis of *haer*. 46,1." In: Emmerick, R.E. et al. (eds.): *Studia Manichaica. IV. Internationaler Kongreß zum Manichäismus, Berlin, 14.–18. Juli 1997*. Berichte und Abhandlungen der Berlin-Brandenburgischen Akademie der Wissenschaften, Sonderband 4. Berlin, 451–463.

Oort, J. van (2002): "Manichäismus." In: Betz, H.D. et al. (eds.): *Die Religion in Geschichte und Gegenwart*. Fourth edition. Band V. Tübingen, 732–741.

Oort, J. van (2008a): "Heeding and Hiding their particular Knowledge? An Analysis of Augustine's Dispute with Fortunatus." In: Fuhrer, T. (ed.): *Die christlich-philosophischen Diskurse der Spätantike*. Philosophie der Antike 28. Stuttgart, 113–121.

Oort, J. van (2008b): "The Young Augustine's Knowledge of Manichaeism. An Analysis of the *Confessiones* and Some Other Relevant Texts." *Vigiliae Christianae* 62, 441–466.

Oort, J. van (2010): "Manichaean Christians in Augustine's Life and Works." *Church History and Religious Culture* 90, 505–546.

Oort, J. van (2013): *Jerusalem and Babylon. A Study of Augustine's* City of God *and the Sources of his Doctrine of the Two Cities*. Supplements to Vigiliae Christianae 14. Second edition. Leiden, Boston.

Oort, J. van (2020): "What Did Augustine See? Augustine and Mani's *Picture Book*." *Augustiniana* (forthc.).

Pettipiece. T. (2009): *Pentadic Redaction in the Manichaean* Kephalaia. NHMS 66. Leiden, Boston.

Poirier, P.-H./Pettipiece, T. (2017): *Biblical and Manichaean Citations in Titus of Bostra's* Against the Manichaeans. *An Annotated Inventory*. Instrumenta Patristica et Mediaevalia 78. Turnhout.

Reck, C. (2009): "A Sogdian Version of Mani's *Letter of the Seal*." In: BeDuhn, J. (ed.): *New

Light on Manichaeism. Papers from the Sixth International Congress on Manichaeism. NHMS 64. Leiden, Boston, 225–239.

Reeves, J.C. (2011): *Prolegomena to a History of Islamicate Manichaeism.* Sheffield.

Schipper, H.G./Oort, J. van (2000): *Sancti Leonis magni romani pontificis sermones et epistulae. Fragmenta selecta.* CFM, Series Latina I. Turnhout.

Scopello, M. (2001): "L'*Epistula fundamenti* à la lumière des sources manichéennes du Fayoum." In: Oort, J. van/Wermelinger, O./Wurst, G. (eds.), *Augustine and Manichaeism in the Latin West. Proceedings of the Fribourg-Utrecht Symposium of the IAMS.* NHMS 49. Leiden, Boston, 205–229.

Tardieu, M. (1980): *Le manichéisme.* Que sais-je? 1940. Paris.

Vanspauwen, A. (2019) "In Defence of Faith, against the Manichaeans. Critical Edition and Historical, Literary and Theological Study of the Treatise *Aduersus Manichaeos*, Attributed to Evodius of Uzalis" (unpublished doctoral dissertation, Faculty of Theology and Religious Studies, KU Leuven, Leuven).

Wurst, G. (2005): "L'état de la recherche sur le canon manichéen." In *Le canon du Nouveau Testament. Regards nouveaux.* Le monde de la Bible 54. Geneva, 237–267.

16

The 'Children' of the Manichaeans: Wandering Extreme Ascetics in the Roman East Compared

Rea Matsangou

Abstract

This chapter investigates how and why in both legal and ecclesiastical sources ascetic groups such as the Encratites and the Messalians are associated with the Manichaeans, as well as the way these ascetics are treated by the state and church authorities. The ultimate aim of the research is to answer the question: what does this link (made by the sources) reveal about the Manichaeans of the Roman East?

In modern scholarship it has been supported that this connection did not actually exist, but only served the rhetoric of the authorities against anarchist asceticism. However, this paper—taking into account (1) that these ascetics shared a series of common features (practices, beliefs behind the practices, and lifestyle) with the Manichaeans; (2) the emphasis of the sources that some of these features have been established by Manichaean leaders; and (3) the organized character of the Manichaean movement in contrast to the anarchist and irregular character of these ascetic groups—argues that the answer to the question whether the 'Manichaean' features of the Messalian or Encratite portrait were a heresiological construction or reflect a Manichaean influence upon anarchist Christian asceticism (as the sources imply) is not one-dimensional. A possible interpretation need not exclude the others.

1 Introduction

In Greek anti-Manichaica and in Roman imperial legislation the Manichaeans are often associated or even identified with several other ascetic groups, namely the Encratites, the Apotactites, the Hydroparastates, the Saccophori, and the Messalians. This paper, aiming to shed light on the profile of east-Roman Manichaeans, investigates what exactly these ascetics meant in the eye of state and church authorities, as well as their relationship with Manichaeans.

The paper will first examine how these ascetics are treated by and associated with Manichaeans by ecclesiastical authors, church synods and imperial laws, and then will point out the similarities or differences, some highlighted by the aforementioned sources, between these ascetics and Manichaeans. Encratites, Apotactites, Hydroparastates, and Saccophori will be considered as one case while Messalians as another. Each of these cases will be examined separately. In the last section, some concluding remarks will be made, bringing together the data for both groups of ascetics as well as the analysis and the discussion.*

2 Encratites, Apotactites, Hydroparastates, Saccophori

In the early 380s Theodosius I launched his anti-heretic campaign with three laws against Manichaeans and four 'groups' of ascetics, namely, Encratites, Apotactites, Hydroparastates, Saccophori (from now onwards: Encratites group). Actually, the aim of the first law (381) was not the Encratites group but the Manichaeans who were hiding behind the names of these ascetics. Indeed, as the law declares, the Manichaeans "desire themselves to be denominated Encratites, Apotactites, Hydroparastates or Saccophori", because these names functioned protectively for Manichaeans, since they denoted "approved faith" and a "rather chaste course of life".[1]

The laws' stance towards the Encratites group changed dramatically in less than a year, as shown by the two subsequent laws (382, 383). The Encratites group now were persecuted alongside the Manichaeans as independent religious groups. According to the revised imperial rationale of the law of 382, both Manichaeans and the Encratites group comprised a "factory" of false doctrines and practices and for this reason were subjected to the penalties imposed by the previous law (against Manichaeans).[2] In the third law the heretics of the day, i.e. those who disagreed with Nicene Triadology (Eunomians, Arians, Macedonians, Pneumatomachians), were added to the Manichaeans and the Encratites group.[3] How can this change of the attitude of the law towards the Encratites group be interpreted?

---

*   I would like to thank Professor Johannes van Oort for his patience and support during the preparation of this paper.
    Where English translations of ancient texts are available, I use them (see Bibliography). Where I have modified them, this is noted. Unless otherwise indicated, translations are mine. Most of the ancient texts in Greek were obtained through *TLG*.

1   *CTh* 16.5.7 (381).
2   *CTh* 16.5.9 (382). Apotactites were not included in the law of 382.
3   *CTh* 16.5.11 (383).

Laws against Manichaeans were not Theodosius' innovation. Diocletian, Valens, Valentinian I, and Gratian had preceded him.[4] The Encratites group, however, became the target of the law for the first time, and the reason for this seems to be their connection with Manichaeans. Yet, one could argue—reversing the cause-and-effect relationship—that the Encratites group were associated with the Manichaeans in order to be persecuted.[5] In any case, important is to note, that the Encratites group after the first wave of persecutions by Theodosius I do not reappear in later laws (except Hydroparastates who are found again in the laws of 428 and 438),[6] while the Manichaeans are persistently persecuted. In addition, their common appearance in the Theodosian laws seems to have been the result of a long discussion that was going on for decades between ecclesiastical authorities (culminating in the 370s–380s), and in which the Manichaeans were systematically associated with various ascetic groups (mainly the Encratites).

The Arian Julian (fourth cent.) is among the first authors who connect Manichaeans and pseudo-Encratites (as he calls them) by attributing to both convictions such as that the human body is evil and food is poisonous (αἱ τροφαὶ φαῦλαι).[7] The discourse concerning the Encratites took off and the testimonies linking them with Manichaeans became frequent during the 370s.

The most detailed description of the Encratites is provided by Epiphanius in his *Panarion* (374–377). The first feature Epiphanius attributes to them is a dualistic worldview. They say, as he states, that "there are certain first principles and that the ⟨power⟩ of the devil [...] is not subject to God; he has power of his own and acts as in his own right [...] For they do not agree with the Church, but differ from its declaration of truth".[8] As Epiphanius points out further on, Encratites speak about "different first principles" (ἀρχαὶ διάφοροι) instead of "one Godhead" (μιᾶς θεότητος).[9] Epiphanius then focuses on their everyday practices. "They

---

4   See Diocletian's rescript in Adam 1954, 82–84; Valens' and Valentinian's I edict in *CTh* 16.5.3 (372); Gratian's decree (378/379) in Socrates *HE*: 5.2.1–8 and Sozomenus *HE*: 7.1.3. Cf. Beskow 1988, 6–11, 6.
5   As Caner (2002, 85) argues, "groups totally unrelated in time or place become assimilated under specific heretical labels (e.g., Apotactites, Encratites) simply because their ascetic practices appear similar, or they become linked to specific heretical leaders (e.g., the "heresiarchs" Tatian, Mani), despite the lack of any demonstrable connection".
6   *CTh* 16.5.65(428)= *CJ* 1.5.5; *NTh* 3.1.9(438).
7   Julianus, *comm. Job* 67.8.
8   Epiphanius, *Pan.* 47.1.4 (Williams 2013, 3 modified): Φάσκουσι δὲ καὶ οὗτοι ἀρχάς τινας εἶναι τήν τε τοῦ διαβόλου (216) ⟨δύναμιν⟩ [...] μὴ ὑποτασσομένου θεῷ, ἀλλὰ ἰσχύοντος καὶ πράττοντος ὡς κατὰ ἰδίαν ἐξουσίαν [...] οὐ γὰρ κατὰ τὴν ἐκκλησίαν λέγουσιν, ἀλλὰ ἄλλως παρὰ τὸ τῆς ἀληθείας κήρυγμα.
9   Epiphanius, *Pan.* 47.2.1.

regard meat as an abomination—though they do not prohibit it for the sake of continence or as a pious practice, but from fear" lest they "be condemned for eating animate beings". "They do not drink wine at all", because they "claim that it is of the devil". "They declare that marriage" serves the Devil's plan.[10] "They pride themselves on supposed continence, but all their conduct is risky. For they are surrounded by women, deceive women in every way, travel and eat with women and are served by them".[11] "As scriptures they use principally the so-called Acts of Andrew, and of John, and of Thomas, and certain apocrypha". They use selectively these texts from the Old Testament whereby the patriarchs (Noah, Lot, etc.), whom they call drunkards, misbehaved under the influence of wine.[12] Two things in particular seem to astonish Epiphanius: (1) that though the heresy was ancient (he dates them to the time of Tatian, considering them his successors), during his days "their numbers are increasing" especially in Pisidia and Phrygia Compusta but also in Asia, Isauria, Pamphylia, Cilicia and Galatia, and (2) that his contemporary Encratites have been 'planted' even in big cities such as Rome and Antioch.[13]

The fact that in the area of Antioch, among the many other monastic communities, Encratites' communities also existed is confirmed by John Chrysostom. The target of one of his homilies addressed to the monks and hermits around Antioch was the Manichaeans and their leaders (ἀρχηγετῶν τούτων), the Encratites, the Marcionites, and the "whole factory" (καὶ παντὸς αὐτῶν τοῦ ἐργαστηρίου) of those apostates from faith, who prevent marriage and abstain from food.[14] Two remarks are necessary at this point. First, it is interesting that Chrysostom refers to their leaders only in the case of the Manichaeans. Second, at about the same time that Chrysostom delivered his sermon, two laws

---

10   Epiphanius, *Pan.* 47.1.6–7 (Williams 2013, 4 modified): τὸν δὲ γάμον σαφῶς τοῦ διαβόλου ὁρίζονται· ἔμψυχα δὲ βδελύσσονται, ἀπαγορεύοντες οὐχ ἕνεκεν ἐγκρατείας οὔτε πολιτείας, ἀλλὰ κατὰ φόβον καὶ ἰνδαλμὸν τοῦ μὴ καταδικασθῆναι ἀπὸ τῆς τῶν ἐμψύχων μεταλήψεως. κέχρηνται δὲ καὶ αὐτοὶ μυστηρίοις δι' ὕδατος· οἶνον δὲ ὅλως οὐ μεταλαμβάνουσι, φάσκοντες εἶναι διαβολικὸν ...

11   Epiphanius, *Pan.* 47.3.1: Σεμνύνονται δὲ δῆθεν ἐγκράτειαν, σφαλερῶς τὰ πάντα ἐργαζόμενοι, μέσον γυναικῶν εὑρισκόμενοι καὶ γυναῖκας πανταχόθεν ἀπατῶντες, γυναιξὶ δὲ συνοδεύοντες καὶ συνδιαιτώμενοι καὶ ἐξυπηρετούμενοι ὑπὸ τῶν τοιούτων.

12   Epiphanius, *Pan.* 47.1.5, 47.2.3–4. Epiphanius (47.2.3) also accuses Encratites of using the NT as it suits them. They even discredit Paul "calling him a drunkard" (τοῦτον μεθυστὴν καλοῦντες) when they disagree with his ideas.

13   Epiphanius, *Pan.* 47.1.2–3.

14   Chrysostom, *Hom. 1 Tim.* (PG 62:557.47–50): Περὶ Μανιχαίων, καὶ Ἐγκρατιτῶν, καὶ Μαρκιωνιστῶν, καὶ παντὸς αὐτῶν τοῦ ἐργαστηρίου τὰ τοιαῦτά φησιν, ὅτι ἐν ὑστέροις καιροῖς ἀποστήσονταί τινες τῆς πίστεως; 558.27–30: Οὐ περὶ Ἰουδαίων λέγει ταῦτα· [...] ἀλλὰ περὶ Μανιχαίων, καὶ τῶν ἀρχηγετῶν τούτων.

against Manichaeans were issued, the content of which reveals an interplay between the rhetoric of church leaders and the language of the law. The first was that of 382, where the term 'factory' for Manichaeans and the Encratites group was also used.[15] The second was another law issued in 383, against the apostates to Manichaeism, Judaism, and paganism.[16] Possibly, this was not a coincidence; Chrysostom's discussion of apostates, which reflects a fear of Manichaean influence on other groups of ascetics, could have been one of the reasons that triggered the promulgation of the law.

Encratites were also associated with Manichaeans by Amphilochius of Iconium (fourth cent.; metropolis of Lycaonia). In his most extensive work, entitled *On False Asceticism* (or *Contra haereticos*) and targeting the Encratites, Amphilochius appears to consider the Manichaeans as mentors of the Encratite 'false' practices. Interestingly he explains that these Manichaean ascetic practices (adopted by the Encratites) were ordained by the Manichaean leaders. As he characteristically says:

> They abstain from eating animate beings (ἐμψύχων) according to the teaching of Manichaeans. Because their leaders have ordained, once and for all, to abstain from eating animate beings (ἐμψύχων), because of the impiety that dwells in them, and have said at the same time that things that grow from the earth have a soul too.[17]

From the above excerpt the following observations can be made: (1) the institutionalized and organized character of Manichaean ascesis and discipline is denoted. For the second time, Manichaean leaders are mentioned in the discourse associating Encratites with Manichaeans; (2) the presumed influence of Manichaean ascetic practices to non-Manichaean ascetics is clearly stated; (3) the inter-connection between ascetic practices and 'heretical' ideas is obvious. These ascetics did not eat animate beings, not because they avoided killing living creatures, but "because of the impiety that dwells in them". In addition, they considered all plants as living beings.

As it appears from Amphilochius' correspondence with Basil of Caesarea, there were many ascetics such as Encratites, Hydroparastates and Catharoi in the region of Lycaonia, and the young Amphilochius needed the guidance of

---

15 *CTh* 16.5.9.1(382).
16 *CTh* 16.7.3(383).
17 Amphilochius, *c. haer.* 1067–1071: πάντων τῶν ἐμψύχων (ἀπέχονται) κατὰ τὴν διδασκαλίαν τῶν ἀκαθάρτων Μανιχαίων. Ἐκείν⟨ων γ⟩ὰρ ⟨οἱ⟩ ἔξαρχοι ἅπαξ νομοθετήσαντες ἐμψύχων ἀπέχεσθαι διὰ τὴν ἐνοικοῦσαν ἐν αὐτοῖς ἀσέβειαν, καὶ τὰ φυόμενα ἐκ τῆς γῆς ἔμψυχα εἶπον.

Basil in order to deal with various challenging pastoral issues. One of these issues was the peculiar baptism of the Encratites. It is noteworthy that while Basil initially (374) (though hesitantly) suggested that their baptism could be accepted, just a year later he changed his mind. As he argues in his letter of 375, the Encratites, Saccophori and Apotactites have to be re-baptized since their sect is an offspring of the Marcionites and other similar heretics, who abhor marriage, abstain from wine, and consider God's creation polluted.[18] Presumably, the expression "similar heretics" included the Manichaeans, since in contemporary literature they were always grouped together with the Marcionites.

Irrefutable witness to the presence of Encratites in the above areas (especially in Pisidia or Lycaonia), as well as of their intense confrontation with the Catholics in the 370s, are two Encratite burial monuments found in Laodicea Combusta and dating to 375.[19] The first tomb, according to its inscription, belonged to Elafia, a deaconess of the religion of the Encratites (Ἐλαφία διακόνισσα τῆς Ἐνκρατῶν θρισκίας). On the burial 'doorstone' of the second tomb, the following provision was engraved: "And if any of the wine-bibbers intrudes (a corpse), he has to deal with God and Jesus Christ".[20] From the above burial inscriptions the following can be deduced: (1) the members of this religious community self-identified as Encratites; thus the appellation 'Encratites' is used as an autonym and not as a label *ab extra*; (2) they called their movement a religion distinguishing it from that of the Catholics (independent self-understanding); (3) they had women active in the class of deaconesses.[21] The second inscription, in addition, confirms Epiphanius' testimony about the nickname 'drunkards' used by Encratites for the Catholics, and reveals the size of their controversy. It sounds like the last word of an Encratite in the debate with the Catholics engraved in eternity.

In spite of the bishops' polemic, it seems that these ascetic practices were adopted by an ever growing number of ascetics. According to Macarius of Magnesia (fourth to fifth cent.), "children of Manichaeans" (Μανιχαίων παῖδες) who are self-proclaimed with names difficult even to pronounce (Encratites, Apotactites and Hermits) mushroomed everywhere in Pisidia, Cilicia, Isauria, Lycaonia and Galatia,[22] i.e. in the same territories mentioned by Epiphanius.

---

18   Basil, *Epistles to Amphilochius* 188.1.63–69 and 199.47.1–16. Both Basil's letters (188 and 199) later became canons of the Church.
19   Some ancient authors situate Laodicea Combusta in Lycaonia (not the Laodicea of Frygia) and others in Pisidia, cf. Socrates, *HE* 6.18.
20   Calder 1929, 645–666.
21   Cecire 1985, 175. Cf. Quispel 1985/2008, 356–360.
22   Macarius, *Apocriticus* 3.151.25–28 (§ 25): Τοιοῦτοι δὲ Μανιχαίων παῖδες ἐξεφοίτησαν· τοιαύτας

"Μανιχαίων παῖδες" literally means Manichaean children, but in our context it could also be translated as the followers/disciples/servants of the Manichaeans, or ascetics who adopt Manichaean practices and attitudes. For Macarius, as for Chrysostom, these ascetics were not Christians but apostates from faith. They abstained from foods and held marriage to be illegal.[23] Macarius also speaks about a certain Dositheus of Cilicia, a leader among them, and about eight books he possessed, by means of which he strengthened his doctrines:

> At the head of their chorus doubtless stands Dositheus, a Cilician by race, who confirms their teaching in the course of eight whole books, and magnifies his case by the splendour of his language, saying again and again that marriage is an illegal act, and quite contrary to the law. Here are his words, "Through communion (*koinōnia*) the world had its beginning; through abstinence it has to be terminated."[24]

According to Goulet (the editor of the text), it is not easy to find out what Macarius presupposes as the historical or dogmatic relationship between Manichaeans, Encratites, and Dositheus. Most likely, so he suggests, Macarius does not consider that such ascetics (including Dositheus) were formally members of the Manichaean movement, but describes them as "Manichaean children" for their similarities with the latter.[25] Without disregarding Goulet's view, it is not unlikely that Macarius had in mind a closer relationship between Manichaeans and the above ascetics, since in his next book he points out that the Manichaean heresy is active and acquires followers "corrupting the *oikoumene*" up to his time.[26] In addition, although we know nothing about the eight books which Macarius claims that Dositheus had at his disposal and

---

αἱρέσεις ἡ τῶν Πισσιδ⸢έ⸣ων ἔχει καὶ τῶν Ἰσαύρων χώρα, Κιλικία τε καὶ Λυκαονία καὶ πᾶσα Γαλατία, ὧν καὶ τὰς ἐπωνυμίας ἐργῶδες ἀπαγγεῖλαι· Ἐγκρατηταὶ γὰρ καὶ Ἀποτακτῖται καὶ Ἐρημῖται καλοῦνται.

23 Macarius, *Apocriticus* 3.151.36–40 (§ 27); 3.151.29–31 (§ 25): οὐ Χριστιανοί τινες, [...] πίστεως μὲν εὐαγγελικῆς ἀποστάται καὶ ⸢ἀπόδημοι⸣.

24 Macarius, *Apocriticus* 3.151.32–36 (§ 26): Ἀμέλει Δοσίθεος ὁ κορυφαῖος παρ' αὐτοῖς, Κίλιξ τὸ γένος ὑπάρχων, δι' ὀκτὼ βιβλίων ὅλων κρατύνει τὸ δόγμα καὶ λαμπρότητι λέξεων μεγαλύνει τὸ πρᾶγμα, ἄθεσμον ἔργον καὶ λίαν παράνομον ἀποθρυλλῶν τὸν γάμον, λέγων· "Διὰ μὲν κοινωνίας ὁ κόσμος τὴν ἀρχὴν ἔσχε· διὰ δὲ τῆς ἐγκρατείας τὸ τέλος θέλει λαβεῖν". English translation by Grafer, modified: http://www.tertullian.org/fathers/macarius_apocriticus.htm#3_36.

25 Goulet 2003, 59–60.

26 Macarius, *Apocriticus* 4.184.8–11(3): Αὐτίκα γοῦν ὁ Μαν⸢ῆ⸣'ς ἐν Περσίδι τὸ ὄνομα τοῦ Χριστοῦ ὑποκρινάμενος πολλὴν μὲν σατραπείαν, πολλὴν δὲ τῆς ἀνατολῆς χώραν τῇ πλάνῃ διέφθειρε καὶ μέχρι τήμερον φθείρει λυμαντικοῖς ὑφέρπων τὴν οἰκουμένην σπέρμασιν.

through which he supported his doctrines,[27] the summary of Dositheus' teachings based on these books (as recorded by Macarius) and their number (eight) inevitably lead us to suspect a closer connection with Manichaeism.[28] Especially, the verbatim quotation of Dositheus' own words that: "Since this world (humanity) had its beginning through communion, it has to be terminated through abstinence" sounds very Manichaean. Dositheus' enigmatic statement can only be fully understood in the light of Manichaean cosmogony and eschatology (see below).

As may be noted, Encratites and Manichaeans are associated by our authors for their common disciplinary regimen (dietary rules and attitude towards marriage). The 'negative rites', as Émile Durkheim named such types of ascetic systems,[29] are common practices that religions share. Through them "individuals prepare themselves for contact with the sacred in 'positive rites'".[30] Such tendencies to self-negation have existed since the beginning of Christianity, from the apostle Paul's era, and earlier in the pagan world. Already from the mid-second century, before the appearance of Manichaeism, there were Encratite groups in the eastern provinces; Eusebius is the first one who mentions them.[31] Their practices initially were, *grosso modo*, within the limits of 'acceptability' for the church leaders,[32] although measures were occasionally taken to limit these practices. For instance, in 340 a synod held at Gangra of Paphlagonia condemned these ascetic practices in case their theoretical background was a theology directed against creation, or when the ascetic discipline was considered an end in itself.[33]

However, the discussion does not stop at practices as such, but our authors also provide the theological rationale on which these practices are grounded; thus, food is abominable because impiety dwells within it, plants have a soul, marriage is illegal because it prevents the end of the world, etc. These assumptions making the above practices meaningful are, according to our authors, of Manichaean origin. The latter is explicitly stated by Amphilochius.[34]

---

27 Goulet 2003, 60.
28 Lists of the titles of the books of the Manichaean canon are recorded in several Manichaean sources. Their number varies between five and seven or eight books (including the *Picture-Book*). Cf. Gardner and Lieu 2004, 151–156.
29 Durkheim 1915/1954, 299–414.
30 Beduhn 2000, 123.
31 Eusebius *HE* 4.28–29. Cf. Lössl 2021, 13 n. 53.
32 See for example the opinion of Dionysius of Alexandria in Basil's letters 188 and 199.
33 Joannou 1962, 85–99, esp. 89–96.
34 '[…] according to the teaching of Manichaeans. Because their leaders have ordained […]', see above.

It is well known that the Manichaeans (mainly the Elect) abstain from meat, meat products and wine, because they consider them full of matter, which in Manichaean cosmo-theory is identified with Evil.[35] The consumption of food with a high 'matter' content, almost inanimate such as meat, should be avoided, because its materiality, when consumed, is like reinforcing the dark (the material) side of the self; it is as if being added to the congenital evil forces within man. "Specifically, meat and wine were regarded as dominated by the dark elements that would re-infect the believer striving for personal purification and lead directly to sensuality and ignorance".[36] Materiality of foods, however, is the one side of Manichaean fasting (*seal of mouth*). The other one, which seems contradictory to the first, is that food contains light particles, and is based on the Manichaean assumption that divine substance (soul) is dispersed in all kinds of plant and animal life.[37] It is probable that Amphilochius' statement that "things that grow from the earth have a soul too" reflects this second dimension of Manichaean fasting, since the latter was criticized by many of his contemporary authors.[38]

The idea that marriage is an illegal and non-institutionalized act (ἄθεσμον ἔργον καὶ λίαν παράνομον), which ecclesiastical authors attribute to our ascetics, could also have had a Manichaean provenance (*seal of breast*). According to

---

[35] Manichaean fasting was a constant target of anti-Manichaean authors. See for instance: Titus of Bostra (*c. Manichaeos* 2.55.2–4): "Mani blames the fruits that come from the earth altogether as nourishment of matter". Chrysostom, *Hom. Matt.* 55 (PG 58:547.55): "Don't think that the Manichaeans abhor wheat as the result of a high philosophy, or that they have defeated gluttony. They fast because they have taken a loathing for God's creation". Augustine, *Haer.* 46.11 (Lieu 2010, 89). As Augustine (*c. Faust.* 30.5–6) points out, the "great difference" between the meaning of Catholic and Manichaean fasting is that—while the character of the former is "symbolic" and aims at "the mortification of the body"—the Manichaeans do not eat because they consider food "naturally, evil and impure" (NPNF[1] 4: 565–567).

[36] Gardner and Lieu 2004, 22.

[37] Both contradictory attitudes were meaningful according to the rationale of Manichaean discipline. As BeDuhn (2000, 230) points out: "Manichaeans erect walls between themselves and the world not just to flee its poison, but also to restrain themselves from harmful action upon its goodness".

[38] As Titus of Bostra (*c. Manichaeos* 2.61.1–4) characteristically comments, the Manichaeans accuse all those who kill animals in order to eat them, because they believe that the animals contain part of the divine soul. They say that the power of good is trapped within them. Cf. *Capita VII contra Manichaeos*, ch. 6 (Lieu 2010, 123); Basil of Caesarea, *Hom. Hexaem.* 8.1–15; Chrysostom, *Natal.* (PG 49:359): "Many heretics dare to bring down God's substance to even more despised beings". Manichaeans are doing the same "introducing the substance of God in dogs and apes and in beasts of all sorts (because as they argue the soul of all these beings originates from the same substance)".

the Manichaean myth, after the pre-cosmic mingling between Light (Good) and Darkness (Evil or Matter), two parallel processes counteracting each other are in progress. The purpose of the forces of Light is the pumping and liberation of the entrapped light (divine substance) from the material world and its dispatch back to the kingdom of Light; a procedure that would also lead to the gradual deconstruction of the cosmos (its drainage). The contrary target of the archons of Darkness is the perpetuation of the material world (Matter) through the continual creation of new bodies (procreation). Marriage, which is 'inextricably tied' to family and childbearing, was regarded as ensuring the success of Matter's plan. In the words of the pagan philosopher Alexander of Lycopolis, the Manichaeans "abstain from marriage and love-making and the begetting of children, lest, because of the succession of the race, the [divine] power should dwell in matter for a longer time".[39] Interpreting Dositheus' statement in a Manichaean perspective, he seems to claim that marriage is illegal because it counteracts the plan of the forces of Light, which is the deconstruction of this world.

Beyond the Manichaean provenance of disciplinary rationales, the emphasis of our authors that these sets of beliefs and practices have been established by Manichaean leaders indicates an additional concern: the organized character of the Manichaean movement in contrast to that of the Encratites group. Despite the self-identification 'Encratite religion' and their self-understanding as an independent religious group in opposition to the Catholics, it is most likely—as suggested by many scholars—that the Encratites group were not organized movements, "closed communities with distinct characteristics", but were "interchangeable names for irregular ascetic groups"[40] which adopted certain ascetic practices, as is revealed by their names: Encratites abstained from animal food and wine, and they condemned marriage; Apotactites renounced marriage and private property; Hydroparastates substituted water for wine in the Eucharist (abstaining from all other drinks but water); and Saccophori wore the sackcloth.

Lastly, apart from the aforementioned common features (practices and ideas) and the organized character of the movement, the Manichaeans used the same apocrypha, especially the Acts of Thomas. They also had women participating in the class of the Elect, who could assume missionary and teaching tasks. Yet, Manichaean women could not assume "any office or ministry which

---

39 Alexander, *Tract. Man.* 4.25–30: ἐπεὶ οὖν ἀπόλλυσθαι τὴν ὕλην ἐστὶ θεοῦ δόγμα, [...] ἀπέχεσθαι δὲ γάμων καὶ ἀφροδισίων καὶ τεκνοποιίας, ἵνα μὴ ἐπὶ πλεῖον ἡ δύναμις ἐνοικήσῃ τῇ ὕλῃ κατὰ τὴν τοῦ γένους διαδοχήν.

40 Beskow 1988, 8–11, esp. 9; Caner 2002, 85. Cf. Gregory 1991, 1350.

belonged to the official hierarchy".[41] Thus, while initially these ascetics were considered 'harmless' (although their practices were condemned), it seems that once they were associated with the Manichaeans, imperial and church leaders were alarmed.

3 Messalians

Right in the middle of the critical decade of the 370s, the Messalians, another ascetic group associated by anti-Manichaean authors with Manichaeism, emerges. As Theophanes the Confessor reports "the heresy of the Messalians, that is of the Euchites and Enthusiasts, sprouted up" during the reign of Emperor Valens (375/6).[42] Like the Encratites group, Messalians were mainly found in the central and southern provinces of Asia Minor (Lycaonia, Pamphylia, etc), and in the city of Antioch.[43]

Epiphanius is the first who provides a detailed description of their profile in his *Panarion*. He presents Messalianism as the most recent heresy of all; therefore it constitutes the last chapter of his book. While he begins his account stating that the Messalian heresy is "inconsistent in its doctrine", he then focuses only on their practices.[44] Their basic features as depicted by Epiphanius' report are the following: (1) they lack principles, leadership, the establishment of a name, or of an institution, or legislation; therefore, they are unstable and anarchist in every respect.[45] (2) Their prayer and fasting are also irregular. Wandering "in the open air" and within cities, "they spend their time in prayer and hymns".[46] Four centuries later, Theophanes adds a touch to their

---

41 Van Oort 2020, 499. See also van Oort 2020, 418–432 and 433–442. For a full treatment of women in Manichaeism, see Kristionat 2013.
42 Theophanes, *Chron.* 63.14–20.
43 Epiphanius (*Pan.* 80.1.3–3.1, 3.6) seems to differentiate the origins of the Messalians of Asia Minor and those of Antioch. Whereas, according to him, the motherland of the latter was Mesopotamia, he considers the former as successors of an earlier movement dated to the reign of Constantius II and called by him pagan Messalians. Cf. ACO 1.1.7, 117–118 (*Ephesenum anno 431*). For differing views on Messalianism, in general, and on when and where they appeared, see Caner (2002 esp. 84–85). About the many heretics who according to Epiphanius were found in Asia Minor, see Young 2006, esp. 244.
44 Epiphanius, *Pan.* 80.1.2.
45 Epiphanius, *Pan.* 80.3.3: νῦν καλούμενοι Μασσαλιανοί, ὧν οὔτε ἀρχὴ οὔτε τέλος οὔτε κεφαλὴ οὔτε ῥίζα, ἀλλὰ τὰ πάντα εἰσὶν ἀστήρικτοι καὶ ἄναρχοι καὶ ἠπατημένοι, μὴ ἔχοντες ὅλως στηριγμὸν ὀνόματος ἢ θεσμοῦ ἢ θέσεως ἢ νομοθεσίας.
46 Epiphanius, *Pan.* 80.3.2.

portrait stating that they "dance and rattle castanets while singing psalms".[47] (3) They "abandoned their homes" and their families under the pretence of the world's renunciation and they cohabit together, males and females.[48] (4) "In the summertime they sleep in the public squares, everybody together in a mixed crowd, men with women and women with men, because, as they say, they own no possession on earth. They show no restraint and hold their hands out to beg, as though they had no means of livelihood and no property".[49] (5) In this way, as Epiphanius comments, they made their life a public spectacle. Thus, even if they do not "have commerce with women as they profess", they provoke "by their silly, extravagant activity".[50] Elsewhere, however, he denotes that "vice or sexual misconduct" among them is probable, but states that he is unable to know it.[51] (6) The appearance of Messalians who, according to Epiphanius, had long hair, were beardless, and wore sackcloth, was outlandish. As Epiphanius stresses, these practices were also adopted by some Catholic monks in the Mesopotamian monasteries. However, as he points out, both the female hairstyle and the sackcloth were practices alien to the Catholic Church.[52]

Most of the aforementioned features (apart from the anarchist character) existed also in Manichaeism. The image of wandering Elect Manichaeans from city to city singing hymns is well known and testified by Manichaean sources, as is also the fact that there were women in the movement, and that they were able to climb to the rank of the Elect.[53] Aesthetics and dress code also played an important role in the movement. Indeed, as Epiphanius indicates, Manichaean men may have had long hair, which they called "the Glory of

---

47 Theophanes, *Chron*. 63.14–20: οὗτοι ψάλλοντες βαλλίζουσι καὶ κροταλίζουσι.
48 Epiphanius, *Pan*. 80.3.4: δοκοῦσι τοίνυν οὗτοι ἐπὶ τὸ αὐτὸ ἄνδρες τε καὶ γυναῖκες [...] λέγοντες, ὡς ἀποταξάμενοι τῷ κόσμῳ καὶ τῶν ἰδίων ἀνακεχωρηκότες.
49 Epiphanius, *Pan*. 80.3.4: ὁμοῦ δὲ ἀναμὶξ ἄνδρες ἅμα γυναιξὶ καὶ γυναῖκες ἅμα ἀνδράσιν ἐπὶ τὸ αὐτὸ καθεύδοντες, ἐν ῥύμαις μὲν πλατείαις, ὁπηνίκα θέρους ὥρα εἴη, διὰ τὸ μὴ ἔχειν, φησί, κτῆμα ἐπὶ τῆς γῆς. ἀκώλυτοι δέ εἰσι καὶ ἐκτείνουσι χεῖρας μεταιτεῖν ὡς ἀβίωτοι καὶ ἀκτήμονες.
50 Epiphanius, *Pan*. 80.8.4–6.
51 Epiphanius, *Pan*. 80.3.7.
52 Epiphanius, *Pan*. 80.6.5–7: οἱ αὐτοὶ τίμιοι ἡμῶν ἀδελφοί, οἱ κατὰ Μεσοποταμίαν ἐν μοναστηρίοις ὑπάρχοντες [...] κόμαις γυναικικαῖς ⟨χρῆσθαι⟩ προβαλλόμενοι καὶ σάκκῳ προφανεῖ ἐπερειδόμενοι [...] ἀλλότριον γάρ ἐστι τῆς καθολικῆς ἐκκλησίας σάκκος προφανὴς καὶ κόμη ⟨μὴ⟩ ἐκτεμνομένη [...].
53 Yet, although Manichaean women "had a significant position within the class of the Elect" "the higher positions, [...] in particular those belonging to the official hierarchy, were closed to them" (Van Oort 2020, 502).

God".[54] It is also possible that apart from the Saccophori and the Messalian monks, Manichaeans wore the sackcloth too.[55]

However, the feature that is the hallmark of both Messalians and Manichaeans, and is the main reason why Epiphanius connects them, is *argia*—the refusal to work—and its consequent begging.[56] What seems to be of primary importance for Epiphanius is that this "horrid" Manichaean custom of idleness had found supporters among certain simple-minded Catholic monks in the Mesopotamian monasteries, who, misinterpreting the evangelical command (Mt. 19:21) believed they should not work, should "⟨be⟩ idle and without occupation and [...] ⟨be like⟩ drones".[57] As Epiphanius states:

> Some of these brethren ⟨refrain from all mundane labor*⟩—as though they had learned this from the Persian immigrant, Mani, if I may say so. They have no business to be that way. The word of God tells us to mark such people, who will not work.[58]

Whoever was against manual labour was considered to have certainly learned it from the Manichaeans.[59]

Over the next few decades, a series of local synods (Antioch, Side, and Constantinople) follows which condemned Messalianism as heretical, and which might have been triggered by the account of Epiphanius. The most important was the synod convened at Side of Lycaonia (in the 380s or 390s),[60] which was presided over by Amphilochius.[61] Next, Messalianism was condemned by the Ecumenical Council of Ephesus in 431. According to the synodal *acta*, which

---

54 Epiphanius, *Pan.*, 66.54.4.
55 Cf. Lieu 1981, 166.
56 Epiphanius, *Pan.* 80.7.5, 3.4.
57 Epiphanius, *Pan.* 80.4.1–2: [...] ⟨εἶναι⟩ ἀργὸν [...] ἄεργον καὶ ἀκαιροφάγον, [...] ⟨ἐοικέναι⟩ τῷ κηφῆνι τῶν μελισσῶν.
58 Epiphanius, *Pan.* 80.4.3: τινὲς δὲ τῶν προειρημένων ἀδελφῶν, ὡς ἀπὸ τοῦ Μάνη μεμαθηκότες τάχα, ἵν' οὕτως εἴπω, τοῦ ἀπὸ Περσίδος ἀναβεβηκότος, * ἅτινα οὐκ ἐχρῆν οὕτως εἶναι· σκοπεῖν δὲ μᾶλλον τοὺς τοιούτους παραγγέλλει ὁ θεῖος λόγος τοὺς μηδὲν ἐργαζομένους.
59 See also Ammonius, *frg. John*, 193.
60 As Anna Silvas (2007, 213) states, "Karl Holl [...] dated this synod of Side as early as 383, with Flavian's synod at Antioch following afterward. More recently however, Klaus Fitschen, [...] places Flavian's council first, and dates the Synod of Side well into the 390s. The maturity of doctrine and phraseology in this letter [...] points perhaps to a later rather than an earlier dating for this letter, so that the year 390 or thereabouts it might be reasonably nominated".
61 Photius, *Bibl.*, codex 52. 12b.7–11.

renewed the decisions of previous synods, Messalians or Euchites, or Enthusiasts (even those suspected of being such), should abjure their 'heresy' by a written statement. Otherwise, clerics forfeited their priesthood and were excommunicated, whereas laymen were anathematized. Noteworthy is the recommendation that the suspects should not be confined into monasteries (a common penalty during the Byzantine era for criminals and heretics) during their interrogation, in order to prevent the spread of Messalianism among the monks. The Synod also condemned the book of the heresy, "the so called *Asceticon*".[62]

The successive local synods against Messalians must have been the reason why three years before the Ecumenical Synod in Ephesus, in 428, a law was issued that persecuted, among many other heretics (twenty-one in number), the Messalians, or Euchites or Enthusiasts. We note that in both the *acta* of the Synod of Ephesus and the law, a new name for the Messalians appears: Enthusiasts. The law ranked heretics according to the severity of their crime and to the corresponding penalty. The Messalians were co-classified along with Hydroparastates and Manichaeans in the third category consisting of the most 'reprehensible' religious groups, who "nowhere on Roman soil should have the right of assembly and of prayer". The Manichaeans—as those who, in the words of the law, "have attained to the lowest villainy of crimes"—had in addition to be exiled from the municipalities.[63] It is worthwhile to note that this is the only law persecuting Messalians that exists in both codes (*CTh* and *CJ*).

A few years after the barrage of measures against the Messalians by the Church and state, around the mid-fifth century, Theodoret of Cyrrhus outlines the next portrait of Messalians in three of his works: *Historia Religiosa* (437–449), *Historia ecclesiastica* (449–450) and *Haereticarum fabularum compendium* (after 453). In the latter two, he gives a detailed account of their basic characteristics.

---

62   *ACO* 1.1.7, 117–118 (*Ephesenum anno 431*): "Ὅρος τῆς αὐτῆς ἁγίας καὶ οἰκουμενικῆς συνόδου τῆς ἐν Ἐφέσῳ κατὰ τῶν δυσσεβῶν Μεσσαλιανιτῶν ἢ γοῦν Εὐχιτῶν: Συνελθόντες [...] ἐπίσκοποι Οὐαλεριανὸς καὶ Ἀμφιλόχιος [...] περὶ τῶν λεγομένων ἐν τοῖς τῆς Παμφυλίας μέρεσι Μεσσαλιανιτῶν εἴτ' οὖν Εὐχιτῶν ἢ γοῦν Ἐνθουσιαστῶν εἴτε ὁπωσοῦν [...] χαρτίον συνοδικὸν περὶ τούτων [...] ὥστε τοὺς ὄντας κατὰ πᾶσαν ἐπαρχίαν τῆς Μεσσαλιανῶν ἢ γοῦν Ἐνθουσιαστῶν αἱρέσεως ἢ καὶ ἐν ὑποψίαις τῆς τοιαύτης νόσου γεγενημένους, εἴτε κληρικοὶ εἶεν εἴτε λαικοί, μεθοδεύεσθαι, καὶ ἀναθεματίζοντας κατὰ τὰ ἐν τῷ μνημονευθέντι συνοδικῷ διηγορευμένα ἐγγράφως, [...] τοὺς [...] καὶ μὴ ἀναθεματίζοντας, τοὺς μὲν πρεσβυτέρους καὶ διακόνους καὶ τοὺς ἕτερόν τινα βαθμὸν ἔχοντας ἐν ἐκκλησίαι ἐκπίπτειν καὶ κλήρου καὶ βαθμοῦ καὶ κοινωνίας, τοὺς δὲ λαικοὺς ἀναθεματίζεσθαι· μοναστήρια δὲ μὴ συγχωρεῖσθαι ἔχειν τοὺς ἐλεγχομένους ὑπὲρ τοῦ μὴ τὸ ζιζάνιον ἐκτείνεσθαι καὶ ἰσχύειν·. See also Photius, *Bibl., Codex 52* Bekker p. 12b–13b.

63   *CTh* 16.5.65(428)= *CJ* 1.5.5.

Theodoret, like Epiphanius, points out that Messalians have neither teachings nor rules regulating their ascetic practices (fasting etc).[64] He also attests that they do not work, calling themselves *pneumatikoi* (spirituals), that they rest the whole day, doing nothing, because they supposedly spend their day praying.[65] Additionally, Theodoret provides the theological explanation for the Messalian *argia*: "they avoid manual labour as evil".[66] The contempt for labour of the Messalian *pneumatikoi* resembles that of the Manichaean Elect. According to the Manichaean *seal of the hands* the Elect had "to avoid injury to water, fire, trees and living things";[67] manual labour in Manichaeism was considered evil, as injuring the divine particles contained within material world: "Harvesters who gather the harvest are compared with the princes" of darkness.[68] As a result, a number of professions were rejected as murderous: "farmers and carpenters and masons and other skilled workers" were "excluded from the good".[69]

Further, apart from their behavioural practices, Theodoret, explaining their appellations, informs us about some of their doctrinal positions. They are called 'Euchites' (Εὐχῖται)[70] because, as they claim, only continual and zealous prayer (εὐχή) drives out from man his "indwelling demon" (τὸν ἔνοικον δαίμονα) "who has been attached to him" from his birth and who incites him to misconduct. They claim that this demon "cannot be driven out of the soul either by baptism or by any other power".[71] Further, they are called Enthusiasts (Ἐνθουσιασταί) because they claim that when the demon is expelled, the Holy Spirit indwells within them and enables them to predict the future.[72] As Caner com-

---

64 Theodoretus, *HE* 231.10–11.
65 Theodoretus, *Haer.* 83.429.41–43: ἔργον μὲν οὐδὲν μετίασι (πνευματικοὺς γὰρ ἑαυτοὺς ὀνομάζουσι), τῇ δὲ εὐχῇ δῆθεν ἐσχολακότες, τῆς ἡμέρας τὸ πλεῖστον καθεύδουσιν.
66 Theodoretus, *HE* 229.9–10: ἀποστρέφονται μὲν τὴν τῶν χειρῶν ἐργασίαν ὡς πονηρίαν.
67 Lieu 2010, xix.
68 Cf. *Acta Archelai* 10.2–5; Epiphanius, *Pan.* 66.28.2–5.
69 Cf. Alexander, *Tract. Man.* 16.29–35.
70 Εὐχῖται is a translation of Messalians in Greek and means 'the people who pray'.
71 Theodoretus, *Haer.* 83.429.25–41: Μεσσαλιανοὶ δὲ (τοὔνομα δὲ τοῦτο μεταβαλλόμενον εἰς τὴν Ἑλλάδα φωνὴν, τοὺς Εὐχίτας σημαίνει), τὸ μὲν βάπτισμά φασι μηδὲν ὀνεῖν τοὺς προσιόντας·ξυροῦ γὰρ δίκην ἀφαιρεῖται τῶν ἁμαρτημάτων τὰ πρότερα, τὴν δὲ ῥίζαν οὐκ ἐκκόπτει τῆς ἁμαρτίας·ἡ δὲ ἐνδελεχὴς προσευχὴ, καὶ τὴν ῥίζαν τῆς ἁμαρτίας πρόρριζον ἀνασπᾷ, καὶ τὸν ἐξ ἀρχῆς συγκληρωθέντα πονηρὸν δαίμονα τῆς ψυχῆς ἐξελαύνει. Ἑκάστῳ γάρ φασιν ἀνθρώπῳ τικτομένῳ παραυτίκα συνέπεσθαι δαίμονα, καὶ τοῦτον εἰς τὰς ἀτόπους πράξεις παρακινεῖν. Τοῦτον δὲ οὔτε τὸ βάπτισμα, οὔτε ἄλλο τι δύναται τῆς ψυχῆς ἐξελάσαι, ἀλλὰ μόνη τῆς προσευχῆς ἡ ἐνέργεια. Some parts between quotation marks in the text are from Cope's (1990, 195) translation.
72 Theodoretus, *HE* 229.6–12: ἔχουσι δὲ καὶ ἑτέραν προσηγορίαν ἐκ τοῦ πράγματος γενομένην Ἐνθουσιασταὶ γὰρ καλοῦνται, δαίμονός τινος ἐνέργειαν εἰσδεχόμενοι καὶ πνεύματος ἁγίου παρου-

ments, "not only had" Messalians "suggested the inefficacy of a basic church sacrament" (baptism), but they "had also conjured the almost Manichaean specter of a congenitally indwelling demon, an innate source of evil that could only be exorcised through constant prayer".[73]

However, Theodoret does not make any comment on this point, but he does link Messalians to Manichaeans in his *Historia Religiosa*. As he remarks, the so-called 'Euchites', under the pretext of monastic life, follow the example and adopt the customs of the Manichaeans.[74] It seems that for Theodoret, what was happening with the Encratites group also happened with the Messalians. Manichaeans hide themselves behind the names of other ascetics.

More than a century later, at the time of Timothy the Presbyter (sixth-seventh c.), Messalianism, to judge from Timothy's lists of converted heretics, does not seem to constitute a problem in the way Manichaeism still did. Grouping the converted heretics according to the procedure for their reception into the Church, Timothy classifies Messalians in the third category (they had only to anathematize their previous heresy) as opposed to Manichaeans whom he places in the first, more deviant, group (they had to be baptized).[75] Timothy, like Epiphanius and Theodoret, criticizes the stance of Messalians towards manual labour, which, as he remarks, they considered abominable. Moreover, Timothy emphasizes that they are against giving alms to the needy (an accusation levelled also against Manichaeans),[76] claiming that everything must be provided for them, because, as they say, they themselves are the truly poor (in spirit).[77] Like Epiphanius, Timothy underlines the prominent role of the Messalian women, specifying further, that the women of the sect assume important offices, such as those of a teacher or of a priest.[78] Timothy also elaborates on information firstly given by Theodoret that Messalians did not hesitate to renounce their faith, by adding that "the permission to perjure and anathematize" their own religion before danger was a tradition of the community

---

σίαν ταύτην ὑπολαμβάνοντες [...] ὕπνῳ δὲ σφᾶς αὐτοὺς ἐκδιδόντες τὰς τῶν ὀνείρων φαντασίας προφητείας ἀποκαλοῦσι; *Haer.* 83.429.45–46: ἀποκαλύψεις ἑωρακέναι φασί, καὶ τὰ ἐσόμενα προλέγειν ἐπιχειροῦσιν.

73 Caner 2002, 91.
74 Theodoretus, *Hist. Rel.* 3.16.7–8: ἀπεστρέφετο δὲ κομιδῇ καὶ τοὺς ὀνομαζομένους Εὐχίτας ἐν μοναχικῷ προσχήματι τὰ Μανιχαίων νοσοῦντας.
75 Timothy, PG 86A, col. 45–52.
76 See for instance: *Capita VII contra Manichaeos*, ch. 7 (Lieu 2010, 122); Theodoretus, *Haer.* 380.31–33; Augustine, *c. Faust.* 6.5 and 15.7.
77 Timothy, PG 86A, col. 49: 13, 52: 15.
78 Timothy, PG 86A, col. 52: 18.

"bestowed upon them by the tradition of their teachers".[79] It is important to note that a similar testimony for Manichaeans is recorded in the last anathema of the *Long Abjuration Formula* against Manichaeans. Here, this attitude towards danger appears to be legitimized by Mani himself.[80] However, the late dating of the text (ninth or tenth century) led scholars to suggest that it is either a slander, or that it targeted Paulicians.[81] Another new and interesting feature in Timothy's report (connected with the latter) is the Messalian concept of *apatheia* (the state of the soul when the indwelling demon is replaced by the Holy Spirit) which provides a kind of immunity against all kinds of sins.[82] Neither perjury, nor anathematization of their own faith, they say, could harm those who achieved *apatheia*, i.e., those who became *pneumatikoi* (spirituals).[83] This need for legitimization of betrayal is striking and may reflect the difficult situation for Messalians due to their persecution.[84]

Evaluating the data of the sources, one observes a change in the profile of the Messalians over time. The image of mixed companies of men and women wandering through the cities, chanting, dancing with castanets and sleeping together in the public squares as sketched by Epiphanius gradually fades out. On the contrary, the Messalians of Theodoret's time are persecuted and interrogated. It seems that after the synodal and legal actions against them, the display of eccentricity they performed (as described by Epiphanius) was scaled down since they were persecuted. Flavian of Antioch was one of the bishops who had been active in limiting the spread of the 'heresy'. He interrogated a certain Adelphius, "an old man on the edge of the grave", who, it is said, was the leader of a group of Messalians who lived in Edessa.[85] It is possible that from such interrogations new evidence emerged, which complemented the Messalian profile and is related to both their doctrine (e.g. baptism, innate demon) and practices (especially their attitude towards danger). Constant elements of the Messalian

---

79 Timothy, PG 86A, col. 52: 19; Theodoretus, *Haer.* 83.432.1–6; Theodoretus, *HE* 229.17–18–230.1–2.
80 *Long Greek Abjuration Formula*, PG 1: 1469C–D.226–234. Cf. Adam 1969, 103; Lieu 1994, 298 and 2010, 142–143.
81 Lieu 1994, 225.
82 Timothy, PG 86A, col. 49: 10.
83 Timothy, PG 86A, col. 52: 19: μήτε τῆς ἐπιορκίας μήτε τοῦ ἀναθεματισμοῦ, βλάπτειν λοιπὸν δυναμένων τοὺς μετὰ τὴν ἀπάθειαν, ὡς οὗτοι λέγουσι, πνευματικοὺς γενομένους.
84 Additional references to Messalian dogmatic theses by Timothy may refer to their successors, namely the Lampetians and Marcianists (end of sixth century). However, the research conducted so far does not allow us to say whether we can consider these groups as direct heirs of the Messalians; cf. Fitschen 1993, 355.
85 Theodeoret, *Haer.* 83.432.6–22; *HE* 432.1–28.

profile remain: (1) the non-institutional character and lack of rules; (2) the participation of women in ministries; and above all (3) idleness and the consequent demand to be nourished by others.

Apart from the highlighted common features between Messalianism and Manichaeism, it should be noted that what appeared to worry most church authorities (e.g. Epiphanius and Theodoret) was the dissemination of Manichaean ideas and practices through Messalian monks to Catholic/'orthodox' monasticism. The question of the Messalian identity and its relationship with mainstream Christianity and spirituality has raised much discussion in scholarship.[86]

Fitschen points out that we must be careful when reading heresiological sources. In his article "Did 'Messalianism' exist in Asia Minor after A.D. 431?", he explains that he had put 'Messalianism' in inverted commas in order to highlight that it was an 'amorphous movement'. Based on the fact that in the condemnatory decision in the records of the Ecumenical Council of Ephesus (431): (1) various names are attributed to Messalians (euchites, enthusiasts), and (2) no one is named as their heresiarch, Fitschen argues that Messalianism was not an organized heresy but a spiritual movement.[87]

Disagreeing with the view that Messalianism was a movement, even a spiritual one, Caner argues that researchers reproduce stereotypes and labels of that era when they treated "such groups as separate historical phenomena", "distinct and isolated historical movements" and tend to "identify objections to manual labour with marginal or heretical ascetic groups such as Manichaeans, Messalians or circumcellions".[88] Further, Caner questions the credibility of the sources as well as the origin and accuracy of the information of the synodal *acta* and argues that the interrogated Messalians from Edessa were not actually Messalians. As he states: "More importantly, the synodal *acta* attest that Adelphius and company did not identify themselves as 'Messalians', but as *pneumatikoi* (Spiritual Ones)".[89] Subsequently, building on this assumption, Caner argues that the specific doctrinal features (attributed to the supposed Messalians) were unfounded additions by the church authorities (of the synods), in order for a dogmatically heretical Messalian profile to be generated.[90] In this

---

86   See for instance: Fitschen 1993, 352–355; Stewart 1999; Louth 2007, 110–121, esp. 112–113; Caner 2002, 97–103; Hunt 2012. Cf. Gregory 1991, 1350.
87   Fitschen 1993, 352–355.
88   Caner 2002, 13.
89   Caner 2002, 92.
90   Caner 2002, 92: "these synods [...] generated an official Messalian profile that added specific heretical doctrines to ascetic behavior that had already caused alarm."

way, Caner dissociates the Messalians of Epiphanius from the *pneumatikoi* of Theodoret, and concludes that the later Messalian profile (by Theodoret, Timothy, etc.), with the doctrinal features, was a heresiological construction aimed at the marginalization of Christian ascetic practices that followed the apostolic paradigm of wandering life and threatened church hierarchies.[91] For this reason Caner also suggests a shift in the focus of the methodology of Messalian scholarship onto "behavioral rather than doctrinal features" of Messalianism.

However, nowhere do the synodal *acta* state that the appellation of this group of Edessians was *pneumatikoi*. Rather, it is said that they refrain from any work, because they call themselves spirituals/*pneumatikoi*.[92] Thus, the word *pneumatikoi* is a parenthetical explanation of their idleness: as spirituals, they were not preoccupied with mundane concerns; in other words, *pneumatikoi* is an equivalent term to that of the Manichaean *Elect*. The above clarification—as well as the fact that neither Theodoret nor Timothy, who wrote after these synods, 'use' the new doctrinal Messalian features in order to associate Messalians with Manichaeans—makes it equally probable that these specific doctrinal features were not heresiological touches drawn from other heresiarchs,[93] i.e. Mani, but instead were the result of the interrogations and the discussions during the synods.

Yet, it is true that heresiological accounts should be interpreted with caution. Furthermore, the data of our sources do not suffice to definitively establish an actual connection between Messalianism and Manichaeism.[94]

4 Conclusions

Taking together the findings of the preceding analysis, I will attempt some concluding remarks regarding the relationship between the Manichaeans and both the Encratites group and the Messalians, with the ultimate aim of answering the question: what does this link (made by our sources) reveal about the Manichaeans?

---

91   According to Caner (2002, 85) "what church leaders were confronting under the "Messalian" label was not in fact a novel movement, but rather a complex of ideals, practices, and assumptions deeply rooted in the apostolic model for Christian ascetic life". Indeed, as Caner (2002, 78) points out, "Manichaeans became the most notorious heirs to the apostolic paradigm for Christian life."

92   ... Οὕτως ἐξαπατηθέντες οἱ τρισάθλιοι ἔργον μὲν οὐδὲν μετίασι (πνευματικοὺς γὰρ ἑαυτοὺς ὀνομάζουσι).

93   Cf. Casiday 2003, 429. Caner 2002, 91–96.

94   Cf. Pettipiece 2014, 40.

First, from the above presentation, it becomes apparent that both the Encratites group and Messalians share a series of common features with the Manichaeans. In both cases, these features primarily concern the behaviour and attitudes of these ascetics, such as the wandering ascetic lifestyle even within the cities, women's active role in the sect, renunciation of property/possessions, outlandish appearance, idleness and begging (Messalians), extreme or anarchous/irregular forms of fasting, etc. Doctrinal issues which also arose, mainly underline the dualistic perspective of these movements. Indeed, both the 'distinct principles' (ἀρχαὶ διάφοροι) of the Encratites (Epiphanius), the devil among them as an independent entity, and the 'innate demon in every man' of the Messalians (Theodoret), echo Manichaean positions. In addition, most of the authors I examined do not condemn the ascetic practices as such, but the theological rationale behind them which also echoes Manichaean theses (food is poisonous, labour is evil etc). Therefore, the key problem with Caner's suggestion to focus only "on behavioral rather than doctrinal features" is that it leaves completely out of the discussion the doctrines, which are those that differentiate and finally make sense of the specific practices.[95]

Secondly, the Manichaeans not only shared with the above ascetics some common features (practices and ideas), but were regarded by our sources as the mentors of the above ascetics. The Manichaeans were presented as the teachers of the false ascetic practices of the Encratites. The Manichaeans were also deemed as the teachers of idleness which was highlighted as the main feature of the Messalians. The 'bad' influence of the Manichaeans was considered to have transformed the above ascetic environments into 'factories' producing apostates. In both cases the fear of a Manichaean influence through these ascetics to Catholic monasticism is emphasized. Moreover, this fear was intensified because, as is recorded in some sources, the appellations of these ascetic groups were used as camouflage (or were considered as such) by disguised Manichaeans.

Thirdly, emphasis is also attributed by our sources to the anarchist and irregular character of these ascetic groups. In contrast, the frequent references to the Manichaean leaders suggest that the Manichaean movement was highly organized. Besides, as is entailed by the legislation, the state also held the same view. There is only one law against Messalians (428) and three against the Encratites group, in one of which the Encratites group are portrayed just as masks of Manichaeans (the target is Manichaeans, not the Encratites group),

---

[95] On the question of whether the 'problem' was just the practices in themselves or/and the doctrines behind them, see also Beskow (1988, 10) and Goodrich (2004, 209).

while the twenty-five laws against Manichaeism (eighteen in *CTh* and seven in *CJ*) are more numerous than those against any other religious group. Hence, it is not legitimate to put Manichaeans into one basket with Messalians and Encratites, by arguing that these names were used just as alternative labels for various trends within Christian asceticism, which church and state authorities of the era wished to marginalize.[96]

Let us put the events in a sequence in order to return to our initial question: How can the change of the attitude of the law towards the Encratites group be interpreted?

The outbreak of the phenomenon of radical asceticism during the decades 370s and 380s, and the increasing number of anarchist ascetics (Encratites etc) in combination with the simultaneous appearance of the Messalians, was linked by the official Church and state to Manichaean influence. Therefore, the laws against both Manichaeans and the Encratites group constituted the first priority of Theodosius' religious policy. And while, initially, the terms Encratites etc referred to practices "of approved faith and of rather chaste course of life", this link with the Manichaeans alarmed both the Church and the state. It seems as if in their eyes there were two versions of Encratites: the old and the new ones; the pre-Manichaean and the post-Manichaean. This is illustrated by the ambivalence of both state (laws of 381 and 382) and Church (Basil's letters in 374 and 375) regarding their treatment of the Encratites group. In addition, it is logical to assume that for the (civil and ecclesiastical) authorities the independent and amorphous groups of ascetics, such as Encratites and Messalians, were suspected of being attracted, influenced, and even swallowed up by the highly organized sect of the Manichaeans. Their common practices and outlook were a serious reason for the appeal of the Manichaean movement and the consequent recruitment into it. All the above—in combination with the fact that such practices (and ideas) were adopted by a growing number of Catholic ascetics—explains the sudden shift of the law which rendered the Encratites group illegal in their own right (law of 382). The new imperial religious policy indicates that it was soon realized that the boundaries between various ascetic groups were blurred. In practice, it was difficult to judge whether someone who adopted radical ascetic practices was a Manichaean or a non-heretical Christian ascetic. It is noteworthy that the religious pluralism that existed in the Eastern Roman Empire made the lines between orthodoxy and heresy, Christian and non-Christian, more obscure.

---

96   See the opposite view of Caner (2002 *passim*, esp. 15, 101).

Furthermore, besides the religious side effects, the lifestyle promoted through those ascetics—even in urban areas—was a threat to the social values and social institutions of the Empire.

Therefore, the link between these ascetics and the Manichaeans, in the minds of church and state leaders, seems to have been of crucial importance. Whether or not this link actually existed or was only in their minds, or whether the authorities sought to discredit the Encratites etc. and the Messalians by linking them to the Manichaeans, are all probable alternative interpretations, and it is more likely that to a certain extent all had happened together at the same time. Thus, the question whether the post-Manichaean profile of the Encratites and the profile of Messalians enriched with doctrinal features were just heresiological constructions serving the Church's strategy against anarchist asceticism, or whether they reflect an actual change in the identity of irregular Christian asceticism (towards Manichaeism) cannot be answered in an absolute manner.[97]

What can be said though, is that despite the persistence of church authorities in associating groups of anarchist ascetics with the Manichaeans, the law targeted only the Manichaeans. In combination with the fact that the Manichaean issue had never been addressed in ecumenical or other church synods, while on the contrary a number of synods dealt with Encratites and Messalians, shows that—for the authorities—Manichaeism was an issue of a higher order. It went beyond ecclesiastical jurisdiction and extended to the socio-political sphere, whereas for the state the issue of Encratites and Messalians was an intra-ecclesiastical affair. The latter, I believe, is crucial for the perception of the group identity of the Manichaeans in the Roman East.

List of Abbreviations

ACO	*Acta Conciliorum Oecumenicorum*
Alexander, *Tract. Man*	Alexander Lycopolitanus, *Tractatus de placitis Manichaeorum*
Ammonius, *frg. John*	Ammonius Alexandrinus, *Fragmenta in Joannem*
Amphilochius, *c. Haer.*	Amphilochius Iconiensis, *Contra haereticos*
Augustine, *c. Faust.*	Augustine, *Contra Faustum*
Basil, *ep.*	Basilius Caesariensis, *Epistulae*

---

[97] On the question whether Manichaeism exerted an influence on Western Catholic Christianity see van Oort 2009.

Basil, *Hom. Hexaem.*	Basilius Caesariensis, *Homiliae in Hexaemeron*
Chrysostom, *Natal.*	Joannes Chrysostomus, *In diem natalem*
Chrysostom, *Hom. 1 Tim.*	Joannes Chrysostomus, *In epistulam 1 ad Timotheum*
Chrysostom, *Hom. Matt.*	Joannes Chrysostomus, *In Matthaeum*
CJ	Codex Justinianus
CTh	Codex Theodosianus
Epiphanius, *Pan.*	Epiphanius, *De Haeresibus (Panarion)*
Eusebius, HE	Eusebius Caesariensis, *Historia Ecclesiastica*
Julianus, *comm. Job*	Julianus Arianus, *Commentarius in Job*
Macarius, *Apocriticus*	Macarius Magnes, *Apocriticus seu Μονογενής*
Photius, *Bibl.*	Photius, *Bibliotheca*
Socrates, HE	Socrates Scholasticus, *Historia Ecclesiastica*
Sozomenus, HE	Sozomenus, *Historia Ecclesiastica*
Theodoretus, HE	Theodoretus Cyrrhensis, *Historia Ecclesiastica*
Theodoretus, *Hist. Rel.*	Theodoretus Cyrrhensis, *Historia Religiosa*
Theodoretus, *Haer.*	Theodoretus Cyrrhensis, *Haereticarum fabularum compendium*
Theophanes, *Chron.*	Theophanes the Confessor, *Chronographia*
TLG	*Thesaurus Linguae Graecae*
Timothy	Timotheus Presbyter, *De receptione haereticorum*
Titus, *c. Manichaeos*	Titus Bostrensis, *Contra Manichaeos*

Primary Sources

Alexander Lycopolitanus, *Tractatus de placitis Manichaeorum*: Brinkmann, A. (ed.) (1895). *Alexandri Lycopolitani contra Manichaei opiniones disputatio*. Leipzig: Teubner. Translation by: Horst, P.W. van der & Mansfeld, J. (1974). *An Alexandrian Platonist against dualism: Alexander of Lycopolis' treatise "Critique of the doctrines of Manichaeus"*. Leiden: Brill.

Ammonius Alexandrinus, *Fragmenta in Joannem*: Reuss, J. (1966). *Johannes-Kommentare aus der griechischen Kirche (Texte und Untersuchungen 89)*. Berlin: Akademie Verlag: 196–358.

Amphilochius Iconiensis, *Contra haereticos*: Datema, C. (ed.). (1978). *Amphilochii Iconiensis opera: orationes, pluraque alia quae supersunt, nonnulla etiam spuria* (pp. 185–214). Turnhout: Brepols.

Augustine, *Contra Faustum*: Schaff, P. (ed.).*The Nicene and Post-Nicene Fathers*, Series 1, vol. 4 http://www.ccel.org/ccel/schaff/npnf104.html.

Basilius Caesariensis, *Epistulae*: Courtonne, Y. (ed. and trans.). (1961). *Saint Basile. Lettres* (vol. 2). Paris: Les Belles Lettres.

Basilius *Caesariensis, Homiliae in Hexaemeron*: Giet, S. (1968). *Basile de Césarée. Homélies sur l'Hexaéméron*, (2nd ed.). (*Sources chrétiennes* 26). Paris: Éditions du Cerf.

Concilium universale Ephesenum anno 431: Schwartz, E. (1927/1929 repr. 1960/1965). *Acta conciliorum oecumenicorum*, (vol. 1). Berlin: De Gruyter.

Epiphanius, *De haeresibus* (*Panarion*): Holl, K. & Dummer J. (eds.). (1980). *Epiphanius II: Panarion, haer. 34–64*. GCS 31. Berlin: Akademie-Verlag. (1985). *Epiphanius III: Panarion, haer. 65–80; De Fide.* GCS 37. Berlin: Akademie-Verlag. Translation by: Williams, F. (2013). *The* Panarion *of Epiphanus of Salamis: Books II and III; De Fide* (2nd revised edition). Leiden-Boston: Brill

Eusebius Caesariensis, *Historia Ecclesiastica*: Bardy, G. (1952). *Eusèbe de Césarée. Histoire ecclésiastique*, 3 vols. (*Sources chrétiennes*). Paris: Éditions du Cerf.

[Hegemonius]: Lieu, S.N.C. (ed.) (2001). *Acta Archelai. The Acts of Archelaus* (M. Vermes, Transl.) (Manichaean Studies 4). Turnhout: Brepols.

Joannes Chrysostomus, *In diem natalem*: PG 49: 351–362. Migne, J.-P. (1857–1866). *Patrologiae cursus completus* (Series Graeca). Paris: Migne.

Joannes Chrysostomus, *In epistulam I ad Timotheum* (*hom*. 1–18): PG 62: 501–600. Migne, J.-P. (1857–1866). *Patrologiae cursus completus* (Series Graeca). Paris: Migne.

Joannes Chrysostomus, *In Matthaeum* (*homiliae 1–90*): PG 57: 13–472; 58: 471–794. Migne, J.-P. (1857–1866). *Patrologiae cursus completus* (Series Graeca). Paris: Migne.

Julianus Arianus, *Commentarius in Job*: Hagedorn, D. (1973). *Der Hiobkommentar des Arianers Julian* (Patristische Texte und Studien 14). Berlin: De Gruyter.

Macarius Magnes, *Apocriticus seu Μονογενής*: Goulet, R. (2003). *Macarios de Magnésie: Le monogénès* (vol. 2). *Paris: Librairie Philosophique J. Vrin*. Translation by: T.W. Grafer: http://www.tertullian.org/fathers/macarius_apocriticus.htm#3_36.

Photius, *Bibliotheca*: Henry, R. (ed. and trans.) (1959). *Bibliothèque*. Paris: Les Belles Lettres.

Socrates Scholasticus, *Historia Ecclesiastica*: Périchon P., & Maraval, P. (eds.). (2004). *Socrate de Constantinople. Histoire ecclésiastique I*. Paris: Éditions du Cerf.

Sozomenus, *Historia Ecclesiastica*: Bidez, J. and Hansen, G.C. (1960). *Sozomenus. Kirchengeschichte* (GCS 50). Berlin: Akademie Verlag.

Theodoretus Cyrrhensis, *Historia Ecclesiastica*: Parmentier, L. & Scheidweiler, F. (1954). *Theodoret. Kirchengeschichte* (2nd ed.) (*Die griechischen christlichen Schriftsteller* 44). Berlin: Akademie Verlag.

Theodoretus Cyrrhensis, *Historia Religiosa*: Canivet, P. & Leroy-Molinghen, A. (1977/1979). *Théodoret de Cyr. L'histoire des moines de Syrie, 2 vols.* (*Sources chrétiennes* 234, 257). Paris: Éditions du Cerf.

Theodoretus Cyrrhensis, *Haereticarum fabularum compendium, De Manete*: MPG 83: 336–556 (pp. 377–382). Migne, J.-P. (1857–1866). *Patrologiae cursus completus* (Series Graeca). Paris: Migne.

Theophanes the Confessor, *Chronographia*: Boor, C. de (ed.). (1883). *Theophanis Chro-

nographia (vol. 1). Leipzig: Teubner, 1883 (repr. Hildesheim: Olms, 1963). Translation by: Mango, C.A., Scott, R., & Greatrex, G. (1997). *The Chronicle of Theophanes Confessor: Byzantine and the Near Eastern History, A.D. 284–813*. Oxford: Clarendon Press.

Theodosian Code: Mommsen, T. & Meyer, P. (eds.) (1954). *Theodosiani Libri XVI cum Constitutionibus Sirmondianis*. Berlin: Weidmann. Translation by Coleman-Norton, P.R. (1966). *Roman State & Christian Church: A Collection of Legal Documents to A.D. 535*, (Vol. 1 & 2). London: S.P.C.K.

Thesaurus Linguae Graecae: A Digital Library of Greek Literature. Online. (www.tlg.uci.edu)

Timotheus Presbyter, *De receptione haereticorum*: PG: 86ᴬ: 12–73 (pp. 20–24). Migne, J.-P. (1857–1866). *Patrologiae cursus completus* (Series Graeca). Paris: Migne.

Titus Bostrensis, *Contra Manichaeos*: Roman, A., Schmidt, T.S., Poirier, P.-H., Crégheur, E., & Declerck, J.H. (eds.) (2013). *Titi Bostrensis Contra Manichaeos. Graece et Syriace Libri IV* (CCSG 82). Turnhout: Brepols. French translation: Roman, A., Schmidt, T.S., & Poirier, P.-H. (2015). *Titus de Bostra. Contre les manichéens* (CCT 21). Turnhout: Brepols.

[Zacharias Mytilenaeus], ⟨*Capita vii contra Manichaeos*⟩: Richard, M. (ed.) (1977). *Iohannis Caesariensis opera quae supersunt* (CCSG 1). Turnhout: Brepols. For a republication of Richard's edition with translation in English and full commentary see Lieu 1983, 152–218 & Lieu 1994, 203–305 and for a further revised translation, see Lieu 2010 (CFM), 116–125, 194.

Bibliography

Adam, A. (ed.) (1954/1969). *Texte zum Manichäismus*. Berlin: De Gruyter.

BeDuhn, J.D. (2000). *The Manichaean Body: In Discipline and Ritual*. Baltimore: Johns Hopkins University Press.

Beskow, P. (1988). The Theodosian Laws Against Manichaeism. In P. Bryder (ed.), *Manichaean studies: proceedings of the first International conference on Manichaeism, August 5–9, 1987, Department of History of Religions, Lund University, Sweden* (Vol. 1, pp. 1–11). Lund: Lund Studies in African and Asian Religions.

Calder, W. (1929). Two Encratite Tombstones. *Byzantinische Zeitschrift*, 30, 645–646.

Caner, D. (2002). *Wandering, Begging Monks: Spiritual Authority and the Promotion of Monasticism in Late Antiquity* (The Transformation of the Classical Heritage 33). Berkeley & Los Angeles: University of California Press.

Casiday, A. (2003). Review of *Wandering, Begging Monks: Spiritual Authority and the Promotion of Monasticism in Late Antiquity*, by Caner, D. *Journal of Early Christian Studies*, 11(3), 428–430. doi: 10.1353/earl.2003.0040

Cecire, R.C. (1985). *Encraticism: Early Christian Ascetic Extremism.* [Doctoral dissertation, University of Kansas]. ProQuest Dissertations Publishing.

Cope, G. (1990). *An analysis of the heresiological method of Theodoret of Cyrus in the "Haereticarum fabularum compendium".* [Doctoral dissertation, The Catholic University of America]. ProQuest Dissertations Publishing.

Durkheim, E.M. (1954). *The Elementary Forms of the Religious Life.* London.

Fitschen, K. (1993). Did "Messalianism" Exist in Asia Minor after A.D. 431? In E.A. Livingstone (ed.), *Biblica Et Apocrypha, Orientalia, Ascetica. Papers Presented at the Eleventh International Conference on Patristic Studies Held in Oxford, 1991.* (Studia Patristica 25, pp. 352–355). Leuven: Peeters.

Gardner, I., & Lieu, S.N.C. (2004). *Manichaean Texts from the Roman Empire.* Cambridge: Cambridge University Press.

Goodrich, R. (2004). Mendicant Monks. Review of *Wandering, Begging Monks: Spiritual Authority and the Promotion of Monasticism in Late Antiquity*, by Caner, D. *The Classical Review, 54*(1), 208–210.

Goulet, R. (2003). Dosithée de Cilicie. *Apocrypha*, 14, 55–72.

Gregory, T. (1991). Messalianism. In A.P. Kazhdan (ed.), *The Oxford Dictionary of Byzantium*, (1st ed., 1349–1350). Oxford: Oxford University Press.

Hunt, H. (2012). *Clothed in the body asceticism, the body and the spiritual in the late antique era* (Ashgate studies in philosophy & theology in late antiquity). Farnham, Surrey, England; Burlington, Vt.: Ashgate.

Joannou, P.-P. (1962). *Discipline générale antique, IIe–IXe s.* [*IVe–IXe s.*]: *I, 1, Les canons des conciles oecuméniques. I, 2, Les canons des Synodes particuliers. II, Les canons des Pères Grecs. Index analytique aux CCO, CSP, CPG* (Vol. I.2). Grottaferrata (Roma): Tip. Italo-Orientale S. Nilo.

Kristionat, J. (2013). *Zwischen Selbstverständlichkeit und Schweigen: die Rolle der Frau im frühen Manichäismus.* (Oikumene: Studien zur antiken Weltgeschichte 11), Heidelberg: Verlag Antike.

Lieu, S.N.C. (1981). Precept and Practice in Manichaean Monasticism. *The Journal of Theological Studies, 32*(1), 153–173. doi: 10.1093/jts/XXXII.1.153.

Lieu, S.N.C. (1994). *Manichaeism in Mesopotamia and the Roman East* (Religions in the Graeco-Roman World, 118). Leiden: Brill.

Lieu, S.N.C. (ed.). (2010). *Greek and Latin Sources on Manichaean Cosmogony and Ethics* (G. Fox & J. Sheldon, Trans. S.N.-C. Lieu Introduction & Commentary). (CFM Subsidia Vol. 6). Turnhout: Brepols & Ancient Cultures Research Centre. Macquarie University, N.S.W. Australia.

Lössl, J. The Religious Innovator Tatian: A Precursor of Mani? In J. van Oort (ed.), *Manichaeism and Early Christianity* (NHMS 99, pp. 1–23). Leiden: Brill.

Louth, A. (2007). *The Origins of the Christian Mystical Tradition: from Plato to Denys* (2nd ed.). Oxford: Oxford University Press.

Pettipiece, T. (2014). Parallel Paths. Tracing Manichaean Footprints along the Syriac Book of Steps. In K.S. Heal & R.A. Kitchen (eds.), *Breaking the Mind* (pp. 32–40): Catholic University of America Press.

Quispel, G. (2008). The Study of Encratism: A Historical Survey. In J. van Oort (ed.), *Gnostica, Judaica, Catholica: collected essays of Gilles Quispel* (NHMS 55, pp. 329–363). Leiden, Boston: Brill.

Silvas, A.M. (2007). *Gregory of Nyssa: The Letters* (A.M. Silvas, trans.). (Supplements to Vigiliae Christianae, 83). Leiden: Brill.

Stewart, C. (1991). *'Working the Earth of the Heart': The Messalian Controversy in History, Texts and Language to AD 431* (Oxford Theological Monographs). Oxford [etc.]: Clarendon Press.

van Oort, J. (2009). Manichaeism: Its sources and influences on Western Christianity. *Verbum Et Ecclesia*, 30(2), 126–130.

van Oort, J. (2020). Manichaean Women in Augustine's Life and Works. In J. van Oort (ed.), *Mani and Augustine: collected essays on Mani, Manichaeism and Augustine* (NHMS 97, pp. 418–432). Leiden, Boston: Brill.

van Oort, J. (2020). Manichaean Women in a Pseudo-Augustinian Testimony: An Analysis of the North African Testimonium de Manichaeis sectatoribus. In J. van Oort (ed.), *Mani and Augustine: collected essays on Mani, Manichaeism and Augustine* (NHMS 97, pp. 433–442). Leiden, Boston: Brill.

van Oort, J. (2020). The Role of Women in Manichaeism. In J. van Oort (ed.), *Mani and Augustine: collected essays on Mani, Manichaeism and Augustine* (NHMS 97, pp. 498–502). Leiden, Boston: Brill.

Young, K. (2006). Epiphanius of Cyprus and the Geography of Heresy. In H.A. Drake (ed.), *Violence in Late Antiquity: Perceptions and Practices* (pp. 235–251). Burlington: Ashgate/Taylor & Francis.

17
The Afterlife of Manichaeism in Neoplatonic Education

Byard Bennett

Abstract

This chapter discusses a short work entitled *The Proposition of a Manichaean* (CPG 6998, 7011), which argues for the existence of two unoriginate first principles, one good and one evil. The *Proposition* has been transmitted in conjunction with three philosophical works written by Christian authors in the sixth to eleventh centuries (Zacharias of Mitylene's *Adversus Manichaeos*, Paul the Persian's *Defensio*, and John Italus' *Quaestiones quodlibetales*). I provide a critical edition and English translation of the *Proposition* and show that the text was revised and adapted several times during the course of its transmission. Although a Manichaean origin cannot be securely established for the *Proposition*, the work was preserved and transmitted because it played a role in later Neoplatonic instruction in logic. The revisions made to the work arose from a need to simplify the text so that students could more easily follow the argument. The discussion and refutation of the *Proposition* by Christian authors can thus be seen as part of a broader trend toward expanding the study of paralogisms (fallacious arguments) in sixth-century teaching of logic.

Several works directed against Manichaean teaching were written in Greek during the early sixth century A.D. This is remarkable because there is little evidence for the existence of Manichaean communities and institutions in Greek-speaking areas of the Roman Empire during this period.[1] The composition of anti-Manichaean works in the early sixth century would therefore appear to be due not to a resurgence of Manichaean missions, but to other factors.

I have shown elsewhere that the composition of anti-Manichaean works in the early sixth century was closely connected with the curriculum and instructional practices of contemporary Neoplatonic education and that this educa-

---

1 See Byard Bennett, "The Eclipse of Manichaeism in the Roman Empire," in *Handbook of Manichaeism*, ed. Jason BeDuhn and Johannes van Oort (Leiden: Brill, forthcoming).

tional framework can help us understand why these anti-Manichaean works were written.[2] The authors writing against Manichaeism in the early sixth century were all closely connected with the final phase of Alexandrian Neoplatonism, which had historically regarded Manichaeism as incompatible with authentic Platonism and sometimes used Manichaeism as a foil to establish the correctness of certain Neoplatonic teachings. In some cases, the sixth-century authors writing against Manichaeism are known to have studied in Alexandria with Proclus' student Ammonius.[3] In other cases, their works show a close dependence upon Ammonius' commentaries on Aristotle and interact with arguments that had been advanced by Proclus and were subsequently discussed by Ammonius' students.[4]

In the present study, sixth-century writers' interest in Manichaeism will be examined by considering a short argument for the Manichaean position which has been preserved in connection with three Byzantine philosophical works. After presenting a critical edition and English translation of this short argument (which I will call the *Proposition*), I will suggest that the argument is best understood as a school exercise which allowed advanced students to demonstrate their competence in Aristotelian logic by responding to a position opposed to orthodox Neoplatonism.

The *Proposition* has been transmitted in connection with three Byzantine philosophical works, the first two dating from the sixth century and the third from the eleventh century A.D. The *Proposition* precedes Zacharias of Mitylene's *Adversus Manichaeos* (Ἀντίρρησις) in most of the extant manuscripts which contain the latter work.[5] Since Zacharias' refutation was clearly intended

---

2   Byard Bennett, "The Physics of Light, Darkness and Matter in John the Grammarian's *First Homily against the Manichaeans*: Early Byzantine Anti-Manichaean Literature as a Window on Controversies in Later Neoplatonism," in *Mani in Dublin: Selected Papers from the Seventh International Conference of the International Association of Manichaean Studies in the Chester Beatty Library, Dublin, 8–12 September 2009*, ed. Siegfried G. Richter, Charles Horton, and Klaus Ohlhafer (Leiden: Brill, 2015), 19–33.

3   Bennett, "Physics," 19–20 with n. 1.

4   For one example, see Bennett, "Physics," 30–31 with nn. 46, 48.

5   In the *Clavis Patrum Graecorum*, the *Proposition* and Zacharias' *Adversus Manichaeos* are treated as a single work and assigned the number CPG 6998, although only the incipit for Zacharias' treatise is given. The *Adversus Manichaeos* may have been written in the late 520's. The Greek texts of the *Proposition* and Zacharias' *Adversus Manichaeos* were first published by Andronikos K. Demetrakopoulos, Ἐκκλησιαστική Βιβλιοθήκη, vol. 1 (Leipzig: Otto Wiegand, 1866), 1–2 (*Proposition*), 2–18 (*Adversus Manichaeos*). The edition of Demetrakopoulos is defective in several respects. It appears that the text of Zacharias' *Adversus Manichaeos* actually concluded at Demetrakopoulos, 4.18 (τῇ μὴ οὔσῃ κακίᾳ), as two of the oldest surviving manuscripts (Moscow, Gosudarstvennyj Istoričeskij Muzej, *Sinod. gr.* 394 and Genoa,

to address and correct the arguments given in the *Proposition*, it is reasonable to think that the *Proposition* preceded Zacharias' refutation in the earliest manuscripts and was intended to be read in conjunction with the refutation.

A slightly different text of the *Proposition* appears before the *Defensio* (Ἀπολογία) attributed to Paul the Persian.[6] Paul's apology presupposes and responds to arguments found in the *Proposition*, but adopts a different strategy from that found in Zacharias' refutation and is not dependent upon the latter.

The *Proposition* also appears as chapter 59 of John Italus' *Quaestiones quodlibetales* (Ἀπορίαι καὶ λύσεις).[7] No title appears before this chapter, which is remarkable, given that nearly all the other chapters are preceded by a title

---

Biblioteca Franzoniana, *Urbani* 27) attest. The text printed after that by Demetrakopoulos (inc. Ἀλλ' ἦν μὲν ἱκανά) is probably derived from another source, since in the manuscripts it also appears independently after the *Defensio* of Paul the Persian (PG 88, 557A11ff.); see Marcel Richard, *Iohannis Caesariensis presbyteri et grammatici opera quae supersunt*, CCSG 1 (Turnhout: Brepols, 1977), XL–XLI. Demetrakopoulos presents his edition as if it were based on *Sinod. gr.* 394 (10 c.), but in reality, it is based on Munich, Bayerische Staatsbibliothek, *gr.* 66 (16 c.); see Johannes Dräseke, "Zu Apollinarios' von Laodicea 'Ermunterungsschrift an die Hellenen,'" *Zeitschrift für wissenschaftliche Theologie* 43 (1900): 235; M.-A. Kugener, "La compilation historique de Pseudo-Zacharie le Rhéteur," *Revue de l'Orient Chrétien* 5 (1900): 208; Wilhelm von Christ, Wilhelm Schmid, and Otto Stählin, *Geschichte der griechischen Literatur, II.2: Die nachklassische Periode der griechischen Literatur*, 6 ed. (Munich: C.H. Beck, 1961), 1485 n.4. Another edition of Zacharias' *Adversus Manichaeos* was published by Jean-Baptiste Pitra, *Analecta sacra et classica spicilegio Solesmensi parata*, vol. 5 (Paris: Roger and Chernowitz, 1888), 67–70 (*Adversus Manichaeos* only). Pitra's edition was based on two manuscripts, Genoa, Biblioteca Franzoniana, *Urbani* 27 (11 c.) and Munich, Bayerische Staatsbibliothek, *gr.* 66 (16 c.). Like Demetrakopoulos, Pitra included in his edition the text incorrectly ascribed to Zacharias (inc. Ἀλλ' ἦν μὲν ἱκανά).

6   The *Clavis Patrum Graecorum* treats the *Proposition* and Paul's *Defensio* as a single work, giving it the number CPG 7011 (*Photini Manichaei propositio cum Pauli Persae responsione*); the Greek works attributed to Paul the Persian appear to have been composed during the reign of Justinian, i.e. between 527 and 565 A.D. The Greek texts of the *Proposition* and Paul's *Defensio* were published in Angelo Mai, *Nova patrum bibliotheca*, vol. 4.2 (Rome: Typis Sacri Consilii Propagando Christiano Nomini, 1847), 91 (*Proposition*), 91–93 (Paul's *Defensio*). Mai's edition, which is not entirely satisfactory, was based on Vatican City, Biblioteca Apostolica Vaticana, *Vat. gr.* 1838 (13 c.) and was subsequently reprinted by Migne (PG 88, 552–557).

7   A critical edition of the text of ch. 59 appears in Perikles Joannou, *Ioannes Italos Quaestiones quodlibetales* (Ἀπορίαι καὶ λύσεις) (Ettal: Buch-Kunstverlag Ettal, 1956), 80–81. On Italus' life and works, see Antonio Rigo, "Giovanni Italo," in *Dizionario biografico degli Italiani*, vol. 56 (Rome: Istituto dell'Enciclopedia Italiana, 2001), 62–67; Katerina Ierodiakonou, "John Italos," in *Encyclopedia of Medieval Philosophy: Philosophy Between 500 and 1500*, ed. Henrik Lagerlund (Dordrecht: Springer, 2011), 623–625; A.E. Karnačev, *Aporii* (St. Petersburg: Svoe Izdatelstvo, 2013), 14–39.

indicating the chapter's content or the problem that is to be resolved.[8] Italus' *Quaestiones* appears to be a philosophical commonplace book that records the opinions of earlier Greek philosophers, noting the tensions and oppositions between their teachings. The work evidently served some purpose related to the instruction of students, since it contains excerpts and paraphrases of works commonly used in the study of philosophy and rhetoric.[9] In several chapters of the work, special attention is given to whether matter is evil and can be regarded as a first principle and productive of other beings. Italus' interest in this question, however, arises from his desire to understand Proclus' criticisms of Plotinus, not from any connection with Manichaeism.[10]

It is clear that the text of the *Proposition* was revised several times during the course of its transmission. The text of the *Proposition* which precedes Zacharias' refutation in four manuscripts will be described as *Versio A*. The earliest witness to this version is a twelfth-century manuscript, Athos, Vatopedi 236 (f. 7ʳ). This manuscript has been extensively studied because it contains a large number of anti-heretical works, including a collection of anti-

---

8   Joannou attempted to supply a title for the chapter (Εἰ δύο εἰσὶν ἀρχαὶ ἀγένητοι) by drawing on a phrase that appears near the end of the *Proposition* (πῶς οὐ ψεύδονται οἱ λέγοντες μὴ εἶναι δύο ἀρχὰς ἀγενήτους;) and justifies this addition by a reference to John of Damascus *De fide orthodoxa* 4.19 (PG 94, 1192B). The addition of a title not found in the manuscript tradition seems unnecessary and the passage cited from John of Damascus has no relation to the chapter in Italus.

9   The works most commonly quoted or paraphrased include Aristotle's works on logic and physics, the commentaries of Porphyry and Ammonius on Aristotle's *Categories*, Proclus' *Elements of Theology*, and John of Damascus' *Dialectica*. The work also includes students' notes on Italus' lectures (ch. 44) and letters written by Italus to several Byzantine dignitaries, answering basic philosophical questions about how one is to harmonize the differences between Plato and Aristotle (ch. 42), how to correctly interpret a passage in Homer (ch. 43), and what virtue is, using key passages in Aristotle's *Nicomachean Ethics* as a point of departure (ch. 63). The connection of the *Quaestiones quodlibetales* with Italus' teaching activities is noted by Pelopidas Étienne Stephanou, *Jean Italos philosophe et humaniste* (Rome: Pontificium Institutum Orientalium Studiorum, 1949), 82–85 and Sergei Mariev, "Neoplatonic Philosophy in Byzantium," in *Byzantine Perspectives on Neoplatonism*, ed. Sergei Mariev (Berlin: Walter de Gruyter, 2017), 10 n.50.

10 See Michele Trizio, "A Late-Antique Debate on Matter-Evil Revisited in 11th-Century Byzantium: John Italos and His *Quaestio* 92," in *Fate, Providence and Moral Responsibility in Ancient, Medieval and Early Modern Thought: Studies in Honour of Carlos Steel*, ed. Pieter d'Hoine and Gerd Van Riel (Leuven: Leuven University Press, 2014), 383–394; Monica Marchetto, "Nikephoros Chumnos' Treatise *On Matter*," in *Aesthetics and Theurgy in Byzantium*, ed. Sergei Mariev and Wiebke-Marie Stock (Berlin: De Gruyter, 2013), 52–55.

Manichaean texts.[11] *Versio A* is also attested in a fourteenth-century manuscript, Wolfenbüttel, Herzog August Bibliothek, *Gud. gr.* 102 (f. 35^v), and in two manuscripts copied in Italy during the middle of the sixteenth century, Vatican City, Biblioteca Apostolica Vaticana, *Ott. gr.* 382 (f. 94^{r-v}) and Munich, Bayerische Staatsbibliothek, *gr.* 66 (ff. 63^v–64^r).

In preparing a critical edition of Zacharias' *Adversus Manichaeos* (forthcoming), I examined the text of both the *Proposition* and Zacharias' refutation in these four manuscripts and collated the variant readings. A detailed discussion of the manuscript tradition will be presented in my edition of Zacharias' treatise. For the present, it will be sufficient to note that *Gud. gr.* 102 is descended from the manuscript from which Vatopedi 236 was copied, but is not an apograph of Vatopedi 236. The two sixteenth-century manuscripts, in turn, are descended from *Gud. gr.* 102.[12] The text of the *Proposition* in chapter 59 of Italus' *Quaestiones quodlibetales* is an abbreviated, lightly adapted form of *Versio A*.

---

[11] A number of these anti-Manichaean texts have also been transmitted in an eleventh-century manuscript, Genoa, Biblioteca Franzoniana, *Urbani* 27. It is clear that Vatopedi 236 and *Urbani* 27 were copied from the same manuscript, which has apparently not survived. *Urbani* 27 includes Zacharias' *Adversus Manichaeos* (ff. 302^v–303^v), but for some reason the scribe did not copy the *Proposition* before Zacharias' refutation. A seventeenth-century apograph of *Urbani* 27—Berlin, Staatsbibliothek zu Berlin (Preussischer Kulturbesitz), *Phillipps* 1484 (80), ff. 125^r–126^v—likewise reproduces Zacharias' refutation without the preceding *Proposition*.

[12] In *Gud. gr.* 102 (f. 35^v) the scribe notes the transition from the works of Theodore Abū Qurrah (directed against Muslim criticisms of the Christian faith) to several short anti-Manichaean works with the rubric Ἀρχὴ σὺν θεῷ τῶν κατὰ τῶν Μανιχαίων. This rubric was subsequently reproduced in *Ott. gr.* 382 (f. 94^r) and *Monac. gr.* 66 (f. 63^v). The texts of the *Proposition* and Zacharias' *Adversus Manichaeos* in *Ott. gr.* 382 and *Monac. gr.* 66 also contain a number of variant readings which are otherwise found only in *Gud. gr.* 102; a summary of the evidence will be given in my forthcoming edition of Zacharias' treatise. Although the precise relationship between these three manuscripts needs further study, it is clear that *Ott. gr.* 382 and *Monac. gr.* 66 are descended from *Gud. gr.* 102. Since *Ott. gr.* 382 and *Monac. gr.* 66 do not provide an independent witness to the text, they will not be included in the edition of *Versio A*.

1   Versio A

A = cod. *Athous Vatopedinus* 236 (saec. XII), fol. 7ʳ
W = cod. *Guelferbytanus Gudianus gr.* 102 (saec. XIV), fol. 35ᵛ
It = Joannis Itali *Quaestiones quodlibetales,* cap. 59 (ed. Joannou, pag. 80–81)

Πρότασις Μανιχαίου παραλογιζομένη τὴν ἀλήθειαν τῆς μιᾶς καὶ μόνης παντοκρατορικῆς ἀρχῆς

Εἰ τὰ μὲν ἐναντία αὐτὰ ἑαυτοῖς οὐ λέγεται ἀντικεῖσθαι, πρὸς ἄλληλα δὲ αὐτὰ ἀνάγκη ἀντικεῖσθαι· οἷον τὸ ἄνω οὐ λέγεται πρὸς ἑαυτὸ ἀντικεῖσθαι ἀλλὰ πρὸς τὸ κάτω καὶ ἡ
5   ἀνδρεία οὐ πρὸς ἑαυτὴν ἀλλὰ πρὸς τὴν δειλίαν. ἄλλως τε καὶ οἷα ἂν εἴη τὰ ἀντικείμενα, τοιαῦτα ἀνάγκη καὶ τὰ τούτοις ἀντιδιαστελλόμενα· οἷον εἰ τὸ ἄνω οὐσία, ἀνάγκη καὶ τὸ κάτω οὐσίαν, εἰ δὲ συμβεβηκὸς τὸ ἕν, ἀνάγκη καὶ θάτερον.

Πῶς οὖν εἰ τὸ πονηρὸν ἀντίκειται πρὸς τὸ ἀγαθὸν καὶ τὸ ἀγαθὸν πρὸς τὸ πονηρὸν καὶ τὸ καλὸν πρὸς τὸ κακὸν καὶ τὸ κακὸν πρὸς τὸ καλόν, οὐκ ἀνάγκη τοῦ ἀγαθοῦ
10 ὄντος καὶ τοῦ καλοῦ, εἶναι καὶ τὸ πονηρὸν καὶ τὸ κακόν; καὶ εἰ οὐσία ἐστὶ τὸ ἀγαθὸν καὶ τὸ καλόν, καὶ τὰ ἀντικείμενα οὐσίας εἶναι, εἰ δὲ συμβαίη θάτερον, καὶ τὸ ἕτερον. εἰ γὰρ ἔστι μὲν τὸ ἀγαθὸν ἢ τὸ καλόν, τὸ δὲ πονηρὸν οὐκ ἔστιν ἢ τὸ κακόν, πρὸς τί δύναται ἀντικεῖσθαι τὸ ἀγαθὸν ἢ καλὸν τοῦ ἀντιδιαιρουμένου αὐτῷ μήτε ὄντος μήτε πρὸς τοῦτο λέγεσθαι δυναμένου; ὅπερ ἄτοπον.

15 Πῶς δὲ καὶ ἡ ἀντιδιαίρεσις ἀληθής ἐστι, τὸ ἀντικεῖσθαι τὸ ἀγαθὸν ⟨πρὸς⟩ τὸ πονηρόν, τοῦ μὲν ὄντος, τοῦ δὲ μὴ ὄντος; εἰ δ' ἐνταῦθα οὕτως ἔχει, ὡς καὶ τὸ ἀληθὲς μαρτυρεῖ καὶ τὰ εἰρημένα παρίστησι, πῶς οὐ ψεύδονται οἱ λέγοντες μὴ εἶναι δύο ἀρχὰς ἀγενήτους; εἰ δὲ ψεύδονται οἱ τὰς δύο ἀρχὰς ἀναιροῦντες, πῶς οὐκ ἀνάγκη τοὺς μετὰ τῆς ἀληθείας ζῆν ἐσπουδακότας δύο ἀρχὰς δογματίζειν;

---

1 post Πρότασις add. Φωτεινοῦ A   1–2 Πρότασις—ἀρχῆς] deest in It   3 τά] τό A   ‖   μέν] om. It   ‖   δέ] om. It   4 post οἷον add. εἰ It   5 post οὐ add. λέγεται It   6 ἀνάγκη¹] om. It   7 οὐσίαν] οὐσία W οὐσίαν εἶναι It   ‖   καί] om. W   8 οὖν] om. A   8–11 πονερὸν ἀντίκειται—τὸ ἕτερον] ἀγαθὸν ἀντίκειται τῷ κακῷ, ἔστι δὲ οὐσία τὸ ἀγαθόν, οὐχὶ καὶ τὸ ἀντικείμενον; It 9 πρός¹] κατά A   12 ἤ¹] καί W om. It   ‖   τὸ καλόν] om. It   ‖   πονηρὸν οὐκ—κακόν] κακὸν ὄν It   ‖   ἤ²] καί W   13 τὸ ἀγαθὸν ἢ καλόν] om. It   14 ὅπερ] τοῦτο γάρ It   15 καί] om. It   ‖   ἐστι] ἔσται It   ‖   τὸ ἀγαθόν] om. W   15–16 ⟨πρὸς⟩ τὸ πονηρόν] κατὰ τὸ πονηρόν A W τῷ κακῷ It 16–17 καὶ τὸ ἀληθές—εἰρημένα] om. It   17 παρίστησι] ἀποδείκνυσι A ἀποδέδεικται It   ‖   δύο ἀρχάς] ἀρχὰς δύο W   18 ἀγενήτους] ἀγεννήτους A W   19 τῆς] om. It

Proposition of a Manichaean misrepresenting the truth of the one and only almighty first principle.

If the contraries themselves are not said to be opposed to themselves, it is necessary for them to be opposed to one another; for instance, up is not said to be opposed to itself, but to down[13] and courage is not [said to be opposed] to itself but to cowardice.[14] Above all, whatever the opposites should be, it is necessary for the things contrasted to them also to be of the same kind; for instance, if up is a substance, it is necessary for down also to be a substance, and if the one is an accident, it is necessary for the other also [to be an accident].

If the bad is opposed to the good and the good to the bad and the beautiful to the ugly and the ugly to the beautiful, how then is it not necessary, since the good and the beautiful exists, for the bad and the ugly also to exist? And if the good and the beautiful is a substance, [it is necessary] also for their opposites to be substances, and if one should be an accident, the other is also [an accident]. For if the good or the beautiful exists but the bad or the ugly does not exist, to what can the good or beautiful be opposed, since what is distinguished in contrast to it neither exists, nor can be said in relation to it? This indeed is absurd.

And how is the contradistinction[15] (the good being opposed to the evil) true when the one exists and the other does not? But if then matters are thus, as indeed the truth attests and what has been said proves, how are they not speaking falsely who say that there are not two unoriginate first principles? But if

---

13 For the opposition of up and down as contraries, see Aristotle *Categoriae* 6, 6a12–15; *De caelo* 1.2, 269a14–15; 1.4, 271a4–5,25–26; 1.6, 273a8–9; 1.8, 277a21–23; *Physica* 1.5, 188a24–25; 5.5, 229b6–7; 5.6, 230b16; 8.8, 261b34.

14 For the opposition of courage and cowardice, see Plato *Protagoras* 360c7–d1; *Alcibiades I* 115d12–13; Aristotle *Categoriae* 11, 13b36–14a1; *Ethica Eudemia* 2.2.4, 1220b19–20; Chrysippus *fr. mor.* 256.25–26 (= Galen *De placitiis Hippocratis et Platonis* 7.2.6.5–6); ps.-Archytas in Simplicius *In Aristotelis categorias commentarium* 392.3–4.

15 "Distinction" (ἀντιδιαίρεσις) refers to the Aristotelian (and later, Neoplatonic) division by dichotomy, in which species result from the genus being divided with respect to opposed differentiae; see William E. Dooley, *Alexander of Aphrodisias. On Aristotle's Metaphysics 5* (Ithaca, NY: Cornell University Press, 1993), 139 n.106. The species thus belong to the same genus (e.g. "living being") and share the same definition, but are distinguished by differentiae that are opposed (e.g. "rational" and "irrational").

those who deny the two first principles are speaking falsely, how is it not necessary for those eager to live with truth to affirm two first principles?[16]

A slightly different text of the *Proposition* (*Versio B*) is found before the *Defensio* (Ἀπολογία) attributed to Paul the Persian in the three manuscripts which contain the latter work: Sinai, Monastery of St. Catharine, *gr.* 383 (Beneševič 513; Kamil 445) (10 c.), f. 137ʳ; Athos, Vatopedi 236 (12 c.), f. 135ʳ⁻ᵛ; and Vatican City, Biblioteca Apostolica Vaticana, *Vat. gr.* 1838 (13 c.), ff. 258ᵛ–259ʳ. These three manuscripts appear to be descended from a common ancestor.

Versio B also appears before Zacharias' *Adversus Manichaeos* in three manuscripts: Moscow, Gosudarstvennyj Istoričeskij Muzej, *Sinod. gr.* 394 (Vladimir 231; Matthaei XXXII), ff. 133ᵛ–134ʳ (10 c. [932 A.D.]); Rome, Biblioteca Vallicelliana, *Allacci* 38, fasc. 8 (12 c.); and Athos, Iviron 555 (14 c.), f. 268ᵛ (excerpt only = PG 88, 553B6–9 καὶ μίαν—δογματίζειν). These three manuscripts are reducible to a single witness, since *Allacci* 38 was copied from *Sinod gr.* 394 and Iviron 555 is descended from *Sinod. gr.* 394 by way of an intermediate manuscript that had been badly damaged.[17]

---

16   For the phrase δύο ἀρχὰς δογματίζειν ("to affirm two first principles"), compare Isaac Comnenus *De malorum subsistentia* 19.1.2–3 (which is dependent on Proclus) and Joannes Scholasticus (Scythopolitanus), *Scholia in Dionysii Areopagitae librum De divinis nominibus* schol. in DN 4.21/169.1 (Beate Regina Suchla, *Corpus Dionysiacum IV.1: Ioannis Scythopolitani prologus et scholia in Dionysii Areopagitae librum De divinis nominibus* [Berlin: De Gruyter, 2011], 279.3–4).

17   The texts of the *Proposition* and Zacharias' *Adversus Manichaeos* in *Allacci* 38 and Iviron 555 contain a number of variant readings which are otherwise found only in *Sinod. gr.* 394; a summary of the evidence will be given in my forthcoming edition of Zacharias' treatise. *Allacci* 38 also reproduces the marginal scholia of Arethas found in *Sinod. gr.* 394 (and is the only extant manuscript that reproduces all of Arethas' marginal scholia on this text). It is therefore reasonable to assume that *Allacci* 38 was copied from *Sinod. gr.* 394. Iviron 555 does not appear to have been copied directly from either *Sinod. gr.* 394 or *Allacci* 38. In Iviron 555, f. 268ᵛ, Zacharias' treatise is preceded by a paragraph whose source is not identified. Although the scribe presents the paragraph as a unity, it is obviously composed of disparate and unrelated arguments. The first part of the paragraph reproduces the text of a scholium originally written by Arethas in the margin of *Sinod. gr.* 394, 133ᵛ (εἰ πάντα—φθορᾶς); the text of this scholium was published by L.G. Westerink, "Marginalia by Arethas in Moscow Greek MS 231," *Byzantion* 42 (1972): 240. The second part of the paragraph reproduces the last few lines of the *Proposition* (*Versio B*) (καὶ μίαν—δογματίζειν), which is not the text under discussion in the preceding scholium. It is possible that Iviron 555 was copied from a manuscript that had been badly damaged and the scribe responsible for Iviron 555 simply salvaged all the text that was legible on the damaged page. In doing this, the scribe may have failed to understand that the text given in the margin of the damaged manuscript was a scholium and not sentences inadvertently omitted from the main text and then supplied in the margin.

2 Versio B

A = cod. *Athous Vatopedinus* 236 (saec. XII), fol. 135^(r–v)
M = cod. *Mosquensis Sinod. gr.* 394 (saec. X), fol. 133^v–134^r
S = cod. *Sinaiticus gr.* 383 (saec. X), fol. 137^r
V = cod. *Vaticanus gr.* 1838 (saec. XIII), fol. 258^v–259^r

Φωτεινοῦ Μανιχαίου πρότασις καὶ Παύλου τοῦ Πέρσου ἀπολογία

Εἰ τὰ ἐναντία αὐτὰ ἑαυτοῖς οὐ λέγεται ἀντικεῖσθαι, πρὸς ἄλληλα δὲ ἀνάγκη αὐτὰ ἀντικεῖσθαι· οἷον τὸ ἄνω οὐ λέγεται πρὸς ἑαυτὸ ἀντικεῖσθαι ἀλλὰ πρὸς τὸ κάτω καὶ ἡ ἀνδρεία οὐ λέγεται πρὸς ἑαυτὴν ἀντκεῖσθαι ἀλλὰ πρὸς τὴν δειλίαν. ἄλλως τε δὲ καὶ οἷα
5 ἂν ᾖ τὰ ἀντικείμενα, τοιαῦτα ἀνάγκη εἶναι καὶ τὰ τούτοις ἀντιδιαστελλόμενα· οἷον εἰ τὸ ἄνω οὐσία ἐστίν, ἀνάγκη πάντως καὶ τὸ κάτω οὐσίαν εἶναι καὶ πάλιν εἰ συμβεβηκός ἐστι τὸ ἄνω, ἀνάγκη καὶ τὸ κάτω συμβεβηκὸς εἶναι.

Πῶς οὖν εἰ τὸ ἀγαθὸν πρὸς τὸ πονηρὸν ἀντίκειται καὶ τὸ πονηρὸν πρὸς τὸ ἀγαθὸν καὶ τὸ καλὸν πρὸς τὸ κακὸν καὶ τὸ κακὸν πρὸς τὸ καλόν, οὐκ ἀνάγκη τοῦ ἀγαθοῦ ὄντος,
10 καὶ τὸ πονηρὸν εἶναι καὶ τοῦ καλοῦ ὄντος, καὶ τὸ κακὸν εἶναι; καὶ πάλιν εἰ οὐσία ἐστὶ τὸ ἀγαθὸν ἢ τὸ καλόν, καὶ τὸ πονηρὸν καὶ τὸ κακὸν οὐσίαν εἶναι καὶ εἰ συμβεβηκὸς τούτων θάτερόν ἐστι, καὶ τὸ ἕτερον συμβεβηκὸς εἶναι. εἰ γὰρ ἔστι μὲν τὸ ἀγαθὸν ἢ τὸ καλόν, τὸ δὲ πονηρὸν οὐκ ἔστιν ἢ τὸ κακόν, πρὸς τί δύναται ἀντικεῖσθαι τὸ ἀγαθὸν ἢ τὸ καλὸν τοῦ ἀντιδιαιρουμένου αὐτῷ μήτε ὄντος μήτε πρὸς τοῦτο λέγεσθαι δυναμένου;
15 ὅπερ ἄτοπον.

Πῶς δὲ καὶ ἡ ἀντιδιαίρεσις ἀληθής ἐστι τοῦ ἀντικεῖσθαι τὸ ἀγαθὸν πρὸς τὸ πονηρόν, τοῦ μὲν ὄντος, τοῦ δὲ μὴ ὄντος; εἰ δὲ ταῦθ' οὕτως ἔχει, ὡς καὶ τὸ ἀληθὲς μαρτυρεῖ καὶ τὰ εἰρημένα ἀποδείκνυσιν, πῶς οὐ ψεύδονται οἱ λέγοντες μὴ εἶναι δύο ἀρχὰς ἀγενήτους, μίαν μὲν ἀγαθήν, μίαν δὲ πονηρὰν καὶ μίαν καλὴν καὶ τὴν ἑτέραν κακήν; εἰ
20 δὲ ψεύδονται οἱ τὰς δύο ἀρχὰς ἀναιροῦντες, πῶς οὐκ ἀνάγκη τοὺς μετὰ τῆς ἀληθείας συζῆν ἐσπουδακότας δύο ἀρχὰς δογματίζειν;

---

1 Φωτεινοῦ—ἀπολογία] Πρότασίς τινος [*in marg. add.* Φωτεινοῦ] Μανιχαίου παραλογιζομένου τὴν ἀλήθειαν τῆς μιᾶς καὶ μόνης παντοκρατορικῆς ἀρχῆς M   2 οὔ] οὐδέποτε A V οὐδέποται *sic* S   6 οὐσία] οὐσίας M || πάντως] om. A   8 Πῶς οὖν] Καὶ ἔτι M   9 *ante* οὐκ *add.* πῶς M || *post* ἀνάγκη *add.* καὶ V   10 *post* εἰ *add.* ἡ A || οὐσία] οὐσίᾳ M   11 τὸ²] om. V || *post* καλόν *add.* ἀνάγκη M || οὐσίαν] οὐσίᾳ M || εἰ] ἡ S   12 ἐστι] εἶναι M   13 ἔστιν] ἔστι S ἔσται A V || τί] τίνα M   16 τοῦ] τὸ M   18–19 ἀγενήτους] ἀγεννήτους A V   19 εἰ] οἱ S   20 τὰς] *legi non potest* V   21 ἐσπουδακότας] *legi non potest* V

Proposition of Photinus, a Manichaean, and Defense of Paul the Persian

If the contraries themselves are not said to be opposed to themselves, it is necessary for them to be opposed to one another; for instance, up is not said to be opposed to itself, but to down and courage is not said to be opposed to itself but to cowardice. But above all, whatever the opposites might be, it is necessary for the things contrasted to them also to be of the same kind; for instance, if up is a substance, it is absolutely necessary for down also to be a substance, and again, if up is an accident, it is necessary also for down to be an accident.

If the good is opposed to the bad and the bad to the good and the beautiful to the ugly and the ugly to the beautiful, how then is it not necessary, since the good exists, also for the bad to exist, and since the beautiful exists, for the ugly also to exist? And again, if the good or the beautiful is a substance, [it is necessary] also for the bad and the ugly to be a substance, and if one of these is an accident, [it is necessary for] the other also to be [an accident]. For if the good or the beautiful exists but the bad or the ugly does not exist, to what can the good or the beautiful be opposed, since what is distinguished in contrast to it neither exists, nor can be said in relation to it? This indeed is absurd.

And how is the contradistinction (with the good being opposed to the evil) true, when the one exists and the other does not? But if these things are so, as indeed the truth attests and what has been said demonstrates, how are they not speaking falsely who say that there are not two unoriginate first principles, one good and one bad, and one beautiful and the other ugly? But if those who deny the two first principles are speaking falsely, how is it not necessary for those eager to live in union with the truth to affirm two first principles?

Although the differences between *Versio A* and *Versio B* are relatively minor, it is likely that *Versio A* preserves more features of the original form of the text. For example, the optative εἴη in *Versio A* is replaced in *Versio B* by the more familiar subjunctive ᾖ. The compressed phrases commonly used in logical texts are expanded in *Versio B* to help the reader follow the argument. Thus, εἰ δὲ συμβεβηκὸς τὸ ἕν, ἀνάγκη καὶ θάτερον (*Versio A*) is expanded into καὶ πάλιν εἰ συμβεβηκός ἐστι τὸ ἄνω, ἀνάγκη καὶ τὸ κάτω συμβεβηκὸς εἶναι (*Versio B*) and εἰ δὲ συμβαίη θάτερον, καὶ τὸ ἕτερον (*Versio A*) is expanded into καὶ εἰ συμβεβηκὸς τούτων θάτερόν ἐστι, καὶ τὸ ἕτερον συμβεβηκὸς εἶναι (*Versio B*). Phrases involving parallelism are reduced to simpler constructions in *Versio B*, so that the reader can more readily understand the structure of the argument. For example, ἀνάγκη τοῦ ἀγαθοῦ ὄντος καὶ τοῦ καλοῦ, εἶναι καὶ τὸ πονηρὸν καὶ τὸ κακόν (*Versio A*) is rewritten as ἀνάγκη τοῦ ἀγαθοῦ ὄντος, καὶ τὸ πονηρὸν εἶναι καὶ τοῦ καλοῦ ὄντος, καὶ τὸ κακὸν εἶναι (*Versio B*).[18]

A more extensive revision of the text appears in Italus' reworking of *Versio A*. Rather than rephrasing constructions involving parallelism, Italus simply eliminates the parallelism. For example, εἰ γὰρ ἔστι μὲν τὸ ἀγαθὸν ἢ τὸ καλόν, τὸ δὲ πονηρὸν οὐκ ἔστιν ἢ τὸ κακόν (*Versio A*) becomes εἰ γὰρ ἔστι μὲν τὸ ἀγαθόν, τὸ δὲ κακόν οὔ (Italus). Where *Versio A* contained a repetition of similar phrases, Italus treated these as redundant and recast the sentence to eliminate anything that was not strictly necessary to grasp the argument:

> *Versio A*: Πῶς οὖν εἰ τὸ πονερὸν ἀντίκειται πρὸς τὸ ἀγαθὸν καὶ τὸ ἀγαθὸν πρὸς τὸ πονηρὸν καὶ τὸ καλὸν πρὸς τὸ κακὸν καὶ τὸ κακὸν πρὸς τὸ καλόν, οὐκ ἀνάγκη τοῦ ἀγαθοῦ ὄντος καὶ τοῦ καλοῦ, εἶναι καὶ τὸ πονηρὸν καὶ τὸ κακόν; καὶ εἰ οὐσία ἐστὶ τὸ ἀγαθὸν καὶ τὸ καλόν, καὶ τὰ ἀντικείμενα οὐσίας εἶναι, εἰ δὲ συμβαίη θάτερον, καὶ τὸ ἕτερον.
>
> Italus: Πῶς οὖν εἰ τὸ ἀγαθὸν ἀντίκειται τῷ κακῷ, ἔστι δὲ οὐσία τὸ ἀγαθόν, οὐχὶ καὶ τὸ ἀντικείμενον;

In reviewing the argument given in the *Proposition*, it is remarkable that Manichaeism is not specifically named within the argument, nor are teachings

---

18 The simplification of the text to facilitate comprehension has also affected the physical arrangement of the text in *Sinod. gr.* 394 (the earliest manuscript in which *Versio B* is attested). There the arguments are grouped into separate text blocks, with a space occurring before and after the phrase καὶ πάλιν. In that manuscript, the interrogative πῶς οὖν is also replaced by καὶ ἔτι, which is similarly separated by space before and after it, preparing the reader for the introduction of a new argument.

unique to Manichaeism defended there. There is in fact nothing in the *Proposition* that might connect the argument with Manichaean teaching other than the assertion that there are two unoriginate first principles and that evidence is of uncertain value. The phrase "two unoriginate first principles" was primarily associated with a debate within the Platonic tradition about whether unformed matter could be regarded as having existed eternally alongside God.[19] Writers who had a detailed knowledge of the Platonic tradition sometimes used the phrase "two unoriginate first principles" to describe Manichaean teaching, treating the latter as though it were a heterodox form of Platonism.[20] The phrase "two unoriginate first principles" therefore can only situate the *Proposition* within a broader debate in the Platonic tradition, but cannot confirm that the argument was originally intended specifically to represent Manichaean teaching.

The association of the *Proposition* with Manichaeism must thus depend upon evidence external to the text itself. In refuting the argument made in the *Proposition*, Zacharias' *Adversus Manichaeos* does not refer to Manichaeism and Paul the Persian's *Defensio* mentions Manichaeism only once, so it is difficult to assess how committed they were to identifying the argument in the *Proposition* with specifically Manichaean teaching.[21] It is also remarkable that

---

19 For the debate, see Proclus, *In Platonis Timaeum commentaria* 384.2–12: "... [O]ne may ask with regard to matter itself whether it is ungenerated by [any] cause, as Plutarch and Atticus claim, or whether it is generated, and [if so] from what cause. Aristotle indeed has demonstrated that it is ungenerated in other ways, [namely] as being incomposite, as not coming into existence out of other matter, and as not being resolved back into other [matter]. [Our] present argument, for its part, [first] asserts that it is everlasting, [then] goes on to ask whether it is ungenerated by [any] cause, and whether in Plato's view one should posit two principles of the universe, [namely] matter and God, with neither God producing matter nor matter God, so that [matter] will be totally everlasting and without God and [God] totally without matter and simple" (ET David T. Runia and Michael Share, *Proclus. Commentary on Plato's Timaeus*, vol. 2 [Cambridge: Cambridge University Press, 2008], 252–253). Compare Isaac Comnenus, *De malorum subsistentia* 19.1.2–5, which is dependent on Proclus: Καὶ γὰρ οἱ μὲν δύο ἀρχὰς δογματίσαντες, τούτων τὴν μὲν μίαν εἶπον πηγὴν τῶν κακῶν (προάγοντες πᾶν τὸ ὁπωσοῦν κακὸν ἀπ' αὐτῆς), τὴν δ' ἑτέραν τῶν ἀγαθῶν (James John Rizzo, *Isaak Sebastokrator's Περὶ τῆς τῶν κακῶν ὑποστάσεως* [*De malorum subsistentia*] [Meisenheim am Glan: Anton Hain, 1971], 47).

20 See Didymus Caecus *Commentarii in Zachariam* 4.125.1–3 (Louis Doutreleau, *Didyme l'Aveugle. Sur Zacharie*, vol. 3 [Paris: Cerf, 1962], 864 [309.21–23]); Joannes Grammaticus *Adversus Manichaeos* (*Homilia I*) 251–253 (Richard, 91); Michael Psellus, *Opusculum* 55.122–130 (Paul Gautier, *Michaelis Pselli Theologica*, vol. 1 [Leipzig: B.G. Teubner, 1989], 216–217). The writings of the last two authors show a strong dependence on Proclus.

21 Paul refers in passing to Manichaeism at PG 88, 556C11–D1.

John Italus does not supply a chapter heading or introduction linking the proposition with Manichaeism.

The connection between the *Proposition* and Manichaeism therefore rests almost exclusively on a single source, a prefatory note that appears in a tenth-century manuscript, *Sinod. gr.* 394 (f. 134^{r-v}) after the *Proposition* and before Zacharias' *Adversus Manichaeos*:[22]

> Ἀντίρρησις Ζαχαρίου ἐπισκόπου Μιτυλήνης, τὸν παραλογισμὸν τοῦ Μανιχαίου διελέγχουσα καὶ τῇ ἀληθείᾳ τῆς μιᾶς καὶ μόνης ἀρχῆς συνισταμένη, ἣν ἐποιήσατο σχολαστικὸς ὢν ἔτι καὶ συνήγορος τῆς ἀγορᾶς τῆς μεγίστης τῶν ὑπάρχων καὶ συμπονῶν τῷ κόμητι τοῦ πατριμονίου, ἡνίκα Ἰουστινιανὸς ὁ εὐσεβέστατος ἡμῶν βασιλεὺς διάταξιν ἐξεφώνησε κατὰ τῶν ἀθεωτάτων Μανιχαίων. τότε γὰρ τινες ἐξ αὐτῶν προκειμένης τῆς κατ' αὐτῶν διατάξεως, ἐν Κωνσταντινουπόλει εἰς βιβλιοπρατεῖον διακείμενον ἐν τῇ βασιλικῇ ἔρριψαν τὸν τοιοῦτον χάρτην καὶ ἀνεχώρησαν. ἐζήτει οὖν ὁ βιβλιοπράτης τὸν ὀφείλοντα ἀνατρέψαι τὴν Μανιχαϊκὴν πρότασιν καὶ εὑρὼν Ζαχαρίαν, τὸν μετὰ ταῦτα γενόμενον ἐπίσκοπον Μιτυλήνης, ταύτην αὐτῷ δέδωκεν, αἰτήσας αὐτὸν τὴν ἀντίρρησιν ταύτης ποιήσασθαι. ᾔδει γὰρ αὐτὸν ἐκ τῶν ἑπτὰ κεφαλαίων τῶν παρ' αὐτοῦ κατ' αὐτῶν συντεθέντων εἴτ' οὖν ἀναθεματισμῶν ἐπιτηδείως ἔχειν πρὸς ἀνατροπὴν τῶν τοιούτων παραλογισμῶν. ὁ δὲ λαβὼν οὕτως ἀνέτρεψεν.[23]

Refutation of Zacharias, bishop of Mitylene, utterly refuting the paralogism of the Manichaean and allying [itself] with the truth of the one and only first principle, which he [sc. Zacharias] composed when he was still a *scholastikos*[24] and advocate of the supreme assembly of the hy-

---

22 The prefatory note is most likely the source of the summary information given in the titles which precede the *Proposition* in *Versio A* and *Versio B*. The titles contain nothing that is not found in the prefatory note and similar keywords appear in both the titles and the prefatory note (Μανιχαϊκὴν πρότασιν/Πρότασις Μανιχαίου, παραλογισμὸν ... τῇ ἀληθείᾳ τῆς μιᾶς καὶ μόνης ἀρχῆς/παραλογιζομένη τὴν ἀλήθειαν τῆς μιᾶς καὶ μόνης παντοκρατορικῆς ἀρχῆς).

23 This prefatory note was first published by Christian Friedrich von Matthäi, *Accurata codicum graecorum mss. bibliothecarum Mosquensium Sanctissimae Synodi notitia et recensio*, vol. 1 (Leipzig: Joachim, 1805), 294–295 and subsequently reproduced by Demetrakopoulos, γ'-δ'. Sebastian Brock and Brian Fitzgerald (*Two Early Lives of Severos, Patriarch of Antioch* [Liverpool: Liverpool University Press, 2013], 16) attribute the note to Arethas of Caesarea, although there is no evidence for this in the manuscript itself.

24 The word σχολαστικός originally signified a person who had the leisure to study and, by the Roman imperial period, was increasingly used to describe persons who studied and taught rhetoric. In the fifth and sixth centuries A.D., *scholastikos* often referred to persons who had legal training and served in various administrative positions. See Orion of Thebes, *Etymologicum* (G.H.K. Koës, *Orionis Thebani etymologicon*, ed. F.G. Sturz [Leipzig: Weigel,

parchs[25] and working together with the count of the patrimony,[26] when our most pious Emperor Justinian promulgated a decree against the most impious Manichaeans. For at that time when the decree against them was set forth, some of them threw the sheet in the booksellers' market[27] which is situated in the Imperial Portico[28] in Constantinople and

---

1820; repr. Hildesheim: Olms, 1973], 183.21–22): Σχολαστικός· διὰ τὸ σχολάζειν τοῖς ἀστικοῖς ἢ τῷ δικαίῳ. There was, however, no absolute distinction between the realms of rhetoric and law in this period, since speaking before a court was one of the responsibilities of an advocate and this presumed prior training in rhetoric. Furthermore, it is clear that some persons had taught grammar and rhetoric before becoming an advocate and that even persons holding high judicial offices sometimes taught advanced rhetoric (i.e. epideictic and forensic oratory) and logic to a small circle of students. For further discussion, see Marina Loukaki, "Σχολαστικός. Remarques sur le sens du terme à Byzance (IVe–XVe siècles)," *Byzantinische Zeitschrift* 109 (2016): 41–72; idem, "Le profil des enseignants dans l' Empire Byzantin à la fin de l' Antiquité tardive et au début du Moyen Âge (fin du VIe-fin du VIIe siècle)," in *Myriobiblos: Essays on Byzantine Literature and Culture*, ed. Theodora Antonopoulou, Sofia Kotzabassi, and Marina Loukaki (Berlin: Walter de Gruyter, 2015), 225–226, 229.

25 The hyparchs would presumably be the praetorian and city prefects. Advocates of the judicial assembly convened by the praetorian prefect are mentioned in Justinian *Novellae* 82.1 (W. Kroll and R. Schöll, *Corpus iuris civilis*, vol. 3 [Berlin: Weidmann, 1899], 401.29–35). There is also a reference to advocates at the court of the hyparchs in *Collectio tripartita* 1.3.32 (N. van der Wal and B.H. Stolte, *Collectio Tripartita: Justinian on Religious and Ecclesiastical Affairs* [Groningen: Egbert Forsten, 1994], 39.25–40.2).

26 The count of the patrimony was a short-lived office, created by Anastasius and abolished by Justinian at the beginning of his reign. The count of the patrimony managed private property, especially agricultural land, which had become the property of the imperial government, typically through confiscation. See Athanasius Scholasticus, *Novellae constitutiones* 3.4 (Dieter Simon and Spyros Troianos, *Das Novellensyntagma des Athanasios von Emesa* [Frankfurt am Main: Löwenklau Gesellschaft, 1989], 172.19) and J.B. Bury, *The Imperial Administrative System in the Ninth Century* (London: Oxford University Press, 1911), 79–80. If the accentuation of συμπονῶν ("working with") were changed to συμπόνων (σύμπονος = "assessor," i.e. a judicial advisor), one might translate the text as "of the supreme assembly of the hyparchs and the assessors for the count of the patrimony." The role of the σύμπονοι/*adsessores* of the eparchs (prefects or governors) in the administration of justice is mentioned in *Codex Justinianus* 1.51.11,13 (Bruce W. Frier, *The Codex of Justinian: A New Annotated Translation with Parallel Latin and Greek Text*, vol. 1 [Cambridge: Cambridge University Press, 2016], 388–389); *Novellae* 119.5 (Kroll and Schöll, vol. 3, 574.30–31).

27 Since βιβλιοπρατεῖον appears to be a *hapax legomenon*, this translation is conjectural. Even the noun πρατεῖον is exceedingly rare; see *Vita Aesopi Westermanniana (recensio 2)* 21.3,5 (Ben Edwin Perry, *Aesopica*, vol. 1 [Urbana: University of Illinois Press, 1952], 84.23,25); Theodore Studites, *Catechesis maior* 87 (A. Papadopoulos-Kerameus, Τοῦ ὁσίου Θεοδώρου τοῦ Στουδίτου μεγάλη κατήχησις [St. Petersburg: Kirschbaum, 1904], 622.3).

28 The Imperial Portico was originally a quadriporticus agora (a large rectangular open courtyard that was surrounded on all four sides by a continuous colonnade). After much ren-

departed. The bookseller was therefore looking for the person who ought to refute the Manichaean proposition and, finding Zacharias, who afterward was bishop of Mitylene, gave the proposition to him, asking him to compose a refutation of it, for he [sc. the bookseller] knew, from the seven chapters or rather anathemas composed by him [sc. Zacharias] against them,[29] that he was well suited to refute the paralogisms of such persons. And he, taking it, refuted it as follows.

The purpose of this prefatory note was to establish for the reader that Zacharias had the specialized knowledge needed to refute paralogisms and could therefore be regarded as an authority on logical matters.[30] While the prefatory note may include some accurate information regarding the official positions once held by Zacharias, the historicity of the events described in the prefatory note has been questioned. The story of a bookseller requesting a response to a pamphlet is a literary device previously used by Zacharias himself at the beginning of his earlier work, the *Vita Severi* (*Life of Severus*). In the beginning of the *Vita Severi*, just as in the prefatory note preceding the *Adversus Manichaeos*, Zacharias is given a pamphlet handed out by a bookseller in the Imperial Portico and asked to read and refute it.[31] After analyzing these

---

ovation, it became an imperial monument that housed the juridical court, a library, and the schools that provided higher education; see Dimitrios Chatzilazarou, Η Βασίλειος Στοά και η σύνθεση του μνημειακού κέντρου της Κωνσταντινούπολης. Τοπογραφία, λειτουργίες, συμβολισμοί (PhD diss., National and Kapodistrian University of Athens, 2016).

29 Marcel Richard and Samuel N.C. Lieu have argued for identification of the *Seven Chapters against the Manichaeans*, attributed here to Zacharias, with an anonymous early Byzantine formula for the abjuration of Manichaeism found in Athos, Vatopedi 236; see Richard, XXXI–XXXII and Samuel N.C. Lieu, "An Early Byzantine Formula for the Renunciation of Manichaeism—The *Capita VII contra Manichaeos* of ⟨Zacharias of Mitylene⟩," in Samuel N.C. Lieu, *Manichaeism in Mesopotamia and the Roman East* (Leiden: Brill, 1999), 203–305. A critical edition of this text (CPG 6997: *Capita vii contra Manichaeos*) is given in Richard, XXXIII–XXXIX. An English translation and a helpful commentary on the text appear in Lieu, 234–254, 256–296.

30 In Zacharias' philosophical dialogue *Ammonius*, the Christian disputant, who presents the position favored by Zacharias, similarly comments, "So in order that we may fight together for … the truth … we must quickly and simply dissolve this whole edifice made from sand of your paralogisms" (Maria Minniti Colonna, *Zacaria Scolastico. Ammonio. Introduzione, testo critico, traduzione, commentario* [Naples: Tipolitografia "La Buona Stampa," 1973], 113.567–569; ET Sebastian Gertz, John Dillon and Donald Russell, *Aeneas of Gaza: Theophrastus with Zacharias of Mitylene: Ammonius* [London: Bloomsbury Academic, 2012], 118, slightly modified).

31 The *Vita Severi* begins with an appeal from Zacharias' friend to write a response to a fallacious pamphlet received from a bookseller in the Imperial Portico: "I've come to you

two parallel accounts, Ernest Honigmann rejected the historicity of the events described in the note preceding Zacharias' *Adversus Manichaeos*.³² Peter Nowell has recently come to a similar conclusion, regarding the narrative introductions to both the *Vita Severi* and the *Adversus Manichaeos* as literary constructions with no historical value.³³

The reservations of Honigmann and Nowell seem well founded, as this is the one point where the account given in the prefatory note lacks verisimilitude. Byzantine law took a dim view of anyone who found a document that contained unfounded accusations and did not immediately destroy it;³⁴ this included documents that had been thrown in a public place.³⁵ Any person who read and communicated the content of such a document was to "be subjected to a capital sentence ... as though he were the author" of the document.³⁶ If the story of finding a document was recognizable as a mere literary device, it might have been treated as harmless, but if it had been thought to reflect actual events, a far more severe judgment might have been rendered.

Setting aside the vexing question of historicity, one might consider the prefatory note's assertion that the *Proposition* is a series of paralogisms and that paralogisms can only be detected and refuted by a person who has an authoritative knowledge of logic. One should begin by clarifying what Aristotle meant by "paralogism." At the beginning of the *Topics*, Aristotle discusses syllogistic reasoning. He first defines a syllogism ("an argument in which, when certain

    straight from the Royal Stoa [i.e. Imperial Portico] ... I'm disturbed by a pamphlet which purports to be by someone who is a Christian, but whose real intent is to make fun of Christianity ... I was searching through the books of the booksellers in the Royal Stoa ... and one of the men sitting there selling books handed me the pamphlet in question ... It is not because I have been thrown into any doubt, or that I agree with what has so maliciously been written that I have come to you. But I am upset ... lest people who read it in a simple-minded way might perhaps pick up the wrong sort of idea" (ET Brock and Fitzgerald, 33–34).

32 Ernest Honigmann, *Patristic Studies* (Vatican City: Biblioteca Apostolica Vaticana, 1953), 200: "[T]his bookseller, suggesting him to refute the Manichaean pamphlet, is only a fictitious person."
33 Peter B. Nowell, "Severus of Antioch: Fiction in the Archives?" (forthcoming): "I see both of these introductions as fiction, a literary device to start the piece."
34 *Codex Justinianus* 9.36.1–2 (Frier, vol. 3, 2392–2393).
35 *Codex Justinianus* 9.36.2 (*Si quis famosum libellum ... in publico ... reppererit*), with the commentary in *Synopsis basilicorum major* 21(Φ).4 (Περὶ φλυαριῶν χαρτῶν, τουτέστι τῶν ῥιπτομένων πιττακίων καὶ ἐχόντων κατηγορίας κατά τινων) (Ioannis Zepos and Panagiotis Zepos, *Jus Graecoromanum v: Synopsis Basilicorum: ex editione C.E. Zachariae a Lingenthal* [Athens: Fexis, 1931], 567).
36 *Codex Justinianus* 9.36.2; compare the Greek text given in 9.36.1 ("shall be liable to the same penalty as the person who composed it").

things are set down [i.e., as premises], something different from the things set down [i.e., the conclusion] follows necessarily by means of the things set down").[37] Aristotle then divides syllogisms into four types (demonstrative reasoning, dialectical reasoning, eristic reasoning, and paralogisms).

Demonstrative reasoning (ἀπόδειξις) proceeds from true and primary premises that are connected with a particular science. The premises of an argument affirm or deny something (a predicate) of something else (a subject). A premise is "primary" when

a. What it states is previously known as a fact and is indemonstrable[38] (or has been correctly deduced from such a starting point) and
b. It precedes and causes the conclusion that follows from it, so that the latter is necessarily the case.[39]

A paralogism is an argument that appears to have the features that define demonstrative reasoning but, in reality, it does not. A paralogism instead involves fallacious reasoning from premises that are only apparently scientific; consequently, the conclusion does not necessarily follow and the argument fails to prove or refute what it aimed to prove or refute.[40]

In the *Sophistical Refutations*, Aristotle contended that fallacious arguments depend upon a false presupposition about either language (παρὰ τὴν λέξιν) or the extra-linguistic world (ἔξω τῆς λέξεως); identifying that false presupposition was both necessary and sufficient to refute the argument. Aristotle then developed a comprehensive taxonomy of reasoning errors, describing six errors arising from false presuppositions about language and seven errors arising from false presuppositions about the extra-linguistic world.[41] Aristotle argued that it was useful to study fallacious reasoning so that one could avoid being deceived by it and instead make prudent judgments.[42]

---

37   Aristotle, *Topica* 1.1, 100a25–27; ET of Scott G. Schreiber, *Aristotle on False Reasoning: Language and the World in the Sophistical Refutations* (Albany, NY: SUNY Press, 2003), 1. Compare the similar definitions given in *Sophistici Elenchi* 1, 164b27–165a2 and *Analytica priora* 1.1, 24b18–20.

38   A proposition about X is considered "indemonstrable" if it is known immediately, being true by definition in every instance of X, and is essential to understanding what X is; see Aristotle, *Analytica posteriora* 1.2, 71b17–23; *Topica* 1.1, 100a27–b21. Mathematical definitions and geometrical axioms, for example, do not need demonstration but are epistemically basic and serve as the foundational principles from which new knowledge can be produced by means of deduction.

39   Aristotle, *Analytica posteriora* 1.2, 71b20–33; 1.3, 72b19–25; compare *Analytica priora* 1.1, 24b18–22.

40   Aristotle, *Sophistici elenchi* 1, 164a20–22 and Schreiber, 81–84.

41   For a detailed discussion, see Schreiber, 11–166.

42   Aristotle, *Topica* 1.18, 108a18,26–29: "It is useful to have examined in how many ways a word

It is likely that the *Proposition* should be construed as a series of paralogisms. In spite of using sophisticated logical terminology, the *Proposition* contains some elementary errors in logic that would be evident even to a reader who had only a cursory knowledge of Aristotle's *Categories*. Thus, if the original purpose of the *Proposition* was to offer a demonstrative argument, that argument would have been swiftly dismissed due to these elementary errors. One could better account for the presence of these errors by assuming that the *Proposition* is a series of paralogisms that was used to teach students how to detect and resolve fallacious arguments.

To understand how the *Proposition* functions as a series of paralogisms, it will be helpful to expand the three arguments given in the *Proposition* into a dialectical format, so as to achieve greater clarity. The first argument aims to establish that evil is a substance:

(1) Contrary things (τὰ ἐναντία) are defined not by what each is in relation to itself, but by the opposition (ἀντικεῖσθαι) which exists between the two (e.g. up/down, courage/cowardice, etc.).[43]

(2) For things to be contrary, they must have a particular form of opposition, namely, being contradistinguished (ἀντιδιαιρούμενα/ἀντιδιαστελλόμενα) in the following way: Where X and Y are contraries, X is opposed only to Y, and Y is opposed only to X, and X and Y are both members of the same class and are thus things of the same kind.[44]

(3) Since contrary things are defined by their opposition to one another, and their particular form of opposition requires them to be members of the same class and things of the same kind, if one is a substance, the other will also be a substance.

---

is said … It can also be useful … for resisting fallacies (τὸ μὴ παραλογισθῆναι) … For if we know in how many ways something is said, we shall not be taken in by fallacies ourselves (οὐ μὴ παραλογισθῶμεν) but instead will know if the questioner fails to make the argument about the same thing" (ET Robin Smith, *Aristotle. Topics Books I and VIII* [Oxford: Clarendon Press, 1997], 18, slightly modified); compare *Sophistici elenchi* 16, 175a10–12. This rationale for studying paralogisms was accepted by later Neo-Aristotelian and Neoplatonic philosophers; see Alexander of Aphrodisias, *In Aristotelis topicorum libros octo commentaria* 120.13–19; Iamblichus, *Protrepticus* 2 (9.16–10.1); Olympiodorus, *Prolegomena* 8.19–27.

43 On contrariety as a form of opposition, see Aristotle, *Categoriae* 10, 11b17–19; *Metaphysica* 5.10, 1018a20; 10.4,1055a38–b1.

44 The requirement that to each contrary only one thing is contrary precedes Aristotle and is found already in Plato, *Protagoras* 332c. Aristotle defends this requirement by arguing that contraries have the maximum difference within a genus (*Metaphysica* 5.10,1018a27–31; 10.4,1055a3–6); since there are only two species that have the maximum difference within a genus, there can be no more than two contraries (*Metaphysica* 10.4,1055a8–23).

(4) From (3), it follows that if the good is a substance, that which is contradistinguished from it as its contrary (i.e. evil) will also be a substance.

From (2), a second argument is made to prove that evil necessarily exists:

(5) Since contraries are defined by their opposition to one another, and their form of opposition requires that X is opposed only to Y and Y is opposed only to X, the existence of one contrary implies the existence of the other, so if the one exists, the other will also exist.

(6) From (5), it follows that if the good exists, that which is contradistinguished from the good as its contrary (i.e. evil) will also exist.

Having established the existence of evil, the author of the *Proposition* concludes by arguing that evil is unoriginate. This would seem to require some unexpressed premises which, based on parallel arguments in Proclus and the Neoplatonic commentators on Aristotle, might be supplied as follows:

(7) From (5), if the existence of one contrary implies the existence of the other, then it follows that one contrary cannot be prior to or posterior to the other, so evil cannot be posterior to the good, but must always coexist with it.[45]

(8) If evil is not posterior to the good but always coexists with it, then if the good is unoriginate, evil will also be unoriginate.

Premise (1) is true (contrariety is a form of opposition and in opposition two things are opposed to one another) but contributes nothing to the demonstration since, in discussing opposition, it states a tautology. By definition opposition involves two things that cannot hold at the same time, so of necessity they must be different from one another.[46] To say that contraries, as opposites, are opposed not to themselves but to one another adds no new information but simply restates in different words what opposition is.[47] Premise (1) is therefore

---

45   In the *Elements of Theology*, Proclus considers a similar argument, asking whether the one and the manifold can be considered two principles that are coordinate in nature, existing "as contradistinguished [principles] which by nature co-exist, inasmuch as neither is prior or posterior to the other" (ὡς ἀντιδιῃρημένα ἅμα ὄντα τῇ φύσει εἴπερ μηδέτερον θατέρου πρότερον ἢ ὕστερον) (*Institutio theologica* 5; E.R. Dodds, *Proclus. The Elements of Theology*, 2 ed. [Oxford: Clarendon Press, 1963], 4.29–30).

46   See Jonathan Barnes, Susanne Bobzien, Kevin Flannery, and Katerina Ierodiakonou, *Alexander of Aphrodisias: On Aristotle's Prior Analytics 1.1–7* (Ithaca, NY: Cornell University Press, 1991), 26. Aristotle affirmed in *Metaphysica* 5.10, 1018a25–27 that this is true of contraries as a form of opposition.

47   The assertion that a contrary is not opposed to itself is possibly a verbal reminiscence of *Categoriae* 6, 6a7–8: ἀλλὰ τῶν ἀδυνάτων ἐστὶν αὐτὸ ἑαυτῷ εἶναι ἐναντίον (Richard Bodéüs, *Aristote [Catégories]* [Paris: Les Belles Lettres, 2001], 26). Compare also Maximus *Fragmentum ex libro de materia* in Eusebius of Caesarea *Praeparatio evangelica* 7.22.64.1–5: οὐδὲ γὰρ ἐστί τι αὐτῷ ἀντικείμενον· τὰ γὰρ ἀντικείμενα ἑτέροις ἀντικεῖσθαι πέφυκεν. οἷον τὸ λευκὸν αὐτὸ

irrelevant and contributes nothing to the demonstration. In discussing how to resolve fallacies, Aristotle had argued that one must begin by identifying premises that are irrelevant and contribute nothing to the demonstration.[48] Aristotle illustrated this point by discussing a fallacious argument in which the first premise is irrelevant to the demonstration, just as in the *Proposition*.[49]

The example of up and down as contraries, which is given to illustrate premise (1), is invalid because it involves a category mistake. Up and down are in fact opposed not as contraries, but as relatives.[50] The *Proposition* subtly acknowledges this by repeatedly using πρός followed by the accusative, which Aristotle deemed appropriate for relatives, but inappropriate for contraries.[51]

Premise (2) represents the actual beginning of the attempt at demonstration, asserting that contraries must have a particular form of opposition, i.e. being contradistinguished (ἀντιδιαιρούμενα) in a particular way. The verb ἀντιδιαιρέω does not appear in *Metaphysics* 10.4, 1055a17–23, where contraries are defined as having the maximum difference within the same genus. The verb,

---

ἑαυτῷ οὐκ ἀντίκειται, πρὸς δὲ τὸ μέλαν ἀντικείμενον λέγεται· καὶ τὸ φῶς ὁμοίως ἑαυτῷ μὴ ἀντικεῖσθαι δείκνυται, πρὸς δὲ τὸ σκότος οὕτως ἔχον φαίνεται, καὶ ἄλλα γοῦν ὁμοίως πλεῖστα ὅσα (Karl Mras and Édouard des Places, *Eusebius Werke. Achter Band: Die Praeparatio evangelica*, 2 ed., vol. 1 [Berlin: Akademie-Verlag, 1982], 415.20–416.1).

48 See the discussion of Schreiber, 107–110 on the fallacy of non-cause as cause (παρὰ τὸ μὴ αἴτιον ὡς αἴτιον).

49 See *Sophistici elenchi* 5, 167b21 ff. with the discussion of Schreiber, 107–108.

50 Aristotle's discussion of up and down presupposes a certain model (apparently inherited from the Old Academy) of a finite cosmos whose upward and downward limits are separated by a definite distance and movement is conceived as occurring relative to one of the contrary places. See Aristotle, *Categoriae* 6, 6a12–15; *De caelo* 2.2, 285a31–286a2; and the discussion of Porphyry, *In Aristotelis categorias expositio per interrogationem et responsionem* 107.6–9.

51 Cf. Aristotle, *Categoriae* 10, 11b24–38: "Things opposed as *relatives* (τὰ πρός τι) are called just what they are, *of* their opposites or in some other way *in relation to* (πρός) them. For example, the double is called just what it is, (double) *of* the half ... Thus things opposed as relatives are called just what they are, *of* their opposites or in some other way *in relation to* one another (πρὸς ἄλληλα). Things opposed as *contraries* (ἐναντία), however, are never called just what they are, in relation to one another (πρὸς ἄλληλα), though they are called *contraries of* one another. For the good is not called *good of* the bad, but the contrary of it; and the white not *white of* the black, but its contrary. Thus, these oppositions [i.e., relatives and contraries] differ from one another" (ET J.L. Ackrill, *Aristotle. Categories and De interpretatione* [Oxford: Clarendon, 1963; repr. 1993], 32; emphasis his). This distinction in usage is noted and discussed by the Neoplatonic commentators on the *Categories*; see, e.g., Elias *In Aristotelis categorias commentarium* 196.28–31: τὸ μέγα καὶ μικρὸν καὶ πολὺ καὶ ὀλίγον αὐτὰ ἅπερ εἰσὶν ἑτέρων εἶναι λέγονται, τὰ δὲ ἐναντία οὐ πρὸς ἕτερον λέγονται, οἷον τὸ μέλαν οὐ λέγεται πρὸς λευκὸν μέλαν, ἀλλὰ λευκῷ ἐναντίον, καὶ ἐπὶ τοῦ λευκοῦ ὁμοίως· τὸ ἄρα μέγα καὶ μικρὸν οὐκ ἐναντία.

however, does appear in the *Categories* and the *Topics*, where it is used of opposing differentiae that create coordinate species within the same genus; thus, for example, "odd" and "even" are contradistinguished as divisions within the genus of number.[52]

Since things that are contradistinguished belong to the same genus, they are necessarily things of the same type. Thus, Aristotle noted in the *Categories*, "if one of two contraries is a quality, the other will also be a quality."[53] This passage in the *Categories* received an extended discussion in the sixth-century Neoplatonic commentators. Simplicius, for example, says,

> In general if one of a pair of things that are contradistinguished (ἀντιδι-αιρουμένων) as contraries is found in a genus, then what is contradistinguished (ἀντιδιαιρούμενον) to it as a contrary will be found in the same genus ... It would become clear in another way, too, from the definition of contraries. For if contraries are what are furthest apart from each other in the same genus, it is clear that whatever genus the one is referred to, the other will be referred to it too ... So if we ask in which of the categories, in which there is contrariety, anything is to be found, we will discover in the process how we ought to conduct the enquiry. For we shall take the contrary of what we are seeking, if it is the more knowable [of the two]; and if it is known in which category it is to be found, we shall know that that of which it is the contrary should also be put in the same category.[54]

Premise (3) then uses this valid principle to make a fallacious inference: If one of the contraries is a substance, then the contrary that is opposed to it must also be a substance. The inference is obviously fallacious because in the *Categories* Aristotle clearly states that

(a) Contraries are predicated of a substance, but a contrary is not itself a substance[55] and

---

52 *Topica* 6.4, 142b7–10; for odd and even as contraries, see *Categoriae* 10, 11b38–12a8. On the use of ἀντιδιαιρέω, see also *Categoriae* 13, 14b33–36,15a10–11; *Topica* 5.6, 136b3–9; 6.6, 143a34–b10; 6.6, 144a1–3.

53 *Categoriae* 8, 10b17–18.

54 Simplicius *In Aristotelis categorias commentarium* 278.3–15 (ET Barrie Fleet, *Simplicius. On Aristotle's Categories 7–8* [Ithaca, NY: Cornell University Press, 2002], 138–139, slightly modified).

55 *Categoriae* 5, 4a10–22: "It seems most distinctive of substance that what is numerically one and the same is able to receive contraries. In no other case could one bring forward anything, numerically one, which is able to receive contraries. For example, a color which is numerically one and the same will not be black and white, nor will numerically one

(b) A substance has nothing contrary to it.⁵⁶

Premise (3) thus incorrectly extends a rule pertaining to contraries to something that does not admit of contrariety (i.e., substance). The conclusion drawn from this in premise (4)—that evil is a substance—is therefore not valid.

Premise (5) begins a second argument, also based on premise (2), to show that evil necessarily exists: Since contraries are defined by their opposition to one another, the existence of one contrary implies the existence of the other.⁵⁷ Aristotle did assert that if one of a pair of contraries is found to exist in nature, then the other must exist too.⁵⁸ Aristotle noted, however, that the verb εἶναι ("to be" or "to exist") can be said with or without qualification (to be something vs. to be *simpliciter*).⁵⁹ To say that a contrary exists could therefore mean either that (a) the contrary exists as a predicate that can belong to a subject or (b) that the contrary exists as a discrete entity in the extralinguistic world.

Premise (6) then draws the conclusion: If the existence of one contrary implies the existence of the other, and good and evil are contraries, then it follows that if the good and beautiful exists, evil must also exist. If this conclusion

---

and the same action be bad and good; and similarly with everything else that is not substance. A substance, however, numerically one and the same, is able to receive contraries. For example, an individual man—one and the same—becomes pale at one time and dark at another, and hot and cold, and bad and good. Nothing like this is to be seen in any other case" (ET Ackrill, 11).

56 *Categoriae* 5, 3b24–27: "Another characteristic of substances is that there is nothing contrary to them. For what would be contrary to a primary substance? For example, there is nothing contrary to an individual man, nor yet is there anything contrary to man or to animal" (ET Ackrill, 10).

57 A similar argument is discussed in Sextus Empiricus, *Adversus logicos* 1 (= *Adversus mathematicos* 7) 395: ταῦτα γὰρ κατὰ σύμβλησιν νοεῖται, καὶ ὃν τρόπον μὴ ὄντος δεξιοῦ τινος οὐδὲ ἀριστερὸν ἔστι μηδὲ ὄντος τοῦ κάτω οὐδὲ τὸ ἄνω ἔστιν, οὕτω μὴ ὄντος τοῦ ἑτέρου τῶν ἀντικειμένων οὐδὲ τὸ λοιπὸν ὑποστήσεται "For these things are conceived by way of comparison, and in the same way as there is no left if there is no right, and no up if there is no down, so, if there is not one of these opposing things, nor will the other subsist" (Hermann Mutschmann, *Sexti Empirici opera*, vol. 2 [Leipzig: B.G. Teubner, 1914], 91 [276.27–31]; ET of Richard Bett, *Sextus Empiricus. Against the Logicians* [Cambridge: Cambridge Univ. Press, 2005], 78).

58 Aristotle, *De caelo* 2.3, 286a23–35: "For if one of a pair of contraries naturally exists, the other, if it is really contrary, exists also naturally. In some form it must be present, since the matter of contraries is the same" (ET J.L. Stocks, *De Caelo* [Oxford: Clarendon Press, 1922], 50).

59 Cf. *Sophistici elenchi* 5, 167a2–6, where Aristotle is discussing the fallacy of *secundum quid et simpliciter* and the paralogism, "If non-being is an object of thought, then non-being is": "For to-be-something and to-be without qualification are not the same ... They appear to be the same because of the close resemblance of the language and because 'to-be-something' is little different from 'to-be'" (ET of Schreiber, 143).

is understood in accordance with (a)—evil is a predicate that can belong to a subject—it is valid. Premise (6), however, seems to be making a stronger claim. Phrases like "since the good and beautiful exists" and "if the good and beautiful is a substance" suggest that the author of the *Proposition* assumes the good to have an ongoing existence as the cause of other good things. Indeed, if the second argument (evil exists just as the good exists) is to prepare the way for the third argument (evil is unoriginate and a first principle), then "exists" must be given a strong interpretation ("always was and can never pass away"). In this case, the conclusion in premise (6) would depend upon moving illicitly between two senses of "exist," using a valid principle about when a contrary is available for predication to make a fallacious inference (the property which that predicate ascribes to a subject is necessarily instantiated in the physical world).

The author of the *Proposition* then wishes to move from "evil exists just as the good exists" to the conclusion "evil is unoriginate." This assumes a further (third) argument, whose premises are not made explicit here. The unexpressed premises would need to argue as follows:

(7) If the existence of one contrary implies the existence of the other, then one contrary cannot be prior or posterior to the other, but the two are simultaneous; evil therefore cannot be posterior to the good, but must always coexist with it.

(8) If evil is not posterior to the good but always coexists with it, then if the good is unoriginate, evil will also be unoriginate.

Such an argument would be fallacious because "simultaneous" can be said in different ways and the argument would seem to depend upon moving illicitly between two different senses of the word. In the *Categories*, Aristotle makes an important distinction between two ways in which "simultaneous" is used. When "simultaneous" is said without qualification, the reference is to things "which come into being at the same time; for neither is prior or posterior. These are called simultaneous in respect of time."[60]

Aristotle was careful to distinguish being simultaneous in respect of time from being simultaneous by nature:

> But those things are called *simultaneous by nature* which reciprocate as to implication of existence, provided that neither is in any way the cause of the other's existence, e.g. the double and the half. These reciprocate, since

---

60   *Categoriae* 13, 14b24–26 (ET Ackrill, 40).

if there is a double there is a half and if there is a half there is a double, but neither is the cause of the other's existence.[61]

Earlier in the *Categories*, Aristotle offered a further example to illustrate this point: "Slave" implies the existence of "master" and vice-versa.[62] Furthermore, "these things also eliminate one another"; if there is no slave, then there is no master and vice-versa.[63] For Aristotle, being simultaneous by nature is a property that belongs to a subset of the category of relatives, but not to contraries, which belong to the category of quality.

Aristotle admitted that things can also be called "simultaneous by nature" in a weaker sense.[64] By nature, a genus is divided into species and the species (e.g. "winged," "terrestrial," and "aquatic" within the genus of "animal") are conceived as coming into being simultaneously. Although coordinate species within the same genus (τὰ ἐκ τοῦ αὐτοῦ γένους ἀντιδιῃρημένα ἀλλήλοις) can be regarded as simultaneous by nature, they do not reciprocate in the same way as the relatives discussed above; one cannot infer the existence of one species (e.g., "winged") from the existence of another ("aquatic").

Now assuming that premises (7) and (8) correctly represent the unexpressed premises in the *Proposition*, the author would seem to be assuming that

(a) The contraries good and evil are simultaneous in nature and reciprocate as to implication of existence and

(b) The contraries are not prior to or posterior to one another, but are simultaneous in time, so if there is no occasion when the good came into being (and before which the good was not), the same must be true also of evil.

Such an argument would be erroneous for three reasons. First, being simultaneous in nature and reciprocating as to implication of existence is a property of relatives, not of contraries. Second, even if contraries were treated as coordinate species within a genus, the argument would still not hold, because coordinate species do not reciprocate in such a way that one can infer the existence of one species from the existence of another. Finally, the proposed argument would require moving illicitly between two different senses of "simultaneous," using a principle about what is simultaneous by nature to make an inference about what is simultaneous in time. Since the argument rests upon a false premise and a fallacious inference, the conclusion—that evil is unoriginate—is not valid.

---

61 *Categoriae* 13, 14b27–32 (ET Ackrill, 40; italics his).
62 *Categoriae* 7, 7b17–18.
63 *Categoriae* 7, 7b19–20.
64 *Categoriae* 13, 14b33–34.

Given that all the arguments in the *Proposition* contain elementary errors in logic, one might reasonably wonder why the *Proposition* continued to be copied and discussed. If the *Proposition* had originally been intended to defend a position with demonstrative arguments, it would have been judged a failure and, like so many other mediocre arguments, quickly swept into the dustbin of history and forgotten. Instead the opposite seems to have occurred. Zacharias of Mitylene and Paul the Persian felt compelled to write detailed refutations of the *Proposition* in the sixth century, Arethas of Caesarea discussed and responded to its arguments in marginal scholia in the first half of the tenth century, and John Italus included it in a collection of instructional material for advanced students in the second half of the eleventh century. This degree of interest is only comprehensible if the *Proposition* was valuable precisely because it modeled certain fallacies, inviting the reader to identify the false inferences and refute these fallacious arguments.

As an example of this process, one might consider the responses Arethas of Caesarea made to the *Proposition* in his marginal scholia in *Sinod. gr.* 394, f. 133ᵛ.[65] Arethas began by noting that the *Proposition* depends upon several category mistakes and the illustrations given reflect this confusion. Up and down, for example, are not substances but relations concerning a substance.[66] Relatives should be distinguished from contraries, and it is not relatives but rather contraries that involve opposed things separated by maximum difference.[67] The argument that good and evil are unoriginate is clearly fallacious, Arethas noted, and in any case, if it were true, it would prove too much. If the arguments were accepted, one would have to regard accidents as existing prior to and apart from the subjects of which they are predicated; how then could one speak of what comes to be and passes away?[68] Furthermore, if good and evil are self-subsistent and self-sufficient, then rather than being

---

65 The Greek text of the scholia was published by Westerink, "Marginalia," 240–241.
66 Τὸ ἄνω καὶ κάτω οὐκ οὐσίαι ἀλλὰ σχέσεις περὶ οὐσίας ... ἀλλὰ τὸ ἄνω τῷ κάτω σχέσει, οὐκ οὐσίᾳ, τὸ ἐναντίον εἴληχεν.
67 Ἡ δὲ σχέσις οὐ πέφυκε τὰς φύσεις ὅλως πρὸς μαχομένων διαφορὰν καθιστᾶν.
68 Εἰ πάντα τὰ τῇ οὐσίᾳ συμβεβηκότα καὶ ἐν αὐτῇ ὅ τί ποτέ εἰσιν τὸ εἶναι ἀνευρισκόμενα, ἀνάγκη τὴν ποιότητα πρὸ τοῦ ποιοῦ εἶναι· καὶ πῶς τὸ ἑτεροϋπόστατον [i.e. the accident] πρὸ τοῦ ὑφιστάντος; καὶ τί εἴη τὸ γινόμενον καὶ ἀπογινόμενον [i.e. the accident] ὡς ἀνυπόστατον χωρὶς τῆς τοῦ ὑποκειμένου φθορᾶς;
    In this last sentence, Arethas reminds the reader of Porphyry's definition of accident (*Isagoge* 12.24–25) as "what comes to be and passes away without the destruction of the subject" (Συμβεβηκὸς δέ ἐστιν ὃ γίνεται καὶ ἀπογίνεται χωρὶς τῆς τοῦ ὑποκειμένου φθορᾶς).

wholly opposed, good and evil will be seen to have common features and their definitions will concur.[69] In conclusion, Arethas argued, it is better to believe that the divine unity precedes all duality, as both natural reason and mathematical investigations affirm. It is this divine unity, which transcends every first principle and every substance, that brought the world into existence.

The identification of the *Proposition* as a series of paralogisms is perhaps not surprising, since it is clear that paralogisms were studied and discussed by advanced students in the late fifth and early sixth centuries. Proclus, in the prologue to his commentary on Euclid's *Elements*, defended the need for students to study paralogisms: "Since there are many matters that seem to be dependent on truth and to follow from scientific principles but really lead away from them and deceive the more superficial students, he [sc. Euclid] has given us methods for clear-sighted detection of such errors; and if we are in possession of these methods, we can train beginners in this science for the discovery of paralogisms and also protect ourselves from being led astray."[70]

Later in the commentary, Proclus invites his hearers to consider one such case: "This is Ptolemy's proof. It is worth pausing to see whether there may not be a paralogism in the hypotheses that he has adopted."[71] While Ammonius was content to refer his hearers to Aristotle's *On Sophistical Refutations* for a further discussion of paralogisms, the commentaries produced by his students Asclepius and John Philoponus and his successor Olympiodorus contain extended discussions of paralogisms.[72]

---

69 Εἰ μὲν αὐθυπόστατα καὶ αὐθέδραστα τὸ ἀγαθὸν καὶ κακόν, εἶχεν ἂν συνδρομὴν ὁ λόγος.
70 Proclus, *In primum Euclidis elementorum librum commentarii* 70.1–9; ET Glenn R. Morrow, *Proclus. A Commentary on the First Book of Euclid's Elements* (Princeton, NJ: Princeton University Press, 1970), 58. As Morrow (xlviii–l) notes, Proclus' commentary clearly originated as a series of lectures given to advanced students.
71 Proclus, *In primum Euclidis elementorum librum commentarii* 368.1–3; ET Morrow, *Proclus*, 288 (slightly adapted). For other discussions of paralogisms in Proclus' commentaries, see *In Platonis rem publicam commentarii* 1.244.14–16; 1.245.5–6 (on the fallacy of *secundum quid et simpliciter*); 2.365.9–18 (on the ambiguity of "all" in a paralogism); *In Platonis Parmenidem* 2.727.25–728.3 (on Zeno's argument that the same thing is at once both like and unlike).
72 Ammonius, *In Aristotelis librum de interpretatione commentarius* 85.28–86.4; Asclepius, *In Aristotelis metaphysicorum commentaria* 149.35–36; 217.7–8; 342.18–19; 366.11–367.18; 389.33–390.14; 433.30–434.22; Joannes Philoponus, *In Aristotelis categorias commentarium* 5.11–14; *In Aristotelis analytica priora commentaria* 48.27–29; 166.25–167.2; 325.33–326.5; 450.5–11; *In Aristotelis analytica posteriora commentaria* 21.15–29; 151.26–152.1; 152.20–153.2; 154.15–155.3; 158.15–30; 192.3–32; 194.26–195.4; 203.9–10; 272.14–23; Olympiodorus, *Prolegomena* 15.16–20; *In Aristotelis categorias commentarium* 36.16–22; 121.26–37; *In Plato-*

In conclusion, the *Proposition* is best understood as having originated in later Alexandrian Neoplatonism as an instructional device that helped advanced students review and apply logical concepts. The study of paralogisms gave students an opportunity to discern and identify errors in reasoning, demonstrating their competence in Aristotelian logic by responding to a position opposed to orthodox Neoplatonism.

Bibliography

Ackrill, J.L. *Aristotle. Categories and De interpretatione*. Oxford: Clarendon, 1963; repr. 1993.

Barnes, Jonathan, Susanne Bobzien, Kevin Flannery, and Katerina Ierodiakonou. *Alexander of Aphrodisias: On Aristotle's Prior Analytics 1.1–7*. Ithaca, NY: Cornell University Press, 1991.

Bennett, Byard. "The Physics of Light, Darkness and Matter in John the Grammarian's *First Homily against the Manichaeans*: Early Byzantine Anti-Manichaean Literature as a Window on Controversies in Later Neoplatonism." In *Mani in Dublin: Selected Papers from the Seventh International Conference of the International Association of Manichaean Studies in the Chester Beatty Library, Dublin, 8–12 September 2009*, edited by Siegfried G. Richter, Charles Horton and Klaus Ohlhafer, 19–33. Leiden: Brill, 2015.

Bennett, Byard. "The Eclipse of Manichaeism in the Roman Empire." In *Handbook of Manichaeism*, edited by Johannes van Oort and Jason BeDuhn. Leiden: Brill, forthcoming.

Bett, Richard. *Sextus Empiricus. Against the Logicians*. Cambridge: Cambridge Univ. Press, 2005.

Bodéüs, Richard. *Aristote [Catégories]*. Paris: Les Belles Lettres, 2001.

Brock, Sebastian, and Brian Fitzgerald. *Two Early Lives of Severos, Patriarch of Antioch*. Liverpool: Liverpool University Press, 2013.

Bury, J.B. *The Imperial Administrative System in the Ninth Century*. London: Oxford University Press, 1911.

---

nis Gorgiam commentaria 26.2.8–21; 36.4.26–36.5.28. One of the chapter headings in an early Byzantine handbook of logic, apparently based on sixth-century sources, similarly notes the need to study paralogisms, proposing to describe "how a fallacious argument is formulated—what kind is sophistical and how it can be at once false and plausible" (τίς παραλογισμοῦ σύνθεσις, τίς σοφιστικὸς καὶ πῶς ψευδὴς τε ἄμα καὶ πιθανός); see Oksana Goncharko and Dmitry Goncharko, "A Byzantine Logician's 'Image' within the Second Iconoclastic Controversy. Nikephoros of Constantinople," *Scrinium* 13 (2017): 296.

Chatzilazarou, Dimitrios. Η Βασίλειος Στοά και η σύνθεση του μνημειακού κέντρου της Κωνσταντινούπολης. Τοπογραφία, λειτουργίες, συμβολισμοί. PhD diss., National and Kapodistrian University of Athens, 2016.

Christ, Wilhelm von, Wilhelm Schmid, and Otto Stählin. *Geschichte der griechischen Literatur, II.2: Die nachklassische Periode der griechischen Literatur*. 6 ed. Munich: C.H. Beck, 1961.

Demetrakopoulos, Andronikos K. Ἐκκλησιαστική Βιβλιοθήκη. Vol. 1. Leipzig: Otto Wiegand, 1866.

Dodds, E.R. *Proclus. The Elements of Theology*. Oxford: Clarendon Press, 1963.

Dooley, William E. *Alexander of Aphrodisias. On Aristotle's Metaphysics 5*. Ithaca, NY: Cornell University Press, 1993.

Doutreleau, Louis. *Didyme l'Aveugle. Sur Zacharie*. Vol. 3. Paris: Cerf, 1962.

Dräseke, Johannes. "Zu Apollinarios' von Laodicea 'Ermunterungsschrift an die Hellenen.'" *Zeitschrift für wissenschaftliche Theologie* 43 (1900): 227–236.

Fleet, Barrie. *Simplicius. On Aristotle's Categories 7–8*. Ithaca, NY: Cornell University Press, 2002.

Frier, Bruce W. *The Codex of Justinian: A New Annotated Translation with Parallel Latin and Greek Text*. 3 vols. Cambridge: Cambridge University Press, 2016.

Gautier, Paul. *Michaelis Pselli Theologica*. Vol. 1. Leipzig: B.G. Teubner, 1989.

Gertz, Sebastian, John Dillon, and Donald Russell. *Aeneas of Gaza: Theophrastus with Zacharias of Mitylene: Ammonius*. London: Bloomsbury Academic, 2012.

Goncharko, Oksana, and Dmitry Goncharko. "A Byzantine Logician's 'Image' within the Second Iconoclastic Controversy. Nikephoros of Constantinople." *Scrinium* 13 (2017): 291–308.

Honigmann, Ernest. *Patristic Studies*. Vatican City: Biblioteca Apostolica Vaticana, 1953.

Ierodiakonou, Katerina. "John Italos." In *Encyclopedia of Medieval Philosophy: Philosophy Between 500 and 1500*, edited by Henrik Lagerlund, 623–625. Dordrecht: Springer, 2011.

Joannou, Perikles. *Ioannes Italos Quaestiones quodlibetales (Ἀπορίαι καὶ λύσεις)*. Ettal: Buch-Kunstverlag Ettal, 1956.

Karnačev, A.E. *Aporii*. St. Petersburg: Svoe Izdatelstvo, 2013.

Koës, G.H.K. *Orionis Thebani etymologicon*, edited by F.G. Sturz. Leipzig: Weigel, 1820; repr. Hildesheim: Olms, 1973.

Kroll, W., and R. Schöll. *Corpus iuris civilis*. 3 vols. Berlin: Weidmann, 1899.

Kugener, M.-A. "La compilation historique de Pseudo-Zacharie le Rhéteur." *Revue de l'Orient Chrétien* 5 (1900): 201–214, 461–480.

Lieu, Samuel N.C. "An Early Byzantine Formula for the Renunciation of Manichaeism —The *Capita VII contra Manichaeos* of ⟨Zacharias of Mitylene⟩." In Samuel N.C. Lieu, *Manichaeism in Mesopotamia and the Roman East*, 203–305. Leiden: Brill, 1999.

Loukaki, Marina. "Le profil des enseignants dans l'Empire Byzantin à la fin de l'Antiquité tardive et au début du Moyen Âge (fin du vie-fin du viie siècle)." In *Myriobiblos: Essays on Byzantine Literature and Culture*, edited by Theodora Antonopoulou, Sofia Kotzabassi, and Marina Loukaki, 217–243. Berlin: Walter de Gruyter, 2015.

Loukaki, Marina. "Σχολαστικός. Remarques sur le sens du terme à Byzance (ive–xve siècles)." *Byzantinische Zeitschrift* 109 (2016): 41–72.

Mai, Angelo. *Nova patrum bibliotheca*. Vol. 4.2. Rome: Typis Sacri Consilii Propagando Christiano Nomini, 1847.

Marchetto, Monica. "Nikephoros Chumnos' Treatise *On Matter*." In *Aesthetics and Theurgy in Byzantium*, edited by Sergei Mariev and Wiebke-Marie Stock, 31–55. Berlin: De Gruyter, 2013.

Mariev, Sergei. "Neoplatonic Philosophy in Byzantium." In *Byzantine Perspectives on Neoplatonism*, edited by Sergei Mariev, 1–30. Berlin: Walter de Gruyter, 2017.

Matthäi, Christian Friedrich von. *Accurata codicum graecorum mss. bibliothecarum Mosquensium Sanctissimae Synodi notitia et recensio*. Vol. 1. Leipzig: Joachim, 1805.

Minniti Colonna, Maria. *Zacaria Scolastico. Ammonio. Introduzione, testo critico, traduzione, commentario*. Naples: Tipolitografia "La Buona Stampa," 1973.

Morrow, Glenn R. *Proclus. A Commentary on the First Book of Euclid's Elements*. Princeton, NJ: Princeton University Press, 1970.

Mras, Karl, and Édouard des Places. *Eusebius Werke. Achter Band: Die Praeparatio evangelica*, 2 ed. Vol. 1. Berlin: Akademie-Verlag, 1982.

Mutschmann, Hermann. *Sexti Empirici opera*. Vol. 2. Leipzig: B.G. Teubner, 1914.

Nowell, Peter B. "Severus of Antioch: Fiction in the Archives?" (forthcoming)

Papadopoulos-Kerameus, A. Τοῦ ὁσίου Θεοδώρου τοῦ Στουδίτου μεγάλη κατήχησις. St. Petersburg: Kirschbaum, 1904.

Perry, Ben Edwin. *Aesopica*. Vol. 1. Urbana: University of Illinois Press, 1952.

Pitra, Jean-Baptiste. *Analecta sacra et classica spicilegio Solesmensi parata*. Vol. 5. Paris: Roger and Chernowitz, 1888.

Richard, Marcel. *Iohannis Caesariensis presbyteri et grammatici opera quae supersunt*. CCSG 1. Turnhout: Brepols, 1977.

Rigo, Antonio. "Giovanni Italo." In *Dizionario Biografico degli Italiani*. Vol. 56, 62–67. Rome: Istituto dell'Enciclopedia Italiana, 2001.

Rizzo, James John. *Isaak Sebastokrator's Περὶ τῆς τῶν κακῶν ὑποστάσεως (De malorum subsistentia)*. Meisenheim am Glan: Anton Hain, 1971.

Runia, David T., and Michael Share. *Proclus. Commentary on Plato's Timaeus*. Vol. 2. Cambridge: Cambridge University Press, 2008.

Schreiber, Scott G. *Aristotle on False Reasoning: Language and the World in the Sophistical Refutations*. Albany, NY: SUNY Press, 2003.

Simon, Dieter, and Spyros Troianos. *Das Novellensyntagma des Athanasios von Emesa*. Frankfurt am Main: Löwenklau Gesellschaft, 1989.

Smith, Robin. *Aristotle. Topics Books I and VIII*. Oxford: Clarendon Press, 1997.
Stephanou, Pelopidas Étienne. *Jean Italos philosophe et humaniste*. Rome: Pontificium Institutum Orientalium Studiorum, 1949.
Stocks, J.L. *De Caelo*. Oxford: Clarendon Press, 1922.
Suchla, Beate Regina. *Corpus Dionysiacum IV.1: Ioannis Scythopolitani prologus et scholia in Dionysii Areopagitae librum De divinis nominibus*. Berlin: De Gruyter, 2011.
Trizio, Michele. "A Late-Antique Debate on Matter-Evil Revisited in 11th-Century Byzantium: John Italos and His *Quaestio* 92." In *Fate, Providence and Moral Responsibility in Ancient, Medieval and Early Modern Thought: Studies in Honour of Carlos Steel*, edited by Pieter d'Hoine and Gerd Van Riel, 383–394. Leuven: Leuven University Press, 2014.
van der Wal, N., and B.H. Stolte. *Collectio Tripartita: Justinian on Religious and Ecclesiastical Affairs*. Groningen: Egbert Forsten, 1994.
Westerink, L.G. "Marginalia by Arethas in Moscow Greek MS 231." *Byzantion* 42 (1972): 196–244.
Zepos, Ioannis, and Panagiotis Zepos. *Jus Graecoromanum V: Synopsis Basilicorum: ex editione C.E. Zachariae a Lingenthal*. Athens: Fexis, 1931.

Index of Antique and Modern Personal Names

Aaron   198, 319
Abarshahr   45
Abel   77, 86, 310
Abgar   235
Abraham   80, 154, 161, 199, 319
Ackril, J.L.   421, 423, 424, 425, 428
Adam   13, 14, 16, 18, 19, 21, 22, 37, 58, 67, 70, 71, 72, 74, 75, 79, 80, 83, 84, 85, 86, 87, 89, 90, 91, 116, 117, 118, 195, 199, 207, 218, 219, 240, 330, 332, 333, 338, 361
Adam, A.   71, 75, 78, 81, 82, 91, 93, 284, 376, 390, 398
Adam, S.   290, 291, 298
Adda (cf. Addai; Mar Addā)   24, 29, 30, 167, 217, 218, 314, 316, 317, 319
Addai   1, 4, 66
Addōn   55, 77
Adelphius   390, 391
Adeodatus   292
Adler, W.   7, 10
Adonai   55, 56, 58, 59, 63, 64, 77, 78
Aelian   168, 181
Aegialeus   153, 163
Aenesidemus   24, 26, 29
Aesop   25, 214
Agapius of Hierapolis   12
Aland (Ehlers), B.   83, 93, 197, 219
Aland, K.   106
Alcock, A.   141, 148, 366
Alexander (the Great)   155, 181
Alexander of Aphrodisias   25, 419
Alexander of Lycopolis   105, 118, 119, 256, 383, 388, 395, 396
Alfaric, P.   285, 287
Allberry, C.R.C.   67, 110, 111, 112, 120, 122, 147, 255, 265, 276
Allen, P.   225, 250
Altaner, B.   340, 344
Alypius (of Thagaste)   273
Amar, J.P.   196, 207, 219, 222
Amaro   133
Ambrose of Milan   113, 273, 291, 310
Ammianus Marcellinus   155, 179, 180
Ammon   142
Ammonius   386, 395, 396, 402, 404, 427

Amphilocius of Iconium   378, 381, 382, 386, 387, 395, 396
Anastasius   132, 415
Andrew (apostle)   356, 377
Antonopoulou, T.   415, 430
Antonova, S.E.   7, 9
Aphrahat   42, 86
Apollinaris   331, 342
Aravecchia, N.   148
Archelaus   152–154, 157, 160, 163, 164, 168, 169–178, 180, 183, 184, 185, 354
Archytas (Ps.-)   25, 407
Ardabān   45
Ardashir I   155
Arethas   408, 414, 426, 427
Aristophanes   181
Aristotle   25, 30, 119, 208, 402, 404, 407, 413, 417, 418, 419, 420, 421, 422, 423, 424, 425, 427
Arius   192, 199, 243, 331, 332, 334, 342
Arnobius the Younger   339
Arnold, D.W.H.   301
Arnold-Döben, V.   292, 298
Arsinoē   56, 62, 76
Artemis   9
Arts, M.R.   258
Asclepius   427
Atargatis (Dea Syria)   236, 237, 241
Athanasius (Ps.-)   113, 132
Athanasius Scholasticus   415
Athenagoras   7
Atticus   171, 413
Attridge, H.A.   98, 99, 100, 113, 122, 191, 220
Augustine of Hippo   29, 30, 73, 84, 100, 113, 131, 144, 169, 171, 182, 228, 229, 242, 247, 253–287, 288–298, 302–314, 320–323, 326, 327, 330, 332, 335, 336, 337, 338, 339, 340, 341, 342, 343, 344, 351–369, 382, 389, 395, 396
Avi-Yonah, M.   155
Āz   270
Azmeh, A. al   2

Baarda, T.   4, 49
Baat   132
Bagnall, R.S.   129, 137, 140, 147, 148

Bahram I 188
Bahram II 188
Baker-Brian, N.   1, 2, 145, 150, 203, 209, 216, 218, 219, 295, 298, 355, 362, 370
Bammel, E.   311
Bammel, C.P.H.   335, 344
Bardaisan   7, 70, 71, 72, 80, 81, 83–92, 186–189, 191, 192, 193–202, 205–210, 212–218, 235, 247
Bardy, G.   397
Barlaam   31
Barnes, J.   420, 428
Barns, J.W.B.   99, 123
Barses   156, 160, 161, 162
Basil of Caesarea   378, 379, 381, 382, 394, 395, 396, 397
Basilides   78, 180
Bauer, J.B.   298
Bauer, W.   189, 190, 191, 219
Baur, C.   225, 249
Baur, F.C.   328, 344
Beatrice, P.F.   18, 19
Beatty, A.C.   35, 43, 60, 62, 64
Beck, E.   87, 93, 187, 191, 219
BeDuhn, J.(D)   2, 4–5, 36, 47, 48, 51, 60, 67, 68, 79, 81, 88, 93, 101, 103, 124, 131, 144, 145, 147, 148, 149, 169, 189, 190, 219, 221, 225, 228, 229, 234, 236, 238, 249, 254, 276, 286, 287, 294, 299, 304, 308, 316, 317, 323, 361, 371, 372, 381, 382, 398, 401, 428
Beeson, C.H.   153, 194, 219, 285
Behlmer, H.   69
Belial   166
Bellettato, A.   7
Bellinger, A.R.   48
Benjamin, W.   164
Bennett, B.   401, 402, 428
Berg, J.A. van den   29, 135, 149, 217, 219, 299, 300, 366, 370
Berthold, G.C.   188, 221
Berzon, T.S.   245, 249
Beskow, P.   132, 148, 376, 383, 393, 398
Bethge, H.-G.   55, 67, 68, 69, 74, 75, 76, 77, 93, 123
Bett, R.   423, 428
Betz, H.D.   153, 209, 222, 372
Bevan, A.A.   191, 222
Bidez, J.   181, 182, 397

Bidpai   64
Bieringer, R.   252
Bierzo, V. du   160
Biesen, K. den   194, 195, 220
Bīrūnī, al   70, 71, 72, 81, 83, 87, 88, 89, 90, 91, 266, 284
Bishapour   181
Blaise, A.   162
Blatz, B.   101, 102, 103, 104, 105, 123, 127
Blois, F. de   32, 33, 51, 52, 57, 58, 59, 63, 64, 67, 68, 69, 71, 77, 78, 80, 81, 82, 88, 94, 133, 148
Blowers, P.   304
Bobzien, S.   420, 428
Bodéüs, R.   420, 428
Boeft, J. den   126, 299
Böhlig, A.   67, 106, 117, 121, 126, 228, 249, 265, 268, 285, 328, 348
Bohlin, T.   324, 325, 326, 327, 328, 329, 334, 335, 336, 337, 344, 345
Bonner, G.   325, 340, 345
Boor, C.   397
Botha, P.J.   193, 200, 205, 220
Boulding, M.   258, 356, 370
Boulluec, A. Le   194, 222
Bouissou, G.   258
Bousleh, W.   179
Bovon, A.   181
Bowen, G.E.   138, 147, 151
Bowes, K.   132, 148
Boyarin, D.   3
Boyce, M.   32, 45
Brändle, R.   225, 249
Brakke, D.   97
Brand, M.   129, 139, 140, 143, 148
Brankaer, J.   55, 67, 68, 69, 74, 75, 76, 77, 93
Braun, R.   27, 28
Breytenbach, C.   135, 149
Brice, W.   154
Bright, T.   301
Brinkmann, A.   119, 123, 396
Brock, S.   189, 190, 207, 214, 215, 216, 220, 414, 417, 428
Brottier, L.   248
Browder, M.H.   81, 82, 88, 93
Brown, B.   288, 299
Brown, F.E.   48
Brown, P.   132, 149, 188, 220, 226, 249, 280

… INDEX OF ANTIQUE AND MODERN PERSONAL NAMES … 435

Browne, G.M.   99, 123
Browning, D.S.   222
Brutus   168
Bruyn, T.S. de   326, 329, 332, 334, 335, 336, 337, 338, 339, 340, 345
Bryder, P.   93, 132, 148, 172, 398
Buddha   37
Bull, C.H.   123
Bundy, D.   189, 190, 220
Burchill-Limb, K.   254
Burkitt, F.C.   1, 4, 42, 47, 85, 86, 88, 93, 191, 222
Bury, J.B.   415, 428
Burns, D.M.   52, 78, 93, 126
Burrus, V.   132, 150, 246, 249

Caelestius   329, 339, 340, 342, 343
Caiaphas   46
Cain   77, 309–313, 321
Calcidius   82
Calder, W.   379, 398
Calixtus   177
Cameron, A.   145, 149
Camplani, A.   72, 80, 81, 83, 85, 86, 87, 89, 92, 93, 94
Caner, D.F.   235, 249, 376, 383, 384, 388, 389, 391, 392, 393, 394, 398, 399
Canivet, P.   397
Caracalla   155
Casadio, G.   88, 94
Casiday, A.   392, 398
Cassian (Johannes Cassianus)   171
Catilina   165
Cawte, J.   225, 249
Cecire, R.C.   379, 399
Chadwick, H.   257, 328, 338, 345
Charito   14
Chariton   14
Chatzilazarou, D.   416, 429
Chavannes, E.   30
Chelius, K.H.   349
Choat, M.   58, 68
Christ, see Jesus: *passim*
Christ, W. von   403, 429
Chrysippus   168, 232, 407
Ciasca, A.   44
Cicero   26, 30, 168, 170, 171, 183, 184, 254, 257, 260, 266, 280, 282, 289, 295
Cirillo, L.   94, 371, 372

Clackson, S.J.   134, 149, 215, 220, 353, 364, 370
Claudius   153, 163
Cleanthes   232
Clement of Alexandria   3, 4, 6, 7, 12, 15–21, 23
Cleobulos   153, 163
Clivaz, C.   78, 94
Cohen, S.   132, 149
Colditz, I.   299
Coleman-Norton, P.R.   398
Comnenus, Isaac   408, 413
Commodus   11, 155
Constantine   156, 190
Constantius II   156, 384
Constantius (Manichaean)   131, 339
Constantius tractator   339
Conybeare, C.   290, 293, 296, 299
Cope, G.   388, 399
Corrigan, K.   126
Courcelle, P.   281
Courtonne, Y.   396
Coyle, J.K.   102, 113, 123, 139, 149, 153, 164, 356, 370
Cramer, W.   154
Crassus   155
Crawford, M.R.   4, 23
Crégheur, E.   112, 123, 398
Crescens   11
Cress, D.A.   254, 287
Cribiore, R.   148
Crum, W.E.   75, 76, 94
Cumont, F.   181, 182
Cyprian   170, 321
Cyril of Jerusalem   98, 99, 113, 122, 152, 194

Daris, S.   134, 149
Datema, C.   396
Daur, K.-D.   346
David   199, 200, 319, 332
Davis, S.J.   97
Davoli, P.   148
DeBevoise, M.B.   97, 216, 224
Declerck, J.H.   398
DeConick, A.D.   2, 68, 69, 95
Decret, F.   84, 94, 368, 371
Delmaire, R.   158
Demeter (Isis-Demeter)   138
Demetrakopoulos, A.K.   402, 403, 414, 429
Demetrias   330, 341

Demosthenes 180
Dent, J.M. 258
Devillers, O. 179
Devos, P. 161
Díaz y Díaz, M.C. 160
Didymus the Blind 113, 194, 413
Diels, H. 26
Dietrich, A. 197, 219
Dilley, P.(C.) 4–5, 36, 48, 51, 60, 67, 68, 101, 103, 124, 144, 145, 147, 148, 149, 221, 276
Dillon, J. 416, 429
Diocletian 142, 182, 188, 376
Diodore of Tarsus 240
Diodorus (*Acta Archelai*) 316
Diogenes Laërtius 26
Dionysius of Alexandria 381
Dobschütz, E. von 359, 369
Dodds, E.R. 420, 429
Dodge, B 71, 88, 94
Doerfler, M.E. 93
Doignon, J. 290, 291, 297, 299
Dooley, W.E. 407, 429
Doresse, J. 101, 102, 103, 104, 105
Dositheus of Cilicia 380, 381, 383
Doutreleau, L. 413, 429
Drake, H.A. 400
Drake, S. 237, 245, 249
Dräseke, J. 403, 429
Drecoll, V.H. 294, 299
Drijvers, H.J.W 1, 4, 66, 68, 80, 81, 83, 85, 86, 88, 94, 101, 123, 156, 196, 197, 198, 206, 209, 216, 218, 220, 221, 235, 249
Dubois, J.-D. 78, 94, 139, 140, 149
Dummer, J. 285, 353, 369, 397
Dunphy, W. 340, 345
Durkheim, E. 381, 399
Durkin-Meistererernst, D. 32, 215, 223
Dutton, E.P. 258
Duval, Y.-M. 329, 330, 345, 352, 371

Eco, U. 164
Edwards, R.M. 54, 66, 68
Egeria 160–162
Ehrman, B.D. 4
Eirene (Man. catechumen) 65, 135, 139, 146
Elafia 379
Elchasai 29
Elias (comm. on Aristotle) 421
Elijah 28

Elisha 34
Eloim 77
Elpidius 161
Elton, H. 243, 250
Emmel, S. 97, 123, 124
Emmerick, R.E. 142, 149, 153, 372
Empedocles 26
Enoch 37, 75, 318
Enosh 37
Ephrem of Nisibis 28, 42, 43, 70, 72, 83–92, 102, 156, 186–218
Epicurus 86
Epiphanius 7, 11, 12, 13, 77, 152, 164, 169, 173, 174, 241, 242, 285, 318, 353, 376, 377, 379, 384, 385, 386, 388–393, 396, 397
Erler, M. 300
Ernout, A. 167, 168, 171, 177, 178
Euclid 427
Euelpistos 14
Eulogios 156, 162
Eupolis 178
Euripides 181
Eusebius 3, 4, 7, 11, 12, 13, 75, 86, 113, 217, 381, 396, 397, 420
Evagrius Ponticus 328
Evans, E. 27, 28
Evans, R.F. 325, 326, 329, 330, 331, 337, 339, 343, 344, 345
Evans, G.R. 326, 345
Eve 116, 117, 118, 195, 207, 361
Evodius of Uzalis 56, 351–355, 358–361, 363, 366–369

Falkenberg, R. 99, 100, 101, 102, 103, 104, 106, 107, 108, 109, 113, 114, 116, 117, 121, 123, 126, 228, 251
Falvey, L. 149
Faustianos 146
Faustus of Milev 29, 30, 228, 263, 273, 280, 302–310, 313–323, 337
Feder, F. 69
Feldmann, E. 360, 371
Féliers, J.-H. 352, 371
Felix (Roman governor) 170
Felix Manichaeus 356, 358, 359, 361, 362, 366
Ferguson, J. 325, 330, 346
Ferus, K. 300
Fiano, E. 93, 193, 221

INDEX OF ANTIQUE AND MODERN PERSONAL NAMES 437

Field, F.   226, 227, 235, 237, 239, 241, 243, 246, 247, 248, 249
Filastrius of Brescia   354
Fischer, N.   300
Fitschen, K.   386, 390, 391, 399
Fitzgerald, B.   414, 417, 428
Fitzgerald, J.T.   243, 252
Flannery, K.   420, 428
Flavian of Antioch   386, 390
Fleet, B.   422, 429
Fontaine, J.   179, 180
Fontanier, L.-M.   253, 254, 260, 278
Forstner, K.   300
Fournet, J.L.   137, 148, 151
Fournier, E.   143, 148
Fowden, G.   2
Fox, G.   360, 361, 364, 371, 399
Frankfurter, D.   80, 94
Franzmann, M.   73, 74, 78, 79, 84, 94, 135, 149, 229, 230, 249, 294, 299, 366, 371
Frede, H.J.   344
Fredriksen, P.   302–307, 309–314, 321–323
Freeman, P.   172
Frey, J.   125
Friedrich, G.   166
Frier, B.W.   415, 417, 429
Frohnhofen, H.   311
Funk, W.-P.   37, 47, 54, 55, 66, 67, 68, 76, 77, 94, 95, 101, 102, 103, 106, 107, 108, 123, 124, 141, 147, 148, 265, 366
Fuhrer, Th.   259, 289, 290, 291, 294, 295, 296, 298, 299, 300, 372
Fussl, M.   300

Gaffiot, F.   171, 177, 183, 184
Gager, J.   86, 95
Galen   243, 407
Galerius   155
Galletier, E.   180
Gantke, W.   69
Gardner, I.(M.F.)   2, 4, 5, 32, 36, 37, 39, 45, 47, 48, 52, 56, 57, 58, 63, 67, 68, 70, 71–80, 81, 82, 91, 92, 93, 95, 101, 103, 124, 129, 132, 133, 134, 141, 142, 144, 145, 147, 148, 149, 169, 188, 204, 221, 225, 276, 314, 360, 361, 366, 369, 371, 381, 382, 399
Garnier, J.   329, 330
Gärtner, B.   101, 102, 103, 104, 124
Garsoian, N.   156

Gascou, J.   137, 138, 143, 148
Gathercole, S.   99, 112, 113, 114, 115, 118, 124
Gautier, P.   413, 429
Gēhmurd   58
Gena   137, 138
Gennadius of Marseille   329
George the Sinner   99
Gertz, S.   416, 429
Ghanam, 'Iyadh ibn   156
Gibb, J.   257, 258
Giet, S.   397
Giversen, S.   67, 68, 124, 125
Goldhill, S.   300
Gonzaga, M.   225, 249
Goodrich, R.   393, 399
Gorce, D.   160
Gordian III   155
Goncharko, D.   428, 429
Goncharko, O.   428, 429
Goulet, R.   380, 381, 397, 399
Goundesh   4–5, 55, 65
Gradel, I.   9
Graeve, V. von   181
Grafer, T.W.   380, 397
Grant, M.   242, 249
Gratian   376
Greatrex, G.   243, 250, 398
Green, T.M.   154
Green, W.M.   338, 346
Greenslade, S.L.   208, 221
Gregory of Nyssa   206
Gregory of Tours   355
Gregory, T.   383, 389, 391, 399
Greshake, G.   326, 330, 334, 346
Grey, C.   130, 149
Griffith, S.H.   188, 189, 191, 194, 195, 196, 200, 205, 206, 208, 216, 221
Grote, A.E.J.   295, 300
Guidi, I.   198, 221
Guillaumont, A.   31
Gulácsi, Zs.   45, 46, 48, 126, 355, 356, 362, 371

Hagedorn, D.   397
Hahn, H.P.   288, 300
Halm, K.   329, 346
Halton, T.P.   191, 221, 242, 250
Hammerschmidt, E.   101, 124
Hammond, C.J.-B.   258
Hanig, R.   20

Hansen, G.C.   397
Harkins, P.W.   229, 230, 239, 244, 250
Harnack, A. von   25, 28, 29, 325, 346
Harrison, G.   361, 371
Hartel, W.A. von   331, 343, 346
Hartung, B.   192, 221
Harvey, S.A.   189, 220, 346
Harwardt, S.   293, 296, 300
Hata, G.   191, 220
Hattrup, D.   300
Haxby, M.C.G.   54, 68
Hayduck, M.   25
Hayes, A.   194, 221
Heal, K.S.   400
Hegemonius (Ps.-)   152, 153, 154, 157–160, 162–167, 169, 172–173, 176–184, 194, 285, 336, 397
Hegesippus   75
Heiser, A.   95
Helderman, J.   101, 102, 103, 105, 124
Helm, R   7, 11
Hennecke, E.   123, 126, 127
Henning, W.B.   64, 68
Henrichs, A.   147
Henry, R.   397
Heracleides   56, 97, 127, 276
Heraclianus of Chalcedon   153
Heraclitus   26
Herman, G.   144, 150
Hermas (Shepard)   31
Hermes (Trismegistos)   203
Herodian (of Antioch)   155
Herodotus   178, 181
Heyden, W. von   226, 229, 250
Heylen, F.   354, 369
Hierax   14
Hierius   255, 256, 257, 286
Hilarius of Poitiers   336
Hilhorst, A.   139, 150
Hill, J.H.   44, 48
Hill, R.C.   230, 240, 250
Hintze, A.   69, 135, 149
Hippolytus (Ps.-)   12, 26, 113, 217
Hjärpe, J.   156
Hodgins, G.   36, 47
Hoheisel, K.   69
Hoine, P. d'   404, 431
Holl, K.   285, 353, 369, 386, 397
Holmes, M.W.   4

Homer   404
Honigmann, E.   417, 429
Hope, C.A.   138, 147, 149, 151
Horace   167
Horn, C.B.   236, 251
Horst, P.W. van der   119, 124, 396
Horton, C.   190, 222, 239, 251, 402, 428
Houtman, A.   2
Humbert, G.   159
Hunt, E.   4, 12, 22
Hunt, H.   391, 399
Hunt, T.E.   145, 150
Hunter, D.G.   346
Hunter, E.   47, 220, 353, 364, 370
Hutter, M.   294, 300
Hypatius   102, 197, 201, 204, 208, 209, 214, 215, 216, 217
Hystaspes   53, 66, 70, 71, 72, 80, 90, 91

Iamblichus   419
Ibscher, H.   60, 61, 126, 348
Ibscher, R.   60, 61, 62
Ierodiakonou, K.   403, 420, 428, 429
Innocent I   328, 330, 342
Ioasaph   31
Irenaeus   3, 4, 6, 7, 11–19, 22, 23, 34, 78, 79, 194, 202
Iricinschi, E.   69, 97, 287
Isaac of Antioch   156
Isaiah   332
Isis-Demeter   138
Iuppiter Latiaris   9

Jabbār, 'Abd al   319
Jacob (patriarch)   73
Jackson, A.V.W.   79, 95
Jäger, I.   252
Jamnes   182
James   55, 72, 73, 74, 75, 76, 90
James (disciple of Pelagius)   330
Janin, R.   160
Jannes   182
Janowski, B.   222
Jansma, T.   217, 221
Jenott, L.   54, 68, 69, 97, 99, 114, 123, 125, 126
Jerome   7, 11, 12, 13, 86, 113, 162, 307, 326, 328, 329, 330, 340, 341, 342, 343, 354
Jesus (also Christ and Jesus Christ): *passim*

Jōanna 56
Joannes Scholasticus 408
Joannou, P.-P. 381, 399, 403, 404, 406, 429
Job 207
John (Baptist) 198, 199, 218
John Chrysostom 175–176, 225–248, 338, 377, 378, 380, 382, 396, 397
John (Evangelist) 377
John of Damascus 99, 404
John the Grammarian 413
John Italus 401, 403, 404, 405, 406, 412, 414, 426
John Philoponus 427
Johnson, M. 246, 250
Johnson, S.F. 130, 149
Johnson, W.A. 7, 10
Jones, A.H.M. 155, 158
Jones, D. 149
Jones, F.S. 56, 69
Jong, A.F. de 144, 150
Joosten, J. 4
Jördens, A. 136, 150
Joshua 319
Jovinian 326, 328, 331, 340, 342, 343, 344
Judas Iscariot 37, 38, 39, 40, 41, 46, 66, 71, 74, 75, 90
Jugurtha 165, 171
Julia (Manichaean of Antioch) 183
Julian (Arian) 376, 396, 397
Julian (Emperor) 155, 156, 212
Julian of Eclanum 325, 326, 361, 362, 366
Jülicher, A. 367, 368, 370
Jullien, C. 153
Jüngel, E. 222
Jurasz, I. 84, 85, 86, 87, 95
Jürgens, H. 275, 298
Justin Martyr 3, 7, 10, 11, 13, 14, 20, 23, 42, 73, 307, 321
Justinian 131, 158, 403, 414, 415, 417

Kaatz, K.W. 360, 362, 371, 372
Kahlos, M. 144, 150
Kalleres, D.S. 246, 250
Kamesar, A. 18
Kampen, J. 96
Kant, E. 24
Kaper, O.E. 129, 148, 150
Karnačev, A.E. 403, 429

Kartir 188
Katô, T. 253, 254, 278
Kazhdan, A.P. 399
Kelly, J.N.D. 225, 250
Kennedy, D. 172
Kennedy, G.A. 157
Kenyon, E. 290, 297, 300
Kessler, K. 154
King, K.L. 123
Kitchen, R.A. 400
Kittel, G. 166
Klein, W.W. 69, 294, 300
Klimkeit, H.-J. 94, 101, 102, 105, 124, 132, 150
Klockow, R. 289, 300
Klugkist, A.C. 189, 196, 221, 222
Knape, J. 288, 300
Knauer, G.N. 258
Knight, P. 298
Koenen, L. 29, 147, 364, 370
Koës, G.H.K. 414, 429
Koester, H. 49
Koltun-Fromm, N. 4, 15
Kome 140
König, J. 293, 300
Kósa, G. 236, 250
Kotzabassi, S. 415, 430
Kotzé, A.M. 149, 259, 290, 295, 300
Kraeling, C.H. 43, 48
Kraft, R.A. 189, 219
Kranz, W. 26
Krause, M. 124
Kristionat, J. 384, 399
Krodel, G. 189, 219
Kroll, W. 415, 429
Krutzsch, M. 126
Kudella, M. 294, 299
Kuechler, S. 289, 300
Kugener, M.-A. 403, 429
Kukula, R.C. 9, 11

Laffan, M. 70, 71
Lagerlund, H. 403, 429
Laird, R.J. 229, 238, 239, 250
Lamberigts, M. 326, 327, 346
Lampe, P. 11, 14
Landau, B. 51, 67, 68
Larsen, J.M. 48, 100, 101, 102, 103, 104, 106, 107, 108, 109, 113, 115, 116, 117, 121, 126, 228, 251, 371

Lategan, B.C.   135, 149
Lavender, E.D.   326, 339, 347
Layton, B.   106, 107, 108, 109, 110, 111, 112, 114, 122, 124
Leclercq, H.   154
Lee, K.E.   287
Leipoldt, J.   114, 125
Leloir, L.   43, 48
Lemaire, A.   175
Leontius (Ps.-) of Byzantium   99
Leroy-Molinghen, A.   397
Lesêtre, H.   166
Leucius   354, 355
Leurini, C.   32, 58, 69, 77, 95, 100, 101, 102, 103, 104, 106, 107, 108, 109, 113, 116, 117, 121, 125, 126, 228, 251
Levi   66
Lévy, C.   26
Lewis, N.D.   69, 97
Libanius   130, 132
Liberianus   14
Licentius   295
Liddell, H.G.   178
Lied, L.I.   68
Lieu, J.M.   77, 95, 144, 212, 221
Lieu, S.N.C   30, 45, 47, 49, 70, 73, 80, 95, 132, 133, 142, 144, 148, 150, 172, 182, 188, 190, 204, 212, 217, 220, 221, 222, 226, 229, 250, 292, 300, 353, 357, 359, 360, 361, 363, 364, 365, 366, 370, 371, 372, 381, 382, 386, 388, 389, 390, 397, 398, 399, 416, 429
Lim, R.   145, 217, 222
Lithargoel   31
Livingstone, E.A.   399
Livy (Titus Livius)   167, 168
Lloyd, A.B.   136, 150
Lloyd, S.   154
Löhr, W.A.   326, 330, 336, 337, 338, 347
Lollar, J.B.   236, 250
Lona, H.E.   11
Lössl, J.   2, 6, 7, 11, 145, 150, 259, 381, 399
Lot   377
Louchez, E.   346
Loukaki, M.   415, 429, 430
Louth, A.   391, 399
Lucian of Samosata   8
Lucretius   170
Lundhaug, H.   68, 99, 114, 123, 125

Macarius of Magnesia   379, 380, 381, 396, 397
Macrobius   265
Mai, A.   403, 430
Maier, H.O.   132, 150
Malingrey, A.-M.   248
Mambres   182
Manael   66
Mandouze, A.   352, 372
Mango, C.A.   398
Mani, *passim*
Manippus   153, 163
Mansfeld, J.   119, 124, 396
Mar Addā   66
Mār Ammō   45
Mara, M.G.   226, 227, 228, 239, 250
Maraval, P.   160, 161, 397
Marcellus   152, 153–154, 157–160, 163, 165, 167–170, 172–178, 183–184
Marcellus (heretic)   243
Marchetto, M.   404, 430
Marcion   13, 16, 17, 18, 23, 24–30, 32, 33, 34, 56, 59, 63, 86, 177, 180, 186–189, 191, 192, 194, 196, 198–207, 209–218, 227, 228, 230, 231, 236, 237, 239, 243, 247, 314, 315, 316, 317, 331, 334, 335
Marcus Antoninus Verus   11
Marcus Aurelius   155
Marcus Diaconus   183
Mardirossian, A.   166
Maria (Mariam/Marihammē)   56, 62, 63, 76
Mariev, S.   404, 430
Marinus   83, 84
Marius Mercator   340
Marius Victorinus (Ps.-)   356
Marjanen, A.   54, 56, 69, 76, 95
Markschies, C.   95
Marmarji, A.S.   43, 44, 49
Martens, P.   304
Martha   56, 62
Martini, P.C.   329, 347
Mary Magdalene (cf. Maria, Mariam)   56
Mary (mother of Jesus)   58, 59, 62, 73, 77, 243, 332
Mathews, T.F.   156
Matsangou, R.   132, 150
Matthäi, C.F. von   414, 430
Matthews, E.G.   207, 222
Matthews, J.F.   142, 150

INDEX OF ANTIQUE AND MODERN PERSONAL NAMES 441

Mausbach, J.   325, 347
Maximinus   155
Maximus of Turin   144
Maximus   420
May, G.   15
Mayer, C.   289, 300, 349
Mayer, W.   143, 144, 148, 150, 225, 233, 243, 250, 252
Mazur, Z.   126
McCarthy, C.   43, 49
McFadden, S.   148
McGlothlin, T.D.   83, 84, 85, 86, 96
McVey, K.   196, 207, 222
Meillet, A.   167, 168, 171, 177, 178
Melito of Sardis   321
Ménard, J.-É.   101, 102, 103, 104, 105, 125
Menasce, J. de   34
Menoch   271
Mercury   55
Meşallyāne (radical Man. ascetic)   236
Mews, S.   189, 220
Meyer, P.   398
Migne, J.-P.   98, 250, 397, 398, 403
Mikkelsen, G.B.   30
Miller, M.W.   340, 347
Mills, I.N.   4, 23
Minale, V.M.   182
Minniti Colonna, M.   416, 430
Mirecki, P.   101, 102, 103, 125, 169, 189, 190, 219, 228, 249, 316, 317, 371
Miroshnikov, I.   118, 125
Mitchell, C.W.   83, 84, 85, 86, 93, 96, 191, 197, 201, 202, 203, 208, 214, 222
Mithras   175, 179, 181
Mommsen, T.   398
Monnica   292, 295
Montagnini, F.   166
Montgomery, W.   257, 258
Morano, E.   47, 314
Morehouse, R.(J.)   83, 86, 96, 211, 215, 216, 222
Moreschini, C.   26
Morin, G.   347
Morrow, G.R.   427, 430
Moses   28, 80, 182, 196, 198, 199, 206, 302, 308, 318, 319, 333
Moshe bar Kepha   88
Movia, G.   26
Mras, K.   421, 430

Müller, F.W.K.   103, 125
Muhammad   2, 94
Murray, R.   199, 211, 212, 214, 215, 222
Mutschmann, H.   423, 430
Mutzenbecher, A.   366, 370

Nadīm, Ibn al   51, 52, 54, 56, 63, 66, 68, 70–73, 75, 76, 79, 81, 83, 89, 90, 91, 101, 361, 362
Nafshā   133, 143
Nagel, P.   74, 96, 101, 102, 103, 107, 125, 228, 249
Narseh   155
Nasrallah, L.   8
Nesselrath, H.-G.   3, 4, 6, 7, 8, 9, 11, 12
Nestle, E.   106, 367, 368, 370
Nestorius (unknown Man.?)   141
Netzer, A.   135, 149
Neymeyr, B.   232, 250
Nicklas, T.   3, 149
Noah   37, 199, 377
Nöldeke, T.   85, 96
Nongbri, B.   2
Nørregaard, J.   327, 347
Nos   140
Novatus   331
Nowell, P.B.   417, 430

Oates, J.F.   147
Obbink, D.D.   137, 148
Odaenathus   155
O'Donnell, J.J.   256, 257, 266, 277
Odysseus   167
Ohlhafer, K.   190, 222, 239, 251, 402, 428
Olympiodorus   419, 427
O'Meara, J.J.   286
Oort, J. van   19, 24, 30, 31, 49, 84, 94, 119, 126, 127, 129, 131, 139, 150, 153, 164, 166, 209, 222, 225, 232, 234, 240, 242, 247, 251, 259, 270, 272, 274, 295, 299, 301, 302, 310, 314, 323, 353, 355, 356, 357, 360, 362, 365, 366, 368, 371, 372, 373, 375, 384, 385, 395, 399, 400, 401, 428
Optatus (magistrate)   137
Oribasius   242
Origen   17, 21, 113, 114, 206, 328, 335, 336
Orion of Thebes   414
Orosius   341
Osborn, E.   15

Ostanes 182
Otero, A. de Santos 102, 126
Ouzounian, A. 166
Ovid 167

Pachomius 114
Padovese, L. 226, 250
Pagels, E. 69, 97
Paion 14
Palmer, A. 206, 222
Palut 189
Pammachius 340
Pamour, Aurelius 136, 137, 138, 146
Papaconstantinou, A. 137, 148, 151, 188, 222
Papadopoulos-Kerameus, A. 415, 430
Parmentier, L. 397
Partoens, G. 314
Patīg (Patticius) 361, 362, 365, 366, 369
Paul (biblical apostle) 3, 14, 15, 16, 23, 29, 83, 84, 106, 107, 166, 226, 234, 236, 237, 239, 245, 267, 315, 316, 317, 319, 326, 333, 334, 337, 341, 357, 361, 377, 381
Paul the Persian 401, 403, 408, 410, 411, 413, 426
Paul of Samosata 230, 241, 243
Pausanias 128–130, 136–147
Pchoirus 141
Pedersen, N.A. 47, 48, 66, 69, 72, 79, 88, 96, 98, 100, 101, 102, 103, 104, 106, 107, 108, 109, 113, 115, 116, 117, 121, 126, 133, 150, 190, 222, 225, 228, 251, 287, 341, 347, 371
Pegosh 136, 137, 141
Pelagius 324–331, 333–344
Pelliot, P. 30
Pennacchietti, F. 153
Périchon, P. 397
Perkins, A. 48
Pernot, L. 157
Perrin, N. 4
Perry, B.E. 415, 430
Peter of Sicily 99
Petersen, W.L. 4, 42, 43, 44, 49
Petkov, J. 149
Petronius 181
Pettipiece, T. 36, 49, 353, 356, 372, 392, 400
Pfligersdorffer, G. 290, 291, 300
Phenix, R.R. 236, 251

Philammon 141
Philip of Side 113
Philo of Alexandria 25, 26
Philosarapis 141
Photinus 243, 331, 332, 342, 403, 406, 410, 411
Photius 153, 386, 387, 396, 397
Pietruschka, U. 69
Pindar 168
Pirotte, J. 346
Pisistratos 138, 139, 140, 141, 144
Pitra, J.-B. 403, 430
Places, É. des 421, 430
Plato 25, 119, 203, 254, 278, 289, 291, 294, 296, 297, 404, 407, 413, 419
Plautus 173
Plinius Maior 160
Plinval, G. de 325, 327, 330, 347
Plotinus 265, 278, 291, 404
Plutarch 413
Podolak, P. 82, 96
Poirier, P.-H. 353, 372, 398
Polito, R. 26
Polotsky, H.J. 67, 106, 117, 121, 126, 265, 328, 348
Polycarp 202
Popkes, E.E. 94, 125
Porphyry 278, 404, 421, 426
Possekel, U. 83, 84, 85, 86, 87, 96, 191, 206, 216, 223
Possidius 242, 287
Prepon 217
Pretty, R.A. 83, 87, 96
Prieur, J.-M. 355, 370
Priscianus 132
Priscillian 246, 328
Probus 154, 157
Proclus 402, 404, 408, 413, 420, 427
Prostmeier, F.R. 11
Protogenes (of Carrhae) 156, 161, 162
Psais, Aurelius 136, 137, 138, 146
Ptolemy (*Letter to Flora*) 77, 318, 319
Ptolemy (unspecified?) 427
Puech, H.-C. 101, 102, 103, 104, 126, 127
Pusey, E.B. 258
Pythagoras 285

Quintilian, Ps.- 256
Quiroga Puertas, A.J. 298

INDEX OF ANTIQUE AND MODERN PERSONAL NAMES 443

Quispel, G.   44, 49, 100, 127, 379, 400
Quodvultdeus of Carthage   353, 354
Quq   186, 187

Ramelli, I.   7, 80, 83, 84, 86, 87, 88, 92, 96, 197, 206, 216, 217, 218, 223
Rasimus, T.   126
Rasouli-Narimani, L.   360, 361, 371
Rāzī, Abū   80
Reck, C.   362, 372
Reed, A.Y.   189, 222
Rees, B.R.   326, 330, 331, 341, 343, 348
Reeves, J.C.   1, 7, 70, 71, 72, 73, 75, 79, 80, 81, 82, 88, 96, 116, 127, 266, 285, 319, 355, 361, 364, 373
Refoulé, F.   340, 348
Reinink, G.J.   189, 196, 221, 222
Renaut, A.   24
Reuling, H.   240, 251
Rhodon   3, 11, 16
Rice, D.S.   154
Richard, M.   398, 403, 413, 416, 430
Richardson, E.C.   329, 348, 354, 370
Richter, D.S.   7, 10
Richter, S.G.   32, 73, 74, 76, 78, 97, 101, 103, 112, 124, 127, 190, 222, 228, 239, 249, 251, 402, 428
Riedweg, C.   300
Riggi, C.   164
Riggs, C.   129, 136, 150
Rigo, A.   403, 430
Rizzo, J.J.   413, 430
Roman, A.   398
Romanianus   131
Römer, C.   29, 147, 364, 370
Rose, E.   73, 97
Ross, S.K.   190, 223
Rotelle, J.E.   349
Rowlandson, J.   136, 150
Ruani, F.   24, 32, 67, 94, 189, 191, 192, 223
Rubel, D.   300
Ruffini, G.R.   131, 145, 151
Rufinus of Aquileia   335, 336, 340
Runia, D.T.   413, 430
Russell, D.   416, 429
Russell, P.   190, 192, 223
Rutherford, I.C.   10
Ryan, T.   246, 250

Sabellius   243, 342
Ṣādeghi, A.A.   32
Sala, T.   78, 97
Salles, R.   232, 251
Sallust   165, 171, 266
Salōmē   56, 62, 76
Sappira   56
Satan   15, 16, 37–41, 166, 167, 182, 186, 193, 194, 195, 202, 205–210, 213, 214, 218, 219
Saturninus   13, 18, 23
Säve-Söderbergh, T.   273
Schaff, P.   396
Scarpat, G.   166
Schaten, S.   124
Schaub, W.   275, 298
Scheidweiler, F.   397
Scher, A.   116, 127, 266
Schipper, H.G.   365, 373
Schletterer, I.   123
Schmid, U.B.   4
Schmid, W.   403, 429
Schmidt, J.   232, 250
Schmidt, T.S.   398
Schneemelcher, W.   4, 123, 126, 127
Schneider, H.-C.   159
Schneider, J.   166
Schneider, R.M.   181
Schöll, R.   415, 429
Schreiber, S.G.   418, 421, 423, 430
Schröter, J.   95, 125, 252
Schwartz, D.L.   188, 222
Schwartz, E.   340, 348, 397
Schwertschlager, J.   226, 251
Scopello, M.   149, 153, 154, 159, 164, 166, 175, 178, 183, 360, 363, 373
Scott, R.   398
Scythianus   194, 285
Sebastianus   132
Segal, J.B.   156, 189
Segond, L.   175
Seneca   30, 165, 280
Serapion of Thmuis   336, 354
Serapis   138
Seth, Sethel   37, 53, 318
Severus of Antioch   236
Sextus Empiricus   26, 423
Seyrig, H.   181
Shahîd, I.   235, 251
Shahrahstānī   363, 364

Shaked, S.   135, 149
Shapur I   133, 155
Shapur II   155, 181, 188
Share, M.   413, 430
Shaw, T.M.   234, 251
Sheldon, J.   360, 361, 364, 371, 399
Shelton, J.C.   99, 123
Shem   37
Shepardson, C.   193, 215, 223
Shoemaker, S.J.   56
Silius Italicus   173
Silvas, A.M.   386, 400
Simon Magus   194
Simon, D.   415, 430
Simon of Cyrene   78
Simplicius   407, 422
Sims-Williams, N.   63, 68, 215, 223, 314
Sims-Williams, U.   191, 223
Sin (lunar deity)   152, 154
Skjærvø, P.O.   32, 57, 69, 73, 77, 97
Skutella, M.   275, 298
Smagina, E.B.   279
Smith, A.J.   332, 335, 337, 348
Smith, D.E.   293, 300
Smith, G.   51, 67, 68
Smith, K.   189, 223
Smith, K.R.   93
Smith, R.   419, 431
Smith, R.P.   196, 224
Soares Santropete, L.G.   93, 97
Socrates Scholasticus   376, 379, 396, 397
Soffritti, O.   166
Solignac, A.   285, 287, 291, 300
Soranus of Ephesus   82
Sordi, M.   301
Souter, A.   329, 330, 331, 332, 333, 334, 335, 336, 340, 342, 348
Sozomenos   156, 161, 162, 163, 376, 396, 397
Spät, E.   194, 224
Spartianus   155
Spuler, B.   91
Stahl, W.H.   265
Stählin, O.   403, 429
Stanjek, H.   344
Statius   173
Stein, M.   64, 69, 358, 363, 364, 370
Stenger, J.R.   233, 251
Stephanou, P.E.   404, 431
Stewart, C.   391, 400

Stock, B.   238, 251
Stock, W.-M.   404, 430
Stocks, J.L.   423, 431
Stoffel, P.   159–160
Stolte, B.H.   415, 431
Stroumsa, G.G.   2
Sturz, F.G.   414, 429
Suchla, B.R.   408, 431
Sundermann, W.   30, 32, 44, 45, 49, 57, 69, 73, 79, 97, 102, 127, 133, 142, 149, 151, 153, 314
Susanna   56
Swank, J.   129

Tacitus   165
Tagoshe   136
Tapollos   136
Tardieu, M.   45, 50, 71, 73, 74, 75, 76, 79, 80, 81, 91, 97, 156, 216, 224, 225, 355, 356, 362, 373
Tatian   1, 3–23, 35, 40, 42–44, 46, 47, 247, 276, 376, 377
Tayyib, Abul-Farag Abdallah ibn al   43
Teigen, H.F.   137, 140, 151
Tertullian   12, 26, 27, 28, 80, 82, 86, 89, 162, 168, 177, 179, 181, 203, 208, 214, 321, 343
TeSelle, E.   339, 340, 348
Teske, R.J.   289, 301, 312, 317, 321, 338, 342, 349, 356, 357, 358, 361, 362, 363, 366, 370
Testard, M.   260
Thalhofer, V.   226, 251
Thédenat, H.   158
Theodore bar Koni   12, 79, 116, 266
Theodore of Mopsuestia   240
Theodore Abū Qurrah   405
Theodoret   12, 156, 161, 162, 241, 242, 387, 388, 389, 390, 391, 392, 393, 396, 397
Thedorou, C.   239, 251
Theodorus (Flavius Manlius)   291
Theodorus Lector   132
Theodosius   190, 375, 376, 394
Theophanes (the Confessor)   384, 385, 396, 397
Theophilus of Antioch   7
Thesleff, H.   25
Thiele, W.   367, 370
Thier, S.   326, 349
Thom, J.C.   232, 252

INDEX OF ANTIQUE AND MODERN PERSONAL NAMES 445

Thomas (apostle)   74, 106, 110, 377
Thomassen, E.   54, 69, 79, 97
Thomson, R.W.   156
Timasius   330
Timotheos (monk)   140
Timothy of Constantinople   99
Timothy the Presbyter   389, 390, 392, 396, 398
Timuş, M.   24, 32, 67
Titus of Bostra   336, 341, 353, 354, 382, 396, 398
Toom, T.   266
Torchia, J.   296, 301
Townsend, P.   69, 97
Traina, G.   155
Traube, L.   153
Tréhorel, E.   258
Trelenberg, J.   4, 8, 9, 10, 11, 12, 20, 22
Trizio, M.   404, 431
Troianos, S.   415, 430
Trompf, G.W.   96
Trzcionka, S.   225, 249
Tuchel, S.   235, 252
Turbo   154, 159, 167, 168, 170, 171, 173, 174, 176, 177, 183, 184
Turcan, M.   179
Tyconius   307

Uehlinger, C.   129
Unterseher, L.A.   309
Urba, C.   330, 338, 340, 342, 349

Valantasis, R.   190, 220
Valens   162, 376, 384
Valentinian I   131, 376
Valentinus   13, 22, 23, 186, 187, 214, 228, 230, 239, 335
Valerianus (bishop)   387
Valerianus   155
Valerius   128, 129, 136, 137, 141
Van den Kerchove, A.   93, 97
Van der Meeren, S.   293, 301
Van Riel, G.   404, 431
Van Tongerloo, A.   94, 124, 125, 371, 372
Vanspauwen, A.   352, 353, 370, 373
Verheijen, L.   274, 327, 338, 349, 356, 370
Verheyden, J.   229, 252
Vermes, M.   164, 194, 220, 224, 397
Verosta, S.   228, 252

Vigouroux, F.   166
Villey, A.   274
Virgil   171
Vitus   156

Wal, N. van der   415, 431
Wallace-Hadrill, A.   130, 151
Wallraff, M.   10
Walker, J.   190, 224
Waszink, J.H.   82, 89, 97
Weber, D.   290, 293, 301
Wermelinger, O.   330, 343, 344, 349, 371, 373
Westerink, L.G.   408, 426, 431
Wet, C.(L.) de   144, 150, 225, 233, 234, 236, 243, 245, 248, 252
White, L.M.   243, 252
Whitehouse, H.   149
Whittaker, M.   8, 15
Wickes, J.   192, 196, 214, 224
Wießner, G.   94
Williams, F.   242, 252, 376, 377, 397
Willis, W.H.   147
Willman, J.P.   191, 221
Wilson, K.M.   229, 252
Witakowski, W.   198, 224
Woods, D.   226, 252
Woolf, G.   130, 151
Worp, K.A.   136, 137, 138, 139, 140, 141, 147, 148, 149, 151
Wurst, G.   74, 94, 97, 101, 127, 355, 371, 373

Xenophon   181

Yaltabaoth   77
Yamīn, al   71, 75, 90
Yaʿqūbī   80
Yave   77
Young, K.   384, 400

Zacharias of Mytilene   398, 401–405, 408, 413, 414, 416, 417, 426
Zangemeister, C.   341, 350
Zarathustra   37, 182, 190
Zeno of Citium   82, 427
Zenobia   132, 133, 143
Zepos, I.   417, 431
Zepos, P.   417, 431
Zieme, P.   142, 149, 153
Zimmermann, B.   232, 250

Zola, N.J. 4, 23
Zuckerman, C. 166
Zumkeller, A. 294, 295, 301

Zycha, J. 29, 330, 338, 340, 342, 349, 352, 354, 355, 356, 357, 358, 359, 361, 362, 363, 367, 370

Compiled by Aäron Vanspauwen

Printed in the United States
By Bookmasters